Macroeconomics

MICHAEL PARKIN
University of Western Ontario

Prentice-Hall, Inc., Englewood Cliffs, New Jersey 07632

Library of Congress Cataloging in Publication Data

PARKIN, MICHAEL.
Macroeconomics.

Includes index.
1. Macroeconomics. I. Title.
HB172.5.P36 1984 339 83-21273
ISBN 0-13-542589-1

Editorial/production supervision and
interior design: Esther S. Koehn
Cover design: Ben Santora
Manufacturing buyer: Ed O'Dougherty

Printed in the United States of America

10 9 8 7 6 5 4 3 2 1

ISBN 0-13-542589-1

Prentice-Hall International, Inc., *London*
Prentice-Hall of Australia Pty. Limited, *Sydney*
Editora Prentice-Hall do Brasil, Ltda., *Rio de Janeiro*
Prentice-Hall Canada Inc., *Toronto*
Prentice-Hall of India Private Limited, *New Delhi*
Prentice-Hall of Japan, Inc., *Tokyo*
Prentice-Hall of Southeast Asia Pte. Ltd., *Singapore*
Whitehall Books Limited, *Wellington, New Zealand*

TO ROBIN

Contents

PART IV

THE KEYNESIAN THEORY OF INCOME, EMPLOYMENT, AND THE PRICE LEVEL

PART VI

MACROECONOMIC POLICY

PART VIII

THE UNITED STATES AND THE WORLD ECONOMY

Preface

This book presents a comprehensive and up-to-date account of macroeconomics—that branch of economics that seeks to understand and explain inflation, unemployment, interest rates, foreign exchange rates, the balance of payments, and other related phenomena. Unlike any other book currently available at this level, a considerable amount of space and attention is devoted to developments that have taken place in the past ten years. Chief of these developments is the incorporation into macroeconomics of the rational expectations hypothesis. This hypothesis is explained in simple, intuitive terms and its implications for the determination of inflation and unemployment, and the assessment of economic stabilization policies are analyzed.

The book does not deal only with recent developments in macroeconomics; it also deals with mainstream Keynesian and pre-Keynesian theories from which the new macroeconomic theories have grown. More importantly, it shows how new macroeconomics and earlier approaches are related to each other. In addition, attention is paid to the interrelations of the domestic economy with the rest of the world, and to the design and conduct of macroeconomic policy.

In presenting an account of modern macroeconomics I have attempted to avoid the extremes of dry theory and passionate policy advocacy. Theory is presented in such a way that the reader may quickly and easily see its predictive content—the facts that each theory seeks to explain. It also checks the predictions of each theory against the facts, revealing in the process what that theory is capable of explaining well and what its main shortcomings are.

Policy is treated by analyzing the implications of pursuing the policy recommendations of different schools of thought. This is done in a manner that enables the reader to see clearly why different economists reach different conclusions.

The central purpose of the book is to make modern macroeconomics accessible to beginning and intermediate students as well as to the serious general reader. To this end, I have used the simplest available analytical techniques, intuitive explanations and, wherever possible, illustrations drawn directly from the macroeconomic experience of the United States. The book is pitched for the most part at a level that I hope is appropriate for students in their second year of undergraduate study, although large parts of the book will be easily understood by beginning students, and other parts will be found useful by more advanced students looking for a simplified explanation of material that is otherwise available only in journal articles. Indeed, in view of the lack of any alternative exposition (other than original research articles in learned journals) of much of the material that is presented here, the book will be found useful even by beginning graduate students looking for a broad overview of the topics that they will study in greater depth in later postgraduate courses. Finally, the book will be of interest to professional economists in government, industry, and commerce whose formal study of economics was completed before the rational expectations revolution hit macroeconomics and who desire a quick, guided tour of this new material.

Organization

The book is organized around three main themes—facts, theories, and policies. Two introductory sections set out the facts that macroeconomics seeks to explain and also outline the ways in which macroeconomic phenomena are observed and measured. The core of the book deals with theory. It presents a series of progressively more comprehensive models of the economy, each of which has some merits in explaining a limited set of facts, but each of which also has some shortcomings that are highlighted. Following the presentation and evaluation of alternative theories, macroeconomic policy—the problem of stabilizing output, employment and prices—is discussed at considerable length. In addition to a conventional discussion of stabilization policy, there is a detailed exploration of the implications of rational expectations for that policy. Problems of long-term growth and some of the more recent claims of the so-called "supply-siders" are also explained and evaluated. The final five chapters examine linkages between the U.S. economy and the rest of the world.

Macroeconomics is a controversial subject and economists often disagree vehemently on policy issues. Despite this, there is a considerable measure of agreement on most matters. There do, however, remain crucial issues that divide economists and, although it is a slight caricature, it seems reasonably accurate to divide macroeconomists into two camps—Keynesians and monetarists. I am widely regarded as being a monetarist and, as a descriptive matter, cannot seriously quarrel about being so labelled. I have, nevertheless, tried to write a book that avoids falling into the trap of being a monetarist tract. Some, no doubt, will conclude that I have failed. I certainly have not shyed away from presenting alternative views on macroeconomic policy in the sharpest possible focus. I have attempted to do justice to each position and explain precisely what it is that each expounds and why.

Acceptance of the hypothesis that expectations are formed rationally is often regarded as being synonomous with monetarism. Because this book, unlike any other at this level, presents an account of rational expectations (and a sympathetic one at that) no doubt will lead some readers to conclude that this book is a monetarist tract. Such a conclusion will be seen, on careful reflection, to be incorrect for there are rational expectation Keynesians (usually referred to as new Keynesians) as well as rational expectation monetarists (usually referred to as new Classicals). Both of these are presented and explained.

Acknowledgments

This book would not have been completed without the help of a large number of people. First and foremost, I owe an enormous debt to Robin Bade to whom the book is dedicated. From the outset of the project she has been a constant source of help, guidance, and criticism. She has read the manuscript at least as many times as I have, drafted all the diagrams, suggested many of the review questions, handled all the data and primary source needs of the project, corrected my grammar, and caught many inconsistencies and errors.

Michael Cox (of the Virginia Polytechnic Institute) has read and commented upon substantial parts of the manuscript and provided many of the review questions. Valuable comments on earlier versions of the book—in whole or in part—were provided by Ben Bernanke (Stanford University); Paul Booth (Bank of Canada); Laura Feinstone (University of Rochester); David Gordon (University of Rochester); Gary Grant (Acadia University); Jeremy Greenwood (University of Western Ontario); Herschel Grossman (Brown University); Geoffrey Kingston (University of Queensland); David Laidler (University of Western Ontario); Glenn MacDonald (University of Western Ontario); Andrea Maneschi (Vanderbilt University); Stephen Margolis (North Carolina State University); Bob Nobay (University of Liverpool); James Pesando (University of Toronto); Brian Scarfe (University of Alberta); Michael Sumner (University of Sussex); Randall Wigle (University of Saskatchewan), and Ian Wooton (University of Western Ontario). The entire final manuscript was read with meticulous care by John Lapp of North Carolina State University and Andrew Policano of Fordham University. I have not incorporated each and every of their many suggestions and so in no way can hold them responsible for the final product; I am, nevertheless, extremely grateful to them all.

Several generations of undergraduate students and graduate teaching assistants at the University of Western Ontario have been of considerable help in providing comments and criticisms on various parts of the book at different stages in its development. I am especially grateful to Rosalind Wong, Monica van Huystee, David Abramson, Pierfrancesco Cocco, and Promod Sharma.

Expert library assistance was provided by Jane McAndrew, clerical assistance by Ann Parkin, and research assistance by Kevin Dowd and Eddie McDonnell. The many drafts and revisions of this book have been typed with great skill by Yvonne Adams, Brenda Campbell, Leslie Farrant, Marg Gower, Adeline McKeown, and Catherine Parkin. I am deeply indebted to them all.

Michael Parkin

1

Macroeconomic Questions

This book is going to help you to get abreast of the current state of knowledge in macroeconomics. Three tasks in this introductory chapter will start you out on that process. These tasks are to:

(a) Know the questions that macroeconomics seeks to answer.
(b) Know the macroeconomic policy issues on which economists disagree.
(c) Know the views of the leading "schools of thought."

A. Macroeconomic Questions

Macroeconomic questions have changed over the years and have usually been motivated by a concern to understand the economic problems of the day.

Inflation

The oldest macroeconomic question is, What determines the general level of prices? Or the very closely related question, What determines the rate of inflation (or the rate of deflation)? Excitement over this issue dates back at least to Roman times, when a rampant inflation was experienced. The first scientific answer to the problem was not given, however, until the sixteenth century. That answer—which you will meet in Chapter 12—was worked out by the French philosopher-economist Jean Bodin.

Following the period of European (particularly Spanish) colonization of the Americas and the influx into Europe of vast quantities of gold, there was a substantial rise in the general level of prices in Europe and North America. This went on well into the early seventeenth century. There then followed a period of price stability, which in turn was followed (from about 1750 to the early nineteenth century) by further very strong inflation. In the early part of the nineteenth century, following the Napoleonic wars, there was a period of falling prices. The next hundred years saw alternating periods of rising and falling prices, but over the century as a whole, there was remarkable price stability. Since the 1930s, prices have persistently risen and especially strongly so since the late 1960s.[1]

The questions for macroeconomics are: Why have there been periods of prolonged inflation and deflation? What has caused these major movements in the general level of prices? Can we predict future price level movements? And how can we control inflation?

Unemployment

The second major issue for macroeconomics is, What determines the percentage of the labor force that is unemployed? The earliest attempts to answer this question linked movements in unemployment with movements in inflation and sought to understand the process whereby both inflation and unemployment fluctuate in recurrent cycles—known as the *business cycle.*

In the late 1920s and 1930s, a high unemployment rate was established throughout Western Europe, North America, and most of the world, which was very persistent. Unemployment hardly fell below 20 percent for almost fifteen years in several countries. This gave rise, in 1936, to one of the major contributions to modern macroeconomics—*The General Theory of Employment, Interest and Money* by John Maynard Keynes.[2] In that work, Keynes changed the focus of economists away from the hard, and at the time unyielding, question of what causes the business cycle, to the narrower and apparently easier question of what determines the level of unemployment (and levels of other aggregates) at a particular point in time. He also elevated to a position of central importance in macroeconomics a related issue, namely, real national income.

Real National Income

What determines the level of real national income? Roughly speaking, real national income is a measure of the volume of the goods and services that can be bought with the income of all the individuals in the economy. Fluctuations in real national income give rise to fluctuations in the standard of living, and differences in average growth rates of real national income between countries produce large intercountry differences in living standards. Macroeconomics seeks to understand the reasons why there are persistent differences in real income growth rates between countries and why there are fluctuations in real national income around its trend growth rate.

The Rate of Interest

A fourth question that macroeconomics addresses is, What determines the rate of interest? There are, of course, many rates of interest in a modern economy.

---

[1]An excellent account of the long-term movements in prices in North America and Europe may be found in Anna J. Schwartz, "Secular Price Change in Historical Perspective," *Journal of Money, Credit and Banking*, 5, no. 1, pt. II (February 1973), 243–69.

[2]John Maynard Keynes, *The General Theory of Employment, Interest and Money* (London: Macmillan & Co. Ltd., 1936).

In the study of macroeconomics it is customary to distinguish between short-term and long-term rates of interest. *Short-term rates* (or more simply, *short rates*) are the rates of interest paid and received on loans of a short term or temporary nature—up to five years. *Long-term rates* are those on loans of more than five years—and could be on loans that run indefinitely. There is a tendency for all interest rates to move up and down together, but short rates tend to fluctuate more strongly than long rates. An essential problem for macroeconomics is to understand what determines the general ups and downs in interest rates and why short-term rates fluctuate more than long-term rates.

Balance of Payments and Foreign Exchange Rate

A fifth question is, What determines a country's balance of payments vis-à-vis the rest of the world? And a sixth, related question is, What determines the value of one country's currency in relation to another country's currency? That is, What determines the foreign exchange rate?

These questions also have a long history. Countries have been concerned with their balance of payments for as long as there has been international trade. The great Scottish philosopher, David Hume, writing in the middle of the eighteenth century, provided the first properly worked-out scientific explanation for movements in the balance of payments.[3]

U.S. Macroeconomic Questions in the 1970s and '80s It is evident that although some of the macroeconomic questions posed above have been more important at certain stages in history than at others, in recent years they have all taken on a considerable importance.[4] Inflation has been running at close to, and occasionally in excess of, double digits; unemployment has rarely dipped below 7 percent; real national income growth has been much below its longer term average; interest rates have been in the middle to high teens; and the foreign exchange value of the American dollar has fluctuated substantially.

Thus, at the beginning of the 1980s, the macroeconomic questions for the United States are: Why are U.S. interest rates, inflation, unemployment, real income growth, and the foreign exchange rate behaving so badly? Why have we had so much inflation in recent years, and why have interest rates and unemployment been so high? Why is real income growth below its long-term trend, and why have there been such large fluctuations in the foreign exchange value of the U.S. dollar? A related, more important, and yet harder to answer

---

[3]This is still a highly readable piece of work and may be found in David Hume's essay, "Of the Balance of Trade," *Essays Moral, Political and Literary* (London: Oxford University Press, 1963), pp. 316–33.

[4]A good, comprehensive, and up-to-date source for facts about macroeconomic conditions in the United States is the *Survey of Current Business.* This is a monthly publication that may be purchased from the Superintendent of Documents, U.S. Government Printing Office, Washington, D.C. 20402. An alternative (free of charge) source of material is the Federal Reserve Bank of St. Louis monthly data summaries in *National Economic Trends* and *Monetary Trends.* These sources of data may be ordered from the Federal Reserve Bank of St. Louis, P.O. Box 442, St. Louis, Missouri 63166.

set of questions are: What are the effects on these variables of policies that the Administration and the Federal Reserve might adopt, and how might policy be arranged so as to achieve steadier prices, lower interest rates, lower unemployment, higher real income growth, and more stable and predictable value of the dollar in terms of foreign currency?

You will recognize these as questions that are repeatedly posed and discussed in the media and in a variety of social situations. You will also recognize them as questions for which most people, and certainly most journalists, T.V. and radio commentators, and politicians appear to have answers. Pay attention the next time that Dan Rather (or your own favorite newscaster) is telling you about the latest figures on inflation or unemployment or interest rates.

We are usually told something like this:

> Inflation has risen this month *because* of sharp rises in the prices of fuel and food.

or

> Unemployment rose in April *because* of massive layoffs in the auto industry.

or

> Interest rates have eased *because* of a return of investor confidence.

You are going to discover that answers such as these are too superficial or too shallow to be of much value. You are also going to discover that many of the popular answers are wrong! You are further going to discover that even economists often disagree with each other on the answers to these questions, particularly on the answers to the policy questions.

B. Macroeconomic Policy Issues

As you are probably aware, there is widespread belief that the government can and should take actions designed to influence key economic variables such as inflation and unemployment. Economists do not agree amongst themselves, however, on what measures will achieve the desired results. The main reason why there is disagreement is that we still lack a deep understanding of macroeconomic phenomena. Another way of saying this is that we lack good theories; that is, no one particular theory fits the facts so exactly that it is compelling. This means that each of us tends to subscribe to the theory that best supports our predisposition (or perhaps even our prejudices). This should not be taken to mean that macroeconomics is just a matter of opinion. On the contrary, there exists a solid "core" of theory that commands widespread support amongst economists regardless of the policy view that they adopt. There are, however, some areas where agreement on the relevant theoretical approach is still lacking. But even in these cases, there is general agreement amongst economists on the way to proceed to resolve conflicts of view.

The lack of complete agreement and the lack of a close enough correspondence between the current available theories and the facts will be highlighted and emphasized throughout this book. You will come to know and understand the existing theories; you will also learn the facts—both those that the theories "fit" or explain and those that they do not. It is the as yet unexplained facts that provide much of the agenda for future research.

There are two broad macroeconomic policy questions on which economists disagree amongst themselves, as discussed below.

Should Macroeconomic Policy be Global or Detailed?

Global policies are those that are directed at influencing the values of a small number of aggregate variables such as the money supply, the foreign exchange rate, the overall level of government expenditures, the overall level of taxes, and the size of the government's budget deficit. Those who take the view that a small number of aggregate policy instruments should be the central concern of macroeconomic policy generally believe that it is desirable to leave as much scope as possible for individual initiative to be coordinated through the market mechanism.

Detailed policies are directed at controlling the prices of, or other terms concerning the exchange of, a large number of specific goods and services. Such policies are too numerous to list in full. Some examples are: wage and price controls that regulate the wages and prices of a large number of types of worker and individual products; minimum wage policies; interest rate ceilings or other regulations on banks, savings and loan institutions, and insurance companies; regional policies in the form of special subsidies to particular regions; investment incentives; regulation and control of private manufacturing industry; regulation of international trade by the use of tariffs and quotas; and regulation of international capital flows. Those economists (and others) who favor detailed policies generally take the view that there are a large number of important areas in which markets fail to achieve a desirable economic outcome. They believe that detailed government intervention is needed to modify the outcome of the market process.

Often the disagreement between those advocating detailed intervention and those arguing against it is not so much a disagreement about the existence of a problem that the free market is having trouble solving, but rather about whether or not the government can solve the problem better than the market can.

Should Government Policy be Governed by a Set of Rules or be Discretionary?

Those economists favoring rules are not unanimously agreed upon what the rules should be. They are agreed, however, on one crucial point—that controlling an economy is fundamentally different from controlling a mechanical (or electrical, or electronic) system, such as, for example, the heating/cooling system in a building. What makes controlling the economy different is the fact that it is people who are being controlled, and unlike machines, people know that they are being controlled and are capable of learning the procedures that are being employed by the controllers—the government—and of organizing their affairs so as to take the best advantage of the situation created by policy. A policy based on fixed rules minimizes the uncertainty that people have to face and thus enables a better economic performance.

Those who favor discretion argue that if new information becomes available, it is foolish not to use it. By committing itself to a set of rules, the government ties its hands and bars itself from being in a position to exploit the new information.

The key difference between the advocates of rules and those of discretion is a judgment as to whether individuals acting in their own interests, coordinated by markets, are capable of reacting to, and taking account of, new information without the need for government assistance in the matter.

In view of the major source of the disagreement on global versus detailed policies and rules versus discretion, you will not be surprised to be told that, on the whole, those economists who favor global policies also favor rules, whereas those who favor detailed policies also favor discretionary intervention.

C. Leading Schools of Thought

Broadly speaking, economists fall into two schools of thought on macroeconomic policy. There are no widely accepted, neat labels for identifying these two schools; however, the term *monetarist* is often applied to one group and the term *Keynesian* to the other. Monetarists advocate fixed rules, whereas Keynesians favor active intervention. These labels give flavor to, but sometimes fail to do full justice to, some of the subtleties of the distinctions between the two broad schools of thought. Nevertheless, in this book, the terms will be used to identify the two schools.[5]

The Monetarist View

Monetarists advocate that governments should have policies toward a limited number of global macroeconomic variables such as money supply growth, government expenditure, taxes, and/or government deficit. They advocate the adoption of fixed rules for the behavior of these variables. A well-known example is the rule that the money supply should grow at a certain fixed percentage rate year in and year out. Another proposed rule is that the government budget should be balanced, on the average, over a period of four to five years. More strongly, some monetarists urge the introduction of a constitutional amendment mandating Congress to balance its budget and limiting the fraction of peoples' incomes that government may take in taxes. In any event, monetarists argue, the policy interventions that do occur should be announced as far ahead as possible so as to enable people to take account of them in planning and ordering their own economic affairs.

The intellectual leaders of this school are Milton Friedman (formerly of the University of Chicago and now working at the Hoover Institution at Stanford University), Karl Brunner (University of Rochester), who is credited with coining the term *monetarist*, and Robert E. Lucas Jr. (University of Chicago).

---

[5]An excellent, though demanding, discussion of the identifying characteristics of the different schools may be found in Douglas D. Purvis, "Monetarism: A Review," *The Canadian Journal of Economics*, 13, no. 1 (February 1980), 96–122. The twofold classification suggested here is qualified in many subtle ways by Purvis.

Keynesians advocate detailed intervention to "fine tune" the economy in the neighborhood of full employment and low inflation. They would, if necessary, attempt to control inflation by direct controls of wages and prices and to control unemployment by stimulating demand, using monetary and fiscal policy. They would use discretion in seeking to stimulate the economy in a depression and holding it back in a boom, modifying their policy in the light of the current situation. In their view, policy changes are best not pre-announced so as to deter speculation.

The intellectual leaders of this group of macroeconomists are Franco Modigliani (Massachusetts Institute of Technology) and James Tobin (Yale University).

An Analogy Imagine that you are listening to an FM radio station in a crowded part of the wave band. The signals are repeatedly and randomly drifting, so that, from time to time, your station drifts out of hearing and a neighboring station in which you have no interest comes through loud and clear. What should you do to get a stronger and more persistent signal from the station you want to hear?

The Keynesian says:

> Hang on to the tuning knob and whenever the signal begins to fade, fiddle with the knob, attempting, as best you can, to stay with the signal.

The monetarist says:

> Get yourself an AFC (Automatic Frequency Control) tuner; set it on the station you wish to hear; sit back; relax and enjoy your music. Do not fiddle with the tuner knob; your reception will not be perfect; but on the average, you will not be able to do any better than the AFC.

Summary

A. Macroeconomic Questions

There are six main questions in macroeconomics; they are, What determines:

1. The rate of *inflation*?
2. The *unemployment* rate?
3. The level of *real national income*?
4. The *rate of interest*?
5. The *balance of payments*?
6. The *foreign exchange rate*?

B. Macroeconomic Policy Issues

There are two major disagreements among economists concerning macroeconomic policy. One concerns whether policy should use *global* instruments or whether it should involve *detailed* intervention in individual markets. The second concerns whether policy should be governed by fixed *rules* or whether it should be varied from time to time at the *discretion* of the government in the light of current economic conditions.

C. Leading Schools of Thought

There are two major schools of thought: (1) *monetarists* who advocate *global* instruments setting under fixed *rules*, and (2) *Keynesians*, who advocate *detailed* intervention in a large number of individual markets with *discretion* to vary that intervention from time to time.

Review Questions

The following statements by prominent Americans all concern some aspect or other of U.S. economic policy or economic problems. Read the statements carefully and then classify them according to whether they:

(a) Deal with *macro*economics issues or not.
(b) Deal with *detailed* or *global* policy.
(c) Are talking about *rules* or *discretion* in the conduct of policy.

The first ten statements are taken from *Time* magazine in July 1982:

1. "The amendment would rob the government of needed flexibility in adjusting spending and tax plans" (July 26, p. 9).
2. "Virtually every country has curbed its money supply in the fight against inflation" (July 19, p. 38).
3. "Both in the U.S. and Europe, people ... increasingly look to governments for a wide array of social programs: generous old-age pensions, broad medical coverage, education loans and unemployment insurance" (July 19, p. 39).
4. "The decisive political issue for the 1980s will be to get government expenditures under control" (July 19, p. 41).
5. "Wage and price controls can't work ... [because] ... they are self-defeating" (July 19, p. 41).
6. "The steady deterioration of the Western economies has put ever greater pressure on political leaders to find a way to revive growth and reduce unemployment" (July 19, p. 41).
7. "America has also been slow to remove price controls from natural gas. ... With artificially low prices, people consume more than they should. They waste it" (July 19, p. 42).
8. "Another crucial policy issue facing all nations is the proper role of government in revitalizing industry and promoting technology" (July 19, p. 42).
9. "The inflation cycle can be broken only if governments reduce their spending and keep their money supplies expanding at a slow pace" (July 19, p. 41).
10. "Conservation of gasoline in the U.S. should be pushed a bit faster and further than market prices alone have done" (July 19, p. 41).

The following six quotations are from President Reagan's Economic Report to Congress:

11. "My economic program is based on the fundamental precept that government must respect, protect, and enhance the freedom and integrity of the individual" (p. 3).
12. "For several decades, an ever-larger role for the Federal Government and, more recently, inflation have zapped the economic vitality of the Nation" (p. 3).
13. "My commitment to regulatory reform was made clear in one of my very first Acts in office, when I accelerated the decontrol of crude oil prices and eliminated the cumbersome crude oil entitlements system" (p. 7).
14. "I have made clear my support for a policy of gradual and less volatile reduction of the growth of the money supply" (p. 8).
15. "To spur further business investment and productivity growth, the new tax law provides faster write-offs for capital investment and a restructured investment tax credit. Research and Development expenditures are encouraged with a new tax credit" (p. 7).
16. "Across-the-board cuts in individual income tax rates phased in over three years and the indexing of tax brackets in subsequent years will help put an end to making inflation profitable for the Federal Government" (p. 7).

The next three quotations are taken from the Monetary Policy Report to Congress submitted by the Federal Reserve Board in July 1982 (*Federal Reserve Bulletin,* August 1982).

17. "The progress in reducing inflation that began during 1981 continued in the first half of 1982" (p. 443).
18. "Long-term interest rates also remained high during the first half of 1982" (p. 443).
19. "Gasoline prices at the retail level, which had remained virtually flat over the second half of 1981, fell substantially during the first four months of 1982" (p. 447).

2

U.S. Macroeconomic History Since 1900

Too often in the past, economists have disagreed with each other about theory, while paying little attention to the basic questions: What are the facts? And which, if any, of the theories being advanced are capable of explaining the facts? All useful theories begin with *some* facts in need of explanation. Theories are, in effect, "rigged" to explain a limited set of facts. They are subsequently tested by checking their ability to explain *other* facts, facts that are either not known or not explicitly taken into account when "rigging" the theory.

The theories of macroeconomics that are presented in this book have been designed to explain some aspect or other of the facts about inflation, unemployment, real income, interest rates, balance of payments, and foreign exchange rate. The evolution of these variables over time may be called the *macroeconomic history* of a country. This chapter is designed to give you a broad-brush picture of the macroeconomic history of the United States. It should be thought of as a first quick look at some of the facts that macroeconomic theory seeks to explain. It presents the facts in the most direct, uncluttered manner possible and in no way tries to begin the task of explaining the facts.

The chapter will serve two main purposes. First, it will provide you with some basic material that will enable you to reject the more obviously incorrect theories that you may come across. Second, it will provide you with a quick reference source—especially the appendix to this chapter and the data sources listed therein—in the event that you want to pursue a more systematic testing of macroeconomic theories.

This chapter pursues three tasks that are designed to enable you to:

(a) Know the main features of the evolution of the key macroeconomic variables since 1900; these include inflation, unemployment, real income, interest rates, balance of payments, and exchange rate.
(b) Know the main macroeconomic characteristics of each decade since 1900.
(c) Sharpen your focus on the questions that macroeconomics seeks to answer.

A. Evolution of Macroeconomic Variables

In this chapter we shall examine the evolution of the six key macroeconomic variables—inflation, unemployment, real income, interest rates, balance of payments, and foreign exchange rate—one at a time. Some patterns and relationships amongst the variables may become evident to you in the course of this exercise. I shall not, however, at this stage, seek to highlight in any systematic way, what those interrelationships might be. That task will be delayed until the end of the next part of the book, after you have had an opportunity of studying in more detail the precise ways in which the macroeconomic variables to be described here are defined and measured. At that stage, in Chapter 6, we shall look explicitly at some of the relationships amongst the variables. For now, let us familiarize ourselves with the paths that have been taken by these six key variables.

Inflation

Look at Figure 2.1. It presents the key facts about the behavior of the general level of prices in the United States as measured by the Consumer Price Index (CPI). Chapter 5 will explain precisely how this index is calculated and measured. For now it is sufficient if you think of it as being simply an average of the prices of all the different things that people buy. Focus your attention first on frame (a) of the figure. It shows the *level* of prices in each year.[1] It is immediately obvious that the general level of prices has been rising persistently over the period shown in the figure. In fact, the average (or trend) growth rate over this period is a little under 3 percent per annum. You can also see, however, that prices rose during the period up to the end of the Second World War (1946) much less quickly than they did after that. In fact, from 1900 to 1946, the trend rate of inflation as measured by the Consumer Price Index was only 1.3 percent per annum, whereas in the period between 1947 and 1980, the trend rate of inflation increased to 3.5 percent. The two trend lines are shown in the figure as the straight lines labelled with the percentage growth rates that they represent.

Frame (b) focuses attention on the more commonly reported aspect of prices—*inflation*—the rate at which prices are rising. Before considering the behavior of inflation, let us be sure that the connection between frames (a) and (b) are thoroughly understood. Frame (a) shows the level of prices, whereas frame (b) shows the rate at which prices are changing. You can think of this as meaning that the *slope* of the line in frame (a) is measured by the *height* of the line in frame (b). For example, a steep slope in frame (a), such as that marked

---

[1]The price level that appears on the vertical axis of frame (a) of Figure 2.1 is measured on a *logarithmic* scale. If you are familiar with logarithms, this will give you no problems. If your memory of logarithms has faded, you only need to recall that a logarithm is a measure in ratio terms. Thus, for example, a price level of 100 is twice the price level 50, and a price level of 200 is twice the price level 100. On a logarithmic (or ratio) scale, the *distance* measured between 50 and 100 is the same as the distance between 100 and 200. This is a useful way of graphing economic time-series because the steepness of the line graphed represents the *rate* of change of the variable. This same device will appear later in this chapter when we look at real income.

Figure 2.1
The Price Level and Inflation

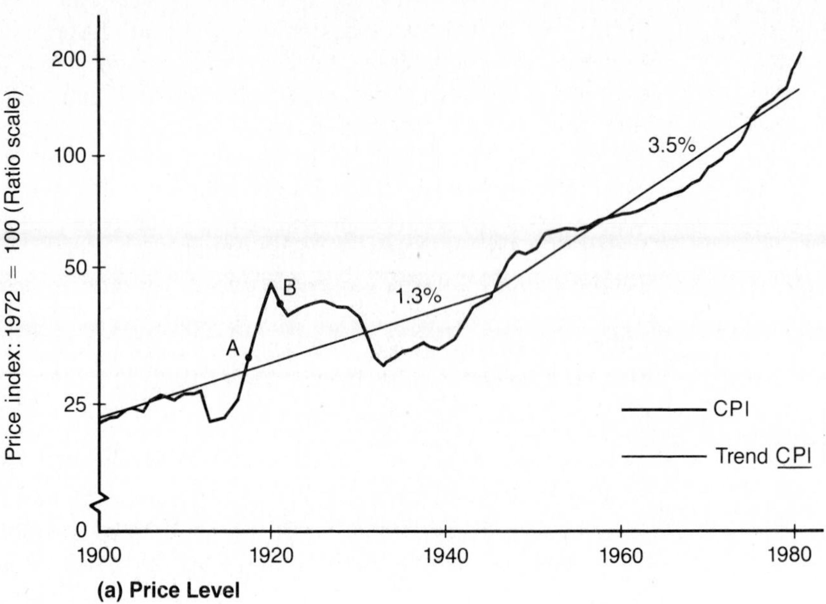

(a) Price Level

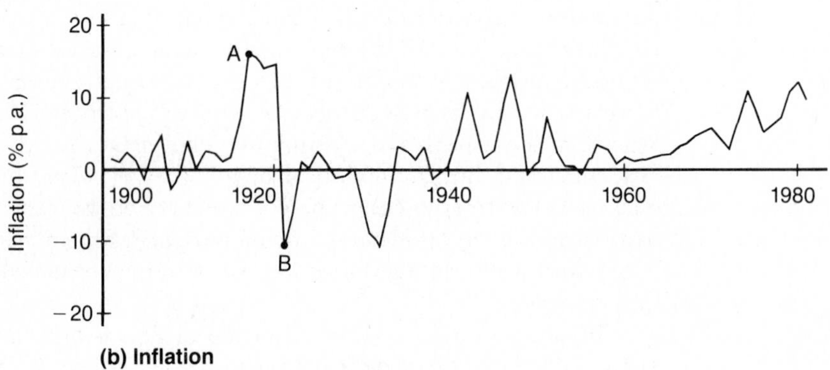

(b) Inflation

The Consumer Price Index (CPI) shows that for the past 80 years, prices have increased at an increasing rate. Inflation was highly erratic before World War II, was less volatile in the 1950s and 1960s, but has become more pronounced in recent years. The last period of sustained falling prices was the Great Depression and the years following it.
SOURCE: Appendix to this chapter.

A, is associated with a high rate of inflation, such as the point marked A in frame (b). To look at another example, when the line in frame (a) is sloping downwards such as at B, this means that prices are falling, or, equivalently, that inflation is negative as shown by the point marked B in frame (b).

Let us now focus on the characteristics of inflation as shown in frame (b). First, it is evident that the *rate* of inflation has itself been on a distinctly rising trend. That is, not only has the price level risen persistently throughout this century, but the rate at which the price level has risen has itself increased. This is particularly noticeable in the period since the early 1930s. Since that time there has hardly been a single year in which the price level has fallen (i.e., in which inflation was negative).

Second, the *range* of inflation is large. The highest inflation rate (of the Consumer Price Index) occurred in 1917, when consumer prices rose by more than 16 percent. Other large inflation rates occurred in 1918 to 1920. In fact, the period from 1917 to 1920 saw the price level almost double. Other high-inflation years were 1942, 1946–1948, 1951, and every year since 1974. With one exception, all these high-inflation years are associated with war or immediate postwar recovery. The highest inflation of all (1917–1920) was associated with the First World War; 1942 and 1946–1948 represented the beginning of the Second World War and its aftermath; and 1951 was the Korean War. The exception is the period since 1974, which is the highest peacetime inflation in U.S. history. At the other extreme, the biggest deflation (falling prices) occurred in 1921 when the Consumer Price Index fell by 11 percent. Other deflationary years were 1927–1933, which span the Great Depression (1929–1933); and prices also fell briefly, although slightly, in 1938–1939; and again, although somewhat trivially, in 1949 and 1955.

The third feature of the inflation rate is its clear tendency to *cycle*. There are no neat regular cycles but rather plenty of irregular swings. There is apparently more volatility in some periods than others, and the period between 1953 and 1966 looks very calm compared with the more turbulent periods before and since that time. The 1970s, in fact, look more normal than did the 1950s and 1960s, which were years of unusually low volatility in inflation. Although as we have noted, there are no regular cycles, there is a very clear cycle that is especially apparent in the 1970s—1970 was a year of peak inflation. For the next two years the inflation rate fell, but then in 1972, it turned up again to reach a new peak in 1974. This was followed by another downturn, reaching a trough in 1976, which in turn was followed by another upturn, which ran for four years, to 1980.

This two-to-four-year cycle in inflation is apparent, although with much smaller up-and-down movements in the 1960s and 1950s, and with even greater volatility than that displayed in the 1970s for the period before World War II.

Although the rate at which the Consumer Price Index is changing is the most commonly used measure of inflation, it is by no means the only measure. Two other commonly used measures are the gross domestic product (GDP) deflator and the personal consumption expenditure (PCE) deflator. The precise meaning of these alternatives and the differences between them and the CPI are explained in Chapter 5. Inflation rates measured by these alternative indexes are set out in the appendix to this chapter. As you will see from inspecting those numbers, although not behaving in exactly the same way as the Consumer Price Index, there is a clear tendency for the other two alternative measures of inflation to follow the Consumer Price Index remarkably closely. This tells us that, although for some purposes we need to be careful in our selection of the appropriate index number with which to measure prices and inflation, at least as regards the main trends and swings in inflation, the major alternatives available to us behave very similarly.

Unemployment

Next look at Figure 2.2, which shows the unemployment rate in the United States since 1900. As with inflation, the precise definition of, and the method of measuring, unemployment will be dealt with in Chapter 5. For the present you may simply think of unemployment as measuring the extent to which people who have indicated that they wish to work are not able to find a job.

The most striking feature about the behavior of unemployment in the United States in this century is its persistently high level from 1931 through to 1940—a decade in which the unemployment rate did not fall below 14 percent. These were the years of the Great Depression and its aftermath.

In addition to the massive unemployment experienced during the Great Depression years, you will also be struck, perhaps, by the rather clear though gentle trend rise in unemployment in the years since World War II (since 1945). It is noticeable that the peaks in unemployment that occurred in 1954, 1958, and 1975 are each successively higher, and the troughs occurring in 1953, 1956, 1973, and 1979 are also each successively higher. A different way of looking at the same thing is to notice that, in the early 1950s, a 5 percent unemployment rate was unusually high and the exception, whereas by the 1970s, a 5 percent unemployment rate had become unusually low and the exception.

Figure 2.2
Unemployment

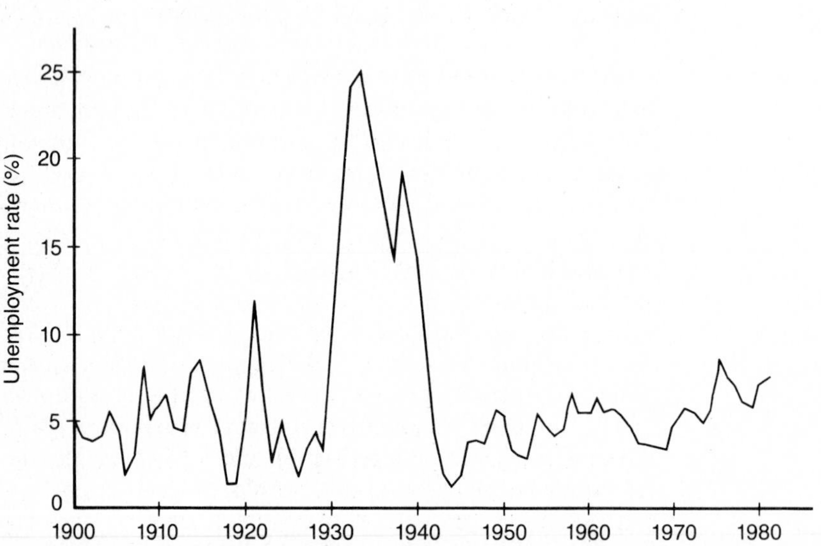

Unemployment is dominated by the Great Depression years of 1929 to 1933 and the period following that up to World War II. There has been a tendency for unemployment to drift upwards in the postwar years. A series of distinct short and irregular cycles are evident in the data. The fluctuations were more pronounced before than after World War II.
SOURCE: Appendix to this chapter.

The range of unemployment experienced in the United States since 1900 is truly enormous. The highest rates have already been identified as being associated with the Great Depression years, and the particular year in which unemployment reached its all-time peak was 1933, when a quarter of the labor force was out of work. The lowest unemployment rates have been below 2 percent, and these occurred during or immediately following the two major world wars (1918–1919 and 1943–1945). The only other year in which unemployment was below 2 percent was 1906. Just as inflation was unusually high in wartime years, so unemployment appears to have been unusually low in those same years.

As with inflation, it is noticeable that unemployment is more volatile in some periods than in others. Also, like inflation, the cycles in unemployment, although distinct, are far from precise and regular. The swings in unemployment are clearly much greater in the period before the Second World War than subsequently, although in the 1970s, the range of movement in unemployment had begun to rise.

Real Income

Figure 2.3 charts the course of real income in the United States since 1900. The particular measure used is the real Gross National Product (GNP). The precise meaning of this aggregate and the way in which it is measured will be described in Chapter 3. For now you may think of it as the total volume of goods and services (valued in constant 1972 dollars) that could be purchased with the aggregate of all incomes earned in the United States in a given year. Figure 2.3 examines the behavior of real income in three different ways. Frame (a) looks at the *level* of income, frame (b) at its *deviations from trend*, and frame (c) at its *growth rate.*

Concentrate first on the *level* of real income—frame (a). Interestingly, the path of real GNP shares a lot of features of the path of prices that we looked at in Figure 2.1. First, it is evident that there is a strong upward trend in real GNP. The overall trend growth rate since 1900 has been 3 percent per annum. Second, like inflation, it is evident that the growth trend after 1946 is higher than before that date. The inflation trends were *very* different between the two subperiods. The real GNP growth trends are not too dissimilar, although they are distinctly different. The growth trend up from 1900 to 1946 was 2.6 percent per annum, and after 1946 was 3.7 percent per annum.

Frame (b) shows the *deviations* of real GNP from the two trend lines shown in frame (a). Before going on to examine these deviations from trend, let us be sure that we understand the connection between frame (b) and frame (a). In frame (a), we are measuring the *level* of real income. In that frame we can see the deviation of the level from its trend as the distance between the trend line and the actual path of real income. That deviation from trend is what is measured in frame (b). Thus, the height of the line in frame (b) is the same thing as the distance between the line and the trend in frame (a).

As an aside, it is perhaps worth emphasizing that the trend lines in frame (a) and the deviations from trend in frame (b) have no independent existence in the real world. They are figments of our imagination. This is not to say that

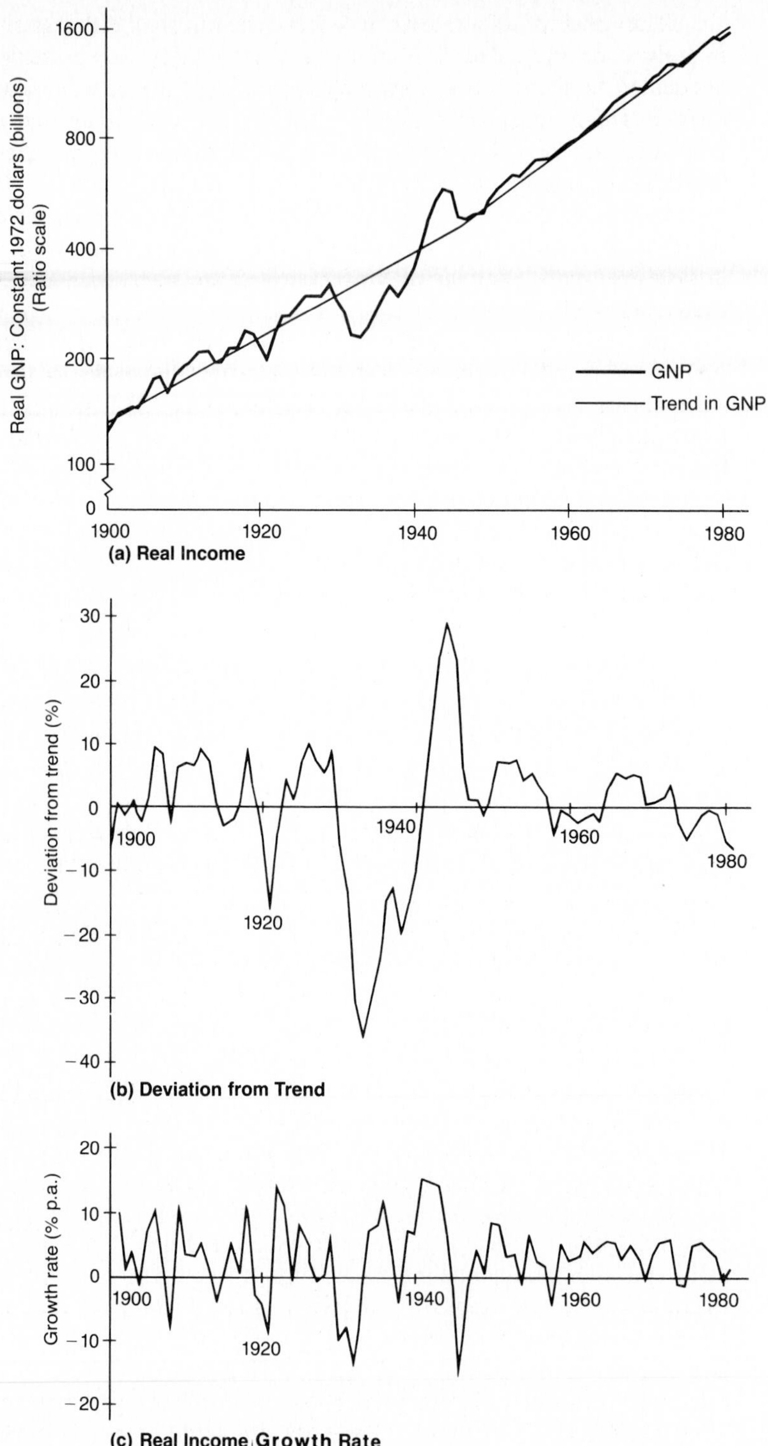
1600
800
400
200
100
0
Real GNP: Constant 1972 dollars (billions)
(Ratio scale)
GNP
Trend in GNP
1900
1920
1940
1960
1980
(a) Real Income
30
20
10
0
−10
−20
−30
−40
Deviation from trend (%)
1900
1920
1940
1960
1980
(b) Deviation from Trend
20
10
0
−10
−20
Growth rate (% p.a.)
1900
1920
1940
1960
1980
(c) Real Income Growth Rate

the decomposition of a time-series into a trend and into deviations from trend is useless. It does, however, say that the usefulness of an exercise such as this resides in the help that it gives us in simplifying the questions that we want to answer. To say that something has a trend, and a cycle around that trend, is just another way of describing the phenomenon itself. It is not the beginning of an explanation of the phenomenon.

Now that the exact meaning of deviations from trend are clear, let us go on to examine their behavior. Evidently the most massive swings in real GNP around its trend occurred in the Great Depression period (the 1930s), when real GNP was substantially below trend, and in the Second World War (the first half of the 1940s), when it was strongly above trend. Aside from these two periods, although real income has fluctuated around its trend, the fluctuations have been relatively mild. As with unemployment and also with inflation, the fluctuations seem to have been less severe in the 1950s and 1960s than at other times.

Frame (c), which shows the percentage change in real income—the *growth rate* of real income—makes this point even more vividly. You can see that the range of fluctuation in real income growth is much smaller in the period after 1950 than it was before that date. When we looked at inflation [Figure 2.1, frame (b)], we noticed a tendency for the rate of inflation itself to rise. No such pattern is visible in the case of real income growth. There is a distinctly higher trend after World War II than before it, but there is no ongoing tendency for the trend rate of growth of real income to change.

Rates of Interest

Figure 2.4 sets out the behavior of two rates of interest. One of them, labelled *long-term*, is the interest that major corporations have to pay on loans that might run for as long as twenty years. The other, labelled *short-term*, is the rate of interest paid by corporations on money borrowed for only three months.

The most noteworthy feature of the behavior of the long-term rate of interest is its lack of volatility as compared with the short-term rate. The long rate is much smoother in its behavior than the short rate.

Both rates of interest follow the same broad trend. They are fairly constant through the first twenty years of the century. Both rates then begin to fall, the short rate strongly so, the long rate slightly so, through the 1930s. They remain low through the World War II years of the 1940s, but then they both begin to rise. The rise is particularly strong in the final years of the 1970s.

Superimposed on these long-term trends are some quite marked cyclical

---

◀ Figure 2.3
Real GNP

Real GNP has grown persistently throughout this century, and the trend growth rate since 1946 has been significantly higher than before that date. The biggest swings of real GNP about its trend are in the Great Depression years (below trend) and in World War II (above trend). Shorter irregular cycles are evident in the data, with bigger fluctuations occurring before than after World War II.
SOURCE: Appendix to this chapter.

Figure 2.4
Interest Rates

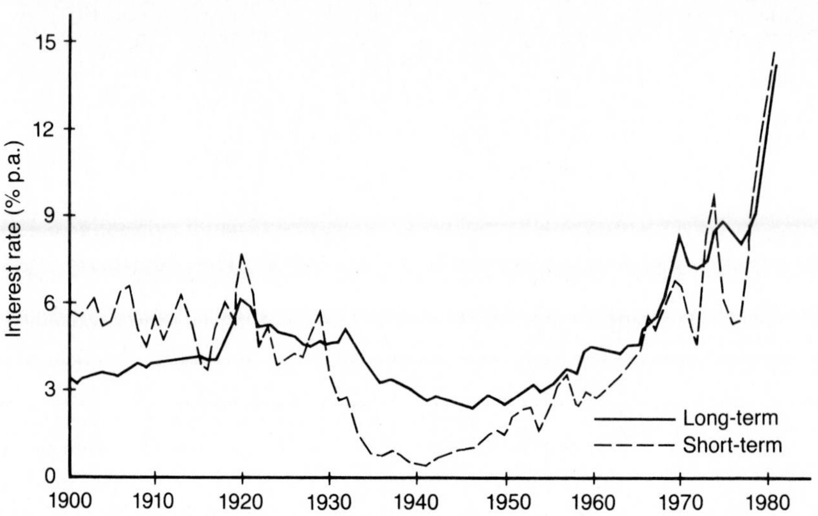

Long-term interest rates have behaved in a smooth fashion compared with the other macroeconomic variables. They were fairly stable until the 1930s, when they began to fall. From their low levels of the Second World War, they rose again at first gently, but then very strongly, in the 1970s. Short-term interest rates follow the same general pattern as long-term interest rates, but they display sharper cyclical fluctuations.
SOURCE: Appendix to this chapter.

movements that are particularly pronounced in the case of the short-term rate. These movements are perhaps most clearly visible in the 1970s, although they are also evident, especially in the short-term rate, in the first twenty years of the century.

Balance of Payments

Let us now turn our attention to the U.S. balance of payments. The precise way in which the balance of payments is defined and measured will not be dealt with until Chapter 40 of this book. For now, you may think of it as a measure of the net payments to, or receipts from, the rest of the world by residents of the United States in aggregate. If, in their economic relations with the rest of the world, the aggregate sales of goods and services plus borrowing of U.S. residents exceeds their purchases of goods and services plus lending, then the balance of payments of the United States would be in *surplus.* The reverse situation in which the sales of goods and services plus borrowing of U.S. residents falls short of their purchases of goods and services plus lending is referred to as a *deficit.*

Figure 2.5 shows the history of the U.S. balance of payments since 1900. During this 82-year period, there have been 50 years in which the balance of payments was in surplus and 32 in which a deficit was experienced. Most of those deficits occurred from 1958 to 1967, a period during which the U.S.

Figure 2.5
The Balance of Payments

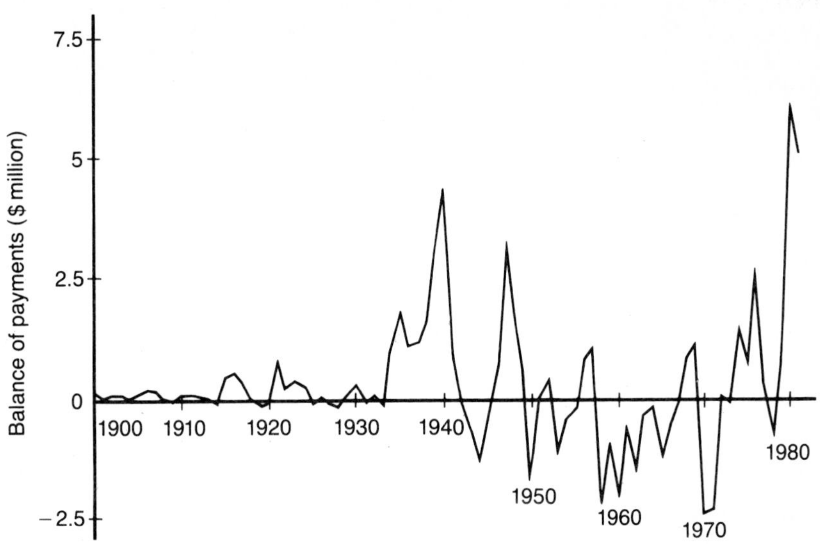

The U.S. balance of payments has, on the average, been in surplus. There was, however, a long run of years in the 1950s and 1960s when the balance of payments was generally in deficit. There is no discernible trend in the U.S. balance of payments.
SOURCE: Appendix to this chapter.

balance of payments was in deficit each and every year. This was a period during which other countries pegged the values of their currencies in terms of the U.S. dollar. Those countries were willing to hold U.S. dollars as their foreign exchange reserves and, at least at first, eagerly accepted U.S. deficits as a means whereby they could acquire their desired increased holdings of foreign exchange.

The biggest single surplus in the U.S. balance of payments occurred in 1980 (8.2 billion dollars) and the biggest deficit in 1970 (2.5 billion dollars). There is no clear tendency for the U.S. balance of payments to follow a trend. The balance fluctuates around zero, lying below zero somewhat less often than it is above zero.

Exchange Rate

Most Americans think less about foreign exchange rates than do residents of any other country. About the only time that a typical American thinks about foreign exchange rates is when he or she is taking a foreign trip. It then becomes necessary to buy some British pounds or French francs, or whatever the required currency might be, and a pleasant surprise or a nasty shock is received when the would-be traveller discovers how much or how little the U.S. dollar will buy in other countries.

Little though the average American thinks about foreign exchange rates, the U.S. dollar price of foreign exchange is an important variable, the movements of which macroeconomists seek to understand and explain. The United

Figure 2.6
The Foreign Exchange Rate

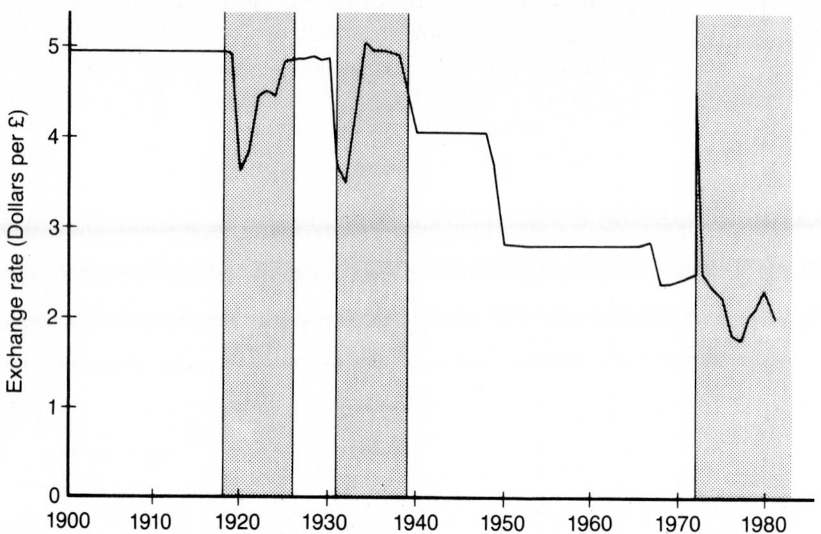

The foreign exchange value of the U.S. dollar in terms of the pound sterling shows that there has been a tendency for the U.S. dollar to rise in value against the pound (fewer dollars will buy one pound). Most of the history of the twentieth century is characterized by a fixed exchange rate between the two currencies. There were three periods when the exchange rates were not pegged (shaded). During these periods, considerable movements in the exchange rate occurred.
SOURCE: Appendix to this chapter.

States does business with practically every other country in the world, and in principal, we are interested in the U.S. dollar price of all other foreign currencies. For present purposes, it is possible to illustrate the U.S. dollar price of foreign currency by considering a single currency and one that, at least until the postwar period, was as important in international trade as the U.S. dollar—the pound sterling or British pound.

Figure 2.6 sets out the exchange rate between the U.S. dollar and the pound sterling since 1900. The value plotted on the vertical axis is the number of U.S. dollars required to buy one pound. The chart highlights two types of exchange rate regime—*fixed* and *flexible.* The unshaded periods are those in which exchange rates were fixed and the shaded periods are those in which the exchange rates were flexible. During the fixed exchange rate periods (1900 to 1918, 1926 to 1931, September 1939 to June 1972), the U.S. dollar value of the pound was determined by the Bank of England, the British central bank. During the flexible exchange rate periods, that value was determined in the marketplace in much the same way that the value of stocks and shares or the prices of soya beans and peanuts are determined. As the chart makes clear, in the period up to the beginning of World War II (1939), although there were times when the U.S. dollar price of a pound fell during the flexible exchange rate periods, there was always a tendency for the exchange rate to return to a fairly steady level in the $4.88 range. During World War II, the pound sterling was pegged at $4.00, but it was devalued to $2.80 in September 1949. It was maintained at that level until November 18, 1967, when it was further devalued to $2.40. Thus, the U.S. dollar has become progressively more valuable in terms of pounds in the postwar period. During the period of floating exchange rates since June 23, 1972, the dollar became even more valuable for a time, but then after 1977, it lost some ground. In the first two years of the present decade, it has regained some of that lost ground.

B. Decade Summaries

In order to present U.S. macroeconomic history in a slightly more compact manner, this section focuses on the decade averages of the key variables since 1900. These are set out in Table 2.1. Also, for comparison purposes, the figures for 1980 and 1981, as well as the long-term average from 1900 to 1981, are presented in the last three rows of that table.

As you can see from the table, the first decade of this century was one of remarkable macroeconomic stability. Inflation was less than 2 percent per annum on the average, unemployment was lower than in any other decade, output growth was very strong (4.1 percent per annum on the average), interest rates were modest (3.5 percent for long-term rates and 5.6 percent for short-term rates), the balance of payments was in a slight average surplus, and the exchange rate between the dollar and the pound sterling was steady.

The second decade of this century saw the world engulfed in the turmoil of war. World War I occurred between 1914 and 1918. During that period, inflation increased sharply, so that the decade average inflation rate was almost 6 percent per annum. Unemployment also increased slightly in this decade, and output growth sagged to a mere 1.5 percent per annum. Interest

TABLE 2.1
The Decade Averages

PERIOD	INFLATION percent per annum	UNEMPLOYMENT percent	REAL INCOME		INTEREST RATES		BALANCE OF PAYMENTS $ million	FOREIGN EXCHANGE RATE $ per £
			Growth Rate percent per annum	Deviation from Trend percent	Long-Term percent per annum	Short-Term percent per annum		
1900s	1.2	4.4	4.1	+1.5	3.5	5.6	+74	4.87
1910s	5.9	5.0	1.5	+4.2	4.1	5.2	+135	4.83
1920s	−1.8	4.7	2.8	+2.3	4.6	5.1	+129	4.52
1930s	−1.7	18.4	1.9	−20.5	3.7	1.6	+1080	4.55
1940s	5.4	5.2	4.4	+9.1	2.7	0.9	+822	4.00
1950s	2.1	4.5	3.2	+3.5	3.3	2.6	−452	2.80
1960s	2.7	4.8	3.9	+1.7	5.0	4.6	−464	2.72
1970s	7.5	6.2	3.1	−0.7	8.2	7.2	+67	2.20
1980	12.7	7.1	−0.2	−5.2	11.9	12.3	+8155	2.33
1981	9.9	7.6	2.0	−6.9	14.2	14.8	+5175	2.03
Average 1900–1981	2.9	6.7	3.1[b]	0[a]	4.6	4.3	+332	3.78

Notes: [a]Defined to be zero by the construction of the series.
[b]1901 to 1981.
SOURCES: See appendix to this chapter.

rates, the balance of payments, and the exchange rate all remained fairly steady.

The 1920s was a decade of falling prices. The average annual inflation rate was close to −2 percent. Unemployment fell slightly compared with the previous decade, and output growth increased. Interest rates, the balance of payments, and the exchange rate all remained fairly steady.

The 1930s was the decade of the Great Depression. It was, in most respects a decade of macroeconomic disaster. Prices continued to fall, although not quite as sharply as they had done on the average in the 1920s. Unemployment climbed to an average of 18.4 percent, and real income (real GNP) averaged more than 20 percent below its trend value. The overall growth rate for the 1930s was 1.9 percent per annum, not quite the worst decade of the century but the second worst. Long-term and short-term interest rates (more so the latter) began to fall, and the U.S. balance of payments moved into a massive surplus of more than one billion dollars. The exchange rate between the U.S. dollar and the pound again remained fairly steady.

The 1940s was another decade of war. World War II, which began in Europe in 1939, and which directly involved the United States from 1942, was the dominant influence on U.S. macroeconomic developments in this period. As in World War I, inflation accelerated to an average of more than 5 percent. Unemployment fell dramatically from the Great Depression heights. Output growth was stronger than in any other decade, and on the average, real GNP was close to 10 percent above its trend level. Interest rates continued to decline, and the balance of payments stayed in a massive surplus position. The U.S. dollar became substantially more valuable against the pound sterling during the 1940s.

The decade of the 1950s looks a lot like the opening decade of the century. It was a time of macroeconomic calm and progress. Inflation was moderate (around 2 percent per annum), unemployment was low (4.5 percent), and output growth was close to its long-term average (a little over 3 percent per annum). Interest rates moved up slightly, but with long-term rates at 3.3 percent and short-term rates at 2.6 percent, this was barely noticeable. It was in the 1950s that the U.S. balance of payments, for the first time in the century, moved into a persistent deficit situation. The exchange rate at this time was pegged and held steady at 2.80 dollars per pound.

The 1960s, on the average, look very much like the 1950s. Inflation remained less than 3 percent, although it did move up somewhat from the 1950s levels of close to 2 percent. Unemployment drifted up slightly, but output growth was up at close to 4 percent. Interest rates also began to rise with long-term rates averaging 5 percent and short-term rates not much below that. This was the second straight decade in a row that the U.S. balance of payments had been in deficit. Toward the end of the decade the pound sterling was devalued slightly against the U.S. dollar.

The 1970s saw an end of the macroeconomic calm and stability of the 1950s and 1960s. Inflation exploded to average around 7 percent, and unemployment also moved up sharply. Output growth sagged slightly, interest rates increased fairly dramatically, and the U.S. balance of payments once again moved into a slight surplus.

The overall 82-year averages provide an even more succinct summary statement of U.S. macroeconomic history in this century. On the average, inflation has been a little under 3 percent, unemployment has averaged close to 7 percent, real GNP has grown at 3 percent, interest rates have averaged around 4.5 percent, and the balance of payments has, on the average, been in a modest surplus.

It is instructive to reexamine the early 1980s against the backdrop of this long-term historical record. You can see, at the present time, although having fallen within the last year, inflation is substantially above its long-term historical average and unemployment even more so. Real income growth is below trend, and interest rates are very much above their long-term average levels. The balance of payments has improved and is in surplus, although the foreign exchange value of the dollar has fluctuated markedly.

This description of the economic condition of the United States at the beginning of the 1980s gives urgency to the task of improving our understanding of the functioning of the economy as a whole and certainly attests to the importance of the study of macroeconomics.

C. Questions

You have now reviewed the behavior of the key macroeconomic variables in the United States and have looked at the main macroeconomic characteristics of each decade in this century. Many questions will be occurring to you, as noted below:

On inflation—Why are there some periods when the inflation rate is very high, others when it is moderate, and yet others when prices are falling? Can the ups and downs in inflation be controlled and perhaps eliminated, or do we have to live with them? What has caused the apparent upward trend in U.S. inflation? Is there anything that can be done to stop it?

We do not know the full answers to any of these questions. We know substantial parts of the answers to all of them, however, and explaining what we do know constitutes one of the prime tasks of this book.

On unemployment—Why was there such an enormous and prolonged burst of unemployment during the 1930s and why is unemployment so high today? You will discover that important though this question is, a satisfactory answer still eludes us. Part IV of this book deals with the most comprehensive and systematic attempt to answer this question and explains why we are still searching for a fully satisfactory answer. Other questions are: Why have there been such marked movements in the unemployment rate, particularly the rather clearly defined short cycles that we have seen in the data? Also, why does there appear to have been a persistent upward trend in the unemployment rate since the end of World War II? Finally, can unemployment be controlled so that the fluctuations in its rate can be removed? These questions will also occupy the center of our attention in what follows.

On output—Why does real income grow in a cyclical but erratic fashion? Why has real income deviated from trend, severely negatively so in the 1930s and strongly positively in the 1940s? Why were the fluctuations in real GNP around its trend value more pronounced before than after the Second World War? What can be done to eradicate the fluctuations in real income?

On interest rates—Why are long-term interest rate movements relatively smooth? Why did interest rates gradually fall from the beginning of the century into the 1940s, and then begin to rise again? Why did interest rates move to all-time high levels in the last few years? Why do short-term interest rates fluctuate more markedly than long-term rates?

On the balance of payments and the exchange rate—Why has the U.S. balance of payments usually been in surplus? Why did a deficit emerge in the 1950s and 1960s? What can the U.S. government do to influence the balance of payments? Why has the foreign exchange value of the U.S. dollar gradually increased over this century? How is it possible for the foreign exchange value of the dollar to be fixed at certain times and to be freely fluctuating at others?

All of these questions concerning the U.S. external macroeconomic relations will be examined in the final part of this book.

It would not be sensible or useful to attempt a more detailed mapping out of the specific parts of the book that deal with each of these questions. Many of the questions turn out to be intimately related to each other in a way that you will find hard to appreciate if you have little or no knowledge of macroeconomics, but that will seem obvious and natural once you have made some progress with your study of the subject. To help you see some of the connections between the questions, after explaining in more detail how the macroeconomic variables that we have just examined are defined, observed, and measured (but before embarking on the task of *explanation* of macroeconomic phenomena), Chapter 6 will explore some of the connections among the variables by defining and describing the phenomenon known as the *business cycle*. In the final section of that chapter you will have a further opportunity to return to the features of the variables described here and to gain some further insights into the way that they behave.

Summary

A. Evolution of Macroeconomic Variables

The main feature of *inflation* has been a distinctly rising trend. There have also been clear but irregular cycles. Inflation was more erratic in the years before the Second World War and in the late 1970s than at other times. There has been a tendency for inflation rates to be higher during war years than in peacetime, although the period since the middle 1970s is an important exception to this. The greatest deflation (falling prices) occurred during the Great Depression years of 1929–1933.

Unemployment was at its worst during the Great Depression and in the years following, up to the beginning of the Second World War. There has been a distinct tendency for unemployment to rise in the postwar years. There are clear though irregular cycles in the rate of unemployment, and like inflation, these cycles are more pronounced in the years before the Second World War.

Real income growth has averaged just over 3 percent per annum in the period since 1900, although the trend growth rate after 1946 was some 1 percent per annum greater than it had been before that date. There is considerable random fluctuation in the growth rate of real income. The highest growth rates were achieved during the Second World War and the lowest during the Great Depression period.

Interest rates remained remarkably steady until the Great Depression years but then fell and remained low throughout the Second World War. In the period since then, interest rates have increased and in the most recent years, dramatically so. Long-term interest rates fluctuate much less than short-term rates. Distinct cycles are visible in the short-term rates, although only slightly so in the long-term rates.

The balance of payments has, on the average, been in surplus, although the 1950s and 1960s were years of sustained deficit.

The foreign exchange rate, measured as the number of U.S. dollars required to buy one pound sterling, shows that the U.S. dollar has tended to increase in value over the long run. During the most recent period of floating exchange rates, there have been sizable fluctuations in the foreign exchange values of the U.S. dollar.

B. Decade Summaries

The averages of the macroeconomic variables in each decade of this century are set out in Table 2.1 and should be studied carefully. The first decade was one of macroeconomic stability with low inflation, low unemployment, high real income growth, moderate interest rates, and a modest balance of payments surplus. The decade of the teens was dominated by World War I and experienced a strong burst of inflation. The 1920s were dominated by falling prices, although in all other respects, this was a fairly average period. The Great Depression was the dominant influence on the 1930s, with output falling below trend and unemployment reaching unprecedented heights. The balance of payments moved into a massive surplus during this decade. The 1940s were dominated by World War II and a return of strong inflation. The 1950s and 1960s were decades of macroeconomic stability, much like the first decade of the century. Inflation was moderate, unemployment low, real income growth strong, and interest rates steady. Through these two decades, the United States had a balance of payments deficit. The 1970s was a decade of macroeconomic problems in most dimensions: Inflation, unemployment, and interest rates all rose; output growth fell; and foreign exchange rates fluctuated markedly. As the 1980s opened, all these problems remained.

C. Questions

Why is there such variation in our inflation experience? Can we control inflation?

Why was unemployment so high and for so long in the 1930s and why is unemployment so high today?

Why does real income grow in a cyclical but erratic fashion?

Why are long-term interest rate movements relatively smooth? Why do short-term interest rates fluctuate more markedly than long-term rates?

Why has the U.S. balance of payments usually been in surplus? Why has the foreign exchange value of the U.S. dollar increased over this century?

Review Questions

1. Briefly describe the history of each of the following macroeconomic variables in the United States since 1945:

(a) Inflation.
(b) Unemployment.
(c) Real income.
(d) Interest rates.
(e) Balance of payments.
(f) Exchange rate.

2. Briefly describe the history of each of the above macroeconomic variables in the United States in the "interwar years"—1920 to 1940.

3. Using later editions of the sources given at the foot of the table in the appendix to this chapter, update the table for each of the variables. Describe how each of these variables has evolved so far in the 1980s.

4. In which decade was inflation the major macroeconomic problem in the United States? Was it associated with any other major macroeconomic problems?

5. What were the major macroeconomic problems of the United States in the 1930s?

6. In which decade since 1900 has the United States suffered the highest average unemployment rate? Compare this average with that so far in the 1980s.

7. In which decade of U.S. history since 1900 has the average long-term interest rate been highest? Compare this with the average long-term interest rate so far for the 1980s.

8. Has the U.S. balance of payments, on the average, been in deficit in any decade since 1900? Would you deduce from this that the United States has had balance of payments problems?

9. Looking at decade averages of the history of the exchange rate and the balance of payments, does there appear to be a relationship between them? If so, what is that relationship?

10. What are the major economic problems of the United States in the 1980s (thus far)?

11. Assume that you are employed as an economic speech writer by President Reagan. Write a short speech that argues as strongly as possible that U.S. macroeconomic performance so far in the 1980s compares favorably with that of earlier decades and is a credit to the economic management of the Reagan administration.

12. Assume that you are employed as an economic speech writer by Senator Ted Kennedy. Write a short speech that argues as strongly as possible that U.S. macroeconomic performance so far in the 1980s compares unfavorably with that of earlier decades and discredits the Reagan administration's economic management.

Appendix to Chapter 2

U.S. Macroeconomic Variables 1900–1981

YEAR	INFLATION			UNEMPLOYMENT percent	REAL INCOME		INTEREST RATES		BALANCE OF PAYMENTS $ million	FOREIGN EXCHANGE RATE $ per £
	CPI	GNP Deflator	Personal Consumption Deflator		Growth Rate percent per annum	Deviations from Trend percent	Long-Term	Short-Term		
	percent per annum						percent per annum			
1900	—	—	—	5.0	—	−7.8	3.30	5.71	91	4.87
1901	1.2	−0.8	−0.6	4.0	11.0	0.5	3.25	5.40	61	4.88
1902	1.2	3.2	3.8	3.7	0.9	−1.2	3.30	5.81	71	4.88
1903	2.3	1.2	0.6	3.9	4.8	1.0	3.45	6.16	71	4.87
1904	1.1	1.2	1.9	5.4	−1.2	−2.8	3.60	5.14	25	4.87
1905	−1.1	2.3	1.7	4.3	7.2	1.7	3.50	5.18	71	4.87
1906	2.2	2.4	1.1	1.7	10.9	10.0	3.55	6.25	171	4.86
1907	4.3	4.0	4.5	2.8	1.6	9.0	3.80	6.66	154	4.87
1908	−2.2	−0.7	0.5	8.0	−8.6	−2.3	3.95	5.00	44	4.87
1909	−1.1	3.4	2.8	5.1	11.5	6.6	3.77	4.67	−18	4.88
1910	4.3	2.6	3.2	5.9	2.8	6.7	3.80	5.72	71	4.87
1911	0.0	−0.3	−1.2	6.7	2.6	6.6	3.90	4.75	90	4.87
1912	2.1	3.8	4.4	4.6	5.5	9.5	3.90	5.41	81	4.87
1913	2.0	0.7	0.5	4.3	0.9	7.8	4.00	6.20	25	4.87
1914	1.0	1.0	1.4	7.9	−4.5	0.6	4.10	5.47	−100	4.88
1915	1.1	3.2	3.1	8.5	−0.9	−2.9	4.15	4.01	499	4.88
1916	7.1	12.0	11.5	5.1	7.6	2.1	4.05	3.84	531	4.88
1917	16.2	20.9	21.6	4.6	0.6	0.1	4.05	5.07	312	4.88
1918	15.9	15.3	14.0	1.4	11.6	9.0	4.75	6.02	5	4.88
1919	14.0	2.5	0.6	1.4	−3.6	2.8	5.49	5.37	−166	4.43
1920	14.6	13.0	11.4	5.2	−4.5	−4.3	6.12	7.50	−68	3.66
1921	−11.4	−16.0	−13.5	11.7	−9.1	−16.1	5.97	6.62	735	3.85
1922	−6.5	−5.7	−5.1	6.7	14.7	−4.0	5.10	4.52	269	4.43
1923	1.7	2.7	1.9	2.4	11.4	4.7	5.12	5.07	315	4.57
1924	0.3	−1.2	−1.2	5.0	−0.2	1.9	5.00	3.98	256	4.42
1925	2.5	1.8	2.3	3.2	8.0	7.3	4.88	4.02	−100	4.83
1926	0.8	0.4	0.4	1.8	5.8	10.4	4.73	4.34	93	4.86
1927	−1.8	−2.4	−2.8	3.3	−0.1	7.6	4.57	4.11	−113	4.86
1928	−1.3	0.8	0.9	4.2	0.6	5.6	4.55	4.85	−238	4.87
1929	0.0	0.3	−0.1	3.2	6.5	9.7	4.73	5.85	143	4.86
1930	−2.5	−2.9	−2.5	8.9	−10.0	−3.0	4.55	3.59	310	4.86
1931	−9.4	−9.5	−10.5	16.3	−8.1	−13.6	4.58	2.60	−133	3.69
1932	−10.7	−11.7	−12.1	24.1	−14.9	−31.1	5.01	2.73	53	3.50
1933	−5.4	−2.1	−3.7	25.2	−2.2	−36.0	4.49	1.73	−131	4.22
1934	3.3	8.3	7.5	22.0	7.4	−31.3	4.00	1.02	1266	5.04
1935	2.5	2.1	2.4	20.3	8.4	−25.5	3.60	.76	1822	4.90
1936	1.0	0.4	1.3	17.0	12.8	−15.4	3.24	.75	1272	4.97
1937	3.5	4.5	3.6	14.3	4.9	−13.2	3.26	.94	1364	4.94
1938	−1.8	−2.2	−1.6	19.1	−4.4	−20.2	3.19	.81	1799	4.89
1939	−1.4	−0.8	−0.7	17.2	7.5	−15.4	3.01	.59	3174	4.46

U.S Macroeconomic Variables 1900–1981 (continued)

YEAR	INFLATION			UNEMPLOYMENT percent	REAL INCOME		INTEREST RATES		BALANCE OF PAYMENTS $ million	FOREIGN EXCHANGE RATE $ per £
	CPI	GNP Deflator	Personal Consumption Deflator		Growth Rate	Deviations from Trend	Long-Term	Short-Term		
	percent per annum				percent per annum	percent	percent per annum			
1940	1.0	2.2	1.3	14.6	7.3	−10.7	2.84	.56	4243	4.03
1941	4.9	7.2	7.2	9.9	15.2	1.8	2.77	.53	719	4.03
1942	10.1	9.4	10.0	4.7	14.2	13.4	2.83	.66	−23	4.03
1943	6.0	5.2	8.9	1.9	14.1	24.9	2.73	.69	−757	4.03
1944	1.7	2.4	5.6	1.2	6.8	29.1	2.72	.73	−1350	4.03
1945	2.3	2.4	3.9	1.9	−1.5	24.9	2.62	.75	−548	4.03
1946	8.2	14.6	8.1	3.9	−15.8	6.4	2.53	.81	623	4.03
1947	13.4	12.2	10.1	3.9	−1.7	1.1	2.61	1.03	3315	4.03
1948	7.5	6.7	5.7	3.8	4.1	1.4	2.82	1.44	1736	4.03
1949	−1.0	−0.9	−0.4	5.9	0.5	−1.7	2.66	1.49	266	3.68
1950	1.0	2.0	2.0	5.3	8.3	2.9	2.62	1.45	−1758	2.80
1951	7.6	6.4	6.3	3.3	8.0	7.3	2.86	2.16	33	2.80
1952	2.2	1.4	2.3	3.0	3.6	7.2	2.96	2.33	415	2.79
1953	0.8	1.5	1.9	2.9	3.7	7.3	3.20	2.52	−1256	2.81
1954	0.5	1.2	0.8	5.5	−1.2	2.4	2.90	1.58	−480	2.81
1955	−0.4	2.1	1.1	4.4	6.5	5.2	3.06	2.18	−182	2.79
1956	1.5	3.2	1.8	4.1	2.1	3.7	3.36	3.31	869	2.80
1957	3.5	3.4	3.3	4.3	1.8	1.8	3.89	3.81	1165	2.79
1958	2.7	1.7	2.0	6.8	−0.4	−2.3	3.79	2.46	−2292	2.81
1959	0.8	2.3	2.0	5.5	5.8	−0.1	4.38	3.97	−1035	2.81
1960	1.6	1.6	1.8	5.5	2.1	−1.6	4.41	3.85	−2145	2.81
1961	1.0	0.9	1.0	6.7	2.6	−2.7	4.35	2.97	−607	2.80
1962	1.1	1.8	1.5	5.5	5.6	−0.8	4.33	3.26	−1535	2.81
1963	1.2	1.5	1.5	5.7	3.9	−0.5	4.26	3.55	−378	2.80
1964	1.3	1.5	1.5	5.2	5.1	1.0	4.40	3.97	−171	2.79
1965	1.7	2.2	1.7	4.5	5.9	3.2	4.49	4.38	−1225	2.80
1966	2.8	3.2	2.8	3.8	5.8	5.3	5.13	5.55	−570	2.79
1967	2.8	3.0	2.5	3.8	2.7	4.3	5.51	5.10	−53	2.83
1968	4.1	4.3	3.9	3.6	4.5	5.2	6.18	5.90	870	2.39
1969	5.2	5.0	4.4	3.5	2.7	4.3	7.03	7.83	1179	2.39
1970	5.8	5.2	4.5	4.9	−0.2	0.4	8.04	7.72	−2481	2.40
1971	4.2	4.9	4.2	5.9	3.3	0.1	7.39	5.11	−2349	2.44
1972	3.2	4.1	3.6	5.6	5.5	1.9	7.21	4.69	4	2.50
1973	6.0	5.5	5.5	4.9	5.7	3.9	7.44	8.15	−158	2.45
1974	10.4	8.4	9.6	5.6	−0.6	−0.3	8.57	9.87	1467	2.34
1975	8.7	8.9	7.4	8.5	−1.1	−5.1	8.83	6.33	849	2.22
1976	5.6	5.1	5.0	7.7	5.2	−3.5	8.43	5.35	2558	1.81
1977	6.3	5.7	5.8	7.0	5.3	−1.8	8.02	5.60	375	1.75
1978	7.4	7.1	6.7	6.0	4.6	−0.9	8.73	7.99	−732	1.92
1979	10.7	8.1	8.5	5.8	3.2	−1.4	9.63	10.91	1133	2.12
1980	12.7	8.6	9.7	7.1	−0.2	−5.2	11.94	12.29	8155	2.33
1981	9.9	8.8	7.9	7.6	2.0	−6.9	14.17	14.76	5175	2.03

◀

SOURCES: The main sources are listed below. Abbreviations for these titles are used in the detailed sources following this list.

Long-Term Economic Growth, 1860–1965 (Washington, D.C.: U.S. Department of Commerce, October 1966). (*LTEG*)

The National Income and Product Accounts of the United States, 1929–1976 Statistical Tables, a supplement to the *Survey of Current Business* (Washington, D.C.: U.S. Department of Commerce, September 1981). (*NIPA1*)

National Income and Product Accounts, 1976–1979: A Special Supplement to the Survey of Current Business (Washington, D.C.: U.S. Department of Commerce, July 1981). (*NIPA2*)

Survey of Current Business, 62, no. 4. (Washington, D.C.: U.S. Department of Commerce, April 1982). (*SCB*)

Economic Report of the President, 1980 (Washington, D.C.: U.S. Government Printing Office, 1980). (*ERP*)

Historical Statistics of the United States: Colonial Times to 1970 (Washington, D.C.: U.S. Department of Commerce, 1976). (*HS*)

Banking and Monetary Statistics 1914–1941 (Washington, D.C.: Board of Governors of the Federal Reserve Board, August 1976). (*BMS*)

1. Inflation:
   - (a) CPI:
     - 1900–1913 Series B70, *LTEG*, pp. 202–3.
     - 1913–1939 CPI all items, Series B71, *LTEG*, pp. 202–3.
     - 1939–1979 CPI all items, *ERP*, p. 289
     - 1980–1981 CPI all items, all urban consumers, *SCB*, S-6.
   - (b) PCE deflator:
     - 1900–1930 Series B65, B66, *LTEG*, pp. 200–201.
     - 1930–1976 Line 1, Table 7.12, *NIPA1*, pp. 345–49, 351.
     - 1977–1979 Line 1, Table 7.12, *NIPA2*, p. 67.
     - 1980–1981 Implicit price deflator, Tables 7.1–7.2, *SCB*, p. 10.
   - (c) GNP deflator:
     - 1900–1929 Series B62, *LTEG*, pp. 200–201.
     - 1929–1976 Line 1, Table 7, *NIPA1*, pp. 318–19.
     - 1977–1979 Line 1, Table 7, *NIPA2*, p. 62.
     - 1980–1981 Implicit price deflator, Tables 7.1–7.2, *SCB*, p. 10.

   The figures in the table are percentage changes in the index over the previous year.
2. Unemployment:
   - 1900–1939 Series B1, *LTEG*, pp. 190–91.
   - 1940–1947 Series B2, *LTEG*, pp. 190–91.
   - 1948–1980 All workers, *ERP*, p. 267.
   - 1981 All civilian workers, *SCB*, S-11.
3. Real Income:

   GNP in constant dollars, real GNP:
   - 1900–1909 Series A1, *LTEG*, pp. 166–67.
   - 1909–1929 Series A2, *LTEG*, pp. 166–67.
   - 1929–1976 Line 1, Table 1.2, *NIPA1*, pp. 6–7.
   - 1977–1979 Line 1, Table 1.2, *NIPA2*, p. 2.
   - 1980–1981 *SCB*, p. 3.

   - (a) Growth rate is the percentage change in real GNP over the previous year.
   - (b) The deviation from trend is the percentage deviation of real GNP from two logarithmic trends fitted to real GNP 1900–1946 and 1947–1981. The 1900–1946 trend line rises at 2.6 percent per annum, and the 1947–1981 trend line rises at 3.5 percent per annum. The two trend lines were constrained to cut in 1946.
4. Interest Rates:
   - (a) Long-term:
     - 1900–1919: 30-year corporate bond yield, Series B75, *LTEG*, pp. 202–3.
     - 1919–1981: Market rate of interest on corporate Aaa bonds (Moody's) for 1919–1941, *BMS*, p. 464; for 1941–1980, *ERP*, p. 308; and for 1981, *SCB*, S-18.
   - (b) Short-term:
     - 1900–1938: Commercial paper rate, Series B80, *LTEG*, pp. 204–5.
     - 1939–1981: Prime commercial paper 4–6 months, *ERP*, p. 308, and *SCB*, S-15.
5. Balance of Payments: Net transactions in U.S. official reserve asset: (+ is a balance of payments surplus)
   - 1900–1945: Series U-24, *HS*, pp. 866–67.
   - 1946–1979: *ERP*, p. 345.
   - 1980–1981: *SCB*, S-1.
6. Foreign Exchange Rate: Annual average exchange rate between the pound sterling and the U.S. dollar, expressed as the number of U.S. dollars per pound.
   - 1900–1964: *British Economy Key Statistics*, 1900–1964, published by the London and Cambridge Economic Service by the Times Publishing Company Ltd., Table F*, p. 15.
   - 1965–1975: *International Financial Statistics*, May 1976, pp. 380–81.
   - 1975–1981: *International Financial Statistics*, May 1982, p. 408.

3

Aggregate Income Accounting

Aggregate income accounting provides one of the major sources of data that are needed in order to do macroeconomic analysis. The other major data needs are met by aggregate balance sheet accounting—which provides a statement of what people in the economy owe and own—and the measurement of inflation and unemployment. This chapter deals with aggregate income accounting, Chapter 4 with aggregate balance sheet accounting, and Chapter 5 with the measurement of inflation and unemployment. As a preliminary to examining aggregate income and balance sheet accounts, this chapter also deals with the distinction between flows and stocks.

You have six specific tasks in this chapter; these are to:

(a) Understand the distinction between flows and stocks.
(b) Know the definitions of: output (or product), income, and expenditure; domestic and national; gross and net; market price and factor cost; nominal and real.
(c) Understand the concepts of aggregate output (or product), income, and expenditure.
(d) Know how aggregate income is measured, using: the expenditure approach, the factor incomes approach, and the output approach.
(e) Know how aggregate income in constant dollars (real) is measured.
(f) Know how to read the national income accounts of the United States.

A. Flows and Stocks

A macroeconomic variable that measures a *flow* measures a rate per unit of time. In contrast, a *stock* is a value at a point in time. Examples of flows are income and expenditures. The dimension of these variables is dollars per unit of time—for example, dollars per month or dollars per year. Examples of stocks are: money in the bank, the value of a car or a house, the value of the airplanes owned by United Airlines, and the value of the telephone lines and exchange switching equipment owned by Bell Telephone. All these variables are measured in dollars on a given day.

Although such items as cars, houses, and physical plant and equipment are stocks, the purchase of additional equipment and the physical wearing out of plant and equipment are flows. Stocks of physical plant and equipment are called *capital.* Additions to capital are called *investment.* The reduction in the value of equipment as a result of wear and tear and/or the passage of time is known as *depreciation.*

Let us illustrate this with something concrete. Imagine that on the 1st of June 1981, you had a 1975 car that had a current market value of $2000. In the year from the 1st of June 1981 to the 1st of June 1982, the market value of the car falls to $1600. The value of the car on the 1st of June each year is a stock. That stock has fallen from $2000 in 1981 to $1600 in 1982. The depreciation (the loss in the value of the car) is a flow. That flow is $400 per year (or, equivalently, $33.63 per month). If, in May 1982, you sold your 1975 car and replaced it with a 1978 car, the value of which is $3000, your capital stock in June of 1982 would, of course, be the same $3000. In that case you would have *invested* a total of $1400. (The $1400 is the difference between the $3000 that your newer car is worth and the $1600 that your old car would have been worth, had you kept it.) The change in your capital stock from June 1981 to June 1982 is, of course, not $1400 but $1000. This is made up of an investment in a new car known as a *gross* investment of $1400, minus the depreciation of the old car of $400. The difference between your gross investment and the depreciation of your capital is known as the *net* investment.

A useful analogy to illustrate the distinction between flows and stocks is a physical one involving a bathtub, a faucet, and a drain. Suppose a bathtub has some water in it, the faucet is turned on, and there is no plug in the drain, so that water is flowing into the bathtub and flowing out of it. The water in the tub is a stock, and the water entering the tub through the faucet and the water leaving the tub through the drain are flows. If the flow through the faucet is greater than the flow through the drain, the stock will be rising. If, conversely, the flow through the drain is greater than the flow through the faucet, the stock will be falling. In this example there are two flows and one stock, and the stock is determined by the flows. Suppose that the rate of outflow through the drain is a constant that cannot be controlled. The stock can be increased by opening the faucet so that the inflow exceeds the outflow, and the stock can be decreased by closing the faucet so that the outflow exceeds the inflow.

In terms of the capital stock, investment, and depreciation concepts illustrated earlier with reference to transactions in used cars, you can think of the water in the bathtub as the capital stock, the outflow through the drain as depreciation, and the inflow through the faucet as gross investment. The difference between the outflow and inflow is net investment, which may, of course, be positive (if the water level is rising) or negative (if the water level is falling).

Suppose that we introduce a human element into the story. Imagine that someone wants to maintain the water level in the tub at a particular depth. That is, they have a desired stock of water. If the actual stock exceeds the desired stock, the corrective action would be to slow down the rate of inflow. If the actual stock was less than the desired stock, the corrective action would be to speed up the rate of inflow. You can see that in this extended story, the stock determines the flow in the sense that individual actions that adjust the flow are triggered by the level of the stock. In the economic analysis that you will be doing shortly, flows (such as national income and expenditure) will be determined by stocks (such as the supply of money).

The remaining tasks in this and the next chapter are a necessary prelude to conducting such economic analyses. The rest of this chapter explains how the national income and expenditure flows are measured, and Chapter 4 deals with the measurement of the stocks of assets and liabilities in the economy. Let us begin by reviewing some of the definitions of the main aggregate income and expenditure flows.

B. Some Frequently Used Terms

You have almost certainly encountered in newspapers or on television current affairs programs, terms like *gross domestic product* or *gross national income*, or, perhaps, *gross national product in constant dollars.* This section will enable you to know what these and a few other important terms mean. Following are five groups of words among which you need to be able to distinguish.

Output (or Product), Income, and Expenditure

Three concepts of aggregate economic activity are commonly used. These are dealt with in some detail in the next section. For now, all that you need to know are the definitions of these terms. *Output* (or *product*) means the value of the output of the economy. *Income* means the sum of the incomes of all the factors of production (labor, capital, and land) employed in the economy. *Expenditure* means the sum of all the expenditures in the economy on final goods and services. (*Note*: See below for the distinction between expenditure on *final* goods and services and expenditure on *intermediate* goods and services.)

Domestic and National

In the preceding paragraph, the term *the economy* is used as if it is unambiguous. There is ambiguity, however, as to what is meant by "the economy." What is the "U.S. economy"? There are two possible answers. One involves the *domestic* economy, which is all economic activity taking place in the geographical domain of the United States. The other involves the *national* economy, which is all economic activity of U.S. residents wherever in the world that activity happens to be performed.

Thus, the concept of *domestic* output (or product), income, and expenditure refers to the aggregate of output, income, and expenditure in the geographical domain of the United States. And the concept of *national* output (or product), income, and expenditure refers to the output produced by, the income earned by, or the expenditure made on goods produced by U.S. residents, no matter where in the world the economic activity takes place.

The difference between these two aggregates is known as "net property income from (or paid) abroad." This amount is not large for most countries and is very small for the United States. Thus, when no special purpose is served by the distinction between the two concepts, this book will use the term *aggregate product, income, and expenditure* to refer to either or both the national and domestic concepts.

Gross and Net

Gross national (or domestic) product (or income or expenditure) means that the aggregate is measured *before* deducting the value of the assets of the economy that have been used up or depreciated in the production process during the year.

Net national (or domestic) product (or income or expenditure) means that the aggregate is measured *after* deducting the value of the assets of the economy that have been used up or depreciated in the production process during the year. Macroeconomics is concerned with explaining the overall scale of economic activity and uses the gross concept. The net concept is of use in measuring standards of living, a topic outside the scope of macroeconomics.

Market Price and Factor Cost

In most modern economies (and certainly in the United States), the government taxes expenditures on some goods and subsidizes expenditures on others. Examples of taxes on expenditures are the excise duties on liquor and tobacco. An example of a subsidy is the sale of water from major irrigation projects at less than cost. There are two ways of measuring the value of a good or service. One is based on the prices paid by the final user (consumer) and is known as the *market price* valuation. The other is based on the cost of all the factors of production used in its production, including the profits made. This is known as the *factor cost* valuation. Market prices include taxes on expenditures and are net of subsidies. Factor costs exclude taxes on expenditures but do not have subsidies netted out.

The various aggregates defined above can be measured on either the market price or factor cost basis. If excise duties were increased and Social Security taxes cut by equal amounts, nothing (as a first approximation) would happen to the level of aggregate economic activity. The market price concept of national income, however, would rise. The factor cost concept would not change. Macroeconomics is concerned with measuring the scale of economic activity and, ideally, would use the factor cost concept. In practice, provided care is taken to interpret any large changes in indirect taxes and subsidies, the market price concept is used.

Nominal and Real

The various aggregates defined above can be measured either in current dollars (nominal) or in constant dollars (real). The *nominal* valuation uses prices of goods or factors of production prevailing in the *current* period to value the current period's output or expenditure. The *real* valuation uses prices of goods or factors that prevailed in a *base* period to value the current period's output or expenditure. Real values are the appropriate ones for measuring the level of economic activity. Since macroeconomics is concerned with both the scale of activity and prices (and inflation), both of these concepts are of importance and will appear again later in this chapter and in Chapter 5.

It is now time to go beyond learning definitions and to develop a deeper understanding of the central concepts of output (or product), income, and expenditure.

C. Aggregate Output (or Product), Income, and Expenditure

In order to help you understand the central concepts of aggregate output (or product), income, and expenditure, it will be convenient to begin by considering an economy that is much simpler than the one in which you live. We will then successively add various features of the economy until we have a picture that corresponds quite closely to the world that we inhabit.

The Simplest Economy

Let us suppose that the economy is one that has no transactions with the rest of the world; that is, no one exports anything to foreigners or imports anything from them. No borrowing or lending takes place across the national borders, either. Indeed, no communications of any kind occur between the domestic economy and the rest of the world.

Next, suppose that there is no government; that is, no one pays taxes; all expenditures by households are voluntary; and all the goods and services that firms produce are bought by households, rather than some of them being bought by governments or their agencies.

The economy consists of just two kinds of economic institutions or *agents*: households and firms. A *household* is an agent that:

1. Owns factors of production.
2. Buys all final consumer goods.

A *firm* is an agent that:

1. Owns nothing.
2. Hires factors of production from households.
3. Sells the goods that it produces to households.
4. Pays any profits that it makes on its activities to households.

This economy can be visualized more clearly by considering Figure 3.1. The households in this economy are represented by the circle labelled *H*, and the firms are represented by the circle labelled *F*. Two kinds of flows take place between households and firms. First, real things are supplied by households to firms and by firms to households. Second, money passes between households and firms in exchange for these real things. The real flows are shown by the dashed lines, and the money flows are shown by the continuous lines. Households are shown as supplying factors of production to firms, and firms are shown as supplying goods and services to households. Moving in the opposite direction to these real flows are the money flows. Firms pay income

Figure 3.1
Real Flows and Money Flows in the Simplest Economy

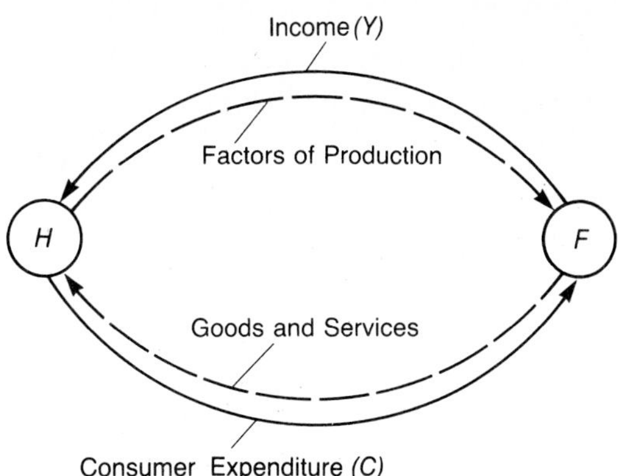

The flow of factors of production from households (H) to firms (F) and the flow of goods and services from firms to households (clockwise dashed lines) are matched by equivalent flows of money—firms paying income to households (Y) and households paying firms (C) for consumer goods and services (counterclockwise continuous lines).

to households, and households spend their income on consumer goods. The aggregate income payment will be denoted by Y and aggregate consumer expenditure by C.

It is evident that in this economy, the value of the income that households receive from firms must be equal to the value of the expenditure that households make on consumer goods. If this were not so, firms would be making either gains or losses that they would not be passing on to the households, who are the ultimate suppliers of factor services. It will also be evident that the *value* of the goods and services produced by the firms—the value of output of the firms—is also equal to the value of the expenditures on those goods and services by the households. In other words,

$$\text{Expenditure} = \text{Income} = \text{Value of output} \qquad \textbf{(3.1)}$$

This very simple economy, which abstracts from much of the detail of the actual world in which we live, has enabled us to establish the equality of income, expenditure, and output, which follows purely from the definitions of the terms involved. We now want to go on to see that this equality also applies to the more complicated world in which we live.

Some More Realistic Economies

There are three features of the "real world" that are not captured in the story above and in Figure 3.1. They are:

1. Households typically do not spend all their incomes on consumer goods—they also save some of their income.

2. Governments are large (and indeed growing) institutions in the modern world that tax individual incomes and use their tax proceeds to buy large quantities of goods and services from firms.
3. Economic activity is not restricted to trading with other domestic residents. International trade, travel, and capital movements are commonplace.

These three characteristics of the world in which we live will be introduced one by one, rather than all at once.

Savings by Households

Since households typically do not spend all their income on consumer goods but also do some saving, it looks as if Figure 3.1 has a serious defect. If households save some of their income, then consumer expenditure must be less than income, and therefore the flow of expenditure from households to firms shown in Figure 3.1 must be smaller than the flow of income received by households from firms. This would mean that firms are continually short of cash because they are paying out more than they are receiving. How does this complicating factor affect the concepts of national income, expenditure, and output and their equality?

The easiest way of dealing with this is to consider a still slightly fictitious (but less fictitious than previously) representation of the economy in which we think of there being two kinds of firms—those that produce consumer goods and those that produce capital goods. (Denote consumer goods firms by the letters F_c, and capital goods firms by the letters F_k.) You can think of F_c firms as being, for example, those that produce food, clothing, and the thousands of commodities that households typically consume; and you can think of F_k firms as those that produce, for example, steel mills, highways, generating stations, and the like. (Of course, in the real world there isn't a clean-cut, hard-and-fast division.)

Figure 3.2 illustrates the real flows and the money flows between the various kinds of firms and households. Households supply factors of production to both consumer goods producers and capital goods producers. These are shown as the two continuous lines representing flows from households to the two kinds of firms. The consumer goods producers, F_c, supply consumer goods to households, and the capital goods producers, F_k, supply capital goods to the producers of consumer goods. (Two further fictions that we will maintain are first, that capital goods firms do not themselves buy capital goods, and second, that households do not buy capital goods. We could easily relax these assumptions, although it would make the pictorial representation of what is going on more complicated.)

To summarize: The real flows in the economy are the two sets of factor services flowing from households to the two kinds of firms, and real goods flowing in the opposite directions, with capital goods flowing from capital goods producers to consumer goods producers, and consumer goods flowing from consumer goods producers to households.

Financial flows move in a direction opposite to the goods and factor flows. Two kinds of firms pay income to households. Households make consumer expenditure, which represent the flow of money from households to

Figure 3.2
Real Flows and Money Flows in an Economy with Savings and Investment

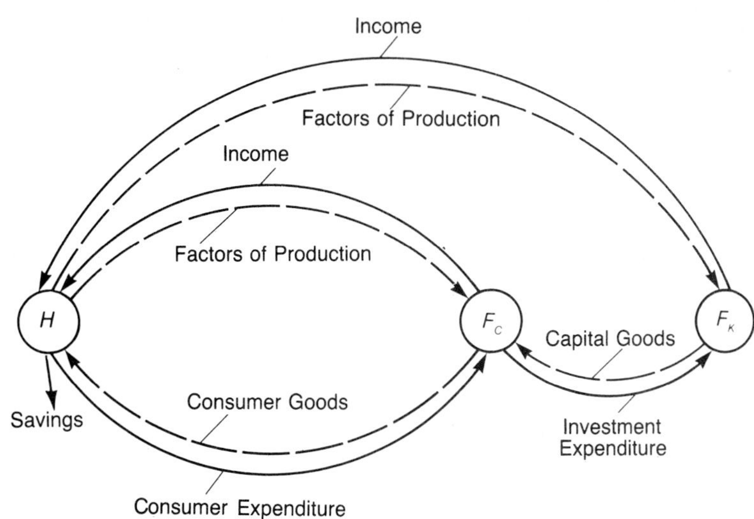

Households (H) supply factor services to producers of consumer goods (F_c) and capital goods (F_k). Consumer goods producers supply households, and capital goods producers supply consumer goods producers with new equipment. These real flows (clockwise dashed lines) are matched by equivalent money flows (counterclockwise continuous lines). Income is paid to households equal in value to the production of both consumer and capital goods. Households pay firms for the purchase of consumer goods. Consumer goods producers pay capital goods producers for their purchases of new equipment. These payments are known as investment expenditure.

consumer goods producers, and consumer goods producers make investment expenditure by paying money to capital goods producers in exchange for the capital goods supplied. In addition, households save some of their income. This is shown in Figure 3.2 as the flow going *from* households (H). Households' savings is not a payment to either capital goods or consumer goods producers directly and therefore is not shown as a flow into either of these two institutions but simply as a flow out of households.

In order to make the picture of the economy simpler, let us now add together the two kinds of firms (F_c and F_k) into a single, aggregate firms sector (F). This is done in Figure 3.3. Now, instead of having two income flows from firms to households, there is one, and this represents the sum of the two flows in Figure 3.2. Also, instead of there being two flows of factor services to firms, there is one, and this also represents the sum of the two flows shown in Figure 3.2. The expenditure by households on goods and services to firms is exactly the same as before, namely, the expenditure on consumer goods. Also, the flow of goods and services from firms to households is the same as the flow from the consumer goods firms to households. By aggregating all the firms in the economy into a single sector, the flow of capital goods from one kind of firm to another and the flow of investment expenditure on those goods have been lost, so to speak, in the aggregation. That is, by only looking at the aggregate of firms and the transactions that they have with households, we are not able

Figure 3.3
Real Flows and Money Flows in an Economy with Savings and Investment—Simplified

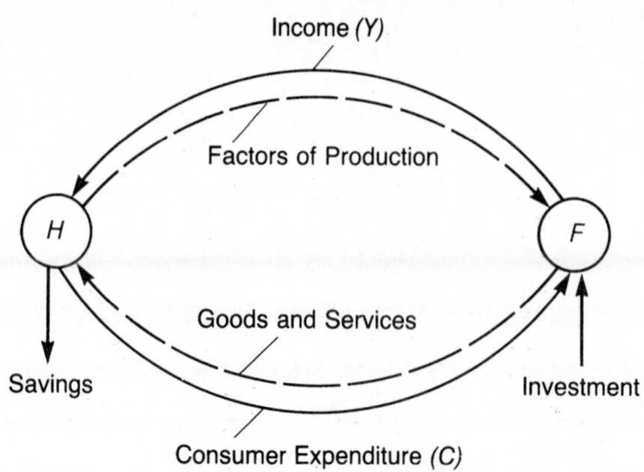

Consumer and capital goods producers are consolidated into an aggregate firm sector (F). Firms in total buy factor services from households (H) in exchange for income. Households buy consumer goods and services in exchange for the money flow of consumers' expenditure. What households do not spend on consumer goods they save. Households' savings are equal in value to firms' investment expenditure.

to "see" in the picture the flow of investment expenditure between the firms and the flow of capital goods between firms. As a substitute for this, and so that we do not forget that it is there, Figure 3.3 shows the flow of investment expenditure as a net receipt by firms.

To simplify things further and to make it easier to move on to the next two stages of complexity, Figure 3.4 reproduces Figure 3.3, but it leaves out the flows of factors of production and real goods and services, showing only the financial flows. Also, it uses only the symbolic names for the flows rather than their full names. Let us now focus on Figure 3.4. What this figure shows us is that income (Y) is paid by firms to households; households' consumption expenditure (C) is received by firms; and households also save (S). This latter activity simply represents the nonspending of income by households and does not represent *direct* transfers of resources to firms. In addition, firms make investment (I) expenditure on new capital goods.

The savings that households make out of their income and the investment that firms make in new capital goods clearly are in some sense related to each other. It is capital markets—in which people borrow and lend—that provide the mechanism whereby these two variables are linked. Households place their savings in various kinds of financial assets, and firms borrow in a variety of ways from households in order to undertake their investment activity. Thus, it is the capital markets that provide the financial flow linkage between savings and investment.

Let us now return to Figure 3.4 and look again at the concepts of income, output, and expenditure embodied in this more complicated representation of the world. To highlight matters, focus first of all on the firms (the circle labelled F). I have put an extra circle (dotted) around F that contains three arrows—two leading into F and one going from F. Recall that every-

Figure 3.4
The Money Flows in an Economy with Savings and Investment—A More Abstract Representation

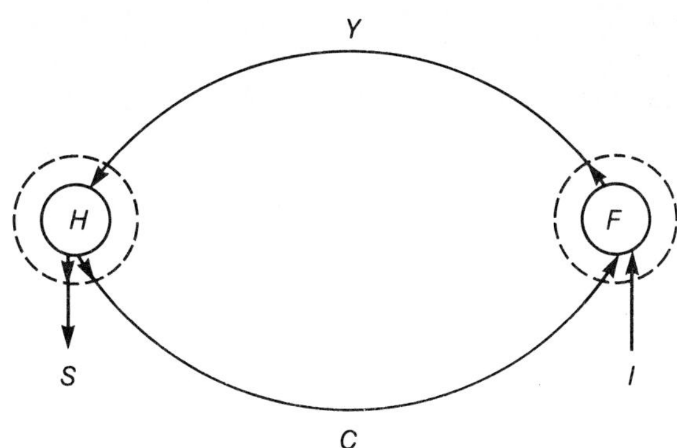

The money flows only are shown, with symbols denoting: income (Y), consumer expenditure (C), savings (S), investment (I). The broken circles around the households (H) and firms (F) contain arrows going to or from households and firms. An arrow leading into a sector represents a receipt. An arrow leaving a sector represents a payment. Total receipts by a sector equal total payments. Thus, for households, $Y = C + S$. For firms, $Y = C + I$. It follows directly that $S = I$.

thing a firm receives it also has to pay out. Firms do not own anything, and the profits they make are paid out to households as factor income. Given this fact, it is clear that the incomes paid out by firms must be equal to the expenditure by households on consumer goods and the expenditure by firms on investment goods; that is

$$Y = C + I \tag{3.2}$$

Next, focus on households (H) and on the dotted circle surrounding H in Figure 3.4. This circle also has three arrows, one leading to H and two leading from H. Since households must, in some way, dispose of their income, either by consuming or saving, it is evident that consumption plus savings (the outflows from households) must be equal to households' income, i.e.,

$$Y = C + S \tag{3.3}$$

Equation (3.2) above tells us that the value of all income in the economy is equal to a value of all expenditure. The expenditure is now broader than it was in the first example and includes investment expenditure as well as consumer expenditure.

Further, just as it was in the simpler example, the value of output in the economy is also equal to income or expenditure. To see this, all you have to do is to recognize that the value of the goods and services produced is equal to the value placed on them by the final demanders of those goods and services. That value is the value of consumer expenditure plus investment expenditure. Thus, income, expenditure, and output are equal again in this more "realistic" representation of the world.

You must be careful to distinguish between expenditure on final goods and services, payment to factors of production, and expenditure on intermediate goods and services. These distinctions are easier to see in this simplified economy, but they apply to all the more complicated economies described later.

The distinction between expenditure on final goods and services, payment to factors of production, and expenditure on intermediate goods and services is most easily understood with the aid of an example. Suppose you buy a chocolate bar from the local university store for 50¢. The university store bought that chocolate bar from its wholesale supplier for 40¢; the wholesaler bought it from the manufacturer for 36¢; the manufacturer bought milk for 2¢, cocoa beans for 4¢, sugar for 4¢, and electricity for 6¢; it paid wages to its workers of 14¢ and made a 6¢ profit, which it paid to its stockholders. The total expenditure in the story of the chocolate bar is $50 + 40 + 36 + 2 + 4 + 4 + 6 + 14 + 6 = \$1.62$. Of this $1.62, only 50¢ represents expenditure on final goods and services. The rest is expenditure on intermediate goods and services or payment to factors of production. The expenditure can be classified as shown in Table 3.1.

Notice that the first column in the table gives the value of expenditure (expenditure on final goods and services) on a chocolate bar, the second column total gives the incomes earned by all those who had a hand in producing the chocolate bar, and the final column simply records some intermediate transactions. From the viewpoint of macroeconomics, these last items are irrelevant. They arise from a particular form of industrial structure and would change if the industrial structure changed. For example, if the manufacturer sold directly to the retailer (for the 40¢ charged by the wholesaler in the above example), the expenditure on intermediate goods and services would fall by 36¢. Nothing important, however, would have changed. Total expenditure on final goods and services would still be 50¢. Also, factor incomes would still be 50¢; the profit of the wholesaler would have been eliminated and transferred

TABLE 3.1
Intermediate and Final Expenditure and Factor Incomes

ITEM	EXPENDITURE ON FINAL GOODS AND SERVICES	FACTOR INCOMES	EXPENDITURE ON INTERMEDIATE GOODS AND SERVICES
Purchase price of a chocolate bar	50¢	—	—
Wholesaler's selling price	—	—	40¢
Manufacturer's selling price	—	—	36¢
Farmer's income (milk)	—	2¢	—
Farmer's income (cocoa beans)	—	4¢	—
Farmer's income (sugar)	—	4¢	—
Electricity producer's income	—	6¢	—
Chocolate producer's wages	—	14¢	—
Chocolate producer's profit	—	6¢	—
Wholesaler's profit	—	4¢	—
Retailer's profit	—	10¢	—
Total	50¢	50¢	

to the manufacturer (by assumption). To count the expenditure on intermediate goods and services as well as the expenditure on final goods and services involves counting the same thing twice (or more than twice if there are several intermediate stages) and is known as "double counting."

Government Expenditure and Taxes

Now let us consider a yet more complicated world—one in which government economic activity plays a role. Figure 3.5 illustrates this type of economy. In addition to households (H) and firms (F), we also have government (denoted as GOV). Figure 3.5, which shows the relationship between households, firms, and government, is drawn on the simplified basis introduced in Figure 3.4. That is, we do not show both the real flows and the money flows. We show only the money flows. Also, we label the various flows with their symbolic rather than their full names. There are two new symbols: T stands for taxes, and G stands for government expenditure on goods and services.

In this more complicated world, households receive income (Y) from firms. They dispose of that income either by buying consumer goods (C), paying taxes (T), or saving (S). Firms, as before, receive households' consumption expenditures (C) as well as investment expenditure (I) (financed by various capital market operations). They also have receipts from the government in exchange for its purchase of goods and services (G). The government itself simply receives taxes (net of any transfers that it makes to households) and makes expenditure on goods and services.

Now, to see the national income accounts that emerge from this more complex world, focus again, first of all, on firms (F) and on the arrows in the broken circle surrounding F. Notice that now the firms pay out income (Y) and receive consumer expenditure (C), government expenditure (G), and investment expenditure (I). Since, as before, they have no ultimate ownership of resources, everything that they receive is paid out to households. Hence,

$$Y = C + I + G \tag{3.4}$$

Next, focus on households (H). They receive income and dispose of that income in the activities of consuming (C), saving (S), and paying taxes (T). Hence,

$$Y = C + S + T \tag{3.5}$$

In this economy, expenditure is still equal to income, but expenditure now incorporates consumer expenditure, firms' investment expenditure, and in addition, government expenditure on goods and services.

It is important that you understand that government payments to households, such as, for example, Social Security benefits, are *not* government expenditure on goods and services; they are the transfer of money from the government to households and are called *transfer payments.* You can think of these as negative taxes, so that total tax payments (denoted as T) need to be

Figure 3.5
Money Flows in an Economy with Savings, Investment, and Government Economic Activity

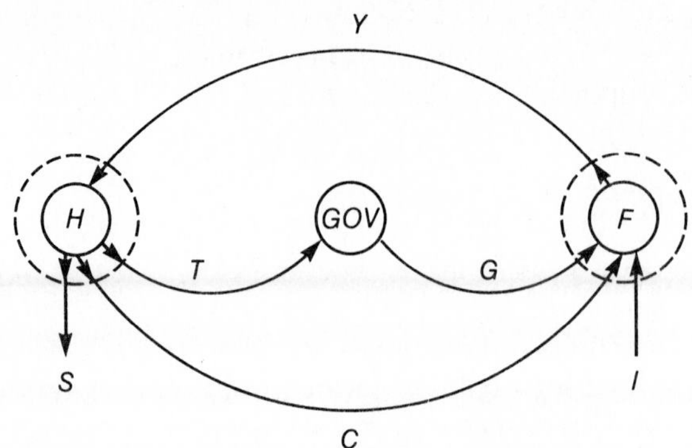

Government (GOV) taxes households (H) and buys goods and services produced by firms (F)—government expenditures on goods and services are shown by G, and government revenues—taxes—are shown by T. When these flows are added to those shown (and defined) in the previous figures, the households' income and expenditure account is modified to become $Y = C + S + T$. The firms' income and expenditure account is modified to become $Y = C + I + G$. It follows directly from these last two statements that $S + T = I + G$. There is no reason why government expenditure should equal taxes. The government may run a surplus ($T > G$) or a deficit ($T < G$).

thought of as being *net* taxes equal to the gross taxes paid by households minus the transfers from government to households.

As in the two simpler economies considered above, not only are income and expenditure equal to each other, but output is also equal to income and expenditure. The value of the goods and services bought by households (C), firms (I), and government (G) represents the value of the goods and services produced in the economy—the output of the economy. Hence, even in this more complex economy, aggregate income, expenditure, and output are one and the same.

The Rest of the World

Now consider the final complication arising from the fact that economic agents do business with their counterparts in the rest of the world. Figure 3.6 will illustrate the story here. Now we have households (H), firms (F), government (GOV), and the rest of the world (R). All the flows are as before, except for some additional flows between the rest of the world and the domestic economy. The left-hand part of Figure 3.6 is identical to Figure 3.5 and does not need to be described again. The additional activities in Figure 3.6 are imports and exports of goods and services. Foreigners buy goods from domestic firms, and, therefore, there is a flow of money from the rest of the world to those firms (EX) for exports. In addition, domestic firms buy goods from the rest of the world, transferring money to foreigners in exchange for those goods—imports (IM). From the way the figure has been drawn, it looks as if only firms do the importing. We know, of course, that sometimes households import goods directly. This could easily be shown in the picture, but it would not add anything of substance.

Figure 3.6
Money Flows in an Economy with Savings, Investment, Government Economic Activity, and Transactions with the Rest of the World

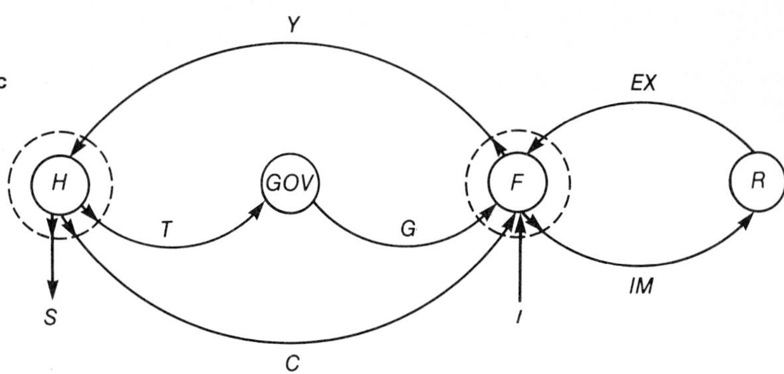

The flow transactions with the rest of the world are exports that give rise to a receipt by the firms doing the exporting (EX), and imports that give rise to payments by firms doing the importing (IM). These receipts and payments run between firms (F) and the rest of the world (R). Extending the flows to include those with the rest of the world leaves the households' income and expenditure unchanged. They remain $Y = C + S + T$. The firms' accounts now become $Y = C + I + G + EX - IM$. It follows directly from this that $S + T + IM = I + G + EX$. There is no requirement that exports (EX) = imports (IM). There may be a trade surplus ($EX > IM$) or a trade deficit ($EX < IM$) with the rest of the world.

Let us see how the national income accounts will look in this economy. There is no change in the flows into and out of households. It is true that households now buy consumer goods, some of which have been imported from the rest of the world by the firms from whom they buy them. That, however, will not show up directly in the households' accounts. Their accounts still say that income (Y) is equal to consumption (C), plus savings (S), plus taxes (T).

We get a slightly different picture, however, when we look at firms. We now have two arrows leading out of the F circle—flows of money from firms to other agents—and four arrows flowing into F. Firms pay factor incomes to households (Y) and pay foreigners for the value of goods and services that have been imported from them (IM). They receive from foreigners the value of exports (EX), from government the value of goods and services purchased by government (G), and from households the value of consumer goods purchased (C). There is also a net inflow of funds to finance the firms' investment expenditure (I). Thus, considering all the arrows showing flows into and out from the firms, it is clear that

$$Y = C + I + G + EX - IM \tag{3.6}$$

The items on the right-hand side of Equation (3.6) are total *net* expenditures on domestic output. Hence, the equality between income and expenditure is retained in the world pictured in Figure 3.6. Income is the flow of money from firms to households, and it represents the value of the factor services supplied by households to firms. Expenditure is equal to the consumption expenditure of households (C), the value of purchases of capital equipment by firms (I), government expenditure of goods and services (G), and the net value of foreigners' expenditure on domestic output. By *net* value we mean the difference between the gross purchases by foreigners (exports) and the purchase of foreign goods by domestic citizens (imports). Also, the value of output is equal to income (and expenditure).

There is an additional interesting implication in the national income accounts in this more "realistic" picture of the world. It follows immediately from the equality between income and expenditure and the fact that income is allocated by households to consumption, savings, and taxes. If you begin by considering Equations (3.5) and (3.6), it will immediately be apparent to you that

$$I + G + EX = S + T + IM \qquad \textbf{(3.7)}$$

Now, deduct savings, taxes, and imports from both sides of this equation and rearrange the order of the terms, so that we obtain:

$$(I - S) + (G - T) + (EX - IM) = 0 \qquad \textbf{(3.8)}$$

The three terms in parentheses in Equation (3.8) have a very natural interpretation. The first term, $(I - S)$, is the excess of investment over savings by the private sector of the economy. The second term, $(G - T)$, is the government's budget deficit, or surplus. The third term, $(EX - IM)$, is the surplus or deficit on the balance of trade with the rest of the world.

What Equation (3.8) says is that the sum of these three items must always be zero. There are various alternative ways in which this could be put. One way, which is perhaps helpful, is to notice that Equation (3.8) implies that if firms are investing more than households are saving, then either it is necessary for there to be a balance of trade deficit—that is, for imports to exceed exports—so that the extra investment goods may indeed be acquired by firms; or it is going to be necessary for government expenditure to be less than taxes, so that, in effect, the government is doing some of the saving that is enabling capital goods to be accumulated by firms. Another way of putting the same thing would be to say that if the government insists on spending more than it generates in taxes—if there is a government budget deficit—then there must either be a shortfall of investment as compared with savings or there must be a balance of trade deficit with the rest of the world to enable the government to acquire the resources in excess of the value of the taxes that it is levying.

D. Measuring Aggregate Income

The Expenditure Approach

In order to measure national income (or expenditure or output), it is necessary to record and add together the appropriate flows that are taking place in the economy. The three most common methods of measuring national income will now be discussed. The first is the *expenditure approach*. You can think of the expenditure approach as an attempt by the national income statisticians to measure the total value of consumer expenditure on goods and services (C), firms' investment expenditure (I), and government expenditure on goods and services (G), as well as exports (EX) and imports (IM). When these items are combined in accordance with Equation (3.6), they provide one estimate of the value of national income, expenditure, or output.

These items can be measured with varying degrees of accuracy. Consumer expenditure is measured partly by taking surveys of what households are spending and partly by observing the value of the sales of consumer goods by producers. Government expenditure is measured directly from the accounts of government itself. Investment expenditure is measured by surveying firms' capital spending programs and inventories. Finally, foreign trade is monitored through the official documentation required to conduct that trade. Most countries have some form of control over international movements of goods and services, and in some cases, these items are subject either to quotas or tariffs. In order to implement these arrangements, governments automatically collect data on the volume of international trade flows.

Thus, by measuring these items, C, I, G, EX, and IM, it is possible to obtain a measure of aggregate income, expenditure, or output by using the previous formula

$$Y = C + I + G + EX - IM \qquad \textbf{(3.6)}$$

By adding the values of expenditure , the aggregate that results will be based on market prices and will include taxes on expenditure less subsidies. To convert this to the factor cost measure needed for macroeconomic analysis, it is necessary to deduct taxes on expenditure and add subsidies to give aggregate income (output or expenditure) at factor cost.

The Factor Incomes Approach

A second method of measuring national income is to measure factor incomes directly. The major sources of such measurements are the returns that individuals and firms make to the tax-collecting branch of government—in the United States, the Internal Revenue Service. Since most taxes are collected as a levy on incomes earned, the reporting of those incomes for the purpose of tax calculations provides the major input for the *factor incomes approach* to the measurement of aggregate income. By using these sources, it is possible to arrive at an estimate of aggregate income. This measure of aggregate income (output or expenditure) is automatically on a factor cost basis and needs no further adjustment.

The two measures of aggregate income—the expenditure approach (adjusted to the factor cost basis) and the factor incomes approach—never quite agree with each other. There is always a statistical discrepancy since it is simply too costly to devote the necessary resources to obtain precise values of these variables.

The Output Approach

A third method of measuring national income is to measure the value of output of each industry and then aggregate those output measures to arrive at an estimate of aggregate output. The major sources of direct output measurement are surveys of production and sales by firms. By using data collected from such surveys, it is possible to arrive at estimates of aggregate output by what is known as the *output approach.* In addition to providing a third way of arriving at an estimate of aggregate economic activity, this approach also provides estimates of the output of each major sector of the economy.

E. Measuring Aggregate Income in Constant Dollars (Real)

The *expenditure approach* to measuring aggregate income provides the basis for the measurement of aggregate income (output or expenditure) in constant dollars, or real terms. A base period is chosen. At the moment, in the United States, that base period is 1972. The average level of prices prevailing in the base period is defined to be equal to 100. The expenditures of a particular year are revalued using the prices prevailing in the base year. They are then aggregated using the formula in Equation (3.6) above to arrive at real income, output, or expenditure.

F. Reading the National Income Accounts of the United States

The U. S. aggregate income accounts are assembled by the Bureau of Economic Analysis in the Department of Commerce. The accounts are drawn up on a quarterly and annual basis and are published in the *Survey of Current Business.*[1] Long historical runs of data are provided in *The National Income and Product Accounts of the United States, 1929–1976 Statistical Tables*; and *National Income and Product Accounts, 1976–1979: A Special Supplement to the Survey of Current Business.*[2] The detailed definitions, concepts, sources, and methods are described (with immense attention being paid to the intricacies involved) in a publication called *Readings in Concepts and Methods of National Income Statistics.*[3]

Reading the U.S. national income accounts and translating them into the aggregate concepts that you have become familiar with in the preceding sections of this chapter is a relatively straightforward business. You may, nevertheless, need some guidance in that task.

If you look at the Commerce Department's, *The National Income and Product Accounts of the United States, 1929–1976 Statistical Tables* (you will find a copy in any university library and in the business/economics section of many public libraries), the first thing that will strike you (probably with mild alarm) is the immense detail presented. There are 55 tables covering over 400 pages. It is hard to know where to begin. Fortunately, for the purposes of macroeconomic analysis, three pairs of tables contain most of what is needed. These are Tables 1.1 and 1.2, which give the details of expenditure on the gross

[1]Monthly publication available from the Superintendent of Documents, U.S. Government Printing Office, Washington, D.C. 20402.

[2]These are supplements to the *Survey of Current Business* and are available from the Superintendent of Documents, U.S. Government Printing Office, Washington, D.C. 20402.

[3]This publication may be obtained from the National Technical Information Service, Springfield, Virginia 22161.

national product; Tables 1.5 and 1.6, which show the relation between the "national" and "domestic" concepts of aggregate income; and Tables 1.7 and 1.8, which give information needed to calculate the "factor cost" concepts, together with capital consumption. The first table in each pair gives data in current dollars, and the second in each pair gives the constant dollar figures.

The contents of the aggregate income accounts are brought together in Table 3.2 in a form that will enable you to see the relationships among the variables, using the concepts developed earlier in this chapter. The name (or names) of the items given in parentheses beneath each major item refers to the details contained in the officially reported national income and product accounts tables. There is little to be gained from committing all this detail to memory. You may, however, find it a useful reference in the event that you want to construct your own accounts for a year, or years other than 1981, the example used here.

TABLE 3.2
U.S. National Income and Expenditure in 1981

		$ BILLIONS
	Consumption (C) (personal consumption expenditures, Table 1.1, line 2)	1,858
add	Investment (I) (gross private domestic investment, Table 1.1, line 6)	451
add	Government expenditure (G) (government purchases of goods and services, Table 1.1, line 21)	591
add	Exports (EX) (exports, Table 1.1, line 19)	366
deduct	Imports (IM) (imports, Table 1.1, line 20)	−341
equals	Gross national product (GNP) at market prices (gross national product, Table 1.1, line 1)	2,925
deduct	Net property income from abroad (rest of world, Table 1.5, line 15)	−54
equals	Gross domestic product (GDP) at market prices (gross domestic product, Table 1.5, line 2)	2,871
deduct	Indirect taxes Less subsidies (Table 1.7, sum of lines 6, 7, and 8, less line 9)	−257
equals	Gross domestic product (GDP) at factor cost (Y) (not shown in official tables)	2,614
	Capital consumption (Table 1.7, sum of lines 2, 3, and 4)	514

Note: The note in parentheses below each item in this table gives the exact name of the item used in the source cited here as well as the table and line numbers where the item may be located.

SOURCE: U.S. Department of Commerce, *Survey of Current Business*, 62, no 2 (February 1982) 1–14.

Looking at the major items in Table 3.2, you will see that consumption (C), *plus* investment (I), *plus* government expenditure (G), *plus* exports (EX), *less* imports (IM), adds up to gross national product (GNP) at market prices. By deducting net property income from abroad, the total of gross domestic product (GDP) at market prices is arrived at. By deducting from that total the value of indirect taxes less subsidies, the factor cost definition of GDP is arrived at.

The bottom of the table notes the amount of capital consumption—that is, depreciation of fixed capital. By subtracting that amount from any of the other *gross* figures, you may arrive at the corresponding *net* national income, expenditure, or product; or *net* domestic income, expenditure, or product. Gross domestic product at factor cost (Y) is the aggregate income variable which macroeconomics seeks to explain.

Summary

A. Flows and Stocks

A flow is a rate per unit of time such as income per annum or expenditure per month. A stock is the value of a variable at a point in time such as the amount of money you have in the bank on a particular day.

B. Some Frequently Used Terms

1. Output (or product), income, and expenditure:

—*Output* (or *product*) is the value of the goods and services produced in the economy.
—*Income* is the sum of all the incomes earned in producing the output of the economy.
—*Expenditure* is the sum of all expenditures on final goods and services in the economy.

2. Domestic and national:

—*Domestic* refers to an aggregation of economic activity taking place in a particular country.
—*National* refers to an aggregation of the economic activity of all residents no matter in which country the activity takes place.

3. Gross and net:

—*Gross* is before deducting the depreciation of assets.
—*Net* is after deducting the depreciation of assets.

4. Market price and factor cost:

—*Market price* valuations are based on the prices paid by consumers and include taxes on expenditure and are net of subsidies.
—*Factor cost* valuations are based on the amounts paid to the factors of production, including profits, and exclude taxes on expenditures and are gross of subsidies.

C. Aggregate Output (or Product), Income, and Expenditure

Aggregate output (or product) is the value of all the goods and services produced in the economy. Aggregate income is the sum of all the incomes of all the individuals in the economy. Aggregate expenditure is the sum of all the expenditures on *final* goods and services produced by the economy. The values of aggregate output, income, and expenditure, are equal to each other.

D. Measuring Aggregate Income

The *expenditure approach* to aggregate income measurement samples the expenditures of households, firms, government, and foreigners and makes an estimate of the sum of those expenditures. From the fact that income, expenditure, and output are equal to each other, this estimate of expenditure is also an estimate of income and output.

The *factor incomes approach* samples the incomes of individuals and from this forms an estimate of aggregate income. From the conceptual equality of income, expenditure, and output, this provides an alternative estimate of aggregate expenditure and output as well as income.

The *output approach* samples the production of individual firms and from this forms an estimate of the value of output in each sector of the economy and in aggregate.

The three approaches never produce identically the same estimate, but they provide a good approximation to the value of aggregate income, expenditure, and output.

E. Measuring Aggregate Income in Constant Dollars (Real)

To measure real income (output and expenditure), the expenditure approach is used. The final goods and services bought in each year are valued at the prices that prevailed in the base year.

F. Reading the National Income Accounts of the United States

The U. S. national income and product accounts are published by the Department of Commerce in the *Survey of Current Business.* The way in which the detailed items supplied in the published tables aggregate into the concepts employed in macroeconomics are set out in Table 3.2, and that table should be used as a reference guide.

Review Questions

1. Indicate which of the following are flows and which are stocks:

(a) The rate at which oil is pumped through the Alaska pipeline.
(b) The amount of oil in Texas.
(c) Gross domestic product.
(d) Real national income.
(e) The value of the airplanes owned by the U.S. Air Force.

2. Review the definition of each of the following terms:

(a) Gross domestic product.
(b) Gross domestic product at market price.
(c) Gross national product at factor cost.
(d) Real national income.

3. Give examples that illustrate the differences between the following terms:

(a) Nominal and real.
(b) Gross and net.
(c) National and domestic.
(d) Factor cost and market price.

4. What are the units of measurement of (a) a nominal variable and (b) a real variable?

5. Using the latest available data from the *Survey of Current Business*, calculate the latest year values of (a) aggregate income, (b) aggregate expenditure, and (c) aggregate output.

6. Using a recent *Survey of Current Business*, calculate aggregate income for 1982 using (a) the expenditure approach, and (b) the factor incomes approach. Is your measure of aggregate income a gross or a net measure? What is the difference between gross aggregate income and net aggregate income in 1982?

7. Using gross aggregate income for 1982 (calculated in Question 6) and other relevant data from the *Survey of Current Business*, calculate 1982 aggregate income in constant 1972 dollars.

8. Suppose that you want to describe the pattern of aggregate output in the United States during the 1970s. Which of the following would be the best series to use, and why?

(a) Aggregate expenditure at market prices.
(b) Aggregate output at factor cost.
(c) Gross domestic product in constant dollars.
(d) Gross domestic product.

Say exactly what *all* the faults are with *all* the series that you would *not* use.

9. The following activities took place in an imaginary economy last year:

	$ MILLIONS
Wages paid to labor	800,000
Consumer expenditure	650,000
Taxes paid on wages	200,000
Government payments to support the unemployed, sick, and aged	50,000
Firms' profits	200,000
Investment	250,000
Taxes paid on profits	50,000
Government purchases of goods and services	200,000
Exports	250,000

Note: There was no property income paid to or received from nonresidents.

(a) Calculate:

Gross domestic income.
Gross national expenditure.
Saving.
Imports.
The government budget surplus/deficit.

(b) What extra information do you need in order to calculate net national income?

10. A troupe of Russian dancers tours the United States. The dancers fly to New York on an *Aeroflot* (Soviet airline) flight at a total round-trip cost of $200,000. They travel inside the United States on domestic airlines at a total cost of $185,000. Their hotel and food bills in the United States amount to $150,000. The receipts from ticket sales for performances of the troupe amount to $1,000,000. The cost of renting theaters is $100,000, hiring American musicians is $200,000, and advertising is $50,000. The Russian dancers' wages amounted to $75,000 for the period of the visit. The dancers bought American-made souvenirs worth a total of $2,500. Any profit or loss on the visit accrued to or was borne by the Soviet government. Show where each of the economic activities described here appears in the national income accounts of the United States.

4

Aggregate Balance Sheet Accounting

This is an unusual topic to appear in an introductory macroeconomics text, and it reflects the unusual nature of the book with which you are working. Keynesian macroeconomics places a great deal of emphasis on the national income accounts and on aggregate income and expenditure flows, and the last chapter dealt with the concepts that lie behind that accounting framework. If you were working with a conventional Keynesian-oriented macroeconomics book, you would now be reading the first "theory" chapter. That chapter would present a theory about how national income is determined, and the theory would be based purely on the items from national income flow accounts. It would postulate hypothetical relationships between various flows—hypotheses that one flow depends in some behavioral way on another flow—and from that it would develop a predictive theory of the determination of national income.

That route is not taken here. The kind of macroeconomics that you are studying in this book is built on the presumption that the most important behavioral relationships are not only those between various flows, but also those between flows and stocks. Accordingly, as a prelude to studying macroeconomic theory, this chapter explains the connections between the main stocks (the assets and liabilities in the economy) and also explains how those stocks are measured.

You have four tasks. These are to:

(a) Understand the meaning of "asset," "liability," and "balance sheet."
(b) Know the definition of money and understand the nature of money.
(c) Know the main items in the balance sheets of households, firms, commercial banks, the central bank, government, and the rest of the world.
(d) Know the main sources of information about aggregate balance sheets in the United States.

A. Asset, Liability, and Balance Sheet

Asset and Liability

An *asset* is simply something that someone owns. A *liability* is what someone owes.

There are two types of assets: financial and real. A *real asset* is concrete, tangible, a real piece of nuts and bolts. Examples of real assets are the desks and tables at which you sit and study; your stereo and records; your car, motorcycle, skis, surfboard, etc. Other examples are highways, steel mills, coal mines, power stations, airplanes.

There is one special real asset that you probably do not ordinarily think of as an asset—that is yourself (and everyone else). The value of this asset in the economy as a whole is the value of all the work that human beings are capable of doing now and in the future. This asset is called *human capital.* Of course, in societies such as our own where slavery is prohibited, it is not possible to buy and sell human capital. It is possible, however, to borrow from a bank against a promise to commit future income (i.e., human capital) to the repayment of the loan.

Financial assets are different from real assets. They are pieces of paper that constitute an asset to one economic agent and a liability to another. That is, they *define a debt relationship* between two agents. Examples of financial assets (which are also someone else's financial liabilities) are: (a) your savings account at the local bank—from your point of view, this is a financial asset (you *own* the deposit), whereas from the point of view of your bank, it is a liability (the bank *owes* you the deposit); (b) an IBM bond—this is an asset to the person who owns it but a liability to stockholders of IBM; (c) a Federal Reserve one-dollar bill—this is an asset to you, but is it anyone's liability? Yes it is: It is a liability of the Federal Reserve System (usually shortened to "Fed")—this country's central bank. The Fed owes you one dollar's worth of goods and services in exchange for that bill and has to hold assets (government securities) that it could sell in order to meet its commitment. In reality, of course, since just about everyone is willing to accept your dollar bill in exchange for goods and services, the Fed never has to!

All financial assets are like the three examples in the above paragraph. Each financial asset has a financial liability that goes with it. It is a piece of paper that specifies that someone X has a claim on someone else Y; it is an asset to X and a liability to Y.

Balance Sheet

A balance sheet is a statement about what is owned by (is an asset of) and what is owed by (is a liability of) a particular individual or agency. It could be an individual like yourself, or it could be an agency like the Fed, a commercial bank like the Bank of America, the U.S. government, or IBM. The best way to get a feel for a balance sheet is to consider the balance sheet of an individual like yourself.

Table 4.1 sets out an example of what an individual student's balance sheet might look like. The balance sheet shown in Table 4.1 lists the assets in

TABLE 4.1
An Individual's Balance Sheet

ITEM	ASSETS ($)	LIABILITIES ($)
1. Bank notes and coins	25	
2. Savings account	150	
3. U.S. savings bonds	200	
4. Bank loan		1,000
5. Mastercard account		200
6. Total financial assets and liabilities	$375	$1,200
7. Car	1,500	
8. Stereo and records	1,000	
9. Total real assets	$2,500	
10. Total assets and liabilities	$2,875	$1,200
11. Wealth		$1,675
12. Totals	$2,875	$2,875

the first column and the liabilities in the second column. The assets are divided between financial items (in the top part of the balance sheet) and real items (in the bottom part of the balance sheet). The person whose balance sheet is shown here has some bank notes and coins, $25 (item #1); a savings account, $150 (item #2); and U.S. savings bonds, $200 (item #3). These are the person's financial assets. The individual has two financial liabilities: a bank loan, $1000 (item #4); and an outstanding balance of $200 with a credit card company—Mastercard (item #5). Item #6 totals the financial assets and liabilities. You will see that this person owes more (has bigger liabilities) than he/she owns (has assets).

The next items are real assets. The individual has a car worth $1500 and a stereo and records worth $1000, giving a total of real assets (item # 9) of $2500. The total assets and liabilities are shown in item #10. This individual has assets of $2875 and liabilities of $1200.

It is a feature of a balance sheet that it must balance. Clearly, as depicted in item #10, the assets of this individual exceed the liabilities. The amount by which the assets exceed the liabilities is $1675. This amount of money is the wealth of this individual. *Wealth* is defined to be a "fictitious" liability (yes, liability) and is shown in item #11 as a liability of $1675. If you add the wealth of the individual to the other liabilities, you will find that total liabilities (item #12) are equal to total assets, $2875. In order to feel more comfortable with the idea of wealth as a liability, you may like to think of it as the amount that is owed by an individual to himself. Another equivalent way of defining wealth, which is perhaps more appealing, is simply: Wealth equals total assets less total liabilities. In the example:

Total assets = $2857
Less total liabilities = $1200
Equals wealth = $1675

Wealth is commonly referred to by the alternative name *net worth.*

B. Definition and Nature of Money

Money is anything that is generally acceptable as a medium of exchange. A medium of exchange is anything that is acceptable in exchange for goods and services. Which precise assets constitute the medium of exchange varies from one society to another and has varied over the years. Gold has commonly served as a medium of exchange; so has silver and so have other metals. In some prisoner-of-war camps in World War II, cigarettes circulated as a medium of exchange. These are all examples of commodity money.

In modern societies, money is a financial asset that is the financial liability either of the central bank or of other banks. There are three widely used alternative measures of the money supply in the United States today. One is sometimes called "narrow money" or M1, another is referred to as "broad money" or M3, and the third is an aggregate that is intermediate between these two and is called M2.

Narrow money (M1) consists of currency (Federal Reserve notes and coins) in circulation, travelers' checks, and demand deposits (checking account balances), together with some other types of deposits that may be instantly converted into spending power.

The intermediate aggregate (M2) consists of M1 plus savings deposits and other very short-term (overnight) deposits at banks and other financial institutions.

Broad money (M3) is M2 plus large-scale and long-term deposits at banks and other financial institutions.[1]

Notice that savings deposits, which are included in the M2 and M3 definitions of money but excluded from the M1 measure, are not directly transferable from one person to another by writing a check, and although it is customary to think of such deposits as "money in the bank," it is important to recognize that only M1 is money in the strict sense that it is a means of payment.

In recent years, deregulation of the banking sector as well as innovations made possible by the advance of computer technology have begun to blur the distinction between M1 and M2. Some of the accounts that banks make available to their customers have some of the properties of a means of payment and, therefore, ought to be regarded as M1, although in other respects they have the properties of savings accounts—which would put them in the M2 category. A good example of such arrangements are the so called NOW account experiments. NOW stands for *N*otice *O*f *W*ithdrawal. Bank customers operating with NOW accounts are, in effect, able to earn interest on bank deposits, while at the same time keeping those deposits available for active transactions use. When NOW accounts were first introduced, they were not included in M1. However, they are now included in that definition. This example serves to highlight the fact that there are no permanent, hard and fast

[1]The definitions given here are designed to give you the main components of the alternative aggregates and are not quite as detailed or precise as those necessary to actually calculate the aggregates. The exact definitions may be found in Note 1 to the table on "Money Stock Measures and Components" in any recent *Federal Reserve Bulletin.*

definitions of money. Thus the precise definition of the aggregate that serves as the means of payment has to be constantly monitored and revised in the light of innovations in the financial sector.

Although there are some imprecise borderline cases between money and nonmoney, there is no doubt at all that money does not include credit cards, such as a Mastercard or Visa card. These cards are convenient identification tags that enable you to create two debts simultaneously. One debt is between yourself and the credit card company and the other is between the credit card company and the seller. These debts are settled when you pay the credit card company and the credit card company pays the seller.

Another innovation in recent years is harder to distinguish from "money" than is the credit card. This is the emergence of money market mutual funds. A money market mutual fund is in many respects like a bank deposit. Individuals and firms place deposits with financial institutions. These financial institutions in turn invest that money in short-term money market securities. The value of one dollar deposited in a money market mutual fund fluctuates with the market fortunes of the fund itself. In this respect, a money market mutual fund deposit is different from a bank deposit. When you deposit a dollar in the bank, no matter what happens to the market value of the investments that the bank acquires using your dollar, you continue to have a one-dollar deposit in the bank. In the case of a money market mutual fund, the value of that one-dollar deposit fluctuates in line with fluctuations in the market value of the assets of the fund. Just as in the case of a checking deposit at the bank, it is possible to transfer a money market mutual fund deposit from one account to another by writing what is, in effect, a check. In this respect, money market mutual funds are like bank deposits. There is, however, a minimum size to the check that may be written on a money market mutual fund, and it is usually of a size such that the fund would be of limited value for ordinary transactions.

Money in the modern world stands in sharp contrast to commodity money in that it is a financial asset not backed by any commodities and not exchangeable by the issuer for anything other than another unit of itself. Its value arises from the fact that it is universally acceptable by all in exchange for goods and services.

C. Main Balance Sheets Items

We are going to look at the balance sheets of six sectors:

Households	H
Firms	F
Banks and other financial institutions	B
Federal Reserve Banks	FED
U.S. Government	GOV
Rest of the world	R

You will identify this as an extension of the sectors whose flow activities we analyzed when dealing with the aggregate income accounts in the previous chapter. There we examined households, firms, government, and the rest of the world. We did not deal with banks and other financial institutions or the Fed. The reason for that is that these institutions are not major actors in the flow of goods and services. They are, however, major actors in the monetary and balance sheet structure of the economy.

Financial Assets and Liabilities

Table 4.2 records the main financial items in the balance sheets of the above listed six sectors. A "+" denotes an asset, and a "−" denotes a liability. Additional explanations for the items and diagrams in Table 4.2 are given below.

Bank Deposits With the Fed Commercial banks maintain checking accounts just as individuals do. The banker to the commercial banks is the central bank—the Fed. As far as the banks are concerned, their deposits with the Fed are like money and are part of their assets. These deposits are a liability of the Fed. A bank can convert its deposits with the Fed into notes and coins, or vice versa, as it chooses.

Currency Currency consists of all the Federal Reserve notes and coins held by (and therefore assets of) households, firms, banks, and other financial institutions. The notes are a liability of the Fed, but the coin is issued by the U.S. Mint, a government agency, and is therefore shown (in Table 4.2) as a liability of the government.

Monetary Base (MB) All the liabilities of the Fed added together, plus the currency liabilities of the government, make up what is known as the *monetary base*. This is shown in the triangle in Table 4.2.

TABLE 4.2
The Structure of Financial Indebtedness

	SECTOR					
ITEM	*H*	*F*	*B*	*FED*	*GOV*	*R*
Bank deposits with the Fed			+	−		
Currency (notes and coins)	+	+	+	−	−	
Demand deposits	+	+	−		+	
Savings deposits	+		−			
Other deposits		+	−			+
Government securities	+	+	+	+	−	+
Loans	−	−	+			
Bonds	+	−				+
Equities	+	−				+
Foreign securities	+	+	+			−
Foreign exchange reserves				+	+	−
Net financial assets	+	−	0	0	−	±

Notes: (+) denotes assets; (−) denotes liabilities. The sectors are: Households (*H*); Firms (*F*); Commercial Banks (*B*); the Federal Reserve System (*FED*); Government (*GOV*); the Rest of the World (*R*). The boxes show the items included in the alternative definitions of the money supply: M1, M2, and M3. The triangle shows the items included in the monetary base.

Demand Deposits Demand deposits are bank accounts from which funds may be withdrawn on demand, typically by writing a check. They are liabilities of banks and assets of households, firms, government, and foreigners.

Narrow Money (M1) The total of currency held by households and firms and demand deposits is "narrow money" or M1. The dotted box in Table 4.2 shows the total of M1. Notice that M1 does *not* include the currency held inside the banking system, nor does it include commercial bank deposits with the Fed. Further, M1 does not include the demand deposits at the commercial banks owned by the government.

Savings Deposits Savings deposits are small-scale or short-term deposits that (mainly) households place with the banks and other financial institutions. They are interest-bearing deposits and typically may only be withdrawn on demand by incurring an interest penalty. Thus, they are not quite as useful as demand deposits as a means of payment.

Other Deposits Other deposits include large-scale deposits and longer-term deposits that (mainly) firms place with the banks. They are not withdrawable on demand, and they earn a larger interest rate than savings deposits.

Broader Measures of Money (M2 and M3) If we add savings deposits to M1, we obtain M2, which is shown as the dashed box in Table 4.2. If we add other deposits to M2, we obtain M3, shown as the unbroken box in the table.

Government Securities Next there is a whole class of financial assets called *government securities.* Many different types of assets are in this category. Examples are: U.S. savings bonds, long-term U.S. government bonds, and Treasury bills. These items are a liability of the federal government and are held by (are assets of) all of the other sectors. The government securities held by the Fed are the assets that provide the backing for the monetary base. In order to raise the size of the monetary base, the Fed buys government securities with newly created money.

Loans The next major item to consider in the sectoral balance sheets is loans. These include the personal and business loans that are assets as far as the commercial banks are concerned and are liabilities of the households and firms that have borrowed the money. This item also includes loans made by other financial institutions to households—for example, for the purchase of homes—usually called *mortgages.*

Bonds Corporations raise money to buy capital equipment by selling bonds. A corporate bond holder, unlike an equity holder (see next item), is not an owner of the company. Rather, such a person has made a loan to the company. All that a corporate bond holder is entitled to is the pre-agreed interest payment on the bond. In contrast, an equity holder is entitled to his share of any residual profits earned by the firm. In terms of balance sheet accounting, a corporate bond appears as a liability to firms and is an asset of households and the rest of the world.

Equities In addition to raising funds to buy capital equipment by selling bonds, corporations also issue equities. An equity holder in a corporation is in fact a part owner of the corporation. That is, the households and foreigners that own equities really own a share of the firm's physical capital stock. In legal terms, of course, the owner of a share in a firm can only sell the share. The owner of a share cannot decide to sell the whole of (or even that individual's share of) the physical plant itself. Thus in legal terms there is an indebtedness between households and foreigners who own firms and the firm itself. The firm has a liability, and the households and foreigners own the corresponding asset.

Foreign Securities There are various securities issued by foreign governments and foreign companies that are held by U.S. households, firms, and banks.

Foreign Exchange Reserves The final item in Table 4.2 is the foreign exchange reserves of the country. These constitute an asset to the Fed and to the government, which hold (and own) the country's foreign exchange reserves. These reserves are in the form of deposits and other short-term securities issued by foreign governments, central banks, and commercial banks. You can think of this item as representing the U.S. bank account with the rest of the world.

Net Financial Assets

If we add up all eleven items in Table 4.2, we arrive at the net financial assets of each of the major sectors in the economy. The net assets for the banks and other financial institutions and for the Fed will approximately add up to zero, reflecting the fact that these institutions have comparatively small holdings of real assets. (They do, of course, have large *absolute* holdings of real assets. For example, they own quite a large amount of real estate and office space. However, compared with their financial assets and liabilities, such items are relatively insignificant and, for our purposes, can be ignored.)

Typically, households and firms, which together constitute what is called the *nonfinancial private sector*, have positive net financial assets. That is, they own financial assets in excess of the liabilities that they have issued. The government, on the other hand, typically has a net financial liability. That liability is sometimes referred to as the *national debt*. The net financial asset position of the country vis-à-vis the rest of the world may be positive or negative. That is, the rest of the world may have a net financial claim on the United States (if the United States has a net liability, it is referred to as a *net debtor*); or the United States may have a net financial claim on the rest of the world (if the United States has a net financial asset, it is referred to as a *net creditor*). In actuality, the United States is a net creditor.

Real and Financial Assets

Table 4.3 shows the net financial assets of the six sectors. It also shows some additional (nonfinancial) items that will be described below. Further, that table contains an extra column that shows the U.S. economy-wide total value of the six sectors' holdings of the various items.

For the world as a whole (not shown in Table 4.3), net financial assets are zero—someone's financial asset is someone else's liability. For the United States, however, net financial assets are positive since foreigners, not counted as part of the U.S. economy, hold the corresponding liability. Thus in the final "economy" column of Table 4.3, the entry "net claims on rest of world" appears.

Real Assets Real assets—plant, equipment, buildings, etc.—are owned by households, firms, and government. (As discussed earlier, the banks' holdings

TABLE 4.3
Financial Assets and Liabilities and Real Assets

ITEM	SECTOR H	F	B	FED	GOV	R	ECONOMY
Net financial assets	+	+	0	0	−	−	Net claims on rest of world
Real assets	+	+			+	(excluded)	Nonhuman wealth
Future tax liabilities	−	−			+		Monetary base
Undistributed profits	+	−					0
Human wealth	+						Human wealth
Wealth	+	0	0	0	0	−	Wealth

Notes: (+) denotes an asset and (−) denotes a liability. The sectors are: Households (*H*), Firms (*F*), Commercial Banks (*B*), the Federal Reserve (*FED*), Government (*GOV*), and the Rest of the World (*R*). The column headed Economy refers to the economy as a whole and is the sum of each of the six sectors. A zero in the table denotes that the item in question *sums* to zero. A blank in the table denotes that the item in question does not appear (or appears negligibly) in a particular sector's balance sheet.

are very small in relation to the total and are ignored.) The "rest of world" holding of real assets is excluded from the table since these do not constitute part of the economy of the country with which we are dealing.

The total of all the real assets held by households, firms, and government constitutes the *nonhuman wealth* of the economy.

Future Tax Liabilities If the government has liabilities that exceed its real assets—which it typically does—then it is the households and firms that pay the taxes that will be responsible for meeting those liabilities. The government will have to levy taxes on households and firms that equal in value the excess of its liabilities over its assets. This may be thought of as an *implicit* financial asset. It is implicit because no explicit paper claim exists to represent this item. It is an asset to the government and a liability to households and firms.

There is one important government sector liability that never has to be repaid and that does not even involve the government in having to raise taxes to make interest payments. This is the currency that the government has issued, together with the value of the government bonds that are held by the Fed as backing for its liabilities—bank reserves and Federal Reserve bank notes. That this currency never has to be redeemed by the government is obvious. That the government securities held by the Fed are in the same category is perhaps less obvious and needs explaining. The reasoning is as follows: First, the Fed is under no obligation to redeem its liabilities, and it does not have to pay any interest on them. Second, the income made by the Fed on its holdings of government securities is, except for having to cover some relatively small expenses, a profit that the Fed pays to the government. In effect, the government does not have to pay interest on that part of its debt held by the Fed because, although it pays interest, it gets nearly all of it back as Fed profits. Since the Fed does not have to redeem its liabilities and since the government gets a free loan that never has to be repaid equal to the value of the Fed's liabilities, those liabilities are exactly like currency in the sense that they do not attract any future tax liability.

The future tax liabilities of households and firms is less than the value of the corresponding asset of the government by the amount of currency and Fed liabilities that never have to be redeemed by the government. The sum of currency and Fed liabilities is the monetary base (see Table 4.2). Therefore, in Table 4.3, the sum of the future tax liabilities for the economy as a whole is shown as being equal to the value of the monetary base.[2]

Undistributed Profits The government and firms are fundamentally different legal entities from households. Households (and the individuals who constitute them) are the ultimate wealth holders. Firms can be regarded as owing to households the net undistributed profits from their activities. These profits (or losses) are exactly equal to the difference between the firms' real assets and net financial liabilities and are shown as an asset to households and as a liability to firms. In the case of firms that have issued equity, undistributed profits are already taken into account (provided that the equity has been valued correctly).

As an example, consider two firms that are identical in all respects except that one of the firms has purchased some plant and equipment with undistributed profits, whereas another has purchased the equivalent amount of plant and equipment with the proceeds from a bond sale. The stock market value of the equity of the firm with undistributed profits will clearly be higher than that of the firm that has financed some of its planned acquisitions with the proceeds of a bond sale. For firms that do not issue equity, however, for example, partnerships and other private firms, the undistributed profits need to be counted as a liability to the firm and as an asset to the owner or owners of the firm even though there is no explicit marketable security representing that asset and liability.

Human Wealth The value of the future income of the individuals in the economy constitutes the economy's human wealth (or human capital). You will probably understand the concept of human wealth most thoroughly if you consider the example of your own human wealth. Your human wealth is the sum of money which, if used here and now to buy an annuity would provide an income each year for the rest of your life equal in value to the income that you will earn each year. It is an *implicit* asset (rather than an *actual* asset) in the sense that (at least since the abolition of slavery) human capital is not traded directly in markets. It is possible, however, for people to borrow using part of their human capital as collateral. This happens whenever an individual borrows purely for consumption purposes and promises to repay the debt out of *future labor income.* Another, and more precise, definition of human capital is the present value of future labor income.

Wealth The sum of all the net claims on the rest of the world, the nonhuman wealth, the monetary base, and human wealth is the economy's wealth. The household sector owns all the wealth because of the implicit asset/liability

[2]You may be thinking that the government is under no obligation to redeem (buy back) any of its debt and could go on issuing additional debt for ever, and further, could issue debt to pay interest on debt. This is certainly true. Nevertheless, each time the government sells a bond that it has no intention of redeeming (except for another like bond), it commits itself to the payment of an interest stream that has the same value as the funds raised by the bond rate and so may be thought of as establishing a *future* liability on households and firms. Chapter 31 will provide a more precise and thorough explanation of this.

items that take account of future tax liabilities and undistributed profits. Government has no wealth on its own account. It owes any excess of assets over liabilities to the households, and the households are liable for its net debts. Similarly, firms have no net wealth because they owe (are liable to) households any undistributed profits (and households have to stand any losses).

National Balance Sheets and National Income Accounts Changes in the net financial asset position of the various sectors are related to flows in the national income accounts that we examined in Chapter 3. The change in the net financial assets of households and firms taken together represents the difference between saving (S) and investment (I) (shown in Table 4.4 as $S - I$). The reason for this is very natural. Saving constitutes the difference between what is earned (the economy's income) and what is spent on consumer goods and paid in taxes. Some of that saving is used to buy physical capital goods. That is, it is invested in real assets. That which is not invested (i.e., not used to buy real assets) is used to buy financial assets. Therefore, the change in the net financial assets of households and firms is the same thing as saving minus investment.

Banks and other financial institutions and the Fed having zero net financial assets also, of course, have zero change in net financial assets.

The change in the government's financial assets is exactly equal to the difference between its current tax receipts and its current expenditures (G). Thus, in Table 4.4 we show $T - G$ as the change in net financial assets of the government.

The change in the net financial assets of the rest of the world is measured by the difference between the flow of expenditures by domestic residents on foreign goods (imports, IM) and the flow of foreign expenditures on domestic goods (exports, EX). We show the change in net financial assets of the rest of the world as being the difference between imports and exports ($IM - EX$).

It is evident that if we aggregate (add up) net financial assets across all the sectors, then we wind up with zero. That is, what is issued as a liability by one sector is held as an asset by another sector, or sectors. If we add up the net financial asset changes, that is, savings minus investment ($S - I$), plus taxes minus government expenditure ($T - G$), plus imports minus exports ($IM - EX$), then we also always come out with zero, reflecting a fact that we discovered when examining the national income accounts, namely, that saving

TABLE 4.4
Change in Financial Assets and the National Income Flows

ITEM	SECTORS				
	H F	*B*	*FED*	*GOV*	*R*
Change in net financial assets	$S - I$	0	0	$T - G$	$IM - EX$

Note: The sectors are Households (*H*), Firms (*F*), Commercial Banks (*B*), the Federal Reserve (*FED*), Government (*GOV*), and the Rest of the World (*R*). *S* is savings; *I* is investment; *T* is total taxes net of transfer payments, *G* is government expenditure on goods and services, *IM* is imports, and *FX* is exports.

plus taxes plus imports are equal to investment plus government expenditure plus exports.

The Sectoral Balance Sheets If you look at each column of Table 4.2 separately, you will see the financial aspects of the balance sheets of each of the six sectors. Usually in macroeconomics we do not separately analyze the balance sheets of households and firms but rather aggregate them together. If we aggregate the two items—currency and demand deposits—across both households and firms (dotted box), the total of those items equals the narrow money supply, M1. If we aggregate the three items—currency, demand deposits, and savings deposits—across both households and firms (the dashed box), then we arrive at a total equal to the intermediate money supply, M2. If we aggregate the four items of currency, demand deposits, savings deposits, and other deposits across both households and firms, then the total (the unbroken box) equals the broad measure of the money supply, M3. These magnitudes are of crucial importance in macroeconomic analysis.

Consider next the third column (*B*) of Table 4.2. This shows the balance sheet of the banks and other financial institutions. It is clear that the liabilities of this sector are the deposits that the financial institutions issue in the form of demand deposits, savings, and other deposits. Their assets consist of reserves at the Fed, currency, government securities, and loans to individuals and firms.

The Fed's balance sheet has a very simple structure. The liability of the Fed consists of all the Federal Reserve notes outstanding, plus the commercial banks' reserve deposits at the Fed. This aggregate, plus the coin issued by the U.S. Mint, is the monetary base. The assets of the Fed that back the monetary base are government securities and foreign exchange reserves. The Fed can change the volume of the monetary base either by buying and selling government securities or by trading in the foreign exchange market. If the Fed wants to increase the monetary base, it will simply buy government securities, paying for the securities with newly created money. It could equivalently buy foreign exchange, that is, buy, say, Japanese yen using newly created U.S. dollars. It could, of course, reduce the monetary base with the opposite operation.

The balance sheets of the government sector and the rest of the world do not in and of themselves have any intrinsic interest for our present purposes and have been presented here merely so that you can have a complete picture of the structure of indebtedness in the economy and the connection between changes in net financial assets and the flows in the national income accounts.

D. Measuring Aggregate Balance Sheets

The Board of Governors of the Federal Reserve System is the main agency responsible for coordinating and publishing information about aggregate balance sheets in the United States. In its monthly *Federal Reserve Bulletin*, the board publishes a large volume of monthly and quarterly data, as well as some annual data, on either complete or part items of balance sheets of the Federal Reserve System itself, the commercial banks, and the federal government, together with institutions dealing with the financing of real estate, consumer credit, and corporations. Historical data on the flow of funds accounts are published by the Federal Reserve in *Flow of Funds Accounts, Assets and Liabil-*

ities Outstanding.[3] These record the flows of funds between nine major sectors of the economy (representing a more detailed sectoral classification than that employed in Table 4.2 above). The flows themselves are classified according to the acquisitions of 5 different types of real assets (consumer durables, residential construction, plant and equipment, inventories, and mineral rights) and 25 financial assets. A good explanation of the flow of funds accounts is contained in *Introduction to Flow of Funds,*[4] published by the Board of Governors of the Federal Reserve System. It provides detailed definitions of the sectors and the transactions categories. It also provides a good intuitive explanation of how the accounts work and how they are linked to the national income accounts.

It is important to take careful note that the flow of funds accounts, although giving information about aggregate balance sheet movements, are not themselves balance sheets. Rather, they give information about changes in assets and liabilities. This means that there are some evaluation problems that are potentially quite difficult to solve. These arise from the fact that the flow of funds accounts show only the values of assets and liabilities acquired or disposed of during a particular period of time and do not give information about changes in the values of previously and remaining outstanding stocks of assets and liabilities.[5]

The Federal Reserve also publishes regularly information on the magnitudes of the three monetary aggregates, M1, M2, and M3.

All these Federal Reserve data are published in the *Federal Reserve Bulletin* each month. In addition, a more comprehensive statement of the flow of funds accounts is published from time to time, giving a long historical run of data.

Our knowledge about aggregate balance sheets is more fragmentary than is our knowledge of the national income and expenditure flows. From the data collected and published by the Fed, we obtain frequent, reliable, and up-to-date information on the Fed itself, the banks, and some key financial institutions. We do not, however, obtain much information from the Fed concerning the balance sheets of households and firms. The flow of funds accounts do, to some extent, help to fill that gap. The flow of funds information is not, however, a balance sheet since, as already noted, it does not allow for changes in the value of outstanding stocks of assets and liabilities.

Despite the fragmentary nature of the information on aggregate balance sheets, it turns out that we do have sufficient material to form the basis of a serious macroeconomic analysis of the determination of the key variables with which the subject is concerned. Specifically, we have good information about

[3]This is an annual publication of the Board of Governors of the Federal Reserve System.

[4]Introduction to the Flow of Funds, Federal Reserve Board of Governors, February 1975.

[5]National accounting procedures are constantly being upgraded and extended, and there is currently under review the possibility of including balance sheets in a wider system of integrated economic accounts for the United States. For more information on these developments, you should consult Richard and Nancy D. Ruggles, "Integrated Economic Accounts for the United States, 1947–1980," *Survey of Current Business*, 12, no. 5 (May 1982).

the money supply (variously defined) and the monetary base, as the two central stocks that feature prominently in the theories of output, employment, and prices that we shall be looking at shortly.

Summary

A. Asset, Liability, and Balance Sheet

An asset is what someone owns. A liability is what someone owes. There are two types of assets, financial and real. A financial asset is always someone else's liability. An individual's wealth equals total financial and real assets less total liabilities. A balance sheet is a statement of assets and liabilities.

B. Definition and Nature of Money

Money is anything that is generally acceptable as a medium of exchange. In the United States today, money is narrowly defined (M1) as the sum of notes and coins in circulation plus demand deposits. Money is defined more broadly (M2) as M1 plus (small-scale or short-term) savings deposits. A broader definition of money (M3) is M2 plus other (long-term or large-scale) bank deposits.

The monetary base is defined as the total liabilities of the Fed—notes outstanding plus banks' reserve deposits with the Fed—together with the stock of coin in circulation with the public.

C. Main Balance Sheet Items

Main balance sheet items are summarized in Tables 4.2 and 4.3. The net value of financial assets in an economy is its net claims on the rest of the world. The change in net financial assets of the economy equals saving minus investment $(S - I)$, plus taxes minus government expenditure $(T - G)$, plus imports minus exports $(IM - EX)$, which is always zero.

The aggregate of net claims on the rest of the world, nonhuman wealth, monetary base, and human wealth is the wealth of the economy.

A major part of the macroeconomic analysis that we shall be doing centers on the relationships between stocks and flows. In particular, it centers on the connection between the stock of money and the flows of expenditure. The theory of aggregate demand that we shall be developing shortly builds on the concepts that have been defined and on the accounting frameworks that are dealt with in this and in the previous chapter.

D. Measuring Aggregate Balance Sheets

The main coordinator of information about aggregate balance sheets in the United States is the Fed. It collects and publishes information about its own balance sheet, about those of the commercial banks, and about those of other financial institutions. It also collects information on and publishes the *Flow of Funds Accounts*. These accounts give information about *changes* in stocks rather than stocks themselves and do not include information about valuation changes.

The key stock variables needed for macroeconomic analysis are those concerning the monetary base and various definitions of the aggregate stock of money, all of which are collected frequently and reported in the *Federal Reserve Bulletin.*

Review Questions

1. Which of the following are *stocks* and which are *flows*?
   (a) A pocket calculator worth $50.
   (b) A bank deposit of $50.
   (c) The *purchase* of a pocket calculator for $50.
   (d) A car.
   (e) The labor used to make a car.
   (f) The consumption of gasoline by a car.
   (g) The labor used to serve gasoline.
   (h) An outstanding bank loan.
   (i) The interest paid on a bank loan.

2. Which items in a balance sheet are stocks and which are flows?

3. What is the difference between an asset and a liability?

4. Construct your own personal balance sheet. What are your total financial assets and liabilities? What are your real assets? What is your wealth?

5. Using the *Federal Reserve Bulletin*, set out, for a recent date, the balance sheets of the Fed and of the commercial banks. What are the net financial assets, real assets, and wealth of the Fed and of the commercial banks?

6. Indicate how you would set about calculating the U.S. national debt.

7. How would you set about calculating the future tax liabilities of the U.S. government? Whose liabilities are these, and why?

8. Which of the following are "money" in the United States today?
   (a) Mastercard cards.
   (b) Savings and Loan deposits.
   (c) Federal Reserve $1 bills.
   (d) Bank of England £1 notes.
   (e) Bank of Japan ¥ 1000 bills.
   (f) Demand deposits at commercial banks.
   (g) Savings accounts at savings banks.
   (h) Checks.
   (i) Bank loans.
   (j) Mortgages.

9. Using data that you will find in the *Federal Reserve Bulletin*, draw a time-series graph from 1970 to the present of: (a) M1 growth rate, (b) M2 growth rate, and (c) M3 growth rate. Describe these three series. Highlight when each grew the fastest and the slowest. Compare and contrast the magnitude and the direction of change of each.

10. What are the links between aggregate balance sheets and aggregate income accounts? In describing the links, be explicit about flows and stocks.

11. Trace the effects on the balance sheets of the seven sectors of Table 4.2 of the following:

You take a bank loan of $2000 from a commercial bank with which you buy a new computer costing $3000 from Radio Shack. You use your savings account to make up the difference between the bank loan and the purchase price. The Radio Shack computer is made in the United States with U.S.-made component parts.

12. Show the effect of the above transaction on the aggregate income accounts. What are the effects on savings and investment? Show the effects also on the net changes in financial assets and show that these are consistent with the aggregate income accounts.

5

Measuring Inflation and Unemployment

Inflation and unemployment are two of the central variables that macroeconomic theory is designed to explain and that macroeconomic policy seeks to control. Your next preliminary tasks before embarking on a study of macroeconomic theory and policy are to:

(a) Know the definition of inflation.
(b) Understand the concept of a price index and its percentage rate of change.
(c) Know how inflation is measured in the United States.
(d) Know the definition of unemployment.
(e) Know how unemployment is measured in the United States.

A. Definition of Inflation

Inflation may be defined, if somewhat loosely, as the percentage rate at which the general level of prices is changing. We refer to the "general level of prices" as the *price level.* You will notice that the dimension of inflation is the percentage rate of change per unit of time. The concept of the general level of prices is a little bit vague, and we will give more precision to this term below.

First of all, it is important to notice that inflation is an *on-going process*—that is, a process of prices rising on a more or less continuous basis rather than on a once-and-for-all basis. Figure 5.1 illustrates this distinction. The price level is measured on the vertical axis, and time is measured in years on the horizontal axis.

Looking at Figure 5.1, suppose that the economy started out in year 0 with a price level equal to 100. If, over the four-year period shown, the price level rose gradually and continuously to the level 200 (as indicated by the continuous, upward-sloping straight line), then we would want to describe that four-year period as a period of inflation. In contrast, suppose that the economy started out at price level 100 and had a stable level of prices, that is, with prices remaining at level 100 all the way through the first two years. Then

Figure 5.1
The Distinction between Inflation and a Once-and-for-All Rise in the Price Level

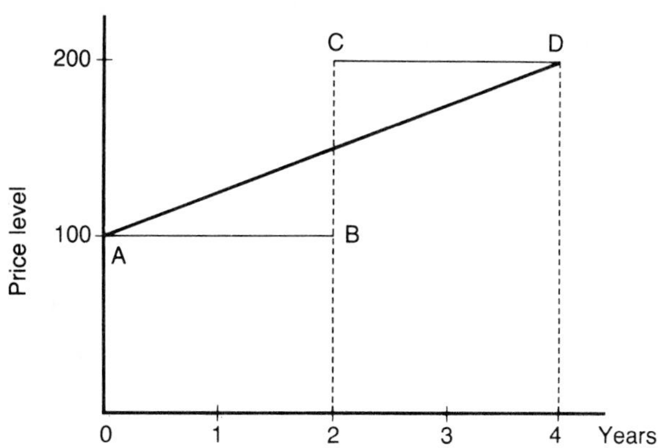

The economy that moves directly along the line AD is one that experiences inflation. The economy that moves along the line ABCD experiences a once-and-for-all rise in the price level in year 2.

suppose that at the beginning of year 2, there was a sudden jump in the price level, from 100 to 200. Suppose thereafter that prices remained at the level 200 and were stable at that level for the remaining two years. We would not normally want to describe this second economy as having had an inflationary four years. Indeed, prices would have been stable in that economy for the first two years at a level of 100 and stable for the second two years at a level of 200.

It is true that the price level starts out at 100 and finishes up at 200 in both cases. However, in the first case, inflation was present in the economy throughout the four-year period. In the second case, we could think of there having been a single instant of inflation when the price level doubled (from 100 to 200) at the beginning of year 2, whereas for the rest of the four-year period the economy was characterized by stable prices. That is, there was a once-and-for-all rise in the price level at the beginning of year 2. In practice, the distinction between a once-and-for-all rise in the price level and inflation may be somewhat blurred because it is possible that a shock to the economy that produces a once-and-for-all rise in prices may have effects that are somewhat drawn out. Thus, although the distinction between inflation and a once-and-for-all rise in prices is an important one in principle, it may in practice often be hard to distinguish one from the other.

The second feature of the phenomenon of inflation that is worth emphasizing at this stage is that it is a rise in the *general* level of prices and not a rise in some particular price or group of prices. The economy may, for example, be experiencing rapid increases in the prices of food and yet not be undergoing an inflation. The rapid increases in food prices may be offset by rapid decreases in prices of some other commodities, such as, for example, electronic data-processing equipment, video games, fuel-efficient cars, and the like. Such price movements, even though they may be very rapid and of great social consequence, are not inflation. They are changes in relative prices.

In order to give more precision to the meaning of inflation, it is now necessary to give more precision to the meaning of the term *the general level of prices*, or *price level*.

B. Price Index and Its Percentage Rate of Change

There can be no unique measure of the price level. The prices of some commodities rise faster than others, and the prices of some things may even fall. Movements in the price level can only be calculated once we have fixed *the basket of goods* to which the price level refers.

A price index measures the amount that would have to be paid for a specific basket of goods in the current period compared with what would have had to have been paid for that same basket in some previous period known as the *base period*. The basket of goods used may be representative of typical consumption patterns in the base period or in the current period. The value of the index in the base period is defined to be 100. Percentage changes in the value of a price index from one year to the next measure the rate of inflation according to the particular index being used.

In order to gain a more concrete understanding of the ideas just set out in summary form, it will be best if we move straight to the next task and illustrate the above propositions.

C. Measuring Inflation in the United States

There are three widely used price indexes for measuring inflation in the United States today. One is known as the Consumer Price Index (CPI), another is known as the Personal Consumption Expenditure (PCE) deflator, and the third is known as the Gross National Product (GNP) deflator.

The Consumer Price Index

The Consumer Price Index (which is calculated and published by the U.S. Department of Labor each month) is an index that attempts to measure movements in the prices of goods and services that are typically consumed by a group of urban American families.

The index is a weighted average of price movements of approximately 400 items. The items themselves and the weights attached to them are chosen to be representative of the goods and services usually bought by urban families.

Each month, price statistics are collected from 56 locations (39 major centers and 17 smaller cities), chosen to be representative of all the urban locations in the United States. Prices are collected from about 18,000 stores, hospitals, gas stations, and other types of establishments. An index is calculated using the following formula:

$$\frac{P_1^t Q_1^0 + P_2^t Q_2^0 + \cdots + P_{400}^t Q_{400}^0}{P_1^0 Q_1^0 + P_2^0 Q_2^0 + \cdots + P_{400}^0 Q_{400}^0} \times 100$$

Although this formula looks formidable, it is in fact very simple. Let us take it piece by piece. The numerator

$$P_1^t Q_1^0 + P_2^t Q_2^0 + \cdots + P_{400}^t Q_{400}^0$$

represents the total amount of money that it would cost in month t at the prices ruling in month t to buy the bundle of commodities that is being used to weight the prices. The term P_1^t is simply the price of expenditure class one in a month t, and the number Q_1^0 is the number of units of expenditure class one in the basket of goods that is being valued. If we simply add up the total outlay on each of the 400 expenditure classes in the index, then we arrive at the number of dollars that would have to be spent to buy the basket of commodities at the prices prevailing in month t. (The dots in the middle of the expression stand for commodities 3 to 399.)

The denominator of the index number calculation

$$P_1^0 Q_1^0 + P_2^0 Q_2^0 + \cdots + P_{400}^0 Q_{400}^0$$

is the amount of money that would have had to have been spent in the base period to purchase the index basket of commodities valued at the prices ruling in the base period. The term P_1^0 is the price of expenditure class one in the base period, period 0. So, $P_1^0 Q_1^0$ is the outlay on commodities in expenditure class one in the base period. Adding the outlays on all commodities that make up the 400 expenditure classes gives the dollar sum of money that would have had to have been spent purchasing the index bundle of commodities in the base period.

The ratio of the outlay in month t to the base period outlay multiplied by 100 gives the index number for the Consumer Price Index in month t. If that index number is 100, then prices have been constant. If the index is greater than 100, prices have risen; and if less than 100, prices have fallen.

Various subsidiary index numbers are available for food, housing, apparel and upkeep, transportation, and health and recreation, and within some of these categories a minute amount of detail is available. Food, for example, is broken down into 117 classes, so that if you are interested, you can find the price indexes of celery and pretzels!

A detailed description of the calculation of the U.S. Consumer Price Index is given in *CPI Detailed Report*, U.S. Department of Labor, December 1976.

Personal Consumption Expenditure (PCE) Deflator

Like the Consumer Price Index, the PCE deflator is also a measure of the inflation of the prices of consumer goods. There are many detailed differences, however, between this index and the CPI. Three differences are important and worth highlighting. First, the PCE deflator measures an average of prices of *all* consumer goods and services, and not just those typical of the consumption patterns of urban families. Second, the PCE deflator uses a current basket of goods and services. That is, it is the expenditure patterns in the current year that are valued in current prices and base period prices. In contrast to this, the

CPI uses a fixed basket of goods and services typical of those consumed (by the relevant group) in the base period.

A third important difference is the way in which the two indexes measure the price of owner-occupied housing services. This is a large item in the index, and, therefore, it does make a material difference to the final calculation. The Consumer Price Index measure is dominated by the current period rate of interest on mortgage loans for owner-occupied housing finance. The PCE deflator measures the cost of owner-occupied housing by attempting to assess the prices that would have to be paid by owner-occupiers to rent a comparable house in the rental market. Conceptually, the PCE deflator is trying to measure the right thing. The Consumer Price Index mismeasures the cost of owner-occupied housing. (You will be in a good position to appreciate precisely why this is so after you have studied Chapter 17.)

The sources of information used in calculating the PCE deflator are, to a large extent, the same as those used for measuring the Consumer Price Index. In addition, however, certain rural prices collected by the U.S. Department of Agriculture and other specialized price indexes calculated by the Bureau of Economic Analysis in the Department of Commerce are also employed.

To see more clearly how the PCE deflator is calculated, take as the starting point the measurement of consumption expenditure in current dollars. In order to calculate that total, it is necessary to take the quantity of each good, Q_i, and multiply it by its price, P_i. We then have to add up the resulting values over all the goods and services in the economy. This gives personal consumption expenditures in current dollars. That is, *personal consumption expenditure in current dollars equals*

$$P_1^t Q_1^t + P_2^t Q_2^t + \cdots + P_n^t Q_n^t$$

The P's and Q's in this formula stand for the prices and quantities of the entire volume of consumption of goods and services in the economy, and not simply for the typical urban consumers' basket that was referred to in the preceding section on the Consumer Price Index. It includes the urban consumers' expenditures as well as all other consumption expenditures.

Now, instead of valuing personal consumption expenditures by multiplying the quantity of each good consumed in a given year by the price of the good in that year, we could multiply consumption in a given year by the prices that prevailed in some base year—for example, year 0. If we pursued such a calculation, we would calculate *personal consumption expenditure in constant dollars equals*

$$P_1^0 Q_1^t + P_2^0 Q_2^t + \cdots + P_n^0 Q_n^t$$

This is a measure of the value of personal consumption expenditures in year t but valued at the prices prevailing in the base year, year 0.

If we divide the constant price personal consumption figure into the current price figure, we obtain the PCE deflator:

$$\text{PCE deflator} = \frac{\text{PCE in current dollars}}{\text{PCE in constant dollars}} \times 100$$

The PCE deflator is sometimes called the PCE *implicit deflator*. The deflator is implicit because we arrive at it from the evaluation of the personal consumption expenditure on the basis of two alternative sets of prices.

GNP Deflator

The third price index often employed to measure inflation is the GNP deflator. It is a similar index in its construction to the PCE deflator. The main difference between these two deflators is the breadth of coverage of the goods and services whose prices go to make up the two indexes. The PCE deflator is a measure of the prices of consumption only. In contrast, the GNP deflator measures the prices of consumption goods and services, capital goods (investment), government purchases of goods and services, and exports and imports as well. It is calculated using a formula exactly like that described above for the Personal Consumption Expenditure deflator. It uses many of the same basic pieces of information as are used in constructing the Consumer Price Index and the PCE deflator. In addition, it uses indexes of building and construction costs and indexes of unit values of imports and exports, as well as other specialized indexes produced in the Department of Commerce.

The Percentage Rate of Change in the Price Index as a Measure of Inflation

We can now define U.S. inflation precisely: U.S. inflation is the percentage rate of change over a specified unit of time (usually a year) in either the Consumer Price Index, the PCE deflator, or GNP deflator.

For example, in December 1981, the Consumer Price Index was 281.5. In December of the year earlier, 1980, the index was 258.4. To calculate the rate of inflation as measured by the Consumer Price Index for the year from December 1980 to December 1981, perform the following calculation:

$$\text{Inflation} = \frac{(281.5 - 258.4)}{258.4} \times 100$$

$$= 8.9\% \text{ per annum}$$

We could perform a similar calculation using the PCE deflator as the GNP deflator.

Both the Consumer Price Index and PCE deflator are available monthly and give a continuous monitoring of the economy's inflation rate. The GNP deflator is available quarterly. Movements in the three broad indexes do not coincide but are not excessively divergent. The table in the appendix to Chapter 2 lists the rate of inflation in the United States each year from 1900 to 1981 as measured by these three indexes, and Figure 2.1 of Chapter 2 shows how they behave.

For convenience, the inflation rates as measured by the three price indexes over the last ten years are reproduced here as Table 5.1. The broad picture presented by each of these three index numbers is of course the same. Inflation was lower in the early 1970s than subsequently. Inflation was at its strongest in 1974–1975 and again in 1979–1981. The detailed picture given by

TABLE 5.1
A Comparison of Inflation Rates as Measured by the Consumer Price Index (CPI), Personal Consumption Expenditure (PCE) Deflator, and Gross National Product (GNP) Deflator

YEAR	CPI	PCE DEFLATOR	GNP DEFLATOR	CPI LESS PCE DEFLATOR	GNP DEFLATOR LESS PCE DEFLATOR
1971	4.2	4.9	4.2	−0.7	−0.7
1972	3.2	4.1	3.6	−0.9	−0.5
1973	6.0	5.5	5.5	0.5	0.0
1974	10.4	8.4	9.6	2.0	1.2
1975	8.7	8.9	7.4	−0.2	−1.5
1976	5.6	5.1	5.0	0.5	−0.1
1977	6.3	5.7	5.8	0.6	0.1
1978	7.4	7.1	6.7	0.3	−1.4
1979	10.7	8.1	8.5	2.6	0.4
1980	12.7	8.6	9.7	4.1	1.1
1981	9.9	8.8	7.9	1.1	−0.9

SOURCE: Appendix to Chapter 2

each index is, however, different. In particular, the Consumer Price Index seems to suggest a faster inflation rate than either of the other two indexes. There are several reasons for this, three of which are worth highlighting.

The first reason for the different measured inflation rates is that different weights are used to compile the index numbers. The Consumer Price Index uses fixed weights. This means that the attempts by consumers to substitute away from relatively more expensive items toward relatively less expensive items are not captured in the CPI. Perhaps an example will make this clearer. Suppose that oranges and apples were consumed in equal quantities in the base year. Suppose that between the base year and the current year, the prices of oranges have doubled, but the prices of apples have increased by only 20 percent. It would be expected that this would lead to a substitution away from oranges toward apples, so that, in the current year, more apples and fewer oranges are consumed compared with the base year. If an index was calculated of the price of fruit that assumed that equal quantities of apples and oranges were consumed in both the base year and the current year, then that would tend to overstate the rise in expenditure (the rise in the average price of) fruit. If the weights attached to oranges and apples were changed, however, in accordance with the changed spending patterns in the current year, then the substitution away from the now more expensive oranges toward the now less expensive apples would be captured. The CPI presumes unchanged weights, whereas the PCE deflator allows for substitutions to take advantage of relatively less expensive items.

The second reason for the differences in the two indexes reflects difficulties that the Consumer Price Index has in coping with quality changes and with the introduction of new products. Again, an example will perhaps make this clear. Suppose that between 1980 and 1981, the price of cars rose by 10 percent. Suppose also, however, that improvements took place in the fuel efficiency of their engines so that their gas consumption was down by 5 percent on the average between the two years. How much have car prices really increased during that year? The answer is that they have increased by less than 10 percent. But how much less? How can one allow adequately for quality improvements of that type? With sufficient ingenuity we could presumably figure out the exact answer to the question and allow for quality improvements in this case. There will be other cases, however, where allowance for quality improvements will be virtually impossible. For example, over the years the quality of the picture and sound delivered by a television set has improved dramatically. How should that be allowed for in calculating the true rate of inflation of television prices? This question (and similar ones in connection with many thousands of other products) are hard to answer, and as a result, there is a general presumption that the Consumer Price Index does not adequately allow for gradual improvements in product quality.

The third reason for the difference in the performance of these two indexes lies in the way in which each measures the cost of owner-occupied housing. Big movements in interest rates show up quickly in the Consumer Price Index but are allowed to be reflected in the PCE deflator only to the extent that they change the rental rates on houses of comparable quality to owner-occupied houses. The difference in the inflation rates of the CPI and the PCE deflator is shown in column 4 of Table 5.1. Since 1971, this difference has ranged from −0.9 in 1972 to 4.1 percentage points in 1980. The reason why the GNP deflator inflation rate differs from that of both the CPI and PCE deflator lies mainly in the fact that it measures the prices of a much broader basket of goods, one that includes capital goods as well as those goods bought by government and net exports. The differences in the GNP deflator and the consumption price indexes, then, can be seen as reflecting changes in the relative price of consumer goods to all other goods. The difference between the inflation rates of the GNP deflator and the PCE deflator is shown in column 5 of the above table. This difference has ranged from −1.5 percentage points in 1975 to 1.2 percentage points in 1974.

We will be analyzing the determination of the rate of inflation as measured by the GNP deflator in our theoretical analysis later in this book. However, since movements in the three index numbers are broadly in line with each other, you can, for most purposes, think of the analysis as relating to the Consumer Price Index or PCE deflator as well, although there may be some specific exercises for which such a presumption would not be warranted.

Let us now turn our attention to the definition and measurement of unemployment.

D. Definition of Unemployment

A person is said to be unemployed when he or she is able and willing to work and is available for work (that is, the person is actively searching for employment) but does not have work. The number of people unemployed in an economy is the number of people whom that description fits. The unemployment rate in an economy is the number of unemployed expressed as a percentage of the total labor force. The total labor force is defined as the number of people employed plus the number of people unemployed.

You will notice that the definition of unemployment says nothing at all about the reasons for unemployment. It simply defines an aggregate or a percent rate based on an explicit and objective criterion for classifying individuals. Much economic analysis of the causes of unemployment and fluctuations in its rate uses terms such as *voluntary* and *involuntary* to describe different types of unemployment.

We shall not have any reason to use such definitions in this book. It may be very interesting for some purposes to know whether a person is voluntarily or involuntarily unemployed. From our point of view, however, it is irrelevant. We are going to be concerned with an objective analysis of the factors that lead to variations in unemployment and to develop theories that will enable us to predict the consequences for unemployment of certain well-defined policies. It will not be necessary for us to inquire into the state of mind of the unemployed person concerning the voluntary or involuntary nature of the unemployment being experienced.

E. Measuring Unemployment in the United States

Unemployment figures are calculated by the Bureau of Labor Statistics in the U.S. Department of Labor and are published each month in a publication called *Employment and Earnings.* A considerable amount of detail concerning the anatomy of unemployment is provided by the Department of Labor's figures. Unemployment is classified by state, sex and age, industry and occupation, and duration of unemployment.

All the unemployment figures are based on information generated from a sample survey of households known as the Current Population Survey. The week that includes the 12th of the month is known as the "survey week." Households are actually interviewed in the week after the "survey week." Close to 50,000 households are in the sample, although about 4 percent of them are, for various reasons, not contacted. The sample changes each month with one-quarter of the households dropping out and being replaced by new households. The precise definition of unemployment measured by the survey is officially given as follows:

> Unemployed persons comprise all persons who did not work during the survey week, who made specific efforts to find a job within the 4 previous weeks, and who were available for work during the survey week (except for temporary illness). Also included as unemployed are those who did not work at all, were available for work, and (a) were waiting to be called back to a job from which they had been laid off; or (b) were waiting to report to a new wage or salary job within 30 days.[1]

To calculate the unemployment rate, the total number of persons that fit the above definition of unemployment are added to the total of employed to

[1] *Employment and Earnings*, 23, no. 1 (January 1978), 136 (Washington, D.C.: U.S. Department of Labor, Bureau of Labor Statistics).

obtain an estimate of the total labor force, and then the unemployed are calculated as a percentage of the total labor force.

No questions are asked concerning the wages at which a person would be willing to work. Thus, although the Current Population Survey counts the number of people who are able and willing to work and who are available for work, it does not check whether there was a willingness to work at any particular wage rate. Fairly clearly, if wages were "high enough," just about everyone would be willing to work, and in that case the entire population not in employment could be regarded as unemployed. Equally clearly, this would not be a very helpful definition of the concept of unemployment. What we really would like to know is the total number of people who are able and willing to work and available to work on terms and conditions currently available. There is a presumption, although there is no explicit means of checking it, that the respondents to the Current Population Survey are implicitly indicating a willingness to work on currently available terms and conditions.

A further shortcoming of the measured unemployment rate arises from the way in which it treats so called discouraged workers and those in part-time employment who would prefer to be in full-time employment. Discouraged workers are people who are unemployed in the sense that they would be willing to work on currently available terms and conditions and are available to work but have given up the active search for work because of their discouraging experience. This type of (unmeasured) unemployment is likely to be most serious when the unemployment rate is high and has remained high for some time. Those in part-time employment who would ideally want to have full-time employment may be thought of as being partially unemployed. The measured unemployment rate misses the fraction of the work effort that such individuals would be willing to supply on current terms and conditions. Broader measures of unemployment than those calculated on the basis of the Current Population Survey, which included discouraged workers and partial unemployment of part-time workers, clearly would show the unemployment rate to be higher than that actually measured. It is likely, however, that the broad up-and-down movements in the broader measure would be similar to those in the official measure.

Summary

A. Definition of Inflation

Inflation is defined as the percentage rate of change in a price index.

B. Price Index and its Percentage Rate of Change

A price index is calculated by valuing a specific basket of goods at the prices prevailing in a base period and at the prices prevailing in a subsequent period. The price index is the ratio of the values of these two baskets multiplied by100. The rate of inflation is measured as the percentage rate of change of the index.

C. Measuring Inflation in the United States

There are three commonly used price indexes in the United States: the Consumer Price Index (CPI), the Personal Consumption Expenditure (PCE) deflator, and the Gross National Product (GNP) deflator. The CPI is based on a fixed basket of goods and services typical of the consumption patterns of urban households. The PCE and GNP deflators are calculated on the basis of a current basket of goods and services, with the PCE deflator covering all consumption expenditures and the GNP deflator covering all consumption plus investment purchases and net exports.

D. Definition of Unemployment

Unemployment is defined as the number of people able and willing to work and available for work but not having work.

E. Measuring Unemployment in the United States

Unemployment is measured in the United States by the Current Population Survey, conducted each month. The survey records as unemployed all those who did not work during the survey week, who made specific efforts to find a job within the four previous weeks, and who were available for work during the survey week. It also includes as unemployed those who were waiting to be called back to a job from which they had been laid off, as well as those waiting to report to a new job within 30 days.

Review Questions

1. What is inflation?

2. What are the three commonly used measures of inflation in the United States?

3. How is the Consumer Price Index in the United States calculated? What is the Consumer Price Index designed to measure?

4. Using a recent *Survey of Current Business*, find the Consumer Price Index (CPI) for the period from 1966 to the present. Be sure you are consistent and collect either midyear (June) or end-of-year (December) figures.

(a) What is the base year of the CPI that you have collected?

(b) Calculate the percentage rate of change of the CPI each year since 1966 and explain exactly what it measures.

5. What does the GNP deflator measure and how is it calculated? Why is it called an *implicit* deflator?

6. From a recent *Survey of Current Business*, collect the GNP deflator for the period from 1966 to the present. Calculate the percentage rate of change of the GNP deflator. Explain exactly what this series measures.

7. From a recent *Survey of Current Business*, collect the PCE deflator for the period from 1966 to the present. Calculate the percentage rate of change of the PCE deflator. Explain exactly what this series measures.

8. The table in the appendix to Chapter 2 gives a comparison of inflation rates as measured by the CPI, the PCE deflator, and the GNP deflator. Plot these three time-series graphs for the period since 1966. Describe these series. Highlight the highest and lowest measures of inflation. Compare and contrast inflation as measured by these three series.

9. What is unemployment?

10. Exactly how does the U.S. Department of Labor define unemployment?

11. How is unemployment in the United States measured?

12. The unemployment rate in the United States varies from state to state. Use the U.S. Department of Labor publication *Employment and Earnings* to collect time-series data starting in 1967 on the unemployment rate of the state in which you live and for the United States as a whole. Plot these two time-series as graphs. Describe, compare, and contrast them. Does your state have higher or lower unemployment than the United States on the average? Try to think of reasons why your state differs in the way that it does from the national average.

13. What are the main problems with the way unemployment is measured in the United States?

6

The Business Cycle

The final chapter of this part is different from the other four. It does not deal with the problem of measuring a single macroeconomic variable (or group of variables). Rather, it is concerned with the problem of observing and discerning patterns in the evolution of the economic aggregates and in the relationships among variables. In short, it is concerned with the business cycle.[1]

Until the middle 1930s, the term *business cycle* was used to describe the phenomenon that students of short-term movements in economic aggregates sought to explain and understand. Scholars saw their task as one of understanding the general recurrent ups and downs in economic activity *viewed as an ongoing process.* In 1936, however, with the publication by John Maynard Keynes of *The General Theory of Employment, Interest and Money,*[2] there was a fundamental redirection of research effort. What Keynes did was to change the question that students of aggregate economic phenomena tried to answer. Instead of trying to understand the recurrent ups and downs of economic activity viewed as an ongoing process, Keynes redirected research efforts to an apparently easier question, namely, that of the determination of output, employment, prices, interest rates, etc., *viewed at a point in time,* taking the past history of the economy and expectations about the future as given.

At about the same time as Keynes's simplification enabled scholars to direct their attention to the simpler question of the determination of the aggregate economic variables at a point in time, strides were being made in the mathematical formulation and statistical testing of economic theories, notably by the Dutch economist Jan Tinbergen. As a result of the pioneering efforts of Keynes and Tinbergen, subsequent scholars were able to develop a considerable refined body of knowledge that came to be known as *macroeconomics.* In

[1]This chapter draws heavily on, and in places will be recognized as a paraphrase of, parts of the important paper "Understanding Business Cycles," by Robert E. Lucas, Jr., in *Stabilization of the Domestic and International Economy*, Carnegie-Rochester Conference Series on Public Policy, 5, eds. Karl Brunner and Allan H. Meltzer (Amsterdam: North Holland Publishing Co., 1977.)

[2]John Maynard Keynes, *The General Theory of Employment, Interest and Money* (London: Macmillan & Co. Ltd., 1936).

this new macroeconomic analysis, there seemed to be no special place for business cycle theory. Indeed, as far as Keynes himself was concerned, the job of explaining what determined the values of economic variables at a moment in time is almost the same thing as explaining the business cycle (or *trade cycle* as it is known in Europe). Keynes said that

> since we claim to have shown... what determines the volume of employment at any time, it follows, if we are right, that our theory must be capable of explaining the phenomena of the Trade Cycle.[3]

Further, not only did it appear that there was no need for a special theory of the business cycle, it even seemed as if the earlier attempts to find a theory of the business cycle were hopelessly muddled and confused in comparison with the clarity that had been brought to the task of understanding the determination of the aggregate economic variables at a point in time.

It was not until the early 1970s, with the seminal work of Robert E. Lucas, Jr. of the University of Chicago, that attention was redirected to the problem of understanding more than what determines income, employment, prices, etc., at a point in time, given their past history. Lucas suggested that the bigger question of what determines the evolution of the aggregate economic variables over time, and viewed as a process, had to be tackled head on if we were to develop a deep enough understanding of aggregate economic phenomena to be able to design policy arrangements that would stand some chance of improving matters.

As Lucas sees things, and as will be elaborated more fully later in this book, the task of understanding what determines income, employment, and prices at a moment in time, given their past history, cannot be accomplished without *analyzing the entire ongoing cyclical process* that determines these aggregate economic variables. The key reason for this is that what people do today depends on their expectations of what is going to happen in the future. To formulate an expectation as to what is going to happen in the future, people have to do the best they can to assess how the economy will evolve in the future. This means that their current action will depend on their expectations of future actions by themselves and by others. Now it is evident that the only guide that is available concerning what will happen in the future is what has happened in the past. This means that if present actions depend on expectations of the future, they must also depend on what has happened in the past. Only by analyzing an entire economic process—past, present, and future—shall we be able to understand what is happening at any given moment.

The redirection of research effort in macroeconomics by Keynes was not, in my view, a blind alley. Rather, it was a necessary stage in the process of developing a satisfactory theory of the business cycle. Not until we had made a great deal of progress with the simpler question posed by Keynes were we able to go back to the harder question to which Lucas has now redirected us.

To progress through the subject matter of modern macroeconomics all the way to the new theories of the business cycle will take most of the rest of

[3]Ibid., p. 313.

this book. Not until we get to Chapter 29 will it be possible to summarize our current understanding of what determines business cycles.

In order to pave the way, this chapter will take you through five tasks that are designed to enable you to understand what we mean by business cycles. These tasks are to:

(a) Know the definition of the business cycle.
(b) Understand the concept of autocorrelation.
(c) Understand the concept of co-movement.
(d) Know the properties of the business cycle.
(e) Know the features of the U.S. business cycle.

A. Definition of the Business Cycle

Although business cycles have been studied for well over a hundred years, it was not until the 1940s that a clear definition of business cycles emerged, due to the efforts of a group of outstanding and careful observers of cycles working under the auspices of the National Bureau of Economic Research in New York. Wesley Clare Mitchell and Arthur F. Burns (Burns subsequently became chairman of the Board of Governors of the Federal Reserve System) defined the business cycle as follows:

> Business cycles are a type of fluctuation found in the aggregate economic activity of nations that organize their work mainly in business enterprises: A cycle consists of expansions occurring at about the same time in many economic activities, followed by similarly general recessions, contractions and revivals which merge into the expansion phase of the next cycle; this sequence of changes is recurrent but not periodic; in duration business cycles vary from more than one year to ten or twelve years; they are not divisible into shorter cycles of similar character with amplitudes approximating their own.[4]

Let us dissect this definition a little bit. Three aspects of the definition are worth highlighting. First, let us ask, What is a business cycle a cycle in? The answer to that is given in the first part of the definition: The business cycle is a cycle (or fluctuation) in aggregate economic activity. Although there are several alternative ways in which "aggregate economic activity" may be measured, the most natural comprehensive measure is the level of real income (output or expenditure)—real GNP. Such a measure summarizes all the many individual producing and spending activities in the economy. Because real GNP, on the average, grows from one year to the next, it is necessary, in defining the cycle, to abstract from that growth trend and define the cycle as "deviations of real GNP from trend." By regarding the deviations of real GNP from trend as defining the cycle, it is possible to examine the ups and

[4]This definition is from Arthur F. Burns and Wesley Clare Mitchell, *Measuring Business Cycles* (New York: National Bureau of Economic Research, 1946), p. 3.

Figure 6.1
A Hypothetical Cycle

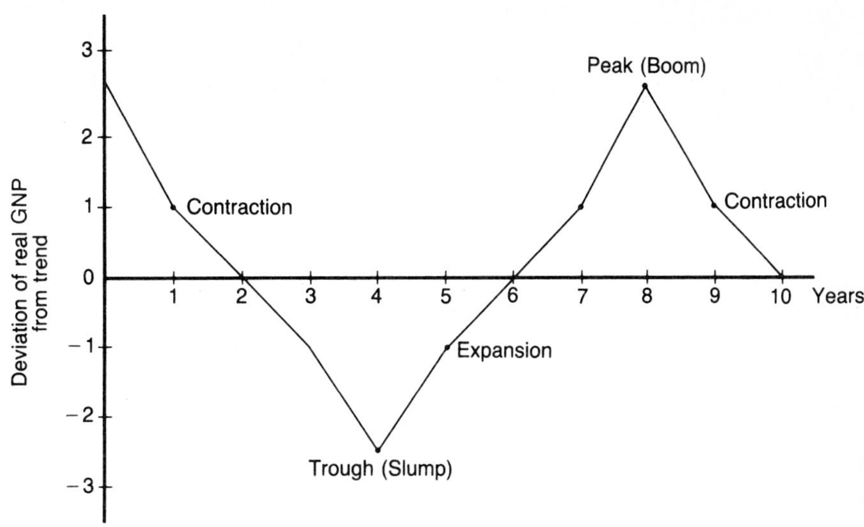

A cycle in the deviation of real GNP from trend begins in the contraction phase, reaches a trough (or slump), moves through an expansion to a peak (or boom), and then turns into a further contraction phase.

downs of other aggregate variables in relation to or *with reference to* the cycle in real GNP.[5]

The second thing to notice about the definition of the cycle is that it involves two turning points, an upper turning point and a lower turning point; and two phases, an expansion phase and a contraction phase. Figure 6.1 illustrates the hypothetical cycle of Table 6.1. The upper turning point is often referred to as the *cyclical peak* and the lower turning point as the *cyclical trough.* The movement from the peak to the trough is the *contraction,* and the movement from trough back to peak is the *expansion.* If a contraction is particularly severe, it is referred to as a *recession.* Technically, a recession is defined as occurring when real GNP falls for two successive quarters. An even more severe contraction and prolonged trough would be known as a *depression,* and if particularly severe, the prefix *great* would be attached to it. The picture of the cycle shown in Figure 6.1 gives just one complete up-and-down movement in the deviation of real GNP from trend.

The third feature of the definition of the business cycle emphasizes the fact that cycles are not regular *periodic* ups and downs but are *irregular* though *recurrent* ups and downs, the duration of which (measured from trough to trough) could run from something slightly more than one year to as long as

[5]In their pioneering work on measuring the business cycle, the National Bureau of Economic Research economists (referred to above) developed a concept of the *reference cycle,* which was somewhat more general than simply using deviations of real GNP from trend. Their methods, however, to some degree involve judgment, and to describe them and fully appreciate them would divert us too far.

Table 6.1
Calculating Deviations of Real GNP From Trend

YEAR	REAL GNP		
	Trend Value	Actual Value	Deviation from Trend
0	100.0	102.5	+2.5
1	104.0	105.0	+1.0
2	108.2	108.2	0
3	112.5	111.5	−1.0
4	117.0	114.5	−2.5
5	121.7	120.7	−1.0
6	126.5	126.5	0
7	131.6	132.6	+1.0
8	136.9	139.4	+2.5
9	142.3	143.3	+1.0
10	148.0	148.0	0

ten or twelve years. To see how we might characterize this in a simple way involves introducing a technical idea that will be developed in the next section of this chapter—the concept of autocorrelation.

The fourth and final feature of the definition of the cycle given above—that "they are not divisible into shorter cycles of similar character with amplitudes approximating their own"—is simply designed to capture the idea that the cycle is a basic unit of observation and analysis. It is not divisible into smaller similar patterns.

Let us now turn to the first of the two technical tasks that face us in this chapter.

B. Autocorrelation

This section and the next one deal with technical matters. They do so, however, in a nontechnical way.[6] It is worthwhile becoming familiar with the concept of autocorrelation because it will give you a more precise, and at the same time very simple, way of viewing a process that may be used to describe the recurrent but nonperiodic ups and downs in economic activity that characterize the business cycle.

Two key ideas are combined in the concept of autocorrelation. First, *the present is influenced by the past*; second, *the present is not completely predictable from knowledge of the past.* An alternative way of capturing the same two ideas would be to say that the current value of some variable may be better predicted by knowledge of its past values but may not be exactly predicted on the basis of such knowledge.

There are many examples in everyday life of autocorrelation. One obvious one is the state of the weather. Wet days and dry days tend to go in runs. If you were to try predicting tomorrow's weather without using refined meterological observations and methods, one possible rule might be to predict

[6]If you want a more technical though still simplified treatment of this topic, you should work through the appendix to this chapter.

that tomorrow will be much like today. If today is wet, you predict that tomorrow will also be wet. And if today is dry, you predict that tomorrow will also be dry. Such a prediction will, of course, often be wrong. It turns out, however, that it will be right more often than it is wrong. It will certainly do better than flipping a coin and calling "dry" for heads and "wet" for tails. How much better it will do will depend in part on where you live and what the longer-term climatic patterns are. Nevertheless, the basic idea of predicting tomorrow's weather on the basis of today's is a sound one (though not the best available) and one that exploits the autocorrelation in weather patterns.

Another example concerns the movements of waves on the ocean surface. Sitting at the ocean side you can predict the pattern and timing of the wave movements breaking on the shoreline by supposing that the next wave will look much like the one that has just preceded it. You will not be exactly right because the wind patterns and the interaction of the waves ensure that no wave is exactly like its predecessor. There is, however, a strong resemblance.

A third example would be the movement of a child's swing or rocking horse. If you wanted to predict the extent of the movement of the horse or the height attained by the swing on a given movement, predicting an outcome similar to that which occurred on the previous rock or swing would be fairly accurate. It would not be exactly right because you wouldn't know exactly how much work the child was doing to keep the motion of the swing or horse at a constant level. An unpredictable surge of effort on the child's part would send the swing or horse on a more extreme course, whereas an unpredicted slackening off of effort would cause the horse or swing to come closer to a rest position.

These are all examples of the existence of autocorrelation in the behavior of variables that we commonly observe in the ordinary course of life. We need to be more precise, however, in specifying how the current value of some variable relates to its previous value or values. The simplest case would be where the value of a variable at a given point in time depends only on its own value at the previous point in time. (The units in which time is measured will vary from case to case and could be as short as an instant or as long as a decade. In economics we typically think of units of time as coming either in calendar quarters or years.) Such a case is given the special name *first-order autocorrelation.* If the current value of a variable depends on its own values at the previous point in time *and* at the time before that, then it is given the special name *second-order autocorrelation.* This idea clearly can be generalized to permit any degree of influence of the past on the present.

The aspect of autocorrelation having to do with imperfect predictability simply reflects the obvious fact that the world is a fairly complicated place and is not capable of prediction by the application of simple (mechanical) rules linking current values of variables to their own past values. A different way of saying the same thing is that, to some extent, the world is *random* (or *stochastic*).

Let us now use the notion of autocorrelation to describe the evolution of real GNP from one year to the next. Real GNP would be autocorrelated if next year's GNP could be better predicted, although not exactly predicted, from knowledge of the current (and perhaps some previous) year's GNP. We can capture this idea by writing an equation that says

$$y_t = 25 + 0.75y_{t-1} + e_t \tag{6.1}$$

The variable y_t represents the value of real GNP in year t. The same variable with the subscript $t - 1$ represents the value of real GNP in the previous year. The variable e_t represents all the random unpredictable influences that affect real GNP that are not predictable on the basis of knowledge of previous values of GNP. What this equation says (and it is of course just an example) is that real GNP in a given year will be equal to three-quarters of its previous year's value, plus 25, plus some unpredictable random amounts.

Such an equation, as we shall see in the final section of this chapter, fairly well describes the movements not in GNP itself but in deviations of GNP from its trend values.

You have now discovered what autocorrelation is. Autocorrelation simply means that the value of some particular variable at some particular date is related to its own value at some earlier date. In the above example, income at date t is related to income at date $t - 1$. The relationship is not perfect. There is a randomness that loosens the link between income at date t and income at date $t - 1$. In rough terms, an autocorrelated series is one that shows systematic and recurrent up-and-down movements.

It is important to realize that *describing* the path of GNP by a low-order stochastic difference equation is not the same thing as *understanding* what *causes* GNP movements—that is, what causes the business cycle. The description is simply a neat and convenient way of thinking about the process. It also directs our attention to potential explanations in the sense that it alerts us to the idea that we shall have to find, in any theory of the business cycle, two things:

1. A source of, or more generally, sources of, random disturbance to the economy.
2. Systematic sources of inertia causing movements of GNP (and other aggregates) from one period to another to be gradual—that is, to display autocorrelation.

Although you are now able to describe the recurrent ups and downs in real income in very simple terms, you need to be aware of some other technical language that will help you to talk about broader aspects of the business cycle. This is the next task.

C. Co-Movement

In fully characterizing business cycles, it is going to be necessary to talk about the way in which different variables move in relation to each other. That is, we shall want to be able to say how employment and unemployment, prices and wages, and money and interest rates all move in relationship to the movements in real income. In other words, we want to be able to characterize the co-movements of various pairwise combinations of variables.

Figure 6.2
Leading and Lagging Procyclical Co-Movements

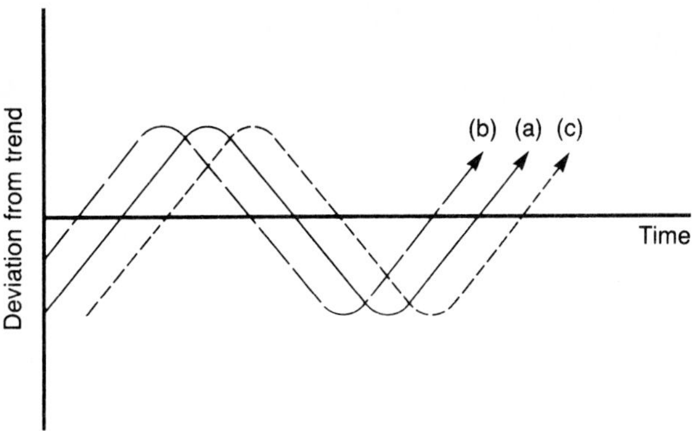

The three series plotted here have procyclical co-movements. If (a) describes the reference cycle of real income deviations from trend, then the variable (b) leads the cycle in income, and the variable (c) lags the cycle.

There are four features of co-movements amongst variables that may be identified. First, co-movements may be either *procyclical* or *countercyclical.* A procyclical co-movement is a movement in a variable that has broadly the same cyclical pattern as the variable with which it is being compared. It tends to rise when the reference variable rises and to fall when the reference variable falls. Since the reference variable for the business cycle is deviation of GNP from trend, procyclical variables are those that rise as GNP rises above trend and fall as GNP falls below trend.

A countercyclical co-movement is a movement in one variable that is in the opposite direction to the movement in the reference variable. Thus, a countercyclical variable is one that falls as real GNP rises above its trend and rises as real GNP falls below its trend.

Usually, variables do not exactly move in a procyclical or countercyclical manner. They tend to either *lead* or *lag* the reference variable. This is the second feature of co-movement that we need to identify. Figure 6.2 illustrates leading and lagging procyclical variables. Suppose that the curve labelled (a) represents the cycle in real GNP. Then the line (b) would represent a variable that leads the cycle, and (c) would represent a variable that lags the cycle. Both variables are generally procyclical. That is, they generally move up with income and down with income, but they don't move at exactly the same time. Figure 6.3 illustrates a countercyclical co-movement. If (a) again is the path of real GNP, then (d) would be the path of a variable that moves countercyclically.

You will recognize that there is a potential element of ambiguity as to whether a variable is countercyclical or procyclical if it leads or lags the reference variable by "too much." You could, as a matter of description, regard a variable that is exactly countercyclical as one that is procyclical but lagged by half a cycle. That would seem to be using language in an awkward way, however. We don't think of leads and lags as being as big as half a cycle.

Figure 6.3
Countercyclical Co-Movements

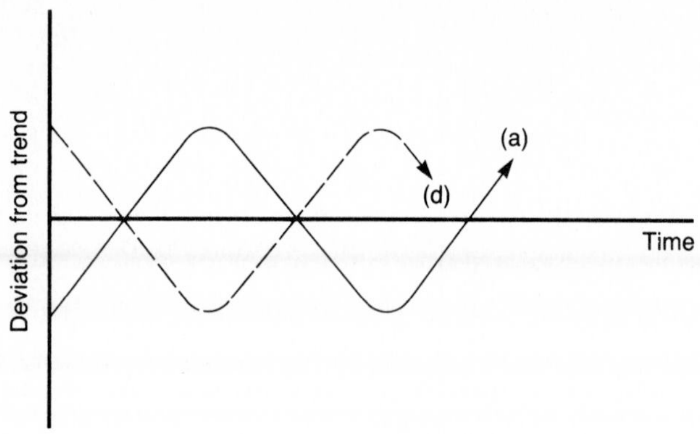

The variable marked (d) displays perfect countercyclical co-movement with the variable marked (a).

A third feature of co-movement has to do with the *amplitude* of fluctuation in one variable relative to another. Roughly speaking, the amplitude of fluctuation in a variable is the distance from the average value to its peak value, or average value to trough value. Figure 6.4 illustrates this. Suppose that the line labelled (a) measures the percentage deviation from trend of real GNP. The thin lines marked (b) and (c) are examples of variables that display smaller amplitude (b), and larger amplitude (c) than the fluctuations in real GNP (a). Of course, there has to be a unit-free method of comparing different variables. It would not do to measure GNP in billions of dollars and interest rates in percentages, for example. The most natural unit-free measure is the percentage deviation of each variable from its trend.

The fourth and final feature of a co-movement that we need to identify is the *conformity* between the two variables. We shall say that co-movement has

Figure 6.4
Amplitude

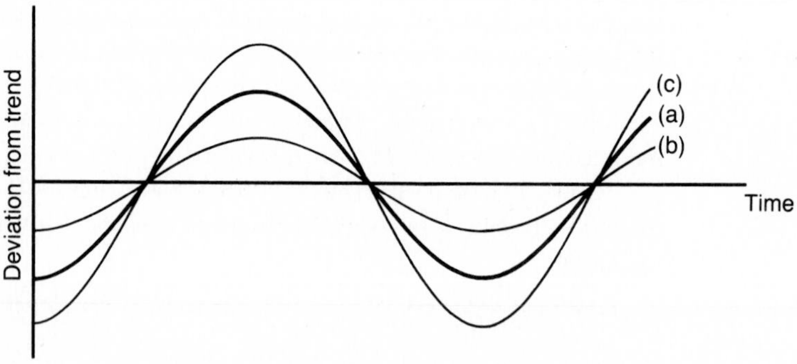

The cycle in (b) has smaller amplitude than the reference cycle (a), and the cycle in (c) has larger amplitude than the reference cycle.

Figure 6.5
Conformity

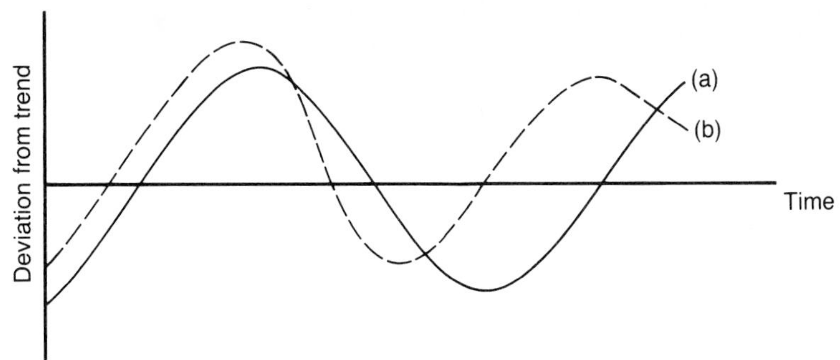

The series (a) and (b) display only a moderate degree of conformity: (b) follows the same general pattern as the reference cycle (a) in the first up- and downswing but begins to lead the reference cycle in the second upswing.

a high degree of conformity if two series "look the same." For example, all the series graphed in Figures 6.2 and 6.3 have a high degree of conformity. A low degree of conformity would occur if one variable sometimes appeared to follow the same cyclical pattern as the reference variable but did not always do so. Figure 6.5 illustrates. Suppose that (a) is the reference variable. We would describe the variable plotted with the broken line marked (b) as displaying a lower degree of conformity. There is obviously some rough procyclical relationship between (a) and (b), but it is by no means exact.

We may thus speak about the co-movements (joint movements, if you like) between two variables as being either procyclical or countercyclical, as involving a lead or a lag of one variable in relation to the other, as displaying greater or less amplitude of fluctuation, and as having a high- or low-degree of conformity. This is merely a language for describing business cycles. It is now possible to go on and use this language to address the more substantive tasks of this chapter. The first of these is to characterize the business cycle more fully.

D. Properties of the Business Cycle

The properties of the business cycle may now be set out more precisely, using the language that has been introduced to you in the previous two sections.

The first feature of business cycles has to do with the movements in the deviations of real GNP from trend.

> Technically, movements about trend in Gross National Product in any country can be well described by a [low-order autocorrelation]. These movements do not exhibit uniformity of either period or amplitude, which is to say, they do not resemble the deterministic wave motions which sometimes arise in the natural sciences.[7]

[7]Lucas, "Understanding Business Cycles," p. 9.

The second feature of business cycles has to do with the co-movements among the various aggregates. The chief regularities that are observed are in the co-movements among different aggregate time-series.

The principal among these are the following:[8]

1. Output movements across broadly defined sectors of the economy move together.
2. Production of durable goods exhibits much greater amplitude than production of nondurables.
3. Production and prices of agricultural goods and natural resources have lower than average conformity.
4. Business profits show high conformity and much greater amplitude than other series.
5. Prices generally are procyclical.
6. Short-term interest rates are procyclical; long-term rates slightly so.
7. Monetary aggregates and velocity measures are procyclical.

For the purpose of what will follow in this book, where the primary emphasis is on economic aggregates, we shall be concerned with five features of the cycle selected from those set out above. First, we shall be concerned to understand why it is that movements in real GNP can be described by a low-order autocorrelation process; second, we shall be concerned to understand why fluctuations in output of durable goods exhibit greater amplitude than those in output of nondurables; third, why prices are generally procyclical; fourth, why interest rates are procyclical; and fifth, why the monetary aggregates and velocity measures of money are procyclical.

These are the central features of the business cycle that macroeconomics seeks to understand. In addition, implicit in the characterization but needing to be made explicit, we shall be concerned to explain why unemployment is countercyclical and employment procyclical. If unemployment is countercyclical and prices (inflation) procyclical, in general there will be a negative relationship between inflation and unemployment.

Before moving on to begin these tasks, let us look at some of the broad facts about the U.S. business cycle.

E. The U.S. Business Cycle

The Movements in Real GNP about Trend

As you have already discovered in Chapter 2, real GNP (real income) in the United States has grown at an average rate of 3.1 percent over the period between 1900 and 1980. You have also discovered that the trend growth rate from 1900 to 1946 was less than the trend after 1946. The deviations of real GNP from the two trends were set out in frame (b) of Figure 2.3 (Chapter 2). Recall that the most dominant feature of those deviations was the large negative deviation during the Great Depression years and the rest of the 1930s and

[8]Ibid., with slight adjustments from the original.

the large positive deviation during World War II (1942–1945). There were also distinct but irregular smaller cycles visible in the data. Can this history of deviations of real GNP from trend in the United States be described by a low-order autocorrelation process? You are about to discover that, as a matter of fact, it can.

The fluctuations around trend in real GNP since 1900 are well described by the following equation:[9]

$$(y_t - y_t^*) = 0.84\,(y_{t-1} - y_{t-1}^*) + e_t \tag{6.2}$$

The way to read this is as follows: y_t represents real GNP in year t, and y_t^* represents the trend value of real GNP in year t. Thus $(y_t - y_t^*)$ represents the deviation of real GNP from trend in year t. The same variable with the subscript $t - 1$ represents deviations from trend in the previous year. As before, e_t represents a random disturbance. Notice that Equation (6.2) is very similar in the magnitude of the coefficient to the one that we used as an example in the section on autocorrelation above (and in the appendix to this chapter). It says that real GNP will deviate from its trend value by 0.84 of its previous deviation plus a random disturbance.

In interpreting Equation (6.2), recall that you discovered that this way of looking at the movements of GNP simply involves breaking the actual movement into two components: (1) a source of (or, more generally, sources of) random disturbance to the economy, and (2) systematic sources of inertia. In the above equation, the inertia is represented by the term $0.84\,(y_{t-1} - y_{t-1}^*)$ and the sources of random disturbance in any one year are represented by the term e_t.

To give you a better feel for what has been going on, Figure 6.6 plots the deviations of real GNP from trend and its two components—the systematic source of inertia and the random component. Frame (a) of the figure shows the deviations of real GNP from trend. [These are exactly the same as those shown in frame (b) of Figure 2.3 in Chapter 2.] This cycle in real GNP is decomposed into a purely random element[10] and an inertia element in frames

[9]Equation (6.2) and Figure 6.6 were constructed in the following way. First, deviations of real GNP from trend were calculated by fitting the two trend lines shown in Figure 2.3, frame (a), to real GNP from 1900 to 1980. The deviations were then analyzed to determine their degree of autocorrelation, and it was discovered that although not quite a perfectly satisfactory relationship, that shown as Equation (6.2) in the text could be regarded as a useful approximate description of the data. The random shock charted in frame (c) of the Figure 6.6 is the calculated residual movements in real GNP about its trend not accounted for by the previous year's value of that variable, multiplied by the coefficient 0.84. As a matter of fact, a *second*-order difference equation—one that says that the deviation of real GNP from trend in year t depends on the deviations in year $t - 1$ and year $t - 2$ as well as a random disturbance—describes the data best. The improvement in the description is not, however, so enormous as to render the first-order description misleading.

[10]What I am calling a "purely random element" is, in fact, only approximately so. The movements in deviations of real GNP from trend not accounted for by a second-order difference equation are indistinguishable from purely random disturbances. The disturbances in Figure 6.5 could be reduced slightly and made "more random" by taking account of this. The broad picture would not, however, be changed by adding this complication.

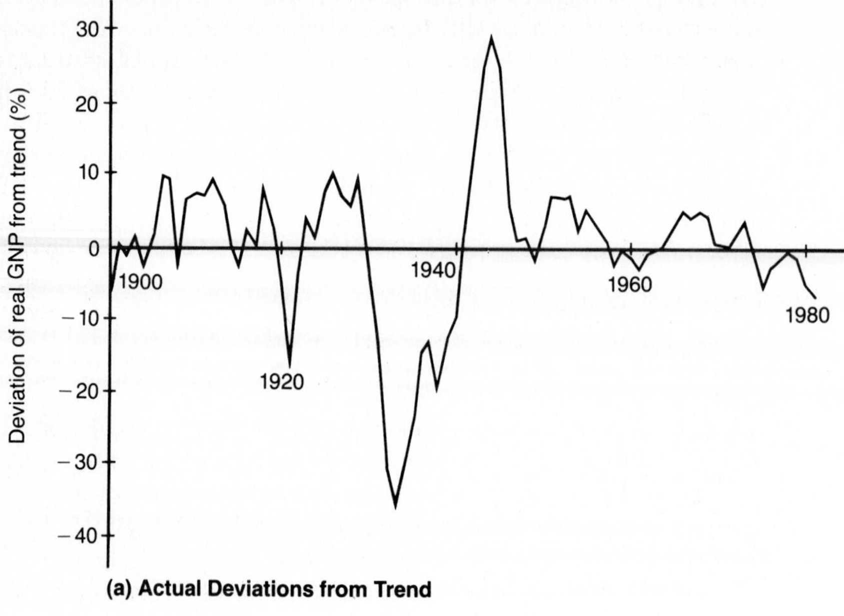

(a) Actual Deviations from Trend

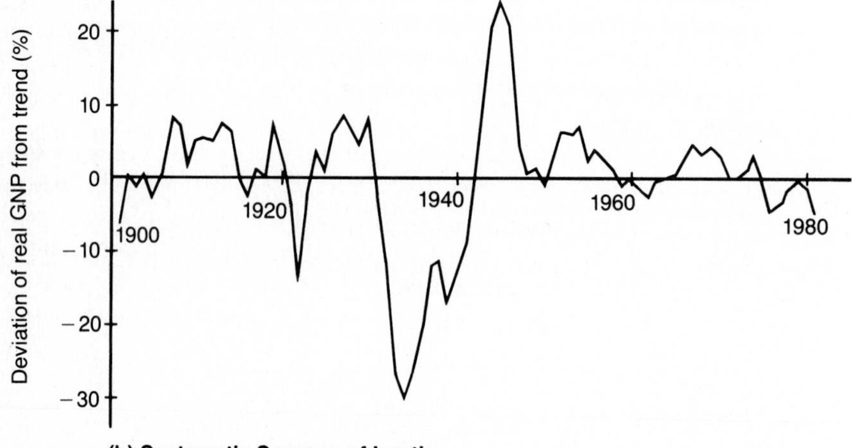

(b) Systematic Sources of Inertia

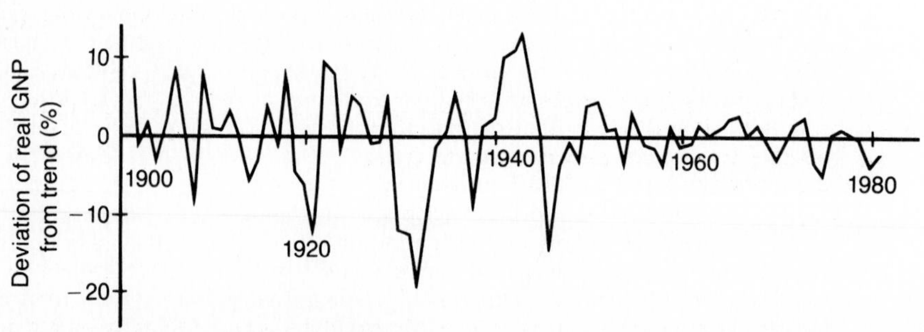

(c) Purely Random Shocks

(c) and (b) of Figure 6.6. Frame (c) of the figure shows the purely random disturbances that have hit the U.S. economy over this time period. These disturbances add up to zero over the entire period. Sometimes they have been as large as a negative shock of 19.7 and a positive shock of 13.6 (percent of GNP). Most of the time, however, the shocks have been small, 33 of them lying between +2 and −2, a further 25 lying between +5 and −5, a further 15 lying between +10 and −10, and only 8 being greater than +10 or −10 (percent of GNP). These shocks impact on the economy to produce the cycle in real GNP described by Equation (6.2) and plotted as frame (a) of Figure 6.6. Frame (b) of Figure 6.6 represents the contribution of inertia to the deviations of GNP from trend. The line in frame (a) of Figure 6.6 represents nothing other than the summation of the lines in frames (b) and (c).

To get a feel for how this works, consider a particular year. The year 1943 will illustrate the story well. According to this description of events, in 1943 there was a positive random shock of 13.7 percent of GNP—the biggest of the positive shocks recorded. The shocks from 1939 to 1942 had also been positive and had accumulated over those years to produce a positive deviation of GNP from trend in 1942 of 13.6 percent. You can read this off in frame (a) of Figure 6.6. This positive deviation in 1942, when multiplied by the coefficient 0.84, gave positive inertia to GNP in 1943 as shown in frame (b) of Figure 6.6. This inertia, other things remaining the same, would have put real GNP above trend by a little more than 11 percent in 1943. Other things, however, were not the same. In 1943, a further large positive shock (13.7 percent of GNP) occurred. This has to be added to the positive inertia and moves the actual value of GNP to 25 percent above trend. Thus, the 25 percent deviation of GNP from trend in 1943 represents the sum of a large positive shock (13.7 percent) and a sizable amount of inertia (11.3 percent) coming from the accumulation of previous positive shocks.

It cannot be emphasized sufficiently that this is merely *a way of describing* the movement of GNP. It does, however, provide us with a valuable way of thinking about what has been happening to the GNP. The economy is bombarded by shocks as described in frame (c) of Figure 6.6, and those shocks affect the level of output (and other variables as well) in a manner that looks much less random than the shocks themselves. We can translate the random shocks into a more systematic up-and-down movement of output by the device of describing output as following a first-order difference equation that is stochastically (randomly) disturbed. The task for explanation is to figure out: (1) what causes the shocks shown in frame (c) of Figure 6.6, (2) what gives rise

◀ Figure 6.6
Random and Systematic Components of the Deviation from Trend in the United States, 1900–1981

The actual deviation of real GNP from trend [frame (a)] is decomposed into a systematic source of inertia [frame (b)] and a purely random shock [frame (c)].
SOURCE: Appendix to Chapter 2.

Figure 6.7
The Production of Durables and Nondurables, 1946–1981

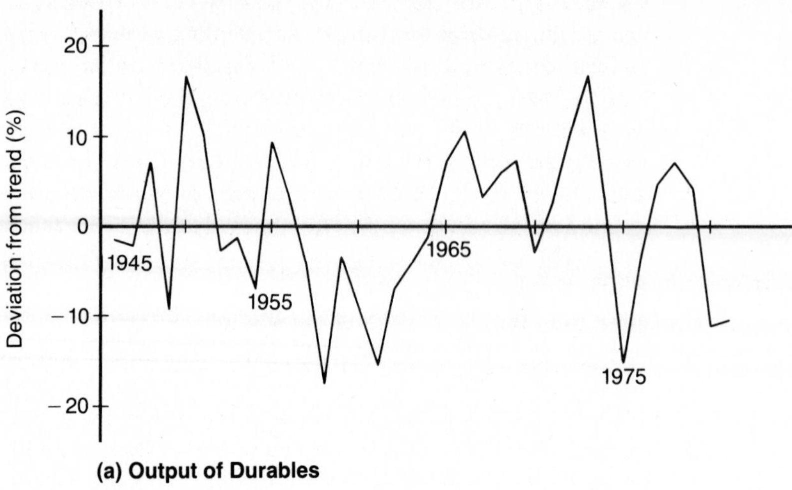

(a) Output of Durables

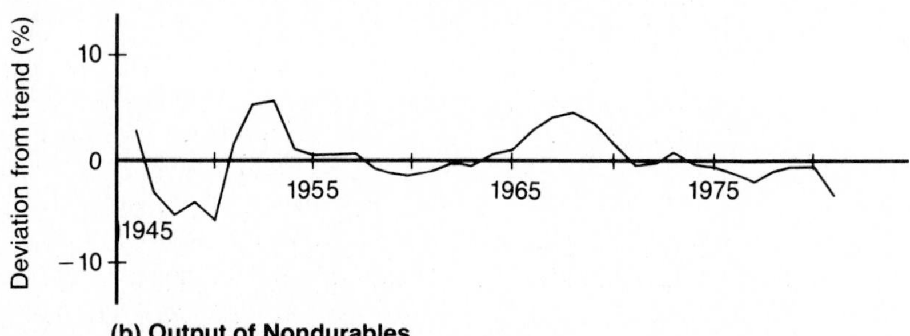

(b) Output of Nondurables

The production of durables [frame (a)] fluctuates with much greater amplitude than the production of nondurables [frame (b)].
SOURCE: Output of durables is the sum of Gross Private Domestic Investment (line 6) and Personal Consumption Expenditure, Durable (line 3) Table 1.2 *NIPA*1 pp. 6–7, *NIPA*2 p. 2. Output of nondurables is real GNP less output of durables. Real GNP is given in the Appendix to Chapter 2.

to the translation of those shocks into movements of output and other variables, and (3) what the sources are that give rise to inertia as described in frame (b).

The Production of Durables and Nondurables

The second feature of the business cycle that was identified above in the section on properties of the business cycle was the tendency for the production of durables (investment goods and consumer durables) to fluctuate with greater amplitude than the production of nondurables (consumer goods and services). This general feature of the business cycle is very evident in the U.S. data, as Figure 6.7 shows. Data for the postwar years only, have been used in this figure because the division of output into durables and nondurables was severely distorted in the war years (1942–1945), and it obscures the basic peacetime pattern. Frame (a), which illustrates the movements in durables, shows fluctuations commonly ranging from as much as 10 percent above or below trend and, on several occasions, going above or below trend by almost 20 percent. In contrast, the production of nondurables [frame (b)] never gets more than 5 percent away from its trend (with the exceptions of 1952–1953 and 1980). The ups and downs in durable production also occur with greater frequency than those in nondurable production.

Output and Unemployment

A further general feature of the business cycle that was identified above was the tendency for output and employment to move together or, equivalently, for output and unemployment to move opposite each other. A useful way of exploring the co-movements among variables is to plot one variable against another in the same diagram, that is, to construct what is called a *scatter diagram.* Figure 6.8 does this for unemployment and deviations of real GNP from trend. Each point in Figure 6.8 represents a year and shows the levels of unemployment and of the deviation of real GNP from trend in a particular year. To be sure that you know how to read Figure 6.8, consider the point marked 33. This is in the bottom right-hand corner of the figure. It represents the observation for the year 1933. In 1933, unemployment was 25.2 percent (which you can read off on the horizontal axis of the diagram), and real GNP was 36 percent below trend (which you can read off on the vertical axis of the diagram). Evidently, there is a clear tendency for unemployment to move in the opposite direction to deviations of real GNP from trend. The relationship is by no means perfect, but it is nevertheless very distinct. One year that evidently was considerably out of line with the generally observed relationship was 1941. In that year unemployment was higher than usual (almost 10 percent), but real GNP was, according to the figures presented here, slightly above trend. For the most part, however, there is a clear systematic tendency for unemployment to move countercyclically with reference to deviations of real GNP from trend.

Price Movements

A general feature of the business cycle is that prices move procyclically. This means that inflation rates are strongest when output is deviating above trend and weakest when output deviates below trend. Equivalently, we could expect to find a negative association between inflation movements and unemployment movements. That is, inflation is generally at its highest when unemployment is at its lowest. Viewing the procyclical nature of inflation as a countercyclical relation between inflation and unemployment enables us to focus on a relationship known as the Phillips relation (named for the New Zealand economist A. W. Phillips who popularized this relationship).[11]

[11]Phillips' original contribution is A. W. Phillips, "The Relation between Unemployment and the Rate of Change of Money Wage Rates in the United Kingdom, 1861–1957," *Economica,* 25 (November 1958), 283–99.

Figure 6.8 Unemployment and the Deviation of Real GNP from Trend

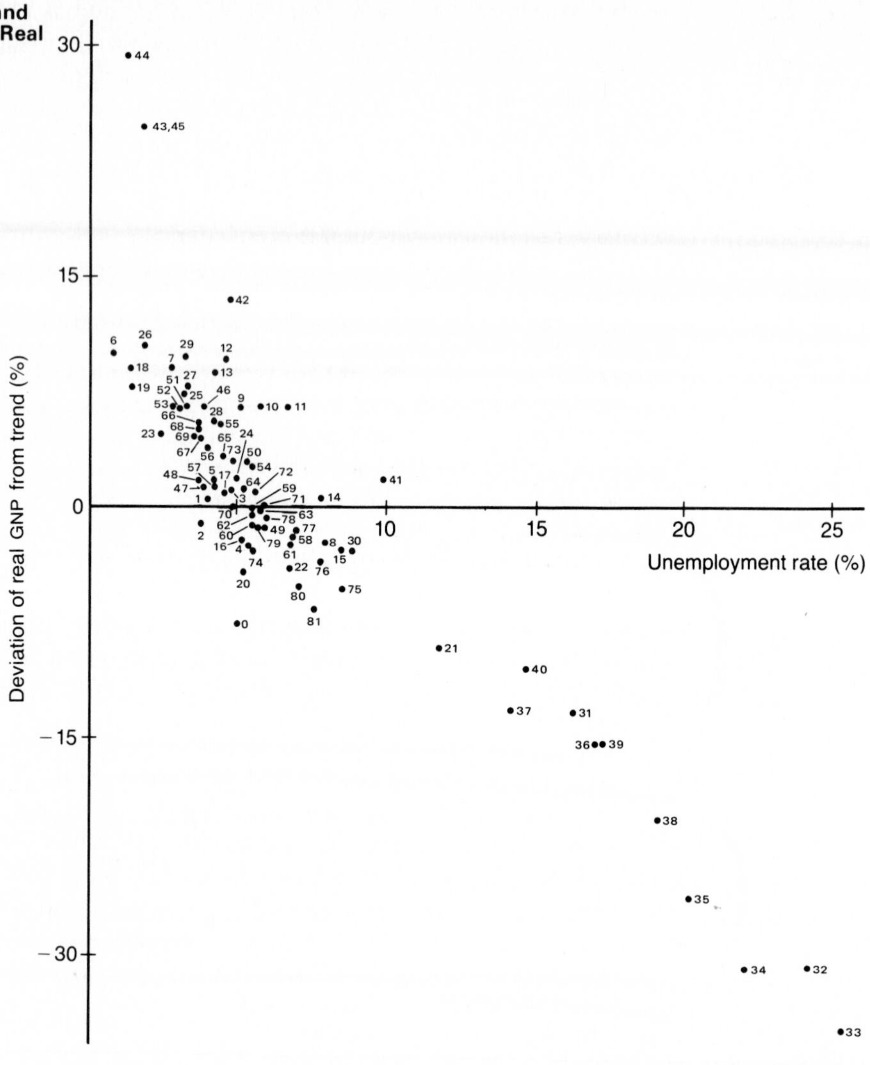

Each point shows the deviation of real GNP from trend and the unemployment rate occurring in a particular year. Years are identified by their last two digits—thus, for example, 1933 is shown as 33. There is a clear tendency for unemployment to be highest when real GNP is furthest below trend and lowest when real GNP is above trend.
SOURCE: Appendix to Chapter 2.

Figures 6.9 and 6.10 show the co-movements of inflation and unemployment in the United States between 1901 and 1945 and between 1946 and 1980. (The reason for plotting these data on two separate figures is that the range of variation in the interwar years is so gigantic that the actual variation in the postwar years would be lost in the corner of the diagram if we were to plot the points shown in Figure 6.10 on the scale used in Figure 6.9.)

Figure 6.9
Co-Movements of Inflation and Unemployment, 1901–1945

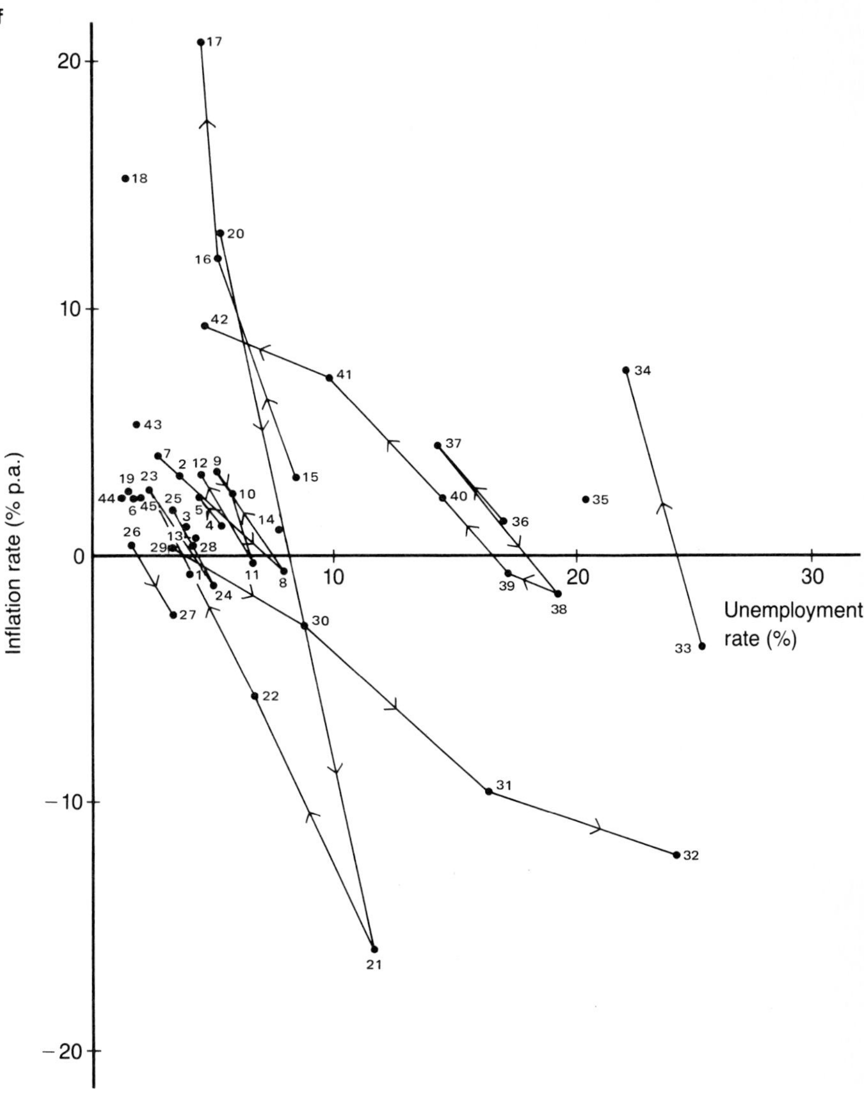

Each point shows the inflation rate and the unemployment rate that occurred in a given year. Years are identified by their last two digits (e.g., 1933 is shown as 33). There have been long periods when inflation and unemployment move in opposite directions (shown by the arrowed lines) and other periods when there is considerable independence in the movements of the two series.
SOURCE: Appendix to Chapter 2.

Notice that there is, from time to time, a clear tendency for inflation and unemployment to move in opposite directions. This is visible between all the years marked with a line in both Figure 6.9 and Figure 6.10. What is also clearly visible, however, is the fact that there is no single relationship that

Figure 6.10
Co-Movements of Inflation and Unemployment, 1946–1981

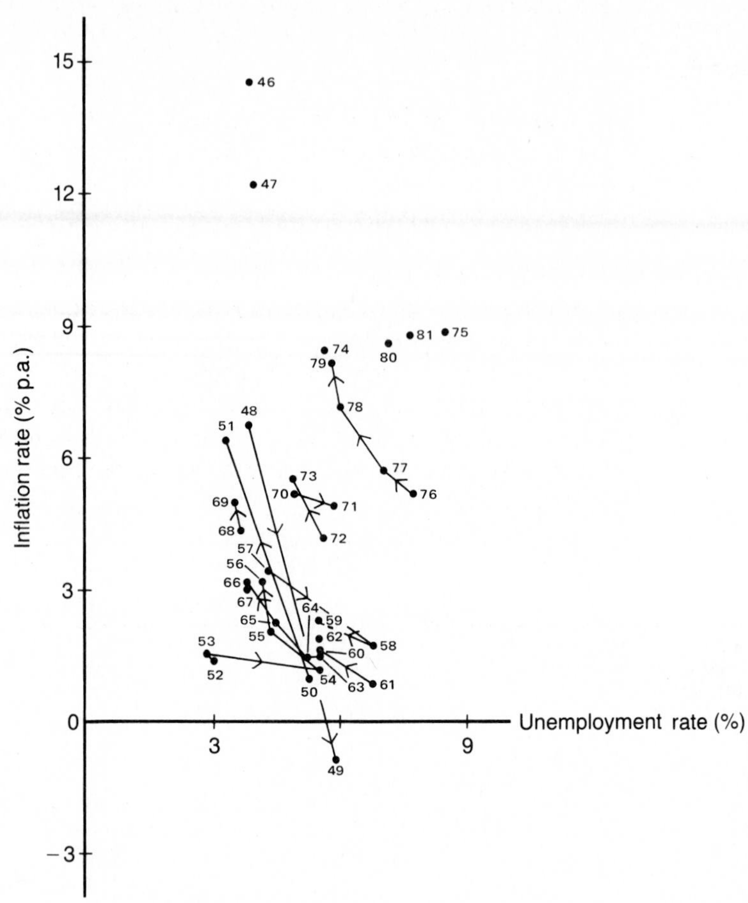

Each point shows the inflation rate and the unemployment rate that occurred in a given year. Years are identified by their last two digits (e.g., 1949 is shown as 49). There have been several periods in which unemployment and inflation have moved in opposite directions to each other (shown by the arrowed lines). There have also, however, been sizable and important positive co-movements of these two variables.
SOURCE: Appendix to Chapter 2.

characterizes all the co-movements of inflation and unemployment. Two-thirds of the movements are *inverse* (i.e., when inflation rises, unemployment falls, or when inflation falls, unemployment rises), but there are significant occasions on which both variables move in the same direction. Consideration of the Phillips relation in the U.S. data raises as many questions having to do with these simultaneous increases in inflation and unemployment (or simultaneous decreases) as it does concerning their negative co-movement. All of these stylized facts will have to be coped with by any viable theory concerning the causes of inflation and unemployment. It will be necessary to understand why, most of the time, the two variables move in opposite directions and why there are other periods when they move in the same direction as each other.

Interest Rates

The general description of the business cycle is that short-term interest rates are procyclical, and long-term rates are only slightly so. A useful way of looking at the cyclical nature of short-term interest rates is to examine how they move with inflation. Since we know that inflation is generally procyclical, then if interest rates and inflation move together, we shall know that interest rates also are procyclical. Figure 6.11 shows the relationship between short-term interest rates and inflation in the United States since 1900. The generally procyclical nature of short-term interest rates is visible in this figure. You can see that although there is not a perfect relationship between interest rates and inflation, there is nevertheless a tendency for these two variables to move in the same direction. This feature of interest rates and inflation rates to move together is also something that our theories are necessarily going to have to be able to account for.

Figure 6.11
Co-Movements of Inflation and Interest Rates

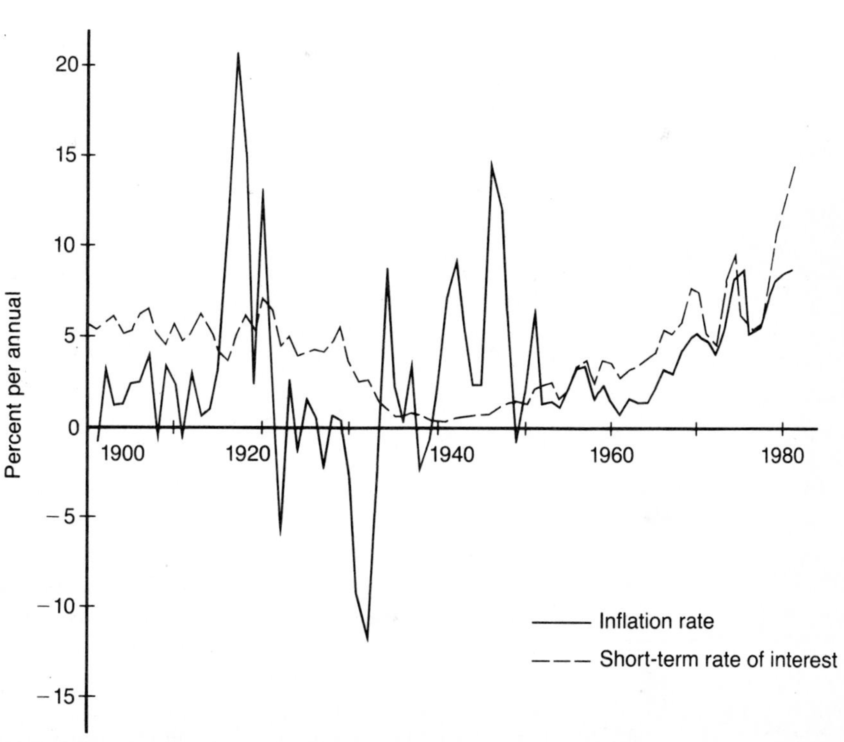

The trends in these two variables are similar, but the volatility in inflation is not seen in the behavior of interest rates.
SOURCE: Appendix to Chapter 2.

There is no need to examine separately the movements of long-term interest rates. You know from Figure 2.4 that long-term interest rates are much smoother than short-term rates. You also know that there is a general tendency for long-term rates to move in the same broad direction as short rates. It immediately follows that long-term interest rates have the general characteristic that they are procyclical, but only slightly so.

These, then, are the major features of the U.S. business cycle that macroeconomic theory needs to be able to explain. The next three parts of this book are concerned with the task of explanation.

Summary

A. Definition of the Business Cycle

Business cycles are recurrent but nonperiodic fluctuations in aggregate economic activity as measured by fluctuation in real GNP about its trend.

B. Autocorrelation

Autocorrelation is a technical term that means that the value of some variable is related to itself at some earlier date (or dates). An autocorrelated variable is described by a difference equation that is stochastically or randomly disturbed.

C. Co-Movement

The term *co-movement* is used in the description of the movement of one variable in relation to another. Co-movements may be procyclical, in which case, two variables move up and down together; or countercyclical, in which case, two variables move in the opposite directions to each other. The cycle in one variable may lead or lag the cycle in another. The cycle in one variable may display a greater or smaller amplitude than the cycle in the other. Co-movement may display high conformity, in which case, the two variables move in a similar manner; or low conformity, in which case, they do not move in close sympathy with each other.

D. Properties of the Business Cycle

Movements in real GNP about trend are well described by a simple difference equation that is stochastically disturbed. In general, employment, prices, and interest rates are procyclical, and unemployment is countercyclical.

E. The U.S. Business Cycle

The general features of the business cycle set out above apply precisely to the U.S. case, with the important observation that movements in inflation, although generally procyclical, are not universally so. There are important co-movements of inflation and unemployment that do not fit a simple pattern.

Review Questions

1. What are business cycles cycles in?
2. Describe the different phases of a cycle.
3. What is a recession?
4. Are all business cycles the same length? If not, why do we use the term *cycle* to describe the phenomenon of nonperiodic economic fluctuations?
5. What is a difference equation? Can a difference equation describe the path followed by deviations of real GNP from trend?
6. Explain how random shocks combine with inertia to describe recurrent but nonperiodic up-and-down movements in economic activity.
7. What is meant by the term *co-movement*?
8. What is meant by the term *conformity*?
9. Try to think of examples (not necessarily economic) of:
   (a) Procyclical co-movements that have high conformity or low conformity.
   (b) Countercyclical co-movements that have high conformity or low conformity.
10. Describe the general character of business cycles.
11. How might the deviation of real GNP from trend in the United States be described in the period since 1900?
12. What have been the co-movements between real GNP and inflation, unemployment, and interest rates in the period since 1960?
13. (You will only want to tackle this question if you have worked through the appendix to this chapter.) Reinforce your understanding of the concept of autocorrelation by conducting the following experiments:
   (a) Using the same "economic shocks" as set out in Table 6A.2 (in the appendix), generate a path for real income if it is described by the processes

$$y_t = 90 + 0.1\ y_{t-1} + e_t$$

   and

$$y_t = 1 + 0.99\ y_{t-1} + e_t$$

   (b) Compare the paths of y_t in the above two equations with each other and with that derived in the appendix using Equation (6A.2). How do the paths differ? What do you learn from this experiment?

Appendix to Chapter 6

Autocorrelation

This appendix deals with the concept of autocorrelation in a slightly more technical way than was done in the preceding text. The appendix contains no fundamentally new ideas that are not treated in an intuitive way in the body of the chapter. It may, however, provide you with a better understanding of the concept of autocorrelation, and certainly the numerical example will provide you with an opportunity to review your understanding of the concept.

It is useful to approach the concept of autocorrelation in two steps. The first is to understand what is meant by a *difference equation.* A difference equation is nothing other than a statement that tells us how some variable evolves over time. We shall only deal with the simplest kind of difference equation and even then only with an example. Let us suppose that we want to describe the evolution of real GNP over time. Let us call real GNP, y. Then, so that we are clear about the date that attaches to the variable, let us denote the value of real GNP in some particular year, the tth year, as y_t. Let us further suppose that real GNP in year t is always related in some way to its own value in the previous year. Never mind why for the present. Specifically, let us suppose that the following equation describes the evolution of real GNP from one year to the next:

$$y_t = 25 + 0.75(y_{t-1}) \tag{6A.1}$$

Let us first of all satisfy ourselves that we can read this equation. What it says in words is that real GNP in year t (y_t) will be equal to 25 plus three-quarters (0.75) of the level of real GNP in the previous year (year $t - 1$), that is, (y_{t-1}). To get a feel for this, imagine that real GNP in year $t - 1$ was equal to 100. You can calculate $\frac{3}{4}$ of 100 (equals 75), add 25 to that, and the result is the value of real GNP in year t. The answer that you have obtained, of course, is that real GNP in year t will be 100. Now imagine going forward to year $t + 1$. At year $t + 1$, the previous year becomes year t. Since real GNP in year t is 100, in year $t + 1$, by the same calculation, it will also be 100. You can quickly convince yourself that real GNP will be 100 in each and every year if the above equation is true and if real GNP in year $t - 1$ was equal to 100.

Now suppose that real GNP in the previous year (y_{t-1}) was not 100 but 110. What does this imply about the value of real GNP in year t? You can calculate that answer by finding $\frac{3}{4}$ of 110 and adding 25 to that to give you the value of real GNP in year t. You should get an answer of 107.5. In the next year, year $t + 1$, real GNP will be 25 plus $\frac{3}{4}$ of 107.5. This will give a level of real GNP of 105.6. By repeating the calculation, you will obtain for the next successive years values of 104.2, 103.2, 102.4, 101.8, 101.3, 101.0, 100.8. ... Thus, in the indefinite future, real GNP will converge to the level of 100. The value of 100 is known as the steady-state value of real GNP. It is that value toward which the above equation always tends.

You are probably now saying to yourself, "Well that's all very simple, but so what?" Clearly, real GNP doesn't behave like either of these paths that have just been calculated. According to the first exercise that we did, if real GNP starts out at 100, it always stays at 100; and according to the second exercise, if it starts out at something other than 100, it monotonically converges toward 100. How does this help us understand the movements of real GNP such as those that occur in an actual economy like that of the United States? The answer is that, on its own, it is of no help at all. With one tiny addition, however, the first-order difference equation (6A.1) (*first order* means that real GNP today depends only on real GNP yesterday) can be capable of

TABLE 6A.1
Converting Die Scores into Economic Shocks

DIE SCORE	ECONOMIC SHOCK
1	−10
2	−5
3	0
4	0
5	+5
6	+10

producing patterns in the evolution of real GNP that are similar in character to patterns that we observe in the data.

This simple addition is to make the difference equation above into a *stochastic* difference equation. A stochastic difference equation is very similar to a difference equation. That is, it has all the properties of the equation that you have just looked at and become familiar with. In addition, however, it adds on to the above equation a *random* shock. In other words, instead of real GNP in one year being uniquely determined, given knowledge of real GNP in the previous year, there is an additional random element that will allow real GNP in the current year to deviate from the prediction of the above equation by a random amount. We could write a stochastic difference equation comparable to the above equation as follows:

$$y_t = 25 + 0.75(y_{t-1}) + e_t \qquad \textbf{(6A.2)}$$

The term e_t at the end of the equation represents a random shock. On the average it will take on the value of 0. From time to time, however, it will take on different values than 0, sometimes positive and sometimes negative.

To keep things simple and concrete, let us generate an example of a random shock (or a series of random shocks) and then see how GNP evolves when the difference equation that describes its path is stochastically disturbed.

I have created a set of random shocks by conducting a simple experiment that you can conduct for yourself. The experiment involves rolling a die and assigning an economic shock depending on the score of the die roll. Table 6A.1 sets out the way that I have converted die scores into economic shocks. You will see that if the die came up 3 or 4, I scored an economic shock of 0, so that there is a 1 in 3 chance that there is no random disturbance to the economy. If the die came up 2, I scored a negative shock of 5 (think of that as a shock that is depressing the economy), and if the die scored 1, then I gave a bigger weight to the depressing effect on the economy (−10). If the die came up 5 or 6, I scored a positive shock to the economy (a boom) assigning a shock of 5 for a die score of 5 and 10 for a die score of 6. Thus you can see that there is a 1 in 6 chance that the economy will be hit with any of the shocks +10, +5, −5, −10, and a 1 in 3 chance of no shock. The shocks, then, that will hit the economy are symmetrical and have an average value of 0 and a range of 20, ranging from +10 to −10.

TABLE 6A.2
Thirty Random Shocks in an Imaginary Economy

DIE ROLL	DIE SCORE	ECONOMIC SHOCK
1	5	+5
2	1	−10
3	6	+10
4	6	+10
5	4	0
6	4	0
7	6	+10
8	4	0
9	2	−5
10	3	0
11	3	0
12	4	0
13	4	0
14	6	+10
15	5	+5
16	5	+5
17	1	−10
18	1	−10
19	3	0
20	2	−5
21	3	0
22	6	+10
23	5	+5
24	6	+10
25	2	−5
26	5	+5
27	2	−5
28	4	0
29	1	−10
30	5	+5

I rolled the die 30 times, and Table 6A.2 records the scores of our 30 die rolls together with the value of the economic shock implied by the scoring scheme set out in Table 6A.1. You will notice that my 30 rolls turned out to have an average value that was greater than 0 (in fact my average was +1), indicating that I rolled rather more 5's and 6's than I did 1's and 2's. Nevertheless, if I had rolled, say, 1000 times, then it is certain that my average would have been very close to 0.

With the series of economic shocks shown in Table 6A.2, it is now possible to see how the economy would evolve if the above stochastic difference equation describes the evolution of real GNP. The calculation for the first ten values of real GNP are set out in Table 6A.3. The first column shows the level of real GNP in year t and the second column in year $t-1$. The third column records the value of the shock, e_t. The values of the shocks listed there are the first ten shocks from Table 6A.2. Imagine that in year 0, the economy started out in its steady state with real GNP equal to 100 and with real GNP in the previous year equal to 100 and with no random shock. The shocks then begin. In year 1, we need to take $\frac{3}{4}$ of the previous real GNP (75) and add 25, which gives 100, and then add the shock of 5 to get the value shown for real

TABLE 6A.3
Calculation of Evolution of GNP in an Imaginary Economy (years 0 to 10 only)

$$y_t = 25 + 0.75(y_{t-1}) + e_t$$

YEAR	y_t	y_{t-1}	e_t
0	100	100	0
1	105	100	+5
2	94	105	−10
3	105	94	+10
4	114	105	+10
5	111	114	0
6	108	111	0
7	116	108	+10
8	112	116	0
9	104	112	−5
10	103	104	0

Note: y denotes real GNP, e denotes the value of the shock and the subscripts t and $(t - 1)$ denote the year of the observation.

GNP of 105. In year 2, year 1's real GNP of 105 becomes the previous year's real GNP level. To calculate year 2 real GNP, we take $\frac{3}{4}$ of 105 and add 25 to that; we then subtract 10, the current year shock of −10, to give a value of 94 for real GNP. This process is repeated throughout the table. Check that you can reproduce the figures listed in column 1 of Table 6A.3 by applying the above-described formula. (The figures given in the table are rounded. To calculate the correct values you should carry the unrounded figures in the memory of your calculator.)

Figure 6A.1 illustrates the values of real GNP over the full 30-year experiment that is described in Tables 6A.2 and 6A.3. The graph of the ups and downs of real GNP in this imaginary economy looks remarkably as if it could have been generated from plotting actual figures for the deviation of real GNP from trend, such as those shown in Chapter 2. Notice that there is certainly a recurrent up-and-down movement, but there is no exact periodicity. The timing from the trough of year 2 to the next trough (year 13) is eleven years. The next trough occurs at year 20—a seven-year cycle. The next trough occurs at year 29—a nine-year cycle. Thus, the cycle lengths in this example, as measured from trough to trough, vary from a short cycle of seven years to a long cycle of eleven years. Notice too that the severity of the down phase varies. The downturn that begins in year 8 continues through year 13 but never gets very deep. The next downturn that begins in year 17 only runs for four years, but it goes all the way to 10 points below the steady-state value.

The particular path of real GNP generated by a stochastic difference equation depends in an important way on the strength of the inertia in the process—that is, on the magnitude of the effect of previous income on current income. In our example, that effect is $\frac{3}{4}$. If, instead of current income depending on previous income with a weight of $\frac{3}{4}$, we were to lower that weight, almost to zero, then real GNP would no longer display much systematic

Figure 6A.1
A Hypothetical Cycle Generated by a First-Order Autoregressive Process

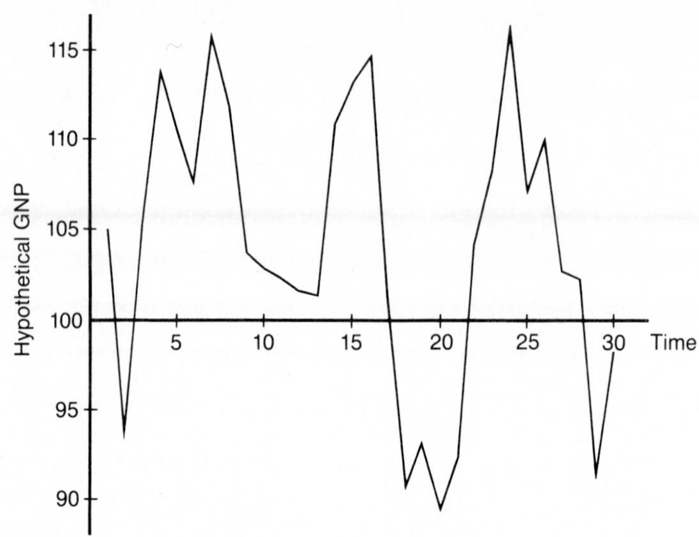

The simple randomly disturbed difference equation $y_t = 25 + 0.75\,(y_{t-1}) + e_t$ generates nonperiodic but recurrent fluctuations that could easily be taken to be real-world deviations of real GNP from trend.

movement but would be purely random (completely unpredictable) like the random shocks, e_t, that are bombarding the economy. At the other extreme, if we were to raise the weight on previous income from $\frac{3}{4}$ to almost 1, then the cyclical swings in real GNP would be much longer (the time from the peak of one cycle to the peak of the next one would be longer).

The key thing to take careful note of is that a very simple process—a stochastically disturbed, first-order difference equation—is capable of generating a path for a variable that is very similar in its characteristics to the recurrent but nonperiodic ups and downs of real GNP (and other variables) over the course of the business cycle. Of course, the specific path of actual GNP movements about trend will only be capable of description by specific shocks and a specific difference equation.

7

Introduction to the Basic Model

You have now reviewed: (a) the questions that macroeconomics seeks to answer; (b) the main facts about the evolution of the key macroeconomic variables in the United States since 1900; (c) the way in which the main macroeconomic variables are measured; and (d) how it is possible to characterize the ups and downs of economic activity and the co-movements among the variables as business cycles.

It is now time to move on to the more challenging problem of explanation of macroeconomic phenomena—*macroeconomic theory*.

The next three chapters develop the simplest available model—what we will call the *basic model*—for the determination of real income, the level of employment, and the price level. What I am calling the *basic model* is usually called the *classical model*.[1] Chapters 11 and 12 will show how unemployment and inflation are explained by the basic model, and Chapter 13 reveals the extent to which that model can and cannot explain the recent macroeconomic history of the United States. You will discover that the explanation given by the basic model is not a completely satisfactory one. There are, however, good reasons for starting out with the basic model even though it is not satisfactory in all respects.

A. Why Study the Basic Model

The first reason for studying *any* model is to improve our understanding of some aspect of the world. We *understand* something when we have a way of *explaining* the past and *predicting* the future that works in all conceivable circumstances. This idea can be made more precise by saying that we understand something when we have a *model* that is capable of explaining the past or predicting the future in all conceivable circumstances.

---

[1]The most comprehensive scholarly treatment of this body of analysis is that done by Don Patinkin in his important book, *Money, Interest and Prices*, 2nd ed. (New York: Harper & Row, Publishers, Inc., 1965). Chapters I to XII of this work are *the* authoritative statement of this body of analysis.

However, models (ways of understanding through explanation and prediction) are not all equally good. Some models are utterly useless. They do not "work"—they do not enable us to explain or predict—in any situations at all. Such models, once they are "found out," clearly need assigning to the scrap heap. They should be remembered only as the useless tools that they turned out to be, so that they may hopefully never again be revived. Other models have *some* value, but that value is limited because they work only in certain narrow special circumstances. The basic model of macroeconomics is in this category. It is a model that works but only in certain special conditions. Nevertheless, and this is the first key reason for studying the basic model, some of its ingredients are present in the more complex and satisfactory theories that you will study later (in Parts IV and V). That is, it will not be necessary to unlearn as wrong, things that you are learning in this simplest of frameworks. On the contrary, you will be able to see exactly in what special circumstances this simplest model yields useful predictions.

A second reason for studying the basic model is that it enables us to understand *some* (though certainly *not all*) of the reasons why unemployment exists and why its rate varies. Indeed, it also helps us to understand why unemployment has increased so persistently in the United States over the postwar years.

Third, and this is of vital importance, the basic model will enable you to see the important distinction between inflation as an ongoing process, and a rise in the price level as a once-and-for-all affair, and to see what can and what cannot cause inflation. There is a great deal of popular mythology to the effect that inflation is the result of all kinds of social pressures, emanating in particular from the behavior of labor unions. You will be able to see with the aid of the basic model that is shortly to be developed, that this popular mythology is misleading and wrong.

B. Weaknesses of the Basic Model

The main areas in which the basic model is deficient arise from its inability to explain the business cycle and the facts of the Great Depression. You will see later the attempts that have been made to modify the basic model so as to remedy these deficiencies.

Summary

A. Why Study the Basic Model

You are studying the basic model for three reasons:

1. Its ingredients are present in more complex and satisfactory models.
2. It shows why unemployment exists and some of the reasons why its rate varies.
3. It enables you to distinguish between inflation and a once-and-for-all rise in the price level, and to understand the causes of inflation.

B. Weaknesses of the Basic Model

The basic model is unable to explain the business cycle and severe and persistent depression.

Review Questions

1. In economics, we use a model as a means of explaining economic phenomena. Why do we use a model in macroeconomics?
2. How would you determine the strengths and weaknesses of a model?
3. What are the strengths and weaknesses of the basic model?

8

Aggregate Supply and the Labor Market

The main objective of this chapter is to enable you to understand what determines the aggregate supply of goods and services in the short run. Three tasks will enable you to achieve that objective. These tasks are to:

(a) Understand the concept of the short-run aggregate production function.
(b) Understand the working of a competitive aggregate labor market.
(c) Understand the concept of the aggregate supply curve.

A. Short-Run Aggregate Production Function

A useful starting point in explaining the concept of the short-run aggregate production function is the production function of an individual producer. A production function is simply a statement about the maximum output that can be produced with a given list of inputs, and more than that, a statement of how that maximum level of output will vary as the inputs themselves are varied.

The maximum output of some particular good that can be produced will depend on the amount of capital employed, the state of technology, the amount of land resources used, and the number and skill of the workers employed.

In the long run, all the inputs used in a production process can be varied. Capital equipment can be purchased, technology can be changed, land use can be modified, and workers can acquire new skills.

In the short run, however, these four factors, which affect the maximum output, are relatively hard to change. They are, of course, changing gradually over time and are the source of the long-term growth trend in output.[1] At any given moment, however, they may, as a useful approximation, be treated as fixed. The input, which can be varied quickly, and whose variations give rise to fluctuations in output around its trend, is the quantity of labor employed. The

[1]Chapter 38 deals with the determination of the long-term growth trend.

Figure 8.1
The Aggregate Short-Run Production Function

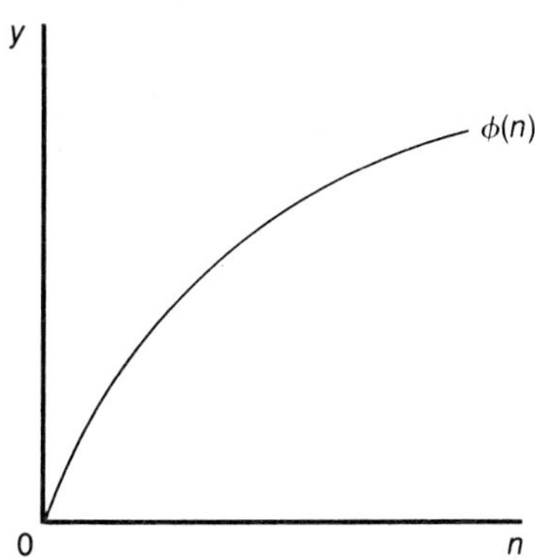

The production function, $\phi(n)$, shows the maximum attainable output level (y) as the level of labor input (n) is varied. The application of more units of labor produces more units of output. However, each additional unit of labor produces less additional output than did the previous unit—there is diminishing marginal product.

short-run production function shows the relationship between the maximum amount of output that can be produced as the quantity of labor employed is varied while holding constant the other inputs into the production process.

So far you have reviewed the short-run production function analysis that is used in microeconomic theory to develop the theory of costs and supply in a competitive industry or to develop a theory of costs and profit-maximizing price and output behavior in a monopolistic industry. It is possible, however, to use this microeconomic production function analysis to derive an *aggregate* short-run production function. The aggregate short-run production function relates the aggregate output to the total number of workers employed. (Recall from Chapter 3 that aggregate output is equal to real expenditure and real income.)

Define output as y, and also define number employed as n. Then, the aggregate short-run production function that we could write as

$$y = \phi(n). \tag{8.1}$$

The symbol $\phi(\ )$ should be read as "is a function of" or, more simply, "is determined by." Thus, Equation (8.1) states that the maximum value of y that can be produced is determined by the level of n and that it varies as n is varied.

The properties of the short-run production function are most easily described by plotting a specific example. This is done in Figure 8.1. The label on the curve, $\phi(n)$, is just a shorthand way of saying that output (y) depends on (or is a function of) the amount of labor employed (n). The short-run production function depicted in Figure 8.1 reflects a common technological fact: that as the number employed is increased, the output of the marginal worker—marginal product—declines.

There is a problem concerning the labor input of which you should take note. It concerns the role of "hours per worker" in the definition of the labor input. Normally, labor is measured in terms of *man-hours*. For example, three people each working for 4 hours a day can produce a similar output to two people each working 6 hours a day. Macroeconomics is more concerned with explaining variation in the *number of people employed* than with explaining the average number of *hours* worked *per worker*. As the economy goes through a cycle of activity from boom to slump, it may be that output drops by, say, 10 percent. That output drop could be accommodated by a cut of 10 percent in the average hours worked by each worker with no one becoming fully unemployed. Typically, however, this does not happen. Average hours per worker employed remains relatively constant, while the number of workers employed declines. It is possible to develop an explanation as to why it is that employment rather than average hours per worker varies with the level of economic activity. Rather than pursue such an explanation, however, we are simply going to assume that each worker works a fairly constant average number of hours, and as economic activity varies, the number of workers employed also varies. The variable n will, therefore, throughout this book, be taken to mean the number of workers employed. It will reflect the number of man-hours employed, provided the number of hours per man is constant, which we will assume to be the case.[2]

This completes the definition of the short-run aggregate production function.

B. Competitive Aggregate Labor Market

The Demand for Labor

First consider the demand side of the labor market. Each competitive firm will demand labor and will produce output up to the point at which the price of its output is equal to the marginal cost of its production. Let us call the output price of an individual firm P_i and its marginal cost of production MC_i. The subscript i is to remind us that we are dealing with an *individual* firm. Thus,

$$P_i = MC_i \tag{8.2}$$

If this condition is satisfied, the firm is making a maximum profit (provided that the marginal cost curve is rising at this point).

Marginal cost is easy to calculate. Recall that in the short run, the only input that can vary is labor. The cost of hiring one extra worker is equal to the money wage per worker (W). However, the money wage is not the marginal cost. The amount produced by the marginal worker is known as the marginal

[2]As a matter of fact, average hours per worker have declined steadily over time at roughly 1 hour per week every seven years. Fluctuations in average hours around that declining trend have usually been less than 1 percent and only very rarely exceeded 2 percent. Thus, the assumption that most of the fluctuations in labor supply are fluctuations in the number of people employed seems to be a reasonable one. For data on average hours, see *Economic Report of the President*, Table B38, p. 276 (Washington, D. C.: U.S. Government Printing Office, 1982).

Figure 8.2
The Marginal Product Curve—The Demand for Labor of a Competitive Firm

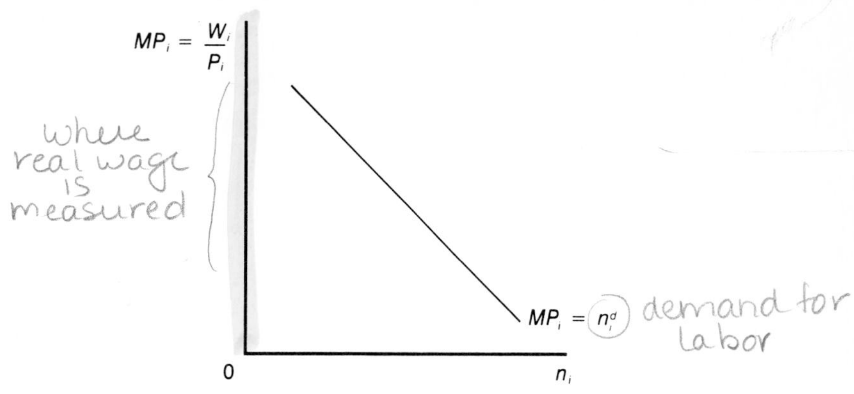

Marginal product (MP_i) declines as labor input (n_i) increases. Profits are maximized when the marginal product is equal to the real wage (W/P_i). The marginal product curve and the demand for labor curve of a competitive firm are, therefore, the same curve.

product (MP_i). The marginal cost is the cost of the marginal worker (W) divided by the output that that marginal worker can produce (MP_i). That is,

$$MC_i = \frac{W}{MP_i} \tag{8.3}$$

For example, if the wage rate was \$10 an hour and if a worker could produce 100 units of output in an hour, the marginal cost (the cost of the last unit of output) would be \$10 ÷ 100 = 10¢. Now, replacing the marginal cost in Equation (8.3) with the price from Equation (8.2), it is clear that

$$P_i = \frac{W}{MP_i} \tag{8.4}$$

If we divide both sides of this equation by P_i and multiply both sides by MP_i, we obtain

$$MP_i = \frac{W}{P_i} \tag{8.5}$$

The Equation (8.5) says that the marginal product of some particular firm will be equal to the money wage (W) divided by the price of the output of that firm (P_i). To see how this condition leads directly to the demand for labor function, consider Figure 8.2, which plots the marginal product of labor of the ith firm against the number of workers employed in that firm. Call this downward sloping relation the marginal product curve.

You have seen that a condition for profit maximizing (Equation 8.5) is that the marginal product of labor must equal the ratio of the money wage to the price level. This ratio is the real wage. You can therefore equivalently

Figure 8.3
The Demand for Labor

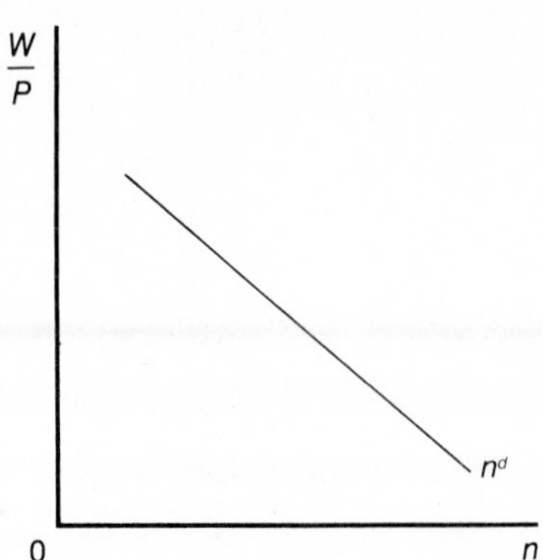

The demand for labor in the economy as a whole n^d is obtained by aggregating the demand for labor in all the individual industries. Like the industry demand curves, the lower the real wage (W/P), the greater the quantity of labor (n) demanded.

measure the real wage on the vertical axis of Figure 8.2. The marginal product curve then automatically becomes the demand for labor curve when thought of as being drawn against the real wage.

So far we have talked only about an individual firm's demand for labor. We now want to move on to consider the economy-wide or aggregate demand for labor. We can obtain this by adding the individual demand for labor curves across all the firms in the economy. There is no difficulty in adding up the quantities of labor demanded across all the firms. The result is the total quantity of labor demanded in the economy as a whole. We have to be careful, however, in interpreting the aggregate demand for labor curve because, on the vertical axis of the diagram describing an individual firm's demand for labor, the real wage that appears is specific to the individual firm. It is the money wage rate divided by the individual firm's output price. If we take an average of the output prices of all the firms in the economy, then what we obtain, of course, is simply the economy-wide average price level. In effect, we obtain the GNP deflator. The economy-wide demand for labor curve, therefore, shows the total quantity of labor demanded in the economy plotted against the economy average real wage, which is the same thing as the money wage rate divided by the average price level. Such a demand for labor curve is shown in Figure 8.3.

The Supply of Labor

Consider next the supply of labor. The theory of household behavior predicts that utility-maximizing households will supply more hours of labor as the real wage increases up to some maximum. Thereafter, as the real wage rises, the number of hours supplied will decline since a higher income will lead the household to want to consume more leisure along with other goods. Thus, the supply of hours per individual household would be represented by a supply

Figure 8.4
The Supply of Labor

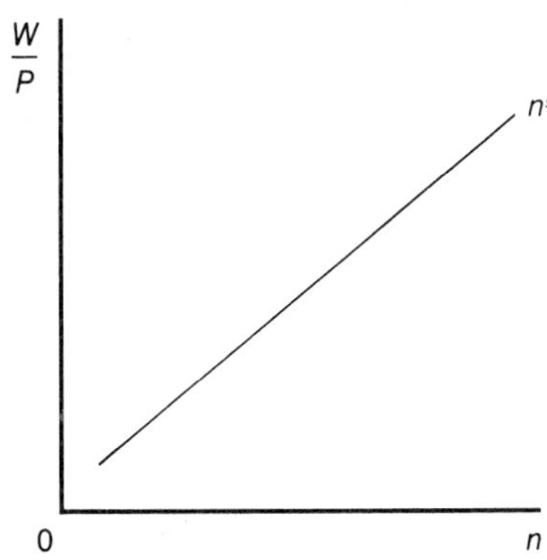

Households choose whether to enter the labor force by comparing the utility they would get from working a fixed number of hours at a certain wage rate with the utility they would derive from taking leisure. The higher the real wage, the larger the number of households that will regard working as yielding superior utility to consuming leisure. Thus the supply of labor (n^s) will rise as the real wage (W/P) rises.

curve that increases with the real wage up to some maximum and then begins to fall off.

For our purposes we are interested in developing a theory of the aggregate supply, not of hours per worker but of the number of workers. In effect, we are interested in analyzing the outcome of an all-or-nothing choice. That is, the potential worker has to evaluate how much utility would be derived from not working and compare this with the utility that would be derived from working for a fixed number of hours per week. If the utility from working exceeds that from not working, the individual will make the decision to be in the labor force and therefore be part of the labor supply. In general, as the real wage rises, more and more people will evaluate the prospect of working as yielding more utility than the prospect of not working. Let us suppose that this is the case and that as a consequence, the aggregate supply of labor increases as the real wage increases. Figure 8.4 shows such a relation.

Competitive Equilibrium

Next, consider the competitive equilibrium in the labor market. Figure 8.5 brings together the demand curve from Figure 8.3 and the supply curve from Figure 8.4. It is supposed that the economy generates sufficient information about supply and demand in the labor market for the real wage *quickly* to achieve a market-clearing or equilibrium value. The economy therefore, on the average, settles down at the real wage $(W/P)^*$ and at the level of employment n^*. Of course, the real wage is the ratio of the money wage rate to the price level, and it is the money wage that will adjust in the labor market to ensure that for a given price level, the equilibrium real wage is attained.

The assumption that the equilibrium real wage is *quickly* achieved is a crucial one for keeping the analysis simple. The presumption is that even

Figure 8.5
Labor Market Equilibrium

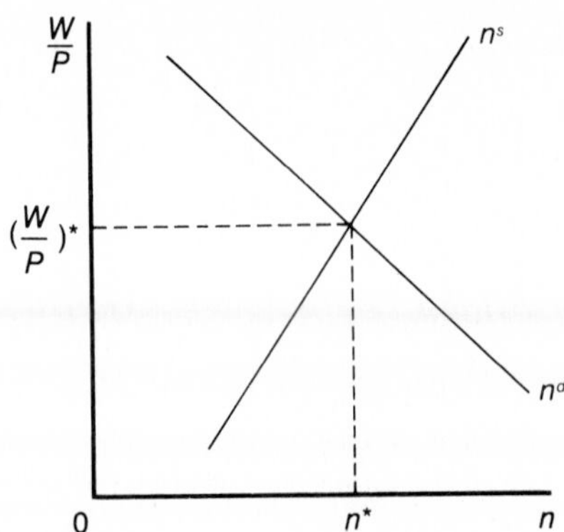

The line labelled n^d is the demand for labor curve and the line labelled n^s is the supply curve of labor. The labor market is in equilibrium when households are maximizing utility (are on their supply curve) and firms are maximizing profits (are on their demand curve). The only such point is where the supply and demand curves cut at the real wage $(W/P)^*$ and the employment level n^*.

though it takes time to attain equilibrium, that time is insignificantly short relative to the length of time for which the equilibrium prevails. This would mean that although we might observe an actual economy that is not in an equilibrium, as depicted in Figure 8.5, that economy would be heading for such an equilibrium, and if we blinked, by the time we opened our eyes again the economy would have settled into such an equilibrium.

We have now determined the equilibrium values of the real wage and the level of employment. You can think of the employment level as the aggregate number employed in the economy and the real wage as the economy's average real wage. Individuals' real wages will be highly variable, depending on individual skills and other factors. If relative wages are fairly stable, however, movements in the average real wage in the economy will also reflect movements in each individual's real wage.

The way in which the analysis has been developed has ignored the phenomenon of unemployment. That is not to say that unemployment cannot exist in this model. It is simply to say that at the present time we are not discussing the implications of the model for the rate of unemployment. This will be taken up at some length in Chapter 11. Furthermore, monopolistic elements in the labor market, such as, for example, the operation of labor unions, have also been ignored. This, too, will be dealt with in Chapter 11.

C. Aggregate Supply Curve

First, a definition of the aggregate supply curve: The aggregate supply curve shows the amount of output that the economy will supply at each different price level, given that firms are maximizing profits, households are maximizing utility, and the labor market is in equilibrium. It is a curve that is drawn in a

Figure 8.6 Derivation of the Aggregate Supply Curve

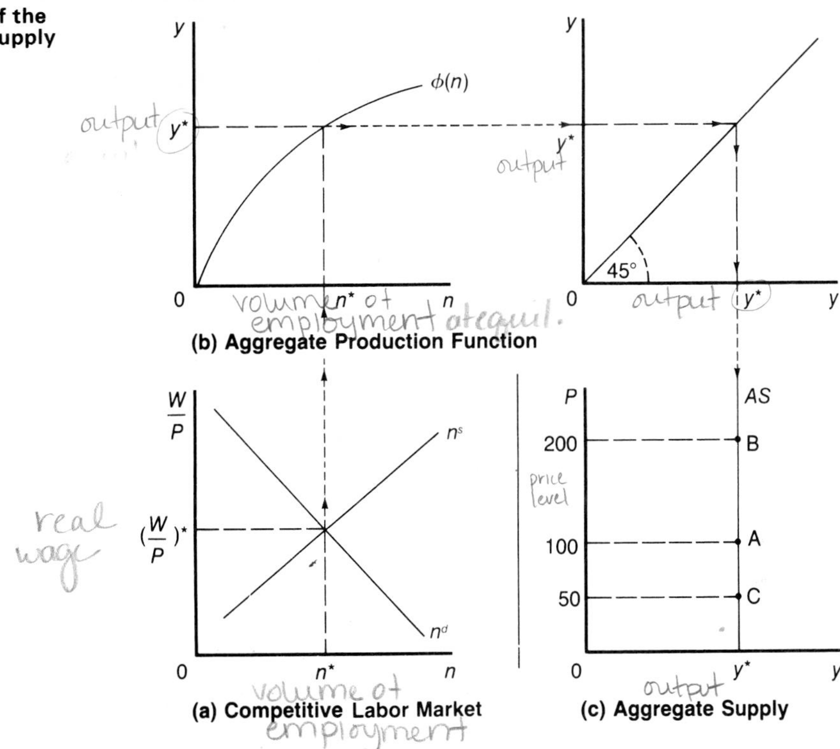

Frame (a) is identical to Figure 8.5 and frame (b) is identical to Figure 8.1. Frame (c) shows the aggregate supply curve (*AS*). This shows the amount of output that will be supplied as the price level varies when firms are hiring the profit-maximizing quantity of labor and households are supplying the utility-maximizing quantity of labor. There is a unique level of output (y*) that will be produced by the equilibrium level of labor input (n*) at the equilibrium real wage (W/P)*. That level of supply will be independent of the price level, so that the aggregate supply curve is vertical.

diagram with the price level on one axis and output on the other. See Figure 8.6.

To derive the aggregate supply curve, it is necessary to bring together the two components of analysis developed above, namely, the short-run production function and the competitive equilibrium in the labor market. This is done in Figure 8.6. Your first quick glance at Figure 8.6 may give you the impression that the analysis on which you are about to embark is going to be difficult. Fortunately, such a first impression would be wrong. The analysis illustrated by Figure 8.6 is actually quite easy, provided you take it step by step.

The first step is to notice that there are four parts to Figure 8.6. The first part, frame (a), is nothing other than Figure 8.5, which you have just been studying. It shows a labor market in competitive equilibrium with the real wage equal to (W/P)* and the level of employment, n*.

The second part of the figure, frame (b), is exactly the same as Figure 8.1, namely, a short-run production function. Notice that the horizontal axes of frames (a) and (b) both measure the same thing—the volume of employment. Adopt the convention that the units of measurement are the same on both horizontal axes. That being the case, you can immediately read off from the horizontal axis of frame (b) the same equilibrium level of employment, n^*, as is determined in frame (a). The dotted line and arrow indicate this.

With the level of employment equal to n^*, the short-run production function in frame (b) determines the level of output y^* as shown on the vertical axis.

So far, you have used frames (a) and (b) to determine the equilibrium values of the real wage, the level of employment, and the level of output.

To complete the derivation of the aggregate supply curve, the question that has to be answered is: How does the equilibrium level of output vary as the price level varies? The answer to this question (and the aggregate supply curve) will be discovered in frame (c). This part of the figure measures the price level on the vertical axis and the level of output on the horizontal axis. Notice that the vertical axis of frame (b) and the horizontal axis of frame (c) measure the same thing—output. The top right part of the diagram has output on both axes and a 45° line. It is just a pictorial device to enable you to read off from the horizontal axis of frame (c) the same quantity as is shown on the vertical axis of frame (b). Notice, by the way, that the vertical axis of frame (c) *does not* measure the same thing as the vertical axis of frame (a)—there are no arrowed lines going from frame (c) directly to frame (a). The arrows (and the analysis) start in frame (a) and go clockwise to finish in frame (c).

Now go back to the question: How does equilibrium output vary as the price level varies? Suppose that the price level initially is equal to 100. We can arbitrarily define our units so that this is true. This would mean that there would be a point at 100 on the aggregate supply curve, which is identified by the letter A in frame (c). Suppose now that the price level was doubled from 100 to 200. What would happen to the amount of output that firms would be willing to supply? The answer is quickly seen—Nothing would happen to it.

If the price level doubled to 200, then the money wage would also have to double to preserve labor market equilibrium [frame (a)]. To see that this is so, suppose that after the price level had increased, the money wage rate remained fixed. In such a case, the real wage would have fallen, and the demand for labor would exceed the supply of labor. Such a situation would force the money wage to rise until the labor market was again in equilibrium. The only real wage consistent with equilibrium is the original one. Thus, the money wage must rise by the same percentage amount as does the price level. In this case, following a doubling of the price level, the money wage would also have to double in order to keep the real wage constant. With the labor market remaining at its original equilibrium, the quantity of employment would remain unchanged as would the amount of output supplied. The economy would move, therefore, to the point identified by the letter B in frame (c).

Next, suppose the price level is halved from 100 to 50. The effects of this on the amount of output that the economy would produce are exactly the same as the effects of the doubling of the price level. In this case, the money wage would have to fall to one-half of its previous level in order to maintain the real wage at its market equilibrium value, and employment and output would remain constant at n^* and y^*. The economy would thus move to the point identified by the letter C in frame (c). These three points (and all the other points above, below, and between them) trace an aggregate supply curve for this economy.

The aggregate supply curve in the basic model is perfectly inelastic. The level of output will be equal to y^* no matter what the price level.

Summary

A. Short-Run Aggregate Production Function

The short-run aggregate production function shows how the maximum amount of output will vary as the number of workers employed varies, holding constant the stock of capital, the state of technology, and the skills of labor. Its properties are the same as the short-run production function of an individual firm in that it displays diminishing marginal productivity.

B. Competitive Aggregate Labor Market

A competitive aggregate labor market will determine an equilibrium real wage and level of employment where the downward sloping demand curve (derived from the marginal product curve) cuts an upward sloping supply curve (derived from utility-maximizing decisions of households).

C. Aggregate Supply Curve

The aggregate supply curve shows how output varies as the price level varies when firms are maximizing profits, households are maximizing utility, and the labor market is in equilibrium. In the basic model developed in this chapter, aggregate supply is perfectly inelastic with respect to the price level.

Review Questions

1. A firm manufactures a good from inputs of labor and capital. Labor is measured by the number of men employed. Use the following data to draw the firm's short-run production function:

No. of men	1	2	3	4	5	6	7	8	9	10
Output	10	21	33	45	56	66	75	83	90	96

If the money wage is \$18 and the firm sells the good it produces for \$2, how many men will the firm employ?

2. If the economy consisted of 1000 firms, all identical and all exactly like the firm described in Question 1, show in a diagram the shape and position of the *aggregate* short-run production function. Also show the aggregate demand for labor curve. If the aggregate labor supply curve is

$$n^s = 2000\left(\frac{W}{P}\right) - 2000$$

how many men will be employed and what will be the economy-wide average real wage?

3. What is an aggregate supply curve?

4. Use your answer to Question 2 to derive the aggregate supply curve for the hypothetical economy described in that question.

5. In drawing the aggregate supply curve, several assumptions have been made. List these assumptions.

6. Labor allocates its time between work and leisure in order to maximize its utility. Along which curve in Figure 8.7 is utility maximized?

7. Firms produce an output level that maximizes profit. Along which curve in Figure 8.7 are all firms maximizing profit?

8. Is the aggregate supply curve fixed in position forever, or does it shift from time to time? If it does shift, list some of the things that would cause it to do so.

Appendix A to Chapter 8

Monopoly and the Demand for Labor

You may be thinking that the analysis just presented is fine for a competitive industry but not for a monopoly. You may also have been taught that we simply *know* that there are no competitive industries in the actual world. If so, you will be regarding the preceding analysis as being about as useful for the task in hand as the flat earth theory would be for charting an air route from New York to Tokyo! Leaving aside the deep question of whether or not it is possible *simply to know* whether or not competitive industries exist, it is perhaps of some interest to notice that for the task at hand, it simply doesn't matter whether the economy is competitive or monopolistic. To see this, consider how the analysis would go for a monopolist.

Now in order to maximize profits, a monopolist will set marginal cost equal, not to price, but to marginal revenue (MR_i). That is,

$$MC_i = MR_i \tag{8A.1}$$

Just as in the case of a competitive firm, the monopolist's marginal cost will be equal to the wage rate divided by the marginal product of labor; that is,

$$MC_i = \frac{W}{MP_i} \tag{8A.2}$$

The monopolist's marginal revenue will be related to price by the formula

$$MR_i = \left(1 + \frac{1}{\eta}\right)P_i,\ \eta < -1 \tag{8A.3}$$

where η is the elasticity of the monopolist's demand curve. (See Appendix B to this chapter.) To get a feel for how the relationship between marginal revenue and price [(Equation (8A.3)] works, notice that if the elasticity of demand (η) was infinite, then MR_i would equal P_i. This, of course, is exactly the case of perfect competition. If η was equal to -1, the demand for the monopolist's output would be unit elastic and the demand curve would be a rectangular hyperbola. In that case, the monopolist's marginal revenue would be zero and the monopolist would not be in business.

In general, the monopolist's marginal revenue will be less than price but a stable fraction of the price.

Using Equations (8A.3) and (8A.2) in (8A.1) enables us to obtain

$$\left(1 + \frac{1}{\eta}\right)P_i = \frac{W}{MP_i} \tag{8A.4}$$

Proceeding as we did in the case of the competitive firm, dividing both sides of (8A.4) by P_i, and multiplying both sides by MP_i, we obtain

$$\left(1 + \frac{1}{\eta}\right)MP_i = \frac{W}{P_i} \tag{8A.5}$$

This says that some fraction [the fraction $(1 - 1/\eta)$] of the marginal product of a monopolistic firm will be equal to the real wage. The monopolist's demand for labor will therefore be *less* than that of a competitive producer (assuming that they have identical production functions) but will still have the crucial property that as the real wage rises, the demand for labor falls. By aggregating across all producers, whether competitive or monopolistic, we shall still end up with an aggregate demand for labor that looks like that shown in Figure 8.3.

Appendix B to Chapter 8

Elasticity of Demand, Marginal Revenue, and Price

Elasticity is a measure of responsiveness. The elasticity of demand measures, in a precise way, the responsiveness of the quantity demanded to a change in the price. The higher the elasticity, the more responsive is the quantity to a price change. Elasticity is a unit-free measure of responsiveness. To be precise, it is the percentage change in the quantity demanded divided by the percentage change in price or, equivalently, the proportionate change of quantity demanded divided by the proportionate change in price. Calling the elasticity η, the change in quantity ΔQ, the change in price ΔP, the quantity Q, and the price P, the elasticity is measured as

$$\eta = \frac{\Delta Q}{Q} \div \frac{\Delta P}{P} \tag{8A.6}$$

This may equivalently be written as

$$\eta = \frac{\Delta Q}{Q} \cdot \frac{P}{\Delta P} \tag{8A.7}$$

For future reference it is useful to notice that one over the elasticity (the inverse of the elasticity) is

$$\frac{1}{\eta} = \frac{\Delta P}{\Delta Q} \cdot \frac{Q}{P} \tag{8A.8}$$

To obtain the formula used in Appendix A, notice that total revenue (R) is equal to price (P) multiplied by quantity (Q); that is,

$$R = PQ \tag{8A.9}$$

Now suppose that there was a change in price that induced a change in quantity and a change in revenue. Then the new revenue that we could call $R + \Delta R$ will be determined as

$$R + \Delta R = (P + \Delta P)(Q + \Delta Q) \tag{8A.10}$$

Multiplying out Equation (8A.10) gives

$$R + \Delta R = PQ + P\Delta Q + \Delta PQ + \Delta P\Delta Q \tag{8A.11}$$

If the change in price (ΔP) is very very small, then Equation (8A.11) is approximately

$$R + \Delta R = PQ + P\Delta Q + Q\Delta P \tag{8A.12}$$

(You see that we are treating the last term in Equation (8A.12) as if it were zero.) Now subtract Equation (8A.9) from Equation (8A.12) to give

$$\Delta R = P\Delta Q + Q\Delta P \tag{8A.13}$$

This can be manipulated by multiplying and dividing the second term on the right-hand side by P to give

$$\Delta R = \left[\Delta Q + \frac{Q}{P}(\Delta P)\right]P \tag{8A.14}$$

Dividing this equation through by ΔQ gives

$$\frac{\Delta R}{\Delta Q} \approx \left[\frac{\Delta Q}{\Delta Q} + \frac{Q}{P}\left(\frac{\Delta P}{\Delta Q}\right)\right]P \tag{8A.15}$$

The left-hand side of Equation (8A.15), ($\Delta R/\Delta Q$) is what is called *marginal revenue*—the change in revenue induced by a change in the quantity sold. Obviously, the first term in the brackets—$\Delta Q/\Delta Q$—in Equation (8A.15) is equal to one. You can also see, by referring back to Equation (8A.8), that the second term in the brackets—$(Q/P)(\Delta P/\Delta Q)$—in Equation (8A.15) is the inverse of the elasticity of demand. Equation (8A.15) may, therefore, be written more simply as:

$$\frac{\Delta R}{\Delta Q} \approx \left(1 + \frac{1}{\eta}\right)P \tag{8A.16}$$

This is the relationship used in Appendix A. In words, it states that marginal revenue equals one plus one over the elasticity of demand multiplied by the price. Clearly if the elasticity of demand is infinitely big (the case of perfect competition), price and marginal revenue are the same as each other.

Another interesting special case is when the elasticity of demand is minus one (the case of a rectangular hyperbola demand curve). In that case, you can verify from Equation (8A.16) that marginal revenue is equal to zero. Notice that, in general, marginal revenue will be positive but less than the price since η, in general, will be negative and will lie between minus infinity (perfect competition) and minus one.

9

Aggregate Demand and the Money Market

You have studied the first ingredient of the basic model—the theory of aggregate supply—and it is now time to move on to the second ingredient—the demand side of the economy. There are two tasks under this topic, which are to:

(a) Understand the concept of aggregate demand.
(b) Understand the monetary theory of aggregate demand.

The second task is the major part of this chapter and is divided into a series of subsidiary tasks that you should work through very carefully.

A. Aggregate Demand

Aggregate demand is the demand for goods and services in total. It is the demand for aggregate output. The *aggregate demand curve* is defined as the relationship between the aggregate quantity of goods and services that people want to buy in a given period of time and the price level.

The questions that we shall be interested in concerning the aggregate demand curve are:

1. What is the shape of the aggregate demand curve? Does it slope downwards? That is, would the level of aggregate demand rise if the price level fell?
2. What variables cause the aggregate demand curve to shift? That is, what variables, other than the price level, cause aggregate demand to vary?

These two questions occupy the rest of this chapter.

B. The Monetary Theory of Aggregate Demand

This section introduces a variety of concepts and is analytically fairly heavy. Therefore, you are encouraged to work through the material several times if necessary, in order to be sure that you have a thorough grasp of the monetary theory of aggregate demand. The starting point for understanding what deter-

Figure 9.1
Money Balances

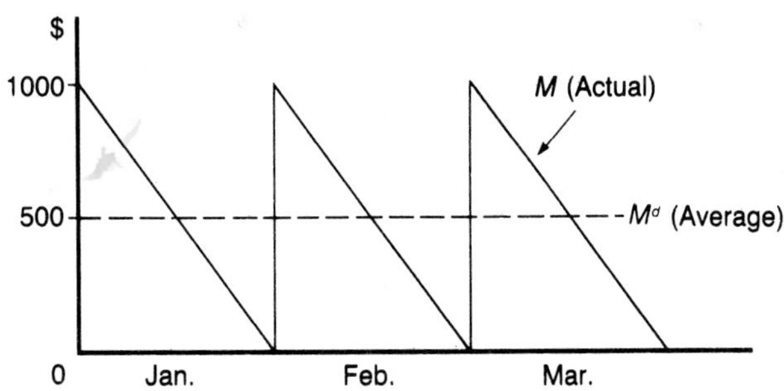

Actual money balances are at their peak at the beginning of each month and are gradually run down to their minimum as expenditure takes place throughout the month. The demand for money refers to the average money holdings (indicated in the diagram by the dashed line).

mines aggregate demand is an analysis of the determination of the demand, not for goods, but for money.

The Demand for Money

First, what do we mean by the demand for money?[1] You already know what money is: It is the *stock* of currency and demand deposits[2] in existence at a given point in time. Most of us acquire money as a *flow* of income that, typically, is received at either weekly or monthly intervals. At the beginning of payday, the amount of money that we are holding is at a minimum, and just after we have been paid, it is at a maximum. In the period between the moment that we have been paid through to the next payday, we typically spend our income gradually, thereby running down our money balances.

Figure 9.1 illustrates the pattern of money holdings for an individual who receives an income of $1000 per month at monthly intervals and who spends that $1000 in equal daily amounts throughout the month. The saw-tooth line shows the actual money holdings of that individual. Those money holdings are $1000 at the beginning of each month and zero at the end of each month. The broken line through the middle of the diagram shows the average money holding of this individual, which, in this case, is $500. It is the average money holding that we refer to as the individual's *demand* for money. The amount of money demanded is an average *stock*, and the income is a *flow*. Call the quantity of money demanded M^d (the superscript d on the M is to remind you

---

[1]The analysis of the demand for money presented here is highly simplified. A comprehensive treatment of this topic may be found in David Laidler, *The Demand for Money: Theories and Evidence*, 2nd ed. (New York: Harper & Row, Publishers, Inc., 1978).

[2]This is the definition of money known as M1 (See Chapter 4.)

that M^d is the *demand* for money), and call money income Py—the price level (P), multiplied by real income (y). Then let us define the ratio of money demanded (M^d) to money income (Py) as k. That is,

$$k = \frac{M^d}{Py} \qquad \textbf{(9.1)}$$

The individual in the above example has an annual income of \$12,000 (\$1000 each month) and a demand for money of \$500. For this individual, therefore, the ratio of average money holdings to annual money income is

$$k = \frac{\$500}{\$12{,}000} = \frac{1}{24}$$

An alternative way of writing Equation (9.1) would be (by multiplying both sides of the equation by Py) as

$$M^d = kPy \qquad \textbf{(9.2)}$$

This says that the demand for money is some fraction k of money income. Let us give a name to k: We will call it the *propensity to hold money*.

The next question to be dealt with is, Will the propensity to hold money be constant? Put slightly differently, would it make sense for individuals to mechanically hold money balances equal, on the average, to one-half of their periodic income? That is, would it make sense for an individual paid weekly to hold money balances equal, on the average, to one-half a week's income; and a person paid monthly to hold money balances equal, on the average, to one-half a month's income; and so on? The answer, in general, is that it would not. Rather it would be sensible to attempt to *economize* on money holdings.

Consider the example of a person who receives \$12,000 a year, paid at quarterly intervals. Specifically, suppose a person receives \$3000 on the 1st of January, April, July, and October. Would it make sense for such a person to run down his money balances at an even rate over each quarter? Notice that if such a person did spread his outlays evenly, the propensity to hold money would be one-eighth. That is, on the average, one-eighth of a year's income would be held in the form of money. The average money holding of such a person would be \$1500. What could such a person do to economize on his money holdings? There are two possibilities: (1) He could make a loan by buying and holding some financial asset other than money, an asset that unlike money, pays interest; or (2) he could bunch the purchase of goods toward the beginning of the income period, thereby holding less money, on the average, but having a higher average inventory of goods.

Under what circumstances would an individual attempt to use one or both of these devices for economizing on money holdings? Obviously, the higher the rate of interest, the more will an individual be losing by holding money rather than buying interest-earning financial assets. Equally obviously, the higher the rate of inflation, the more will an individual be losing by holding money rather than buying and holding inventories of goods. It seems reasonable to suppose, therefore, that the higher the rate of interest, the more will individuals seek to switch out of money holdings and into the holdings of financial assets that earn a return. This action will lower an individual's propensity to hold money.

It also seems reasonable to suppose that the faster prices are rising or, equivalently, the higher the rate of inflation, the more it would pay an individual to bunch purchases of goods so that most goods are bought soon after payday. There is, however, an important difference between the interest rate that an individual can earn on a financial asset and the consequences of inflation that can be avoided by buying goods earlier rather than later. When an individual buys a financial asset, the interest rate that will be paid on that financial asset is known at the time of the purchase. But when an individual seeks to avoid losses from inflation by buying goods early, he does not know with any certainty what the inflation rate will in fact turn out to be over some relevant future period. Thus, what determines the decision to economize on money holdings and buy bigger inventories of goods is not the actual but the *expected* rate of inflation.

In the example that we have just worked through, we dealt with an individual whose income was received at quarterly intervals. This meant that the individual received a fairly sizable amount of money on each payday and therefore would be able to earn a substantial amount of interest income (or avoid losses from inflation) by taking economizing actions of the type discussed. However, the more frequently a person is paid, the less the incentive to take advantage of these economizing actions. In fact, for people paid at very frequent intervals, such as a week, it may well be that the best they can do is to hold money balances that roughly equal one-half a week's income. This is because the interest that could be earned on a half a week's income would not be sufficient to justify the costs of moving between money and interest-earning securities and back again into money all within a week. For these individuals, the propensity to hold money (k) would be 1/104. For such individuals, then, the propensity to hold money would indeed be a constant.

There is another factor working in the direction of reducing the incentive to economize on money holdings and that is the increasing tendency for certain types of monetary assets to bear interest themselves. If all forms of money received interest at a rate that moved up and down in line with movements in other interest rates, then there would be no tendency for the incentive to economize on money holdings to vary with the level of interest rates. In a situation, however, in which not all monetary assets bear interest (such as in today's world), there will remain an incentive to economize on money holdings as interest rates and inflation fluctuate.

Let us now summarize the above: There are two ways of economizing on money holdings—(1) by buying financial assets, and (2) by buying real goods. Buying financial assets is a way of earning interest, and buying goods is a way of avoiding some of the loss in the value of money resulting from inflation. The higher the interest rates and the higher the expected rate of inflation, the more that people will seek to economize on money holdings and the lower will be the propensity to hold money.

Interest Rates and Expected Inflation

The next step in developing the monetary theory of aggregate demand is the simplified theory of the rate of interest. The starting point of the simplified theory is an important definition that states that the real rate of interest equals the nominal rate of interest *minus* the *expected* rate of inflation.

The rate of interest actually paid and received is sometimes called the *money* (or, equivalently, *nominal*) *rate* of interest. This is to emphasize its distinction from the *real* rate of interest. The distinction between real and money (or nominal) interest is a vital and natural one. In an economy in which prices are expected to rise by, say, 10 percent a year, money that is borrowed and lent will be expected to lose value at the rate of 10 percent a year. This means that someone who lends money for a year will expect to be repaid at the end of the year in dollars that are worth 10 percent less than the dollars that were lent. Similarly, the borrower will expect to repay the loan with cheaper dollars. This expected fall in the value of money—*expected inflation*—must be subtracted from the rate of interest—the *money rate of interest*—in order to calculate the interest rate that people expect they will *really* pay and receive.

All this can be summarized in two simple equations. Call the money rate of interest r_m and the real rate of interest r. Then, the real rate of interest is the difference between the money rate of interest and the expected rate of inflation; i.e.,

$$r = r_m - \pi^e \tag{9.3}$$

and equivalently, the money rate of interest is the sum of the real rate of interest and the expected rate of inflation; i.e.,

$$r_m = r + \pi^e \tag{9.4}$$

Two Special Assumptions

The next step in the simplified theory of interest is to make two very special assumptions. These are special in the sense that, in general, there is no reason to suppose that they will be true. In fact, much of what you will be doing in the next two parts of this book will be working out the consequences of avoiding these two special and restrictive assumptions. There is, of course, nothing wrong in principle with special assumptions provided they yield predictions that are not in conflict with the facts. The only way that we shall be able to discover this is to work out the implications of the assumptions—that is, work out the predictions that are the consequences of making particular assumptions, and then see whether or not the predictions and the facts are in agreement. Let us go on now to see what the two special assumptions are that complete the simplified theory of interest.

The first special assumption is that *the expected rate of inflation*, although conceptually distinct from the actual rate of inflation, *is* in fact arithmetically *equal to the actual rate of inflation.* In other words, the simplified theory of interest abstracts from (ignores) any differences that there might be between actual and anticipated inflation. In what follows in the rest of this chapter, we shall, therefore, replace the expected rate of inflation (π^e) with the actual rate of inflation (π).

The second special assumption made is that *the real rate of interest is constant*. That is, changes in the nominal rate of interest occur only as a result of changes in the expected rate of inflation. This does not imply that all borrowers and lenders will pay the same real rate of interest. Rather, it says that whatever real rate of interest prevails between a particular borrower and lender (which will vary across individuals and will depend on the risk of the loan not being repaid), that real rate will not vary because of variations in the expected rate of inflation.

According to this theory, this means that each 1 percent rise or fall in the rate of inflation will be associated with an equivalent 1 percent rise or fall in rates of interest, and no other factors will produce a change in the rate of interest.

Inflation and the Demand for Money

Now that we have a theory about the determination of the rate of interest, it is possible to return to the demand for money and make a simpler proposition about the determination of the propensity to hold money. We started our discussion of the ways of economizing on money holdings by noting that this can be achieved as a result of individuals buying interest-earning assets or buying goods. The higher the rate of interest, the more will it pay people to economize on their money holdings by buying interest-earning assets; and the higher the rate of inflation, the more will it pay people to economize on money holdings by bunching their purchases of goods toward the beginning of the pay period.

The simplified theory of the rate of interest that we have just reviewed implies, however, that although there are two ways of economizing on money holdings, there is only one factor that induces that economizing—inflation. A higher rate of inflation induces a substitution away from money and toward holdings of inventories of goods, and a higher rate of inflation also raises the nominal rate of interest, thus inducing substitution away from money and toward interest-earning assets.

This entire lengthy discussion may thus be summarized with the following statement: The propensity to hold money will vary inversely with the rate of inflation.

We can write this as an equation, which says

$$\frac{M^d}{Py} = \underset{(-)}{k\,(\pi)} \qquad \textbf{(9.5)}$$

where $k(\pi)$ stands for "k is a function of—or depends on—π, the rate of inflation." The minus sign (−) below the equation is there to remind you that as inflation rises, the propensity to hold money falls.

We can also illustrate the proposition with Figure 9.2. The downward

Figure 9.2
The Propensity to Hold Money

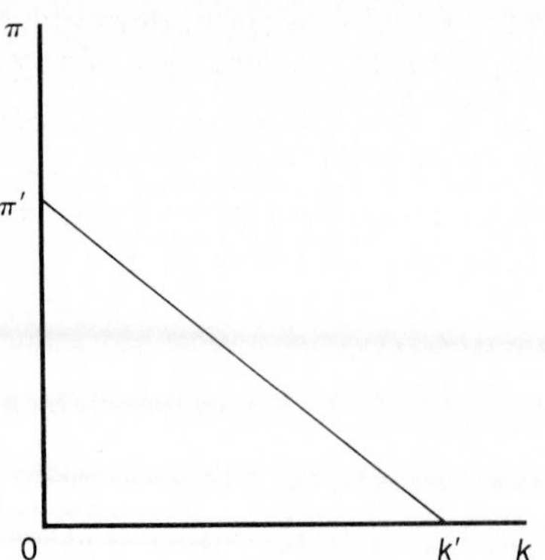

Inflation is a tax on money holdings. The higher is the tax—the higher is inflation—the more people will economize on their money holdings, and the lower, therefore, will be the propensity to hold money.

sloping curve ($\pi' k'$) shows how k rises as π falls. If inflation was as high as π', people would no longer want to use money, and trade would be undertaken with barter or some commodity means of exchange. If inflation was zero, then k would equal k'.

Equivalently, we can write Equation (9.5) in the form of Equation (9.2), as

$$M^d = k \underset{(-)}{(\pi)} Py \tag{9.6}$$

which says that the demand for money (M^d) is a function of (depends on) the level of money income (Py) and the rate of inflation (π). The minus sign (−) below π in Equation (9.6) is there to remind you that a rise in inflation has the effect of lowering the demand for money.

Notice that there is a crucial difference between the effect of *inflation* and the effect of the *price level* on the demand for money. If the price level doubled overnight, and if everything else (including the rate of inflation) remained the same,[3] then the amount of money that people would want to hold would also double. Thus, the demand for money is proportional to the level of prices. This idea, that the amount of money demanded is proportional to the price level, enables us to make use of a simpler statement about the demand for money based on a definition of real money. Real money is the quantity of money (M) divided by the price level (P). That is,

$$\text{Real money} = \frac{M}{P}$$

[3]If the idea of the price level doubling overnight and the rate of inflation remaining constant seems puzzling, recall the distinction between a once-and-for-all change in the price level and inflation—Figure 5.1.

You can express the demand for money as the demand for real money. The demand for real money depends on the level of real income and on the rate of inflation. The higher the level of real income, the more real money will be demanded; and the higher the rate of inflation, the less real money will be demanded.

You can represent this in terms of a simple equation derived directly from Equation (9.6), which says:

$$\frac{M^d}{P} = \underset{(-)}{k(\pi)}\, y \qquad \textbf{(9.7)}$$

For the rest of the material that we are covering in this chapter, it is going to be a convenient simplification to suppose that the rate of inflation is constant. (We shall be dealing with varying inflation rates and the determination of inflation in Chapter 12.) It will also be convenient to set that constant inflation rate equal to zero for the moment, so that the propensity to hold money is k' (see Figure 9.2) and the demand for real money is

$$\frac{M^d}{P} = k'y \qquad \textbf{(9.8)}$$

This simple theory of the demand for money is a central ingredient in developing the monetary theory of aggregate demand. Each individual decides how much money to demand in real terms, relative to his level of income. For the economy as a whole, we may add up all the individual demands to arrive at the economy's aggregate demand for real money balances, which will depend on the economy's aggregate real income.

The Supply of Money

The stock of money in the economy is called the *supply of money*. This supply is determined by the actions of the central bank and the banking system and will be analyzed in some detail in Chapter 32. For present purposes we shall treat the supply of money as being determined exogenously.[4] The private individuals who hold the money have no control over what the supply of money will be. The supply of money will be called M.

Making the assumption that the supply of money (M) is exogenous,

[4]When proper account is taken of the linkages between the domestic economy and the rest of the world, it is not always possible to regard the supply of money as being determined exogenously. If the economy has a floating exchange rate, such an assumption may be in order. In the case of an economy with a fixed exchange rate, however, it is inappropriate to regard the money supply as being determined exogenously. For present purposes, therefore, you should regard the exercise that is being conducted as one that applies to an economy that does not have any trading links with the rest of the world, or you should regard it as applying to an economy that has a floating exchange rate. (The world as a whole is the only interesting example of an economy that does not have trading links with the rest of the world.)

enables us to move on to examine how money market equilibrium determines the level of aggregate demand for goods and services.

Money Market Equilibrium

Suppose that the supply of money was bigger than the amount of money that people wanted to hold. How would people react in such a situation? Since we are thinking of a competitive economy, there would be nothing that any individual could do, acting alone, to affect prices. Every individual, however, has to make a decision about how much to spend and how to allocate wealth between money and interest-earning assets. If the amount of money made available by the central bank was to exceed the amount of money that individuals wanted to hold, then there would be two remedies available *for the individual.* One would be to use the excess money holdings to acquire interest-earning assets, and the other would be to increase spending. Although an individual with excess money holdings could reduce those holdings by acquiring interest-earning assets, the economy as a whole is not in a position to do that—for whenever one individual buys an interest-earning asset, another individual must sell one. Thus, from the point of view of the economy as a whole, the only thing that can be done to get rid of excess money holdings is to increase spending. What one individual spends, however, is the income received by other individuals. Therefore, if the amount of money in the economy exceeded the amount of money demanded, expenditure (and therefore income) would rise.

Conversely, if the amount of money made available by the central bank was less than the amount of money that people wanted to hold, then individuals would cut back their expenditures in order to replenish their money balances. All this may be summarized more compactly using the symbols that were introduced above. Recall that M is the money supply; M^d is the demand for money and Py is aggregate expenditure (equals income). Thus,

1. If $M > M^d$, then Py will rise.
2. If $M < M^d$, then Py will fall.
3. If $M = M^d$, then Py will be constant.

Although we have just conducted a conceptual experiment to analyze what would happen if the amount of money that people wanted to hold was different from the amount of money supplied, a moment's reflection will reveal that in the ordinary course of events these situations will not be observed. Individuals will not ordinarily be holding an excess or a deficiency of money, on the average. Rather, they will vary their expenditures in order to eliminate either a money balance deficiency or an excessive amount of money holdings. In the ordinary course of events, therefore, what we shall observe is a situation in which the amount of money that people want to hold is equal to the amount of money that the central bank has made available. That is,

$$M = M^d \tag{9.9}$$

This is a situation of money market equilibrium.

Another analogy may be useful here. Suppose that Lake Tahoe was arbitrarily divided by a straight line running north-south midway along its length. Now ask the question, What would happen if the water level on the left-hand side of this line was 10 feet higher than the water level on the right-hand side? This is a perfectly sensible question to ask. The answer is that the molecular structure of the water is such that the force of gravity would very quickly act upon the higher level to reduce it to equality with that of the lower level. We would never, in the ordinary course of events, observe such an inequality, although the theory that explains why the lake surface is flat involves conceptually letting the level be temporarily and hypothetically disturbed. It is the same in the money market. The very forces that would lead to money market equilibrium will, in the ordinary course of events, prevent the money market from ever straying very far away from such an equilibrium.[5]

Aggregate Demand

We are now almost at the point of being able to derive the monetary theory of aggregate demand. With money market equilibrium we know from Equation (9.9) that $M = M^d$, and we also know from Equation (9.8) that the demand for money is $M^d/P = k'y$. It follows, therefore, that

$$\frac{M}{P} = k'y \qquad \textbf{(9.10)}$$

That is, we know that the amount of real money being held is, in equilibrium, going to be proportional to real income (continuing to assume for the present that the inflation rate is constant and zero).

The aggregate demand curve is the relationship between the level of planned real expenditure (which equals real income or output) and the price level. To find the aggregate demand curve, we hold the money supply constant and conceptually vary the price level asking the question: How does the level of planned real expenditure (real income or output) vary, while preserving money market equilibrium at each given price level? Call the level of planned real expenditure (real income or output), which maintains money market equilibrium, the level of aggregate demand (denoted as y^d).

The answer to the question just posed is obtained directly by "solving" the money market equilibrium equation for the value of y^d as we conceptually vary the price level P. That is,

$$y^d = \frac{1}{k'}\left(\frac{M}{P}\right) \qquad \textbf{(9.11)}$$

The term $1/k'$ is what is usually referred to as the *velocity of circulation* of money. You can see immediately that as the price level rises, real money

---

[5]David Hume first suggested this water-level analogy. See his essay "Of the Balance of Trade" in *Essays: Moral, Political and Literary* (London: Oxford University Press, 1963), p. 319.

Figure 9.3
The Aggregate Demand Curve

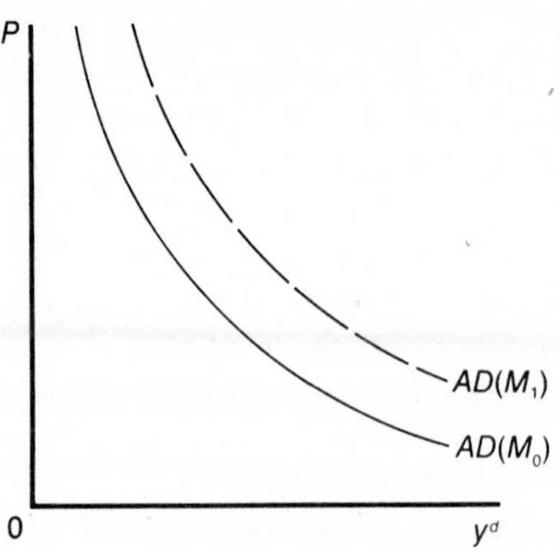

The aggregate demand curve traces the relationship between output demanded (y^d) and the price level (P) when people have equilibrium money holdings—when the supply of money equals the demand for money. The aggregate demand curve has an elasticity of −1. The higher the stock of money, the further to the right is the aggregate demand curve. The dashed curve is associated with a bigger money stock than is the continuous curve.

balances fall (as P rises, M/P falls) and aggregate demand also falls. That is, aggregate demand varies *inversely* with the price level. You can also see that the relationship between aggregate demand and the price level is a very simple one. Because aggregate demand depends on the ratio of the money supply to the price level, a rise in the price level of 1 percent will lower real money balances by the same 1 percent. It will also lower aggregate demand by 1 percent. Thus, the *elasticity* of aggregate demand, according to this simple monetary theory, is equal to *minus one*. The aggregate demand Equation (9.11) is plotted in Figure 9.3 as the curve labelled $AD(M_0)$.

You have now answered the first question posed at the beginning of this chapter. That is, you have discovered that the aggregate demand curve slopes downwards, indicating that aggregate demand rises as the price level falls. More precisely, you have discovered that, according to this simple monetary theory, the elasticity of that demand curve is minus one.

The second question: What variables other than the price level cause aggregate demand to vary? is easily answered. In this simple framework there are two variables. One is the money supply. The higher the money supply, the higher is aggregate demand or, equivalently, the further to the right is the aggregate demand curve. The curve labelled $AD(M_1)$ in Figure 9.3 illustrates the aggregate demand curve for a higher money supply than that in the case of the curve $AD(M_0)$. The second thing that can cause aggregate demand to change is a change in the expected rate of inflation. This will operate by changing the propensity to hold money (k). The higher the expected rate of inflation, the lower is the propensity to hold money and the higher is aggregate demand or, equivalently, the further to the right is the aggregate demand curve. Thus, the curve labelled $AD(M_1)$ in Figure 9.3 could be thought of as illustrating an aggregate demand curve for a higher expected rate of inflation than that in the case of the curve $AD(M_0)$.

Although the aggregate demand curve can shift either as a result of the change in the quantity of money or as a result of a change in the expected rate of inflation, the latter variable is, as we shall see in Chapter 12, itself going to be influenced by the behavior of the money supply. Thus, although two things can in principle shift the aggregate demand curve, it is better to think of the quantity of money as the only truly exogenous force that can shift that curve. This is why the curves in Figure 9.3 have been labelled as representing values of the aggregate demand curve associated with different quantities of money (M_0 and M_1). This is to remind you that money is the only exogenous force underlying the position of the aggregate demand curve.

To summarize: The monetary theory of aggregate demand is based on the idea that equilibrating forces ensure that the supply of money equals the amount of money demanded. This implies that for a given money supply, the amount of real goods and services demanded will fall as the price level rises and will, for a given price level, rise as the money supply rises.

Summary

A. Aggregate Demand

Aggregate demand is the demand for all goods and services—the demand for output. The aggregate demand curve is the relationship between the price level and the demand for output.

B. The Monetary Theory of Aggregate Demand

The monetary theory of aggregate demand states that the level of aggregate demand will fall as the price level rises. It also states that aggregate demand will rise as the money supply rises. These propositions are derived from the assumption that the amount of money that people want to hold is proportional to the price level, rises as real income rises, and falls as the inflation rate rises. Equilibrating forces ensure that the supply of money equals the demand for money and that the amount of goods and services demanded is proportional to the supply of real money balances.

Review Questions

1. What does the term *aggregate demand* mean?
2. What does the term *demand for money* mean?
3. Calculate your own average holding of money. What are the units of this quantity? Is it a stock or a flow?
4. Calculate your own demand for money.
5. Calculate your own propensity to hold money. What are the units of this quantity?
6. If the interval between when you are paid is lengthened (i.e., multiplied by 2 or 4), would your demand for money change? Explain why or why not.
7. Some people "economize" on their money holdings. What does this mean? Explain why they would "economize."

8. If the inflation rate dropped to zero tomorrow and remained there, would your demand for money change? Explain why or why not.
9. If the inflation rate doubled tomorrow and remained at that level, would you "economize" on your money holdings? Explain why or why not.
10. The propensity to hold money is related to the inflation rate. What is this relationship? Draw a diagram to illustrate this relationship.
11. What is the relationship between the demand for money and money income?
12. What is the relationship between the demand for money and the price level?
13. What is the relationship between the demand for money and real income?
14. What is *money market equilibrium*?
15. If the supply of money exceeded the demand for money, what would happen?
16. Explain the connection between aggregate demand and money market equilibrium.
17. Derive the relationship between aggregate demand and the price level. Draw the aggregate demand curve. Where, on this diagram, is the money market in equilibrium? Where is there excess demand for money, and where is there excess supply?
18. What is the effect on the aggregate demand curve of a once-and-for-all rise in the money supply?

10

Equilibrium in the Basic Model

You have now studied all the ingredients of the basic model. Specifically, you have studied the labor market and the determination of aggregate supply, and the money market and the determination of aggregate demand. Your task now is to bring these two aspects of the basic model together and to see how the actual level of output, employment, real wages, and the price level are determined. This chapter builds on the presumption that you have understood the material contained in the two previous chapters. You may find it necessary to refer back, from time to time, to reinforce that understanding.

Your task in this chapter is to:

Understand how the equality of aggregate supply and aggregate demand for goods and for labor determines the level of output, employment, the real wage, the money wage, and the price level.

Equilibrium

It is now possible to combine the theory of aggregate supply and the monetary theory of aggregate demand to determine the price level and the level of output (real income). Figure 10.1 illustrates this. Frame (b) shows the aggregate production function—the relationship between output y and the level of employment n. Frame (a) shows the competitive labor market. The demand for labor curve, labelled n^d, comes from the profit-maximizing decisions of competitive producers. The labor supply curve, labelled n^s, comes from the utility-maximizing decisions of households. (Remember that n is the number of workers and not the number of man-hours.) As the real wage rises, we are assuming that more and more people make an all-or-nothing choice to become workers. Also, as n varies, we presume that there is no variation in hours per worker, but rather a variation in the number of workers, each working a fixed number of hours. Next, the labor market is assumed to equilibrate. That is, the forces of supply and demand are assumed to be strong enough to bring about a real wage that makes the demand for labor equal to the supply of labor. The labor market will settle down at the point indicated by n^* (which denotes equilibrium employment) and $(W/P)^*$, which denotes the equilibrium real wage.

Figure 10.1
Summary of the Basic Model of Output, Employment, the Real Wage, and the Price Level

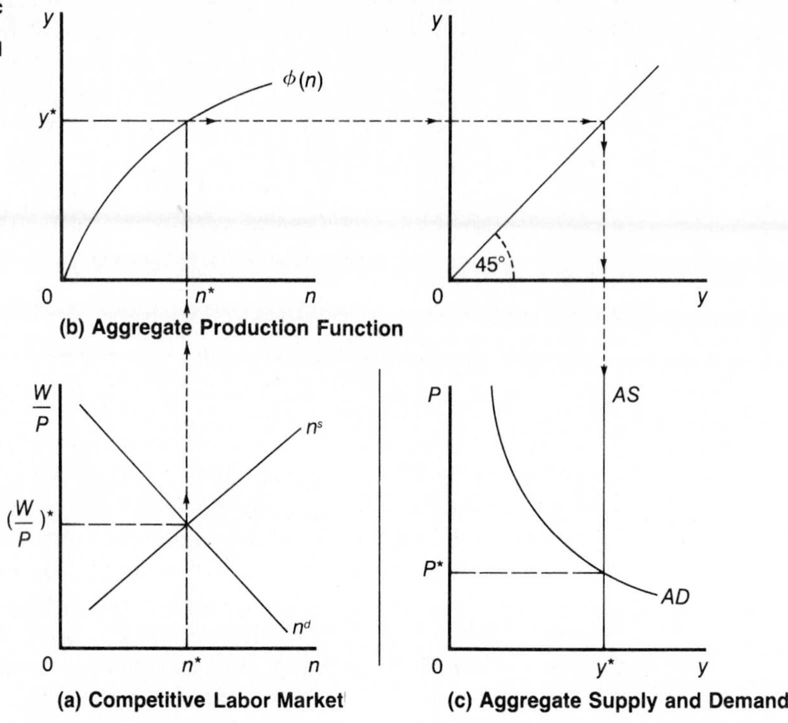

Equilibrium in the labor market [frame (a)] determines the level of employment and real wage rate at which firms are maximizing profits and households are maximizing utility. The equilibrium level of employment generates, through the short-run production function [frame (b)], the equilibrium level of aggregate supply (y^*) in frame (c). This is the equilibrium level of output. The price level is determined by the point at which the aggregate demand curve (AD) cuts the aggregate supply curve (AS)—point P^* in frame (c).

From the equilibrium level of employment determined in frame (a), you can work out the value of the equilibrium level of output (real income) by using the production function shown in frame (b). By transferring the equilibrium level of output shown on the vertical axis of frame (b) to the horizontal axis of frame (c) (follow the dotted line through the 45° line in the top right frame), the aggregate supply curve may be derived. This is shown as the vertical line in frame (c), labelled *AS*. This is the relationship between the price level and the level of output that profit-maximizing producers will want to supply.

The model is completed by the monetary theory of aggregate demand (Chapter 9), which predicts the rectangular hyperbola relationship between the price level and output (real income), labelled *AD*. This curve traces out the levels of prices and output that ensure an equilibrium in the money market. At the combinations of the price level and output traced out by this curve, the amount of money demanded is equal to the supply of money.

The point where the aggregate demand curve (which represents monetary equilibrium) cuts the aggregate supply curve (which represents labor market equilibrium) determines the price level at which all markets are simultaneously in equilibrium. That is, at the price level P^*, the demand for money equals the supply of money. This is indicated because the economy is on its aggregate demand curve. Further, at the price level P^*, the supply of labor is equal to the demand for labor. This is indicated because the economy is on its aggregate supply curve.

The description of the determination of equilibrium in the labor and goods markets given above makes it seem as if there is a complete separation between the two markets. The levels of employment and the real wage are determined in the labor market independently of what is happening in the goods market and the unique level of aggregate supply implied by labor market equilibrium determines the level of output. The only thing that is left for aggregate demand to determine (for money market equilibrium to determine) is the price level.

You may find it helpful, however, to think of the processes that occur in the actual world as involving more interaction than what is implied by this description. The real wage determined by labor market equilibrium is, in effect, a fiction that we have invented for the purpose of doing theory. What gets determined in the labor market in the actual economy is the *money* wage. That is, labor is supplied and demanded on the basis of the money wage that is prevailing in the labor market and the price level that is prevailing in the goods market. If, at a given price level, there was an excess demand for labor, then the money wage would rise to achieve a real wage that gives labor market equilibrium. In equilibrium, the money wage will simply be proportional to the price level. Anything that makes the price level change by x percent will also make the money wage change by x percent, thus preserving the real wage at its equilibrium value.

Some Comparative Static Experiments

It is possible to reinforce your understanding of the equilibrium that we have just examined by performing some experiments that are given the name *comparative static*. These two words indicate that we are going to compare two static equilibrium situations. To do so we shall begin with the equilibrium set out in Figure 10.1. We shall then disturb the economy in some way and examine what happens to output, employment, real wages, and the price level as the result of that disturbance. We shall consider two broad types of disturbance both of which will be analyzed in more detail in the next two chapters. One will concern a disturbance to aggregate supply, and the other will concern a disturbance to aggregate demand. Let us begin with an aggregate demand disturbance.

Aggregate Demand Disturbance Figure 10.2 will illustrate the analysis. Suppose that the economy initially is in a situation that is identical to that depicted in Figure 10.1. Such a situation is one in which the output level is y^*, the price level is P^*, the level of employment is n^*, and the real wage is $(W/P)^*$. We now suppose that this equilibrium is disturbed as a result of the aggregate demand curve shifting to the right from the curve labelled AD to that labelled AD'. (You should think about the underlying shocks that could

Figure 10.2
An Aggregate Demand Disturbance

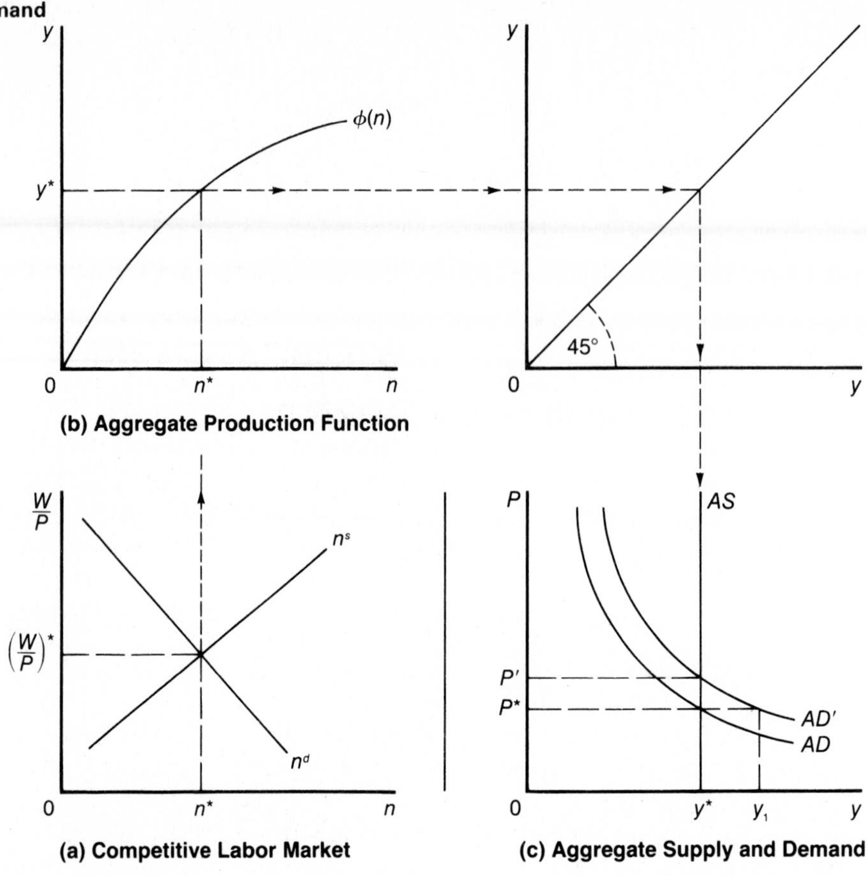

The equilibrium depicted in Figure 10.1 is disturbed as a result of a rise in aggregate demand. The aggregate demand curve increases from *AD* to *AD′*. The result is a rise in the price level from *P** to *P′*, with no other changes.

hit the economy and would lead to a shift in the aggregate demand curve. Some examples would be a rise in the money supply, a rise in the expected rate of inflation, or a fall in the average pay interval.)

What happens to output, employment, real wages, and the price level as a result of a shock of this type? You can read off the answer in Figure 10.2. Clearly the price level rises from P^* to P', but no other changes occur. Why is this? You can easily see why the price level has to rise. If the price level was to remain at P^*, then there would be an excess demand for goods. The quantity of goods that firms would be wanting to supply would remain at y^*, but the quantity that households would be trying to demand would become y_1. Clearly, something would have to adjust in such a situation. According to this equilibrium theory, the variable that adjusts is the price level. The excess demand for goods would force prices to rise from P^* to P'. As a result, the excess demand for goods would be eliminated, and the plans of all economic agents would be compatible with each other. Under this experiment, nothing happens to real income, real wages, or the level of employment. This zero change in the real variables results from the fact that nothing has happened to move either the supply of, or demand for, labor or the production function, so that the vertical aggregate supply curve has remained unchanged.

Let us now consider an aggregate supply shock.

Aggregate Supply Disturbance There are a variety of potential sources of aggregate supply disturbance that we could analyze. The one that will be illustrated here involves a productivity improvement. Specifically, we shall consider what would happen if, for some reason, perhaps because of technological advances or perhaps because of an increase in the amount of capital equipment available, workers are able to produce more output at each level of labor input. Figure 10.3 will illustrate the analysis. First, you should study Figure 10.3 and satisfy yourself that you can find the initial equilibrium of the economy that was illustrated in Figure 10.2. As before, this is shown as the output level y^*, the price level P^*, an employment level of n^*, and a real wage of $(W/P)^*$.

The disturbance that we are going to introduce into the economy involves a rise in productivity. This is illustrated by an upward shift in the economy's production function. Thus, in the initial situation, the economy was on the production function labelled $\phi_1(n)$. The new production function is labelled $\phi_2(n)$. Thus, at each level of labor input, the economy can now produce more output.

We have to be careful to notice that the upward shift in the production function is not the only thing that happens when productivity improves. The marginal product of labor also rises, and, therefore, so does the demand for labor curve. This is shown as the higher demand curve in frame (a) of Figure 10.3. Continuing to focus on frame (a), it is now evident that, with a higher demand for labor, the labor market will achieve an equilibrium at a higher real wage and higher employment level than before. These are illustrated as the real wage $(W/P)'$ and the employment level n'.

With the labor market achieving equilibrium at a higher employment level, evidently the economy's aggregate supply will have increased. This is illustrated in frame (c). To derive the new aggregate supply curve, AS', all that you need to do is repeat the experiment conducted earlier when we derived the aggregate supply curve. To do this, first go back to frame (a) and notice that the level of employment in the new equilibrium is n'. Tracing that level of employment up to frame (b) and reading off the output level from the new higher production function indicates that the economy can now produce the output level y'. Transferring that output level across to the top right frame and down to frame (c) gives the location of the new aggregate supply curve AS'. This new aggregate supply curve cuts the original aggregate demand curve at the price level P' and the output level y'.

Let us now pause and examine how the new equilibrium differs from the original equilibrium. Evidently, the real wage and the levels of output and employment have all increased, and the price level has fallen. To see how this new equilibrium came about, consider what would have happened in the economy if the real wage and the price level had remained initially in their original equilibrium positions. If the real wage had remained at $(W/P)^*$, then

Figure 10.3
Aggregate Supply Disturbance—Productivity Rise

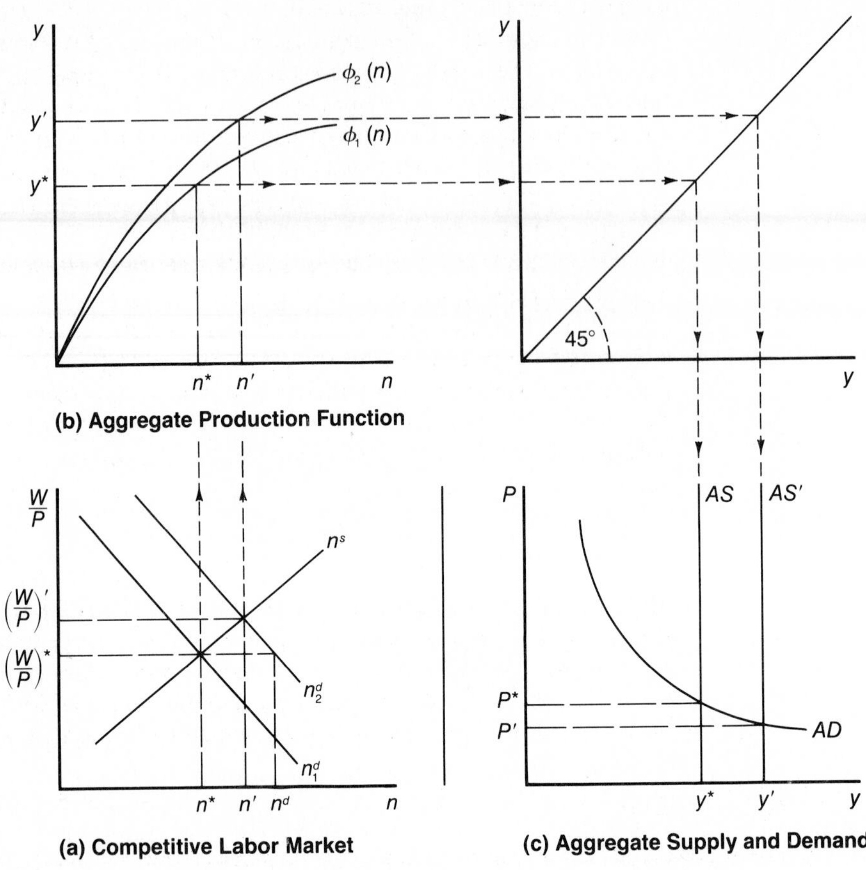

The equilibrium in Figure 10.1 is disturbed by a productivity rise. The production function shifts upwards from $\phi_1(n)$ to $\phi_2(n)$ and so does the demand for labor curve (from n_1^d to n_2^d). The result is a higher equilibrium level of employment (up from n^* to n') and a higher real wage [from $(W/P)^*$ to $(W/P)'$] and a rightward shift in the aggregate supply curve (from AS to AS'). The price level falls from P^* to P'.

the demand for labor would have become n^d, while the supply of labor would have remained at n^*. Clearly such a situation would involve an excess demand for labor. Firms would not have been able to hire all the labor that they wanted to at that real wage. Competitive pressures would force the real wage upwards and keep doing so until the real wage had arrived at its new equilibrium value $(W/P)'$.

Similarly, consider what would happen in the goods market if the price level had remained at its initial equilibrium value P^*. In this case, since the supply curve has shifted to the right, there will be an excess supply of goods. Households would not be willing to buy all the goods that firms were seeking to supply. In this situation, competitive pressures would force the price level downwards and would continue to do so until the excess supply was eliminated. This occurs at the price level P'.

It is the essence of the equilibrium theory that the equilibrating processes described in the above experiments are so strong and rapid that we would never observe the economy at points other than its equilibrium. *Only the equilibrium is observed.* It is worth emphasizing that, in an equilibrium, no one has any incentive to change what is occurring. Each household is satisfied with the amount of labor that it is supplying, the amount of money that it is holding, and the volume of goods purchased. Each firm is satisfied with the amount of labor that it is hiring and the output that it is selling. Households are making maximum utility and firms maximum profits.

This is the basic model of the determination of output, employment, real wages, and the price level. Subsequent chapters in this section will examine in greater depth than has just been done what happens when there are changes in the economy that lead to a change in the equilibrium. The theory will also be used to analyze the effects of certain policy actions on the levels of output and prices.

Summary

When the amount of money that people wish to hold is equal to the money supply and when producers are unable to increase their profits by changing their output and employment, then the economy is in equilibrium. It is the essence of the basic model that the equilibrating forces are sufficiently strong for the economy normally to be observed only at an equilibrium.

Review Questions

1. When aggregate demand and aggregate supply are equal, the economy is in equilibrium. Explain exactly which markets are in equilibrium. Are households maximizing their utility? Are firms maximizing profits? Explain why or why not.

2. At the equilibrium level of output, but at a price level that exceeds its equilibrium level, is there excess supply, excess demand, or equilibrium in the markets for goods, money, and labor?

3. At the equilibrium price level, but at a level of output that is less than its equilibrium level, is there excess demand, excess supply, or equilibrium in the markets for goods, labor, and money? If, for some market or markets you cannot determine whether there is excess demand or excess supply, state what extra information would be needed to resolve the ambiguity.

4. What is the effect of a once-and-for-all rise in the money supply on the price level, output, employment, unemployment, the money wage, and the real wage?

5. What is the effect of technological improvement that raises the productivity of labor on the price level, output, employment, unemployment, the money wage, and the real wage?

6. If the income payment interval for all households was quadrupled, would there be any effect on the price level, output, employment, unemployment, the money wage, and the real wage? Use a diagram to illustrate your answer.

11

Unemployment

You do not need reminding that unemployment is an important problem in the United States today. In November 1982, the rate stood at 10.8 percent. Since the early 1950s, when unemployment was only 3.0 percent, there has been a clear and persistent upward trend in its rate. The objective of this chapter is to help you to understand some of the reasons why unemployment exists, why it persists, and why it has increased over the past decade.

Chapters 8, 9, and 10 developed the basic model designed to explain the determination of the level of output, employment, the real wage, and the price level. That model is now going to be used to analyze the effects of minimum wage laws, labor unions, unemployment insurance benefits, and employment taxes and income taxes on the level of employment and unemployment. In the next chapter, the model will be used to analyze the effects of these things on the level of prices; we shall also, in the next chapter, analyze the effects of changes in the money supply on prices.

The rest of this chapter will help you to understand some of the reasons why unemployment arises and what leads to variations in its rate.

You have four tasks, which are to:

(a) Understand how minimum wage laws create unemployment.
(b) Understand how labor unions raise wages and create unemployment.
(c) Understand how unemployment insurance programs create unemployment.
(d) Understand how taxes affect unemployment.

In Chapter 13, you will have an opportunity to review the importance of these three factors in recent U.S. history. For now, you will find it best to concentrate on the mechanics of the theory.

A. Minimum Wage Laws and Unemployment

Federal minimum wage regulations were first introduced in the United States in the Fair Labor Standards Act of 1938. By the middle 1970s, four-fifths of the U.S. labor force were employed in sectors covered by the updated regulations under this act.

What are the effects of minimum wages on the level of output, employment, unemployment, and real wages? The starting point is to recognize that minimum wages are determined by government regulation at a level higher than what would prevail in competitive labor markets. The minimum wage is set in terms of so many dollars per hour—that is, it is set as a money wage. This money wage is revised from time to time, however, and it is clear that what the legislators have in mind is the establishment of a minimum real wage that is above the competitive equilibrium real wage.

It is also clear that minimum real wages do not directly affect a very large fraction of the labor force. They impinge directly only on those workers who would otherwise have been paid a wage below the minimum. However, *they do affect* the economy *average real wage*, for two reasons. First, since the economy average real wage is an average of all the individual real wages, there is automatically a rise in the economy average real wage resulting from chopping off the bottom end of the wage distribution (those wages that would be lower than the minimum wage). Second, there will be a rise in the economy average real wage as a result of competitive pressures. If the lowest income workers are paid a higher wage than the competitive market would pay, there will be pressure to raise other wages as well. On the supply side, there will be a tendency for people to try to substitute away from slightly higher paid but more demanding jobs and enter those jobs that now attract the minimum wage rate. On the demand side, firms will substitute more expensive but more highly skilled labor for those whose wages have been increased by the minimum wage regulation. These shifts of supply toward lower productivity jobs and of demand toward more highly skilled labor will put upward pressure on real wages all the way up the scale (with the pressure of course diminishing as you move further up the income scale).

For these two reasons, then—(1) chopping off the bottom end of the wage distribution, and (2) the competitive pressures pushing up the real wages in substitute activities—the imposition of a minimum wage will raise the economy average real wage above the competitive equilibrium level. Furthermore, the higher the minimum wage is relative to the competitive equilibrium wage, the bigger will be the rise in the economy average real wage relative to its competitive equilibrium.

It is now possible to analyze the effects of minimum wages. We may conduct the analysis in Figure 11.1. The vertical axis of Figure 11.1 measures the economy average real wage, and the horizontal axis measures the aggregate level of employment, n. The curves labelled n^d and n^s are the labor demand and supply curves, respectively. The competitive equilibrium in this labor market is the real wage $(W/P)^*$ and the employment level n^*.

Now suppose that a minimum wage is established that has the effect of raising the economy average real wage to the level marked in Figure 11.1 as $(W/P)_{\min}$. What is the effect of this minimum wage law?

In a market economy in which all exchange is voluntary, no one can compel employers to hire more workers than they choose to hire. At the minimum wage, the demand for labor is less than the supply of labor. It is, therefore, the demand for labor curve that will determine how much labor is employed. The level of employment will be n_1^d. This is the amount read off

Figure 11.1
How Minimum Wages Create Unemployment

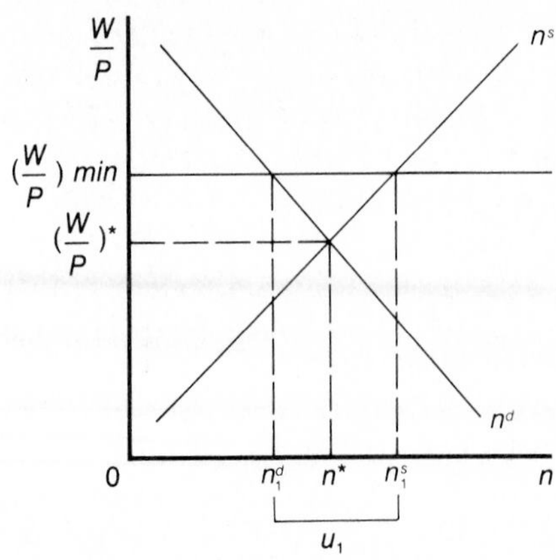

A minimum wage set higher than the competitive equilibrium wage creates a regulated equilibrium at which the quantity of labor employed is equal to the quantity demanded n_1^d, which is less than the quantity supplied n_1^s. The gap between the quantity supplied and the quantity demanded, u_1, measures the quantity of unemployment.

from the demand curve at the average real wage induced by the minimum wage legislation. The supply of labor at that real wage rate will be n_1^s.

The gap between the supply of labor n_1^s and the demand for labor n_1^d represents the number of people who will be unemployed, u_1. If you recall the definition of unemployment and the way in which unemployment is measured in the United States, you will verify that the people in the group u_1 will be recorded as unemployed. When surveyed, they will show up as being available for work—willing to work and able to work—but not having work. The higher the minimum wage is relative to the competitive equilibrium wage, the greater will be the reduction in employment, the larger will be the supply of labor, and the greater will be the amount of unemployment created.

The economy will now be in a regulated equilibrium. It is important to realize that an equilibrium is nothing more than a state of rest or, equivalently, a state in which all the forces acting on a variable exactly offset each other. One of the forces acting on the economy in this case is the minimum wage regulation, and so the real wage and employment level come to rest at a different point from the competitive equilibrium that would be reached in the absence of the regulation.

If you recall the water-level analogy (Chapter 9), a minimum wage regulation is like a dam that alters the equilibrium levels of water on either side of it.

To summarize: A minimum wage that raises the economy average real wage above its competitive equilibrium level will generate a regulated equilibrium in which there is lower employment, a larger labor supply, and persistent unemployment.

B. Labor Unions and Unemployment

Labor unions are a dominant institution in the labor market. They act as an agent for households in the negotiation of employment and wage contracts. However, a much larger fraction of the labor force works on contracts negotiated by unions than are members of unions. Thus, in analyzing the effects of unions on the macroeconomic variables, it will be convenient to proceed in two steps. First, we will analyze the effect of an economy-wide union—one that embraces the entire labor force; and second, we will analyze the effects of unions in an economy where there is a nonunion as well as a union sector in the labor market.

An Economy-Wide Union

The economy will be described using Figure 11.2. First, focus your attention on the competitive equilibrium. The curves labelled n^d and n^s are the demand and supply of labor curves (identical to those in Figure 11.1), and the real wage $(W/P)^*$ and the employment level n^* are the competitive equilibrium values for those variables. Now suppose that all the workers in this economy join an economy-wide labor union that seeks to raise real wages.

There are two types of things that the labor union could do in order to raise the real wages of its members. One possibility would be to declare that no one may work for a real wage of less than, say, $(W/P)_u$, and then to enforce this rule either by having some sort of legal protection or by using more indirect pressures. Alternatively, the union could restrict the supply of labor by, for example, defining minimum acceptable qualifications for particular jobs such that the number of people able to meet the minimum qualifications was less than the labor supply in the absence of the union. In that event, supply

Figure 11.2
Labor Market Equilibrium with an Economy-Wide Union

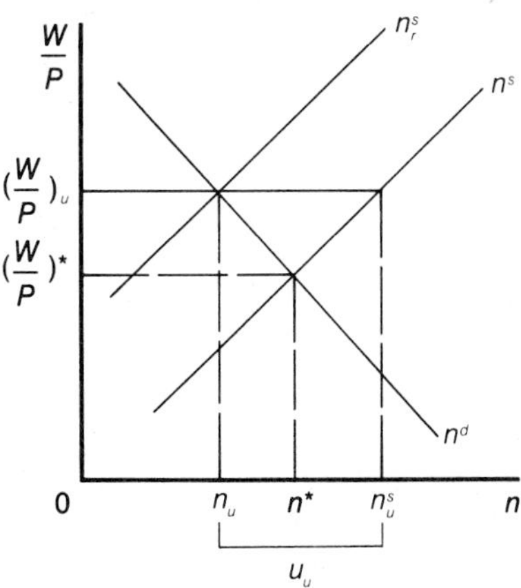

An economy-wide union would either restrict the supply of labor below the competitive supply n^s_r or would raise the wage rate above the competitive equilibrium rate $(W/P)_u$. The effect would be the same in either case. It would lower the quantity of employment from n^* to n_u but raise the supply from n^* to n^s_u. The gap between the quantity of labor supplied and the quantity demanded would be the amount of union-induced unemployment, u_u.

would be artificially restricted, and the supply curve would move to the left of the nonunion supply curve.

Either way, the result would be a higher real wage and a lower level of employment. Figure 11.2 illustrates this. In examining Figure 11.2, keep the competitive equilibrium firmly in mind as a reference point. We can illustrate what happens if the union declares a *minimum wage* below which no one may be employed by recording that wage, say, $(W/P)_u$, on the vertical axis of the figure. That wage will be above the competitive equilibrium real wage. Then, simply by reading off from the demand for labor curve, you can see that at the real wage, $(W/P)_u$, the level of employment becomes n_u. This is less than the competitive employment level n^*. At the real wage set by the union, n_u^s people would like to have a job, and the difference between n_u^s and n_u represents the level of unemployment induced by this economy-wide labor union.

If, alternatively, the union enforced *minimum qualifications* that had the effect of shifting the labor supply curve to the left—to a position such as that shown as n_r^s—the effect would be raised wages and lowered employment. (The diagram is drawn so that the same result arises from either of these policies. This has been done only to simplify the diagram. There is no presumption that both union strategies would have exactly the same effect.)

In this case, the people unemployed are unemployed because they do not meet the minimum qualification standards for the job. This can often be made to look semirespectable, for example, by dressing up the restriction as "protecting the consumer," and is therefore a much more commonly employed practice among labor unions than that of simply declaring that no one may work for less than a certain wage. It is especially widely practiced by professional labor unions such as those in the legal and medical industries. It is an easier restriction to enforce.

Either way, whether it sets a minimum real wage or restricts supply, an economy-wide labor union will have the same kind of effect on employment and real wages as would a government-enforced minimum wage law. The economy-wide union will raise the real wage above its competitive equilibrium level, will lower the level of employment, will raise the quantity of labor supplied, and will generate unemployment. The greater the ability of the union to raise the real wage above the competitive equilibrium level, the bigger these effects will be.

An Economy with a Union and a Nonunion Sector

Analyzing the effects of labor unions in an economy where the unions do not control the entire labor force and where there is a nonunion sector is not quite as straightforward as the case that we have just dealt with. By working carefully through this section, however, it will be possible for you to get a good understanding of how unions operate in this case and what their macroeconomic effects will be. Figure 11.3 is going to be the vehicle through which you gain your understanding, and it will be described to you in stages.

First of all, imagine that the economy can be divided into two identical sectors, so that we can represent the labor market of the economy with two diagrams that are identical to each other. This is a fiction, of course, but one that makes the understanding of the principles clearer. Frames (a) and (b)

Figure 11.3
An Economy with a Union and a Nonunion Sector

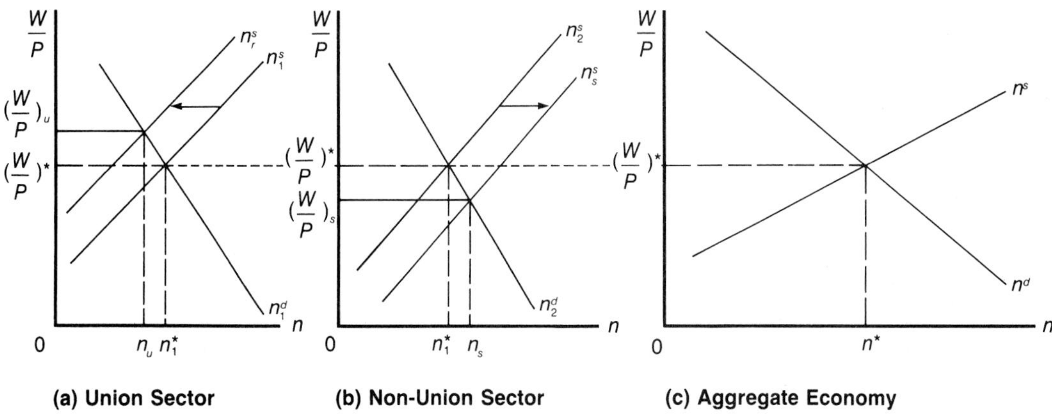

The union restricts the supply of labor n^s_r or raises the union wage rate above the competitive rate $(W/P)_u$ [frame (a)]. This results in a drop in employment in the union sector n^*_1 to n_u. Those who cannot find work in the union sector spill over to the nonunion sector, shifting the supply curve there from n^s_2 to n^s_s. The result is a drop in the real wage below the competitive equilibrium level and a rise in employment. In this example, where the union and nonunion sectors are of identical size, aggregate employment and average real wages remain unchanged [frame (c)].

represent these two sectors. The aggregate labor market (the sum of the two sectors) is shown in frame (c). If you ignore the curve n^s_r in frame (a) and the curve n^s_s in frame (b), you will see that a competitive equilibrium is shown in the three separate parts of that figure. Each labor market is in equilibrium, and each has an identical real wage and employment level.

Now suppose a labor union gets established in one of these markets [that shown in frame (a)] and establishes some minimum qualifications for employment in that part of the economy. Next, suppose that the effect of this is to shift the effective labor supply curve in the union sector leftwards, so that it is represented by the curve n^s_r. The real wage in the union sector and the level of employment will now move to $(W/P)_u$ and n_u, as indicated in the diagram. Thus, in the union sector, the real wage will rise, and the level of employment will fall.

However, this is not the end of the story. The people who do not qualify for work in the union sector, now that the qualifications have been increased by the union, spill over into the nonunion sector. The supply curve in the nonunion sector will therefore shift rightwards by an amount equal to the leftward shift of the supply curve in the union sector. This is shown as the supply curve n^s_s in frame (b). The real wage in the nonunion sector will now fall, and the number of people employed in that sector will rise to the amounts shown as $(W/P)_s$ and n_s in frame (b).

From a macroeconomic point of view [frame (c)], *nothing has happened in this economy*. The real wage, on the average, will still be $(W/P)^*$, and the level of employment will still be n^*. The union has simply redistributed income away from nonunion workers toward union workers. No unemployment is created. All that the unions have done is to redistribute incomes.[1]

To summarize: An economy-wide labor union that restricts the supply of labor or raises the real wage above the competitive equilibrium level by other means will lower the aggregate level of employment and raise the level of unemployment. A union that does not control the entire economy will have the effect of raising the real wages of unionized workers and lowering the real wages of nonunion workers, leaving the macroeconomic magnitudes—the average real wage and the average levels of employment and unemployment—undisturbed.

You will now be able to understand better why minimum wage laws are so popular, and especially among labor union leaders. If a labor union behaved in the way described in the above section, raising the wages of its own members at the expense of the wages of nonmembers, it would become extremely unpopular. Labor unions, therefore, lobby for minimum wage regulations. This has the effect, of course, as we analyzed in the above section on minimum wage laws, of creating unemployment. However, it is possible to blame this unemployment on the selfishness of the employer for refusing to pay a "fair" wage or on the incompetence of the government in failing to provide an adequate level of overall demand. This diverts attention away from the unions, and because they are pressing for better wages and working conditions for the poorest members of the labor force, it makes them look highly virtuous!

C. Unemployment Insurance Benefits and Unemployment

Job-Search Unemployment

As a prelude to analyzing the effects of unemployment insurance benefits, it is necessary to introduce the idea of job search. People allocate their time to three major economic activities: work, leisure, and job search.

Jobs cannot be found without search, and search is costly. Thus it is useful to think of job search as being an investment. There is a cost and an expected return. The higher the cost, the smaller will be the amount of job-search activity undertaken. The higher the expected return or payoff, the bigger will be the amount of job-search activity undertaken.

Much job searching is done on a casual basis while a person is employed. Some job searchers, however, specialize in searching; that is, they cease to be workers for a period in which they spend all their nonleisure time in job-

[1]The conclusion that there are no macroeconomic effects resulting from labor union actions is not a completely general one. It arises in the example used here because the supply and demand curves in the two sectors are identical. The same result would arise if the two sectors were of unequal size but had the same elasticities of supply and demand. Since there can be no presumption that union and nonunion sectors differ significantly in this respect, the result may be regarded as a useful approximation to the actual outcome in the "real" world.

Figure 11.4
The Supply of Job Search

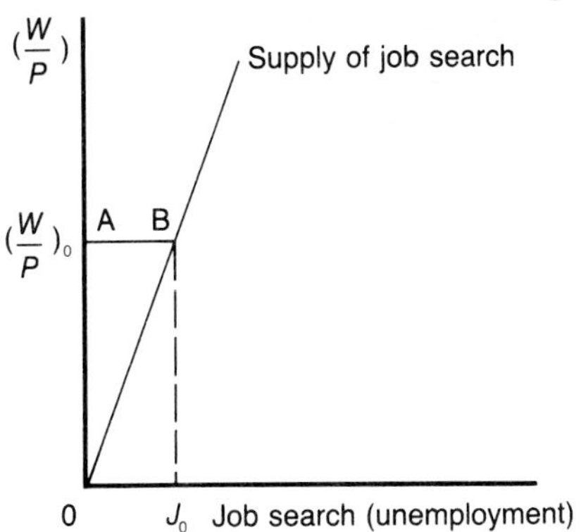

Job search is an alternative activity to working and consuming leisure. The higher the real wage, the more people will join the pool of job searchers. At the real wage $(W/P)_0$, J_0 workers will join the labor force and search for jobs.

search activities. These job searchers are interesting from a macroeconomic point of view because they will be recorded as unemployed.

For a given cost of job search, it seems reasonable to suppose that the larger the labor force, the greater will be the number of people engaged in full-time job search. Further, the higher the real wage, the bigger the labor force is. This would lead us to suppose that the supply of job search would increase as the real wage increases. We need to be careful, however, before we accept that conclusion. Caution is needed because increases in the real wage will also affect the costs and benefits of job search.

You can think of the wage as being part of the opportunity cost of job search. That is, over and above the direct costs involved (phone calls, travel, etc.), there is the cost of foregone earnings measured by the wage that would have been obtained from accepting the first job that comes along. The higher the average real wage, the higher would be that portion of the opportunity cost of job-search activity. On the other side of the calculation, the real wage obtained from the best job that could be found after an appropriate search process is part of the benefit from job search. Again, the higher the average real wage, the higher that benefit on the average will be. Thus, the higher the real wage, the higher are both the cost and expected benefit from job-search activity.

It will be assumed that these two forces working in opposite directions to each other approximately offset each other, so that, as real wages rise, the ratio of costs to benefits stays fairly constant, and the fraction of the labor force engaging in full-time job-search activity remains fairly constant. This implies that the *number* of people involved in job-search activity will rise as the labor force rises, which in turn means that the number of people engaged in job-search activity will rise as the real wage rises.

The supply of job search embodying the above considerations is shown in Figure 11.4. If the real wage rate was $(W/P)_0$, there would be J_0 full-time job searchers recorded as unemployed (equivalently shown as the distance AB).

Figure 11.5 Equilibrium Employment, Unemployment, and Real Wage

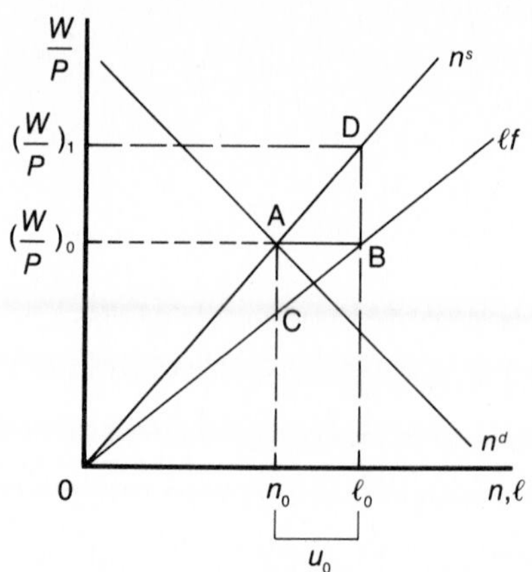

If the supply of job search is added to the supply of labor n^s, the labor force supply curve ℓf is derived. (The distance AB in Figure 11.5 is the same as the distance AB in Figure 11.4.) With the demand curve n^d, the equilibrium is at $(W/P)_0$ and n_0. The labor force at that equilibrium wage will be ℓ_0, and the unemployed job searchers will be u_0. The distance AC measures the value placed on job search by the last person to be employed. The real wage would have to drop by AC to induce that person to leave the labor force. The distance DB measures the value placed on job search by the last person to join the labor force. The real wage would have to rise by DB to $(W/P)_1$ in order to induce that person to take a job.

Next, let us distinguish between the supply of labor and the labor force. The *labor force* is defined as the supply of labor plus the supply of job search. The *supply of labor* is defined as the number of people who, at a given real wage, are willing to supply their labor services to a full-time job immediately without further search.

Figure 11.5 shows how these magnitudes will be related to the real wage. The curve n^s is the supply curve that was used in the above analysis of Chapters 8 and 10. It shows the number of people immediately available for work without further search at each real wage. Adding horizontally to that curve the amount of job search that would be undertaken at each real wage gives the labor force (the curve ℓf). This shows the total number of people available for work right now, plus the total number of people at each real wage who will still be searching for a job. The distance AB in Figure 11.5 is equivalent to the distance AB in Figure 11.4. Thus, the curve ℓf simply adds the supply of job-search curve to the supply of labor curve. If the real wage was $(W/P)_0$, the supply of labor would be n_0, and the labor force would be ℓ_0.

The vertical distances AC and BD are interesting economic magnitudes. The marginal person in employment (the last person to become employed at the employment level n_0) who is just willing to work for the wage rate $(W/P)_0$ is on the margin of indifference between accepting a job and continuing to search for a job. If the real wage was marginally below $(W/P)_0$, that person would quit and start to search for a new job. The distance AC measures the value that that marginal worker places on job search.

There is another margin, that between being in the labor force and not being in the labor force. This individual is at ℓ_0. At a real wage $(W/P)_0$, such an individual feels that it is just worthwhile searching for a job. The value that this individual places on job search is the distance DB. A real wage equal to $(W/P)_1$ would be necessary to induce this marginal worker to actually accept a job instantaneously with no further search.

Given the demand curve n^d, the real wage $(W/P)_0$ will be the competitive equilibrium real wage. The economy will be in an equilibrium characterized by less than complete knowledge about job opportunities, so that there is always a certain number of people searching for jobs. The labor force will be ℓ_0, the employment level n_0, and there will be u_0 unemployed job searchers.

It is important that you realize that the labor market as depicted in Figure 11.5 is not in a static state, with a certain number of people being permanently employed and another group being permanently unemployed. Rather, there is a continuous turnover, with people quitting jobs to search for new ones, other people entering the labor force to search for jobs, others leaving the labor force, and still others being hired. Thus, the flows of hires and quits will be matched, and the flows of people into and out of the labor force will be balanced, so that the individuals involved are continuously in a state of flux, although the economy, on the average, is in the position shown in Figure 11.5.

How Unemployment Insurance Benefits Affect the Level of Employment, Unemployment, and the Real Wage

Suppose the government introduces an unemployment insurance program that makes it possible for people, while searching for a new job, to receive an income from the government equal to some fraction of the wage that they had previously been earning while employed. What effects would this have?

It is immediately clear that such a policy would lower the cost of job search. It would therefore make job-search activity, at the margin, more attractive. You have already seen that there are two relevant margins of job search. One is the margin between search and employment, the other is the margin between employment and complete leisure (withdrawal from the labor force). Improving unemployment insurance benefits would alter both of these margins. There would be a tendency for people to search longer before accepting employment, thereby lowering the amount of work that people in aggregate would be willing to do at any given real wage. This would have the effect of rotating the labor supply curve n^s upwards. This is shown in Figure 11.6 as the movement from n_0^s to n_1^s. Additionally, people who previously were not in the labor force will now be induced to enter the labor force and take a temporary job to qualify for unemployment insurance benefits, and then later search for a more acceptable long-term job. There will, therefore, be a rotation of the labor force curve in a rightward direction. This again is illustrated in Figure 11.6 as the movement from ℓf_0 to ℓf_1.

The curves n_0^s and ℓf_0 and the equilibrium $(W/P)_0$ and n_0 represent the economy with no unemployment compensation and are the same as those illustrated in Figure 11.5. The curves n_1^s and ℓf_1 represent the new labor force and the labor supply curve induced by an unemployment insurance program.

It is now possible to read off the effects of an unemployment insurance

Figure 11.6
How Unemployment Insurance Benefits Increase Unemployment

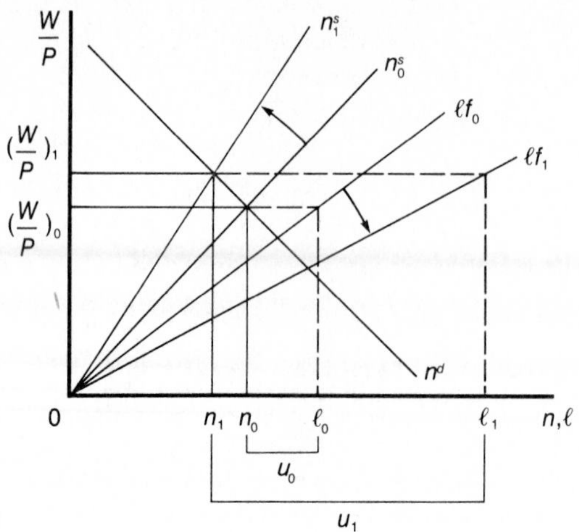

Unemployment benefits make job search a more attractive activity relative to either working or consuming leisure. The supply of labor falls from n_0^s to n_1^s and raises the labor force supply curve from ℓf_0 to ℓf_1. The real wage rises, the employment level falls, the labor force rises, and the number unemployed rises.

program on the variables. The labor market will be in equilibrium at the real wage $(W/P)_1$ and the employment level n_1. The labor force will rise to ℓ_1, and unemployment will be u_1, which is $\ell_1 - n_1$. Thus, an unemployment insurance program raises the real wage, lowers the level of employment, raises the size of the labor force, and increases the number unemployed.

The analysis just conducted has ignored the question of who pays the taxes that provide the unemployment insurance benefits. The next section of this chapter will go on to analyze the effects of employment taxes and income taxes on the level of employment, unemployment, and real wages. This analysis applies more generally than just to those taxes used to pay unemployment insurance benefits. It applies to any taxes. The analysis just conducted may be augmented by an analysis of the effects of taxes, to which we now turn.

D. Taxes and Unemployment

It will be convenient, in analyzing the effects of taxes, to abstract from the considerations of job search that were the central feature of the analysis of the previous section. This is not to say that the above analysis is irrelevant when considering the effects of taxes. It is simply a convenient way of considering one thing at a time. Once you have thoroughly mastered the material in this and the preceding sections, it will be a straightforward matter for you to consider both effects simultaneously. There is no gain, however, in presenting them as a simultaneous analysis.

The questions that we want to address now are: First, what are the effects of income taxes—taxes on labor income—on real wages, employment, and

Figure 11.7
The Effects of Taxes on the Labor Market

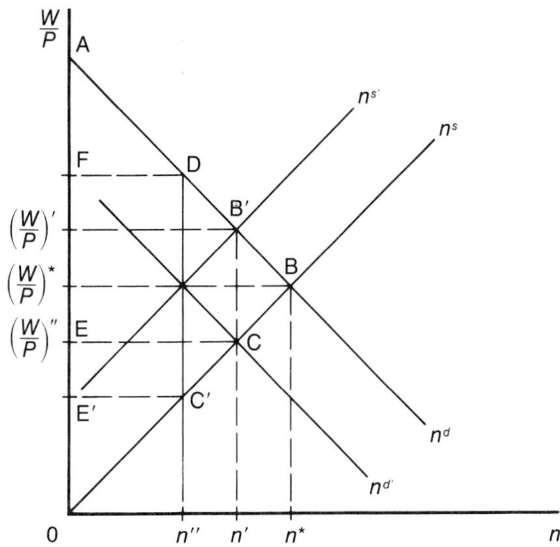

A competitive equilibrium is shown at the real wage $(W/P)^*$ and employment level n^*. This equilibrium is disturbed by the introduction of a tax on labor income or by a tax on consumption that shifts the labor supply curve to $n^{s'}$. The real wage rises to $(W/P)'$, and employment falls to n'. After-tax wages fall. Alternatively, the equilibrium is disturbed by the introduction of an employment tax that shifts the labor demand curve down to $n^{d'}$. Again the level of employment falls to n', and wages become $(W/P)''$, equivalent to the after-tax wage level of E in the previous experiment. Both sets of taxes introduced together lower the level of employment to n''. As taxes on employment are successively increased, labor's share in national income (defined to include the taxes) increases, while the share accruing to the owners of capital decreases.

unemployment? Second, what are the effects of employment taxes—taxes on firms that vary with the number of workers they employ—on the level of employment, unemployment, and real wages? And third, what are the effects of expenditure taxes—taxes on consumption—on the level of employment, unemployment, and real wages?

As a starting point, let us begin with an economy that has no taxes and then consider what happens as we introduce these alternative taxes first separately and then simultaneously. Figure 11.7 will illustrate the analysis. The curves labelled n^s and n^d are the supply and demand curves for labor in a world in which there are no taxes. The competitive equilibrium in this economy is at point B, where the real wage is $(W/P)^*$ and the employment level is n^*. This is exactly the position shown as the competitive equilibrium in Figure 11.1, with which we started this analysis of the labor market.

There is one additional thing that you can work out about the economy, to which attention has not previously been drawn but which is of some interest for the purpose of the present exercise—that is, the distribution of national income between labor and the owners of capital. Labor income will be equal to the rectangle $0(W/P)^*\,Bn^*$. You can readily verify that this is so by noting that the number of workers is n^*, and the wage per worker is $(W/P)^*$, so that labor income, being the product of employment and wages, is given by the area of that rectangle.

The income accruing to the owners of capital is the triangle $(W/P)^*$ AB. This is a less obvious proposition than the previous one. You may, however, verify that that triangle represents the part of total product not paid to labor. To do this, begin by recalling that the demand for labor curve measures the marginal product of labor. Thus, the first worker hired would produce a marginal product of A (that is, where the demand curve hits the real wage axis). As more and more workers are hired, the marginal product declines until the final worker is hired at the equilibrium level of employment n^*, by which time the marginal product has fallen to B. For each extra worker hired, the extra output produced is equal to the marginal product, and the total product accruing to the producer is given by the entire area underneath the marginal product curve all the way up to the level of employment n^*. Total product in the economy, then, is the trapezium $0ABn^*$. That which is paid to labor is $0(W/P)^*$ Bn^*, and that which is paid to the owners of capital is $(W/P)^*$ AB. (In the economy shown in Figure 11.7, labor gets two-thirds and capital one-third of the economy's output.)

Now consider the introduction of an income tax. Instead of keeping all the wages they earn, workers now have to pay some fraction of their labor income to the government in the form of a tax. This means that the wage received by workers is less than the real wage paid by employers. Assuming, as we are, that a higher real wage always brings forth a higher supply of labor, this will imply that for any given real wage paid by the employer, there will now be a lower supply of labor. This can be represented by shifting the labor supply curve to the left. For simplicity, the figure has been drawn on the presumption that the labor supply curve shift is a parallel one, so that the new curve after allowing for taxes is the one labelled $n^{s'}$. The way to read $n^{s'}$ is as follows: For any given level of employment, without taxes, the wage that would have to be paid would be read off from the n^s curve; with the taxes in place, however, the wage that would have to be paid to call forth the same level of employment would be read off from the higher curve $n^{s'}$.

To determine the equilibrium in this case, we have to find the point where the new effective labor supply curve $n^{s'}$ intersects the demand for labor curve n^d. This occurs at the point B′, with the real wage equal to $(W/P)'$ and an employment level n'. Thus, the real wage has risen, and the employment level has fallen as a result of the introduction of a tax on labor income. The after-tax income of workers will have fallen from a wage rate of $(W/P)^*$ to a wage rate given by the position E on the vertical axis. In fact, total wages will be $0ECn'$. The tax receipts of the government will be $E(W/P)'$ B′C, and the income accruing to capital will be the triangle $(W/P)'$ AB′. The overall effects, then, of the imposition of a tax on labor income are for there to be a drop in after-tax real wages, a rise in pretax real wages, a fall in labor income, a rise in the government's income, and a fall in the income accruing to the owners of capital. There is also a fall in the level of employment.

The drop in employment from n^* to n' cannot, properly speaking, be regarded as unemployment. Although there are fewer people in employment in the situation n' as compared with n^*, the situation that prevails is a competitive equilibrium. Nevertheless, it may be the case that the workers who withdraw from the labor force as the effective wage rate falls from $(W/P)^*$ to E will be entitled to unemployment insurance benefits and will, therefore, appear to swell the ranks of the unemployed job searchers—if not forever, at least for a period. In this limited sense, the raising of taxes on labor income can be said to "create unemployment."

Next consider the effects of imposing a tax on the other side of the labor market—on the employers. Imagine that firms have to pay a tax on each worker that they employ. This will mean that the firm no longer regards the marginal product of labor as being equivalent to the value of labor. Rather, firms will regard labor as being worth its marginal product minus the tax that it has to pay on each worker employed. This means that the demand for labor curve will shift downwards. The curve $n^{d'}$ in Figure 11.7 illustrates such a demand curve.

What will be the effect of this tax on employment, unemployment, and wages? Let us first answer this question in the absence of income taxes. In that case, the new equilibrium will be where the curve $n^{d'}$ cuts the original supply curve n^s. This occurs at the wage rate $(W/P)'' = \text{E}$ and at the employment level n'.

Notice that this experiment has been set up so as to yield an identical amount of revenue for the government as the income tax did in the previous experiment. In principle, we could analyze cases where different amounts of revenue are raised. It does, however, seem to be more instructive to hold the government revenue constant for the purpose of comparing the effects of alternative taxes.

It is now possible to read off all the effects of this employment tax on the level of employment and wages. These effects are, evidently, exactly the same as in the previous case. Employment falls from n^* to n'; the share of labor in national income falls to the same level as before, namely, 0ECn'; and the government revenue is exactly the same as before, as is the share of income accruing to the owners of capital. The only difference between the two cases is that the wages paid by firms fall, and firms pay the taxes to the government. In the first experiment conducted, the wages paid by firms increased, but after workers had paid their taxes, the effective net of tax wage decreased. Workers had exactly the same net of tax income in the previous situation as they do in this one.

Next, consider what happens when taxes are imposed on the expenditure on consumer goods by workers. From the perspective of the analysis conducted here, this will have identical effects to the first tax analyzed—the tax on labor income. The easiest way to see this is to see the way in which both income taxes and expenditure taxes affect the relative price between labor and consumption. Equivalently, we may ask how income taxes and expenditure taxes affect the rate at which labor may be traded for consumption goods. The wage rate that a worker receives is equal to the gross wage paid, scaled down by the income taxes levied by the government. Suppose that we call the income tax rate t_y. Then, the effective wage rate is $W(1 - t_y)$. When a worker purchases consumer goods, the price paid is equal to the price received by the producer, P, plus any taxes levied by the government. Call the rate of tax on expenditure t_c. This means that the price paid by the consumer will be equal to $P(1 + t_c)$. Evidently, the ratio of the price received by the worker to the price paid for goods by the worker is equal to:

$$\frac{W(1 - t_y)}{P(1 + t_c)} \qquad \textbf{(11.1)}$$

You may think of the expression $(1 - t_y)/(1 + t_c)$ as the wedge that taxes drive between the price that firms have to pay for their labor, W, and the price that they receive for their output, P. From the household's point of view, for any given real wage, W/P, the bigger the tax wedge, the smaller will be the supply of labor. Thus, you may think of the shift in the labor supply curve from n^s to $n^{s'}$, analyzed in the first experiment conducted above, as arising from either the imposition of an income tax or an expenditure tax having an equivalent total yield.

Finally, consider what happens when all of these tax measures are introduced simultaneously. In this case, the relevant supply curve is $n^{s'}$, and the demand curve is $n^{d'}$. The equilibrium employment level falls still further to n'', but by the construction of the example, the real wage remains at the no tax equilibrium level of $(W/P)^*$. [To avoid having too many equilibrium positions on the one diagram, we have caused these two curves to intersect at the original real wage, $(W/P)^*$.] Workers' incomes will now be $0E'C'n''$, the government's tax receipts will be $E'FDC'$, and the income accruing to capital owners will be FAD. Employment will have fallen from n^* to n''.

It is worth highlighting what is happening to the relative shares of labor and capital in national income as we move from the initial no-tax equilibrium to the after-tax equilibrium. To do this, it will be most convenient to use the accounting conventions employed in the national income accounts. In those accounts, labor income is defined to include the payments of employment taxes by firms to the government. The fiction is that this is really part of the wages of the workers that is being deducted as a tax at source and handed over to the government in much the same way as the workers' income taxes are also withheld by the employer and paid to the government.

Thus, in the no-tax situation, labor income is $0(W/P)^*\ Bn^*$, and in the after-tax situation (after all taxes), labor income is $0FDn''$. Using this accounting convention, it is evident that, as taxes are increased, the share of national income accruing to labor increases. You can see this visually in Figure 11.7. In the initial situation, labor income was equal to two-thirds of total income, whereas in the after-tax situation, it is equal to six-sevenths. What is happening as taxes are increased is that although the number of workers employed declines, the average wage per worker (defined in the gross sense in which it is being defined here) increases. Total product, of course, declines in the experiment conducted here.

The experiments just reviewed have started with an economy that had zero taxes and then introduced some positive taxes. The same results could have been generated, however, starting out with an economy with a given level of taxes and then raising those taxes. Thus, if taxes on labor (whether paid by workers or employers) are increased, the prediction is that there will be a drop in the level of employment, a rise in labor's share in the national product, and, a temporary rise in the measured rate of unemployment.

Summary

A. Minimum Wage Laws and Unemployment

Minimum wage laws raise the economy average real wage above the competitive equilibrium level. With voluntary exchange, this means that the number of people employed will be less than the competitive equilibrium quantity, and the number of people who would like jobs will be greater than the competitive equilibrium quantity. There will, therefore, be a rise in the real wage, a fall in employment, a rise in the labor force, and a rise in unemployment.

B. Labor Unions and Unemployment

An economy-wide labor union has exactly the same kind of effect as a government-enforced minimum wage law.

A labor union that does not control the whole economy, but leaves some part of the economy competitive, will have the effect of raising the real wage in the union sector and lowering employment in that sector, while the real wage will fall and employment will rise in the nonunion sector. In such a case, no unemployment will be created. If, however, the labor union successfully lobbies for minimum wages, then unemployment will arise but because of the minimum wage, not because of the union wage-setting activity.

C. Unemployment Insurance Benefits and Unemployment

The introduction of an unemployment insurance program lowers the cost of job search and makes job search more attractive than both work and leisure at the margin. Therefore, it raises the labor force and cuts the supply of labor; the equilibrium real wage rises, employment falls, the labor force rises, and unemployment rises.

D. Taxes and Unemployment

If the level of taxes is increased, there will be a fall in the level of employment and a rise in labor's share of national income. The fall in employment will manifest itself as measured unemployment if the workers who withdraw from labor avail themselves of unemployment insurance benefits to which they have earned an entitlement.

Review Questions

1. Suppose the labor market in some particular industry is described in the following way. The demand for labor is

$$n^d = 100 - 5\left(\frac{W}{P}\right)$$

and the supply of labor is

$$n^s = 5\left(\frac{W}{P}\right)$$

(a) Plot the demand curve and state in words what the demand equation means.
(b) Plot the supply curve and state in words what the supply equation means.
(c) Calculate (either algebraically or graphically) the equilibrium real wage and level of employment.
(d) How much unemployment is there in the equilibrium calculated in (c)?
(e) If the price level is 1.2, what is the equilibrium money wage?
(f) If a minimum wage of $15 is set in this industry, what is the new equilibrium money wage, and how much unemployment is created in this industry?
(g) Suppose that all the workers in this industry become unionized, and the union sets its wage at $18. What is the money wage that is paid, and how many workers are now employed and how many cannot find work in this industry?

2. An economy consisting of 1000 firms has a labor demand given by

$$n^d = 4000 - \frac{1}{2}\left(\frac{W}{P}\right)$$

and a labor supply given by

$$n^s = 3000\left(\frac{W}{P}\right) - 2000$$

(a) What is the equilibrium real wage?
(b) If the price level is 2, what is the money wage?
(c) If a minimum wage of $5 is legislated, how many workers are employed and how many unemployed?
(d) If there is no minimum wage, but half of all the firms become 100 percent unionized and the union sets the union wage at $5, what is the average money wage paid in this industry, and how many unionized workers are employed and unemployed, and how many nonunion workers are employed and unemployed?
(e) Assume that there is no minimum wage and no unionization of labor but that the government introduces an unemployment insurance program that compensates any unemployed worker 75 percent of the money wage paid to employed workers. Using a diagram, show the impact of this program on the money wage paid, the number of workers employed, the number of workers unemployed, and the cost to the government of this program.

3. An economy with a competitive labor market has a demand curve given by

$$n^d = 1008 - 4\left(\frac{W}{P}\right)$$

and a labor supply given by

$$n^s = 960 + 2\left(\frac{W}{P}\right)$$

(a) What is the equilibrium real wage?

(b) Assume the price level to be 1, so that the equilibrium real wage is the equilibrium money wage. Now assume that the government imposes an employment tax of \$1 per worker. Calculate the new equilibrium level of employment and the money wage.

(c) Calculate the level of real national income and the share of national income accruing to labor, government, and the owners of capital.

(d) Now suppose that the government introduces a tax on labor income that shifts the labor supply curve to

$$n^s = 954 + 2.0\left(\frac{W}{P}\right)$$

What is the new equilibrium real wage, employment level, and share of national income accruing to labor, government, and the owners of capital?

12

Inflation

U.S. inflation has, throughout the 1970s, been historically unusually high. The average inflation rate over the past 80 years has been close to 3 percent per annum, whereas for the decade of the 1970s the average was more than twice that.

The question of what causes inflation and what can be done to control it is one that is surrounded by a great deal of mythology as well as sheer nonsense. The material that is presented in this chapter is designed to help you arrive at a clear understanding of what can and what cannot cause inflation and also to help you understand and avoid some of the principal mistakes that are made in the popular press and by noneconomist commentators.

You have three tasks, which are to:

(a) Review the distinction between a once-and-for-all rise in the price level and inflation.

(b) Know the effects on the price level of the following labor market shocks: a rise in the legislated minimum wage, a labor union-induced wage rise, a rise in the scale of unemployment insurance benefits, and a rise in taxes.

(c) Understand how a continuing growth in the money supply leads to inflation.

A. Once-and-for-All Price Level Rises and Inflation

Inflation is an ongoing process whereby prices are rising persistently year after year. A once-and-for-all rise in the price level occurs when the economy experiences a price level that is generally stable but occasionally jumps to a new level. Recall Figure 5.1 in Chapter 5. Two economies were illustrated. One had a price level that increased from 100 to 200 over a period of 4 years. In the other economy, the price level suddenly rose from 100 to 200, and for the rest of the time prices were stable. The first economy was one that was experiencing inflation. The second economy experienced a once-and-for-all price rise. This distinction is important in analyzing the effects of various shocks on prices.

Figure 12.1
How a Labor Market Shock That Raises the Real Wage Affects Employment, Output, and the Price Level

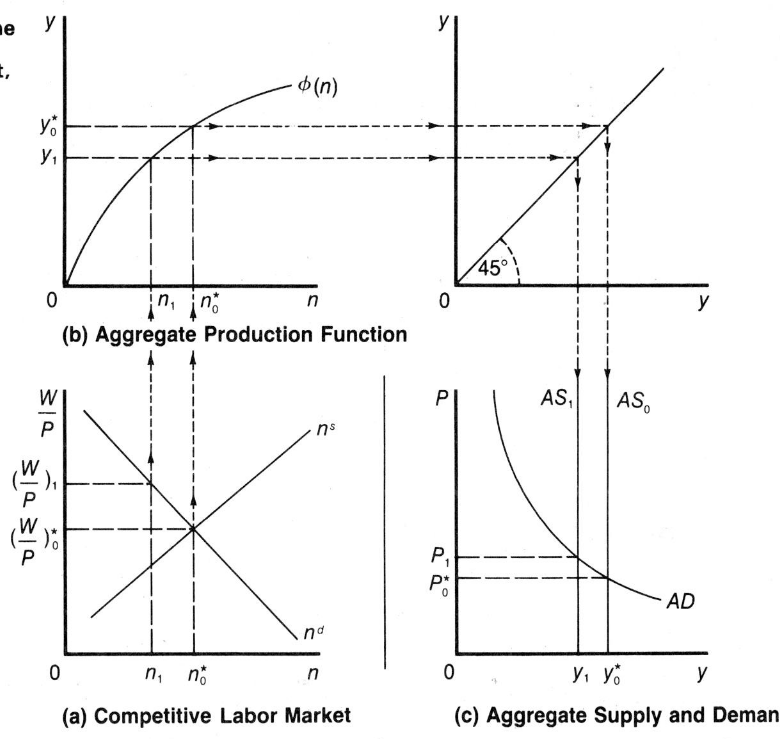

A rise in the minimum wage, a rise in union wages, a rise in taxes or an improvement in unemployment compensation raises the equilibrium real wage and lowers the level of employment [frame (a)]. This lowers the level of aggregate supply [frame (b)]. The shift in aggregate supply from y_0^* to y_1 [frame (c)] leads to a rise in the price level. Because the aggregate demand curve is unit elastic, the percentage rise in the price level equals the percentage drop in output.

B. The Price Level and Labor Market Shocks

The analysis that was presented in the previous chapter can now be extended to enable you to work out the effects of labor market shocks on the level of output and prices. This is illustrated in Figure 12.1. Frame (a) shows the labor market with a competitive equilibrium at n_0^* and $(W/P)_0^*$. This competitive equilibrium level of employment will generate a level of output equal to y_0^*, which is calculated by reading off the level of output from the short-run production function at the equilibrium level of employment [frame (b)]. The competitive equilibrium level of output is then translated into frame (c) to give the vertical aggregate supply curve AS_0. The equilibrium price level P_0^* is the point at which the aggregate demand curve AD cuts the aggregate supply curve AS_0.

Before going further be sure that you understand the basic model. If necessary, review Chapters 8, 9, and 10.

Each of the four shocks that we are considering—a rise in the legislated minimum wage, a labor union-induced real wage rise, a rise in unemployment insurance benefits, and a rise in taxes on labor—will have qualitatively the same effect on the real wage and employment. They each raise the real wage above its competitive equilibrium level, and they each lower the level of employment below its competitive equilibrium level. Frame (a) captures these effects by showing a rise in the real wage to $(W/P)_1$ with a drop in employment to n_1. This may be thought of as having arisen from any one of the four labor market shocks that we are considering. The lower level of employment n_1 will generate a lower level of output y_1, as read off from the production function in frame (b). This, in turn, following the dotted line to frame (c), implies that the aggregate supply curve will shift to the left to position AS_1 as shown in frame (c).

With a fixed money supply, and therefore a fixed aggregate demand curve, you can now read off the effect on the price level. Unambiguously the price level will rise.

Can anything be said about the *amount* by which prices will rise? It can. Within the framework of the basic model, the price level will rise by the same percentage as that by which output falls. How is this known? It follows directly from the assumption made about the relationship between the level of income and the amount of money that people will choose to hold—the demand for money function. Specifically, it was assumed that

$$\frac{M^d}{P} = k'y \tag{12.1}$$

Further, it was assumed that planned expenditure y^d adjusts so that the demand for money M^d is equal to the supply of money M. This gives us the aggregate demand curve described by the following equation:

$$y^d = \frac{1}{k'}\left(\frac{M}{P}\right) \tag{12.2}$$

This aggregate demand curve is unit elastic with respect to the price level. Since the aggregate demand curve is unit elastic with respect to the price level, if the money supply is held constant, a labor market intervention that lowers real income by 1 percent will raise the price level by 1 percent.

With a constant money supply, the price level rise induced by a rise in the legislated minimum wage, a labor union-induced wage rise, a rise in the scale of unemployment insurance benefits, or a rise in taxes on labor is clearly a once-and-for-all rise. The only way in which these "shocks" could cause an ongoing inflation would be if the minimum wage, union wage, scale of unemployment insurance benefits, or tax on labor was persistently increased in the face of rising unemployment, falling employment, falling output, and rising real wages. Thus, if we observed an economy experiencing this combination of events, we might infer that the inflation had its origins in labor market conditions or what are sometimes called *wage push* forces.

Although these labor market shocks—a rise in the legislated minimum wage, a rise in the scale of unemployment insurance benefits, a rise in taxes or a labor union-induced wage rise—have the effect of raising the price level in a once-and-for-all manner, it may be that it will take some time for the price level to rise from its initial equilibrium level to its new equilibrium level. If it does indeed take a sizable amount of time to move from the initial level to the new level, then it would not be unreasonable to describe the economy as going through an inflation. However, once the price level has reached its new equilibrium level, there would be no further tendency for it to increase. That is, these labor market "shocks" have no capacity to generate a *permanent* or *ongoing inflation*.

To summarize: Legislated rises in the real wage in the form of minimum wage laws, real wage rises induced by labor unions, a rise in the scale of unemployment insurance benefits, or a rise in taxes on labor will have the macroeconomic effect of lowering output relative to its competitive equilibrium level and raising the price level. The price level will rise by the same percentage as that by which output falls. With a constant money supply, however, none of these labor market "shocks" is capable of generating ongoing inflation.

C. Money Supply Growth and Inflation

It will help your understanding of how inflation is generated by money supply growth if the problem is broken up into three parts. First, consider the effects of a once-and-for-all rise in the money supply on the price level; second, determine the behavior of the price level when the money supply is growing at a constant, steady rate; and third, work out what happens to the rate of inflation when the rate at which the money supply is growing changes—that is, for example, analyze what would happen if the money supply had been growing at 5 percent per annum and then suddenly increased to a growth rate of 10 percent per annum.

A Once-and-for-All Rise in the Money Supply

Suppose the economy is in equilibrium as shown in Figure 12.2, where the aggregate demand curve AD_0 cuts the aggregate supply curve at the price level P_0^* and the level of output y^*. Let us call the value of the money supply in that situation M_0. Now imagine that there is a rise in the money supply to a higher level (call the new level M_1). The aggregate demand curve will shift upwards as a result of this rise in the money supply. In Figure 12.2, AD_1 represents the new aggregate demand curve. If the price level remained at P_0^*, the amount of output demanded would exceed the amount that firms would be willing to supply. The level of demand would be y_1, and the supply would be y^*. Firms could not be induced to supply the level of output y_1, consistent with expenditure plans being at point A. In a situation like A, firms would be making less than maximum profits and would have every incentive to contract production from y_1 to y^*. They would therefore never find it profitable to be at point A.

The excess demand pressures that would be operating on the economy if

Figure 12.2
A Once-and-for-All Rise in the Money Supply

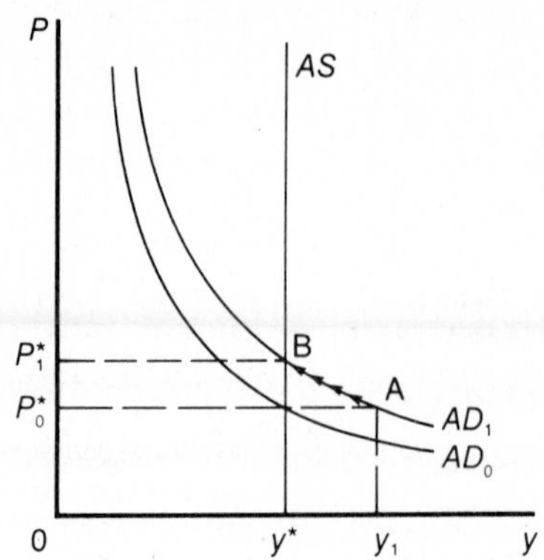

A once-and-for-all rise in the money supply shifts the aggregate demand curve from AD_0 to AD_1. At the price level P_0^*, there would be excess demand ($y_1 > y^*$). The price level would have to rise to P_1^* to restore equilibrium.

the level of demand was at point A would raise prices. There would be chronic shortages, and prices would quickly be marked up in order to eliminate the shortages. The price level at which the shortages would be eliminated is P_1^* at point B. It is the essence of the equilibrium theory that the equilibrating forces are strong enough for the price level to move from P_0^* to P_1^* (point B) quickly enough for only the new equilibrium P_1^*, y^* to be observed following the money supply increase.

You should think of the rise in the price level that follows a once-and-for-all rise in the money supply as being a sudden affair that catches people by surprise and does not lead them to attempt to economize on their money balance holdings. (We shall deal with the complications that arise in this case later in this chapter.)

Can anything be said about the amount by which the price level rises? Just as in the case analyzed in the previous section, the amount by which the price level rises is known precisely. The percentage rise in the price level will be the same as the percentage rise in the money supply. How is this known? Consider the equation for the aggregate demand curve that was derived in Chapter 9. That equation is

$$y^d = \frac{1}{k'}\left(\frac{M}{P}\right) \tag{12.3}$$

Alternatively, write the aggregate demand equation with the price level on the left-hand side. This is the way in which it is most natural to write the aggregate demand equation as plotted in Figure 12.2. Rewriting the aggregate demand equation with the price level on the left-hand side, it becomes

$$P = \frac{M}{k'y^d} \tag{12.4}$$

But in equilibrium, aggregate demand y^d is equal to aggregate supply y^*. Replacing y^d in Equation (12.4) with y^* gives

$$P = \frac{M}{k'y^*} \tag{12.5}$$

Simply by inspecting Equation (12.5), it is now obvious that the price level is proportional to the money supply; the proportion is equal to $1/k'y^*$.

Thus, it is evident that a 1 percent rise in the money stock will move the aggregate demand curve upwards by 1 percent, and since the aggregate supply curve is totally inelastic (vertical), the equilibrium price level will rise by that same 1 percent.

A Constant Rate of Growth of the Money Supply

Now that you understand what happens to the price level in the event of a once-and-for-all rise in the money supply, consider the more complicated case and ask what will happen to the price level if the money supply is increasing at a constant rate of, let us say, 5 percent per annum. So as to get some important principles clear, suppose that the money supply has been increasing at 5 percent per annum for as long as anybody can remember, and that everybody fully expects that it is going to continue to increase at 5 percent per annum into the indefinite future.

The situation to be analyzed is called the *steady state.* The steady-state value of a variable is the value at which the variable eventually settles after it has been disturbed. If the rate of inflation has settled at some particular value, then it is called the *steady-state rate of inflation.* Notice that if the steady-state rate of inflation is not equal to zero, then the price level is continuously rising. However, the price level may be an equilibrium level in the sense that, at each moment in time, it is determined by the intersection of the aggregate demand and aggregate supply curves. In that case, the position of the aggregate demand curve will be rising at a constant rate.

Returning to the substance of our analysis, you have already seen that a once-and-for-all rise in the money stock of a certain percentage generates a once-and-for-all rise in the price level of the same percentage provided the level of aggregate supply remains constant. Does this once-and-for-all result extend to the case of an ongoing money supply growth? The answer is that it does: With a constant level of real income (with a fixed aggregate supply curve), the rate of inflation will equal the rate of growth of the money supply. In the case of our example, if the money supply is growing at 5 percent per annum and if the aggregate supply curve is fixed, then the price level will be inflating at a rate of 5 percent per annum.

This proposition about an ongoing inflation may seem to follow directly and obviously from the analysis of the effects of a once-and-for-all rise in the money stock. We do have to be careful, however, to convince ourselves that the result is correct in the case of an ongoing money supply growth process. You will recall that when analyzing the determination of the demand for money, we noticed that at higher rates of inflation there would be an incentive for individuals to economize on their holdings of money balances. Specifically,

Figure 12.3
The Effect of Inflation on the Demand for Money

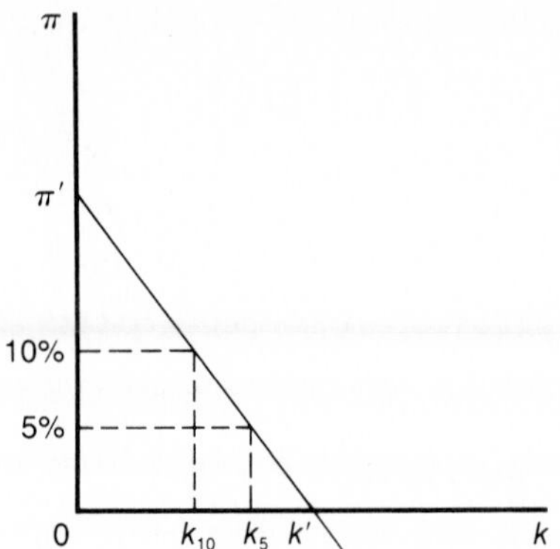

At an inflation rate of 5 percent, the propensity to hold money (M/Py) would be k_5. At an inflation rate of 10 percent, the propensity to hold money would be the smaller quantity k_{10}. Although the propensity to hold money falls as the inflation rate rises, for a given rate of inflation the propensity to hold money is a constant. If M/Py is constant then M must be changing at the same rate as Py. This could only occur if the rate of inflation (the rate of increase in P) was equal to the growth rate of the money supply (the rate of increase in M) less the growth rate of output (the rate of increase in y).

we postulated that the demand for real money would depend positively on the level of real income (output) and negatively on the rate of inflation. Thus, if the economy experiences a 5 percent rate of inflation year in and year out, individuals will, on the average, hold a smaller quantity of real money balances than they would if the economy experienced price stability.

You can think of this in the following way: If there is no inflation in the economy, the propensity to hold money, k, will take on a particular constant value. If, however, that same economy has a 5 percent rate of inflation, then the propensity to hold money would take on a lower value than in the zero inflation economy as Figure 12.3 illustrates. Recall that the propensity to hold money, k, is simply the ratio of the money supply to the flow of nominal GNP. That is,

$$k = \frac{M}{Py} \tag{12.6}$$

Figure 12.3 shows the value of k (equivalently, the value of M/Py) plotted against the inflation rate. The relationship is downward sloping, showing that at higher rates of inflation, people will economize on their money holdings and hold a smaller quantity of money relative to the flow of money expenditures that they seek to undertake. If the rate of inflation was zero, then the value of k would be k'. If the rate of inflation was 5 percent, then the value of k would be the smaller number read off on the horizontal axis of Figure 12.3, indicated as k_5.

You are now almost able to see that an ongoing rate of growth of the money supply of, say, 5 percent will indeed lead to an ongoing rate of inflation of 5 percent. Let us first write Equation (12.6) with the specific value of k relating to a 5 percent rate of inflation; that is,

$$k_5 = \frac{M}{Py} \tag{12.7}$$

This may be rearranged (multiplying both sides by P and dividing both sides of k_5), as

$$P = \left(\frac{1}{k_5\, y}\right)M \tag{12.8}$$

If income is equal to its equilibrium value, y^*, this can be written as

$$P = \left(\frac{1}{k_5\, y^*}\right)M \tag{12.9}$$

This looks exactly like Equation (12.5), which we used to establish the proposition that a rise in the price level will be proportional to the rise in the money supply. If the money supply is growing at 5 percent per annum and if real income is constant, there is only one rate at which the price level can be increasing to maintain equilibrium. That rate is the same rate at which the money supply is growing—5 percent per annum. To convince yourself that this is so, consider what would be happening in the economy if the price level was not inflating at the same rate as the money supply was growing. Suppose the money supply is growing by 5 percent per annum, real income is fixed, and the price level is only inflating by, say, $2\frac{1}{2}$ percent per annum. In such a case, the amount of *real money* in the economy would be increasing. We know that if the amount of real money in the economy increases (if the money supply rises relative to the price level), then aggregate demand rises. This would cause an excess demand for goods, thereby forcing the inflation rate upwards.

Consider the opposite extreme. Suppose that with the real money supply growing at 5 percent per annum and real income constant, the inflation rate is 10 percent per annum. In this case, the amount of real money in the economy is falling. With the money supply in real terms falling, people will cut back on their demand for goods and services to try to build up their money balances to the desired level, and this will have the effect of lowering the rate at which prices are rising.

Thus, if the inflation rate is lower than the rate of growth of the money supply, excess demand for goods will force the inflation rate up. If the money supply growth rate is lower than the rate at which inflation is proceeding, an excess supply of goods will force the inflation rate down. There is only one inflation rate that is consistent with maintaining equilibrium, and that is the rate at which the money supply is growing.

In general then, an ongoing steady rate of growth of the money supply of x percent will, with constant real income (output), lead to an x percent rate of inflation.

The above conceptual experiment has been conducted in the context of an economy that has no real income growth. That is, the aggregate supply curve has been assumed to be fixed. However, it is more natural to think of an economy that experiences output growth over time. You can think of capital accumulation and technical progress as shifting the short-run production function upwards and therefore continuously moving the aggregate supply curve out rightwards at a steady trend rate.

From our analysis about the once-and-for-all effects of labor market shocks on the aggregate supply curve and on the price level, you already know that a 1 percent drop in aggregate supply leads to a 1 percent rise in the price level. It follows immediately, therefore, that a 1 percent rise in aggregate supply will lead to a 1 percent drop in the price level. If the economy experienced continuing real income growth, with the aggregate supply curve moving rightwards at a constant rate of, say, 3 percent per annum, and if the money supply was held constant so that the aggregate demand curve did not move, then it is immediately obvious that the price level would be falling by 3 percent per annum.

It is an easy matter now to allow for output growth in calculating the relationship between the rate of growth of the money supply and the rate of inflation. You have seen that with no output growth, that is, with a fixed aggregate supply curve, a 5 percent growth rate in the money supply leads to a 5 percent rate of inflation. You also have seen that a 3 percent rise in real aggregate supply with a fixed money supply leads to a 3 percent per annum fall in the price level. These two offsetting effects can be brought together. If the money supply is growing at 5 percent per annum, and at the same time output is growing at 3 percent per annum, the rate of inflation will be 2 percent per annum. You have just used the *fundamental steady-state inflation equation*. That equation says that the rate of inflation equals the rate of growth of the money supply minus the rate of growth of output.

If we call the rate of inflation π, the rate of growth of the money supply μ, and the rate of growth of output ρ, then we can write this in a more compact form:

$$\pi = \mu - \rho \qquad \textbf{(12.10)}$$

The Effects of a Rise in the Rate of Growth of the Money Supply

Now that you understand the effects of a once-and-for-all rise in the money supply on the price level and the effects of a constant ongoing rate of growth of the money supply on the steady-state rate of inflation, you are in a position to tackle the most difficult part of the analysis, that is, to analyze the effects of a *change* in the rate of growth of the money supply. You are now going to discover a very important proposition, the *overshooting proposition*, which states that a rise in the rate of growth of the money supply will lead to a rise in the rate of inflation that will initially overshoot its steady-state value and approach its steady-state value from a *higher* rate of inflation. The proposition can be stated equivalently for a fall in the growth rate of the money supply; that is, a fall in the rate of growth of the money supply will lead to a fall in the rate of inflation that will overshoot its steady-state value and approach its steady-state value from a *lower* rate of inflation.

Figure 12.4
The Overshooting Proposition

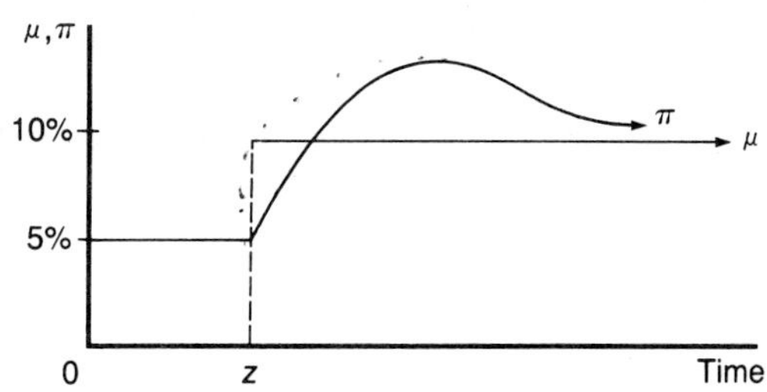

When the money supply growth rate suddenly and unexpectedly rises, the rate of inflation also rises. On its route to a new steady-state level, however, inflation overshoots the growth rate of the money supply. This happens because the higher rate of inflation induces economizing on money holdings, so that a drop in the demand for money adds to the effects of a rise in the supply of money on the level of aggregate demand and prices.

To explain the overshooting proposition, the rest of the chapter concentrates on the first case—a rise in the growth rate of the money supply. To be sure that you thoroughly understand the overshooting proposition, let me state it again in a slightly more long-winded, though simpler, way. If the money supply has been growing at a steady rate of 5 percent per annum, and if the inflation rate has settled down at 5 percent per annum (the steady-state inflation rate with a constant level of real income), and if the money supply *growth rate* is then increased to 10 percent per annum, the inflation rate will eventually settle down at 10 percent per annum. However, in the process of reaching the 10 percent inflation rate, inflation will go higher than 10 percent, i.e., will overshoot the 10 percent rate and will approach 10 percent from that higher level.

Figure 12.4 illustrates a possible path for the inflation rate. The figure shows the rate of inflation and the rate of growth of the money supply (π and μ) on the vertical axis and measures time on the horizontal axis. Let us suppose that from time 0 to time z, the rate of inflation and the rate of money supply growth were both 5 percent per annum. Then, at the time marked z, the money supply growth rate is suddenly increased to 10 percent per annum and is maintained at that level forever thereafter. The inflation rate will begin to increase and at some stage (perhaps very early in the process or even instantly) will overshoot the 10 percent rate and move to yet higher levels. Eventually the inflation rate will approach its steady-state value, but from above the steady-state value, 10 percent, not from below it.

Why does this happen? The key to the answer is contained in Figure 12.3. You will notice (turning back to that figure) that if we move from a 5 percent inflation rate to a 10 percent inflation rate, the propensity to hold money, k, which is the same thing as the ratio of money supply to nominal income, M/Py, falls from k_5 down to k_{10}. Therefore, if the economy moved from a 5 percent inflation rate to a 10 percent inflation rate, it would be necessary during that process for the ratio of the money supply to nominal income, M/Py, to fall. Remember that in the basic model, real income is constant, so that the only way in which the ratio of the money supply to nominal income can fall is for the price level to rise by a larger percentage amount than the money supply rises. Therefore, in moving from k_5 to k_{10}, the price level must rise by a larger percentage than does the money supply. This could not happen if the inflation rate was never to exceed the growth rate of money supply. If the inflation rate was always equal to the rate of growth of the money supply, and with real income (output) constant, M/Py could not change. But M/Py does change: It falls when the inflation rate rises. It follows directly, then, that the inflation rate must overshoot the money supply growth rate in order to achieve this.

Now let me try to give you some simple economic intuition as to what is going on here. The above argument has been a purely abstract, logical one. It is a correct argument, but perhaps it will be better appreciated if it is filled out with an economic story.

Imagine the economy with a 5 percent steady-state rate of inflation such as depicted at time z in Figure 12.4. Then suppose that at time z, the money supply growth rate is increased to 10 percent per annum. This will have the immediate effect of increasing the demand for goods since the money supply is now growing at a faster rate than the rate of inflation. With a fixed level of aggregate supply, this will force up the price level and force up the inflation rate. The higher inflation rate will now lead people to start economizing on their holdings of money balances. They will seek to hold a smaller quantity of money relative to income. There will, therefore, be an even bigger excess demand for goods as a result of people economizing on their money holdings than there would otherwise have been. This will put additional upward pressure on prices as people try to lower their money balances by increasing their expenditures. This additional rise in the rate of inflation will lead to still further economizing on money balances.

It sounds as if the process just described could be unstable. In fact, there are some conditions under which it might be unstable, although they do not appear to occur in the real world. Rather, what happens eventually is that the inflation rate exceeds the money supply growth rate by such a large amount that the amount of real money balances in the economy is falling at a rate even faster than the rate at which people want to reduce their real money balances. When this happens, people will cut back on their expenditures and attempt to increase their real money balances. At this stage, the rate of inflation will begin to fall. This part of the process will continue until the steady-state rate of inflation is reached.

The precise path followed will depend on how quickly people's expectations of inflation adjust to the changed money growth rate. If that expectation adjusts slowly (perhaps because of uncertainty as to whether the new higher money supply growth rate is going to be maintained), then the path illustrated is representative of the path the economy would take. If, at the other extreme, inflation expectations adjust instantly and completely to the new money supply growth path, the price level would "jump"—the inflation rate would be infinitely large for an instant—to lower real money balances to their new equilibrium level, and thereafter the inflation rate would immediately settle down at its new steady-state rate.

Summary

A. Once-and-for-All Price Level Rises and Inflation

Inflation is an ongoing process of persistently rising prices. A once-and-for-all rise in the price level occurs when the price level moves from one steady-state level to another steady-state level.

B. The Price Level and Labor Market Shocks

A rise in the legislated minimum wage, a labor union-induced wage rise, a rise in the scale of unemployment insurance benefits, and a rise in taxes on labor all have the effect of raising the real wage and lowering the level of employment. A lower level of employment will generate a lower level of output, and therefore, aggregate supply will fall. A lower level of aggregate supply will induce a higher price level. The percentage rise in the price level will equal the percentage fall in output. Thus, these shocks will have the effect of generating a once-and-for-all rise in the price level.

C. Money Supply Growth and Inflation

A continuing growth in the money supply leads to inflation. The steady-state rate of inflation will equal the rate of growth of the money supply minus the rate of growth of output. A rise in the rate of growth of the money supply will cause the rate of inflation to "overshoot" its steady-state value and to approach the steady state from above.

Review Questions

1. From the following, label those that are a once-and-for-all rise in the price level and those that are inflation:

- (a) The price of beef this week rose by 10 percent.
- (b) The Consumer Price Index, after having been steady for one year, jumped 10 percent at the beginning of last winter but has been steady ever since.
- (c) Over the past decade the Consumer Price Index has gradually and consistently increased, so that today it is double what it was a decade ago.
- (d) Over the last decade the Consumer Price Index doubled, but this is the result of two big jumps, one in 1974 and one in 1979.

2. What happens to the price level when a strong labor union successfully raises the money wage rate? Does inflation ensue? What happens to employment, unemployment, real wages, and the level of output?

3. Imagine an economy that has been experiencing stable prices for as long as anyone can remember. Suddenly there is a doubling in the quantity of money. The money supply then remains constant at its new level. What happens in that economy to output, employment, real wages, and the price level? Why? Trace out all the effects and fully set out your reasoning.

4. Does the price level "overshoot" the money supply in the situation described in Question 3? If so, why? If not, why not?
5. Imagine an economy that has experienced 10 percent inflation for as long as anyone can remember. Output has been constant, and the money supply has grown at the same 10 percent rate as inflation. Suddenly there is a doubling in the growth rate of the money supply, after which the new higher (20 percent) growth rate is maintained. What happens in this economy to output, employment, real wages, and inflation?
6. Does the inflation rate "overshoot" the money supply growth rate in the economy described in Question 5? If so, why? If not, why not?
7. Describe what would happen to interest rates in the event of monetary shocks such as those set out in Questions 3 and 5 above.

Appendix to Chapter 12

The Algebra of Inflation

This appendix sets out in a slightly more rigorous form some of the ideas developed in the text of this chapter. You might find this treatment helpful. However, if you find algebraic arguments difficult, you can safely ignore this appendix. The important thing is that you have understood the text.

The starting point for an algebraic analysis of inflation is to recall the theory of the demand for money developed in Chapter 9. You will recall that we worked out that the demand for real money will be higher when the level of real income is higher and will be lower when the rate of inflation is higher. Specifically, we wrote

$$\frac{M^d}{P} = k(\pi)y$$

We could make this slightly more general by writing

$$\frac{M^d}{P} = g(\underset{+}{y}, \underset{-}{\pi}) \qquad \textbf{(12A.1)}$$

If we have equilibrium in the money market, then we can remove the superscript d and set the demand for money M^d equal to the supply of money M, so that

$$\frac{M}{P} = g(y, \pi) \qquad \textbf{(12A.2)}$$

Take the logarithms of both sides of this equation to give

$$\log M - \log P = \log [g(y, \pi)] \qquad \textbf{(12A.3)}$$

Now suppose that the demand for money function takes on a very specific form and, in particular, is given by

$$\log [g(y, \pi)] = \alpha \log y - \beta\pi \quad \textbf{(12A.4)}$$

This is simply making the demand for money function take on the special functional form that the logarithm of real money balances demanded be equal to a constant, α, times the logarithm of real income minus another constant, β, times the rate of inflation. Substitute the right-hand side of (12A.4) into the right-hand side of (12A.3) to give

$$\log M - \log P = \alpha \log y - \beta\pi \quad \textbf{(12A.5)}$$

Now consider how Equation (12A.5) changes over time. Use the operator Δ to denote a change, so that

$$\Delta \log M - \Delta \log P = \alpha\Delta \log y - \beta\Delta\pi \quad \textbf{(12A.6)}$$

Note that the change in a logarithm of a variable is nothing other than its growth rate. Therefore we will define

$$\begin{aligned} \log M &\equiv \mu \\ \log P &\equiv \pi \\ \log y &\equiv \rho \end{aligned} \quad \textbf{(12A.7)}$$

We are defining μ as the growth rate of the money supply, ρ as the growth rate of output, and π as the inflation rate. We then obtain

$$\mu - \pi = \alpha\rho - \beta\Delta\pi \quad \textbf{(12A.8)}$$

If the inflation rate is constant, then $\Delta\pi$ is equal to zero, and we obtain the steady-state rate of inflation as

$$\pi = \mu - \alpha\rho \quad \textbf{(12A.9)}$$

This is the fundamental steady-state inflation equation developed in the text. The equation differs slightly from that in the text in that the growth rate of output is multiplied by a constant α, which is nothing other than the elasticity of demand for money with respect to income. We assumed this to be equal to unity—not a bad approximation as it turns out—in the text and in Chapter 9.

13

U.S. Macroeconomic History: How Well Is It Explained by the Basic Model?

The last six chapters have taken you through the basic model and have generated a variety of predictions about the determination of output, unemployment, inflation, and interest rates. This chapter provides you with an opportunity to go back to the facts and to examine the extent to which the basic model is in conformity with those facts and, perhaps more importantly, the extent to which it is not.

This chapter will take you through five tasks, which are to:

(a) Review the facts that the basic model seeks to explain.
(b) Summarize the predictions of the basic model.
(c) Examine the main labor market shocks in the United States and their effects.
(d) Examine the growth rate of the money supply and its effects.
(e) Understand what the basic model does and does not explain.

Let us begin with the first of these tasks.

A. The Facts

The most useful way in which you can review the facts about the U.S. economy is to go back and reexamine the charts shown in Chapter 2 and those in Section E of Chapter 6. It will be useful if you specifically concentrate on the four variables—output (real income), unemployment, inflation, and interest rates. These are the four variables on which this chapter will focus. I will begin by highlighting the key features of these variables.

First, inflation, unemployment, and the deviations of real income around its trend all fluctuated much more before World War II than in the period since then. In contrast to these three variables, the rate of interest has behaved much more smoothly. That is, interest rate fluctuations have had a much smaller amplitude than the fluctuations in the other three variables.

The second feature to highlight is the trends in these variables. There is no discernible trend in unemployment before World War II, although of course the Great Depression dominates the behavior of that variable in that period. However, since World War II there has been a distinct though gentle rising trend in the rate of unemployment. The trend in inflation was very gently upwards until World War II; then it was falling through the 1950s; and it has been increasing at an increasing rate through the 1960s and 1970s. The trend in interest rates has been much like that in inflation, although less prominently so.

The third feature to highlight is the co-movements of these variables. The co-movement between unemployment and the deviation of output (real income) from trend is particularly strong and displays countercyclical behavior of the unemployment rate. It is so strong that we can speak of the cycle in real economic activity interchangeably as a cycle in either of these variables. The relationship between inflation and unemployment or equivalently between inflation and deviations of output from trend does not show a simple, single pattern. About two-thirds of the time, inflation rises as unemployment falls (or equivalently inflation rises as output deviates above its trend); whereas one-third of the time, inflation and unemployment move in the same direction as each other. Finally, interest rates and inflation tend to move together, although the fluctuations in inflation have bigger amplitude than those in interest rates.

These, then, are the broad facts concerning U.S. macroeconomic history that we would like to be able to explain:

- Bigger fluctuations in activity before World War II than afterwards
- A trend rise in the unemployment rate since the war
- A fall in trend inflation in the 1950s and a rising inflation trend in the 1960s and 1970s
- Countercyclical co-movements between unemployment and deviations of output from trend
- Procyclical co-movements between inflation and unemployment most of the time, although interspersed with occasionally strong countercyclical movements
- A tendency for interest rates to move with, although to understate, movements in the inflation rate.

Let us begin our attempt to see how well the basic model performs in explaining these facts by summarizing its key predictions.

B. Predictions of the Basic Model

Let us first review the predicted effects of the labor market shocks that we analyzed in Chapter 11. There we established that the introduction of a minimum wage, of an economy-wide labor union, of an increase in unemployment insurance benefits, or of an increase in the tax wedge (the tax on labor income or on employment) all would have the effect of raising the real wage, lowering the level of employment, lowering the output level, and raising the price level. In addition, the first three of these shocks would also raise the unemployment rate. A rise in the tax wedge might also produce a rise in the unemployment rate if workers who voluntarily withdrew from employment as a result of higher taxes remained for a time in the job-search pool. We also established that the introduction of a labor union that does not embrace the whole economy would have, as a first approximation, no macroeconomic effects but rather would influence the distribution of wages and employment between the union and nonunion sectors.

In Chapter 12 we analyzed the effects of monetary shocks and discovered that a rise in the money supply would lead to a rise in aggregate demand and a rise in the price level but would have no effects on such real variables as output, employment, and unemployment. A rise in the growth rate of the money supply would lead to a rise in the rate of inflation and would display overshooting—that is, the inflation rate would, for a period, exceed the growth rate of the money supply.

The basic model makes no distinction between the actual and expected rates of inflation. It predicts that interest rates will move one-for-one with the *actual* rate of inflation. The model predicts that there will either be, in general, no relationship between inflation and output (or equivalently inflation and unemployment) or, to the extent that output fluctuations are generated by labor market shocks, there will be a negative co-movement between prices and output (positive co-movement between prices and unemployment). To generate positive co-movements between prices and output it would be necessary, in the event of a negative labor market shock that reduced output, that there be a coincident fall in the money supply to ensure that as output falls, the price level also falls. In other words, the basic model can only generate procyclical co-movements between prices and output as a result of simultaneous shocks occurring on both the supply and the demand side of the economy. The size of the movements of output and prices would, according to the basic model, depend on the size of the shocks occurring in the labor market to affect the aggregate supply of goods and services, or in the money market to affect the aggregate demand for goods and services. Thus, big fluctuations would be the result of big shocks.

None of the shocks is predicted to lead to a *systematic cycle* in output and unemployment. Further, none of the shocks taken alone leads to the prediction that prices will be procyclical. For the basic model to generate cycles in output and unemployment, it would be necessary for the labor market shocks themselves to be cyclical in character.

The key predictions of the basic model that we shall check out in the rest of this chapter are as follows: Labor market shocks that cut the supply of or demand for labor will lower output and raise prices. They may also raise the unemployment rate. Changes in the growth rate of the money supply will lead to changes in the rate of inflation, which will also lead to changes in interest rates.

Let us now turn to an examination of the shocks, the effects of which we have analyzed in Chapters 11 and 12, beginning with those that affect the labor market.

C. Labor Market Shocks

We analyzed four labor market shocks in Chapter 11: minimum wages, labor unions, unemployment insurance programs, and taxes on employment. Let us now review the actual behavior of these shocks in the U.S. economy.

Figure 13.1
Real Minimum Wages and Unemployment, 1940–1981

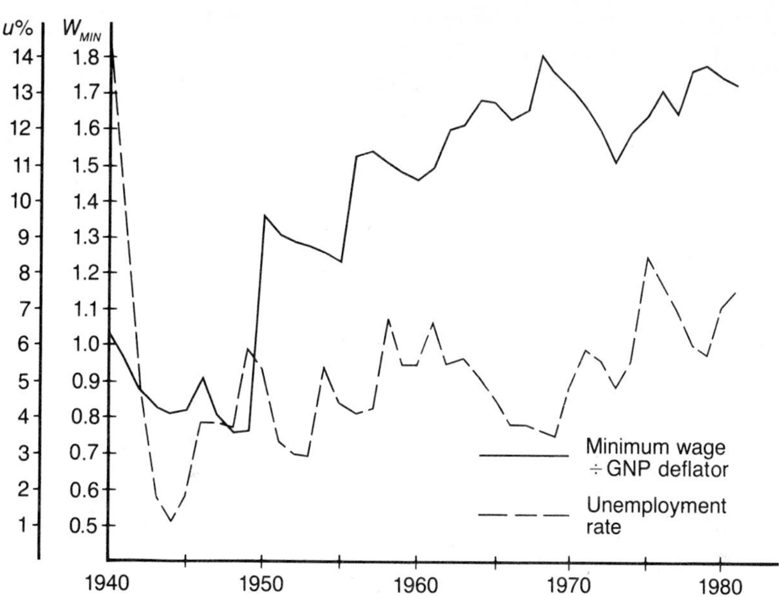

Real minimum wages (continuous line) have grown in spurts since minimum wages were first introduced in 1938. Although both the trend of real minimum wages and that of unemployment are broadly upwards, the detailed timing of changes in real minimum wages does not seem capable of accounting for variations in unemployment. Further, the strongest upward trend of the real minimum wage rate ended in the middle 1960s at about the time that the unemployment rate was beginning to trend upwards more quickly.

SOURCE: Appendix to Chapter 2 for the GNP deflator and the unemployment rate. The minimum wage is minimum rates for nonfarm workers, *Monthly Labor Review*, 102, no. 7 (July 1979), 11, and *Statistical Abstract of the United States*, 1980, 425.

Minimum Wages

The United States has had federally enforced minimum wages since 1938. In that year, President Franklin D. Roosevelt signed into law the Fair Labor Standards Act. This act, which covered one-fifth of the U.S. labor force at the time, provided for a minimum hourly wage of 25¢ and a maximum work week of 44 hours. The 1938 act has been amended six times, providing periodic increases in the minimum wage and also extending the range of employment covered. By 1976, over 80 percent of the U.S. labor force was employed in sectors covered by the act. The 1977 amendment to the act covered 52 million workers and raised the minimum wage to $2.90 an hour effective January 1, 1979. It also provided a further increase to $3.35 an hour on January 1, 1981.[1]

You discovered in Chapter 11 that what matters is not the dollar value of the minimum wage but the *real minimum wage*. The real minimum wage has

[1]A useful, brief, and factual account of the act and its amendments may be found in Peyton K. Elder and Heidi D. Miller, "The Fair Labor Standards Act: Changes of Four Decades," *Monthly Labor Review*, 102, no. 7 (July 1979), 10–16.

been calculated (by dividing the dollar minimum wage by the GNP deflator),[2] and the result is set out in Figure 13.1 (the continuous line). Evidently the real minimum wage has gradually increased in the period since its introduction in 1938. By no means has there been a uniform increase in its rate, however. In fact, it has tended to jump in certain years and then sag in the intervening years. Sizable jumps occurred in 1946, 1950, 1956, 1961–1962, 1967–1968, and 1974–1976. In the years between these dates, there was a slight erosion in the real minimum wage.

How has the minimum wage affected the level of unemployment? This is a controversial and unsettled question. Nevertheless, let us see how much we can learn by examining the relationship between the minimum wage and unemployment in the light of the basic model. Using the predictions of that model, if the minimum wage has affected unemployment, then we would expect to see the following: First, the unemployment rate would be higher on the average after 1938 than before that date; second, unemployment would be higher in the years just after a jump in the real minimum wage and would tend to decline in the years in which the real minimum wage was declining; third, there would be a general tendency for the unemployment rate to trend upwards in sympathy with the general upward trend in real minimum wages. What do we see in the data?

First, the average unemployment rate before 1939 was higher than afterwards. In fact, the average for the four decades 1900 to 1939 was 8.1 percent and for the four decades 1940 to 1979 was 5.2 percent. If the Great Depression is regarded as something special and unusual and is therefore taken out of the calculation so that we compare only the 30 years 1900 to 1929 with the 40 years 1940 to 1979, the averages are almost identical (4.7 percent for the first 30 years of this century compared with 5.2 percent for the years since 1940). Thus, on this test the minimum wage appears to have had only trivial effects on unemployment in the period since its introduction and certainly cannot be held responsible for the massive unemployment of the Great Depression years because this occurred before federal minimum wages existed.

What do we learn from the timing of the changes in real minimum wages and the movements in unemployment? Of the five occasions on which real minimum wages increased (1946, 1950, 1961–1962, 1967–1968, and 1974–1976), only one (1946) was associated with a rise in unemployment. In all the other cases, unemployment actually fell either in the year in which minimum wages increased or very soon thereafter (see the broken line in Figure 13.1 that measures unemployment). This is almost the exact opposite of what the theory would predict and points strongly, therefore, to the conclusion that minimum wages are not the key source of movements in the unemployment rate. Exam-

[2] An alternative definition of the real minimum wage could have been calculated by dividing the minimum wage by the Consumer Price Index. This would measure the value of the real minimum wage to workers. The number shown in Figure 13.1 represents the real minimum cost of labor, on the average, to employers. It is the relevant number for determining the effects of the real minimum wage on the level of employment. Both definitions are relevant for determining the effects of minimum wages on unemployment. However, the two definitions show similar behavior, and little would be gained here from examining each definition separately.

ination of the trends strengthens this conclusion. It is clear that there is a general tendency for both real minimum wages and unemployment to trend upwards. The main upward thrust in real minimum wages, however, takes place between 1949 and 1968, a period during which the trend in the unemployment rate is hardly observable. Unemployment sees most of its increases occurring in the 1970s, a period during which the real minimum wage is reasonably well described as having had no trend at all.

This examination of minimum wages and unemployment in the United States seems, then, to lead us to the conclusion that minimum wages have not been a major factor in influencing the *aggregate* unemployment rate. This conclusion does not mean that the basic model is necessarily wrong. It may well be that the level at which minimum wages have been set is not very different from what would have occurred in the market. Also, it must be borne in mind that the analysis of Chapter 11 presumed a minimum wage regulation that was economy-wide and binding on all members of the labor force, whereas the U.S. minimum wage regulations, even today, do not extend to the entire labor force.

The conclusion that minimum wages are not a major factor in influencing aggregate unemployment in the United States does not mean that they do not have any effects. In fact, many detailed studies of the effects of minimum wages on the unemployment rates of particular groups of workers and on relative earnings have concluded that these regulations are indeed influential in significant and important ways. For example, higher than average unemployment amongst young people almost certainly arises from the operation of the minimum wage laws.[3]

Let us now go on to examine the role of labor unions.

Labor Unions

We saw in our analysis of the effects of labor unions in Chapter 11 that in the event of the establishment of an economy-wide labor union it is possible for unemployment to be created and output to fall as a result of union actions. We also saw, however, that if only part of the economy is unionized, the effect will not only be to raise real wages in the union sector and cut employment in that sector but also to lower real wages and raise employment in the nonunion sector. As a first approximation, there will be no aggregate effects of union actions in such a situation.

Obviously the U.S. economy is not one that has complete labor unionization. Nevertheless, does it usefully approximate such a case? The facts would seem to point strongly against that. In 1930, as the economy was moving into

---

[3]One recent study by Robert H. Meyer and David A. Wise, "The Effects of the Minimum Wage on the Employment and Earnings of Youth," *Journal of Labor Economics*, 1, (Jan. 1983), 66–100, has estimated that, during the period 1973–1978, the minimum wage added 4 points to the unemployment rate of young (16 to 24 years old) white men and 6 points to that of young black men. A good survey of the studies of this aspect of minimum wages is Charles Brown, Curtis Gilroy, and Andrew Kohen, "The Effect of the Minimum Wage on Employment and Unemployment," *Journal of Economic Literature*, 20, no. 2 (June 1982), 487–528.

the depths of the Great Depression, only 6.8 percent of U.S. workers belonged to labor unions. The fraction of the labor force belonging to unions has increased over the years, reaching a peak of just over one-quarter in 1953. Since then, union membership, in relation to the size of the labor force, has declined so that only approximately one-fifth of the labor force belonged to unions in the latter part of the 1970s. Thus, it is clear that a small, and in recent years, declining, fraction of the U.S. labor force belongs to labor unions. This leads immediately to the prediction that labor unions are likely to have had only a negligible impact on aggregate unemployment in the U.S. economy. Their main effects would be predicted to be on the distribution of income, raising real wages of union members, and lowering the real wages of others. Indeed, such effects have been found in numerous studies, showing that union members' wages are higher than those of nonunion workers with similar characteristics, to the extent of between a fifth and a quarter.[4]

Thus, it seems that labor unions, although extremely important institutions in the U.S. economy, are principally important for their effects on the distribution of jobs and incomes and not on the overall level of output, employment, and unemployment.

Unemployment Insurance Benefits

Evaluating how unemployment insurance benefits affect unemployment in the United States is very hard because programs concerning these benefits differ enormously from state to state. Programs vary in many different dimensions: for example, the minimum number of weeks of prior employment required to qualify for benefits, the maximum duration of benefits, the scale of benefits and their relation to previous earnings, and the tax rates that apply to benefits.[5] What we can do, however, despite these many differences, is look at two overall measures of the extent to which the state and the federal programs provide income replacement for the unemployed and, therefore, provide incentives to engage in lengthier job-search activities than would be the case in the absence of such programs.

The first measure that we shall look at is the extent to which unemployment insurance benefits replace lost earnings for the workers covered by such programs. The second measure is the fraction of the labor force covered by such programs. Clearly, an increase in either of these variables ought, according to the basic model, to be associated with a rise in the unemployment rate. A rise in the ratio of unemployment insurance benefits to average earnings, often referred to as the "replacement ratio," would provide a bigger incentive for insured members of the labor force to engage in longer average job-search activities between employment. A rise in the fraction of the labor force covered

[4]An interesting survey of findings on this matter, together with comprehensive references to other literature, is contained in Paul M. Ryscavage, "Measuring Union–Nonunion Earnings Differences," *Monthly Labor Review*, 97, no. 12 (December 1974), 3–9.

[5]A good, fairly comprehensive, and up-to-date study of unemployment insurance in the United States can be found in Daniel S. Hamermesh, *Jobless Pay and the Economy* (Baltimore: The Johns Hopkins University Press, 1977).

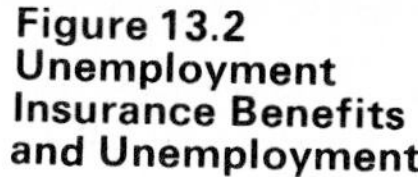
Figure 13.2 Unemployment Insurance Benefits and Unemployment

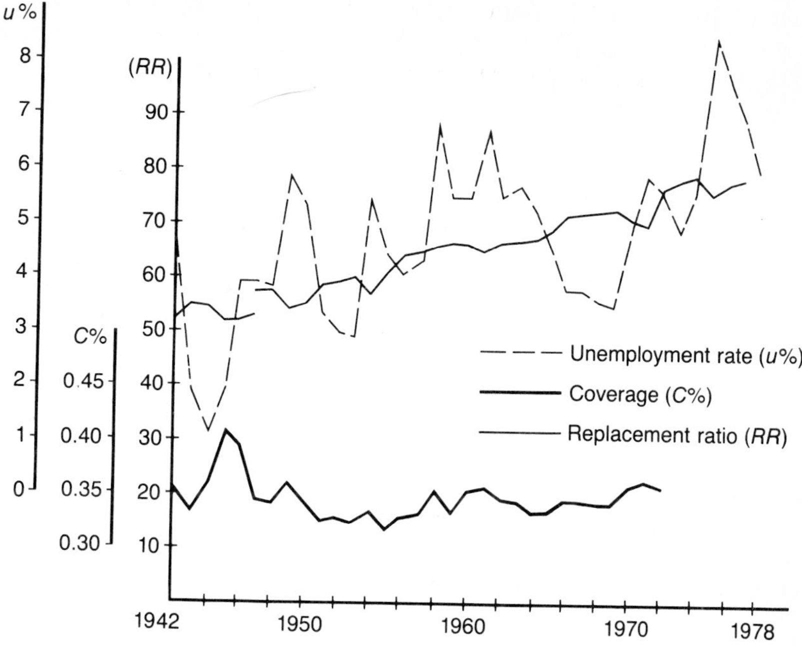

The replacement ratio (ratio of unemployment benefits to average earnings of insured workers) has been remarkably constant in the postwar years and has actually declined from its level in the late 1930s. The fraction of the labor force covered by unemployment insurance programs has steadily increased, and strongly so in the 1960s and 1970s. The trend in coverage seems to be clearly related to the trend in unemployment, although none of these unemployment insurance benefit programs can account for the cycles in unemployment.
SOURCES: Unemployment rate: Appendix to Chapter 2. Replacement ratio: David L. Edgell and Stephen A. Wadner, "Unemployment Insurance: Its Economic Performances," *Monthly Labor Review*, 97, no. 4, (April 1974), 34–5, Table 2, column 4. Coverage, 1942–1947: Edgell and Wadner, *op. cit.*, Table 1, column 6 divided by civilian labor force, *Economic Report of the President*, 1970, Table C–22, column 4, 202. Coverage, 1947–1979: *Economic Report of the President*, 1980, Table B–33, column 1, 241 divided by Table B–27, column 3, 234.

by such programs would increase the number of people having the incentive to search more extensively and, therefore, perhaps for a longer period of time.

For either or both of these characteristics of unemployment insurance programs to have been a major source of movements in U.S. unemployment, it must be the case that one or both of them have increased over the postwar years and have displayed systematic cycles. Examination of the relevant data, displayed in Figure 13.2, suggests that one of these things has certainly happened but not the other. What is apparent is a clear tendency for the fraction of the labor force covered by unemployment insurance programs to have increased systematically over the postwar period. There is, however, no clear recurrent cycle in that variable or in the replacement ratio. Furthermore, the replacement ratio itself has been remarkably constant since the late 1940s and has actually fallen compared with its 1938 value.

Although the rise in coverage can, in no way, explain the cycles in unemployment in the United States, it does not seem likely that the trend rise in coverage may well account, at least in part, for the trend rise in unemployment that has occurred. This conclusion is reinforced by noticing that some of the biggest increases in coverage occurred in the middle 1960s and early 1970s, a period that coincides with the clearest tendency for the unemployment rate to trend upwards.

It is also possible that the replacement ratio data shown in Figure 13.2 are misleading. Those data are averages across all workers. As unemployment insurance programs expand their coverage, they typically extend from the higher paid to the lower paid workers. Therefore it is possible that the available benefits represent a bigger fraction of the wages of those most recently included in the coverage rather than the wages of those who have been covered for a longer period of time. As a result, the effective marginal replacement ratio may well have risen, even though the average replacement ratio has not. If this was the case, it too would be a possible source of a trend rise in the rate of unemployment.

It seems likely, then, that changes in unemployment insurance programs in the United States are one of the sources of the trend rise in unemployment in the postwar years. They clearly are not, however, in any way, a source of the cycles in unemployment that are to be seen in the data.

The Tax Wedge

There have been literally hundreds of changes in tax regulations that may be expected to have effects on the supply of and demand for labor in the United States. It would be a mammoth task to describe and summarize them all. What can be done, however, is to provide an overall summary measure of the tax wedge by calculating the total taxes paid by employers and employees expressed as a fraction of the total wage bill. This has been done and is shown for the postwar period in Figure 13.3.

As noted in the figure, there is a clear tendency for the tax wedge to rise throughout the postwar years (although with occasional slight downward movements). The basic model predicts that the increasing size of the tax wedge will have led to a lower level of employment and lower output than would otherwise have occurred. However, it would be hard to see such effects in the data. The reason for this is that the tax wedge has gradually increased and, therefore, may be predicted to have gradually lowered the levels of employment and output *relative to what they otherwise would have been.* Since we cannot observe what output and employment otherwise would have been, we cannot directly see the effects of the tax wedge on the data.

Furthermore, the tax wedge itself is not predicted to affect the level of unemployment, except perhaps as a result of a *change* in the tax wedge leading to a withdrawal from employment and possibly a temporary period of unemployment before withdrawing from the labor force. Figure 13.3 plots the change in the tax wedge (measured as the percent change from year to year). It also plots the unemployment rate for comparison purposes. Evidently, there is no appearance of a relationship of any kind between changes in the tax wedge

Figure 13.3
The Tax Wedge and Unemployment

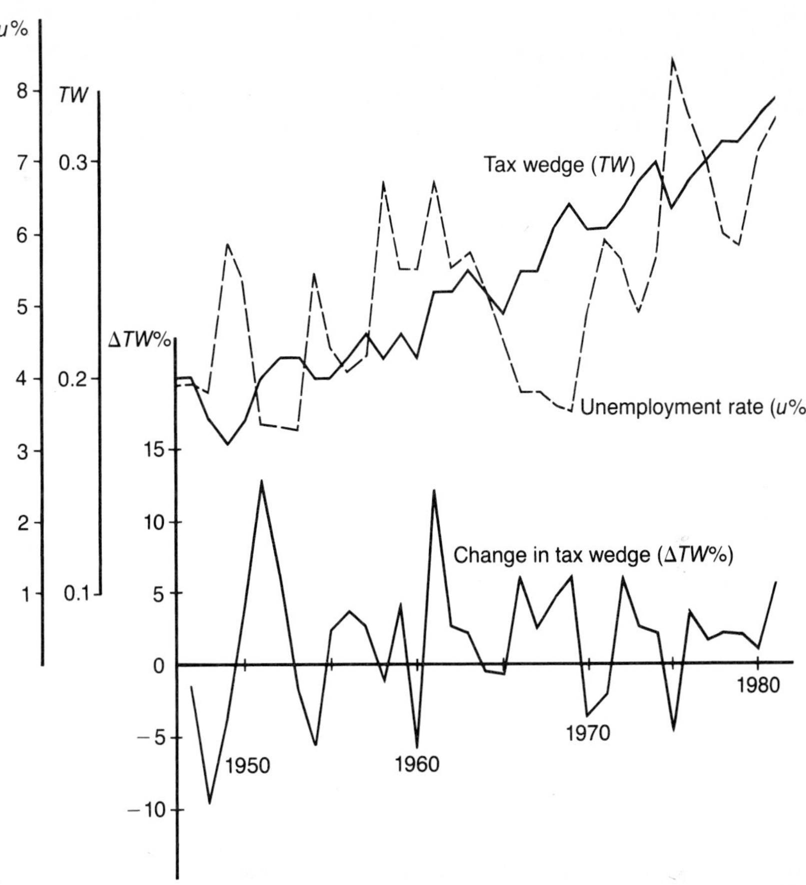

The tax wedge increased quickly during World War II and, having declined slightly immediately after the war, has gradually increased all through the period since the early 1950s. Although the trends in unemployment and the tax wedge agree with each other, the years in which the tax wedge decreased most are typically those in which unemployment was high. Thus there is no clear year-by-year relation between these variables.

SOURCES: Unemployment rate: Appendix to Chapter 2. Tax wedge: *National Income and Product Accounts*, 1976, 73, 123–129. The tax wedge is $\{[(t_c + t_y)/(1 + t_c)] + t_e\}$ where t_c is the sum of excise duties (Table 3.2, line 8) and sales taxes (Table 3.3, line 8) as a fraction of personal consumption expenditures (Table 2.1, line 27); t_y is the sum of personal contributions for social insurance (Table 2.1, line 23) and personal income taxes (Table 3.2, line 3 plus Table 3.3, line 3) as a fraction of personal income (Table 2.1, line 1); t_e is the difference between contributions for social insurance (Table 3.1, line 5) and personal contributions for social insurance as a fraction of wage and salary disbursements (Table 2.1, line 2).

Change in the tax wedge is the growth rate of the tax wedge.

and the unemployment rate. Indeed, the years when unemployment surges are more often than not years in which the tax wedge declined (1948–1949, 1954, 1958, 1970, 1975).

Summary

You have now discovered that of all the labor market shocks analyzed in Chapter 11, shocks that are capable of influencing the levels of output, employment, and unemployment, only one appears to be capable of accounting for just one aspect of the behavior of unemployment, and presumably also of the behavior of real GNP, in the U.S. economy. This exception is the increased breadth of coverage of unemployment insurance programs. The postwar trend in unemployment may well be accounted for by the trend rise in the coverage of unemployment insurance programs, although the cycles in its rate cannot be accounted for in that way.

Minimum wage and labor union actions as well as changes in the tax wedge do not show up as having had clear effects on the swings in the rate of unemployment and, therefore, on the levels of employment and output. The trend in unemployment, the trend in the tax wedge, and the trend in real minimum wages are in broad terms related to each other, but the detailed timing of movements in these variables do not add up to a convincing story that the labor market shocks identified have been the major forces at work in moving the unemployment and output rates around. Indeed, the most glaring example of a swing in economic activity—the Great Depression—occurred at a time when there were no minimum wages, when hardly anyone belonged to labor unions, when unemployment insurance benefits were much less comprehensive than they became in the later 1930s, and when the tax wedge was negligible.

Furthermore, the overall greater volatility in unemployment and output in the years before World War II can in no way be accounted for by greater volatility in these labor markets shocks at that time than subsequently. If anything, more has been going on in these directions in the postwar years than previously. Despite this fact, unemployment and output fluctuations have been less in the postwar era than previously.

Thus, the basic model seems to be of limited use in assisting our understanding of the changes in the level of economic activity that we have observed. It may account for the postwar trend in unemployment, but in no way can it account for the cyclical movements observed.

Let us turn now to examine the performance of the basic model concerning the predicted effects of changes in the quantity of money.

D. Money Supply Growth and Inflation

The basic model predicts that variations in the growth rate of the money supply will lead to variations in the rate of inflation, and variations in the inflation rate are predicted to overshoot variations in the growth rate of the money supply. Furthermore, the basic model predicts that variations in the growth rate of the money supply will have no effects on the real variables in the economy—output, employment, and unemployment.

Let us look at the facts about U.S. money growth. Data on the growth rate of narrow money—M1—are available only after 1915. The growth rate of M1 for each year since then is shown as the continuous line in Figure 13.4.

Figure 13.4
Money Supply Growth and Inflation

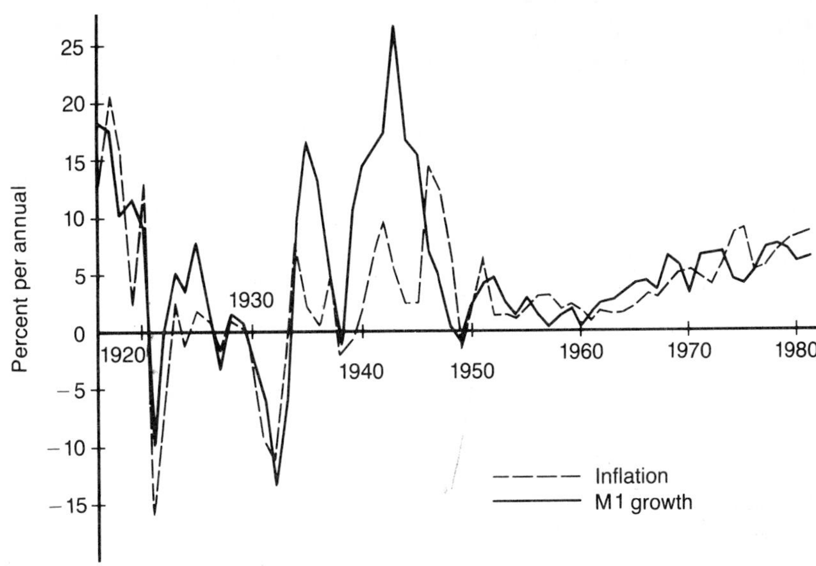

The money supply growth rate and the inflation rate are remarkably closely related to each other, with the exception of the years of World War II when money supply growth strongly exceeded the inflation rate, and immediately after that war when the money supply growth rate fell short of the inflation rate. Both variables are much more volatile before World War II than after. Inflation and money supply growth move together before World War II, and money supply growth tends to lead inflation in the 1950s and 1960s. There is no clear tendency for money supply growth to overshoot the rate of inflation.
SOURCE: Inflation: Appendix to Chapter 2. M1 1915–1958: *Historical Statistics of the United States, Colonial Times to 1970*, U.S. Department of Commerce, Series X414. M1 1959–1981: *Revised Money Stock Data*, Board of Governors of the Federal Reserve System (March 1982), Table 1.

The pattern of M1 growth shown in that figure has some features that will strike you as being remarkably like the features of some of the graphs in Chapter 2. The growth of M1 evidently was very much more volatile before 1948 than it has been since that date. There were, in the period between 1916 and 1948, three and a half major cycles in the growth rate of M1, and the range of growth rates in that period was truly enormous, going from a high of 26 percent in 1943 to a low of minus 18 percent in 1921. It is hard to see any trends over that period, although there is a tendency for the growth rate to move downwards from 1916 to 1932 and then back up again after that date through to the middle of World War II.

In contrast, the period since 1948 has been one of remarkably smooth money supply growth. The range of fluctuation in this period has been from a low of minus 1.0 percent to a high of 7.2 percent. There was, in the postwar period, a tendency for the money supply growth rate to decline from 1951 through 1960 and to increase thereafter. Also there have been cycles, although much less pronounced than those experienced before World War II.

In addition to showing the growth rate of the money supply, Figure 13.4 also shows the rate of inflation of the GNP deflator over the same period 1916 to 1981 (the dashed line). This makes it possible for you to see some of the patterns in the relationship between money supply growth and inflation. You will immediately be struck by the remarkable similarity in the two time-series. There is not, by any means, a one-to-one correspondence between the annual rate of growth of the money supply and the annual rate of inflation. Nevertheless, certain features are shared by both series. They are both much more volatile before than after World War II. The cyclical swings in the growth rate of the money supply are also apparent in the rate of inflation and with remarkable closeness up to 1938. In contrast, during World War II there is a strong burst of money supply growth that is *not* matched by a rise in the inflation rate. Immediately after the war, as the money supply growth rate falls, the inflation rate accelerates. However, in the period after World War II, although the detailed cycles in money growth and inflation do not coincide with each other, the broad trends line up remarkably closely. Furthermore, there is a general tendency for the inflation rate to follow rather than coincide with the rate of growth of the money supply.

Figure 13.5 illustrates this tendency for inflation to lag the money supply growth for the period after 1956. In this figure, the rate of inflation is shown as the continuous line, and the growth rate of the money supply two years earlier is shown as the broken line. Thus, for example, in the year 1956 the points shown are that for the rate of inflation in 1956 and the money supply growth rate in 1954 (2 years earlier). It is apparent that not only is there a remarkable similarity between the trends in inflation and money supply growth but the cycles also line up fairly closely as well. Prior to this period, the relationship between money supply growth and inflation was more contemporaneous than appears in this later period.

Figures 13.4 and 13.5 make it clear that one of the major predictions of the basic model (that changes in the money supply growth rate either coincide with or precede similar changes in the inflation rate) is in broad terms, although not exactly, borne out by the facts. Changes in the growth rate of the money supply do indeed seem either to coincide with or to precede similar changes in the rate of inflation.

In contrast, there are two features of the relationship between money growth and inflation that are slightly at odds with the basic model and one that is very much at odds. The two features that are slightly out of line with the predictions of the model have to do with timing and overshooting. First, the basic model does not predict that there will be a time lag in the relationship between money supply growth and inflation. Rather, it predicts that changes in the money supply will lead instantly to changes in the price level. What we see in the data, and especially clearly in the period since the middle 1950s, is a distinct delay in the effects of money supply growth on inflation. The second detailed prediction of the basic model not quite borne out is the overshooting proposition. There is no clear tendency for the inflation rate to overshoot the growth rate of the money supply, with the possible exception of

Figure 13.5 Inflation, and Money Growth Two Years Earlier

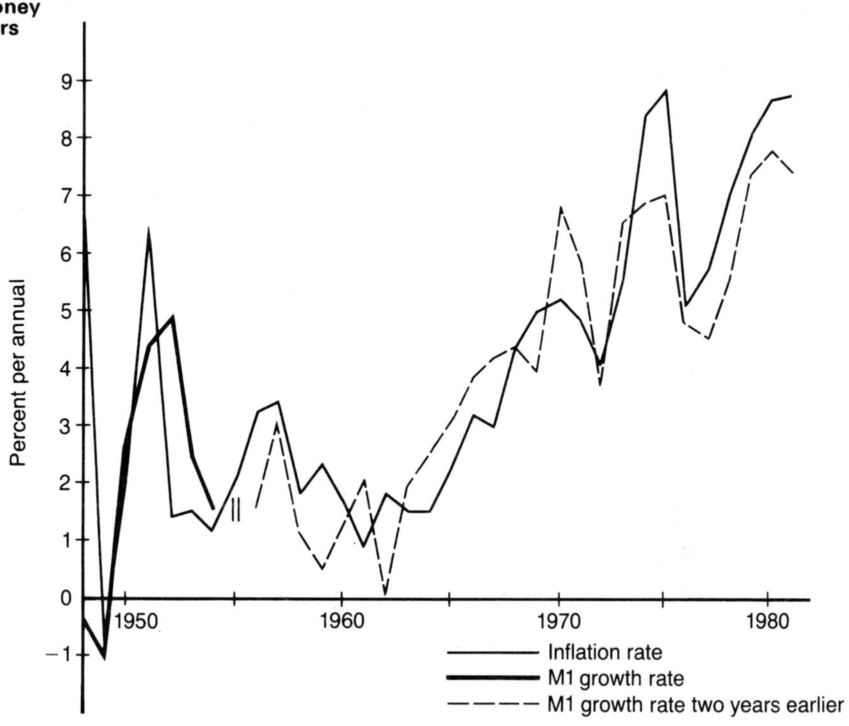

Inflation (the continuous line) is shown alongside money supply growth (the dashed line) two years earlier. There is a remarkably close relationship between these two variables, both in their trends and cycles.

the most recent strong upturn in money growth between 1970 and 1972, which was followed by an overshooting in the rate of inflation two years later (1972–1974).

There is an additional feature of the implications of Figures 13.4 and 13.5 that is very disquieting for the basic model. It arises from the fact (already established in Chapter 6) that, in two-thirds of the years of the twentieth century, movements in the inflation rate are in the opposite direction to movements in unemployment. Figures 13.4 and 13.5 show that movements in the inflation rate are closely related to movements in money supply growth. The implication from these two facts is that unemployment is also closely related (although inversely so) to money supply growth. That is, when the money supply growth rate accelerates, the unemployment rate tends to fall; and when the money supply growth rate falls, unemployment tends to rise. Although this is not revealed directly in Figures 13.4 and 13.5, by combining the relationship shown in those figures with the relationships between inflation and unemployment shown in Section E of Chapter 6, you can readily verify that in approximately two-thirds of the years of this century, the above pattern exists between changes in the growth rate of the money supply and the unemployment rate.

These facts are very awkward for the basic model because it predicts that there will be *no* relationship between the money supply and such real variables as unemployment. According to that model, variations in the quantity of money lead to movements in the aggregate demand curve, which change the price level but not the level of real economic activity. Of course, the discovery that there is a relationship between money supply growth and unemployment does not mean that variations in the money supply growth rate lead to variations in the unemployment rate. It does, however, suggest that potential linkages between those two variables might be worth investigating. This conclusion is reinforced when one realizes that the real variables, which according to the basic model are supposed to affect the unemployment rate, have been discovered (as reviewed in the preceding section) to have no ability to explain the cycles in that variable.

Variations in the money supply growth rate, then, unlike the various labor market shocks that we investigated in the previous section, do seem to have an interesting relationship with inflation as predicted by the basic model and, more than that, with variations in unemployment as well—a finding that is the opposite of what the basic model predicts.

E. What the Basic Model Does and Does Not Explain

We have now reviewed the main facts about labor market shocks and variations in the money supply growth rate in the United States. We have seen that one labor market shock is capable of explaining the postwar trend in the unemployment rate, but none of them is capable of accounting for the cycles that have been observed in unemployment and real GNP. Neither the cycles nor the trends in unemployment are clearly accounted for by changes in minimum wages, by labor union actions, or by changes in the tax wedge. However, the coverage of unemployment insurance benefits may account for the trend. In contrast to this, variations in the growth rate of the money supply are seen to provide a powerful explanation for variations in the rate of inflation. Furthermore, for much of the time, variations in the growth rate of the money supply are also closely related to variations in such real variables as real GNP and unemployment.

From this, we can conclude that the basic model provides us with some useful insights into the phenomenon of inflation, but it furnishes little help in understanding the reasons for variations in the rate of unemployment. The basic model is able to explain why unemployment exists, as well as providing some clues as to why it trended upwards in the postwar years, but the model does not seem to be capable of accounting for the cyclical variations in the rate of unemployment.

The greater volatility of economic activity before World War II, compared with more recent years, is highly related to volatility in money supply growth. The basic model explains why variations in money supply growth influence variations in the rate of inflation, but it does not explain why real economic activity also fluctuates in sympathy with fluctuations in the rate of inflation and money supply growth.

In addition to failing to explain the cycle in real economic activity, it is evident that the basic model also fails to capture the co-movements between inflation and interest rates that are observed in the data. Those co-movements displayed in Figure 6.12 (Chapter 6) evidently involve interest rates moving less than would be necessary if they were to fully reflect changes in the rate of inflation.

It is possible to summarize the main strengths and weaknesses of the basic model in the following way: The main strength of the model is that it provides a useful account of the inflationary process and explains why variations in the growth rate of the money supply lead to variations in the rate of inflation. Its second strength is that it provides a possible explanation of why unemployment exists and why it has trended upwards. Its main weakness is its failure to explain any other aspects of the business cycle. It does not account for the cyclical fluctuations in real income and unemployment, nor does it account for the failure of interest rates to fluctuate as much as inflation does.

Summary

A. The Facts

The dominant facts of U.S. macroeconomic history that the basic model seeks to understand are as follows: (1) Inflation, unemployment, and output all fluctuated much more before World War II than afterwards, and interest rate movements have been much smoother than fluctuations in these other three variables. (2) Unemployment displayed a gentle upward trend after World War II, whereas inflation displayed a downward trend in the 1950s but an upward trend in the 1960s and 1970s. (3) Unemployment and output are strongly countercyclical; inflation and unemployment move in opposite directions two-thirds of the time and in the same direction one-third of the time.

B. Predictions of the Basic Model

The basic model predicts that movements in output and unemployment will be caused by labor market shocks induced either by minimum wage laws, labor union actions, unemployment insurance programs, or other government tax changes. Inflation and interest rates will be determined by the growth rate of the money supply. Changes in the growth rate of the money supply will have no effects on the real variables—output, employment, and unemployment.

C. Labor Market Shocks

Minimum wages were introduced in 1938 and have increased in spurts over the period since then. Labor unions have never represented more than a quarter of the U.S. labor force and have, since 1953, represented a declining fraction. Unemployment insurance benefits, expressed as the fraction of earnings replaced, have been remarkably constant over the period since the late 1930s and have provided unemployed workers with a benefit rate in the neighborhood of one-third of average weekly earnings. The coverage of programs has increased dramatically, however, from less than one-third in 1938 to more than four-fifths by the late 1970s. The tax wedge has gradually increased over the postwar years but was remarkably small prior to World War II.

Only one of these labor market shocks, increased coverage of the unemployment insurance programs, seems capable of accounting for the trend observed in the rate of unemployment, and none of them seems capable of accounting for the cycles.

D. Money Supply Growth and Inflation

Variations in the growth rate of M1 have been remarkably closely related to variations in U.S. inflation. The cycles and broad trends in inflation are well-explained by cycles and trends in money supply growth. The only period when there was a marked departure between the two variables occurred during and immediately after World War II, when wartime price controls bottled up an inflation that was only allowed to unwind at the end of the war.

E. What the Basic Model Does and Does Not Explain

The basic model explains movements in the rate of inflation and explains the existence of, and postwar trend rise in, unemployment. The model does not explain the fluctuations in output and unemployment, nor the persistent tendency for inflation to be related to changes in these real variables. Further, the model does not capture the facts about the relationship between inflation and interest rates.

Review Questions

1. How well does the basic model account for the co-movements between the decade averages of inflation, unemployment, real GNP, and interest rates, as set out in Chapter 2?
2. Examine the facts about the years of the Great Depression (see Appendix to Chapter 2), and set out in detail the aspects of that period that are in line with the predictions of the basic model and those that are not.
3. Using recent issues of the *Federal Reserve Bulletin*, obtain data on money supply growth more up-to-date than that reviewed in this chapter. Using the new data on money growth, examine whether or not the basic model is capable of explaining what has happened to inflation in the United States since the end of 1978 up to the present time.
4. Try to think of labor market shocks other than those analyzed in this chapter that could account for the continuing trend increase in unemployment through the 1970s. How might you go about testing whether or not such factors were important?
5. Why does it seem as if minimum wages in the United States have not had a major impact on aggregate unemployment?
6. What is the main reason for concluding that unemployment insurance programs probably have led to a rise in the rate of unemployment in the postwar years?
7. What is the single most devastating failure of the basic model?

14

Introduction to the Keynesian Model

You have studied the basic model of output, employment, and the price level and have discovered that there is a good deal in our macroeconomic history that the model is capable of explaining. You also know, however, that the basic model has some serious shortcomings. It cannot explain several features of the business cycle. Nor can it account for the long and deep depression that the United States and the rest of the world suffered throughout the entire decade of the 1930s.

You are now going to embark upon the study of an important modification to the basic model. When you see the major feature of that modification in the next chapter, you will think it very trivial. In a sense, it is a trivial modification. It does, however, have radical implications, both for our understanding of macroeconomic phenomena and for the design and conduct of macroeconomic policy. The modification to the basic model that you are about to study is one suggested by John Maynard Keynes in the middle 1930s.

The implications of Keynes's modification of the basic model are so radical, in fact, that it is worthwhile giving the resulting model a name of its own. We shall call it the *Keynesian model.*

You have just two tasks in this short chapter, which are to:

(a) Know why you are studying the Keynesian model.
(b) Know the main strengths and weaknesses of the Keynesian model.

A. Why Study the Keynesian Model

There are three main reasons why you are studying the Keynesian model. First, it is the model that has, more than any other, shaped the thinking and understanding about macroeconomic phenomena of several generations of economists and policy makers, and more important, it is the model that has shaped the views of many of those who are in positions of authority and power today. Keynes's revolutionary ideas were published in 1936 in his book *The General Theory of Employment, Interest and Money.* In the closing paragraph of that book (pp. 383–84) Keynes wrote:

> The ideas of economists and political philosophers, both when they are right and when they are wrong, are more powerful than is commonly understood. Indeed the world is ruled by little else. Practical men, who believe themselves to be quite exempt from any intellectual influences, are usually the slaves of some defunct economist. Mad men in authority, who hear voices in the air, are distilling their frenzy from some academic scribbler of a few years back. I am sure that the power of vested interests is vastly exaggerated compared with the gradual encroachment of ideas. Not, indeed, immediately, but after a certain interval; for in the field of economic and political philosophy there are not many who are influenced by new theories after they are 25 or 30 years of age, so that the ideas which civil servants and politicans and even agitators apply to current events are not likely to be the newest. But, sooner or later, it is ideas, not vested interests, which are dangerous for good or evil.[1]

As you see from this passage, Keynes was not just a brilliant economist but also an incredibly perceptive observer of the human condition in the broadest sense. Keynes was writing in 1936 of the ideas held by politicans and civil servants at that time. He would have been the last to be surprised that his own ideas, radical and revolutionary though they were in 1936, were regarded by the leading economists of today in the same way as he regarded the ideas of his precursors. Nevertheless, the very fact that the ideas of Keynes are so pervasively believed in today and so widely used as the justification for much current economic policy making requires that you, as a student of modern macroeconomics, understand that body of knowledge and understand its major strengths and weaknesses. This then, is the first and perhaps most important reason why you are embarking upon a study of what is, in many ways, an outdated way of looking at macroeconomics.

The second reason for studying the Keynesian model is that it remains the only, even if rudimentary, explanation that we have for the event known as the Great Depression. The persistence, for more than a decade, of unemployment rates in excess of 10 percent with little tendency for prices to fall remains a challenge to those who seek a rational explanation for economic phenomena. Keynes did not offer a rational explanation of that phenomenon. It remains a task for a future generation of students of economics. Nevertheless, Keynes does provide us with an explanation that, rudimentary and unsatisfactory though it may be, is the only one available. Even though Keynes's explanation for the Great Depression is not a satisfactory one, by understanding that explanation you will be better able to understand the current research challenge that remains ahead of us.

The third reason for studying the Keynesian model is that, in the process of attempting to explain the phenomenon of the Great Depression, Keynes made some innovations in macroeconomics that have stood the test of time and remain a useful part of modern macroeconomics. This is the area of generalizing the theory of aggregate demand. In this area, Keynes made inno-

[1] John Maynard Keynes, *The General Theory of Employment, Interest and Money* (London: Macmillan & Co., Ltd., 1936)

vations that are today almost universally accepted by economists of all schools of thought and shades of opinion. Part of the Keynesian model is therefore a central ingredient in mainstream modern macroeconomics.

B. Strengths and Weaknesses of the Keynesian Model

The main strength of the Keynesian model is that is provides an explanation (although unsatisfactory) of the phenomenon of the Great Depression. This phenomenon of high and persistent unemployment with rather stable prices is hard to explain with the basic model. The main strength of the Keynesian model is that it does provide an internally consistent rationalization for the Great Depression.

The major weakness of the Keynesian model is that the explanation of the Great Depression that it provides seems to involve irrational behavior. That is, it seems to involve behavior that is inconsistent with profit and utility maximization on the part of firms and individuals. Modern Keynesians (new Keynesians) seek to show that although the Keynesian model in fact *appears* to involve irrational behavior, it actually does not. You will be given a brief account of some of this work in Part V of the book, when the new macroeconomics is developed.

Summary

A. Why Study the Keynesian Model

You are studying the Keynesian model for three reasons:

1. It is the model that governs the thinking of those in positions of authority and power today and is the basis of most current macroeconomic policy making.
2. It provides the only available, if rudimentary, explanation of the phenomenon of the Great Depression.
3. It contains some modifications to the basic theory of aggregate demand that have been absorbed into the mainstream body of macroeconomics.

B. Strengths and Weaknesses of the Keynesian Model

The main strength of the Keynesian model is that it provides a rudimentary explanation for the Great Depression.

The main weakness of the Keynesian model is that the explanation of the Great Depression that it provides seems to be inconsistent with the notion that individuals and firms seek to maximize utility and profits.

Review Questions

1. What are the three main reasons for studying the Keynesian model?

2. Examine the facts about unemployment, output, and inflation in the years of the Great Depression (1930–1933) set out in the Appendix to Chapter 2 and contrast those facts with the predictions of the basic model.

3. One of the outstanding difficult tasks for economists is to find an explanation of the Great Depression that does *not* involve assuming that people behave irrationally—that they do not maximize profits and utility. Why do we regard explanations that involve assuming irrational behavior as unsatisfactory?

15

The Keynesian Theory of Aggregate Supply

The objective of this chapter is to enable you to understand the Keynesian theory of aggregate supply. You have four detailed tasks. They are to:

(a) Know Keynes's modification of the basic model's theory of aggregate supply.
(b) Understand the nature of the Keynesian aggregate supply curve.
(c) Know how to derive the Keynesian aggregate supply curve.
(d) Understand the approximate Keynesian aggregate supply curve—the inverse "L."

A. Keynes's Modification of the Basic Model

If your memory of the analysis in Chapter 8 on aggregate supply and the labor market is not fresh, you will perhaps find it helpful before going any further to review the material in that chapter. It is possible to illustrate Keynes's major modification of the basic model by recalling the labor market equilibrium of the basic model. Figure 8.6 illustrated that equilibrium, and it is reproduced in Figure 15.1.

You will recall that the real wage is measured on the vertical axis of the diagram, and the number of people employed is measured on the horizontal axis. The curve labelled n^d represents the demand for labor that will be forthcoming from profit-maximizing firms. In order to achieve a maximum profit, firms hire labor up to the point at which the real wage is equal to the marginal product of labor. This curve is downward sloping, reflecting diminishing marginal product of labor. The upward sloping curve, labelled n^s, represents the supply of labor that will be forthcoming from utility-maximizing households. To induce more people to work (that is, to induce more people to consume less leisure), a higher real wage has to be offered. The labor market of the basic model achieves an equilibrium at the real wage $(W/P)^*$ and n^*. At that real wage, the demands for labor by firms and the supplies of labor by households

Figure 15.1
The Labor Market in the Keynesian Model

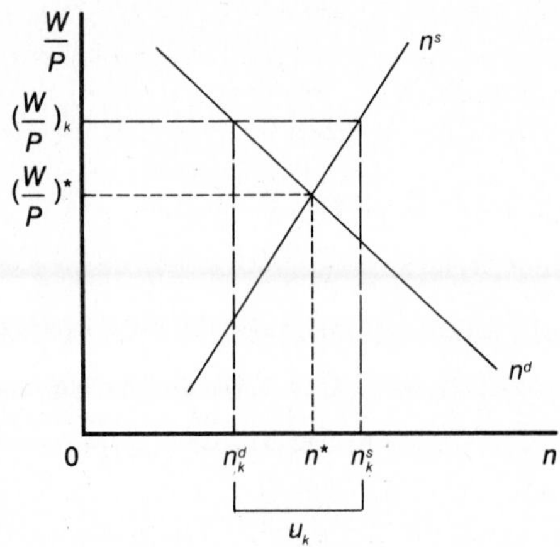

The money wage rate will rise quickly to achieve an equilibrium in the labor market if the quantity of labor demanded exceeds the quantity supplied. When, however, the quantity of labor demanded is less than the quantity of labor supplied, the money wage rate does not fall—it is rigid in a downward direction. This means that the real wage can become stuck at a level like $(W/P)_k$, so that there is an excess supply of labor and unemployment u_k.

are exactly balanced, and no forces are at work to make either households or firms want to change the situation.

Keynes's modification of the basic model is to deny that the labor market always achieves an equilibrium at the point at which the demand for labor equals the supply of labor. For Keynes, the equilibrium represented in Figure 15.1 as the real wage $(W/P)^*$ and the level of employment n^* is just a special case.

Keynes dropped the assumption of the basic model that the real wage adjusts quickly to achieve a labor market equilibrium in which the quantity of labor supplied equals the quantity demanded. In place of that assumption, Keynes introduced a far-reaching modification. Keynes's modification is that the money wage rate will *rise* quickly to achieve an equilibrium in the labor market if the quantity of labor demanded exceeds the quantity of labor supplied. When, however, the quantity of labor demanded is less than the quantity of labor supplied, the money wage rate will not fall quickly. Indeed, Keynes made the stronger assumption that *the money wage rate is rigid in a downward direction.*

You can think of this as meaning that the money wage rate behaves a bit like a ratchet. It will move in one direction but not in the other. Excess demands for labor will never be observed because the money wage rate will always rise quickly enough to achieve equality between the quantity of labor supplied and the quantity demanded. Excess supplies of labor, however, will be observed, and they will arise in situations in which the real wage is too high. And they will persist as long as the real wage stays too high. Since, by Keynes's assumption, the money wage rate will not fall, a situation of excess supply of labor can only be cured by a fall in the real wage being brought about by a rise in the price level.[1]

The above remarks can be illustrated with the help of Figure 15.1. The basic model solution is shown in Figure 15.1 as n^* and $(W/P)^*$. Now imagine that because the money wage rate is downwardly rigid, the real wage is stuck at $(W/P)_k$ as shown in the figure. At this real wage rate, n_k^d workers will be demanded by firms. The quantity of labor that households want to supply at that real wage is shown as n_k^s. Evidently, the quantity of labor supplied exceeds the quantity demanded. Since trade is voluntary, firms cannot be forced to hire more workers than they wish to hire, and the quantity of labor actually employed will equal the quantity of labor demanded. The difference between the quantity of labor supplied and the quantity demanded will be the quantity of labor that is involuntarily unemployed. This is shown in the diagram as u_k. This is Keynesian unemployment.

Keynesian unemployment is different from the type of unemployment that you met in Chapter 11. It is a consequence of the assumption that the money wage rate will not move downwards in order to clear the labor market. In contrast to this, in the basic model, the money wage rate was assumed to have unlimited flexibility in both directions so as always to achieve an equality of supply and demand in the labor market. Unemployment arose in that model as a result of utility-maximizing withdrawals from work in order to undertake job search or as the result of government- or union-imposed real wage rigidities.

The situation depicted in Figure 15.1 as $(W/P)_k$ and n_k^d is just one of the possible Keynesian unemployment positions. The higher the real wage, the lower will be the demand for labor and the higher the supply of labor. The lower, therefore, would be the level of employment, and the higher the level of unemployment.

According to Keynes's theory, the real wage can never be lower than $(W/P)^*$. If it momentarily was below $(W/P)^*$, the money wage would rise quickly to restore the real wage to $(W/P)^*$, thereby choking off any excess demand for labor.

B. The Keynesian Aggregate Supply Curve

Recall the definition of the aggregate supply curve given in Chapter 8. The aggregate supply curve shows the amount of output that the economy will supply at each different price level. In the basic model, the aggregate supply curve embodies the profit-maximizing decisions of producers and the utility-maximizing decisions of households. When drawn in a diagram with the price level on the vertical axis and output on the horizontal axis, the basic model's

[1] A thorough working out of the implications of the assumption of wage rigidity has been provided by Robert W. Clower in his essay, "The Keynesian Counter-Revolution: A Theoretical Appraisal," in F. Hahn and F. Brechling, eds., *The Theory of Interest Rates* (London: Macmillan & Co. Ltd., 1965) and by Herschel I. Grossman and Robert J. Barro in *Money, Employment and Inflation* (Cambridge, England: Cambridge University Press, 1976).

aggregate supply curve is simply a vertical line at the output level that is associated with the quantity of labor employed being equal to the quantity of labor demanded *and* supplied.

The Keynesian aggregate supply curve, like the basic model aggregate supply curve, is the amount of output that the economy will supply at each different price level. It is, however, importantly different from that in the basic model. The Keynesian aggregate supply curve, like that of the basic model, recognizes that output will not be supplied in excess of that capable of being produced by profit-maximizing firms. Because, however, the labor market does not necessarily achieve an equilibrium between the quantity of labor supplied and demanded, the utility-maximizing decisions of households do not, except in the special case of full employment, affect the amount of output that will be supplied. The only thing that matters for the Keynesian aggregate supply curve is the profit-maximizing decisions of firms.

C. How to Derive the Keynesian Aggregate Supply Curve

The Keynesian aggregate supply curve may be derived in a manner quite similar to that used to derive the aggregate supply curve of the basic model. The four-quadrant diagram illustrated in Figure 15.2 provides the basis for derivation.

First, focus on frame (a), in which the Keynesian labor market is illustrated. The demand for labor is shown by the curve n^d. The supply of labor curve is shown with the broken line n^s. This curve has been drawn with breaks to remind you that the supply curve of labor does not, except at the special point of full employment, determine the real wage in the Keynesian analysis. As a reference point, however, let us first focus on the full-employment equilibrium case. If the labor market is cleared (as it is in the basic model), then the quantity of employment will be n^* and the real wage will be $(W/P)^*$. (For the moment, ignore the subscript numbers on W and P. They come into the story below.)

Now, focus on frame (b). It displays the short-run production function that tells us how much output will be supplied at each level of employment. By transferring the equilibrium quantity of employment n^* from the horizontal axis of frame (a) to the same axis of frame (b), you may read off from the aggregate production function the quantity of output that will be supplied at full employment. That quantity is shown on the vertical axis of frame (b) as y^*.

So far, you have used Figure 15.2 simply to do an exercise that is identical to the one that you did with Figure 8.7 in Chapter 8. That is, you have discovered that at full-employment equilibrium, the level of employment is n^*, and the level of output that will be produced is y^*. It is now possible to obtain a single point on the Keynesian aggregate supply curve. To do this, focus on frame (c). Define the price level to be equal to 1. Then, with the price level equal to 1 and with the quantity of labor employed n^* and output y^*, the point A is obtained as a point on the aggregate supply curve. That is, with a price level of 1 and with an equilibrium real wage, the quantity of output supplied is equal to y^*. Define the money wage rate in the economy also as 1.

Figure 15.2
The Derivation of the Keynesian Aggregate Supply Curve

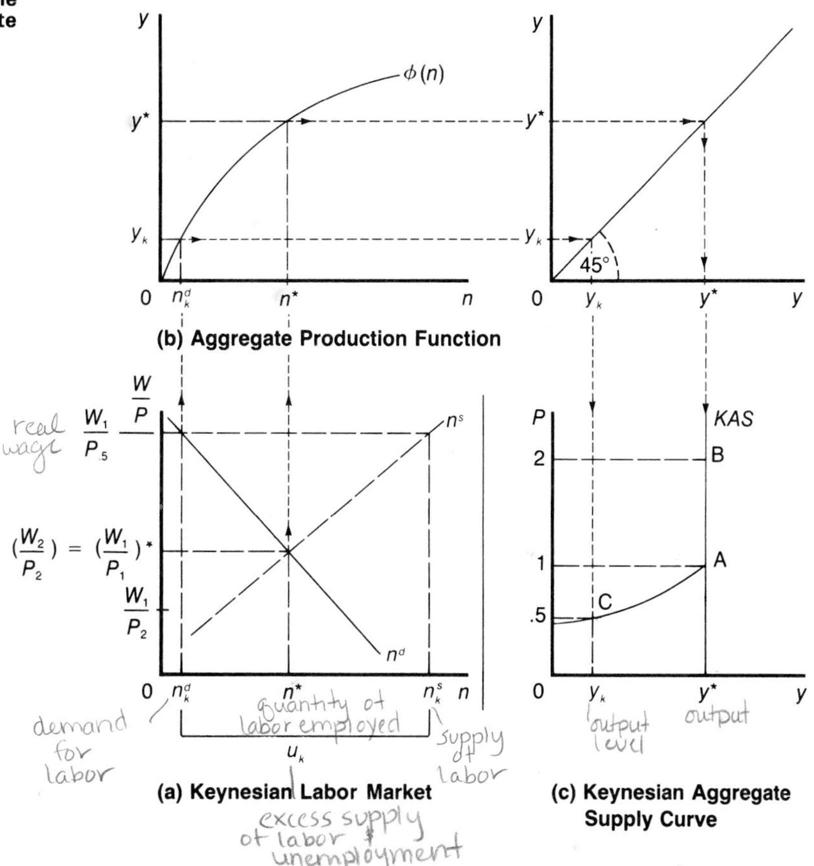

This figure is similar to Figure 8.7 (Chapter 8). If the real wage is $(W/P)^*$, then the employment level will be n^* and output y^*. The money wage rate is downwardly rigid but flexible upwards. By setting things up so that when the price level is 1, the real wage is at its full-employment equilibrium level, the Keynesian aggregate supply curve may be derived. At price levels higher than 1, the money wage rate is dragged up, with the price level maintaining full-employment equilibrium, so that output remains at y^*. At price levels below 1, the real wage rises, and the level of employment declines (following the demand for labor curve). For example, at a price level of 0.5, the real wage is $W_1/P_{0.5}$, and the level of employment is n^d_k. The output level is y_k. The curve *CAB* traces the Keynesian aggregate supply curve (*KAS*).

The equilibrium real wage, therefore, is equal to (W_1/P_1). This is equal to $(W/P)^*$, the equilibrium real wage.

Now imagine that the price level doubles to 2. This is shown on the vertical axis of frame (c). Also imagine, for the moment, that the money wage rate is held rigid at 1. This means that the real wage will halve to W_1/P_2 as shown in frame (a). At that low real wage, there will be an excess demand for labor. You can read this off the diagram in frame (a) by noting that at the real wage W_1/P_2, the quantity of labor demanded exceeds the quantity of labor supplied. By the assumptions discussed in the first section of this chapter, a situation in which there is a bigger demand for labor than supply will quickly lead to a rise in the money wage rate. The situation in which the real wage is equal to W_1/P_2 could only be temporary and would quickly disappear. It would disappear because the money wage rate would rise and would continue rising until the excess demand for labor had been eliminated.

You can easily work out the required rise in the money wage rate. You know from the initial assumption that the price level has doubled from 1 to 2. The only way the economy can get back to a situation in which there is no excess demand for labor is for the money wage rate also to double. The Keynesian theory predicts that this will happen and that the real wage will be restored to $(W/P)^*$, with the money wage rate rising to 2, so that the equilibrium real wage is given by W_2/P_2, which of course, equals W_1/P_1, and which in turn equals $(W/P)^*$.

As a result of the analysis just performed, it is now possible to find another point on the Keynesian aggregate supply curve. You have just discovered that if the price level doubles, the money wage rate also doubles, and the real wage remains constant. Not only does the real wage remain constant, but so do the levels of employment and output. They remain at n^* and y^*, respectively. The point B in frame (c) is therefore another point on the Keynesian aggregate supply curve. Further, all the points between A and B joined together by the vertical continuous line are points on the Keynesian aggregate supply curve. Indeed, over the range AB (and at price levels above 2—i.e., at points above B), the Keynesian aggregate supply curve is identical to the aggregate supply curve of the basic model.

Next, consider the opposite experiment. Imagine that instead of rising to twice its initial value, the price level fell to one-half that initial value. (This is a fairly unlikely thing to actually happen, but by imagining an extreme shock, we see more clearly the implications of a smaller, more likely one.) What would then happen in the Keynesian model? The first step toward the answer is contained in frame (a). If the price level halves, with the wage rate stuck at 1, the real wage would rise to $W_1/P_{0.5}$, as shown on the vertical axis of frame (a). The quantity of labor demanded at this higher real wage would be n_k^d, which, of course, is less than n^*. In the basic model, with the demand for labor being less than the supply of labor, there would be downward pressure on the wage rate. We are, however, now using the Keynesian assumption that the money wage rate does not fall. The economy would, therefore, be stuck with a real wage that was too high, and the employment level would remain at n_k^d. The amount of output that would be produced at the level of employment n_k^d is obtained by travelling up to frame (b) and reading off from the vertical axis of that frame the quantity of output that n_k^d can produce. The quantity is shown as y_k. The quantity y_k may now be transferred (through the 45° line in the top right) to frame (c), so that the point C is arrived at. Point C is the point at which the price level is 0.5 and the level of output is y_k.

You might find it helpful to your understanding to trace out another point or two and satisfy yourself that you can follow the analysis that led up to point C. For example, put in a price level of 0.25 and then work out the quantity of output that would be supplied at that price level. Also, put in a price level of 0.75 and work out what the level of output is in that case. You will discover that the output levels achieved trace out a line similar to the continuous upward sloping line shown in frame (c).

The continuous line that slopes upwards through point C to point A and then becomes vertical above A labelled *KAS*, is the Keynesian aggregate supply curve. It says that because the money wage rate is stuck at a point below which it will not move, at very low price levels the real wage is so high that the firms are unwilling to hire as many workers as are available for work. The output that firms are willing to produce is, therefore, less than the full-employment quantity of output. As the price level rises, the real wage falls, and the quantity of labor demanded rises. As the quantity of labor demanded rises, the quantity of output produced rises. This process can go on until the quantity of labor demanded is equal to the quantity supplied. This happens when the real wage has fallen to $(W/P)^*$ and the level of output has risen to y^*. If the price level rises beyond that level, the money wage rate also will rise in sympathy with it, maintaining the equilibrium real wage $(W/P)^*$ and therefore leading the economy to produce the full-employment quantity of output y^*, regardless of how high the price level goes.

At all output levels below y^* there is unemployment. This is illustrated for the price level of 0.5 and the output level y_k in frame (a). At a price level of 0.5 with the real wage $W_1/P_{0.5}$, the quantity of labor supplied is n_k^s, which exceeds the quantity demanded by the amount shown as u_k.

D. Approximate Keynesian Aggregate Supply Curve—the Inverse "L"

There is a useful approximation to the Keynesian aggregate supply curve. It is an approximation that considerably simplifies the analysis of the determination of output and employment in the Keynesian model. It is also an approximation that is not violently at odds with the Keynesian story. That approximation is shown in Figure 15.3. It is an aggregate supply curve that is

Figure 15.3
The Inverse "L" Aggregate Supply Curve

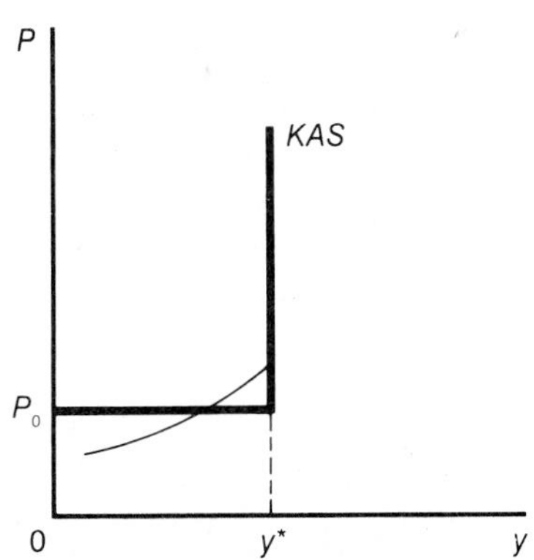

An approximation to the Keynesian aggregate supply curve is the inverse "L." This implies that the price level itself is downwardly rigid (at P_0), but that, at full-employment output (y^*), any higher price level is possible.

Figure 15.4
Output Determined by Aggregate Demand in the Keynesian Model

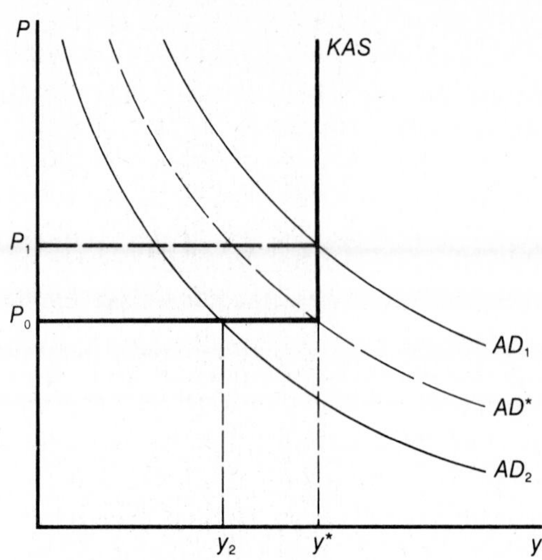

At full employment, the Keynesian model behaves exactly like the basic model. Aggregate demand AD_1 cuts the vertical part of the aggregate supply curve to determine the price level, P_1. If aggregate demand is below the critical curve AD^*, for example at AD_2, then it is the position of the aggregate demand curve alone that determines the level of output and employment, such as the level y_2 where the aggregate demand curve AD_2 cuts the inverse "L" aggregate supply curve.

horizontal at the price level P_0 for all output below y^*, and at y^*, it becomes the vertical aggregate supply curve of the basic model. This is the inverse "L" approximation to the Keynesian aggregate supply curve. It says that, as an approximation, we may think of the price level as being downwardly rigid, so that it will not fall below P_0.

It is an important implication of the Keynesian theory of aggregate supply that at full employment, aggregate demand determines the price level, but that at less than full employment, aggregate demand determines the level of output and employment. You can see this very clearly with the inverse "L" supply curve in Figure 15.3. It is approximately true with the general Keynesian aggregate supply curve as depicted in frame (c) of Figure 15.2.

If you were to draw in an aggregate demand curve (as derived in Chapter 9) in Figure 15.3, you would be able to determine the price level and the level of output as the point at which that aggregate demand curve cuts the Keynesian aggregate supply curve. This is illustrated in Figure 15.4.

The curve KAS is the inverse "L" approximation to the Keynesian aggregate supply curve. The curves AD_1 and AD_2 are aggregate demand curves of the type derived in Chapter 9. The curve AD_1 is drawn for a larger money supply than the curve AD_2. If the money supply was such that the aggregate demand curve was indeed AD_1, then the economy would be at a point depicted by the price level P_1 and the output level y^*. If, however, the money supply was the lower amount such that the aggregate demand curve was AD_2, then the economy would be stuck at the price level P_0 and with an output level equal to y_2. Fluctuations in the level of aggregate demand that did not take the aggregate demand curve as high as the dashed curve AD^* would lead to fluctuations in the level of output and leave the price level unaffected. Rises in the aggregate demand curve above AD^* would lead to rises in the price level and would leave output unchanged at y^*.

You can now see that on the horizontal part of the Keynesian aggregate supply curve, the level of aggregate demand is the all-important matter determining the level of output and employment in the economy. For this reason, the theory of aggregate demand becomes very important for understanding the forces that generate fluctuations in output and employment. Much of what Keynes went on to do in modifying the basic model had to do with the theory of aggregate demand, and these matters will be taken up in the next two chapters.

Summary

A. Keynes's Modification of the Basic Model

The major modification of the basic model suggested by Keynes was to replace the assumption that at all times the labor market achieves an equilibrium where the demand for, and supply of, labor are equal, with the assumption that the money wage rate is downwardly rigid. The money wage rate will rise to achieve an equality between supply and demand if there is an excess demand for labor. The money wage rate will not fall if there is an excess supply of labor. Instead, the economy gets stuck with a real wage that is "too high" and with a level of employment below the quantity of labor supplied. There is unemployment in such a situation.

B. The Keynesian Aggregate Supply Curve

The Keynesian aggregate supply curve, like that in the basic model, shows the maximum amount of output that firms, in the aggregate, will supply at each different price level. If the price level is high enough to ensure that the real wage is not above the full-employment real wage, the Keynesian aggregate supply curve is identical to that in the basic model. At price levels below that, however, when the real wage is "too high," the Keynesian aggregate supply curve is derived entirely from the demand for labor by profit-maximizing firms and is not influenced by households' labor supply decisions.

C. How to Derive the Keynesian Aggregate Supply Curve

The Keynesian aggregate supply curve is derived in a four-quadrant analysis that links the demand for labor by profit-maximizing firms through the production function to the quantity of output that will be supplied at each price level. Figure 15.2 illustrates the derivation and should be fully understood.

D. Approximate Keynesian Aggregate Supply Curve—the Inverse "L"

The inverse "L" approximation to the Keynesian aggregate supply curve presumes that it is the price level rather than the money wage that is downwardly rigid. This gives a horizontal segment to the aggregate supply curve at the fixed price level up to full-employment output, and then gives a vertical segment at the full-employment level of output.

The important implication of the Keynesian aggregate supply curve (made most clear in the inverse "L" approximate case) is that below full employment, the quantity of output and employment are determined by aggregate demand alone and do not in any way depend on the aggregate supply conditions since the aggregate supply curve itself is horizontal (or nearly so).

Review Questions

1. What is the modification that Keynes made to the basic model's theory of aggregate supply?
2. Suppose that an economy was at full employment and that suddenly the price level fell to one-half of its previous level. Trace out what would happen in the labor market according to the basic model and the Keynesian model.
3. Between 1929 and 1933, prices in the United States (measured by the GNP deflator) fell by 23.1 percent. Using your answer to Question 2 above and any other relevant facts in the Appendix to Chapter 2, compare the predicted effects of such a price fall in the basic and Keynesian models with the actual performance of the U.S. labor market.
4. Define the Keynesian aggregate supply curve. What happens as the economy moves along that curve? Which markets are in equilibrium? Are firms maximizing profits and households maximizing utility?
5. Why is there no difference between the Keynesian and basic theory of aggregate supply at full employment?
6. Why is the inverse "L" aggregate supply curve only an approximation to the Keynesian theory of aggregate supply?
7. Why does the Keynesian aggregate supply curve slope upwards at output levels below full employment?
8. What will cause the Keynesian aggregate supply curve to shift?
9. What is the main *implication* of the Keynesian theory of aggregate supply that distinguishes it from the basic model's theory?

16

Aggregate Demand, Consumption, and the Keynesian Cross Model

The subject matter of this and the next four chapters was, for the 20 years from the late 1950s through to the late 1970s, the heart of macroeconomics. Several generations of intermediate textbooks on the subject, many important research monographs, and literally thousands of important articles in learned journals have dealt with various aspects of the material presented here. It is the Keynesian theory of aggregate demand. You should be aware that the material presented in this book covers only the essential features of that theory. As a result of the developments in macroeconomics in the past 10 to 15 years—developments that will be explained in some detail in Part V of this book—we now have a much better perspective than ever before on the Keynesian theory of aggregate demand. It no longer stands as the whole of macroeconomics. It does not even provide the centerpiece of the explanation for macroeconomic fluctuations. That is not, however, to say that the Keynesian theory of aggregate demand is wrong. Like the basic model, there is nothing wrong with an analysis that is but one part of the complete story. The basic model, with which you are now familiar, contains some of the complete story. The Keynesian theory of aggregate demand contains more of the story. The part of the story that the Keynesian analysis contains deals with the determination of aggregate demand at a given price level.

To embark upon your study of the Keynesian theory of aggregate demand, you have five tasks, which are to:

(a) Know the components of aggregate demand.
(b) Know the theories of the consumption function proposed by Keynes, Friedman, and Modigliani.
(c) Understand the connection between wealth and income and why current income is a major determinant of consumption.
(d) Know how to represent the consumption and savings functions in simple equations and diagrams.
(e) Understand the Keynesian cross model.

First, it will be useful to know the components into which aggregate demand is divided.

A. Components of Aggregate Demand

Just as a matter of arithmetic, aggregate demand could be divided up in an infinite number of different ways. It would be possible to distinguish between the demand for beer, for pretzels, for steak, for ketchup, ..., for power stations, for nuclear submarines, and so on. For some purposes, such a detailed disaggregation of the total volume of demand in the economy is essential. For the purpose of the questions addressed in macroeconomics, however, such a detailed classification of the components of aggregate demand appears to be unnecessary. It has turned out to be useful, nevertheless, to divide aggregate demand into a small number of key components, the determination of each of which involves different considerations. Specifically, for the purpose of doing macroeconomic analysis, aggregate demand is divided into four components. They are:

1. Consumption demand
2. Investment demand
3. Government demand
4. Net foreign demand

These four components of aggregate demand are closely related to the components of aggregate expenditure dealt with in Chapter 3. [For example, see Equation (3.6.)] There are, however, two important distinctions between the components of aggregate expenditure and the components of aggregate demand. One of these distinctions will be explained now and the other reserved until we have examined the four components of aggregate demand.

One distinction between the components of aggregate expenditure and those of aggregate demand turns on the distinction between the terms *expenditure* and *demand*. *Expenditure* refers to what people have actually *spent*. *Demand* refers to what people are *planning* to spend. Expenditure is an actual *quantity*. Demand is a *schedule*—a statement about how much would be spent under certain specified conditions. Keep this distinction in mind when dealing with the theories that you will meet in this chapter and later in the book.

Let us now go on to briefly describe the four components of aggregate demand. When we have completed our description of consumption and investment demand, it will be possible to come back and emphasize another distinction between the components of aggregate demand and those of aggregate expenditure.

Consumption Demand

Consumption demand is the aggregate demand by households for goods and services to be used up for current consumption purposes. Examples of consumption demand would be the demand for beer and pretzels and for steak and ketchup. Other examples would be expenditures on vacations, travel, movies, and entertainment; rent of houses and apartments; the purchase of electricity, gas, or oil; and the purchase of haircuts, skiing lessons, etc.—indeed, any of the many thousands and thousands of activities on which we spend our income.

Investment Demand

Investment demand is distinguished from consumption demand by the fact that an *investment is the purchase of a new capital good*—defined as a new piece of equipment that is durable and that provides services over a number of years. Sometimes the services will be in the form of consumption services, and sometimes they will be in the form of production services. Both households and firms make investment expenditures. Examples of investment expenditures made by households are the purchase of a new house, a new car, a new refrigerator, or any of the other many thousands of new consumer durable goods. Examples of investment expenditures by firms are the purchase of a new steel mill, a hydroelectric generating plant, a car assembly line, a computer, or again, any of the many thousands of different types of new capital goods used in the production process.

It is important that you clearly understand the distinction between consumption and investment. *Consumption* is the purchase of goods and services for current use. *Investment* is the purchase of goods and services for current and future use. When you buy a consumption good, you buy a current flow of services. When you invest, you buy a capital good that is a stock of equipment that gives rise to a current and future flow of either production or consumption services.

It is also important to distinguish clearly between the term investment in the sense in which economists use it when doing macroeconomic analysis and the way in which the term is used in everyday speech. In everyday usage, investment often means the purchase of a stock or a share or a bond. That is not investment in macroeconomic analysis. Such an activity is a portfolio reallocation and has very different causes and consequences from the purchase of newly produced capital equipment.

Before going on to deal with the other components of aggregate demand, let us also notice a further distinction between the components of aggregate demand and the components of aggregate expenditure set out in Chapter 3. We are here distinguishing between consumption and investment in terms of the *durability* of the goods purchased. Consumption is the purchase of goods and services that are going to be used up in the current period regardless of whether they are bought by households or by firms. Investment is the purchase of goods that are more durable than a single period and that will provide either productive or consumption services into the future.

In Chapter 3, we did not make that distinction. Rather, we talked of consumers' expenditure as being the purchase of all goods and services by households regardless of whether they were durable or not, and we referred to investment as the purchases of capital equipment by firms only. There are two reasons why Chapter 3 used the definitions that it did. First, that is the way the National Income Accounts are put together. Second, the flow diagrams used in that chapter would have been more cumbersome if we had allowed both households and firms to invest in capital equipment. (You may find it beneficial to go back to Chapter 3 and develop for yourself some flow charts that take into account this additional investment activity.) Now that we are about to embark upon an analysis of the determination of the demand for consumer and capital goods, it becomes necessary to be more careful in distinguishing between the demand for consumption services and the demand for capital goods.

Let us now go on to consider the remaining two components of aggregate demand.

Government Demand

The third component of aggregate demand is government expenditure on goods and services. Much of government expenditure represents the demands by the government for goods and services produced by the private sector of the economy. Examples of the demand by the government for goods and services produced by the private sector are the demand for a nuclear submarine, for a highway, for a new administrative building, or for paper clips and paper. Notice that the examples just given include both capital and consumption goods. No distinction is made between what might be termed government investment demand (nuclear submarines, highways, and buildings) and what might be termed government consumption demand (paper clips and paper).

For the purpose of macroeconomic analysis, there is no advantage to be gained from dividing government expenditure into its investment and consumption components. Indeed, such a decision is, to a large extent, arbitrary. For example, two of the big items of expenditure by the government, health and education expenditure, could be regarded as either consumption or investment. They are consumption in the sense that they provide an immediate flow of services—of good health and knowledge. They are also interpretable as investment expenditures because a healthy and educated person has an asset—human capital—which is capable of generating an income stream not just at the present but in the future as well. For some purposes it is crucial to be able to correctly distinguish the investment component from the consumption component of government expenditure. For present purposes, however, there is no gain from pursuing that distinction.

In addition to buying goods and services produced by the private sector, the government also demands goods and services that it supplies itself. Examples are administrative services, police and law-enforcement services, and military services. In its undertaking of these activities, you may think of the government as being like a firm. It hires labor from households (soldiers, sailors, bureaucrats, judges, and so on) and produces goods and services—goods and services that it uses itself.

Government expenditure on goods and services is treated as being exogenous. That is, the quantity of government expenditure on goods and services is treated as something that it is not our task to explain and that can be determined by the government at whatever level the government so chooses, independently of the values of any of the other variables in our macroeconomic model.[1]

---

[1] As a matter of fact, in some very elaborate statistical models of the economy, government expenditures on goods and services are broken into two parts, those that are exogenous and those that respond to the state of the economy. Such a dichotomization of government expenditure is important for some purposes, but is not essential to the task upon which you are currently embarked.

Much of government expenditure in the modern world is excluded from the above definition of government demand. For example, government Social Security expenditures on pensions and welfare programs, and subsidies to various industries, although vast in volume, do not represent government expenditures on goods and services. Rather, they represent transfers of money—of purchasing power—from the government to private individuals and firms. These expenditures are called *transfer payments.* Their effects on aggregate demand are analyzed by examining their effects on private consumption and investment demand. They are not ignored, therefore, but they are not treated as direct demands for goods and services by the government.

Net Foreign Demand

Net foreign demand for goods and services is the difference between exports and imports. Foreigners place demands on the domestic economy by demanding those goods and services that are exported from the domestic economy. Residents of the domestic economy place demands on the rest of the world, and these are measured by the quantity of imports of goods and services. The difference between these two magnitudes represents net foreign demand. For the purposes of what follows, it will be assumed that net foreign demand is always exactly zero. This, of course, does not correspond with the facts. But by making the assumption, it turns out to be possible to considerably simplify the task of understanding the main elements of the Keynesian theory of aggregate demand. In the final part of this book, attention will be paid specifically to the determination of international trade as well as international investment flows.

Aggregate demand has been divided into four components—consumption, investment, government, and net foreign demand for goods and services. The last item is being ignored for the present, and government demand is being treated as exogenous and, therefore, does not have to be explained. The other two items, however, do need explanation. The rest of this chapter deals with the determinants of consumption demand, and the next chapter, with investment.

B. Theories of the Consumption Function Proposed by Keynes, Friedman, and Modigliani

In his analysis of the determination of aggregate demand, the so-called theory of the consumption function was regarded by Keynes as the centerpiece of his new theory of income and employment. We now suspect that Keynes had an exaggerated opinion of the importance of this innovation. It is, nevertheless, an important ingredient in the theory of aggregate demand.

Keynes's Theory of the Consumption Function

Keynes's theory of the determinants of consumption was that of the many possible factors that influence the level of consumption demand, the most important is the level of real disposable income.[2] By real disposable income is

[2]Keynes set out his theory of the consumption function in Chapters 8 and 9 of *The General Theory of Employment, Interest and Money* (London: Macmillan & Co. Ltd., 1936). The two quotations in this paragraph are taken from p. 96 of this source.

meant real income (real GNP), minus the real value of taxes levied by the government. The way in which consumption demand is influenced by real disposable income is, according to Keynes, based on what he called "the fundamental psychological law upon which we are entitled to depend with great confidence." That law, Keynes went on to outline, is the proposition "that men are disposed, as a rule and on the average, to increase their consumption as their income increases, but not by as much as the increase in their income." What Keynes is saying is that consumption depends on income such that, for a given rise in income, consumption will rise by some fraction of the rise in income.

Following the first statement of Keynes's consumption function hypothesis, a great deal of statistical work was undertaken that sought to test Keynes's theory with the newly available national income accounting data. It was discovered, as a result of this work, that although Keynes's basic ideas seemed well-founded, there was an important difference in the relationship between consumption and income in the short run (year by year) as compared with the long run (decade by decade). The long-run data revealed that consumption was proportional to income. The short-run data revealed that although consumption and income move in the same direction, the relationship between the two is nonproportional. Furthermore, when individual consumption and income data were examined, it was discovered that although people with higher incomes consumed more, the variations in consumption were much smaller in proportionate terms than the variations in income. Also, these individual variations in income and consumption were less than those observed for variations in aggregate income and consumption over time.

These puzzles and problems revealed by the data led to a more refined formulation of the theory of the consumption function. The two leading architects of the refining were Milton Friedman, who developed the permanent income hypothesis,[3] and Franco Modigliani, who developed the life-cycle hypothesis.[4] These two contributions have more similarities than differences and hark back to the work of one of the greatest pre-Keynesian economists, Irving Fisher. They can be conveniently summarized by treating them as if they are a single theory.

Friedman's and Modigliani's Theory of the Consumption Function

Friedman and Modigliani reasoned as follows. If people can borrow and lend freely through financial institutions, then their consumption in any one particular period will not be constrained by their income in that particular period. If for some reason income is *temporarily* high, it will be possible to save a larger than normal fraction of that temporarily high income, so that consumption

---

[3]Milton Friedman, *A Theory of the Consumption Function* (Princeton, N.J.: Princeton University Press, 1957).

[4]Franco Modigliani gave a useful and comprehensive appraisal of his work in his paper "The Life-Cycle Hypothesis of Saving Twenty-Five Years Later," in Michael Parkin and A. R. Nobay, eds., *Contemporary Issues in Economics* (Manchester, England: Manchester University Press, 1975), pp. 2–36. This paper also contains a fairly comprehensive bibliography on the consumption function.

would be a low fraction of income. If, in some other year, income was temporarily low, it would be possible to consume the whole of income and perhaps also to consume some previous savings (or, if previous savings were inadequate, to borrow against future income).

Recognizing the possibility of breaking the direct link between income and consumption through borrowing and lending, Modigliani and Friedman suggested that the ultimate constraint upon how much consumption an individual can undertake is the amount of that individual's wealth. They proposed the hypothesis that the wealthier an individual is, on the average, the more that individual will consume. In Modigliani's version of the theory (called the *life-cycle* hypothesis), the individual would attempt to smooth out the path of consumption over the life span, even though income received would vary from year to year. In Friedman's version of the theory (called the *permanent income* hypothesis), families are assumed to live forever and seek to smooth consumption both over the lifetimes of individual family members and across the generations.

Upon careful investigation of the data, it turns out that both the *permanent income* hypothesis and the *life-cycle hypothesis,* which say that consumption depends on wealth, are theories that fit the facts better than the Keynesian hypothesis that consumption depends primarily on disposable income.

C. Connection Between Wealth and Income and Why Current Income is a Major Determinant of Consumption

Wealth and income are related to each other in a simple way. As you already know, wealth is a stock, and income is a flow. The relationship between income and wealth can be put in terms of stocks and flows. Income is the flow that is generated by the stock of wealth.

You have already seen in Chapters 3 and 4 how the main macroeconomic flows and stocks are defined and measured. You are now going to be able to deepen your understanding of the relationship between these stocks and flows. The easiest way to see the connection is in the case of a financial asset. Suppose that you own a savings deposit in a bank that has a value of $1000 and pays interest at the rate of 5 percent per annum. (Think of this rate of interest as the real rate of interest and check back to Chapter 9 if you are not sure of the meaning of that.) Evidently, if you have a deposit of $1000 yielding a rate of return of 5 percent per annum, you will receive an income from that deposit of $50 per annum. The deposit of $1000 is a *stock* and is part of your *wealth.* The income of $50 per annum is a *flow* and is part of your *income.* The rate of interest is what converts the stock of wealth into the flow of income. We could write an equation to describe this, which would read as follows:

$$\text{Wealth} \times \text{Interest rate} = \text{Income}$$

This same type of relationship holds between *all* forms of wealth and all forms of income. For example, the stocks of physical assets held—plant and equipment—and their rate of return generate an income. Also, the stock of human capital (see Chapter 4) and its rate of return generate a labor income. That is,

$$\text{Human wealth} \times \text{Interest rate} = \text{Labor income}$$

Of course, financial assets are traded in markets and pay an explicit rate of interest. Human wealth is unlike other forms of wealth in that it does not (at least in societies that do not have slavery) trade directly in markets. Nevertheless, conceptually the relationship between human wealth and labor income is identical to that between other forms of wealth and the income stream that they generate.

If we were to add up all the forms of wealth owned by an individual, the individual's total wealth would be obtained. The rate of return on that total wealth would generate the individual's total income.

The concept of *permanent income*, which gives the name to Milton Friedman's theory of the consumption function, can now be understood. It is the level of income that would be sustained on the average through the infinite future, while maintaining a constant stock of wealth. It could be thought of as the stock of wealth multiplied by the normal long-run average real rate of return. Actual income will fluctuate from year to year as a result of random fluctuations in the actual rate of return.

So far we have talked about how to convert wealth into income. We do this by multiplying the relevant wealth stock by a rate of return. We could equivalently convert a future stream of income into its equivalent current stock of wealth. In performing such a calculation it is important to notice that the value today (today's wealth) of $1 of income earned in the future depends on how far in the future that income is earned. One dollar earned in the next 5 minutes is worth much more than $1 earned in the last 5 minutes of your life. The reason for this is easy to see. One dollar earned in the next 5 minutes could be used to buy an interest-bearing security that would lead to the accumulation of more dollars in the future from interest receipts. One dollar earned 50 years in the future would be worth less than $1 earned in the next 5 minutes simply because it would be incapable of earning interest for you over the next 50 years. To calculate the wealth equivalent of future income, the future income stream has to be converted to a common valuation basis.

The most useful common valuation basis is known as the *present value*. The present value of a future sum of money is simply the sum of money that, if you were to receive it today, would, when invested at the average rate of interest, accumulate to the prestated future value. For example, if the rate of interest is 10 percent, $100 invested today would accumulate in 1 year to $110. It would be said, therefore, that the present value of $110 to be received 1 year hence, at a 10 percent rate of interest, is equal to $100. The sum of $100 invested today at a rate of interest of 10 percent for 2 years would, at the end of that period, accumulate to $121—$10 interest in the first year accumulating to $110, plus $11 in the second year ($10 interest on the principal and $1 interest on the $10 of interest earned in the first year). It would be said, therefore, that the present value of $121 to be received 2 years hence, at a 10 percent rate of interest, is equal to $100.

It is important that you recognize the distinction between real and nominal or market interest rates when performing present value calculations. The purpose in calculating a present value is not simply to cancel out the effects of inflation. It would be necessary to calculate a present value even in a world in which there was no inflation.

The arithmetic example given in the preceding paragraph, where the rate of interest is 10 percent, could be thought of as applying to a world in which there is no inflation (although in such a case the rate of interest used is unrealistically high). What is being said in this example is that $110 received 1 year hence would be worth less to someone today than would $110 received today, even though one year from now it would have the same purchasing power in terms of goods as $110 would today. The reason for this is that if the individual had $110 today, it would be possible to invest the money and earn a real rate of interest so that in 1 year from now more goods than $110 worth could be bought. With constant prices and a real rate of interest of 10 percent, $100 today is the equivalent of (would be regarded by anyone as being just as good as) $110 to be delivered 1 year from today. The calculation of a present value, therefore, is a *real* calculation. It is the conversion of a real stream of future income into a present value.

If we add up the present values of the incomes that an individual will (or expects to) receive each year in the future, we arrive at a total that is the individual's wealth. That is, we arrive at a sum of money that is a present stock and that has an equivalent value to the future (discounted) income flow.

Now that you understand the connection between income and wealth, you will be aware that the life-cycle and permanent income hypotheses of consumption are, in effect, generalizations of the Keynesian theory of consumption. They both say that consumption will depend on today's disposable income and on all future (discounted) disposable income. Other things being equal, the larger that today's disposable income is, the larger wealth is, and the greater will be the level of consumption. The larger that future disposable income is, other things being equal, the larger wealth is, and the greater will be today's consumption.

There are two lines of reasoning that lead to the proposition that the most important factor determining current consumption is current disposable income. The first reason follows directly from the discussion above concerning the relationship between wealth and income. Although it is true that if borrowing and lending in free capital markets are possible, then it is wealth rather than income that is the ultimate constraint on consumption. There is nevertheless good reason for elevating the level of current disposable income to a more important status than wealth.

As you saw above, wealth can be equivalently thought of as current disposable income plus all future disposable income converted to a present value. There is an important distinction, however, between the present and future that arises from the information that we have about them. The present is known and certain, whereas the future is unknown and probabilistic. It is very likely that what is happening in the present to an individual's disposable income is going to be treated as a signal concerning what is likely to happen to it in the future. It seems sensible to hypothesize, therefore, that wealth, as

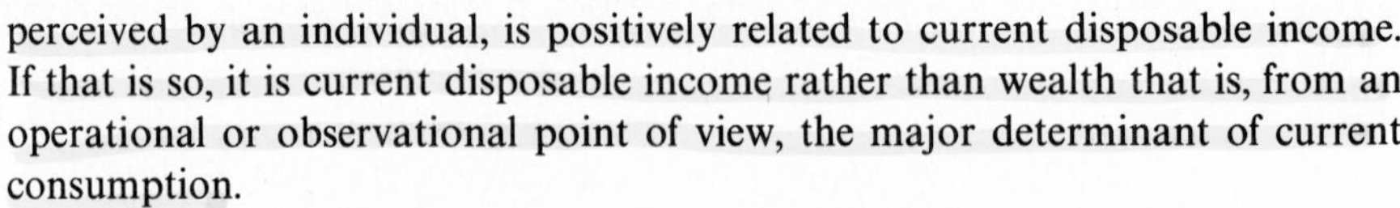

perceived by an individual, is positively related to current disposable income. If that is so, it is current disposable income rather than wealth that is, from an operational or observational point of view, the major determinant of current consumption.

Another way of putting this would be to say that to a large extent, wealth is not a directly observable and measurable variable. It contains, in part, future expected income flows that are not yet known. Those future expected income flows must be forecasted on the basis of things that are known, one important ingredient of which is current disposable income.

There is a second reason why current disposable income is an important determinant of consumption. The permanent income and life-cycle hypotheses both reach the conclusion that consumption will depend on wealth by assuming that individuals may borrow and lend unlimited amounts in order to smooth out consumption over their lifetime. However, there are good reasons why this will not, in general, be possible. It is difficult to borrow unlimited funds against future labor income. It may be possible, therefore that an individual is constrained in the amount of consumption that can be undertaken by the amount of current disposable income, since that amount will be used as an indication to a potential lender concerning the individual's ability to repay the loan and pay the interest on it.

For two reasons, then, (1) because current income provides good information to an individual about future income and therefore about wealth and (2) because current disposable income provides good information to potential lenders, it seems reasonable to suppose that it is current disposable income that is the most important single factor determining current consumption demand.[5]

D. Consumption and Savings Functions in Simple Equations and Diagrams

The discussion and analysis that have been conducted above may now be summarized in a very compact form by writing a simple equation to describe the determination of consumption demand. Such an equation would be

$$c = a + b(y - t) \qquad a > 0, \qquad 1 > b > 0 \tag{16.1}$$

The value of aggregate real consumption demand is represented by c, real income (real gross national product) is represented by y, the total collection of real taxes by the government net of transfer payments is represented by t, and a and b are *constants* or *parameters*. According to Keynes's "fundamental

[5]The account of the theory of the consumption function given in this chapter has been highly condensed and selective. The best, lengthy textbook treatment of the subject that will fill in a lot of the detail for you is Gardner Ackley, *Macroeconomic Theory* (New York: Macmillan Publishing Co., Inc., 1961), Chapters 10–12. An up-to-date survey of the empirical issues, from a U.S. perspective, is Walter Dolde, "Issues and Models in Empirical Research on Aggregate Consumer Expenditure," in Karl Brunner and Allan H. Meltzer, eds., *On the State of Macro-Economics*, 12 (Spring 1980), 161–206, Carnegie-Rochester Conference Series on Public Policy.

Figure 16.1
The Consumption Function

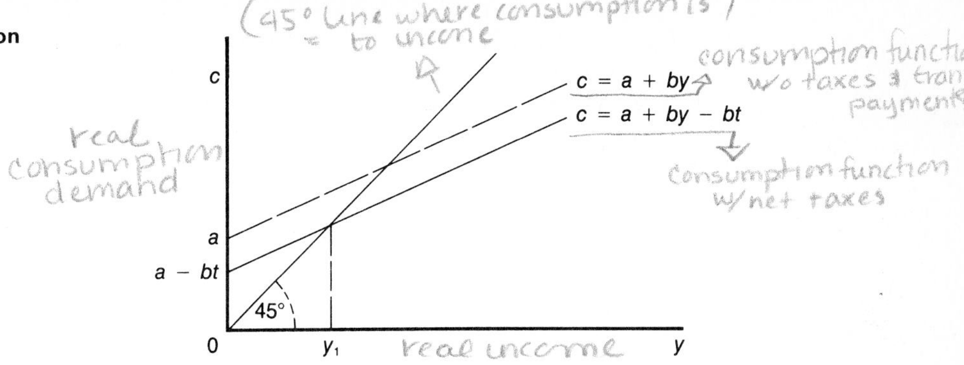

Consumption is a function of disposable income. When consumption (c) is graphed against income (y), the consumption function slopes upwards at the rate of the marginal propensity to consume (the parameter b). If the level of taxes (t) is zero, the intercept of the consumption function on the vertical axis is equal to a. If the level of taxes is nonzero, the intercept of the consumption function on the vertical axis is equal to a minus the marginal propensity to consume (b) times the level of taxes (t).

psychological law," the parameter b will be a positive fraction; an example would be, say, $\frac{3}{4}$. The parameter a captures the effects of all the things that influence consumption other than disposable income. There are, of course, many such things. The assumption being made, however, is that all the other influences upon consumption have effects that may be ignored either because their effects are slight or because they are factors which are themselves changing slowly. These other factors will include such things as demographic trends and tastes. The parameter a will presumably be positive, indicating that if people had very low current income, they would seek to consume more than their income, thereby using up part of their past accumulated savings.

The consumption function written as an equation above may be shown in a simple diagram. Figure 16.1 illustrates the consumption function. The vertical axis measures real consumption demand, and the horizontal axis measures real income. In order to show the relationship between consumption demand and income on a diagram, it is necessary to be precise about how taxes vary as income varies. For present purposes, it will be assumed that taxes are set by the government to yield a certain total amount of revenue, t, independently of what the level of income is. In other words, taxes will be treated as a constant. This is not the only assumption that could have been made, nor is it necessarily the most natural one. Permitting taxes to vary with income would be more natural, but it makes the presentation of the analysis slightly more cumbersome and does not modify the results that we shall get in any qualitative way.

Proceeding then with the assumption that taxes are constant, we can now illustrate the relationship between real consumption demand and real income in Figure 16.1. The dashed line labelled $c = a + by$ represents the consumption function in an economy in which taxes and transfer payments add up to zero. The continuous line labelled $c = a + by - bt$ represents the consumption function in an economy that has net taxes at the level t. The other line in the diagram is a 45° line and can be read as telling you that at each point on that line, consumption would be exactly equal to income. You may use this as a reference line, therefore, to figure out whether or not consumption demand will exceed, equal, or fall short of current income. You see, for example, that at the income level y_1 and the level of net taxes (t), consumption demand exactly equals income. At income levels above y_1, consumption is less than income, and at income levels below y_1, consumption exceeds income.

This equation and diagram summarize the theory of the determinants of consumption demand. The slope of this line (represented by the parameter b) is given a name, and that name is the *marginal propensity to consume*. If the marginal propensity to consume is high (close to 1), the consumption function will be steep (almost as steep as the 45° line). The lower the marginal propensity to consume, the flatter will be the consumption function.

Notice that the consumption function as drawn in Figure 16.1 will shift each time there is a different level of taxes. You can see this directly in Figure 16.1 by comparing the dashed line drawn for zero taxes with the continuous line drawn for a tax level of t. This tells you that the higher the level of taxes, the further downwards the consumption function shifts. What this means is that the higher the tax level, the lower the level of disposable income, and therefore, the lower will be the level of consumption associated with each level of gross national product. The amount by which the consumption function shifts down for a \$1 rise in taxes is the fraction b. The reason why the consumption function shifts down by only the fraction b and not by the whole amount of the increase in taxes is that some of the increase in taxes come from a reduction in savings, and only fraction b of the increase in taxes comes from a reduction in consumption. You will be able to see this more clearly by considering the relationship between consumption, savings, and taxes, which is the next and final task in what has been a long section of this chapter.

A household can do only three things with its income: It can (1) consume, (2) save, or (3) pay taxes. This can be written as an equation, namely,

$$y = c + s + t \tag{16.2}$$

Savings are what are left over after meeting consumption expenditures and paying taxes. Clearly, in planning its consumption, the household is also implicitly planning how much saving to undertake. If consumption is determined by Equation (16.1) above, that is, if $c = a + b(y - t)$, it must be the case that the household is planning to save an amount given by another equation, namely,

$$s = -a + (1 - b)(y - t) \tag{16.3}$$

How do we know that Equation (16.3) tells us about the household's savings plans? The answer is simply that if we add together the household's consumption plan Equation (16.1) and its savings plan Equation (16.3), we get the proposition that

$$c + s = y - t \tag{16.4}$$

Figure 16.2
The Consumption and Savings Functions

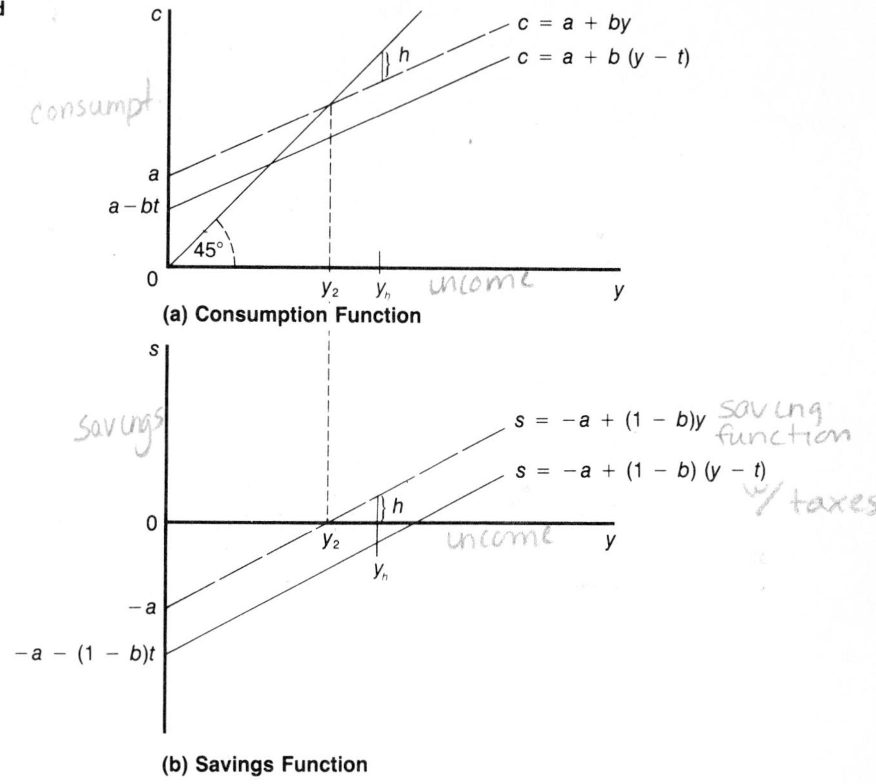

Since income must be disposed of either by consuming, saving, or paying taxes, the consumption function implies a savings function. When savings and consumption plans are added together, they exactly exhaust disposable income. For example, if taxes are zero (the dashed lines) and if income is y_h, then the amount saved, h may be read off directly from the savings function in frame (b) or as the distance marked h in frame (a). When taxes are t the consumption function is lower by bt [frame (a)] and the savings function is lower by $(1 - b)t$ [frame (b)].

namely, that consumption plus saving is equal to disposable income. You will recognize this as simply a rearrangement of Equation (16.2) above. Equation (16.3) is usually referred to as the *savings function*, and the slope of the savings function $(1 - b)$ is the *marginal propensity to save*. The marginal propensity to save plus the marginal propensity to consume always add up to unity.

You may find it helpful to represent the consumption function and the savings function in a diagram that shows how the two are related. Figure 16.2 does just this. Frame (a) shows consumption plotted against income, and frame (b) shows savings plotted against income. Indeed, frame (a) is nothing other than Figure 16.1. The two frames are related to each other in the following way. Look first at the dashed lines that represent an economy with no taxes, so that disposable income and aggregate income are the same number. In this case, the vertical distance between the consumption function and the 45° line in frame (a) is equal to the vertical distance between the horizontal axis and the savings function in frame (b). As an example, at the income level y_2, consumption exactly equals income, and savings exactly equals zero. At an income level above y_2, say, y_h, savings can be represented on frame (a) by the vertical line marked h and equivalently in frame (*b*) by the vertical distance h.

Next, consider the economy in which taxes are not zero. In this case, the consumption function has shifted downwards by an amount equal to b times taxes. The savings function has also shifted down, but this time by an amount equal to $1 - b$ times taxes. What does this mean? It means simply that for each $1 rise in taxes, consumption drops by fraction b of a dollar, and savings drop by fraction $1 - b$ of a dollar—the drop in savings and consumption taken together being enough to make up the $1 of taxes. The after-tax consumption and savings functions are parallel to the pretax functions.

Adding the consumption function and the savings function together gives a number equal to disposable income, that is, a number equal to income minus taxes.

You have just covered the major aspects of the theory of consumption demand and the related theory of savings. It is now possible to explore the simplest flow theory of income determination, the Keynesian cross model.

E. The Keynesian Cross Model

The essence of the Keynesian theory of aggregate demand—which has come to be called the *Keynesian cross model*—may now be understood. We already know that in the simplest Keynesian framework, output is determined by aggregate demand. That is, except in the special case of full employment, and using the inverse "L" approximation to the aggregate supply curve, the price level is fixed, and variations in actual output are determined entirely by movements in the aggregate demand curve.

In Figure 16.2, you have already become familiar with a diagram in which output is measured on the horizontal axis (recalling that output and real income are equal to each other) and one of the major components of aggregate demand (consumption demand) is measured on the vertical axis. We don't have to move very far from the content of Figure 16.2 to determine aggregate demand and aggregate output (real income) in the simplest Keynesian framework. We can do this by broadening our view slightly, as we do in Figure 16.3, and measuring on the vertical axis of the diagram not just consumption demand but all the components of aggregate demand added together, that is, y^d. We continue to measure actual output, y, on the horizontal axis.

The first thing to understand about the diagram in this slightly modified form is the meaning of the 45° line. This line has been labelled $y = y^d$. You may interpret the 45° line as saying that actual output, y, will be determined as the quantity of output that is actually demanded, y^d. There is a sense in which this might be thought of as the aggregate supply curve, although you must be careful not to confuse it with the aggregate supply curve derived in Chapter 15. Since, in terms of Figures 15.3 and 15.4 of the previous chapter, the price level is fixed and we are operating on the horizontal section of the inverse "L"

Figure 16.3
The Keynesian Cross Model

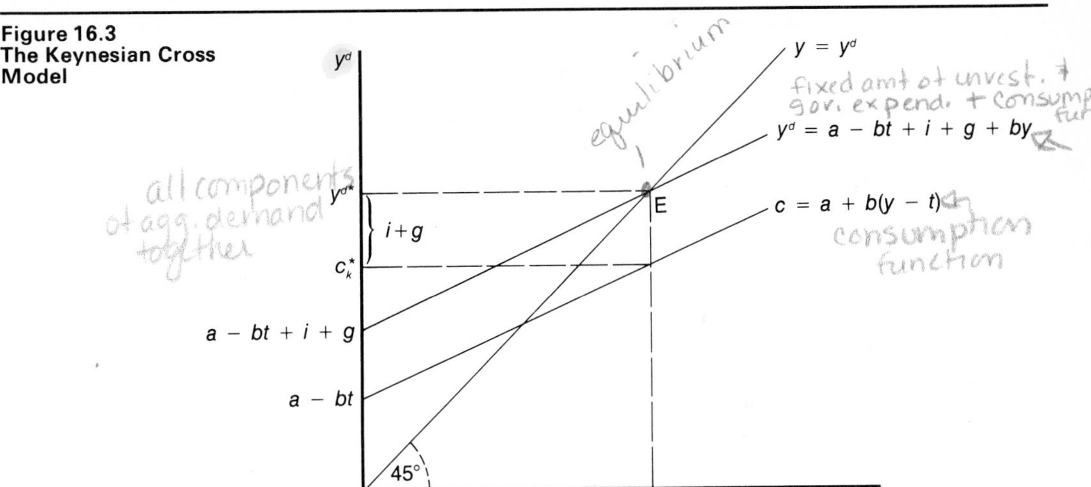

The Keynesian cross model is the essence of the Keynesian theory of output determination. Actual output (y) is equal to aggregate demand (y^d) (the 45° line). Aggregate demand is the sum of consumption demand (c) and autonomous expenditure ($i + g$). The point where the aggregate demand line ($y^d = a - bt + i + g + by$) cuts the 45° line determines the equilibrium level of real income (y_k^*).

aggregate supply curve, we may plot variations in the actual quantity of output supplied (the horizontal axis of Figure 16.3) against the quantity of output demanded (the vertical axis of Figure 16.3). So much for the 45° line, which tells us that the actual quantity of output will be equal to the quantity demanded. Let us now turn to the demand side of the economy itself.

The consumption function, the line labelled $c = a + b(y - t)$, already introduced in Figure 16.2, is reproduced in Figure 16.3. Consumption demand is only part of total demand. The other elements of aggregate demand (ignoring net foreign demand) are investment and government expenditure on goods and services. We have already agreed to treat government expenditure as exogenous. Let us, for the moment, treat investment in the same way. That is, let us suppose that investment is given. (The next chapter actually goes on to discuss the factors that determine investment.) Aggregate demand, then, can be written as

$$y^d = c + i + g \qquad \textbf{(16.5)}$$

where i and g are real investment and real government expenditure on goods and services, respectively. In order to graph aggregate demand y^d in Figure 16.3, all that we have to do is to add the fixed amount of investment and government expenditure to the consumption function. That is, we need to displace the consumption function upwards by an amount equal to investment plus government expenditure. This is done in the diagram and is represented by the line labelled

$$y^d = a - bt + i + g + by$$

This curve tells us what the total level of demand will be at each level of income. Total demand will rise as income rises. It will not, however, rise by as much as income since the consumption function itself has a slope of less than 1. At low income levels, total demand would exceed income, and at high income levels, total demand would fall short of income. There is only one income level, y_k^*, that generates a level of aggregate demand equal to itself. This is the equilibrium level of aggregate demand in the Keynesian cross model.

Income, rather than prices, is the variable that adjusts to achieve the equilibrium. To see this, consider hypothetically what would happen if income was greater than y_k^*. This is a purely hypothetical experiment, one that could not actually happen in the world described in Figure 16.3. In such a case, the level of demand would be less than the level of income. You can see this is true because the curve labelled y^d is lower than the 45° line at all points to the right of y_k^*. This would mean that total spending (gross national product) was less than income. However, you know this to be impossible. Hence, the conjectured income level greater than y_k^* could not occur. Similarly, income levels below y_k^* could not occur. There is one, and only one, income level that is compatible with the relationships hypothesized here, and that is the income level y_k^*, or the point E at which the aggregate demand curve cuts the 45° line.

The analysis that you have just gone through is the essence of Keynes's general theory.[6] (Keynes himself was explicit about this on page 29 of *The General Theory of Employment, Interest and Money*.)

An important and interesting implication of this analysis is the so-called autonomous expenditure multiplier. Investment and government expenditure (and taxes) are all variables that change their values autonomously with respect to (independently of) real income. Only consumption changes as income changes. If there is a change in the value of taxes, investment, or government expenditure, there will be induced changes in consumption and income, and the change in income will be larger than the initial change in autonomous expenditure.

To see this, consider, by way of an example, the effects of a rise in investment. Suppose that taxes and government spending are held constant, but investment rises. We know that any change in income that occurs will be equal to the change in investment plus any induced change in consumption. That is, using the symbol "Δ" to denote "change in," we have

$$\Delta y = \Delta c + \Delta i \qquad \textbf{(16.6)}$$

[6]The presentation of this model on pp. 28 and 29 of *The General Theory* is slightly disguised by the fact that Keynes uses the level of employment rather than the level of output (income) as the variable determined by the analysis, but if you work carefully through these two pages of Keynes's book, you will find the above model there.

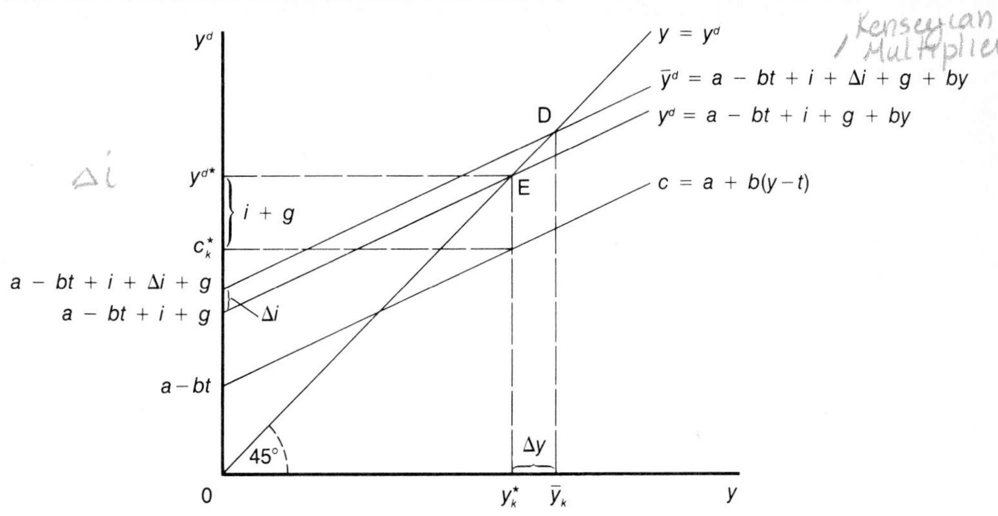

Figure 16.4
The Multiplier in the Keynesian Cross Model

A rise in autonomous expenditure (for example, a rise in investment by Δi) raises aggregate demand and raises equilibrium income (output) by Δy, an amount equal to $[1/(1-b)]\,\Delta i$.

But we know from the theory of the consumption function that the change in consumption will be equal to the change in income multiplied by b, the marginal propensity to consume; that is,

$$\Delta c = b\Delta y \tag{16.7}$$

Substituting this equation into the previous one tells us that the change in income will be equal to b times the change in income plus the change in investment. That is,

$$\Delta y = b\Delta y + \Delta i \tag{16.8}$$

Rearranging this equation by moving the term $b\Delta y$ to the left-hand side and then dividing through by $(1 - b)$ gives

$$\Delta y = \left(\frac{1}{1-b}\right)\Delta i \tag{16.9}$$

You have just worked out the famous Keynesian *multiplier*. The change in income that is induced by a change in autonomous expenditure (investment in this case) is equal to 1, divided by the marginal propensity to save, times the initial change in autonomous expenditure. If the propensity to consume is, for example, 0.8, then the multiplier would be 5.

Figure 16.4 illustrates the multiplier. It is possible to mark the rise in investment (Δi) on the vertical axis of the figure, thereby generating a new aggregate demand curve—the curve labelled

$$y^d = a - bt + i + \Delta i + g + by$$

The new equilibrium level of income is at point D at an income level y_k. The rise in income is marked in the figure as Δy, and the initial rise in investment is Δi. A change in government expenditure induces a change in income that is identical to that induced by a change in investment expenditure and shown in Equation (16.9).

A change in taxes, however, induces a change in income that has a different multiplier from that on investment and government spending. Why is that? It is for two reasons: First, a rise in taxes will lower income, whereas a rise in investment and a rise in government spending will raise income. This occurs because when taxes rise, disposable income and, therefore, consumption, fall. However, a rise in taxes of $1 will in part be paid out of lower savings. Savings will be cut by $1 times the marginal propensity to save (by $1 - b$), and consumption will only be cut by b. Thus, a $1 rise in taxes leads to a fraction b of $1 cut in consumption. It is this number that has to be scaled up by the standard multiplier so that the change in income induced by a tax change is

$$\Delta y = \left(\frac{-b}{1 - b}\right) \Delta t \qquad \textbf{(16.10)}$$

Continuing with the example of a marginal propensity to consume of 0.8, the multiplier for a tax change would be -4. Thus a $1 rise in taxes would cut income by $4.

You have now discovered that in the simplest version of the Keynesian theory of aggregate demand, the level of demand (which equals the level of actual income and output) is determined by the level of autonomous expenditure. Change taxes, government spending, or investment and there will be a change in income that is bigger than the initial change in autonomous expenditure.

You may be wondering what has become of the monetary theory of aggregate demand in the basic model. How is it that the level of aggregate demand can be determined entirely by the relationship between consumption and income and the level of autonomous expenditure? What is going on in the money market? What has become of money market equilibrium—the fundamental condition giving rise to the aggregate demand curve in the basic model? These questions will be answered shortly. It will be best, however, if the answer is approached in stages and left until we get to Chapter 20.

Summary

A. Components of Aggregate Demand

The components of aggregate demand are consumption, investment, government purchases of goods and services, and net exports.

B. Theories of the Consumption Function Proposed by Keynes, Friedman, and Modigliani

Keynes hypothesized that the major determinant of consumption was current disposable income. Keynes supposed that the level of consumption would rise as income rose, but the fraction of income consumed would decline. Friedman and Modigliani developed the permanent income and life-cycle hypotheses, which emphasized the role of wealth as the ultimate constraint upon consumption.

C. Connection Between Wealth and Income and Why Current Income is a Major Determinant of Consumption

Wealth is the present value of current and future income. By borrowing and lending, it is possible to break the direct connection between current income and current consumption. Nevertheless, current income is an important indicator of potential future income and therefore will influence the extent to which an individual can borrow against future labor income and will influence the individual's own assessment of what represents a desirable, sustainable consumption and savings plan. Therefore, current income is a major determinant of consumption.

D. Consumption and Savings Functions in Simple Equations and Diagrams

The consumption function may be written as

$$c = a + b(y - t)$$

Since savings plus consumption must equal disposable income, it follows that the savings function must be

$$s = -a + (1 - b)(y - t)$$

If savings and consumption are added together, they always add up to disposable income $(y - t)$.

E. The Keynesian Cross Model

The essence of the simple Keynesian theory of aggregate demand can be summarized in the Keynesian cross diagram. Aggregate demand is measured on the vertical axis and actual output on the horizontal axis. The 45° line says that the level of actual output will equal the quantity demanded. The aggregate demand curve plotted in the diagram shows the consumption function plus the assumed fixed level of investment and government expenditure. The point where the aggregate demand line cuts the 45° line determines the equilibrium level of income. It is an equilibrium in the sense that it is the only income level that generates a level of consumption that, when added to investment and government spending, equals that same level of income.

A rise in investment or government spending will shift the aggregate demand curve upwards and produce a higher equilibrium income level. The rise in income will be equal to the rise in investment or government expenditure multiplied by $1/(1 - b)$, where b is the marginal propensity to consume. A rise in taxes will change income by $-b/(1 - b)$ times the rise in taxes (i.e., a tax rise will lower income).

Review Questions

1. What are the components into which aggregate demand is separated in order to study the determination of aggregate demand?

2. Classify the following according to whether they are consumption (c), investment (i), government expenditure (g), none of these and not part of aggregate demand (n), or not enough information to say (?):

(a) Your purchase of lunch today.
(b) The purchase of a new car.
(c) The purchase of a used car.
(d) The purchase of a new office block by the U.S. federal government.
(e) The payment of unemployment compensation by federal and state governments.
(f) The purchase by American Airlines of a Boeing 747 airplane.
(g) The purchase by American Airlines of food for in-flight service. (*Hint:* Be careful—look at Chapter 3 on the distinction between final and intermediate expenditure.)
(h) Your purchase of a ticket on an American Airlines flight.
(i) The purchase of a computer by Chase Manhattan Bank.
(j) Your income tax payments to the U.S. federal government.

3. What is Keynes's theory of the consumption function?

4. What, according to the permanent income and life-cycle hypotheses, is the fundamental constraint on consumption?

5. What is the connection between income and wealth?

6. If a person's income was to rise in 1982 by $1000, but thereafter to return to its original path, and if the rate of interest was 10 percent, by how much would that person's wealth rise in 1981?

7. Why is it that despite the fact that wealth is the fundamental constraint on consumption, disposable income is regarded as the major determinant of consumption?

8. What is the meaning of the term *marginal propensity to consume b*? Why is b less than one?

9. What is the savings function? What is the relationship between the savings function and the consumption function?

10. You are given the following information about a hypothetical economy:

$$c = 100 + 0.8(y - t)$$
$$i = 500$$
$$g = 400$$
$$t = 400$$

There is unemployment, and the price level is fixed.
(c = consumption, i = investment, g = government expenditure on goods and services, y = real income, t = taxes)

(a) Calculate the equilibrium level of output and consumption.
(b) If government expenditure is cut to 300, what is the *change* in income and the *change* in consumption?
(c) What is the size of the multiplier effect of government expenditure on output?

17

Investment Demand

You already know from the definitions given at the beginning of the last chapter that investment demand is the purchase of durable goods by both households and firms. You also know from your examination of the characteristics of the business cycle in Chapter 6 that fluctuations in the output of durables have much greater amplitude than those in nondurables. Understanding what determines investment is, therefore, of crucial importance in understanding some of the major sources of fluctuations in aggregate demand. What determines investment, and why does it fluctuate so much? These are the principal questions for this chapter.[1] Answering these questions is a fairly big task and one that is going to be more easily approached by breaking it up into a series of specific subtasks, which are to:

(a) Understand the distinction between investment and the capital stock.
(b) Understand what determines the demand for capital.
(c) Understand what is meant by the rental rate of capital.
(d) Understand how investment demand is related to the demand for capital.
(e) Know how to represent the investment demand function in a simple equation and diagram.

A. Distinction Between Investment and the Capital Stock

Investment demand is the demand for capital goods for use in production or consumption-yielding activities. Investment may be undertaken for two purposes:

1. To add to the existing stock of capital
2. To replace capital equipment that has depreciated (that has worn out)

---

[1]The development of the theory of investment presented in this chapter is based very closely on Dale W. Jorgensen, "Capital Theory and Investment Behavior," *American Economic Review Papers and Proceedings*, 53 (1963), 247–59.

You already know that investment is a flow. It is the flow of additions to the capital stock or replacements for worn-out capital. In any one year, the amount of investment is likely to be small relative to the size of the capital stock. For example, in the United States in 1980, gross investment was $402.3 billion. Of this, $293.2 billion was replacement investment, so that the rate of net investment (addition to the capital stock) was $109.1 billion. The capital stock in 1980 was estimated to be $7001 billion, which means that net investment was 1.6 percent of the capital stock.

To summarize: The capital stock is the total value of the capital equipment located in the economy at a particular point in time. The level of investment is the rate of flow of additions to that capital stock, plus the rate of flow of expenditure on capital goods to replace worn out capital equipment.

What determines the rate of investment? This question is best answered in a slightly roundabout manner. Rather than answering it directly, we are going to approach it by asking first of all, what determines the amount of capital stock that, in the aggregate, the agents in the economy want to hold. Let us now examine this question.

B. The Demand for Capital

In any productive or consumption-yielding activity, there is a range of choice of techniques available. For example, it would be possible to undertake almost any imaginable task by using only labor as the resource and using no capital at all. At the other extreme, it would be possible to undertake almost any imaginable task by using a very capital-intensive technology, that is, a technology that involves very little labor and large amounts of capital. (It is, of course, true that there are some tasks that one could not imagine doing in any way other than by using large amounts of capital—for example, putting a satellite into earth orbit.) Nevertheless, over a very large range of economic activities, it is possible to visualize differing degrees of intensity of the use of capital. A classical example would be the building of a dam, which could be undertaken with massive earth-moving equipment and a small amount of labor or with masses of labor working by hand or using small wooden shovels, themselves made by hand. A technology that uses a lot of capital and a small amount of labor is called a *capital-intensive technology*. The opposite, which uses large amounts of labor and very little capital, is called a *labor-intensive technology*.

What determines the extent to which a capital-intensive technology will be used rather than a labor-intensive technology? A moment's reflection suggests that the choice will depend on the relative costs of the alternative techniques of production, which in turn will depend on the relative costs of capital and labor. If capital is cheap relative to labor, then it would seem efficient to use a capital-intensive technology. If, on the other hand, labor is cheap relative to capital, then a labor-intensive technology would seem to be indicated.

All this seems obvious enough until one reflects a little further and begins to wonder how to calculate whether or not capital is cheap relative to labor. After all, buying a piece of equipment is buying something that is durable and that is going to be usable over a long period of time, whereas hiring labor is something that is more in the nature of a consumption activity. How can we compare the price of capital and the price of labor in order to know whether capital is cheap or not? The answer lies in a concept called the *rental rate* of capital. By comparing the rental rate of capital with the wage rate of labor, we can establish the relative price of capital and labor.

The term rental rate of capital suggests the notion of a price that has to be paid for the *use* of a piece of capital and not the price that has to be paid to *buy* a piece of capital. Most capital equipment is not, however, rented at all; it is bought and used, as needed. It is convenient to think of the owner of a piece of capital equipment as wearing two hats; one hat is that of the owner, the other is the hat of the user. Put differently, the owner rents the equipment and is the renter of the equipment. We call the rent *implicit* because no actual rent is explicitly paid.

There are, of course, many examples of *explicit* renting—when the owner and user of a piece of capital are different people. Examples include the rental of a car at an airport, or, more commonly, the rental of an apartment or house. Firms often rent equipment, for example, the rental of heavy earth-moving and other specialized equipment by civil engineering contractors.

Whether capital equipment is explicitly rented by its user from its owner or implicitly rented by its owner from himself for his own use makes no difference to the general concept of the rental rate of capital.

C. Rental Rate of Capital

The best way of understanding what is meant by the rental rate of capital is to proceed by example. How much would you be willing to pay each year to rent a house that you could otherwise buy for $60,000? To answer that question, you need to know a little bit more information than you have just been given. Let's supply some more pieces of information.

The house will last for 50 years, so that if you bought the house, it would wear out at a rate of 2 percent a year.[2] The interest rate that you would face is 15 percent per annum. That means that you would have to pay 15 percent per annum for any money that you borrowed (any mortgage money) to buy the house. Equivalently, if you sold some existing securities to buy the house, you would have to forego a 15 percent rate of interest on those securities. Either way, the opportunity cost of funds that you would use to buy the house is going to be 15 percent. House prices are also rising and are expected to rise indefinitely through the future at a rate of 10 percent per annum.

---

[2]Actually, to say that a house will last 50 years and that it will wear out at the rate of 2 percent a year is slightly contradictory. The two statements are approximately equivalent, however. If a house wore out in 50 years at exactly a rate of 1/50 of the initial house each year, then the depreciation expressed as a percentage of the remaining value of the house would rise. If we express the depreciation rate as a constant percent each year, what we are really saying is that the asset will never finally wear out. This is known as radioactive depreciation. It makes the arithmetic easier and is approximately the same as a constant absolute amount of depreciation.

You now have enough information with which to answer the question, How much would you pay each year to rent a house that you could otherwise buy for \$60,000? The answer is you wouldn't pay any more rent than the amount that you would implicitly have to pay to yourself if you were to buy the house and live in it for as long as you needed it and thereafter sell the house. How much is that amount? To figure it out, consider the following three costs of owning the house and renting it to yourself. First, there is a cost in the form of physical depreciation on the house; second, there is a cost in the form of the interest that you would have to pay in order to acquire the \$60,000 needed to buy the house; and third, there is a negative cost, the gain, that arises from the fact that the value of the house on the housing market will rise at a rate at which house prices are expected to rise (in the example, 10 percent per annum).

If you are going to buy a \$60,000 house, the depreciation of 2 percent per annum would cost you \$1200 a year. The interest payment at 15 percent would cost a further \$9000 a year. Thus your total cost so far is \$10,200. However, offset against this is the fact that the house value will appreciate by 10 percent a year, which will give you a capital gain of \$6000. This has to be offset against the \$10,200 to give a net annual cost of \$4200. Ignoring tax considerations and ignoring the costs of searching for a house and of transacting to buy and sell a house—abstracting from all those things—\$4200 per annum is the implicit rental rate that you would have to pay to yourself if you were to buy the house. If houses actually rented for less than \$4200 a year, it would pay you to rent rather than buy. If houses of this type rented for more than \$4200 a year, it would pay you to buy rather than rent.

Since everyone is capable of doing the kinds of calculations that you have just performed, it might be expected that there would be some equilibrating forces at work in the marketplace ensuring that the actual rental rates on houses did not stray too far away from the implicit rental rate that we have just calculated. That is, if the implicit rental rate was less than the actual market rent, there would be a rise in the demand for houses to buy and a fall in the demand for houses to rent. This would tend to raise the purchase price of houses and to lower house rental rates. The process would continue until people were indifferent between owning and renting. The same considerations apply in the opposite case. If the implicit rental rate was greater than the market rental rate on houses, then there would be a drop in the demand for houses to buy and a rise in the demand for houses to rent. This would have the reverse effect on rents and purchase prices and, again, would bring about an equality between the actual and implicit rental rates. Thus, the actual rent of capital goods (a house in this example) and the implicit rent may be regarded as the same.

You have now calculated a formula that can be stated in general terms; namely, the rental rate of a piece of capital equipment is equal to the price of the capital multiplied by the sum of the rate of depreciation plus the market rate of interest minus the expected rate of change of the price of the piece of capital equipment. Let us write this as an equation, defining P_k as the price of capital, δ as the depreciation rate, r_m as the market rate of interest, and $\Delta P_k^e/P_k$ as the rate at which the price of capital is expected to rise. The formula for the rental rate becomes:

$$P_k\left[(\delta + r_m) - \left(\frac{\Delta P_k^e}{P_k}\right)\right] \tag{17.1}$$

Let us check that this formula gives us the right answer for the annual rental rate of a house. Using the numbers introduced above, P_k equals $60,000, and δ is 2 percent per annum, expressed in proportionate terms as 0.02. The interest rate, r_m (again expressed as a proportion), is 0.15, and the expected rate of increase of house prices, $\Delta P_k^e/P_k$ (also expressed as a proportion), is 0.10. Putting these numbers into the formula, we have:

$$\begin{aligned}\text{Rent} &= \$60{,}000\ (0.02 + 0.15 - 0.10)\\ &= \$60{,}000 \times 0.07\\ &= \$4200 \text{ per annum}\end{aligned}$$

Evidently the formula works.

Now that you have got the basic idea of how to calculate the rental rate on a piece of capital equipment, let us return to the task of figuring out how a producer will choose how much capital and labor to employ in the production process. You already know that, in order to maximize profits, a producer will set the marginal product of a factor of production equal to its real price. In the case of labor, this involves setting the marginal product of labor equal to the real wage. For capital, the producer has to set the marginal product of capital equal to the real rental rate. What we have just calculated above is the nominal rental rate. The real rental rate (RR) is obtained by dividing the nominal rental rate by the price level (P) to give:

$$RR = \frac{P_k}{P}\left[(\delta + r_m) - \left(\frac{\Delta P_k^e}{P_k}\right)\right] \tag{17.2}$$

Since we are interested in aggregate economic phenomena, we are interested in the economy average real rental rate. In terms of the above equation, this means that we want to interpret P_k/P as the relative price of capital goods to goods and services in general. It is a reasonable approximation to regard that ratio as constant. (During the period between 1948 and 1981 in the United States, capital goods prices increased by 0.4 of a percent per annum relative to consumer good prices.) By calculating a price index for capital goods (P_k) and for consumer goods in general (P) with the same base, we can regard the relative price as being equal to one. Further, since capital goods prices inflate at approximately the same rate as prices in general, we can replace the term $\Delta P_k^e/P_k$ with the expected rate of inflation, π^e. This enables us to write the formula for the real rental rate of capital in a simpler way:

$$RR = (\delta + r_m - \pi^e) \tag{17.3}$$

Figure 17.1
The Demand for Capital Stock

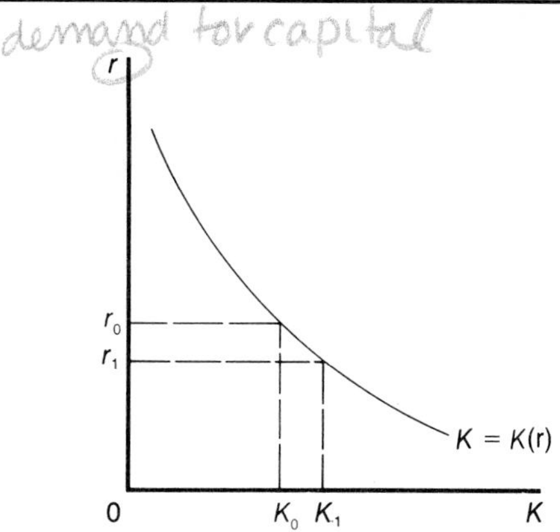

The demand for capital stock (K) will depend inversely on the rental rate of capital. The rental rate will be equal to the technologically given rate of depreciation plus the difference between the money rate of interest and the rate of inflation of asset prices. The difference between the money rate of interest and the rate of inflation of asset prices is the real rate of interest (r). The demand for capital (K) will therefore depend inversely on the real rate of interest (r). If the real interest rate fell from r_0 to r_1 the demand for capital would rise from K_0 to K_1.

Notice that the expected change in the price of capital now becomes π^e, the expected rate of inflation.

You have met a term very similar to $r_m - \pi^e$ before (in Chapter 9). Actually, the term used there was $r_m - \pi$. If the actual rate of inflation, (π), equals the expected rate of inflation, (π^e), these two terms are identical. The term $r_m - \pi^e$ is the real rate of interest and will be denoted as r. Using this we can simplify the formula for the real capital rental rate as:

$$RR = \delta + r \qquad \textbf{(17.4)}$$

If the rate of depreciation is a technologically given constant, it is clear that the only *variable* that affects the real capital rental rate is the real rate of interest. Thus, the higher the real rate of interest, the higher will be the real capital rental rate.

If producers utilize capital and labor resources in an efficient way, at a lower real rate of interest they will seek to use a more capital-intensive technology. Figure 17.1 illustrates the relationship between the desired capital stock (K) and the real rate of interest (r), the demand for capital. If the real rate of interest was the level r_0, then the capital stock that producers would wish to have is shown as K_0. If the interest rate was lower, at r_1, then the higher capital stock K_1 would be desired.

Now that you understand the relationship between the real rate of interest and the rental rate of capital and also the relationship between the real rate of interest and the demand for capital stock, it is possible to take the next step and see how the rate of investment is determined.

D. Investment and the Demand for Capital

As already stated earlier in this chapter, investment demand is the demand for capital goods for use in productive (or consumption-yielding) activities. Investment is a flow that represents either additions to the existing stock of capital or replacement of worn-out (depreciated) pieces of capital equipment. Capital equipment that is wearing out will be proportional to the stock of capital in existence, and from the discussion that we had above concerning the rental rate of capital, the depreciation rate, denoted as δ, implies that the rate at which the capital stock is being worn out is equal to δK. The rate at which the capital stock is changing is equal to ΔK. Therefore, investment, i, is the sum of these two things; that is,

$$i = \delta K + \Delta K \tag{17.5}$$

There are some very elaborate theories that explain the speed with which firms will seek to add to their capital stock. For our purposes, it seems sufficient to remark that if firms added to their capital stock too quickly, they would incur a variety of high costs in the form of organizational problems and planning bottlenecks. If, on the other hand, they added to their capital stock too slowly, then they would have to put up with having too little equipment for too long. There would seem to be some optimum rate at which to add to the capital stock, which might be thought of as depending on the extent to which the capital stock currently in place falls short of (or exceeds) the desired capital stock.

We know what the preferred capital stock is. It is shown in Figure 17.1 and depends on the real rate of interest. If the change in the capital stock proceeds at some rate that depends on the gap between this preferred capital stock and the actual capital stock, then the rate of investment will depend on two things: first, the rate of interest, since this determines the desired capital stock; and second, the existing capital stock, since this affects how much capital shortage or surplus there is. How do these two variables, the real rate of interest and the stock of capital, affect the investment rate? A moment's reflection will reveal, other things being constant, that they each have a negative effect on investment. We have already seen that the higher the real rate of interest, the smaller will be the desired capital stock. The bigger the actual capital stock, the smaller, other things being equal, will be the gap between the desired and the actual capital stock that firms seek to close. Both of these forces, then, would work to reduce the rate of investment.

To summarize, then, the rate of investment will depend on the real rate of interest and the capital stock. The higher is either of those two variables, the lower will be the rate of investment.

There is one final simplification that it will be useful to introduce into the analysis, and this concerns the approximation arising from the fact that investment is a small number relative to the capital stock, so that even though positive investment is being undertaken at all times, the capital stock is a very slowly changing variable and may be regarded as approximately constant. This being so, it is possible to simplify the theory of investment still further by ignoring, at least for short-run purposes, the effect of the capital stock on the rate of investment. Thus, the theory of investment used in short-run macroeconomic models is one that supposes that investment depends only on the real rate of interest.

In developing the proposition that investment depends only on the real rate of interest, a great deal has been set aside. Indeed, it would not be an exaggeration to say that the major sources of fluctuation in investment are ignored by focusing exclusively on the real rate of interest as a determinant of investment. There are obviously many things other than the real rate of interest that will influence the pace of investment. Such things as taxes; changes in technology that make some types of equipment outmoded and stimulate massive demand for new, previously unknown types of capital; changes in population (both in terms of its size, age, and sex distributions); and changes in entrepreneurs' perceptions of profit opportunities, as well, of course, as the slowly changing capital stock itself, are all examples of things that undoubtedly exert a major influence on investment.

Furthermore, because investment is the *flow* by means of which the *stock* of capital is changed, anything that changes the desired stock of capital will have a magnified effect on the flow of investment. When the demand for capital (a stock demand) rises, the flow of investment will jump. When the stock of capital reaches its desired level, the pace of investment will slacken off to a rate consistent with replacing worn-out capital.

The bathtub analogy that we have used before illustrates this phenomenon well. The desire to soak in a tub leads to a rise in the demand for a *stock* of water. This results in opening the tap to maximum pressure—a *flow*—for as long as necessary to achieve the desired water level. Then the tap is closed and the flow stops—although the stock remains. Thus, a flow rises from zero to its maximum rate and back to zero very quickly. The flow displays large fluctuations. It is exactly the same with the variables that lead to changes in the desired capital stock. These variables result in large fluctuations in investment. This, indeed, is the reason why the cycles in durables have greater amplitude than those in nondurables.

The key to understanding the theory of investment as used in macroeconomic analysis is the realization that all the factors that influence investment, other than the real rate of interest, may, as a reasonable approximation, be taken to be independent of all the other variables that a macroeconomic model determines. This means that when such factors change, a shift occurs in the investment demand curve, and this sets up repercussions for income, prices, interest rates, and other macroeconomic variables. It is assumed, however, that there are no significant feedbacks onto the rate of investment itself other than those that go through the real rate of interest.

E. The Investment Demand Function

The entire discussion in this chapter can now be summarized very compactly. The investment demand function implied by the previous discussion may be written as a simple equation, which is

$$i = i_0 - hr \qquad i_0, h > 0 \tag{17.6}$$

Figure 17.2
The Investment Function

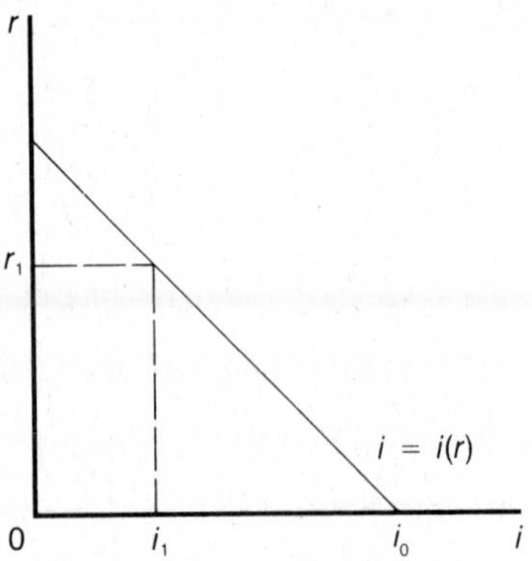

Investment (i) will be undertaken to replace existing capital and to close the gap between the desired and actual capital stock. Since the desired capital stock depends inversely on the real rate of interest (r), and since the actual capital stock changes only slowly over time, investment (i) itself will be a function, $[i(r)]$, of the real rate of interest (r). Many other factors, summarized in the intercept i_0, will influence investment. None of the variables that influence the position of the investment demand function, i_0, is determined in the macroeconomic model. Rather, shifts in the investment demand function may be important exogenous sources of fluctuation in aggregate demand. At the real rate of interest r_1 investment demand is i_1.

This equation says that the level of investment will be equal to some amount that is independent of all the other variables in our macroeconomic model, i_0, and, over and above that, will vary inversely with the real rate of interest. The way that the equation is specified makes the relationship linear. A one percentage point rise in the real rate of interest would produce an h-million dollar drop in the rate of investment. The same relationship as appears in Equation (17.6) is shown in Figure 17.2. You should think of the volatility of investment as being reflected in shifts in the investment function as shown in Figure 17.2, or equivalently, in exogenous changes in the intercept of the investment function, i_0. These changes could arise from many factors such as changes in taxes, technology, population size and composition, entrepreneurs' perceptions of profit opportunities, and the (slowly evolving) capital stock itself.[3]

[3]As in the case of the consumption function, the theory of investment presented here is highly condensed and selective. A superb treatment of the subject at a more advanced level, however, may be found in Frank Brechling, *Investment and Employment Decisions* (Manchester: Manchester University Press, 1975). A good, up-to-date, though again fairly demanding survey is Andrew B. Abel "Empirical Investment Equations: An Integrative Framework," in Karl Brunner and Allan H. Melzer, (eds.) *On the State of Macro-Economics*, Carnegie-Rochester Conference Series, Vol. 12 (Spring 1980), pp. 39–92.

Summary

A. Distinction Between Investment and the Capital Stock

Investment demand is the demand for capital goods for use in production or consumption-yielding activities. It represents additions to the stock of capital or replacement of depreciated capital. Thus, investment is the *flow* that augments or maintains the *stock* of capital.

B. The Demand for Capital

The demand for capital is determined by cost-minimizing or profit-maximizing considerations. Capital will be demanded up to the point at which its marginal product equals its rental rate.

C. Rental Rate of Capital

Where capital equipment is explicitly rented, as is often the case with houses, and occasionally with cars, T.V. sets, and industrial equipment, the rental rate of capital is simply the rate per hour that has to be paid for the use of a particular type of equipment. Most capital is not rented explicitly but is owned by the individual or firm that uses it. In such a case, the rental rate on capital is *implicit*. The individual implicitly rents the equipment from him/herself. That implicit rental rate will be equal to the price of the capital multiplied by the sum of the rate of depreciation plus the market rate of interest (nominal rate of interest) minus the rate of appreciation of the asset in question.

D. Investment and the Demand for Capital

The rate of investment will be determined by the size of the capital stock relative to the profit-maximizing capital stock. The bigger the stock of capital relative to the desired stock, the slower will be the rate of investment. Since the capital stock is a slowly changing variable, as an approximation, the rate of investment may be presumed to depend only on the rental rate of capital. The rental rate will in turn depend primarily on the real rate of interest. Thus, the simple macroeconomic theory of investment is that it depends on the real rate of interest. A higher real rate of interest will induce a lower rate of investment. This theory leaves out more than it includes. What is left out, however, may be presumed to be independent of (exogenous with respect to) the other variables that macroeconomics seeks to understand. It is fluctuations in those other variables, however, that are responsible for some of the major swings in investment activity.

E. Investment Demand Function

The investment demand function can be written in a simple equation

$$i = i_0 - hr$$

This equation states that as the real rate of interest, r, rises, the level of investment, i, falls. The constant, h, is the degree of responsiveness of investment to interest rate changes. Volatility of investment is reflected in changes in i_0 that shift the investment demand function.

Review Questions

1. What is the difference between investment and the capital stock?
2. What is the difference between a change in investment and a change in the capital stock?
3. How do firms decide on the size of the desired capital stock?
4. What is the rental rate of capital? How does it relate to the price of capital goods?
5. A car that you are thinking of buying costs $6000 and will, after one year, have a resale value of $5000. The rate of interest on the bank loan that you would take if you did buy the car is 15 percent. A friend who already owns an identical car offers to lease you that car for one year for $1800 (you buy the gas and pay for maintenance). Should you accept the offer from your friend, or should you buy the car? What is the rental rate that your friend is asking? What is the implicit rental rate if you buy?
6. What determines the rate of investment?
7. What is the investment demand function? What is being held constant, and what is varying as we move along the investment demand function?
8. What causes shifts in the investment demand function?
9. Use the *National Income and Product Accounts* and obtain data on investment expenditure over the last 10 years. (Refer back to Chapter 3 if you are not sure how to do this.) Draw a time-series graph of investment. Describe the main movements. What relationship, if any, can you find between investment and the difference between the long-term rate of interest and the actual rate of inflation? (Use the Appendix to Chapter 2 for data on interest rates and inflation rates.) Is the difference between the long-term rate of interest and the rate of inflation the real rate of interest?

18

The *IS* Curve

There are various stages in the process of learning economics that involve mastering certain steps of analysis that seem, at the time, completely pointless. It is as if analysis is being mastered for its own sake, rather than to achieve some objective in terms of having greater insights or better understanding of how the economy works. It is not until a later stage in the learning process that the point of a particular piece of analysis becomes fully apparent. You are about to embark on such a piece of analysis in this chapter. The objective toward which you are working is to have an understanding of what determines aggregate demand and how aggregate demand is affected by such things as government expenditure, taxes, and the money supply.

Achieving a level of expertise and understanding that is worthwhile involves mastering a body of analysis that, in its entirety, is hard to grasp the first time through (and even the second or third time for some of us). It is easier to grasp and understand if it is broken down into a series of individually easy-to-manage steps. This makes the process of comprehension and understanding easier. At the same time, it does give rise to the problem that I describe above; namely, that while a series of small intermediate steps are being taken, the final objective, the point to where it is all leading, may be lost from sight.

Try to keep in mind where you are going. You are going to end up after another two chapters with a clear understanding of the Keynesian theory of aggregate demand. You are going to see how the various bits and pieces, one of which is now going to be developed in this chapter, all fit together.

The part of the aggregate demand story that you are going to master in this chapter involves a relationship called the *IS* curve. *I* stands for investment and *S* for savings. You are going to undertake four tasks, which are to:

(a) Know the definition of the *IS* curve.
(b) Know how to derive the *IS* curve.
(c) Understand what determines the slope of the *IS* curve.
(d) Understand what makes the *IS* curve shift and by how much.

A. Definition of the *IS* Curve

The *IS* curve is a relationship between the level of output and the real rate of interest. It is the relationship that links the level of income and the real rate of interest such that investment demand plus government demand equals savings plus taxes.[1] Equivalently, it is the relationship between the level of real income and the real rate of interest that ensures that aggregate demand (consumption demand plus investment demand plus government demand) is equal to the level of real income.

It might be helpful to put this slightly differently and more long-windedly. Since consumption depends on income, different levels of income will bring forth different levels of consumption. When consumption is added to investment and government spending, the result is a particular level of total demand for output (real income). The *IS* curve traces the relationship between the level of output (real income) and the real rate of interest when the level of aggregate demand is equal to the level of real income that generates that level of aggregate demand.

The *IS* curve is not a description of the desires or decisions of any single agent or group of agents. Rather, it is the same kind of relationship as the aggregate demand curve that you have already met. It is an equilibrium locus. It traces the locus of points that give an equality between the aggregate demand for goods and services and the level of output of goods and services. Indeed, you can think of the *IS* curve as a kind of aggregate demand curve. The aggregate demand curve as we defined it in Chapter 9 is a relationship between the total demand for goods and services and the price level. That meaning of the term aggregate demand curve is a useful one, and we shall reserve it, even in the Keynesian context, for something other than the *IS* curve. Nevertheless, the *IS* curve tells us what the total demand for goods and services is as we vary, not the price level, but the real rate of interest.

It is important not to interpret the *IS* curve as implying anything about causality. The *IS* curve emphatically does not say that different levels of aggregate demand are caused by different levels of the real rate of interest. All that it is telling us is that the real rate of interest and the level of real income cannot be just any values that they like. They must be restricted to lie on the *IS* curve. The two variables will be determined simultaneously (by a procedure that we shall get to in Chapter 20).

What you are going to be looking at next, then, is the way in which the *IS* curve is derived.

B. Derivation of the *IS* Curve

The easiest way to learn how to derive the *IS* curve is to begin by refreshing your memory about the components of aggregate demand for goods and services and the ways in which aggregate income may be allocated by house-

[1]You may think that the *IS* curve is peculiarly named since it is a curve that describes the equality of investment (*I*) plus government spending (*G*), and savings (*S*) plus taxes (*T*). Aside from *IGST* being a clumsy name, when the analysis presented here was first invented by Sir John Hicks in 1936, he illustrated the analysis for an economy in which government spending and taxes were assumed to be zero; hence the name *IS*.

holds. Recall that aggregate income may be allocated in three ways. It may be spent on consumption, saved, or paid in taxes; that is,

$$y = c + s + t \tag{18.1}$$

[Recall that c is consumption demand, s is savings, t is taxes, and y is real income (output).] Also recall that aggregate demand is decomposed into three components—consumption demand, investment demand, and government demand for goods and services. That is,

$$y^d = c + i + g \tag{18.2}$$

You subtract c from both sides of Equation (18.1) to obtain

$$y - c = s + t \tag{18.3}$$

This simply says that income minus consumption demand must be equal to savings-plus-taxes. This does not say anything about behavior, of course. It is simply a statement about the necessary relationship between income and expenditure. It is nothing other than the household sector's budget constraint.

Next, subtract c from both sides of Equation (18.2) to obtain

$$y^d - c = i + g \tag{18.4}$$

What this says is that the difference between aggregate demand and consumption demand is equal to investment-plus-government spending. Equation (18.1) says exactly the same thing as Equation (18.3), and Equation (18.2) says the same thing as Equation (18.4). They are simply different ways of looking at the same thing.

The *IS* curve, the derivation of which you are now embarking upon, traces the relationship between the level of aggregate demand and the real rate of interest when the level of aggregate demand is equal to the level of real income. In other words, the *IS* curve has to be derived satisfying the condition

$$y = y^d \tag{18.5}$$

This says that points on the *IS* curve are points such that aggregate demand is equal to aggregate real income (output).

You will notice, if you replace y with y^d in Equation (18.3), that the left-hand side of Equation (18.3) is exactly the same as the left-hand side of Equation (18.4). It follows, therefore, that the right-hand side of Equation (18.3) must be equal to the right-hand side of Equation (18.4) when we are on the *IS* curve. That is,

$$s + t = i + g \tag{18.6}$$

Equation (18.6) says that planned savings-plus-taxes must equal investment-plus-government spending at all points on the *IS* curve. It is Equation (18.6) that gives the name to the *IS* curve. If there was no government, so that t and

Figure 18.1
Investment-plus-Government Spending

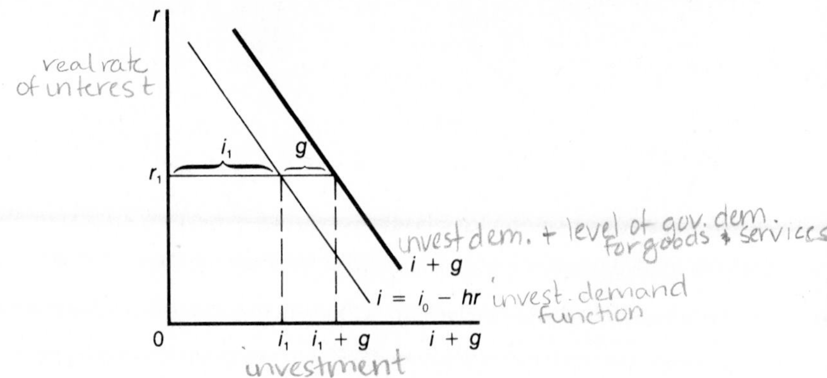

Investment (the thin line) varies inversely with the real rate of interest. Government spending is fixed independently of the rate of interest. Investment-plus-government spending (the thick line) has the same slope as the investment line but is shifted to the right by the amount of government spending (g). For example, at the real interest rate r_1, investment is i_1 and investment-plus-government spending is $i_1 + g$.

g were equal to zero, it would simply say that to be on the *IS* curve, savings plans must equal investment demand. With government spending and taxes not being zero, these have to be added to private savings and investment to obtain the equivalent flow equilibrium condition in the goods market that underlies the *IS* curve.

With this background it is now possible to proceed to derive the *IS* curve. It will be helpful to proceed in easy stages, however, and first to examine the right-hand side of Equation (18.6)—investment-plus-government spending. Figure 18.1 illustrates this aspect of the demand for goods. The real interest rate is measured on the vertical axis, and investment is measured on the horizontal axis. The thin curve labelled $i = i_0 - hr$ is the investment demand function, the derivation of which was discussed in Chapter 17. It shows that the level of investment demand increases as the real rate of interest falls. For example, at the interest rate r_1, the level of investment demand will be i_1. At higher interest rates, the level of investment demand will be less than i_1.

The thicker line in the figure, which is drawn parallel to the investment demand curve, is the level of investment demand plus the level of government demand for goods and services. You will recall that the level of government demand is assumed to be exogenous. It is determined independently of the level of the interest rate or of any other of the variables in the model. The horizontal distance between the investment demand curve and the curve labelled $i + g$ is the fixed level of government expenditure. It is illustrated by the horizontal line g at the interest rate r_1. You can see, however, that the distance between i and $i + g$ is the same at all rates of interest. The thick line $i + g$ represents the total amount of investment demand and the total demand for goods and services by the government added together—investment-plus-government spending. This diagram will be returned to later.

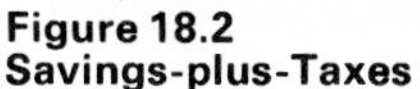

Figure 18.2
Savings-plus-Taxes

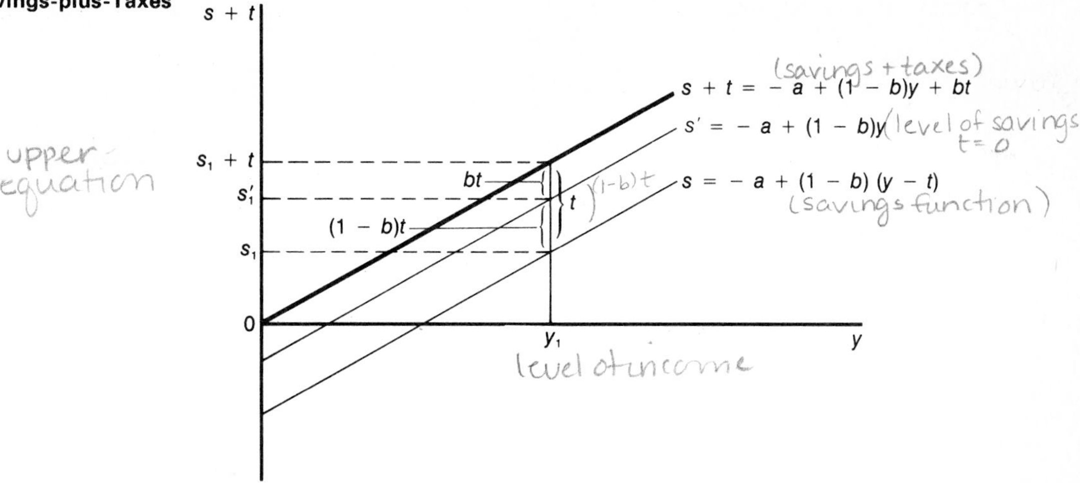

In the absence of taxes, savings would be s', the center thin line. With taxes at level t, the savings function is the lower thin line. It is displaced downwards by the propensity to save $(1-b)$ times taxes. Taxes are treated as constant. The savings-plus-taxes function therefore is displaced upwards above the savings function by the amount of taxes and is shown as the thick line. If taxes rise, the savings-plus-taxes line rises by the marginal propensity to consume (b) times the rise in taxes.

Next, consider the other side of Equation (18.6), savings-plus-taxes. This is slightly trickier than the previous analysis. The reason that it is trickier is that savings depend on *disposable* income. Disposable income, in turn, depends in part on taxes, so taxes have a double influence on the volume of savings-plus-taxes. That is, higher taxes mean lower savings, but higher taxes also mean bigger savings-*plus*-taxes all taken together. You need to be careful, therefore, in sorting out the relationships involved here. Figure 18.2 illustrates what goes on. Looking at Figure 18.2, first focus on the middle line. This line shows the level of savings that would be forthcoming at each level of income if taxes were equal to zero. It is simply describing the equation $s = -a + (1 - b)y$. This is the savings relation implied by the consumption function that was discussed in Chapter 16. Now, focus on the income level y_1 and notice that if taxes were indeed zero, savings would be equal to s'_1 at the income level y_1.

Now, drop the assumption that taxes are zero and allow taxes to be some positive number, t. You will recall, from the discussion in Chapter 16, that with taxes at level t, the savings function will shift downwards by an amount equal to $(1 - b)$ times the level of taxes. This is because when taxes go up, consumption and savings must fall by an amount equal to the tax rise. Fraction b of the taxes is paid for by reducing consumption, and fraction $1 - b$ is paid for by reducing savings. The bottom line in Figure 18.2 illustrates the savings function, allowing for taxes at level t. With taxes at level t and income at y_1, savings will be equal to s_1. The vertical distance between the line labelled $s = -a + (1 - b)y$ and the line $s = -a + (1 - b)(y - t)$ is equal to $(1 - b)t$.

Now, according to Equation (18.6), it is savings-plus-taxes that must be equal to investment-plus-government spending, and it is therefore the total of savings-plus-taxes that we are interested in. The top line of Figure 18.2 is a graph of savings-plus-taxes. It is nothing other than the level of taxes, t, added (vertically) to the lowest of the three lines in the diagram. This is illustrated at the income level y_1 by the distance indicated by t.

You are now in a position to understand the nature of the relationship between savings-plus-taxes and income. This relationship is similar to the relationship between savings and income. If you start from the curve describing the relationship between savings and income when taxes are zero, the savings-plus-taxes curve is equal to that original savings curve, plus taxes times the marginal propensity to consume. What this says is that a rise in taxes does not raise savings-plus-taxes one-for-one. A rise in taxes raises savings-plus-taxes by less than the rise in taxes because there is going to be a drop in savings in order to meet part of the tax payments.

You are now in a position to derive the *IS* curve graphically. Figure 18.3 is the source of the derivation. It looks much more formidable than it is, so try not to be put off by your first glance at that figure. Just follow the text carefully and slowly as it leads you through what, as you will soon see, is a straightforward derivation.

Frame (a) is nothing other than Figure 18.1—investment-plus-government spending. The interest rate r_1, the investment level i_1, and the government spending level g shown in that frame are the same as the values shown in Figure 18.1. Frame (c) is exactly the same as Figure 18.2—savings-plus-taxes. Again, the income level y_1, the savings level s_1, and the tax level t are the same in frame (c) as those shown and already discussed in Figure 18.2. The new frames of Figure 18.3 are frames (b) and (d). Frame (b) of the figure is just a graphical representation of the equilibrium condition that defines the *IS* curve. It is a 45° line. You will readily verify that measuring investment-plus-government spending on the horizontal axis in the same units as savings-plus-taxes are measured on the vertical axis implies that at each point on that 45° line, savings-plus-taxes are equal to investment-plus-government spending.

You can think of the *IS* curve now as being a relationship between the level of real income and the real rate of interest such that the economy is located on each of the three curves depicted in frames (a), (b), and (c). One point on the *IS* curve is the point A depicted in frame (d). Notice that the axes of frame (d) measure the real rate of interest and real income. Opposite this real interest rate axis, in frame (a), the real interest rate is also measured. Transferring the real interest rate r_1 across from frame (a) to frame (d) takes us horizontally across to point A. You will also notice that the level of real income on the horizontal axis of frame (d) is the same as the horizontal axis of frame (c) immediately above it. Transferring the income level y_1 down from frame (c) to frame (d), we shall reach the same point A. Notice that the level of savings-plus-taxes generated by income level y_1 is exactly equal to the level of investment-plus-government spending generated by the interest rate r_1. You can verify this by tracking up vertically from frame (a) to frame (b) and across

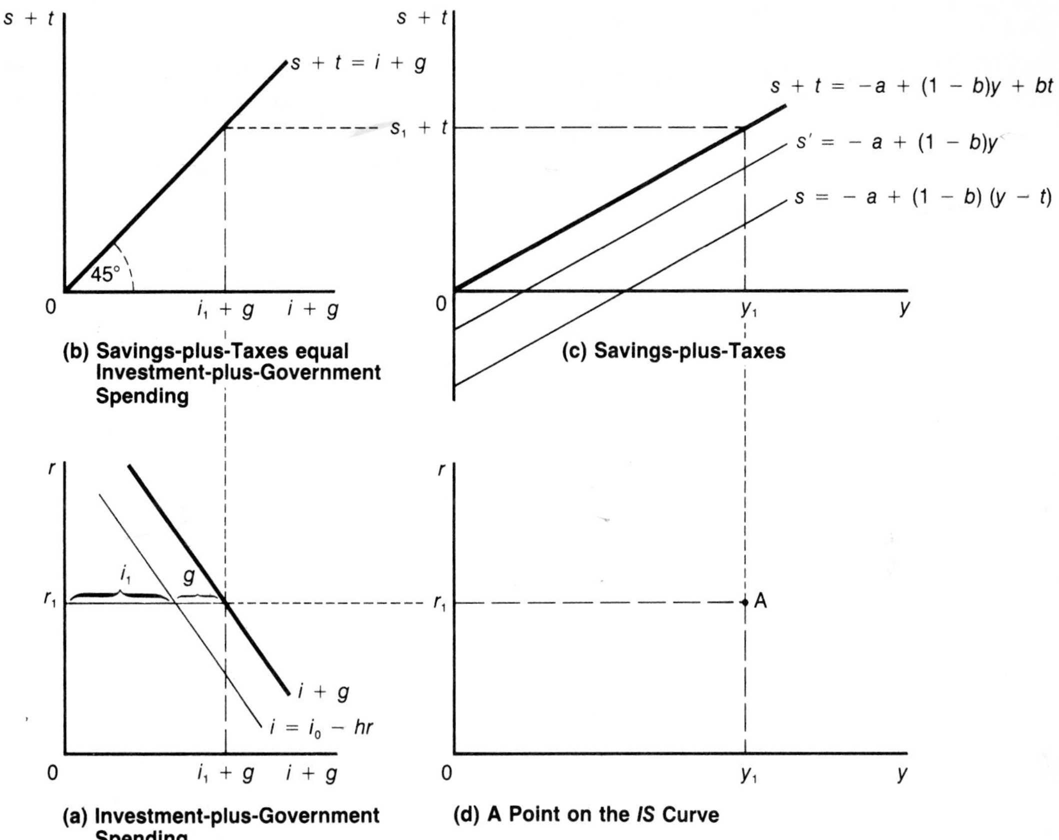

Figure 18.3
The Derivation of a Point on the *IS* Curve

The *IS* curve traces the relationship between the real rate of interest and the level of real income at which investment-plus-government spending equals savings-plus-taxes. Point A is a point on the *IS* curve. At point A, real income is y_1 [horizontal axis of frames (d) and (c)], so that savings-plus-taxes are $s_1 + t$. At A, the interest rate is r_1 [vertical axis of frames (d) and (a)], so that investment-plus-government spending is $i_1 + g$. Looking at frame (b), you see that $s_1 + t$ equals $i_1 + g$, so that point A satisfies the definition of the *IS* curve.

horizontally from frame (c) to frame (b). Point A, then, is a point on the *IS* curve.

Let us complete the derivation of the *IS* curve in a slightly less cluttered-up diagram but one that is in every respect identical to Figure 18.3 except that it has some of the lines removed for clarity. Figure 18.4 reproduces the curves $i + g$ and $s + t$ from Figure 18.3. First of all, familiarize yourself with Figure 18.4 and satisfy yourself it is identical to Figure 18.3 except that some lines have been left off to give the diagram a fresher and clearer appearance.

Now choose a higher interest rate than r_1, such as r_2. Notice that at r_2, the level of investment-plus-government spending is $i_2 + g$, which is less than

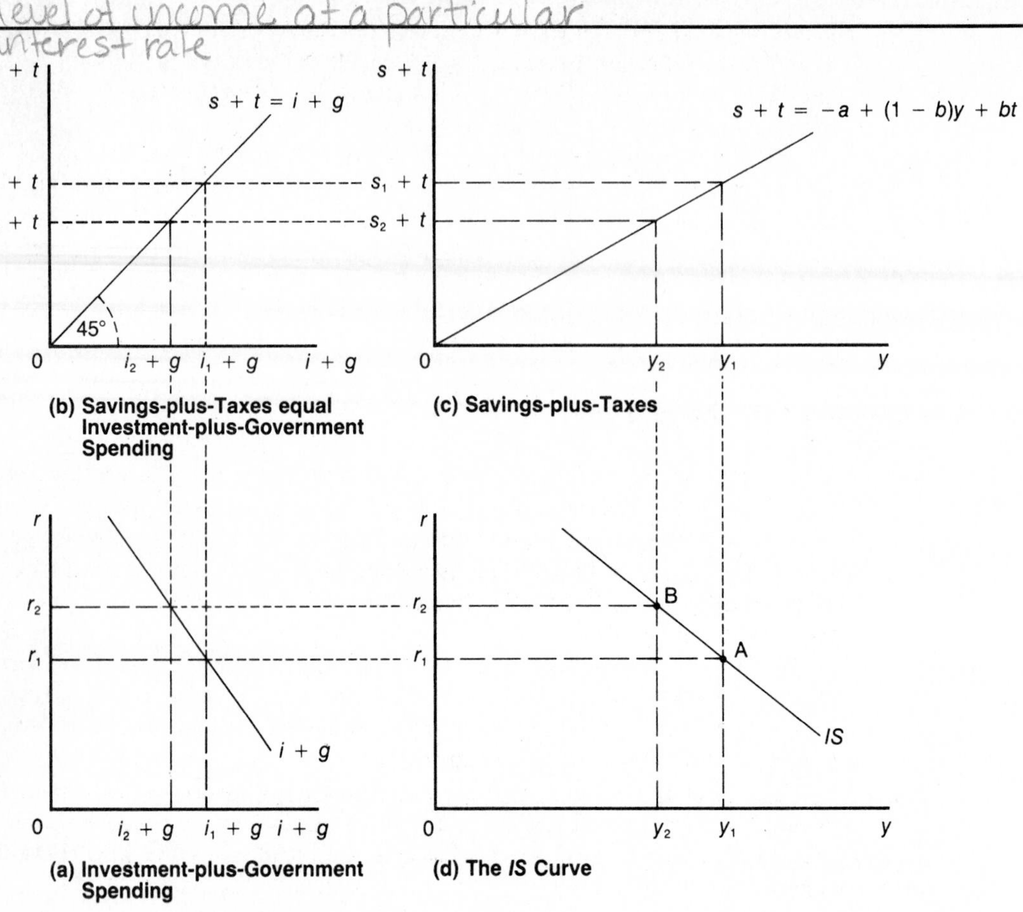

Figure 18.4
The Derivation of the *IS* Curve

This figure is exactly like Figure 18.3 except that in frames (a) and (c), only the $i + g$ and $s + t$ curves are plotted. Point A in this figure is the same as point A in Figure 18.3. Point B [in frame (d)] is equivalent to point A but relates to the income level y_2 and the interest rate r_2. At point B the income level is y_2 and savings-plus-taxes are $s_2 + t$. The interest rate at point B is r_2, so that investment-plus-government spending is $i_2 + g$. By looking at frame (b), you can see that $i_2 + g$ equals $s_2 + t$, so that B is also a point on an *IS* curve. Joining up A and B and extending the line beyond those points traces out the *IS* curve.

$i_1 + g$. Then track up from frame (a) to frame (b) and record the level of investment-plus-government spending $i_2 + g$ on the horizontal axis of frame (b). Notice that if investment-plus-government spending is equal to savings-plus-taxes (if we are going to be at a point on the *IS* curve), the level of savings-plus-taxes must equal $s_2 + t$ as shown on the vertical axis of frame (b). Now transfer that amount of savings-plus-taxes horizontally across to frame (c). You may now read off from frame (c) the level of real income that is necessary to ensure that the volume of savings-plus-taxes equals $s_2 + t$. That level of income is given by y_2. Now transfer the income level y_2 down to the horizontal axis of frame (d) and transfer the interest rate level r_2 horizontally across from frame (a) to frame (d). Where these two lines join, labelled B, is another point on the *IS* curve. Joining together points A and B with other intermediate points traces out the *IS* curve.

You will probably find it helpful to derive an *IS* curve for yourself by setting up the diagrams shown as frames (a), (b), and (c), and then deriving explicitly points on the *IS* curve for a series of interest rates such as r_1, r_2, and other intermediate rates. Be sure that you are thoroughly conversant with the way in which the *IS* curve is derived before moving on to the next two sections of this chapter.

C. Determination of the *IS* Curve Slope

You already know that the *IS* curve slopes downward. You can see this simply from frame (d) of Figure 18.4 in which you have derived an *IS* curve. You can also see from inspecting Figure 18.4 and comparing frame (d) with frame (a) that the *IS* curve is flatter than the slope of the investment demand curve. What does this mean? It means that as the interest rate falls from, say, r_2 to r_1, the investment rise from i_2 to i_1 is less than the amount by which income rises from y_2 to y_1. Call the change in investment Δi and call the change in income Δy. What is the relationship between the change in income and the change in investment when the interest rate is (hypothetically) allowed to drop from r_2 to r_1? Figure 18.5 illustrates this relationship.

You can figure this out by using a small amount of high-school geometry. A thickened triangle is shown in frame (c). What are the properties of that triangle? Its base clearly has length Δy, and its height has length Δi. You also know that the hypotenuse of that triangle has a slope equal to $1 - b$, the marginal propensity to save or, equivalently, one minus the marginal propensity to consume. Now recall your high-school geometry. The proposition that you need is the one that goes "slope equals rise over run." The "slope" in this case is $1 - b$, the "rise" is Δi, and the "run" is Δy. Translating "slope equals rise over run" into the numbers that represent the "slope," "rise," and "run" of the triangle in frame (c), we have:

$$\text{“slope”} = 1 - b$$

$$\text{“rise”} = \Delta i$$

$$\text{“run”} = \Delta y$$

so that

$$1 - b = \frac{\Delta i}{\Delta y}$$

Now multiply both sides of this equation by the change in income (Δy) to give

$$\Delta y(1 - b) = \Delta i$$

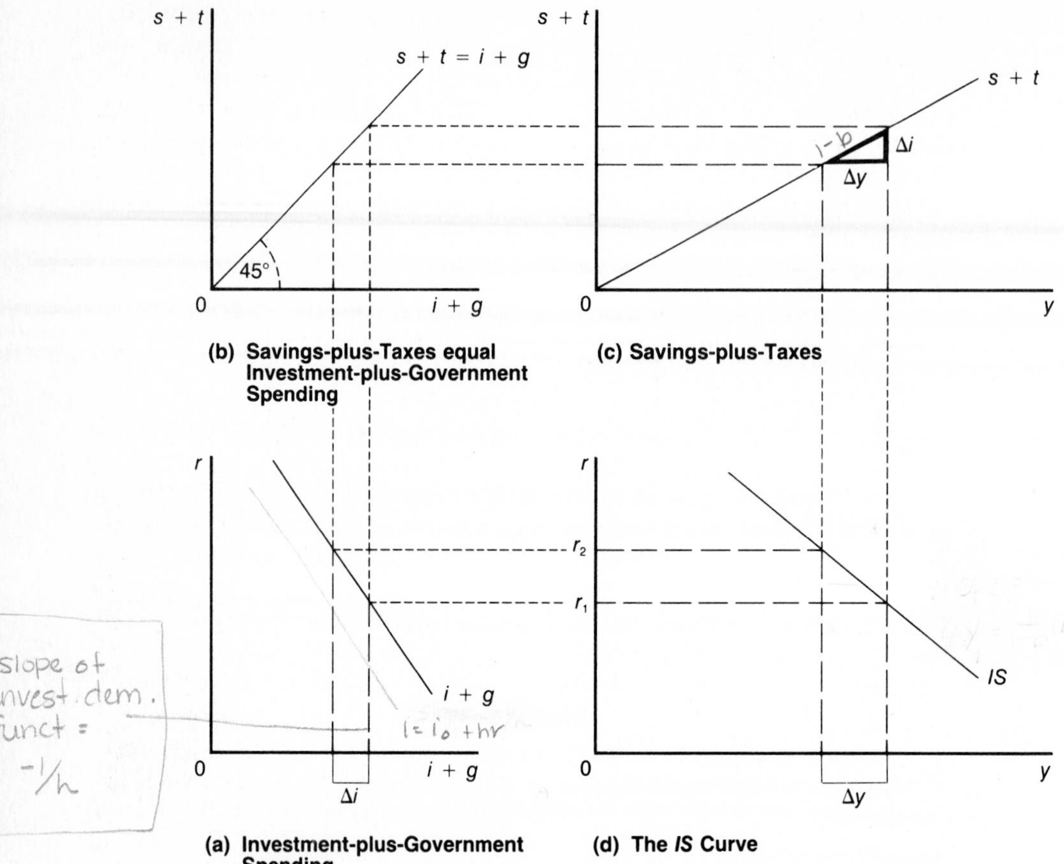

Figure 18.5
The Slope of the *IS* Curve

The *IS* curve slopes downwards. The lower the real rate of interest, the higher the level of investment, and since investment-plus-government spending must equal savings-plus-taxes, the higher too must be the level of savings. Since savings depend on income, higher savings will require higher income levels. Hence, to be on the *IS* curve, the lower rate of interest will have to be associated with a higher level of income. For a given drop in the rate of interest, the rise in income will be equal to the rise in investment divided by the marginal propensity to save or, $\Delta i/(1 - b)$.

Then divide both sides of the equation by the marginal propensity to save, $(1 - b)$, to give

$$\Delta y = \frac{1}{1-b}(\Delta i)$$

This is the famous Keynesian multiplier that you have already met in Chapter 16. It says that the change in income will be related to the change in investment by the amount $1/(1 - b)$. Clearly, since b is a fraction, $1 - b$ is also a fraction, and $1/(1 - b)$ is a number bigger than one, a multiple giving rise to the name *multiplier*.

You have now discovered that the slope of the *IS* curve is negative and that it is flatter than the slope of the investment demand curve. The slope of the investment demand curve is $-1/h$ (the ratio of the change in the interest rate to a one percentage change in investment). The slope of the *IS* curve is equal to the slope of the investment demand curve multiplied by the marginal propensity to save, or one minus the marginal propensity to consume.

D. Shifts in the *IS* Curve

The *IS* curve will shift if government spending changes, if taxes change, and if autonomous expenditure, i_0 or a, changes. Notice that this implies that the *IS* curve will shift due to a change in any of its determinants that is not itself induced by a change in either real income or the rate of interest. We shall focus only on changes in government spending and taxes. Changes in i_0 and a have identical effects on the *IS* curve to changes in government spending, as you will be readily able to verify for yourself once you are familiar with the analysis.

First, let us look at the effects of a change in government spending. Figure 18.6 will illustrate the analysis. The thickened curves simply reproduce the curves already introduced here and used in Figures 18.4 and 18.5. Now suppose that there is a rise in government spending by an amount that will be called Δg. What does that do to this diagram? The answer is shown in frame (a). The curve labelled $i + g$, which shows investment-plus-government spending, shifts to the right by an amount equal to the rise in government spending. This is illustrated by the thinner line in frame (a) that is displaced horizontally to the right from the original $i + g$ line by an amount indicated as Δg.

Holding taxes constant for the moment, there are no changes to be recorded in frame (c). All that remains is to work out the implications of the shift in the curve $i + g$ for the *IS* curve. You can do that by deriving a new *IS* curve, using the new $i + g + \Delta g$ line in frame (a). Applying the method that you have learned in the previous section on derivation of the *IS* curve, you will discover that the new *IS* curve is the one labelled IS_2 in frame (d). (If you are not sure how to derive the *IS* curve, you should go back to that section and reinforce your understanding of how to derive the *IS* curve.)

What is the effect on the *IS* curve of the rise in Δg? Suppose that g rises by an amount that will be called Δg. You can see by inspecting Figure 18.6 what happens to the *IS* curve. It shifts to the right. Further, it shifts to the right by more than the rise in government spending (Δg). You can see this by visual inspection of frames (a) and (d).

By how much more to the right has the *IS* curve shifted than the rise in government spending? The answer to this question turns out to be identical to the answer that you have already derived concerning the relationship between the slope of the $i + g$ curve and the slope of the *IS* curve. You can see this directly because of a visual trick that I have used in selecting the amount by which to raise government spending, Δg. Notice that I chose the rise in government spending, Δg, to be an amount such that when the interest rate is r_2

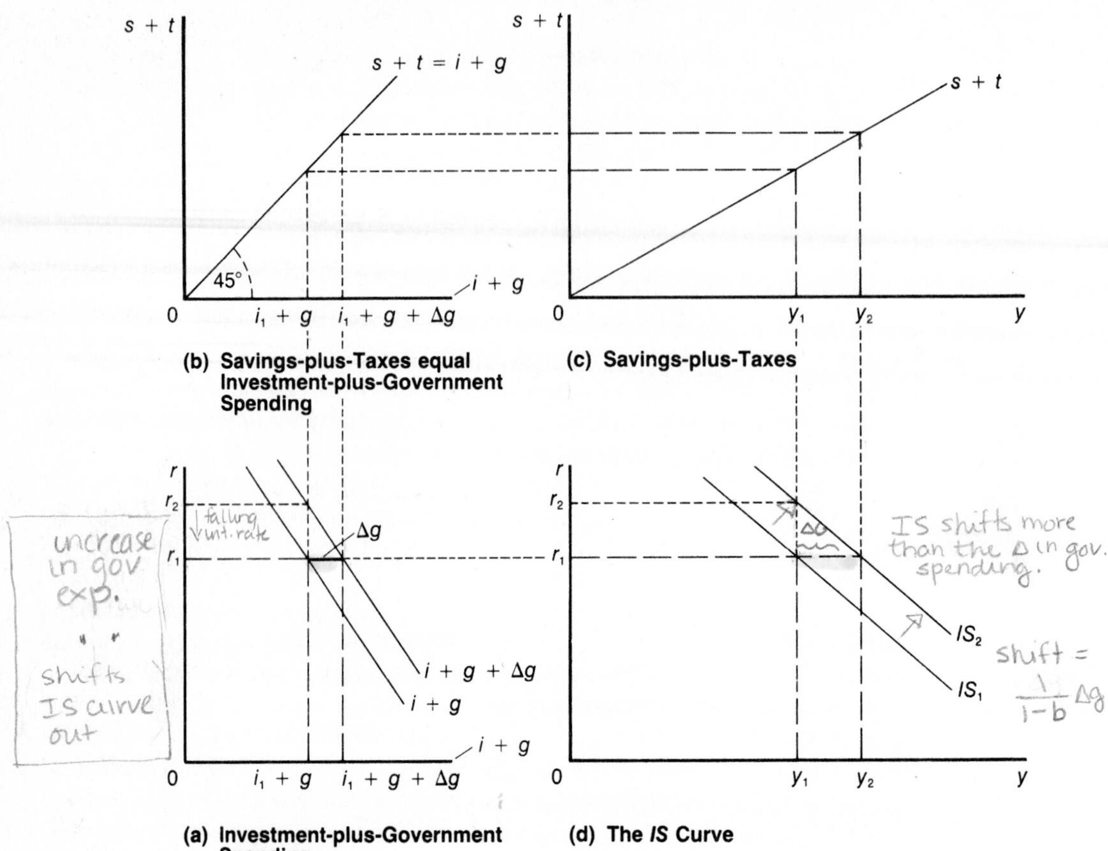

Figure 18.6
A Change in Government Spending Shifts the *IS* Curve

A rise in government spending of Δg shifts the investment-plus-government spending function to the right by the amount Δg. The *IS* curve is shifted to the right as a result of this by an amount equal to $\Delta g/(1 - b)$.

with the new higher level of government spending, the total level of investment-plus-government spending is identical to what had been previously at the interest rate r_1. You have already established that a fall in the rate of interest from r_2 to r_1 (a movement along the *IS* curve) raises income by $1/(1 - b)$ times the induced rise in investment. In Figure 18.5, this is labelled Δy [frame (d)]. In Figure 18.6, you can see this same amount shown as $y_2 - y_1$ (moving along the curve IS_2). You can see by further inspecting Figure 18.6 that the rise in income induced by a fall in the rate of interest from r_2 to r_1 along IS_2 is exactly the same as the rise in income, at the constant interest rate r_1, induced by a rise in government expenditure of Δg. Thus, you have established that the rise in income at a given rate of interest—the shift in the *IS* curve—induced by a rise in g is the rise in g multiplied by $1/(1 - b)$.

Now let us turn to an analysis to the effects of a rise in taxes on the *IS*

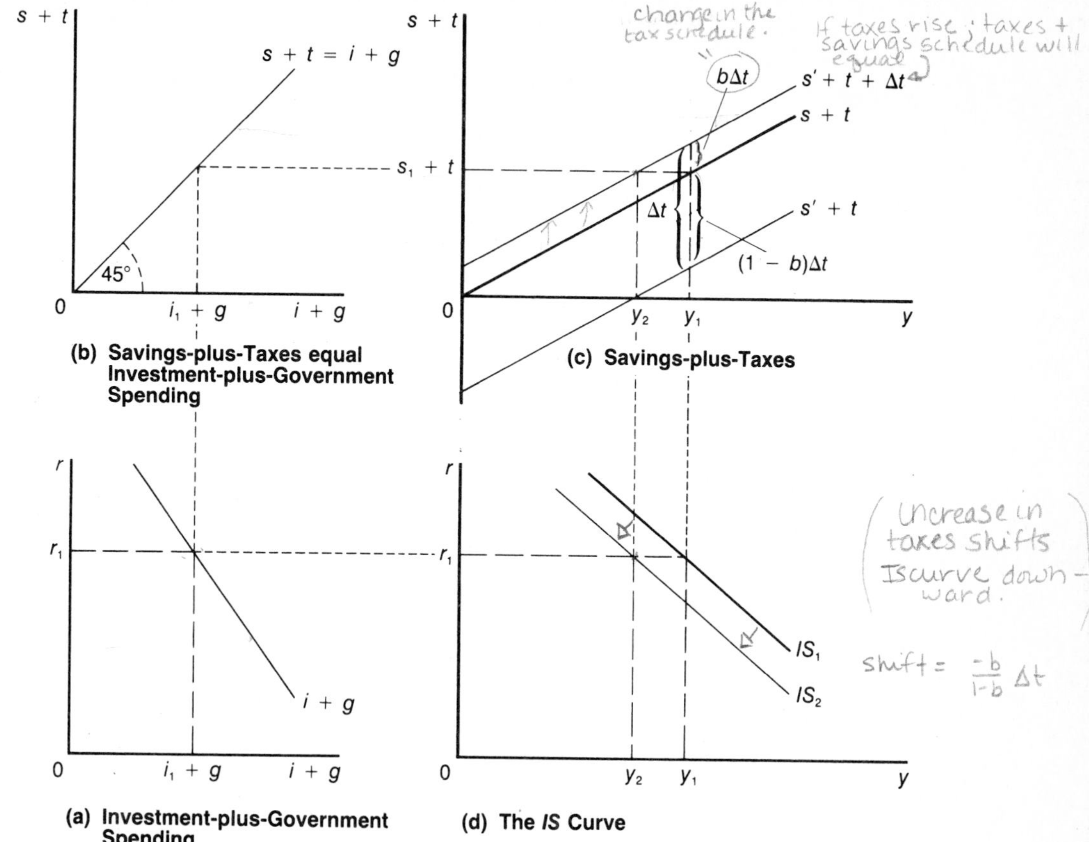

Figure 18.7
A Change in Taxes Shifts the *IS* Curve

A rise in taxes of Δt will raise the savings-plus-taxes curve by $b\Delta t$. This will result in a *backward* shift in the *IS* curve.

curve. This is slightly more complicated, and the extra complexity arises from the fact that the savings-plus-taxes schedule is a slightly more tricky relationship than the investment-plus-government spending schedule. Figure 18.7 will illustrate the analysis. Let us again familiarize ourselves with the setup by noting that the thick curves in Figure 18.7 are identical to those used in Figure 18.4. The *IS* curve labelled IS_1 is the *IS* curve that would be derived under the conditions prevailing in Figure 18.4.

We now want to ask what happens to the *IS* curve if taxes rise by an amount that will be called Δt. The impact effect of the rise in taxes is to be seen in frame (c). You know from the material that you have already mastered earlier in this chapter that if taxes rise, this will raise the savings-plus-taxes schedule but not by the full amount of the tax rise. This is because savings themselves will fall somewhat. If taxes rise by Δt, the savings-plus-taxes schedule will move to the schedule labelled $s' + t + \Delta t$. You should satisfy yourself that this new schedule is higher than the original schedule by an amount equal

Figure 18.8
The Size of the Shift in the *IS* Curve Resulting from a Change in Taxes

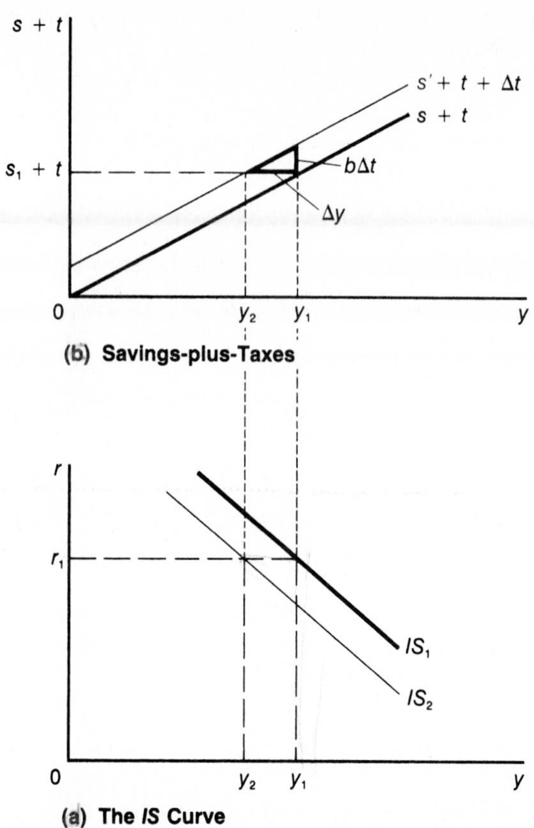

A tax rise of Δt will raise the savings-plus-taxes curve by $b\Delta t$. The backward shift in the *IS* curve that results from this will be equal to $b\Delta t/(1-b)$. The effect of a tax change on the *IS* curve is less than the (opposite) effect of an equivalent change in government spending. Government spending affects aggregate demand directly, whereas taxes affect aggregate demand indirectly through their effect on consumption. A \$1 change in taxes produces a \$$b$ change in spending. Thus, the tax multiplier is $-b/(1-b)$, whereas the government spending multiplier is $1/(1-b)$.

to $b\Delta t$. Savings will have dropped to s', which is $(1-b)\Delta t$ lower than originally. The total rise in taxes is the distance between the top line and the bottom line in frame (c).

Now let us figure out what this change in taxes has done to the *IS* curve. Derive a new *IS* curve, using exactly the same technique as before but using the curve labelled $s' + t + \Delta t$, the new savings-plus-taxes curve in frame (c). This *IS* curve, you will discover, is the one labelled IS_2 in frame (d).

How does this *IS* curve compare with the curve IS_1? First, you will notice that a rise in taxes leads to a shift in the *IS* curve but in the opposite direction to the shift resulting from an increase in government spending. By how much does the *IS* curve shift leftwards when the level of taxes is increased? You can answer this question with another piece of high-school geometry illustrated in Figure 18.8. Figure 18.8 reproduces frames (c) and (d) of Figure 18.7. Focus on the interest rate at r_1 with the income level at y_1. Notice that at the interest rate r_1, the tax rise shifts the *IS* curve such that, if the interest rate was to remain constant at r_1, income would fall to y_2. Call the change in income from y_1 to y_2, Δy. That income change is labelled Δy in frame (a). Transferring that income change up to frame (b), you see that it forms the base of a triangle whose height is given by b times the change in taxes. Again, use the formula "slope equals rise over run" to figure out what the change in income is in this case. You know that the "slope" of the hypotenuse of that triangle is $1 - b$, the "rise" is $b\Delta t$, and the "run" is $(-\Delta y)$, so you may establish that "slope equals rise over run" becomes

$$1 - b = \frac{b\Delta t}{(-\Delta y)}$$

(Why have I put a minus sign in front of Δy? Because income *falls* as taxes *rise*, so they move in opposite directions.) Now multiply both sides of this equation by the change in income (Δy) to give

$$\Delta y(1 - b) = -\, b\Delta t$$

Then divide both sides of this equation by $1 - b$, the marginal propensity to save, and obtain

$$\Delta y = \left(\frac{-b}{1 - b}\right)\Delta t$$

What does this say? It says that a change in taxes changes income in the opposite direction and by an amount that is equal to the marginal propensity to consume divided by the marginal propensity to save, times the change in taxes.

Summary

A. The Definition of the *IS* Curve

The *IS* curve is the relationship between the aggregate demand for goods and services and the real rate of interest when flow equilibrium prevails in the goods market, that is, when investment-plus-government spending is equal to planned savings-plus-taxes.

B. Derivation of the *IS* Curve

The *IS* curve is derived from the investment-plus-government spending curve, the planned savings-plus-taxes curve, and the equality of investment-plus-government spending and savings-plus-taxes. Figures 18.1 through 18.4 illustrate this and should be thoroughly understood.

C. Determination of the *IS* Curve Slope

The *IS* curve slopes downwards. That is, at lower real interest rates, higher levels of real income are required to maintain flow equilibrium in the goods market. This arises because at lower interest rates there is more investment spending, and with higher investment there needs to be higher savings to maintain equilibrium. Higher savings require a higher level of income, so that lower interest rates require higher income levels. More precisely, the slope of the *IS* curve is equal to the slope of the investment demand curve multiplied by $1/(1-b)$, where b is the marginal propensity to consume.

D. Shifts in the *IS* Curve

The *IS* curve shifts when government spending and taxes change. A rise in government spending will lead to a rightward shift in the *IS* curve by an amount equal to $1/(1-b)$ times the change in government spending. A rise in taxes will cause the *IS* curve to shift leftwards. The amount of the shift will be equal to the rise in taxes times $b/(1-b)$.

Review Questions

1. What is the *IS* curve?
2. Which markets are in equilibrium along the *IS* curve?
3. Why does the *IS* curve slope downwards?
4. Why is the *IS* curve flatter than the investment demand curve?
5. What happens to the position of the *IS* curve if there is a \$1 million rise in government expenditure on goods and services?
6. What happens to the position of the *IS* curve if there is a \$1 million rise in government transfers to individuals in the form of increased pensions and unemployment benefits?
7. What happens to the position of the *IS* curve if the government cuts pensions and raises defense spending by \$1 million?
8. You are given the following information about a hypothetical economy:

$$c = 100 + 0.8(y - t)$$
$$i = 500 - 50r$$
$$g = 400$$
$$t = 400$$

(c = consumption; i = investment; g = government expenditure on goods and services; t = taxes; y = real income; r = real rate of interest)

(a) Find the equation for the *IS* curve.
(b) Show that the slope of the *IS* curve is the same as the slope of the investment demand curve multiplied by one minus the marginal propensity to consume.
(c) Show that a rise in g shifts the *IS* curve to the right by five times the rise in g.
(d) Show that a rise in t shifts the *IS* curve to the left by four times the rise in t.

Appendix to Chapter 18

The Algebra of the IS *Curve*

This appendix sets out the algebra of the *IS* curve. The material presented here is simply another way of looking at the derivation given in the body of the chapter. For those who prefer an algebraic treatment, this may be found to be more compact and straightforward. It does not, however, contain anything of substance that is not stated in words and diagrams in the chapter.

Aggregate demand for goods and services is shown by

$$y^d = c + i + g \qquad \textbf{(18A.1)}$$

Consumption demand is determined by

$$c = a + b(y - t) \qquad a < 0, \qquad 0 < b < 1 \qquad \textbf{(18A.2)}$$

and investment demand is determined by

$$i = i_0 - hr \qquad i_0, h > 0 \qquad \textbf{(18A.3)}$$

Substituting c and i from Equations (18A.2) and (18A.3) into Equation (18A.1) gives

$$y^d = a + b(y - t) + i_0 - hr + g \qquad \textbf{(18A.4)}$$

To be on the *IS* curve,

$$y = y^d \qquad \textbf{(18A.5)}$$

so replacing y^d with y in Equation (18A.4) gives

$$y = a + b(y - t) + i_0 - hr + g \qquad \textbf{(18A.6)}$$

which may be rearranged as

$$(1 - b)y = a + i_0 + g - bt - hr \qquad \textbf{(18A.7)}$$

and dividing both sides by $1 - b$, we have

$$y = \frac{1}{1 - b}(a + i_0 + g - bt - hr) \qquad \textbf{(18A.8)}$$

or, equivalently,

$$y = \frac{a + i_0}{1 - b} + \frac{1}{1 - b}(g) - \frac{b}{1 - b}(t) - \frac{h}{1 - b}(r) \qquad \textbf{(18A.9)}$$

Equations (18A.8) and (18A.9) are alternative ways of writing the equation for the *IS* curve. The second of these is perhaps the clearest way of writing the *IS* curve and the one that makes interpretation of it most straightforward. The variables that enter the *IS* curve are government spending (g), taxes (t), and the rate of interest (r). The parameters that affect the *IS* curve are the constant in the consumption function (a), the constant in the investment demand function (i_0), the responsiveness of investment to a change in the rate of interest ($-h$), and the marginal propensity to consume (b). The way in which these various parameters enter the *IS* curve is made very precise in Equation (18A.9). First, the level of output that would obtain, even if government spending, taxes, and the rate of interest were all zero, is the first term in Equation (18A.9); that is,

$$\frac{a + i_0}{1 - b}$$

The slope of the *IS* curve (the change in the rate of interest that occurs when income changes) is given by the inverse of the coefficient in front of the rate of interest, namely,

$$\frac{-(1 - b)}{h}$$

Since $-1/h$ is the slope of the investment curve, you can immediately verify the proposition derived in the text that the slope of the *IS* curve is equal to the slope of the investment curve multiplied by $1 - b$.

A change in government spending shifts the *IS* curve by an amount indicated by the coefficient that multiplies g in Equation (18A.9). That coefficient is $1/(1 - b)$ and agrees with the derivation in the text.

A rise in taxes lowers the level of income (shifts the *IS* curve leftwards) since the coefficient in front of taxes has a minus sign attached to it. The size of the change in income that results from a rise in taxes will be equal to $b/(1 - b)$ times the change in taxes. This also agrees with the derivation in the text.

19

The Demand for Money, The Supply of Money, and the *LM* Curve

The subject matter of this chapter is very closely related to that of Chapter 9. If it is a little while since you studied that chapter, you will probably find it helpful to review its contents again before proceeding any further.

In the basic model, the analysis of the demand for money, the supply of money, and monetary equilibrium gave rise to the basic model's aggregate demand curve. The aggregate demand curve of the Keynesian model is a bit more complicated than that. Fundamentally, the additional complication arises because in the Keynesian model, unlike the basic model, the real rate of interest is not regarded as fixed but rather is a variable to be determined in the analysis. The real rate of interest is determined simultaneously with the level of output in the Keynesian model. The determination of consumption and investment summarized in the *IS* curve is one of the ingredients in the Keynesian theory of interest and income. An analysis of the demand for money and money market equilibrium summarized in the *LM* curve is the other ingredient in the Keynesian theory. This chapter deals with this second ingredient. You have four tasks ahead of you in this chapter, which are to:

(a) Know the definition of the *LM* curve.
(b) Know how to derive the *LM* curve.
(c) Understand what determines the slope of the *LM* curve.
(d) Understand what makes the *LM* curve shift and by how much.

A. Definition of the *LM* Curve

Like the *IS* curve that you have already studied, the *LM* curve is also a relationship between the rate of interest and the level of real income. Specifically, the *LM* curve is the relationship between the rate of interest and the level of real income that makes the demand for money equal to the supply of money.[1] Thus, like the *IS* curve, the *LM* curve is an equilibrium locus. It is

[1]You may be wondering why the *LM* curve is so called. The name was first used by Sir John Hicks who invented the *IS-LM* analysis. The letter *L* stands for "Liquidity Preference," the name that Keynes gave to the demand for money (what we are calling M^d). The letter *M* stands for the supply of money. Thus, the label *LM* reminds us that this curve depicts values of the rate of interest and the level of income at which the demand for money (*L*) equals the supply of money (*M*).

worth emphasizing again that the *LM* curve does not imply any causal relationship from the rate of interest to the level of income or in the reverse direction. Like the *IS* curve, it places further restrictions on the values that these two variables may take on. Let us now proceed to see how the *LM* curve is derived.

B. Derivation of the *LM* Curve

The starting point for the derivation of the *LM* curve is to recall the theory of the demand for money.[2] This theory, set out in Chapter 9, says that the amount of real money balances that people will want to hold in the aggregate will vary directly with the level of real income and inversely with the level of the market or *money* rate of interest and the rate of inflation. In Chapter 9, we went on to hypothesize that the market rate of interest would be equal to a *constant real* rate of interest plus a potentially variable rate of inflation. This led us to focus on the rate of inflation as the sole determinant of the propensity to hold money. In the Keynesian model, the price level is fixed, so that inflation is constant and zero, whereas the real rate of interest is a variable to be determined in the analysis. This difference of focus between the Keynesian model and the basic model does not mean that the Keynesian theory has to have a different theory of the demand for money. It does, however, lead us to write the demand for money function in the Keynesian model in a way that focuses attention on the variables that that model seeks to determine and explain.

Purely for the convenience of manipulating the Keynesian model, the demand for money function will be treated as *linear* in real income and in the rate of interest.[3] Specifically, we shall suppose that the demand for money is determined by the equation

$$\frac{M^d}{P} = ky + m_0 - lr_m \tag{19.1}$$

Exactly the same as in Chapter 9, M^d stands for the quantity of nominal money balances demanded, P is the price level, y is real income, r_m is the market rate of interest, and k, m_0, and l are constants. This equation says that

---

[2]There are several excellent discussions of the theory of, and empirical evidence on, the demand for money function. In my view, you can do no better than study David Laidler's *The Demand for Money: Theories and Evidence*, 2nd ed. (New York: Harper & Row, Publishers, Inc., 1978). An excellent and even more up-to-date study is David Laidler, "The Demand for Money in the United States—Yet Again," in Karl Brunner and Allan H. Meltzer, eds., *On the State of Macro-Economics*, 12 (Spring 1980), 219–71, Carnegie-Rochester Conference Series on Public Policy.

[3]The precise functional form of the demand for money that best fits the facts is a logarithmic function that says that the logarithm of real money demanded is a linear function of the logarithm of real income and the level (not logarithm) of the rate of interest. The different forms of the function used in Chapter 9 and here are selected for analytical convenience and may be regarded as holding approximately for small enough movements in the variables.

for each extra dollar of real income in the economy, k real dollars of extra money balances would be demanded. For every 1 percentage point rise in the market rate of interest on bonds, the demand for bonds would rise and the demand for money balances would drop by l dollars. Even at a zero level of income and a zero rate of interest, there would be some rock-bottom level of money balances demanded equal to m_0.

As reviewed and explained in Chapter 9, the market rate of interest will be equal to the real rate of interest plus the inflation rate. That is,

$$r_m = r + \pi \tag{19.2}$$

In the Keynesian model that you are now studying, the price level is assumed to be fixed at some number P_0, so that the inflation rate, π, is equal to zero. Taking account of this and calling the fixed price level P_0 enables us to write the demand for money function as follows:

$$\frac{M^d}{P_0} = ky + m_0 - lr \tag{19.3}$$

This equation incorporates the fact that the amount of nominal money demanded is deflated by a particular fixed price level, the price level called P_0, and the market rate of interest, r_m, is exactly the same as r, the real rate of interest, since with a fixed price level the inflation rate, π, is equal to zero.

Equilibrium in the money market requires the demand for money to be equal to the supply of money. Calling the supply of money that is determined by the actions of the monetary authorities M, the equilibrium condition in the money market may be written as:

$$M^d = M \tag{19.4}$$

Just as in the previous chapter, government spending and taxes were regarded as exogenous, so in this chapter, M is treated as being exogenous. That is, the money supply, M, does not respond directly to the values of any of the variables in the model, but rather is determined externally to the model and influences the values of those variables.

If M^d is replaced in Equation (19.3) with M, we obtain

$$\frac{M}{P_0} = ky + m_0 - lr \tag{19.5}$$

which is the equation for the *LM* curve. Notice that there are two variables in this equation, y and r. All the other terms in the equation are constants. The money supply, M, is a constant determined by the monetary authorities, P_0 is a constant determined by the Keynesian assumption about the money wage rate (using the approximation of the inverse "L" aggregate supply curve), and m_0, l, and k are constants, being parameters of the demand for money function.

Figure 19.1 illustrates the derivation of the *LM* curve. To draw Figure 19.1, first break the amount of money demanded into two parts. Define the

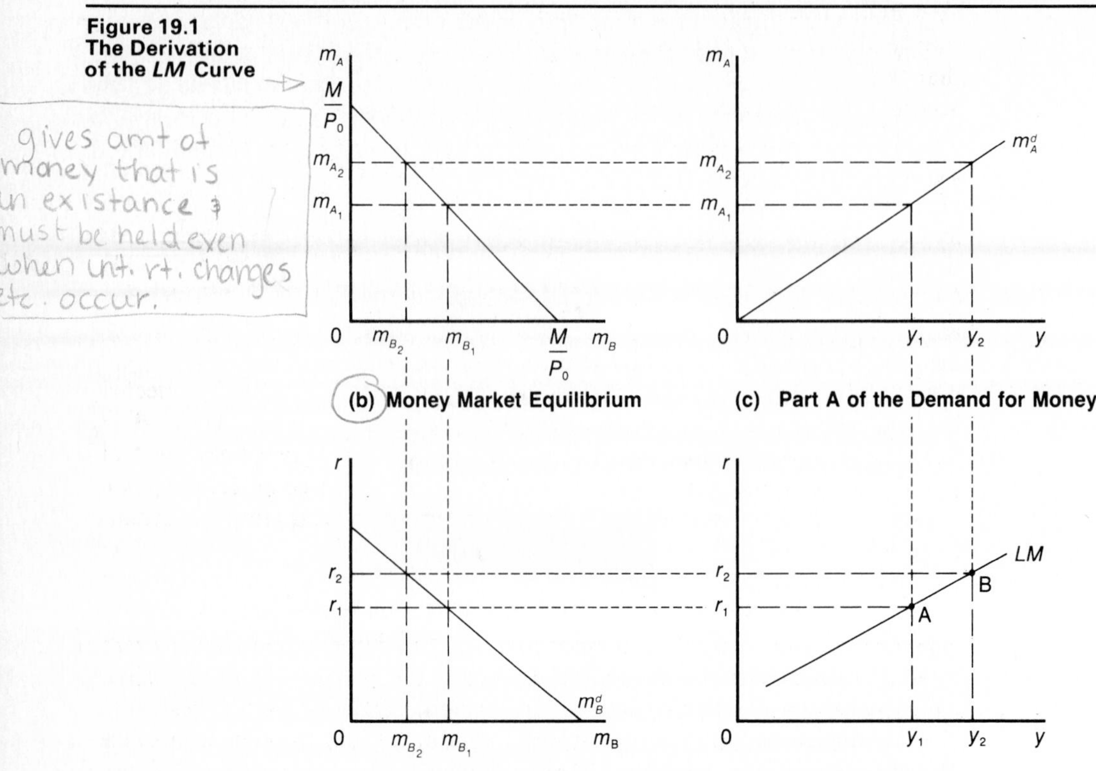

Figure 19.1
The Derivation of the *LM* Curve

The *LM* curve traces the relationship between the rate of interest and the level of income that ensures that the demand for money equals the supply of money. The *LM* curve slopes upwards. For a given amount of money, a higher income level (which gives rise to a higher demand for money) can only be sustained if there is more economizing on money balances. A higher rate of interest is needed to induce such economizing.

first part, ky, as m_A^d and the second part, $(m_0 - lr)$, as m_B^d. The demand for money may then be written as:

$$\frac{M^d}{P_0} = m_A^d + m_B^d$$

Now turn to Figure 19.1. The figure has four parts. Frame (c) contains a graph of the part of the demand for money m_A^d. Frame (a) contains the other part of the demand for money m_B^d. Notice that frame (a) is very similar to Figure 9.2 that you studied in Chapter 9. Frame (b) measures m_B^d on the horizontal axis and m_A^d on the vertical axis. The line drawn in frame (c) slopes at "minus one" and is located in the following way. Measure on the horizontal axis the total exogenously given amount of money divided by the price level P_0; then measure the same distance on the vertical axis, and join together the two points. What that line tells us is the amount of money that is in existence and that must be held and "allocated" to either m_A^d or m_B^d. In effect, it is the supply of money. The *LM* curve, derived in frame (d), is a relationship such that the supply of money depicted in frame (b) is held and is demanded in accordance with the two-part demand function plotted in frames (a) and (c).

To derive the *LM* curve, proceed as follows. First, pick an interest rate—say, r_1. Focus on frame (a) and notice that at the interest rate r_1, the amount of money demanded under the *B* part of the demand for money is m_{B_1}. Transfer that amount of money demanded up to frame (b) and notice that if m_{B_1} is demanded under part *B*, then under part *A*, m_{A_1} money must be demanded ($m_{B_1} + m_{A_1}$ exactly equals the supply of money available). Then transfer m_{A_1} across to the vertical axis of frame (c), and using the curve drawn in that figure, work out the level of income that is necessary to ensure that m_{A_1} is demanded. That level of income is y_1. Now transfer the initially selected interest rate r_1 rightwards across to frame (d), and transfer the income level y_1 vertically downwards from frame (c) to frame (d). These two lines meet at point A, indicating that with the interest rate r_1, the income level y_1 will generate a sufficient demand for money to ensure that the quantity of money in existence is willingly held.

Now repeat the above experiment with the interest rate r_2. At interest rate r_2, m_{B_2} balances are demanded in part *B*. That leaves m_{A_2} balances to be demanded in part *A* of the demand for money. According to frame (c), in order that m_{A_2} balances be demanded, the income level would have to be y_2. Thus, the interest rate r_2 and the income level y_2, taken together, would lead to a demand for money equal to the supply of money. This gives point B in frame (d). The points A and B are both points on the *LM* curve as defined above. Joining these points together and extending the curve beyond these points plots the *LM* curve.

The *LM* curve that you have just derived graphically can be derived by a simple piece of algebra that involves nothing more than a slight rearrangement of Equation (19.5). By dividing through Equation (19.5) by *k*, the equation for the *LM* curve can be written with real income, *y*, on the left-hand side, as

$$y = \frac{1}{k}\left(\frac{M}{P_0}\right) - \frac{m_0}{k} + \left(\frac{l}{k}\right)r \qquad \textbf{(19.6)}$$

Alternatively, by dividing Equation (19.5) through by *l* and rearranging things slightly, the equation for the *LM* curve can be written as

$$r = -\frac{1}{l}\left(\frac{M}{P_0}\right) + \frac{m_0}{l} + \left(\frac{k}{l}\right)y \qquad \textbf{(19.7)}$$

which is an equation relating *y* to *r*. Equations (19.6) and (19.7) are identical and, indeed, are identical to Equation (19.5).

You have now seen how the *LM* curve may be derived graphically, and you have seen how it can be represented in a simple equation. Equation (19.7) is a direct representation of the *LM* curve shown in frame (d) of Figure 19.1. Let us now go on to explore more thoroughly the properties of the *LM* curve.

Figure 19.2
How a Change in the Interest Slope of the Demand for Money Affects the Slope of the *LM* Curve

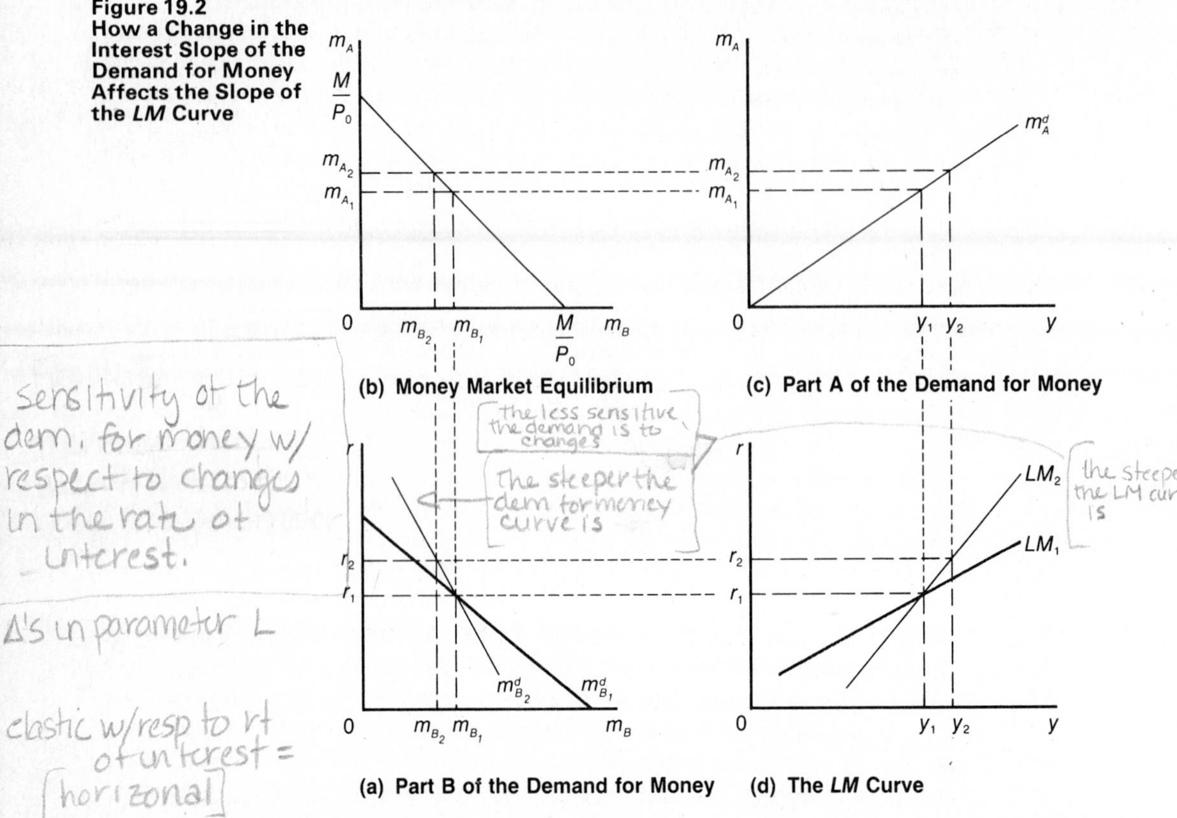

The less sensitive the demand for money to interest rate changes, the steeper will be the slope of the *LM* curve. As the demand for money becomes steeper [frame (a)], the *LM* curve rotates to become steeper [frame (d)]. In the extreme, if the demand for money was completely elastic [horizontal demand in frame (a)], the *LM* curve would be horizontal; whereas if the demand for money was totally inelastic [vertical in frame (a)], then the *LM* curve would become vertical.

C. Determination of the *LM* Curve Slope

The slope of the *LM* curve has considerable importance for the relative effectiveness of changes in the money supply and changes in government spending and taxes on the level of aggregate demand. You will see this in the next chapter. For now, let us focus on the factors that determine the slope of the *LM* curve. You can see from inspecting frame (d) in Figure 19.1 that the *LM* curve slopes upwards. What determines how steep or flat the *LM* curve will be? There are only two things that underlie the slope of the *LM* curve—the parameters k and l. These determine the sensitivity of the demand for money with respect to changes in the level of real income and the rate of interest.

Figure 19.2 illustrates the effects on the *LM* curve of changing the sensitivity of the demand for money function to changes in the rate of interest, by changing the parameter l. The curve LM_2 is derived from the steeper demand

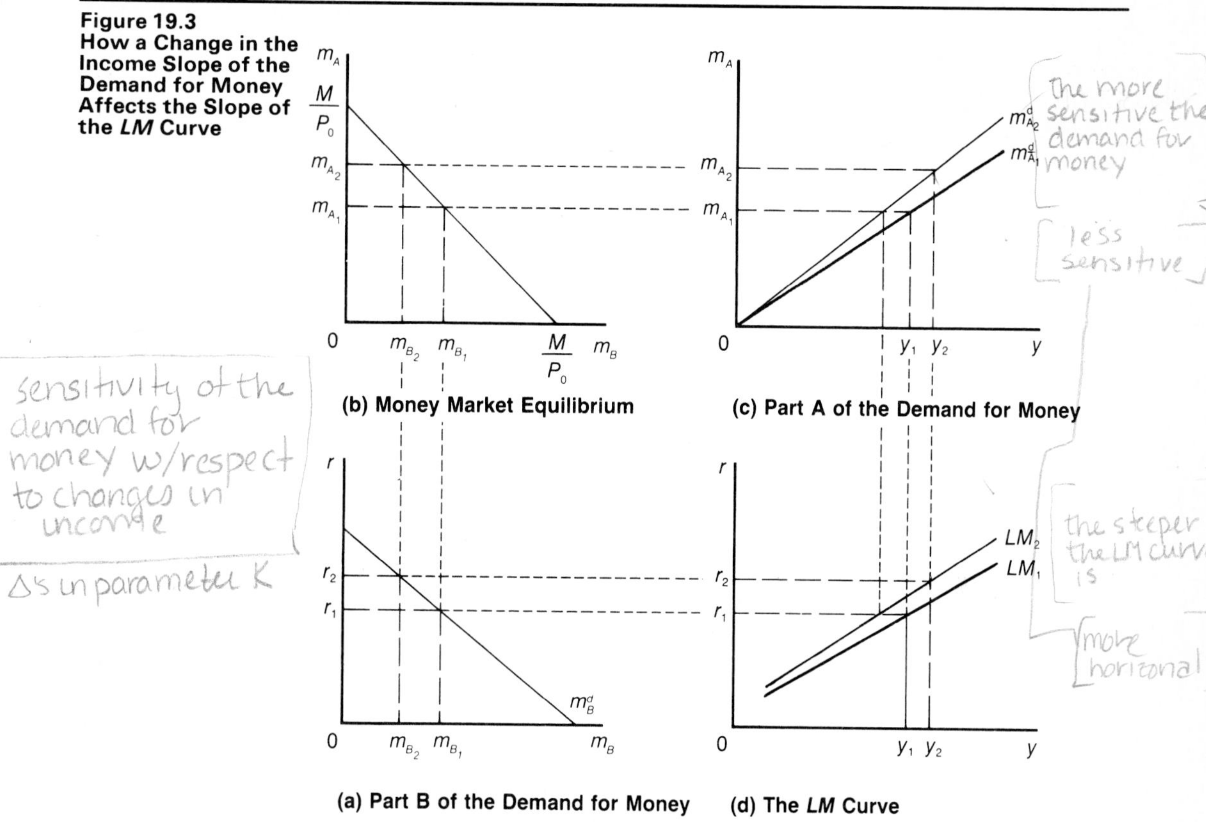

Figure 19.3
How a Change in the Income Slope of the Demand for Money Affects the Slope of the *LM* Curve

The bigger the effect of a change in income on the demand for money, the steeper will be the slope of the *LM* curve. As the demand for money becomes more sensitive to the level of income [frame (c)], the *LM* curve becomes steeper [frame (d)].

for money function plotted in frame (a). Notice that the steeper demand for money function makes the *LM* curve steeper. That is, the less sensitive the demand for money to changes in the interest rate, the steeper will be the *LM* curve. In the limit, if the demand for money became perfectly elastic with respect to the rate of interest, the *LM* curve would become horizontal; and if the demand for money became completely inelastic with respect to the rate of interest, the *LM* curve would become vertical. Check that you can derive those two extreme cases.

Figure 19.3 illustrates the effects of changing the sensitivity of the demand for money to changes in income, by changing the parameter k. Again, LM_1 is identical to the *LM* curve in Figure 19.1. The curve LM_2 is derived for the steeper m_A^d demand curve in frame (c). Notice that the more sensitive the demand for money to changes in income (the bigger the value of k), the steeper is the *LM* curve.

You can obtain these results that we have just derived directly from Equation (19.7), the equation to the *LM* curve. Notice that the *LM* curve equation says that the rate of interest is equal to some constants that involve only the money supply, the prive level, and the parameters l and m_0, plus a term equal to $(k/l)y$. Clearly, the ratio k/l measures the slope of the LM curve. The bigger that k is, the steeper the slope; and the bigger that l is, the flatter the slope.

What this all means is very simple. If money is a poor substitute for bonds, so that the demand for money is inelastic with respect to the rate of interest (l is very small), then the LM curve will be very steep. Thus small changes in income will require big changes in the rate of interest in order to preserve money market equilibrium. Conversely, if money and bonds are very close substitutes for each other, so that the demand for money is elastic with respect to the rate of interest, big variations in income will be possible with only small variations in the rate of interest, while maintaining money market equilibrium.

D. Shifts in the *LM* Curve

There are three things that can make the LM curve shift. One is a shift in the demand for money (a change in one of the parameters, m_0, l, or k), another is a change in the money supply, and the third is a change in the price level. We shall focus attention on the second and third factors. Notice that in the equation that defines the LM curve, the money supply is divided by the price level. In other words, the position of the LM curve depends on the real money supply. It follows immediately from this that a 1 percent rise in the money supply will have exactly the same effect on the position of the LM curve as a 1 percent cut in the price level. It is possible, therefore, to discuss both the factors that shift the LM curve by considering what would happen to the LM curve if the money supply changed. Once you know how the LM curve shifts when the money supply changes, you also know, by implication, how the LM curve shifts in response to price level changes.

Figure 19.4 illustrates the effects on the LM curve of a rise in the money supply. The thick curves in Figure 19.4 are identical to those in Figure 19.1. Now suppose that there is a rise in the money stock of an amount ΔM. This is shown in the diagram in frame (b) by the parallel shift of the money supply curve. Notice that it is shifted horizontally by an amount $\Delta M/P_0$, indicating that at all interest rates and income levels there is an extra $\Delta M/P_0$ of real money balances to be held. You can derive the new LM curve for this new higher quantity of money in exactly the same manner as the original LM curve, LM_1, was derived. You will notice that this new LM curve, LM_2, is to the right of LM_1. Thus, a rise in the quantity of money shifts the LM curve to the right. The amount by which the LM curve shifts to the right is evidently equal to $(1/k)$ times the rise in the quantity of real money balances. How do we know that? We know it by exactly the same line of reasoning that led us to work out the size of the shift in the IS curve in the previous chapter. Notice that the thickened triangle in frame (c) provides the detailed calculation of the amount of the shift in the LM curve. The rise in the money stock $\Delta M/P_0$ measures the height of that triangle. We know that its slope is equal to k, and we know that its base is the change in income that would occur at a given

Figure 19.4
The Effect of a Change in the Money Supply on the *LM* Curve

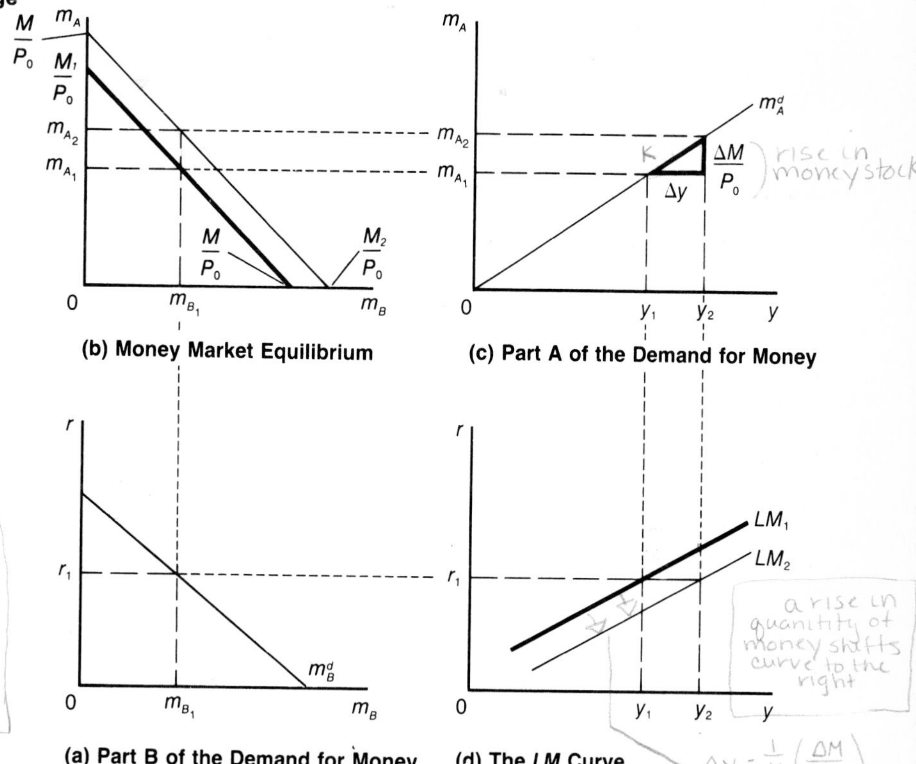

A rise in the supply of money shifts the *LM* curve to the right. The rise in the money supply ($\Delta M/P_0$) is illustrated with a horizontal shift in the money supply curve [frame (b)]. The resulting shift in the *LM* curve is equal to ($1/k$) times the rise in the money supply.

interest rate. Using the formula "slope equals rise over run," we can see that

$$k = \frac{\Delta M/P_0}{\Delta y}$$

Dividing both sides of that equation by k and multiplying both sides by Δy gives "run equals rise over slope," or

$$\Delta y = \frac{1}{k}\left(\frac{\Delta M}{P_0}\right)$$

That is, the size of the shift of the *LM* curve to the right, Δy, equals ($1/k$) times the rise in real money supply, $\Delta M/P_0$.

A percentage fall in the price level equal to the rise in the money stock just considered would shift the *LM* curve in exactly the same way.

Summary

A. Definition of the *LM* Curve

The *LM* curve is defined as an equilibrium locus that traces out the relationship between the rate of interest and the level of real income when the money supply is equal to the amount of money demanded.

B. Derivation of the *LM* Curve

The *LM* curve is derived graphically in Figure 19.1. This derivation should be thoroughly understood.

C. Determination of the *LM* Curve Slope

The *LM* curve slopes upwards. This is due to the fact that as the interest rate rises, people economize on their holdings of money. With a given quantity of money in existence, the only way that monetary equilibrium can be maintained at higher interest rates is for there to be a higher level of real income to induce a rise in the demand for money to offset the economizing on money holdings. The less elastic the demand for money with respect to the rate of interest, the steeper will be the *LM* curve. Also, the more responsive the demand for money to income changes, the steeper will be the *LM* curve.

D. Shifts in the *LM* Curve

The *LM* curve will shift if the money supply changes or if the price level changes. A rise in the quantity of money will make the *LM* curve shift to the right by an amount equal to $(1/k)$ times the rise in the real money supply. A rise in the price level will have an equivalent but opposite effect on the *LM* curve to that of a rise in the money supply.

Review Questions

1. What is the *LM* curve?
2. Which markets are in equilibrium along the *LM* curve?
3. Why does the *LM* curve slope upwards?
4. If money was a perfect substitute for bonds, what would be the slope of the *LM* curve?
5. If money and bonds were completely nonsubstitutable, what would be the slope of the *LM* curve?
6. What happens to the position of the *LM* curve when the money supply rises?
7. What happens to the position of the *LM* curve when the price level rises?
8. What happens to the position of the *LM* curve if the money supply grows at a constant rate?
9. Why does the demand for money depend on the money rate of interest rather than on the real rate of interest?

20

Equilibrium in the Keynesian Model

It is now possible to see the light at the end of the Keynesian tunnel![1] You may feel that you have been groping in the darkness of that tunnel for the last two chapters. Very soon you should be able to see the light! You are going to do five things in this chapter. They are as follows:

(a) Understand why the intersection of the *IS* and *LM* curves determines the equilibrium levels of output and the interest rate in the Keynesian model.
(b) Know the properties of the *IS*-*LM* equilibrium.
(c) Understand the effects of changes in government expenditure and taxes in the Keynesian model.
(d) Understand the effects of a change in the money supply in the Keynesian model.
(e) Understand how to interpret the Keynesian model as a more general theory of aggregate demand than that of the basic model.

A. Equilibrium at the *IS*-*LM* Intersection

From the discussion in Chapter 15 concerning the Keynesian theory of aggregate supply, you will recall that, at least as an approximation, the Keynesian aggregate supply curve is perfectly elastic at the price level P_0 for all income levels up to the full-employment income level, y^*. At y^* the aggregate supply curve becomes the same as that of the basic model and is perfectly inelastic with respect to the price level. The Keynesian theory refers to the determination of economic magnitudes in the region of output between zero and full employment. As was explained in the final part of Chapter 15, the fact that the

[1]This chapter presents the analysis developed by J. R. (now Sir John) Hicks in "Mr. Keynes and the 'Classics': A Suggested Interpretation," *Econometrica*, 5 (April 1937), 147–59. I vividly recall the sense of amazement and admiration I felt for John Hicks when, as a student struggling to understand Keynes's *General Theory* and getting nowhere, I came across this now very famous paper by Hicks. It seemed incredible that the complexities of the *General Theory* could be made so simple, and so soon after the work appeared.

Keynesian aggregate supply curve is perfectly elastic over the relevant range means that the level of output is determined purely on the demand side of the economy.

In the last two chapters we have, in fact, developed a theory of aggregate demand that is capable of telling us what the level of real income will be. The first part of this theory is the *IS* curve analysis, which tells us what the level of aggregate demand will be at each level of the rate of interest. The second ingredient is the *LM* curve analysis, which tells us the relationship between the level of real income and the level of the interest rate at which the amount of money supplied will equal the amount demanded. In effect, the *IS* curve and the *LM* curve give us two equations in two unknown variables—the level of real income and the rate of interest. When the economy is on both the *IS* curve and the *LM* curve, a unique level of real income and of the rate of interest is determined.

According to the Keynesian analysis, we shall never observe the economy "off" either of these two curves. If the economy was, in an imaginary sense, "off" the *IS* curve, investment-plus-government spending would not be equal to savings-plus-taxes. Equilibrating forces (which will be described below) would be set up that would quickly produce an equality between these two variables. If the economy was "off" the *LM* curve, the demand for money would not be equal to the supply of money. Again, strong equilibrating forces would be set up to bring about this equality. Only when the demand for money and the supply of money are equal and when savings-plus-taxes are equal to investment-plus-government spending will individuals' plans be compatible with each other, and will the economy be in equilibrium. The equilibrating forces will be so strong that the economy will only be observed in equilibrium. These remarks are very similar to the remarks made in Chapter 10, which discussed equilibrium in the basic model.

Notice that an equilibrium is a position of rest. It is a position in which, given the assumptions made, the plans of all economic agents are compatible with each other, and no one has any incentive to behave in a different manner. In the Keynesian model, this equilibrium may involve nonmarket clearing in the labor market as a result of the assumption that the money wage rate is incapable of downward adjustment to achieve a balance between supply and demand in that market. The very forces that, by assumption, hold the money wage rate fixed are, of course, part of the forces describing the overall equilibrium. Thus, you must distinguish sharply between *equilibrium* in the economy and *market clearing*. The two terms are not synonymous.

Let us now go on to characterize the equilibrium level of output and interest rate in the Keynesian model.

B. Properties of the *IS*-*LM* Equilibrium

Equilibrium

The *IS* curve derived in Figure 18.4 and the *LM* curve derived in Figure 19.1 are brought together and shown in the same diagram in Figure 20.1. Since the *IS* curve slopes downwards and the *LM* curve slopes upwards, these two curves cut in just one place. Label this point y_1, r_1. It is a property of the

Figure 20.1
Equilibrium in the Keynesian Model

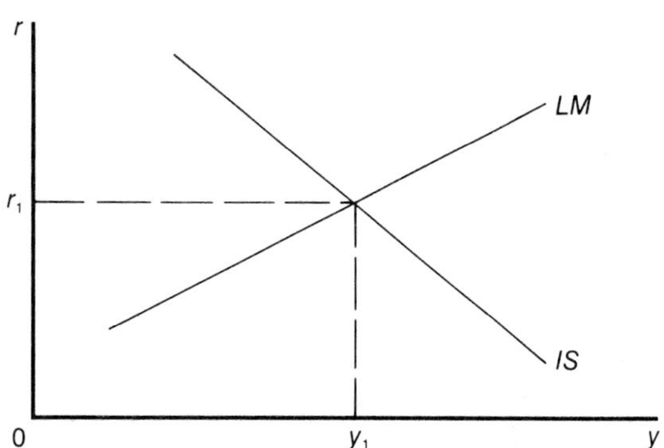

When investment-plus-government spending equals savings-plus-taxes (on the *IS* curve), and when the demand for money equals the supply of money (on the *LM* curve), then the economy is in equilibrium. Such an equilibrium is shown as y_1, r_1 in the diagram.

interest rate r_1 and the income level y_1 that two sets of equilibrium conditions are simultaneously satisfied. First, planned savings-plus-taxes are equal to investment-plus-government spending. Second, the stock of money in existence is equal to the stock of money demanded. The point at which the income level is y_1 and the interest rate is r_1 is the only point at which these two equilibrium conditions are simultaneously satisfied. This position is the equilibrium level of real income and the interest rate in the Keynesian model.

To determine the values of the other variables in the economy—the level of investment and savings—all that is necessary is to use a diagram like Figure 18.4 and work backwards from the quadrant that displays the *IS* and *LM* curves. Figure 20.2 illustrates the values of investment and savings. In frame (d), the *IS* and *LM* curves from Figure 20.1 are reproduced. The *IS* curve itself is derived from the underlying savings and investment decisions that are shown in frames (a) and (c). By working backwards from frame (d), we can work out the equilibrium levels of savings and investment. Transfer the equilibrium income level y_1 from frame (d) to frame (c), and you can read off immediately the equilibrium level of savings in the economy. Tracking leftwards across to frame (a), you can read off the equilibrium level of investment that is generated by the equilibrium interest rate r_1. By tracking this level of investment-plus-government spending vertically upwards to frame (b) and by tracking the level of savings-plus-taxes horizontally leftwards across from frame (c) to (b), you can see that the position depicted is indeed in equilibrium, for the two lines meet on the 45° line that describes the equality of $i + g$ with $s + t$.

Convergence to Equilibrium

Just what are the forces that bring about the equilibrium between investment-plus-government spending and savings-plus-taxes on the one hand and the supply of and demand for money on the other? To answer this question it is necessary to perform a conceptual experiment. Suppose, in a hypothetical

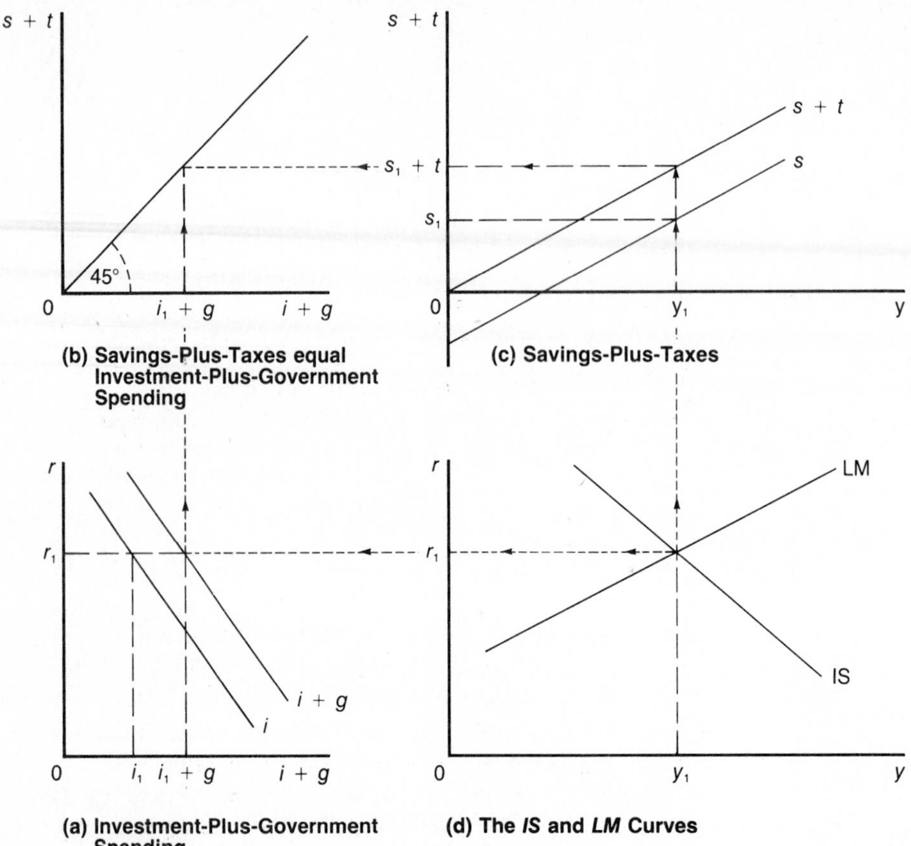

Figure 20.2
Equilibrium in the Goods Market

Once the equilibrium level of income and the rate of interest are determined by the intersection of *IS* and *LM* [frame (d)], it is possible to trace backwards to establish the levels of savings [frame (c)] and investment [frame (a)]. When taxes are added to savings and government spending to investment, as frame (b) shows, investment-plus-government spending is equal to savings-plus-taxes.

sense, that the economy was "off" the *IS* curve. Frame (a) of Figure 20.3 can be used to illustrate the discussion. If the economy was "off" the *IS* curve and to its right, investment-plus-government spending would be less than savings-plus-taxes. That is, you could view the interest rate as being too high, thereby depressing investment to too low a level, or income could be too high, raising savings to too high a level. Either way, savings-plus-taxes would exceed investment-plus-government spending. On the left side of the *IS* curve, the reverse inequality will hold. The interest rate is too low and is stimulating too much investment, or conversely, income is too low and is generating too little saving. Either way, investment-plus-government spending exceeds savings-plus-taxes.

Suppose the economy is in this second situation of too much investment-

Figure 20.3
The Keynesian Equilibrating Story

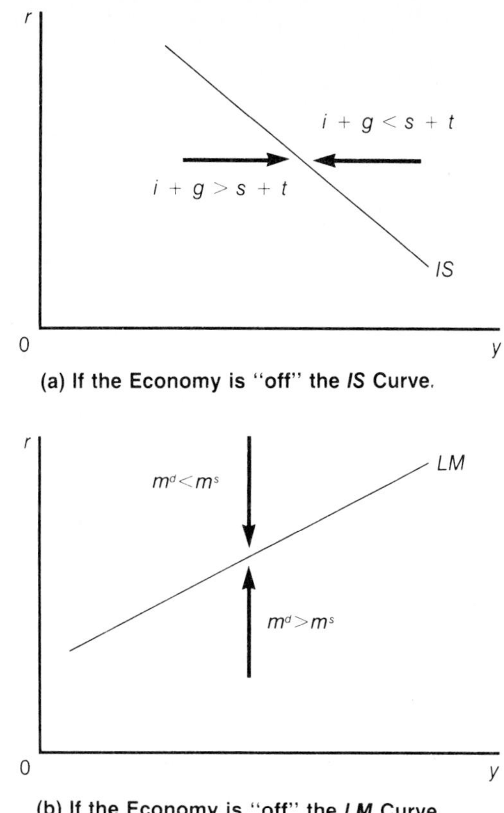

(a) If the Economy is "off" the *IS* Curve.

(b) If the Economy is "off" the *LM* Curve

If the economy is "off" the *IS* curve, planned expenditures will differ from income. In such a case, income would have to rise ($i + g > s + t$) or fall ($i + g < s + t$). The movement in income would be rapid, and the economy quickly would be brought to a point on the *IS* curve. If the demand for money was not equal to the supply of money, the economy would be "off" the *LM* curve. This would lead to the buying or selling of securities, which would produce a rise or fall in the interest rate, so that money market equilibrium was achieved. These equilibrating forces are assumed to operate quickly, so that the economy is not, in the normal course of events, observed to be "off" either the *IS* or the *LM* curves.

plus-government spending relative to the amount of savings-plus-taxes. What would happen? According to the Keynesian story, this would be a situation in which income would not be stationary but would be rising. The reason why income would be rising is that the total amount of spending that individuals are attempting to undertake exceeds the level of income out of which they are attempting to undertake that spending. To see this, recall that consumption is simply income minus savings minus taxes; this means that if savings-plus-taxes are less than investment-plus-government spending, the sum of consumption and investment-plus-government spending must be a bigger number than income. Such a situation clearly cannot be because we know that, as a matter of fact, income is equal to consumption plus investment-plus-government spending.

We can illustrate this point with a story (analogous to the story told earlier in the book about different levels of water on Lake Tahoe). The story would go like this. As people *tried* to spend more than current income, income would rise and keep on rising until it had reached a high enough level to be equal to the total level of spending that individuals were undertaking. We know where this point is. For any given interest rate, it is the point at which income is read off from the *IS* curve.

To reinforce your understanding, consider the reverse situation. Suppose the economy was to the right of the *IS* curve, with savings-plus-taxes bigger than investment-plus-government spending. In this case, total spending plans would add up to a number less than income, and income would be falling and would continue to fall until it had reached a low enough level for spending plans to have reached equality with income. Again, this would be a point on the *IS* curve.

Thus, part of the Keynesian equilibrating story is one that says that if investment-plus-government spending is different from savings-plus-taxes, income will adjust and will achieve an equality between those two variables, putting the economy on the *IS* curve. Income, not the price level or the interest rate, is the equilibrating variable in the goods market.[2]

Next, consider a conceptual experiment in the money market. Suppose that the economy is "off" the *LM* curve, as shown in frame (b) of Figure 20.3. If it was below the *LM* curve, then the demand for money would exceed the supply of money. That is, the interest rate would be too low or income would be too high, generating a larger demand for money than the amount of money available. If the economy was above the *LM* curve, the demand for money would be less than the supply of money. That is, the interest rate would be too high and/or the income level too low, making the amount of money demanded fall short of the amount available to be held.

What would happen if the economy was in one of these situations? Imagine that it is in a situation in which the demand for money was less than the supply of money. Obviously, since the supply of money is physically present in the economy, even though the amount demanded is less than the amount supplied, the amount supplied would have to be the same as the amount being held. In other words, individuals would have in their pockets, purses, and bank accounts more money than they would want to be holding in current conditions. What would they do in such a situation? The answer is they would try to get rid of the excess money.

The Keynesian story is that in order to lower their money holdings, people would buy bonds and other kinds of financial assets. Of course, each

---

[2]Don Patinkin (of the Hebrew University in Jerusalem), the world's leading Keynes scholar, believes that the essential originality in Keynes's *General Theory* was this idea—that income rather than prices plays the equilibrating role in the economy. If you wish to pursue this matter in greater depth and also get some experience of how a first-rate historian of economic thought works, you can do no better than read two of Don Patinkin's pieces on this subject. They are: "A Study of Keynes' Theory of Effective Demand," *Economic Inquiry*, 17 (April 1979), 155–76; and "The Process of Writing *The General Theory*, A Critical Survey," pp. 3–24, in *Keynes, Cambridge, and The General Theory*, eds., D. Patinkin and J. C. Leith (London: Macmillan, 1977).

individual can get rid of unwanted excess money holdings by buying bonds. Individuals in aggregate, however, cannot do this because there is a certain fixed amount of money in existence in the economy. One individual's purchase of bonds is another individual's sale of bonds. The reduction in one individual's holdings of money will be matched by an increase in someone else's. For the economy as a whole then, the attempts by individuals to rid themselves of excess money balances cannot result in a drop in the amount of money being held. Something else has to do the adjusting. What is it that adjusts? The answer is the rate of interest. The effect of buying bonds is to raise the demand for bonds and bid up their prices. Bidding up the price of a bond has the effect of bidding down its rate of return—the rate of interest.

You might find it helpful to have this spelled out. Suppose a bond pays $5 a year in interest in perpetuity, and suppose that the bond has a current market price of $50. The rate of interest clearly, then, is 10 percent—$5 divided by $50 expressed as a percent. Now suppose that instead of being $50, the bond price is $25. The interest payment is still $5 a year, but now the interest rate has increased to 20 percent ($5 divided by $25). Yet again, suppose that instead of being $50, the bond price is $100. In this case, with an interest payment of $5 a year, the interest rate would be 5 percent ($5 divided by $100). You see, then, that the rate of interest on a bond (the market rate of interest in the economy) is inversely related to the price of a bond.

Continuing now with the story—as people tried to get rid of their unwanted excess money balances by buying bonds, they would bid up the price of bonds and bid down the rate of interest. This process would continue until a situation arose in which the excess supply of money was eliminated. The interest rate would fall far enough to eliminate the excess supply of money because people would continue to buy bonds, bidding up their price and bidding down the interest rate, until they were satisfied that the money they were holding was equal to the amount that they wanted to hold.

The same mechanism would work in the opposite direction. If the demand for money exceeded the amount of money in existence, individuals would seek to add to their money balances. They would do this by selling bonds. As they sold bonds, the price of bonds would fall, and the interest rate on them would rise. This process would continue until the interest rate had risen sufficiently to make the amount of money in existence enough to satisfy people's demand for money. Either way, then, an excess demand or an excess supply in the money market would lead to a movement in the rate of interest by an amount sufficient to place the economy on the *LM* curve.

Now bring these two stories together. If the economy was "off" the *IS* curve, income would adjust to bring about an equality between savings-plus-taxes and investment-plus-government spending. If the economy was "off" the *LM* curve, the interest rate would adjust to bring about an equality between the demand for money and the supply of money. These two forces, operating simultaneously, ensure that both the stock equilibrium in the money market and the flow equilibrium between investment-plus-government spending and savings-plus-taxes are simultaneously achieved. It is an assumption of the Keynesian analysis that these forces operate with sufficient speed for the economy to be observed only at points of intersection of the *IS* and *LM* curves.

Figure 20.4
The Effect of Fiscal Policy on the Interest Rate and Real Income

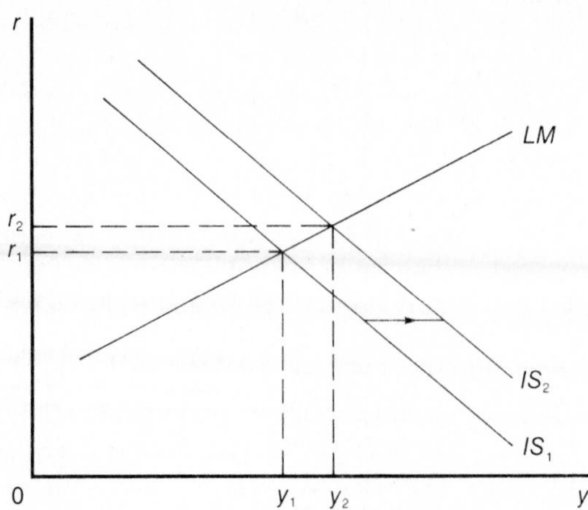

A rise in government spending or a tax cut will shift the IS curve from IS_1 to IS_2. The result will be a higher income level (y_1 to y_2) and a higher interest rate (r_1 to r_2).

C. Changes in Government Expenditure and Taxes

You have now studied all the key ingredients of the Keynesian model and are in the position to analyze in a fairly straightforward manner the effects of changes in government spending and taxes on the level of real income and the rate of interest. You should not confuse such an exercise with an analysis of macroeconomic policy. Properly understood, it is just one ingredient in a full policy analysis—the ingredient that tells us how changes in the government's monetary and fiscal policies influence the level of aggregate demand. A comprehensive analysis of macroeconomic policy cannot be performed using only the aggregate demand side of the economy. We shall conduct a thorough analysis of macroeconomic policy in Part VI of this book. Nevertheless, this is a useful stage of your study at which to analyze the effects of changes in government macroeconomic policy variables on the level of aggregate demand. Let us now turn to that task.

Changes in Government Expenditure

First, let us analyze the effects of a change in government spending. You already know that a change in government spending leads to a shift in the *IS* curve. Specifically, you know that a rise in government spending leads to a rightward shift of the *IS* curve by an amount equal to the change in government spending multiplied by one over one minus the marginal propensity to consume. What is the effect of the change in government spending, not on the shift in the *IS* curve but on the equilibrium level of income and the rate of interest? Figure 20.4 provides the basis for answering this question. Assume that initially the level of government spending is such that the *IS* curve is represented by IS_1. This intersects the *LM* curve at the interest rate r_1 and the

Figure 20.5
Fiscal Policy and the Steepness of the *LM* Curve

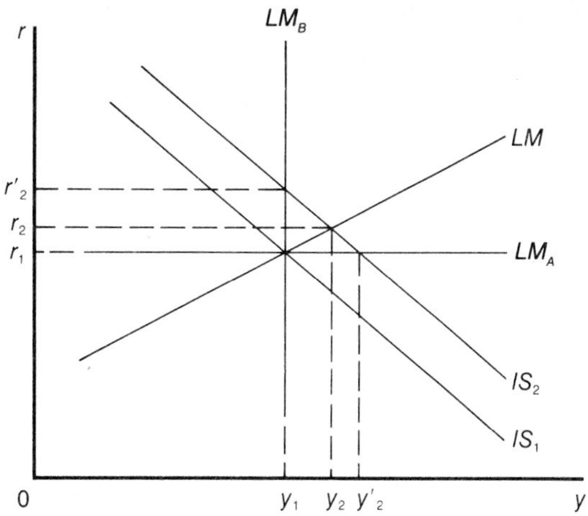

The flatter the *LM* curve, the bigger is the effect of a fiscal policy change on income, and the smaller will be its effect on the interest rate. In the extremes, a horizontal *LM* curve (LM_A) income will rise from y_1 to y'_2, and the interest rates stay constant; and with a vertical *LM* curve (LM_B), the interest rate will rise from r_1 to r'_2, and real income will remain unchanged at y_1.

income level y_1. Now imagine that there is a rise in government spending by an amount sufficient to shift the *IS* curve from IS_1 to IS_2. Recall that the horizontal distance of the shift in the *IS* curve is equal to the change in government spending multiplied by one over one minus the marginal propensity to consume. You can discover, by inspecting Figure 20.4, that the effect on the equilibrium levels of income and the rate of interest of this shift in the *IS* curve is to raise the interest rate from r_1 to r_2 and to raise income from y_1 to y_2. This result, depicted in Figure 20.4, is a general result. A rise in government spending raises both real income and the rate of interest.

The amounts by which income and the interest rate rise depend on the slopes of both the *LM* and *IS* curves. To see how the slope of the *LM* curve affects the outcome, consider Figure 20.5. In this figure are shown two extreme slopes for the *LM* curve. The curve labelled LM_A is horizontal. This would be one limiting case of the slope of the *LM* curve—that is, if money and nonmoney assets were such perfect substitutes for each other that people really didn't care how much money they were holding relative to other assets. If the interest rate was slightly above r_1, they would want to hold entirely nonmoney assets. If the interest rate was slightly below r_1, they would want to hold nothing but money. So r_1 represents the interest rate at which people are entirely indifferent as to whether they want to hold money or other assets. This is a pretty unlikely case, but one that serves to illustrate one of the extreme values of the effects of a change in government spending. In this particular case, you can see that the effect of a change in government spending would be to raise income and leave the interest rate unchanged. The rise in income would be equal to the full amount of the horizontal shift of the *IS* curve. That is, it would be

Figure 20.6
Fiscal Policy and the Steepness of the *IS* Curve

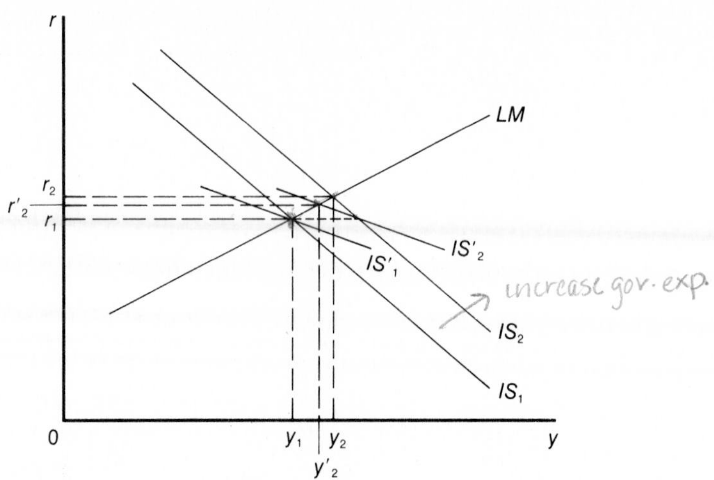

The flatter the *IS* curve is, the smaller will be the effect of fiscal policy on both interest rates and income. If the *IS* curve is *IS'*, the rise in income and the interest rate will be y'_2 and r'_2 compared with the unprimed *IS* curve and unprimed income and interest rate solutions.

equal to the rise in government spending multiplied by one over one minus the marginal propensity to consume.

The other extreme case illustrated in Figure 20.5 is that of the *LM* curve labelled LM_B. The *LM* curve would be vertical if the demand for money did not depend on the interest rate at all. This would be the case if people regarded nonmoney assets as completely useless as substitutes for money, so that regardless of the opportunity cost of holding money, there would be a certain amount of money that they felt it absolutely necessary to hold. In that not so unlikely but nevertheless exaggerated case, the rise in government spending that shifts the *IS* curve to IS_2 would raise the interest rate to r_2 but would leave the level of real income unaffected. What is going on here is that the amount of money that people want to hold is, in effect, a rigid fraction of the level of income. Since the amount of money in the economy has not been changed, then neither can the level of income change. Any change in government spending is fully "crowded out" by a rise in the interest rate choking off an equal amount of private investment demand.

The analysis in Figure 20.5 serves to illustrate the propositions that the effect of a change in government spending on real income is smaller when the interest elasticity of the demand for money is smaller, and the effect of a change in government spending on the rate of interest is larger when the interest elasticity of the demand for money is smaller.

The size of the government spending multiplier is also affected by the slope of the *IS* curve. This is illustrated in Figure 20.6. Consider first the *IS* curve labelled IS_1 and the equilibrium y_1, r_1. Now imagine that government spending increases, shifting the *IS* curve to IS_2. This produces a change in income to y_2 and a change in the interest rate to r_2. Now imagine that the *IS* curve is flatter than those depicted as IS_1, IS_2. In particular, let the initial IS curve by IS'_1. Now conduct the same experiment of raising government spending. Raise it by exactly the same amount as before. We know that the new IS curve will be parallel to the original one and will shift to the right by the same absolute amount, so that at the interest rate r_1, the curve IS'_2 intersects the curve IS_2. Now the new equilibrium income level is y'_2, and the interest rate level is r'_2. Notice that y'_2 is lower than y_2, and r'_2 is lower than r_2.

The analysis in Figure 20.6 shows that the flatter the IS curve, the smaller will be the effect of a change in government spending on income and on the rate of interest.

The consequences of the slopes of the LM and IS curves may now be summarized succinctly. The smaller the interest elasticity of the demand for money and the greater the interest elasticity of investment demand, the smaller will be the effect of a change in government spending on the level of real income. The smaller the interest elasticity of demand for money and the smaller the interest elasticity of investment demand, the larger will be the effect of a change in government spending on the interest rate.

Changes in Taxes

Considering the effects of tax changes is a straightforward extension of the exercise that you have just conducted. You already know from Chapter 18 that a rise in taxes shifts the IS curve in the *opposite* direction to that of a rise in government spending. That is, a rise in taxes will shift the IS curve to the left, whereas a rise in government spending will shift the IS curve to the right. You also know that the distance of the shift is fraction b (marginal propensity to consume) of the shift for an equivalent change in government spending. The differences between the effects of changes in government spending and taxes end here. The other effects of each of the two changes are identical in this Keynesian setup. All the remarks made above concerning the effects of the slopes of the LM and IS curves on the size of the government expenditure multipliers apply identically to the tax multipliers. The effects of a tax rise on income and the rate on interest are opposite in direction and fraction b of the magnitude of the effects of changes in government spending.

D. Change in the Money Supply

You already know that a change in the money supply will shift the LM curve. The effects of an LM curve shift on the equilibrium level of real income and the interest rate will, like the effects of the IS curve shift just analyzed, depend on the slopes of both the IS and LM curves. Let us consider first the general case. Figure 20.7 illustrates the effects of a change in money supply on the equilibrium level of real income and the rate of interest. The economy is initially in equilibrium, with the IS curve intersecting LM_1 at the interest rate r_1 and the output level y_1. Now imagine the money supply is increased, so that the LM curve moves to LM_2. The new intersection of the IS and LM curves is at the income level y_2 and the interest rate r_2. You can see by inspection of Figure 20.7 that the rise in the money supply leads to a rise in real income and

Figure 20.7
The Effects of Monetary Policy on Real Income and the Rate of Interest

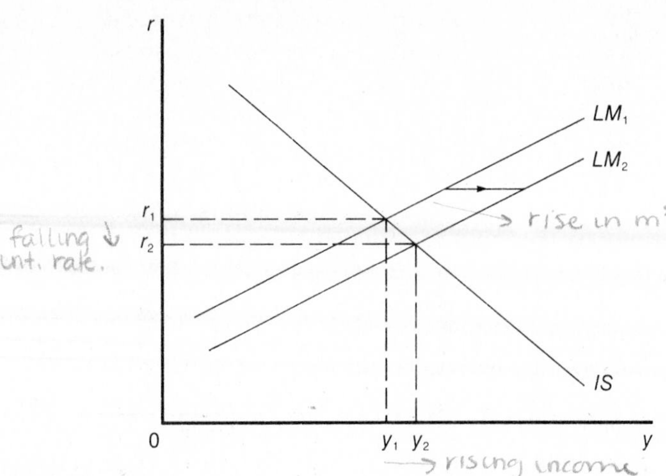

A rise in the money stock shifts the *LM* curve to the right, lowering the rate of interest and raising the level of income.

a fall in the rate of interest. This is the general prediction of the Keynesian model.

Now consider what happens to these effects when the slope of the *IS* curve is allowed to vary. The relationship between the effects of a change in monetary policy and the slope of the *IS* curve is illustrated in Figure 20.8. Just as in the previous case, two extreme slopes for the *IS* curve are shown. If the *IS* curve is the horizontal curve IS_A, the effect of a change in the money stock is to raise real income by the full amount of the horizontal shift of the *LM* curve. The interest rate remains unchanged. This result would arise if the marginal productivity of capital was completely constant, independent of the size of the capital stock. The opposite case, depicted as the vertical curve IS_B, leads to the prediction that the interest rate would drop to r'_2, and income would remain unchanged at y_1. This would arise if, no matter how much the rate of interest changed, firms saw no reason to change their capital stock.

What is going on in these two cases is straightforward to interpret. With a horizontal *IS* curve (with a fixed rate of interest), we are, in effect, in the world of the basic model. The level of aggregate demand moves one-for-one with the level of the money stock. We are not, of course, in the world of the basic model in all respects since, in this Keynesian world, the price level is fixed at P_0, and it is real income rather than the price level that does the adjusting as a consequence of the shift in aggregate demand. Nevertheless, as regards the specification of aggregate demand, this case is identical to that of the basic model. In the case of a vertical *IS* curve, the change in the money supply merely changes the rate of interest, leaving the level of aggregate demand unaffected. This arises because, with investment being completely insensitive to interest rates, the level of investment will remain unchanged no matter what the interest rate is. Since the level of government spending is also constant (by assumption), and since consumption demand depends only on income, there is

Figure 20.8
Monetary Policy and the Steepness of the *IS* Curve

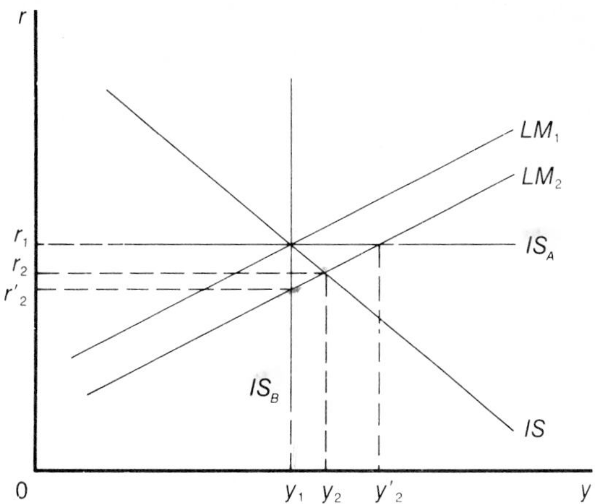

The flatter the *IS* curve, the bigger is the effect of a change in the money stock on the level of income and the smaller is its effect on the rate of interest. If the *IS* curve was horizontal (IS_A) the shift in *LM* from LM_1 to LM_2 raises income from y_1 to y'_2 and leaves the interest rate unchanged. If the *IS* curve was vertical (IS_B), a rise in the money stock that shifts the *LM* curve from LM_1 to LM_2 lowers the interest rate from r_1 to r'_2 and leaves income unchanged.

nothing being altered on the expenditure side of the economy to produce any change in the quantity of output demanded. All the adjustment, therefore, has to come out in a lower interest rate.

What Figure 20.8 illustrates is the general proposition that the more elastic the demand for investment with respect to the rate of interest, the bigger is the effect of a change in the money stock on income, and the smaller is the effect of a change in the money stock on the rate of interest.

Next, consider the effect of the slope of the *LM* curve on the size of the change in the real income and the rate of interest resulting from a change in the money stock. This is illustrated in Figure 20.9. Again, let the economy initially be in an equilibrium where the *IS* curve intersects the curve LM_1 at the interest rate r_1 and the income level y_1. Now let the money stock increase, so that the *LM* curve shifts to LM_2. As in the case of Figure 20.7, this produces a rise in income to y_2 and a drop in the interest rate to r_2. Now imagine that instead of the *LM* curve being $LM_1(LM_2)$, it is steeper than that, indicating a less elastic demand for money with respect to the rate of interest. Specifically, suppose the *LM* curve initially is LM'_1. When the money stock rises, the *LM* curve will shift to LM'_2. (Remember that the horizontal shift at a given interest rate, in this case r_1, is independent of the steepness of the *LM* curve.) What is the effect of an equivalent change in the money stock in this case? It is to raise income to y'_2 and lower the interest rate to r'_2. Notice that the change in both income and interest rate is bigger in this case than it was in the previous case. This serves to illustrate the general proposition that the smaller is the interest elasticity of the demand for money, the bigger will be the effect of a change in the money supply on both the rate of interest and the level of income.

Figure 20.9
Monetary Policy and the Steepness of the *LM* Curve

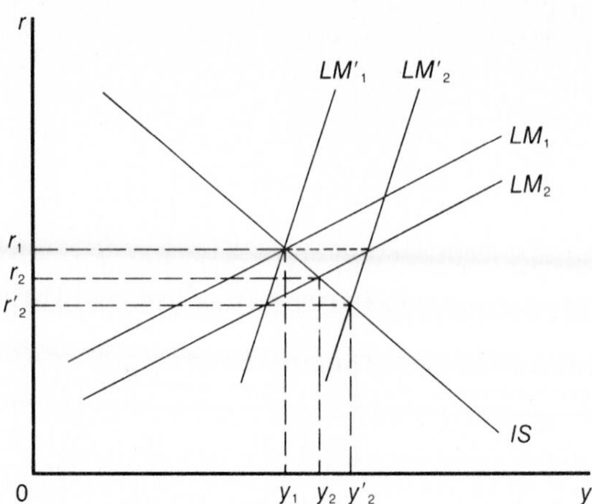

The steeper the *LM* curve, the bigger are the effects of a change in the money supply on both the level of income and the rate of interest. If the *LM* curve is *LM'*, then the changes in income and in the rate of interest are from y_1 to y'_2 and r_1 to r'_2. These are larger than the shifts arising in the case of the flatter unprimed *LM* curves.

You have now completed your investigation of the properties of the Keynesian model. The final section of this chapter is designed to help you see the connection between the Keynesian model and the basic model with which you are already familiar and also to prepare the way for helping you to understand how the useful and valid parts of the Keynesian model carry over and form an integral part of the new macroeconomics that you will be studying in the next part of this book.

E. The Keynesian Model as a General Theory of Aggregate Demand

Just as there are various stages in the process of learning economics that involve mastering some steps of analysis that seem, at the time, completely pointless so also there are times when everything seems to be falling into place. You have now reached one such point. It is as if a major section of a complicated jigsaw puzzle is just about to have the final piece put in, and a single pattern connecting previously seemingly distinct sections is revealed. Specifically, you are now going to be able to see not only the Keynesian model in its entirety but also how that model relates to the basic model with which you are already familiar. You can do more than this, however. You can also summarize the entire Keynesian analysis as a theory of aggregate demand that itself represents a generalization of the theory of aggregate demand as developed in the basic model and one that will carry over and remain an integral part of the new macroeconomics that you will study in Part V of this book.

Begin by recalling the concept of the aggregate demand curve. As set out in Chapter 9, the aggregate demand curve is defined as the relationship be-

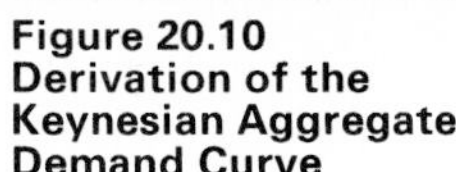

Figure 20.10
Derivation of the Keynesian Aggregate Demand Curve

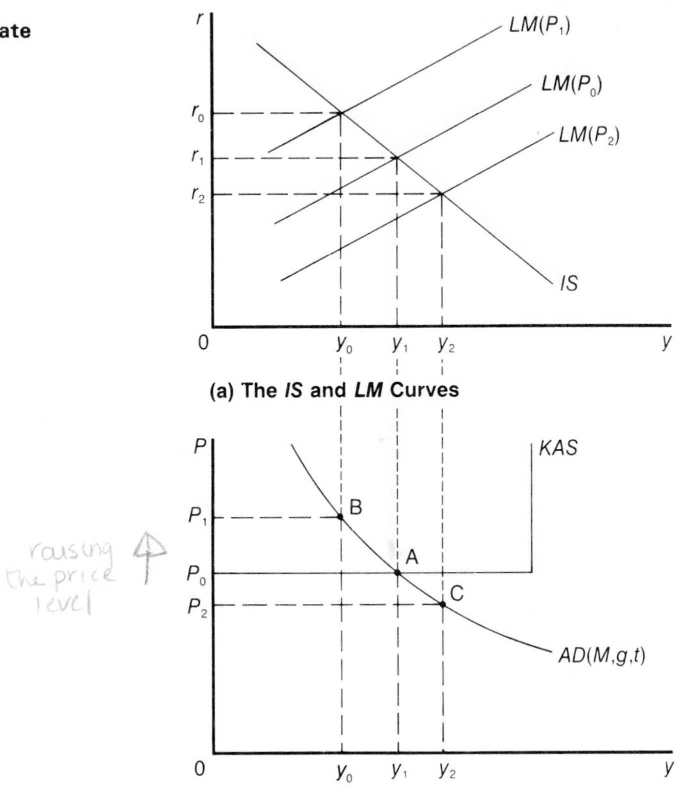

By hypothetically allowing the price level to vary, the *LM* curve will shift [frame (a)], generating different equilibrium interest rate and real income levels. These real income solutions and price levels may be mapped into a standard aggregate supply and aggregate demand diagram [frame (b)] to trace out the Keynesian aggregate demand curve. In general, aggregate demand will depend on the money supply, government spending, and taxes.

tween the aggregate quantity of goods and services that people want to buy in a given period of time and the general price level. This definition (and concept) is sufficiently general to embrace all conceivable theoretical frameworks and certainly that of the Keynesian model. We have, so far, not bothered to derive the aggregate demand curve of the Keynesian model primarily because, although it does exist, it is not very useful in the framework of analysis employed by Keynes. It *is* useful, however, in seeing the connection between the Keynesian and basic models. It is also a vital ingredient in the new theories of macroeconomics that we shall get to shortly. Let us begin by deriving the Keynesian aggregate demand curve and, from that exercise, understanding precisely why, within the context of the Keynesian analysis, the curve is not really needed.

It is easy to derive the Keynesian aggregate demand curve in a two-part diagram, as set out in Figure 20.10. Frame (a) shows the rate of interest on the vertical axis and real income on the horizontal axis. Frame (b) shows the price level on the vertical axis and real income on the horizontal axis. In frame (a) are shown an *IS* curve and an *LM* curve labelled $LM(P_0)$. These two curves intersect at the income level y_1 and interest rate r_1. This is exactly the solution that we have been working with throughout this chapter. That solution point can also be characterized in frame (b). It is point A. We know that it is point A because we know that the Keynesian aggregate supply curve is horizontal at the predetermined price level P_0, and we know that the model has determined for us, on the demand side, an output level of y_1.

It is possible, to ask, hypothetically, what the level of aggregate demand would be in the Keynesian framework if the price level was different from P_0. Suppose the price level was higher than P_0, say at P_1. What then would be the quantity of goods and services demanded if everything else was the same? From the analysis of the *IS* curve in Chapter 18 you can quickly verify that the position of the *IS* curve is independent of the price level. It is entirely a real curve that relates real income to the rate of interest and depends only on other real variables, namely, real taxes and real government spending. The *LM* curve, in contrast, is not independent of the price level. You can quickly verify from its definition and derivation that a change in the price level has the same type of effect (but opposite in direction) on the *LM* curve as does a change in the money supply. If we *lower* the money supply, we shift the *LM* curve to the left. If we *raise* the price level to P_1, we know that the *LM* curve will also shift to the left. Let us suppose that it shifts to become the curve $LM(P_1)$ in frame (a).

This new *LM* curve intersects the *IS* curve at the interest rate r_0 and the output level y_0. Since we know the price level that gave rise to that *LM* curve is P_1, we can read off from frame (b) the point at which the income level y_0 is associated with the price level P_1. That point is B. Point B is, like point A, another point on the Keynesian aggregate demand curve. However, unlike point A, point B is not a point at which we shall observe the economy. Point A is the economy equilibrium. Nevertheless, simply tracing out the locus of points that link the price level and level of output that simultaneously satisfy equilibrium in the money market and in investment and savings plans yields point B.

Next, imagine that the price level is at some lower level than P_0, say, P_2, as shown on the vertical axis of frame (b). With a lower price level we know that the *LM* curve would shift to the right (equivalent to a rise in the money stock). Suppose, in fact, that the *LM* curve shifts to the curve labelled $LM(P_2)$, which generates the income level y_2 and the interest rate r_2. Dropping that income level y_2 down to frame (b) shows that point C is also a point on the Keynesian aggregate demand curve. Joining up points B, A, C and extrapolating to points beyond B and C traces out the Keynesian aggregate demand curve.

In conducting the Keynesian analysis of the determination of output, it was possible, of course, to focus only on point A. By looking at what happens to the *IS* and *LM* curve intersections, we are simply examining how point A travels horizontally along the aggregate supply curve. This is why there is no need, in the Keynesian framework, to derive the aggregate demand curve. Nevertheless, the curve is there, and we can use it to help us understand the relationship between the Keynesian and basic models of output and employment determination. It is also going to be used in the work that follows in the next part of the book.

The key thing to understand about the analysis of aggregate demand that we have conducted in the Keynesian framework is that the entire analysis may be interpreted as telling us about the factors that cause horizontal shifts in the aggregate demand curve. Anything that shifts point A will also shift point B and point C in the same horizontal direction. Thus, a rise in government spending or a cut in taxes or a rise in the money stock will all produce a rightward shift of the aggregate demand curve. The *AD* curve in frame (b) in Figure 20.10 is labelled *AD*(M, g, t) to remind us of this. The size of that shift will depend on the slopes of the *IS* and *LM* curves. Those slopes will in turn depend on the slopes of the demand for money function and the investment demand function. In general, the steeper the demand for money function with respect to the interest rate and/or the flatter the investment demand function with respect to the interest rate, the bigger will be the effect of a change in the money supply on the horizontal shift of the aggregate demand curve, and the smaller will be the effect of a change in government spending or taxes.

In the limiting case where the *IS* curve is horizontal (the interest rate is fixed) or where the *LM* curve is vertical (money is completely nonsubstitutable for other assets), then only changes in the money supply will lead to changes in the aggregate demand curve, and changes in government spending and taxes will leave the aggregate demand curve unaffected.

At the other extreme, if money is a perfect substitute for other assets so that the *LM* curve is horizontal, or if investment demand is completely unresponsive to interest rate changes so that the *IS* curve is vertical, then only changes in government spending and taxes will lead to shifts in the aggregate demand curve, and changes in the money stock will leave the aggregate demand curve unaffected.

You can now see that the monetary theory of aggregate demand developed in Chapter 9 is, in effect, a special case of this more general Keynesian theory of aggregate demand. It is the case in which the *IS* curve is horizontal—when the real rate of interest is constant. In this case, as was illustrated in Figure 20.8, only changes in the money stock lead to changes in real income. Within the broader framework of the aggregate demand analysis just examined, we could say, equivalently, that only changes in the money stock will shift the aggregate demand curve.

The Keynesian cross model that we examined in Chapter 16 may be seen as another special case. That model is the case in which either the *IS* curve is vertical or the *LM* curve is horizontal, so that changes in the rate of interest do not affect the level of investment.

There is one final special case—a vertical *LM* curve—that generates results similar to those of the basic model (Chapter 9). In this case, as in the basic model, only changes in the money stock will shift the aggregate demand curve. Unlike the basic model, however, changes in the money stock or in fiscal policy variables will change the real rate of interest. Thus, the vertical *LM* curve is not the same as the basic model. Only the horizontal *IS* curve is equivalent to the basic model.

In general, none of these extremes will be a relevant description of an actual economy and the aggregate demand curve will shift both because of changes in the money stock and because of changes in the levels of government spending and taxes.

Summary

A. Equilibrium at the *IS*-*LM* Intersection

Because the price level is fixed in the Keynesian analysis, the level of output is determined purely by the level of aggregate demand. The *IS* curve shows at each level of the interest rate the level of real income that equates savings-plus-taxes with investment-plus-government spending. The *LM* curve gives another relationship between real income and the interest rate, that which equates the supply of and the demand for money. There is just one level of the interest rate and of real income at which both of these relationships are simultaneously satisfied. This point is the equilibrium of the Keynesian model.

B. Properties of the *IS*-*LM* Equilibrium

The *IS-LM* equilibrium occurs when both the demand for money equals the supply of money and savings-plus-taxes equal investment-plus-government spending. It is assumed that the forces making for equality of both these sets of magnitudes are strong enough to ensure that the economy is never observed away from equilibrium. If savings-plus-taxes were to exceed investment-plus-government spending, real income would fall quickly enough and far enough to restore the equality. If the demand for money exceeded the supply of money, the act of attempting to reduce money balances and acquire bonds would put downward pressure on interest rates to the point at which the amount of money in existence was willingly held. Both sets of forces will occur sufficiently quickly for the economy never to be observed "off" either the *IS* or *LM* curves. Thus, the intersection point of the *IS* and *LM* curves is the point that describes the state of the economy.

C. Changes in Government Expenditure and Taxes

In general, a rise in government spending or a cut in taxes will raise the level of real income and the rate of interest. The steeper the *IS* curve the greater will be the rise in both variables. The flatter the *LM* curve the greater will be the rise in real income and the smaller will be the rise in the interest rate.

D. Change in the Money Supply

In general, a rise in the money supply will lead to a rise in real income and a fall in the rate of interest. The steeper the *LM* curve the larger will be the change in both variables. The flatter the *IS* curve the greater will be the change in real income and the smaller will be the change in the interest rate.

E. The Keynesian Model as a General Theory of Aggregate Demand

Although there is no need to derive a Keynesian aggregate demand curve for the purpose of conducting Keynesian analysis, such an aggregate demand curve is implied by the Keynesian theory. By hypothetically varying the price level, a Keynesian aggregate demand curve may be traced out. Like that of the basic model, the Keynesian aggregate demand curve will be downward sloping. In general, the aggregate demand curve will shift when the money stock changes, when government spending changes, or when taxes change. There are special extreme cases in which some of the variables under government control have no effect on the aggregate demand curve. If the *IS* curve is vertical or if the *LM* curve is horizontal, only government spending and taxes will shift the aggregate demand curve; changes in the money supply will leave the curve unaffected. This is the Keynesian cross model. At the other extreme, if the *IS* curve is horizontal or if the *LM* curve is vertical, then changes in the money supply will shift the aggregate demand curve, but changes in government spending and taxes will leave it unaffected. This is the basic model.

Review Questions

1. Which markets are in equilibrium at the point of intersection of the *IS* and *LM* curves?
2. What would be happening if the economy was "off" its *IS* curve?
3. What would be happening if the economy was "off" its *LM* curve?
4. Show the effects in the *IS-LM* model of a rise in government expenditure on the level of real income and the rate of interest. What conditions would lead to only the rate of interest changing? What conditions would lead to only real income changing?
5. Suppose there was a rise in the government's budget deficit (g rises relative to t). What does the *IS-LM* model predict will happen to the rate of interest?
6. Could your answer to Question 5 be part of the reason for high interest rates in the United States in recent years? (Be careful to distinguish between real and money rates of interest in your answer to this question.)
7. Show the effect in the *IS-LM* model of a rise in the money supply on the rate of interest and the level of real income. What conditions would lead to only the level of real income changing?
8. What is the Keynesian aggregate demand curve? Which markets are in equilibrium along that aggregate demand curve? What is being held constant along the aggregate demand curve? Why does the curve slope downwards? Are there any conditions that would make the aggregate demand curve vertical?
9. You are given the following information about a hypothetical economy:

$$c = 100 + 0.8(y - t)$$
$$i = 500 - 50r$$
$$g = 400$$
$$t = 400$$
$$M/P = 0.2y + 500 - 25r$$

There is unemployment.
The price level is fixed at 1.
The money supply is 520.
(c = consumption; i = investment; g = government expenditure; t = taxes; r = rate of interest; M = money supply; P = price level; y = real income)

(a) Find the equilibrium values of real income, consumption, investment, and the rate of interest.

(b) Find the effect on those equilibrium values of a unit rise in M, g, and t.

Appendix to Chapter 20

The Algebra of the Keynesian Model

This appendix takes you through the algebra of the determination of the equilibrium levels of output and the rate of interest in the Keynesian model. Like the Appendix to Chapter 18, it contains nothing of substance that is not explained in words and diagrams in the body of the chapter. It may, nevertheless, provided that you feel comfortable with algebraic formulations, give you a clearer picture of how the Keynesian model works. The case analyzed in this appendix is that in which the price level is fixed at P_0, so that output is varying only in ranges up to, but not including, full-employment output.

Aggregate demand is determined by the sum of consumption, investment, and government demand. That is,

$$y^d = c + i + g \tag{20A.1}$$

Consumption demand is determined by the consumption function, which is

$$c = a + b(y - t) \qquad a < 0,\ 0 < b < 1 \tag{20A.2}$$

Investment demand is determined by

$$i = i_0 - hr \qquad i_0,\ h < 0 \tag{20A.3}$$

Flow equilibrium prevails in the goods market when aggregate demand equals actual income. That is,

$$y^d = y \tag{20A.4}$$

The above four equations taken together constitute the equation for the IS curve. That equation may be derived by using Equations (20A.2), (20A.3), and (20A.4) together with Equation (20A.1) to give

$$y = a + b(y - t) + i_0 - hr + g \tag{20A.5}$$

This may be rearranged or "solved" for real income as

$$y = \frac{1}{1 - b}(a + i_0 + g - bt - hr) \tag{20A.6}$$

Equation (20A.6) is the equation for the IS curve.

The demand for money function is given by

$$\frac{M^d}{P_0} = m_0 + k_y - lr \qquad k > 0, l > 0 \qquad \textbf{(20A.7)}$$

Monetary equilibrium requires that the demand for money be equal to the supply of money; that is,

$$M^d = M \qquad \textbf{(20A.8)}$$

Substituting Equation (20A.7) into Equation (20A.8) yields an equation for the *LM* curve that may be "solved" for real income as

$$y = \frac{1}{k}\left[\frac{M}{P_0} - (m_0 + lr)\right] \qquad \textbf{(20A.9)}$$

Equation (20A.9) describes the *LM* relation.

Equations (20A.6) and (20A.9), the equations for the *IS* and *LM* curves, contain two unknowns—real income and the rate of interest. By setting the real income level in Equation (20A.6) equal to the real income level in Equation (20A.9) and solving for the rate of interest, you readily obtain

$$r = \frac{1}{1 - b + (kh/l)}\left[\frac{k}{l}(a + i_0 + g - bt) - \frac{1 - b}{l}\left(\frac{M}{P_0} - m_0\right)\right] \qquad \textbf{(20A.10)}$$

Equation (20A.10) is an algebraic expression for the equilibrium value of the rate of interest in the Keynesian model. By substituting Equation (20A.10) back into Equation (20A.9) to eliminate the rate of interest, you may obtain an expression for the level of real income. It is possible to "tidy up" the expression to give

$$y = \frac{1}{1 - b + (kh/l)}\left[(a + i_0 + g - bt) + \frac{h}{l}\left(\frac{M}{P_0} - m_0\right)\right] \qquad \textbf{(20A.11)}$$

Equation (20A.11) is the solution of the Keynesian model for the equilibrium level of real income.

In order to obtain a better understanding of what these equations are saying, let us examine Equations (20A.10) and (20A.11) to see how the interest rate and the level of income vary as we vary the three policy instruments—government spending, taxes, and the money supply. Imagine that each of those three policy variables took on a different value from g, t, and M. Specifically, suppose that g was to increase to g', t to t', and M to M'. In that case, we know that the solutions for the interest rate and the level of income could be expressed as

$$r' = \frac{1}{1 - b + (kh/l)}\left[\frac{k}{l}(a + i_0 + g' - bt') - \frac{1 - b}{l}\left(\frac{M'}{P_0} - m_0\right)\right] \qquad \textbf{(20A.12)}$$

and

$$y' = \frac{1}{1 - b + (kh/l)} \left[(a + i_0 + g' - bt') + \frac{h}{l} \left(\frac{M'}{P_0} - m_0 \right) \right] \qquad \textbf{(20A.13)}$$

Equations (20A.12) and (20A.13) are, of course, identical to Equations (20A.10) and (20A.11) except that the values of the variables (r and y on the left-hand side and g, t, and M on the right-hand side) have all changed from their original values to their new (primed) values.

Now subtract Equation (20A.10) from Equation (20A.12) to obtain Equation (20A.14). Also subtract Equation (20A.11) from Equation (20A.13) to obtain Equation (20A.15). Notice that in Equations (20A.14) and (20A.15) the terms a, i_0, and m_0 have disappeared since they are common to both the original solutions and the new solutions for y and r. Thus,

$$r' - r = \frac{1}{1 - b + (kh/l)} \left[\frac{k}{l}(g' - g) - \frac{bk}{l}(t' - t) - \frac{1 - b}{l} \left(\frac{M'}{P_0} - \frac{M}{P_0} \right) \right] \qquad \textbf{(20A.14)}$$

and

$$y' - y = \frac{1}{1 - b + (kh/l)} \left[(g' - g) - b(t' - t) + \frac{h}{l} \left(\frac{M'}{P_0} - \frac{M}{P_0} \right) \right] \qquad \textbf{(20A.15)}$$

Now call the gap between y' and y the change in y and label it Δy. Similarly, call the gap between r' and r, Δr, and likewise for the policy variables. That is, $g' - g$ is Δg, $t' - t$ is Δt, and $M' - M$ is ΔM. Using this convention, you can write equations (20A.14) and (20A.15) slightly more compactly as Equations (20A.16) and (20A.17); that is,

$$\Delta r = \frac{1}{1 - b + (kh/l)} \left[\frac{k}{l} \Delta g - \frac{bk}{l} \Delta t - \frac{1 - b}{lP_0} \Delta M \right] \qquad \textbf{(20A.16)}$$

and

$$\Delta y = \frac{1}{1 - b + (kh/l)} \left[\Delta g - b\Delta t + \frac{h}{lP_0} \Delta M \right] \qquad \textbf{(20A.17)}$$

You can now interpret Equations (20A.16) and (20A.17) very directly. Notice that the expression

$$\frac{1}{1 - b + (kh/l)}$$

will be a positive coefficient relating the changes in the policy variable to the changes in the rate of interest and the level of real income. (You know that it will be positive because, since b is a positive fraction, $1 - b$ is also a positive fraction, and k, h, and l are all positive parameters.) You can immediately see that Equation (20A.16) says that, in general, a rise in g will raise the interest rate, whereas a rise in t and a rise in M will cut the interest rate. From Equation (20A.17) you can see that in general, a rise in g or a rise in M will raise real income, but a rise in t will cut real income. Equations (20A.16) and (20A.17) are nothing other than algebraic expressions for the equivalent propositions obtained in Chapter 20 by direct inspection of the diagrammatic solution for equilibrium output and the interest rate.

In this chapter some extreme cases were presented, and the way in which the policy instrument multipliers are affected by the slopes of the *IS* and *LM* curves was examined. This can now be done fairly precisely with the algebraic solutions in Equations (20A.16) and (20A.17). Let us now look at this.

Some Special Cases

First, suppose that the parameter h became infinitely big. An infinitely big h means that the investment demand curve and, hence, the *IS* curve are horizontal; it also means that the rate of interest remains constant. This, in effect, is the special case that we have called the *basic model.* What do the multipliers become when h is infinitely big? By inspecting Equations (20A.16) and (20A.17), you can establish that the multipliers are as follows:

$$\Delta r = 0 \tag{20A.18}$$

and

$$\Delta y = \frac{1}{kP_0} \Delta M \tag{20A.19}$$

What this says is that the aggregate demand curve will shift (y will change by Δy) only as a result of a change in the money stock. The shift will be equal to $1/(kP_0)$ times the change in the money stock. Changes in government spending and taxes will have no effect on aggregate demand in this special case.

Consider as the next special case that in which $l = 0$. This would be where the demand for money is completely insensitive to interest rates. You can think of this situation as arising when money is such a unique asset that it is completely nonsubstitutable for any other assets. In this case, by inspection of Equations (20A.16) and (20A.17), you will discover that the multipliers become

$$\Delta r = \frac{1}{h}\left(\Delta g - b\Delta t - \frac{1-b}{kP_0} \Delta M\right) \tag{20A.20}$$

and

$$\Delta y = \frac{1}{kP_0} \Delta M \tag{20A.21}$$

In this case, the interest rate will change when government spending, taxes, and the money stock change. It will rise with a rise in government spending, and it will fall with a rise in taxes or in the money supply. The change in y will be exactly the same as in the previous special case.

Now consider the opposite special case to the first one, where instead of h being infinitely big, it becomes infinitely small, specifically, zero. This would be the case where firms' investment plans were completely unresponsive to interest rates. In this case, the changes in the rate of interest and in the real income level will be given by

$$\Delta r = \frac{1}{1-b}\left(\frac{k}{l}\,\Delta g - \frac{kb}{l}\,\Delta t - \frac{1-b}{lP_0}\,\Delta M\right) \qquad \textbf{(20A.22)}$$

and

$$\Delta y = \frac{1}{1-b}\,(\Delta g - b\Delta t) \qquad \textbf{(20A.23)}$$

This tells you that, in this case, a rise in government spending will raise the interest rate, and a rise in taxes or the money supply will cut the interest rate. Unlike the two previous special cases, a rise in government spending or a cut in taxes will raise real income, but a change in the money stock will leave real income unaffected. Equation (20A.23) says that in the special case $h = 0$, the aggregate demand will change only as a result of changes in fiscal policy variables and will remain unchanged when the money stock changes.

Now consider the opposite special case to the second one above, in which we let the parameter l become infinitely big. This would be the case where money is regarded as a perfect substitute for other nonmoney assets. Substituting an infinite value for l in Equations (20A.16) and (20A.17) gives the solutions for the change in the interest rate and the change in the real income as

$$\Delta r = 0 \qquad \textbf{(20A.24)}$$

and

$$\Delta y = \frac{1}{1-b}\,(\Delta g - b\Delta t) \qquad \textbf{(20A.25)}$$

This time the interest rate is entirely unaffected by changes in any of the variables. Real income changes, however, as a result of changing government spending or taxes (rises when government spending rises and falls when taxes rise) but is unaffected by a change in the money stock.

Notice that Equations (20A.23) and (20A.25) are identical, just as Equations (20A.19) and (20A.21) are identical. Equations (20A.19) and (20A.21) say that only money affects aggregate demand, whereas Equations (20A.23) and (20A.25) say that only fiscal policy variables affect aggregate demand.

These two sets of results are the two extreme cases that arise as the parameter values l and h are allowed to vary. The effect of a change in government spending, taxes, or the money supply on real income actually depends only on the ratio of h to l. As that ratio goes from zero to infinity, the value of the fiscal policy multipliers falls from $1/(1-b)$ to 0, and that of the money multipliers rises from 0 to $1/k$.

21

The Neoclassical Synthesis

After studying the basic model, we went on in Chapter 13 to examine how the predictions of that model compared with the facts. We attempted to establish the facts that the basic model explained well and those for which it could not provide a satisfactory account. It would seem natural, perhaps, to do the same kind of thing with the Keynesian model—that is, to establish how the Keynesian model compares with the facts and what its main strengths and weaknesses are. We are not, however, quite ready to do that. The Keynesian model as presented in the previous six chapters, with its fixed money wage rate (and in the approximate version with its fixed price level), is clearly at odds with the actual behavior of wages and prices. You know from your study of the facts presented in Chapter 2 that periods in which prices are constant are very exceptional. For example, during the Great Depression, prices were falling and, with trivial exceptions, since World War II they have been rising and at an increasing rate.

Clearly, the Keynesian model needs some modification to cope with both the facts of falling prices in the Great Depression and of persistently rising prices in the postwar world. It was under the pressure of the facts of stubborn, persistent inflation that the Keynesian model came to be modified by the contributions of a series of scholars. The resulting system is known as the *neoclassical synthesis*. This chapter explains this body of analysis. In effect, the content of this chapter is a summary of the mainstream way of looking at macroeconomic problems that developed sometime in the late 1950s and the early 1960s. This mainstream analysis gave rise to countless important and lasting contributions to our subject.

Let us now go on to understand the nature of the important extensions to the Keynesian model that resulted in the development of the neoclassical synthesis. Six tasks will achieve this objective. They are to:

(a) Know what is meant by the term *neoclassical synthesis*.
(b) Understand how the Keynesian theory of aggregate demand works at full employment when the price level is rising.
(c) Understand the neoclassical theory of price adjustment.

(d) Understand the role of price level expectations in the neoclassical theory of price adjustment and understand the "natural rate" hypothesis.
(e) Understand the explanation of the business cycle given by the neoclassical synthesis.
(f) Understand the policy implications of the neoclassical synthesis.

A. Definition of "Neoclassical Synthesis"

The term *neoclassical synthesis* describes a body of analysis in macroeconomics that deals with the determination of the level of output, the rate of interest, and the price level (including its rate of change—the inflation rate). It incorporates three elements:

1. The Keynesian theory of aggregate demand.
2. The basic model's theory of aggregate supply.
3. A theory of how prices adjust in a situation in which aggregate demand does not equal aggregate supply.

The equality of aggregate demand and aggregate supply is the state of rest (or equilibrium) of the neoclassical system. Such a state is not, however, according to the neoclassical theory, the only one in which the economy will be observed. Starting from any given rate of inflation, if aggregate demand exceeds aggregate supply, inflation will accelerate. If aggregate demand is less than aggregate supply, inflation will slow down. The actual level of output and the actual rate of change of prices will be determined by a rather complicated dynamic adjustment process.

Before it is possible to explain in full detail the characteristics of the neoclassical synthesis, it is necessary to become familiar with the way in which the Keynesian theory of aggregate demand behaves at full employment when the price level is changing.[1] Let us now turn to that task.

B. The Keynesian Theory at Full Employment

How the Keynesian Theory of Aggregate Demand Determines the Price Level at Full Employment

Figure 21.1 illustrates the determination of the price level. Notice that frame (a) contains an *IS-LM* analysis, and frame (b) contains an aggregate supply and demand analysis. The level of real income is measured on the horizontal axis of each diagram and refers to the same magnitude in each case.

[1]A seminal treatment of this material is Franco Modigliani, "Liquidity Preference and the Theory of Interest and Money," *Econometrica*, 12 (January 1944), 45–88. The definitive presentation, however, with attention being paid to many issues ignored here, is Don Patinkin, *Money, Interest and Prices*, 2nd ed. (New York: Harper & Row, Publishers, Inc., 1965), chaps. 9, 10, and 11.

Figure 21.1
The Effect of a Once-and-For-All Rise in the Money Supply On Output and the Price Level

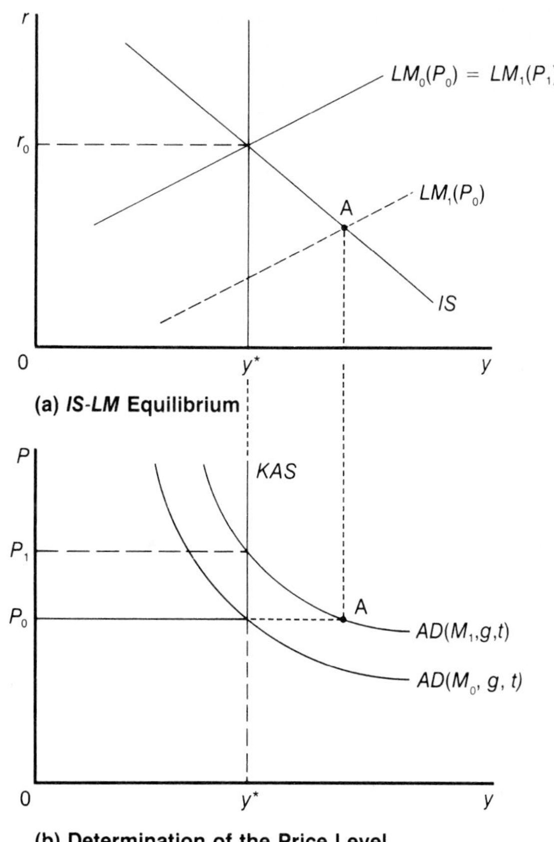

At full employment in the Keynesian model, as in the basic model, a rise in the money supply produces a proportionate rise in the price level. The initial equilibrium (y^*, r_0, P_0) shown is the intersection of *IS* and *LM* in frame (a) and the intersection of *AD* and *KAS* in frame (b). This equilibrium is disturbed by a rise in the money stock. If the price level stayed constant, the *LM* and *AD* curves would shift, and the economy would move to the position A. But at A the economy cannot be in equilibrium because output cannot exceed y^*. The price level has to rise to P_1 [frame (b)], and the *LM* curve shifts back to its original position [frame (a)].

Begin by focusing on an initial equilibrium that, by a happy accident, is exactly at full employment and the price level P_0. Such an equilibrium is depicted in frame (a) as the intersection point of the curve $LM_0(P_0)$ and the *IS* curve, that is, the income level y^* and the interest rate r_0. The same equilibrium is depicted in frame (b) as the point at which the aggregate demand curve labelled $AD(M_0, g, t)$ intersects the corner of the inverse "L" aggregate supply curve *KAS*. The price level is P_0 and the output level is y^*.

Now imagine that the money supply rises from M_0 to some higher level, say, M_1. If the price level remained at P_0, the *LM* curve representing a money stock of M_1 and the price level of P_0 would be to the right of the original *LM* curve. Such an *LM* curve is shown in frame (a) as that labelled $LM_1(P_0)$. It intersects the IS curve at point A. This higher money stock (M_1) can be represented in frame (b) by showing an aggregate demand curve that is wholly to the right of the original aggregate demand curve. Such an aggregate demand curve is shown as that labelled $AD(M_1, g, t)$. Notice that the point on this aggregate demand curve marked A in frame (b) corresponds to point A in frame (a) and is at the price level P_0, but is displaced horizontally to a higher level of real income. That level of real income corresponds to the intersection of the IS and $LM_1(P_0)$ curves.

Now recall that according to the Keynesian model, wages and prices are completely flexible in an upward direction. They are only rigid downwards. It is evident that a position like point A cannot be sustained, given the Keynesian assumptions. At point A there is an excess demand for goods and therefore an excess demand for labor. Such a situation would produce higher wages and prices. How much higher? The answer can be seen by looking in frame (b) at the point at which the new aggregate demand curve, $AD(M_1, g, t)$ [the one drawn for a money stock of M_1] cuts the full-employment vertical section of the aggregate supply curve. That point is at the price level indicated in frame (b) as P_1. It is a price level that is higher than P_0 by the same percentage amount that the money stock M_1 exceeds the money stock M_0. At the higher price level, the LM curve would not be the curve shown as $LM_1(P_0)$ but rather would be the curve $LM_1(P_1)$. This LM curve is, of course, identical to the curve $LM_0(P_0)$. (If you are not sure about this, check back to Chapter 19, where the LM curve was derived and where the factors that cause the LM curve to shift were analyzed.)

You have now analyzed the effects of a once-and-for-all rise in the money stock at full employment in the Keynesian analysis. These effects are so simple and yet so important that they are worth emphasizing and highlighting. In frame (a) of Figure 21.1 the initial equilibrium is r_0 and y^* on the IS curve and on the LM curve labelled $LM_0(P_0)$. Now there is a one-shot rise in the money stock, from M_0 to M_1. If the price level remained constant, the LM curve would move to the dashed LM curve, $LM_1(P_0)$. The price level will not, however, remain constant at full employment. It will have to rise, and by an amount such that the LM curve shifts back (as indicated by the arrow) to the original position, so that it becomes the same curve as before, relabelled $LM_1(P_1)$.

What are the effects of this one-shot rise in the money stock at full employment in the Keynesian model? The answer is very clear from the diagram. There is no effect on the rate of interest and no effect on output: The price level rises proportionately to the one-shot rise in the money stock.

Where have you seen that result before? Answer: In the analysis of the effects of a one-shot rise in the money stock in the basic model. At full employment the Keynesian model predicts precisely the same things as the basic model does. This is what Keynes meant when he called his theory a *general theory*. He meant that the basic model was simply a special case of his more general theory.

Let us now analyze what happens at full employment when money and prices are continuously rising and, more difficult and important, when the growth rate of the money supply (and the inflation rate) changes.

How a Continuously Rising Money Supply Generates Inflation and a Gap between the Market Rate of Interest and the Real Rate of Interest

The starting point for this analysis is to recall that the demand for money depends on the rate of interest that is available on other financial assets. That is, the demand for money will vary inversely with the market rate of interest. The market rate of interest will equal the real rate of interest when there is no inflation. In an inflationary world, however, as you have already discovered, the market rate of interest will be higher than the real rate of interest by precisely the same amount as the expected rate of inflation. That is,

$$r_m = r + \pi^e \tag{21.1}$$

Since the demand for money depends on r_m and not on r, it is necessary to be rather careful in figuring out how to determine equilibrium at full employment when the expected inflation rate is not zero. Figure 21.2 will help you understand how to determine a full-employment equilibrium with inflation that is not zero.

First, of all, notice that the vertical axis of Figure 21.2 measures two rates of interest, the real rate, r, and the market rate, r_m. The diagram also shows the full-employment output level, y^*. We shall conduct the analysis entirely in terms of the economy being at that output level. Since the demand for money depends on the market or nominal rate of interest, it is necessary to plot the *LM* curve against that market rate of interest. You should be careful to remember that the *LM* curve is indeed plotted against the market rate of interest.

Figure 21.2
The Effect of a Continuously Rising Money Supply

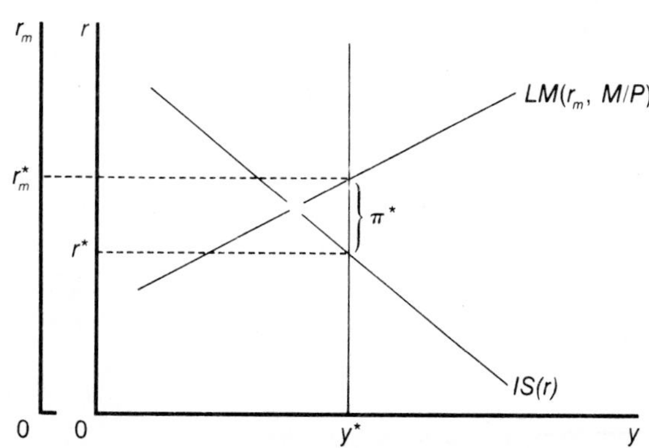

A continuously rising money supply drives a wedge of inflation between the real rate of interest and the money rate of interest. The *IS* curve is drawn against the real rate of interest r, and the *LM* curve is drawn against the money rate of interest r_m. The real interest rate r^* is determined where the *IS* curve cuts the full-employment line, and the money rate of interest r_m^* is determined where the *LM* curve cuts the full-employment line. The vertical distance between the *IS* and *LM* curves at full employment is the rate of inflation, π^*.

The position of the *LM* curve depends, as you know, on the real money supply, M/P. If we are going to analyze a situation in which both M and P are rising, it is evident that the *LM* curve will be continuously shifting unless M and P are growing at the same rate. When M and P are growing at the same rate, M/P will be constant, and as a result the *LM* curve will be stationary. To remind you that the *LM* curve is plotted against the market rate of interest, r_m, and that it depends on the real money supply, M/P, the *LM* curve has been labelled $LM(r_m, M/P)$.

The *IS* curve, depending as it does on the equality of investment-plus-government spending with savings-plus-taxes, depends on the real rate of interest. To remind you of this, I have labelled the *IS* curve $IS(r)$. Notice that the *IS* and *LM* curves have been drawn with a break in them. The break coincides with the point at which those two curves would have intersected if they had been drawn continuously. This has been done to remind you that the point at which those two curves cut in this diagram is irrelevant for the analysis. (Strictly speaking, there is no point at which these two curves cut because one of them is plotted against the market rate of interest and the other against the real rate of interest. So, in effect, the two curves are not really drawn in the same space at all.) You may perhaps find it helpful to think of there being two diagrams, one with an *IS* curve plotted against the real interest rate and another one with an *LM* curve plotted against the market rate of interest. Nevertheless, it is useful to draw the two curves in the same picture because we do know that there is a simple link between the two interest rates. This link, of course, is the rate of inflation. The market rate of interest is equal to the real rate of interest plus the expected rate of inflation.

When studying the link between real and market rates of interest in the basic model (Chapter 9), we assumed that the expected rate of inflation and the actual rate of inflation were equal to each other. Let us for the present continue to make that assumption. This means that the gap between the market rate of interest and the real rate of interest is also represented by the actual rate of inflation. If there is a given level of income (marked on the horizontal axis of Figure 21.2), and if the economy is on both the *IS* and *LM* curves, then we can think of the vertical gap between the two curves as measuring the (expected and actual) rate of inflation. Such an inflation rate is shown as the distance π^* in the diagram, when income is at y^*.

Figure 21.2 now can be interpreted as characterizing a full-employment equilibrium with an expected and actual inflation rate of π^*. The real interest rate is r^*, and with an income level y^*, this puts the economy on the *IS* curve, so that there is an equality between the expenditure and income flows in the goods market. The market interest rate is the real interest rate plus π^* which equals r_m. This market rate of interest, along with an income level of y^*, puts the economy on its *LM* curve, so that there is an equality between the supply of and demand for money.

There is just one further thing that you need to be aware of and that concerns the money supply and price level that lie behind the *LM* curve. If the price level is rising at a rate π^*, other things being equal, the *LM* curve would be moving leftwards. If the *LM* curve is not moving, there must be that something else happening that is just offsetting the pressure to move the *LM* curve as a result of rising prices. It is rather clear what this is; it is a continuously rising money supply. Underlying the *LM* curve, when inflation is proceeding at the rate π^*, there is a rising money stock and a rising price level. Each is rising by precisely the same percentage amount so that the real money supply is unchanged. That is, a continuously rising money supply generates a fully anticipated inflation and a gap between the market rate of interest and the real rate of interest.

You have seen this result before in the basic model. Recall that the fundamental inflation equation says that the rate of inflation is equal to the growth rate of the money supply minus the growth rate of real income. In the analysis depicted in Figure 21.1, the growth rate of real income is zero (y^* is a constant), so that the rate of inflation equals the growth rate of the money supply.

What Happens When the Growth Rate of the Money Supply Is Increased from Its Initial Level to Some New Higher Level?

What would happen to the equilibrium depicted in Figure 21.2 if there was a rise in the growth rate of the money supply? The answer is illustrated in Figure 21.3. It is evident that the increasing rate of money supply growth, other things being equal, would tend to make the *LM* curve move to the right. If the inflation rate stayed constant at π_0, this would lower the market rate of interest and the real rate of interest and would generate an excess demand for goods. The excess demand for goods would put pressure on the inflation rate, and the rising inflation rate would offset the rightward movement of the *LM* curve and start the *LM* curve moving in the opposite direction. The only new equilibrium that is possible is the one that arises when the *LM* curve has shifted, not to the right at all, but to the left and by enough to have raised

Figure 21.3
The Effect of a Rise in the Growth Rate of the Money Supply

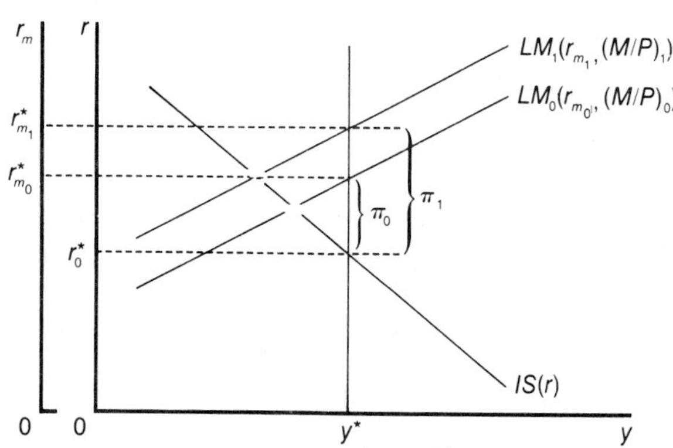

The initial equilibrium (subscripted 0) is disturbed by making the money supply grow at a faster rate. This produces a faster rate of inflation that initially overshoots the growth rate of the money supply, thus lowering real balances (shifting the *LM* curve to the left). The new equilibrium is subscript one. The result is exactly the same as that in the basic model.

the market rate of interest above the real rate of interest by the amount of the new, higher rate of money growth and rate of inflation. By the time the economy settles down on the LM curve labelled $LM_1(r_{m1}, (M/P)_1)$, such as situation will have arisen. In this situation, the real interest rate is unaffected, and the output level is unaffected; but the market rate of interest is higher, the inflation rate is higher, and the money supply growth rate is higher, all by the same amount as each other.

How does the economy get from the curve LM_0 to LM_1? The answer must be that the real money supply has fallen between these two situations. How could this have happened? The answer lies in the proposition that you have also met before in the basic model, namely, the overshooting proposition. As the economy moves from a low inflation rate to a high inflation rate, the price level must overshoot the rate of inflation in the process. It necessarily has to do this in the Keynesian model for exactly the same reasons as discussed in the basic model. At a higher rate of inflation and higher nominal rate of interest, the opportunity cost of holding money balances has risen. There is, therefore, an incentive to economize on those money holdings. The demand for *real* money falls, and equilibrium can only be restored when the supply of real money has also fallen by the same amount. Since the nominal money supply is now increasing at an increasing rate, it must be the case that the price level rises during the adjustment process to the higher inflation rate by more than the rise in the money supply itself. (You may find it useful to refresh your memory and understanding of this process by referring back to the discussion of overshooting in Chapter 12.)

It is of some importance to notice that an implication of the analysis that we have just conducted is that it is not possible for the monetary authority to permanently lower the rate of interest by increasing the money supply. We have seen that if there is only a once-and-for-all rise in the money stock, this produces a once-and-for-all rise in the price level with no change in the rate of interest. We have also now seen that if the growth rate of the money supply is increased, this produces a rise in the rate of interest and a rise in the rate of inflation in equilibrium. Initially, it is possible that a rise in the growth rate of the money supply would create a fall in the rate of interest, but such a fall could only be temporary.

You now have a much richer understanding of the Keynesian theory of aggregate demand. This theory simplifies when the price level is fixed and output is less than full-employment output, to become a theory of the determination of output and employment. At full employment the Keynesian theory of aggregate demand becomes a theory of the price level. This analysis is slightly more complicated because a distinction has to be made between the market rate of interest, upon which the demand for money depends, and the real rate of interest, upon which the demand for investment depends. Therefore, the equilibrium at full employment is not determined by the intersection of IS and LM curves, but rather at the point at which there is a vertical gap between the IS and LM curves that measures the rate of inflation.

You are now in a position to go on to see how the neoclassical theory of price adjustment operates and how it smooths the transition between the two states of the Keynesian model.

Figure 21.4
The Neoclassical Theory of Price Adjustment

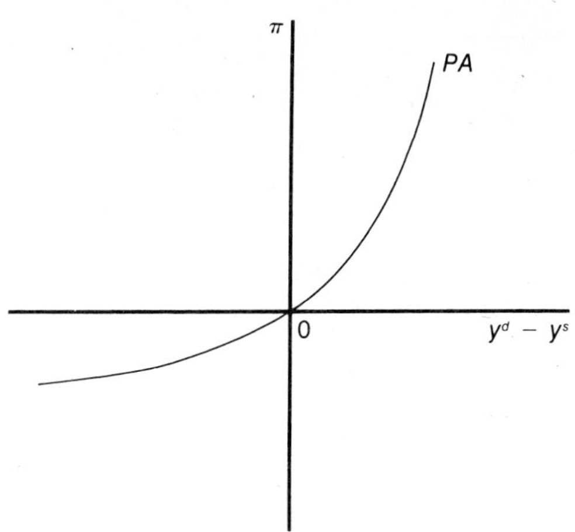

Two propositions are embodied in the neoclassical theory of price adjustment: (1) Prices rise when there is excess demand ($y^d > y^s$) and fall when there is excess supply ($y^d < y^s$). (2) Prices rise faster for a given percentage of excess demand than they fall for an equivalent percentage of excess supply. Thus, the adjustment process is asymmetrical.

C. The Neoclassical Theory of Price Adjustment

Price Adjustment

The neoclassical theory of price adjustment consists of two propositions.[2] The first proposition is that when demand is greater than supply, prices rise. (Or, equivalently, when supply is greater than demand, prices fall.) The second proposition of the neoclassical theory of price adjustment is that the adjustment process is asymmetrical. A given percentage amount of excess demand will produce a bigger price rise than the price fall that would be generated by the same percentage of excess supply. As an example, suppose that a 1 percent excess demand produced a 5 percent rise in prices. Then a 1 percent excess supply would produce something less than a 5 percent fall in prices, perhaps, say, a 2 percent fall in prices.

These two propositions can be summarized in a simple diagram such as Figure 21.4. The vertical axis measures the rate of inflation (the percentage change in prices), π, and the horizontal axis measures excess demand, $y^d - y^s$. The curve that slopes upwards, and increasingly so, illustrates the two propositions. The first proposition says that the curve slopes upwards; the second proposition says that it slopes upwards at an increasing rate.

[2]The neoclassical theory of price adjustment, as a macroeconomic proposition, was introduced by A. W. Phillips in "The Relation between Unemployment and the Rate of Change of Money Wages in the United Kingdom, 1861–1957, "*Economica*, New Series, 25 (November 1958), 283–99. The price adjustment function is often referred to simply as the "Phillips curve."

Often, the neoclassical theory of price adjustment is applied specifically to the labor market and to the adjustment of money wages. Instead of supposing that prices adjust in response to the excess demand for goods, it is assumed that it is the price of labor (money wages) that adjusts to the excess demand for labor. If the demand for labor exceeds the supply of labor, money wages will rise; and if the supply exceeds the demand, money wages will fall. The second proposition—that of asymmetric price adjustment—is asserted to hold with even greater force in the labor market. That is, the percentage fall in wages that would result from a given percentage of excess supply will be much less than the percentage rise in wages that would occur in the face of the same percentage of excess demand. Indeed, you can think of Keynes's assumption that money wages are rigid downwards as an extreme form of asymmetry—one that says that in the face of excess demand for labor, wages will rise, but in the face of excess supply, wages will not fall.

Two further propositions are needed to generate the Phillips curve version of the neoclassical theory of price adjustment. One of these links wage change to inflation, and the other links the excess demand for labor to unemployment. Let us examine them one at a time.

The link between wage change and inflation employed in the simplest theory is one that is built on the notion that prices bear a fixed relationship to costs, so that as costs rise, prices also rise by the same percentage amount. Since labor costs represent a fairly stable proportion of total costs, the percentage by which prices rise will, other things given, equal the percentage by which labor costs rise. Labor costs themselves are influenced by two things: (1) the rate at which wages rise, and (2) the rate at which labor productivity rises. If we think of labor productivity as something that grows at a rather constant rate, then we can think of variations in the rate of wage change as the key factor that influences variations in the rate of price change (i.e., in the rate of inflation).

Thus, on the basis of the above linkage between wage change and inflation, we can restate the neoclassical theory of price adjustment as: The greater the excess demand for labor, the higher will be the rate of inflation.

The second thing we need to look at is the connection between the excess demand for labor and unemployment. When the labor market is in equilibrium (as in the basic model), output is at its full-employment level (y^*), and therefore there would be no excess demand for goods or for labor. This does not mean, however, that there would be no unemployment. Unemployment would arise from the job-search activities that we investigated in Chapter 11. Its amount would depend on a variety of factors—some concerning the demographic characteristics of the populations and others concerning such impediments to full employment as minimum wage regulations or other search-inducing measures such as unemployment compensation.

The amount of unemployment that occurs when the labor market displays neither excess supply nor excess demand and when output is at its "full-employment" level is called the *natural rate of unemployment*. You should not take this to mean that there is anything natural about unemployment. Nor should you take it to imply that the natural rate of unemployment is somehow

Figure 21.5
The Phillips Curve Version of the Neoclassical Theory of Price Adjustment

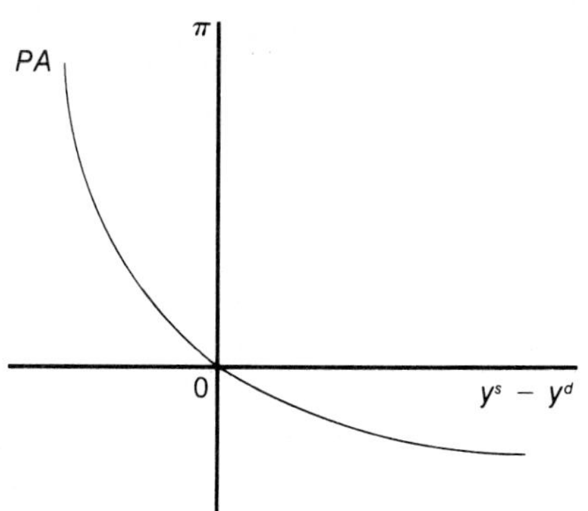

(a) Neoclassical Price Adjustment

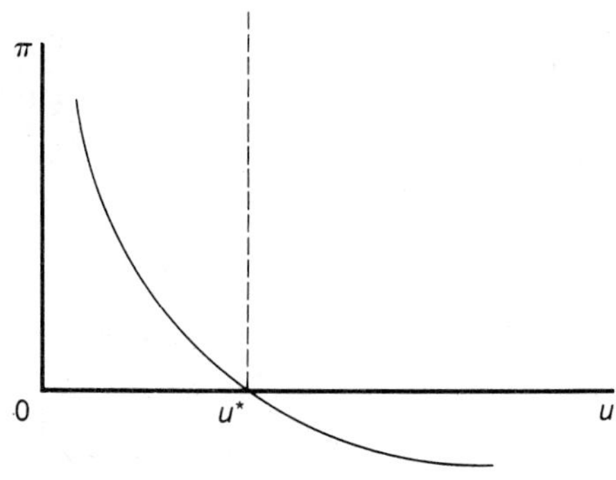

(b) The Phillips Curve

Frame (a) is the same as Figure 21.4 but in mirror image. The horizontal axis of frame (a) measures the excess supply of goods. If unemployment and excess supply moved together, the neoclassical theory of price adjustment in frame (a) implies the Phillips curve in frame (b).

a natural constant. The natural rate of unemployment will vary as a result of variations in the factors that we analyzed in Chapter 11.

Let us denote the natural rate of unemployment as u^*. When unemployment is at the rate u^*, excess demand for goods and excess demand for labor will be zero. If the demand for labor falls short of its full-employment level, then unemployment will rise above its natural rate. If the demand for labor was to rise above its full-employment level, then temporarily, people who were otherwise unemployed and searching for better jobs might be sucked into employment more quickly than would otherwise have happened, and unemployment will temporarily fall below its natural rate. Thus, variations in the rate of unemployment around its natural rate will be associated with variations (in the opposite direction) in the level of employment and output. The bigger the excess demand for goods and labor, the lower will be the unemployment rate; and the bigger the excess supply of goods and labor, the higher will be the unemployment rate.

It is possible to summarize the above discussion and analysis in a simple diagram. Figure 21.5 illustrates how the Phillips curve might be derived. Frame (a) shows the same thing as Figure 21.4, but looked at through a mirror. The horizontal axis measures excess supply rather than excess demand. Frame (b) plots the rate of inflation on the vertical axis and the unemployment rate on the horizontal axis. The natural rate of unemployment, u^*, is lined up with a zero excess supply of goods. Think of the horizontal axis of frame (b), which measures unemployment, and the horizontal axis of frame (a), which measures the excess supply of goods, as having a correspondence with each other. As the excess supply of goods increases [frame (a)], the unemployment rate increases [frame (b)]. The relationship between inflation and unemployment shown in frame (b) then is seen as being equivalent to that between inflation and the excess supply of goods shown in frame (a). When there is an excess supply of goods, unemployment is above its natural rate, and prices fall. When there is an excess demand for goods—excess supply less than zero in frame (a)—unemployment is below its natural rate, and prices rise.

You should be clear that these neoclassical propositions about price and wage adjustment are different from Keynes's theory. Keynes assumed that wages and prices would not move downwards at all and that they would move upwards instantaneously to clear any excess demand. What the neoclassical theory of price adjustment does is to weaken that proposition. It says that wages and prices will fall, but only slowly, and they will rise faster than they will fall, but not at an infinitely fast rate. In terms of Figure 21.5, frame (b), you can think of the Keynesian theory of price adjustment as an "L"-shaped relationship, the vertical part of which would coincide with the dotted line above u^* and the horizontal part of which would correspond with the horizontal axis to the right of u^*.

D. Inflation Expectations and the "Natural Rate" Hypothesis

The neoclassical theory of wage and price adjustment that has been set out in the previous section became widely accepted as a useful description of the processes at work in the real world in the late 1950s and early 1960s.[3]

In the middle 1960s, however, two independent but closely related contributions, one by Milton Friedman of the University of Chicago and the other by Edmund Phelps of Columbia University, pointed out that there was a logical flaw in the proposed price adjustment theory.[4] The flaw arose from a misapplication of the neoclassical theory of price adjustment. According to the neoclassical theory, if there is an excess demand for some commodity, its price

[3] To see why this is so, take some graph paper and plot the rate of inflation against the unemployment rate using the data in the Appendix to Chapter 2 and covering the years 1950 to 1965. Pass the best free-hand line you can through the points and compare your results with frame (b) of Figure 21.5.

[4] Milton Friedman, "The Role of Monetary Policy," *American Economic Review*, 58 (March 1968), 1–17; and Edmund S. Phelps, "Money Wage Dynamics and Labor Market Equilibrium," *Journal of Political Economy*, 76 (July/August 1968), 687–711. These two papers represent the watershed between the neoclassical synthesis and new macroeconomics.

rises *relative* to the prices of other commodities; and if there is an excess supply, its price falls *relative* to the prices of other commodities. In other words, neoclassical theory is a theory of *relative* prices, and the neoclassical theory of price adjustment is a theory about the adjustment of relative prices. It is not a theory about the adjustment of the absolute level or money level of prices.

Suppose, for example, that, on the average, all prices were rising at 10 percent a year. In this situation, suppose there was a bumper orange harvest that increased the supply of oranges to an abnormally high level. If the *relative* price of oranges remained constant, there would be an excess supply of oranges. As a result, the *relative* price of oranges would fall. This does not mean, however, that the money price of oranges would necessarily fall. To see why that is so, remind yourself that, in the absence of a bumper harvest, the money price of oranges would have increased at a rate of 10 percent—the rate at which prices on the average are rising. Provided the bumper harvest did not lower the relative price of oranges by as much as 10 percent, the price of oranges would still rise but by an amount less than 10 percent, reflecting the fact that the relative price of oranges has to fall because of the increase in supply.

The neoclassical theory of price adjustment—described in the previous section as a theory of the response of the absolute price level to aggregate excess demand—is an attempt to incorporate into a macroeconomic model a theory that was developed to explain movements in relative prices. The idea was that if all goods and services were in excess demand, then the prices of all goods and services would rise—but rise in relation to what? As we have seen, we can only make sense of the neoclassical theory of the adjustment of the price of oranges in terms of an adjustment in one price relative to some other prices. How can the general price level adjust relative to some other price? There are no other prices! The price level is, by definition, an average of all prices.

Before answering this question, let me draw your attention to something else. You have already seen above that in the Keynesian theory at full employment, prices can be continuously rising even though there is no excess demand. Figure 21.2 depicts an economy at the full-employment output level—with no excess demand—and yet it has an ongoing inflation. Prices are rising at the rate π^* and the money supply is also rising at the same rate. The market rate of interest exceeds the real rate by that same amount. How is it possible to have prices continuously rising and yet for there to be no excess demand? It is because the prices are rising at a rate at which they are *expected* to be rising. This ensures that the market rate of interest exceeds the real rate of interest by the actual rate of inflation and ensures money market and goods market equilibrium at full employment.

You may by now have guessed the answer to the question that I left hanging at the end of the previous paragraph: It is possible for there to be an ongoing inflation with no excess demand provided that the inflation is expected. Properly understood, the neoclassical theory of price adjustment when applied to aggregate excess demand and the general level of prices would state that the greater the excess demand for goods in total, the faster will be the rate of inflation *relative to the expected rate of inflation.*

The role of inflation expectations will perhaps be seen more clearly by telling the story in the way that Edmund Phelps told it.[5] Phelps began with the notion that firms and workers determining prices and wages would want to have their prices (or wages) set at a level that was compatible with an equilibrium in the market in which they were trading. Neoclassical economic theory tells us that the relevant prices for achieving equilibrium are relative prices, not absolute prices. (Recall from Chapter 8 that it is the real wage that determines the demand for and supply of labor. The real wage is, of course, a relative price—the price of labor relative to goods—and not an absolute price. Similarly, the standard microeconomic analysis of the consumer and producer predicts that demands and supplies will depend on the price of the good in question relative to the prices of all other goods.) It follows from this that the amount by which an individual firm or union would want to change the price of its output or the price of its labor would, in general, be equal to the rate at which it was expecting prices and wages, on the average, to be changing.

It would not always be the case, however, that a desired price change would equal the expected rate at which prices were changing elsewhere. If an individual sector of the economy viewed itself as being in a boom situation and likely to experience some excess demand, then that sector would seek to raise its price (or wage) by more than it was expecting prices and wages, on the average, to rise. Conversely, if an individual sector of the economy thought it was going into a depression phase, with a shortage of demand for its output or labor, then it would seek to raise its prices (or wages) by less than it was expecting wages and prices to rise, on the average. What this amounts to, at the individual sector or market level, is the proposition that the percentage change in prices (or wages) will be equal to the expected percentage change in average prices (or wages) plus an amount reflecting the state of excess demand in that sector or market. This adjustment will be positive if there is excess demand and negative if there is excess supply.

If now we consider the aggregate movements in prices (or wages) that would result from these individual wage and price adjustment decisions, the average change in prices (or wages)—inflation—would equal the expected change in prices (or wages)—the expected rate of inflation plus an amount representing the contribution of excess aggregate demand. In a situation in which there was no excess aggregate demand—in which the economy was at the full employment level of output, y^* (i.e., at its natural rate of unemployment)—the actual and expected rates of inflation would be equal. If there was excess demand, that is, if aggregate demand exceeded aggregate supply, the actual rate of inflation would exceed the expected rate of inflation. If there was excess supply—if aggregate supply exceeded aggregate demand—there might still be inflation, but the actual rate of inflation would be less than the expected rate of inflation.

Viewed in this way, the original Phillips curve version of the neoclassical theory of price adjustment can be regarded as having confused relative and absolute price adjustments. What the Phelps-Friedman proposition amounts to is a statement that the rate of change of a relative price will be a function of

[5] Phelps, "Money Wage Dynamics and Labor Market Equilibrium."

Figure 21.6
The Expectations-Augmented Phillips Curve

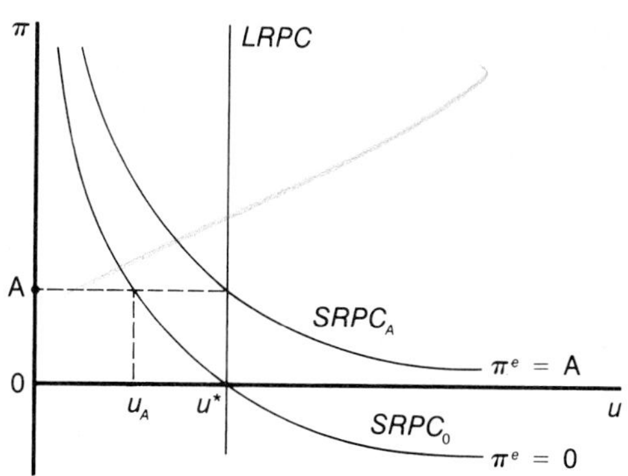

The neoclassical theory of price adjustment is a theory of *relative* price change. When translated into a theory of movements of the *absolute* price level, it has to be augmented. There is a short-run Phillips curve (*SRPC*) for every expected rate of inflation: $SRPC_0$ refers to a zero expected rate of inflation, and $SRPC_A$ refers to a rate of inflation of A. The long-run Phillips curve (*LRPC*) is vertical.

excess demand—the relative price being the general price level relative to its expectation. This means that the rate of inflation will change one-for-one with the expected rate of inflation. This can be illustrated in a diagram such as Figure 21.6. The lower curve in Figure 21.6 is exactly the same as the curve shown in Figure 21.5. It is a Phillips curve. It is a Phillips curve, however, drawn for an expected rate of inflation equal to zero. If, on the average, no inflation is expected, then when there is an unemployment rate of u^* (and therefore zero excess demand for labor), there will actually be no inflation. If, however, the unemployment rate was as low as u_A, so that there was a large amount of excess demand but if no inflation is expected, then inflation will in fact occur and at the rate of A.

The Phelps-Friedman story now asks us to suppose that this rate of inflation A continues for a long period of time and becomes fully anticipated. What will happen to the price adjustment process? The answer is that if more people come to expect the rate of inflation to be A, they will build that expectation into their price and wage adjustments. If everyone expects that prices will rise at the rate A, then the Phillips curve would shift upwards by the whole amount A, so that the new Phillips curve, drawn for an expected rate of inflation equal to A, is directly above the point u^* at the inflation rate A. The two Phillips curves shown in Figure 21.6 are known as *short-run Phillips curves* and are labelled *SRPC* to remind you of that. The vertical line at u^* is sometimes called the *long-run Phillips curve (LRPC)*. It embodies the so-called natural rate hypothesis. The natural rate hypothesis is nothing other than the proposition that if inflation is fully anticipated, unemployment is equal to its "natural rate." Only when the rate of inflation is different from the expected rate will the unemployment rate be different from its natural rate.

In the neoclassical synthesis, the expected rate of inflation is assumed to be a slowly evolving variable and one that imparts a great deal of inertia to the actual rate of inflation. Although it is a slight exaggeration, it is not a serious distortion to assert that the expected rate of inflation is exogenous in the neoclassical synthesis.[6] The expected rate of inflation plays a very similar role to the exogenous money wage assumption of the narrower Keynesian model. This is not to say that the expected rate of inflation does not change. Rather, it is viewed as a variable that changes as a result of forces that are independent of the variables determined within the neoclassical synthesis.

You are now in a position to understand how the neoclassical synthesis explains the business cycle.

E. The Neoclassical Explanation of the Business Cycle

The business cycle—the autocorrelation of output, the countercyclical co-movements in unemployment, and the procyclical co-movements of employment, inflation, and interest rates—is explained, in qualitative terms at least, by the neoclassical synthesis. To see this, I will take you through two exercises that disturb an economy that is initially at rest at full employment with no inflation. In one case, a slump will be generated, and in the other case, a boom. These exercises are designed to show you the mechanisms that are at work in the process. The actual cycle is generated by swings to and fro in either the *IS* curve or the *LM* curve or in both. The illustration that I shall give here visualizes the stimulus coming from a shifting *IS* curve.

From Full-Employment Equilibrium to Slump and Back

Figure 21.7 is used to illustrate the mechanisms at work as the economy is disturbed from a full-employment equilibrium, put into a recession, and then allowed to adjust gradually back to a new full-employment equilibrium. Frame (a) contains the *IS-LM* analysis. Frame (b) contains the aggregate demand and supply analysis, and frame (c) contains the neoclassical price adjustment process (with a zero expected rate of inflation throughout the analysis).

The curves IS^*, LM^*, and AD^* represent the initial equilibrium curves for the economy. The interest rate is, therefore, initially r^*, the income level y^*, and the price level P^*. Now let the economy be disturbed by a shock in the form of a drop in either government spending or investment demand that shifts the *IS* curve from IS^* to IS_0. The impact effect is to lower the rate of interest from r^* to r_0 and to lower income from y^* to y_0. This is the new *IS-LM* equilibrium. Equivalently, the impact effect can be shown in frame (b) as the shift in the aggregate demand curve from AD^* to AD_0, with the income level being y_0, read off as the point at which the new aggregate demand curve AD_0 cuts the horizontal section of the aggregate supply curve, indicating that the price level momentarily is held constant at P^*. The economy is now in a slump condition.

[6]Often, the so-called adaptive expectations hypothesis is employed in neoclassical models. This hypothesis says that expectations of inflation change by some fraction of the most recent error in forecasting inflation. For a rather thorough, although already dated, discussion of expectations, see David Laidler and Michael Parkin, "Inflation: A Survey," *Economic Journal*, 85, no. 340 (December 1975), 741–809.

Figure 21.7
From Neutral to Slump and Back in the Neoclassical Model

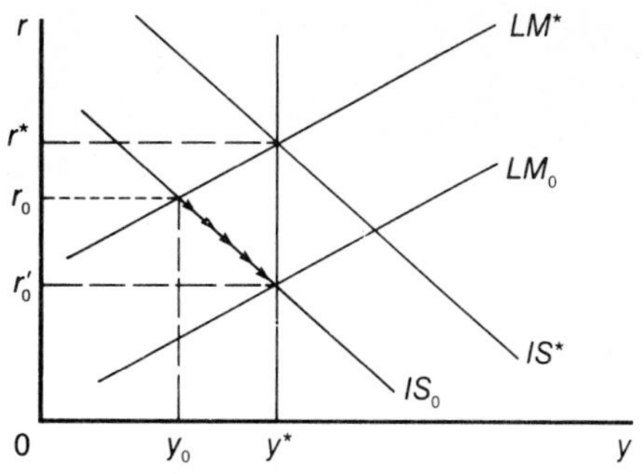

(a) *IS-LM* Equilibrium

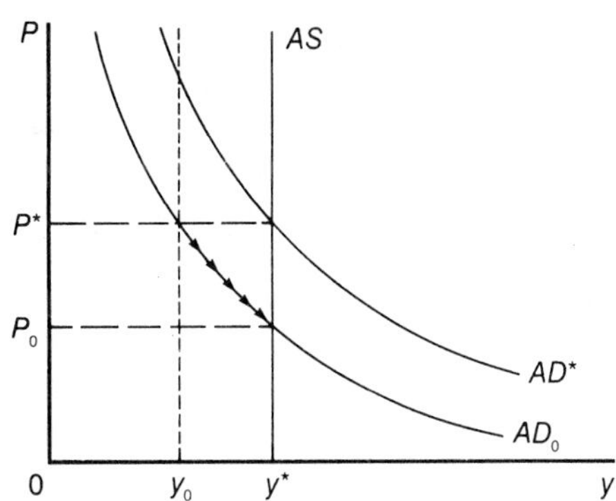

(b) Aggregate Supply and Demand

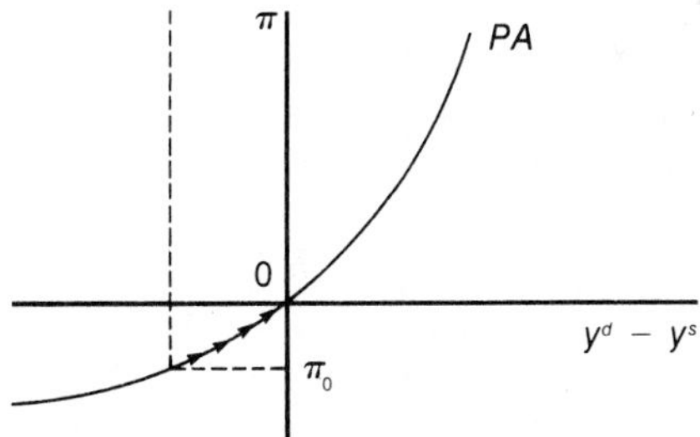

(c) Price Adjustment Process

An initial equilibrium (r^*, y^*, P^*) is disturbed by a leftward shift in the *IS* curve from IS^* to IS_0. Equivalently, the aggregate demand curve shifts from AD^* to AD_0. The impact is for there to be a fall in income and the interest rate to (r_0, y_0) and for prices to start to fall at the rate π_0. As prices fall, the *LM* curve shifts to the right, and the economy follows the arrowed track down the *IS* curve, down the *AD* curve, and up the price adjustment curve, and back to full-employment output, but with a lower price level and interest rate (P_0, r'_0).

If we were analyzing the simple Keynesian model of the previous chapters, this would be the end of the story. The economy would stay there until something else happened to aggregate demand. In the neoclassical synthesis, however, this is not the end of the story. Frame (c) shows why. With output less than y^*, there is excess supply, and prices will begin to fall. They will not fall by much, but they will begin to fall—by π_0 in frame (c). As prices fall, the quantity of real money balances in the economy begins to rise, and the *LM* curve begins to shift rightwards. As this happens, the *LM* curve intersects the *IS* curve at lower and lower rates of interest and at higher and higher levels of real income. The arrows on the *IS* curve indicate the adjustment path the economy takes with a falling interest rate and a rising income level. The same path is illustrated in frame (b) of the diagram. As the price level falls, in effect, the economy is travelling down its new aggregate demand curve. Again, the arrows show that adjustment process. As the output level rises and approaches full employment, the rate at which prices are falling slackens off. This is illustrated in frame (c), showing that the economy travels up the price adjustment curve. A new equilibrium will eventually be reached at full employment with a real interest rate of r'_0, with a price level of P_0, and with prices constant again.

What you have just analyzed is one-half of a business cycle, the half that takes the economy from a neutral position into a slump and back again to a neutral position. Now consider the other half of the cycle.

From Full-Employment Equilibrium to Boom and Back

Figure 21.8 will illustrate the analysis. The initial setup is exactly the same as that in Figure 21.7. Interest is r^*, income is y^*, the price level is P^*, and the inflation rate is zero.

Now let there be a shock to the *IS* curve [frame (a)] as a result of a rise in government spending or a boom in investment demand that shifts the *IS* curve to IS_1. The impact of this shift in the *IS* curve is for it to intersect the *LM* curve at the higher interest rate r_1 and the income level y_1. The same effects can be illustrated in frame (b). There, the aggregate demand curve is shown to have shifted from AD^* to AD_1, and the economy is at point A on that aggregate demand curve. Frame (c) illustrates what is happening to the inflation rate at this moment of shock. With an excess demand equivalent to $y_1 - y^*$, prices are rising at a rate π_1. The economy is in a boom.

In the Keynesian analysis, the economy could never be observed in this position. What would happen is that prices would rise immediately and instantly choke off the excess demand. That is, the price level P_1 in frame (b) and the interest rate r'_1 in frame (a) would be established instantaneously and there would be no further movement from that position. In the neoclassical synthesis, this position would eventually be reached, but not instantaneously.

The neoclassical view is that it takes time for the economy to arrive at the new full-employment equilibrium with a higher price level. Through the process of adjustment, actual output remains above the full-employment level and unemployment below its natural rate. You can think of this as happening as a result of people who would otherwise have been spending time engaged in job search accepting attractive-looking jobs more quickly. Thus, unemployment in the form of job search is lower, employment is higher, and output is also higher than in its full-employment equilibrium. From its initially shocked position, the economy gradually adjusts back to full-employment equilibrium.

Figure 21.8
From Neutral to Boom and Back in the Neoclassical Model

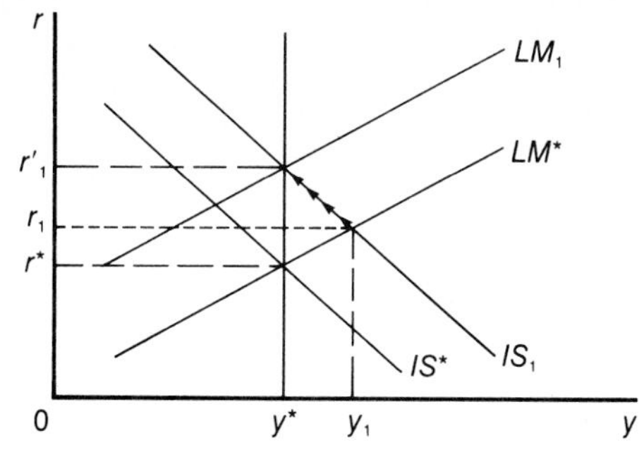

(a) *IS-LM* Equilibrium

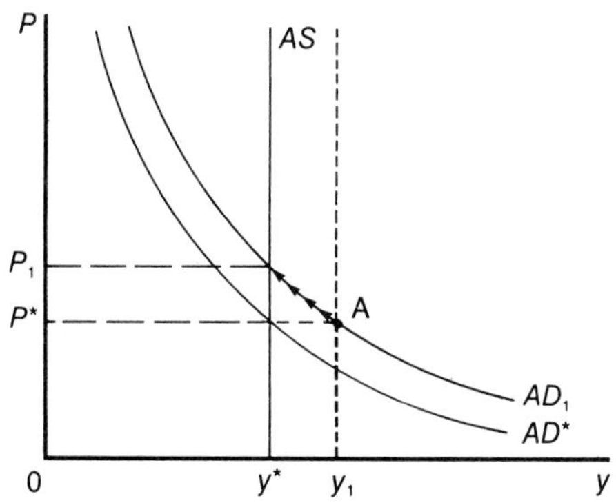

(b) Aggregate Supply and Demand

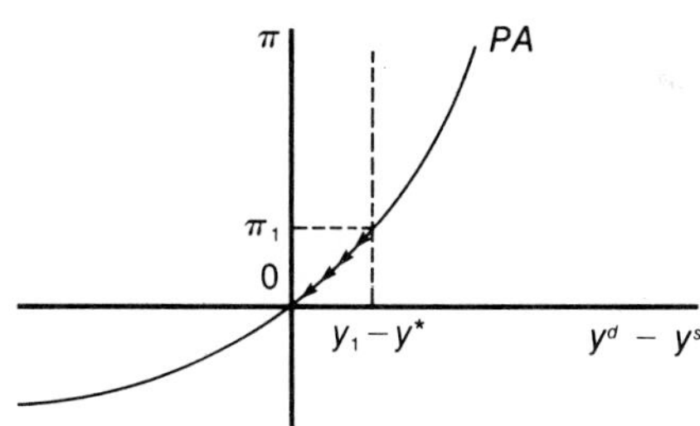

(c) Price Adjustment Process

An initial equilibrium (r^*, y^*, P^*) is disturbed by a rightward shift in the *IS* curve from IS^* to IS_1. Equivalently, the aggregate demand curve shifts from AD^* to AD_1. The impact is for there to be a rise in income and the interest rate (r_1, y_1) and for prices to start to rise at the rate π_1. As prices rise, the *LM* curve shifts leftwards, and the economy moves up the *IS* curve and up the *AD* curve and back down the price adjustment curve to a stable price full-employment equilibrium in which the price level has increased to P_1 and the interest rate to r'_1.

The inflation rate gradually slows, but the price level rises from P^* to P_1, the output level gradually falls from y_1 back to y^*, and the interest rate gradually rises from r_1 to r'_1. The economy has gone from a neutral position into a boom and back again to a neutral position, half a business cycle.

A Complete Cycle

Now, a complete cycle would involve a swing in investment or government spending, so that the IS curve would swing from IS_0 through IS^* to IS_1 and back again. If you visualize the IS curve systematically swinging to and fro between the limits IS_1 and IS_0, you can easily visualize the generation of an ongoing cycle in output and inflation and the rate of interest.

If, superimposed on such a cycle, the money supply is growing at a positive constant rate, then superimposed on the process described here will be an ongoing, positive average rate of inflation. All the diagrams would need modification to incorporate the considerations discussed in the previous section on the Keynesian theory at full employment. There is nothing new in principle, however, to understand in that case.

F. Policy Implications of the Neoclassical Synthesis

The policy implications of the neoclassical synthesis are clear. If inflation and unemployment are to be avoided, swings in aggregate demand must be avoided. Such swings can in principle be avoided by making government spending, taxes, and the money supply move in ways such that whatever is happening to investment demand and perhaps to consumption demand is offset by equivalent changes in the government policy instruments, so that aggregate demand remains steady. By preventing aggregate demand from moving, the cyclical forces described in the previous section can themselves be prevented.

Summary

A. Definition of "Neoclassical Synthesis"

The term *neoclassical synthesis* describes a body of macroeconomic analysis designed to explain the determination of output, prices, employment, and interest rates and to account for the cyclical fluctuations in those variables. It is an amalgamation of the basic model, the Keynesian model, and a gradual price and wage adjustment hypothesis.

B. Keynesian Theory at Full Employment

The Keynesian theory of aggregate demand, which determines output at less than full employment, becomes a theory of the price level at full employment. It yields all the same predictions as those generated by the basic model. A once-and-for-all rise in the money stock raises the price level proportionately. A continuing rise in the money stock generates an inflation rate that is equal to the growth rate of the money stock (minus the growth rate of output). A rise in the growth rate of the money supply produces a rise in the inflation rate, but the inflation rate overshoots the money supply growth rate en route to the new equilibrium.

C. The Neoclassical Theory of Price Adjustment

The neoclassical theory of price adjustment asserts that prices rise when there is excess demand and fall when there is excess supply. The adjustment process is asymmetrical. A 1 percent excess demand would produce a faster price rise than the price fall that would be generated by a 1 percent excess supply.

D. Inflation Expectations and the "Natural Rate" Hypothesis

Properly understood, the neoclassical theory of price adjustment is a theory of relative price adjustment. Nominal price adjustment will therefore be greater at each and every level of excess demand, one-for-one as the expected inflation rate rises. The expected rate of inflation is a slowly evolving variable that may be treated as exogenous in the neoclassical analysis.

E. The Neoclassical Explanation of the Business Cycle

The neoclassical synthesis explains the business cycle as the working out of the effects of swings in the aggregate demand curve generated either by shifts in the *IS* curve or by shifts in the *LM* curve. These shifts themselves arise from changing investment demand, changes in government spending and taxes, and changes in the money supply.

F. The Policy Implications of the Neoclassical Synthesis

The neoclassical synthesis implies that by moving government spending, taxes, and the money supply in a manner that offsets the changes in aggregate demand arising from private behavior, the aggregate demand curve can be stabilized, and as a result, so can the level of output, prices, and interest rates.

Review Questions

1. What is the neoclassical synthesis?
2. What distinguishes the neoclassical synthesis from the Keynesian model?
3. What happens, according to the Keynesian model, if at full employment, there is:

(a) A rise in government expenditure?
(b) A once-and-for-all rise in the money supply?
(c) A rise in the growth rate of the money supply?
(d) A rise in both the excess of government spending over taxes and in the growth rate of the money supply?

4. What is the neoclassical theory of price adjustment?
5. Why do actual price adjustments depend, one-for-one, on expected price adjustments?
6. Trace the effects in the neoclassical model of the following shocks (assume the economy to be at full employment initially):

(a) A once-and-for-all rise in investment demand.
(b) A once-and-for-all rise in the money supply.
(c) A cycle in investment demand.
(d) A cycle in the money supply.

22

Recent U.S. Economic History: How Well Is It Explained by the Neoclassical Synthesis?

The neoclassical synthesis is the post-Keynesian orthodoxy that has reigned supreme in macroeconomics for more than 25 years. It has defined the rules that have governed the research programs over that period. Questions have been posed and answered in terms of the concepts of the *IS-LM* framework for analyzing aggregate demand and of the expectations-augmented Phillips curve (or neoclassical price adjustment hypothesis) for analyzing aggregate supply. Examples of such questions are: How steep are the *IS* and *LM* curves? Is the long-run Phillips curve vertical? How much inflation reduction can be obtained for a given percent of excess supply (or unemployment)? What is the magnitude of the marginal propensity to consume? These are but examples of a long list of similar questions that have been posed and answered within the framework of analysis set out in Chapters 15 to 21.

More than this, the system has formed the basis for complete econometric models. These were pioneered in the interwar years by the Dutch economist Jan Tinbergen.[1] Developments in macroeconometric modelling in the postwar years have been highly innovative and have employed some of the best minds on the subject. Lawrence Klein of the University of Pennsylvania and Arthur Goldberger of the University of Wisconsin developed the first of what was to become a flood of quantitative models of the U.S. economy designed for forecasting and policy evaluation exercises.[2]

There are literally thousands of learned papers written and published on the topic of this chapter—the correspondence of the predictions of the neoclassical synthesis with the facts—and there is no way in which it is going to be possible to do justice to this large, and in many respects exemplary, scientific literature. It would not be sufficient arbitrarily to pull out examples from the literature, nor would it be possible to attempt a faithful and comprehensive summary of it.

[1]Jan Tinbergen, *Business Cycles in the United States of America* (Geneva: League of Nations, 1939).

[2]Lawrence R. Klein, *Economic Fluctuations in the United States, 1921–1941*, Cowles Commission Monograph II (New York: John Wiley and Sons, 1950). Also Lawrence R. Klein and Arthur S. Goldberger, *An Econometric Model of the United States, 1929–1952* (Amsterdam: North Holland, 1955).

Therefore, what this chapter is going to do is to try to give you a general feel for what parts of the neoclassical synthesis are a success and, in the current state of knowledge, must stand as the best explanation available (although almost certainly not the last word on the subject), and what parts are in some sense failing us. In pursuit of this objective, we shall:

(a) Review the main predictions of the neoclassical model.
(b) Examine the way in which the neoclassical model accounts for the Great Depression.
(c) Examine how the model explains the high years of neoclassical macroeconomics in the decade from 1958 to 1967.
(d) See how the model fails to account for the facts in the 1970s.
(e) Understand the main strengths and weaknesses of the neoclassical model.

A. Predictions of the Neoclassical Model

Chapter 21 has already taken you through an analysis of how the neoclassical synthesis works by setting out the model and examining what happens when that model is subjected to various types of shocks. We are now going to expand that analysis somewhat in order to track out the time-series predictions of the neoclassical model when subjected to four types of shocks. These shocks are: (1) a shift in the *IS* curve generated either by fiscal policy or by a shift in investment demand, (2) a shift in the *LM* curve generated by a rise in the growth rate of the money supply, (3) a shift in the neoclassical price adjustment function generated by a drop in the trend value of aggregate supply, and (4) a rise in the expected rate of inflation. Before embarking on these exercises, however, some general introductory remarks may be found helpful.

Some Preliminary Remarks

The analysis is going to be illustrated in figures like Figure 22.1, and it will be best to begin by familiarizing yourself with the various parts of that figure. First, notice that frames (a) and (b) on the left-hand side are exactly the same as frames (a) and (c) of Figure 21.7, p. 293. Frame (c), on the right, is going to track the evolution over time of the variables determined by the neoclassical model. Look at the labelling below those time graphs. We are going to be dealing with four distinct periods of time. The first, referred to as the *initial state*, is the period prior to the shock that we are going to administer to the economy. The second is a single point in time, labelled t_0 on the graph. This is the *point of impact* of the shock that we shall administer. The third block of time is the *adjustment path* of the economy. In general, this will be an infinitely long path, and the time axis is broken to indicate that fact. Finally, beyond the point labelled $t = \infty$, we shall be concerned with the *steady state* of the economy following the shock that we shall administer.

Before we begin any analysis, you should be clear that these time intervals are constructions of the theory and do not refer to any specific units of

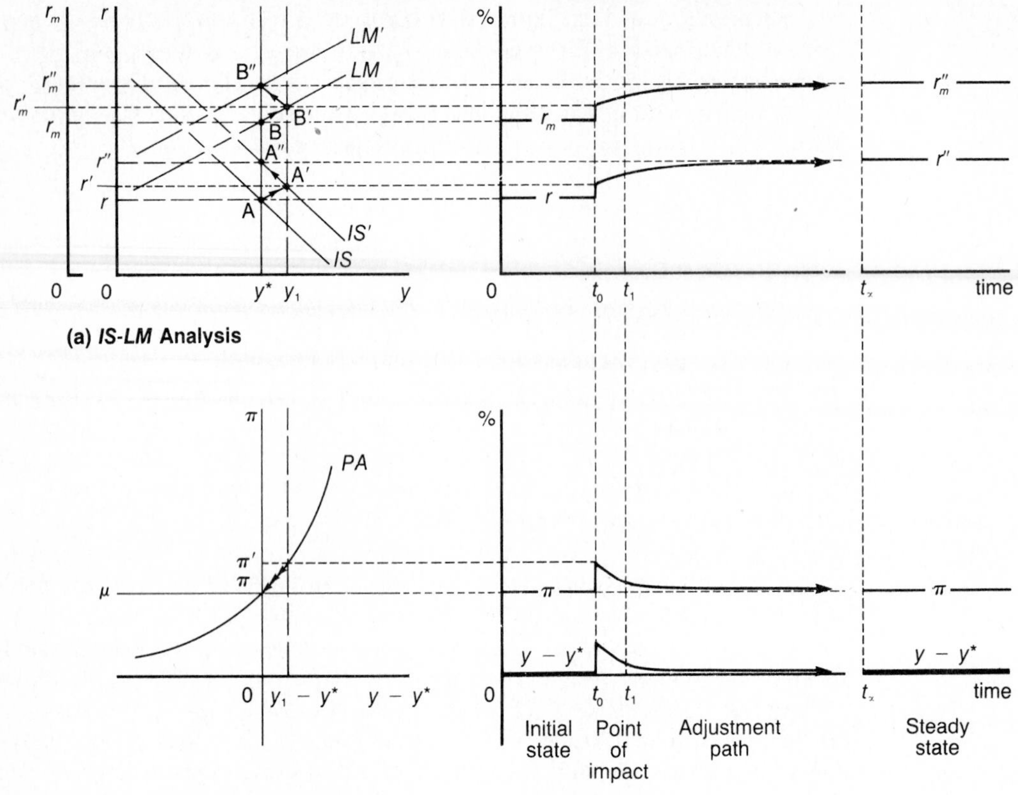

Figure 22.1
The Predicted Effects of an *IS* Curve Shock in the Neoclassical Model

The economy starts out with an interest rate r, money interest rate r_m, inflation rate π the money supply growth rate μ and at full employment. At time t_0, it is disturbed with an *IS* curve shift to the right (to *IS'*). This immediately raises interest rates and the inflation rate and creates excess demand for goods. With inflation higher than the growth rate of the money supply, the *LM* curve starts to drift to the left, raising interest rates still further but choking off the excess demand and lowering the inflation rate. Eventually the economy reaches a steady state with higher interest rates, the initial inflation rate, and full-employment output.

calendar time. How long it would take to get from the point of impact to a position like t_1 on the adjustment path is an empirical matter on which the neoclassical theory is silent. Likewise, how long it would take in calendar time to reach the steady state is a matter on which the theory does not place restrictions. Nevertheless, it is important that you recall that the steady-state predictions of the neoclassical model are identical to the predictions of the basic model. If the neoclassical theory is to be of any interest, therefore, it must be that it is asserting that the steady state does not occur until a long period of time has elapsed. This is the view that will be taken of the neoclassical synthesis in this chapter. That is, the neoclassical synthesis will be treated as being concerned primarily with impact effects and early adjustment paths following the administration of a shock and not with steady states. In terms of the Figure 22.1 and the subsequent figures, that part of the adjustment path on which the neoclassical synthesis focuses will be taken to be the interval between t_0, the point of impact, and the point marked as t_1 along the adjustment path. With these general introductory remarks, let us now consider the effects of an *IS* curve shock.

IS Curve Shock

Imagine that the economy is in an inflationary equilibrium on the *IS* and *LM* curves shown in Figure 22.1. The real rate of interest is r, the money rate of interest is r_m, the inflation rate is π, and output is equal to its full-employment level y^*. Imagine that the economy runs along on this path with constant real and money rates of interest and with prices constantly rising at rate π. A constantly rising money supply at rate μ keeps the *LM* curve in a fixed position. Now imagine that at t_0 there is a rise in government spending or a cut in taxes or a rise in investment spending that shifts the *IS* curve from *IS* to *IS*′. What happens in this economy as a result of this shock? In answering this question we are going to assume, for simplicity, that the expected rate of inflation remains constant at the initial rate of inflation π, and that the gap between the money rate of interest and the real rate of interest also remains constant at that same expected rate of inflation π. This seems a reasonable assumption to make in this model because the neoclassical theory makes no specific predictions concerning movements in the expected rate of inflation, and also with the growth rate of the money supply being held constant, the equilibrium inflation rate does not change. Thus, in effect, we are assuming that the expected rate of inflation remains constant at its equilibrium rate.

With this assumption we can work out the effects of the shift in the *IS* curve in frame (a). The impact of the shift in the *IS* curve to *IS*′ will be to raise interest rates, income, and inflation. To see this, first note that the gap between the *IS* and *LM* curves at full employment (the distance AB) is the initial actual and expected rate of inflation π. Hold that gap constant when the *IS* curve shifts. To do this, focus on the points A′ and B′ on the *IS*′ and *LM* curves. At position A′ on the curve *IS*′, you can read off the impact real rate of interest as r', and at position B′ on the *LM* curve, you can read off the impact money rate of interest as r'_m. The vertical gap between B′ and A′ represents the expected rate of inflation. Only at the level of income y_1 is the vertical gap between the *LM* and *IS* curves equal to the initial anticipated inflation rate. The income level y_1, then, is the amount of demand at the point of impact. Excess demand becomes $y_1 - y^*$, read off on the horizontal axis of frame (b), and π' is the impact inflation rate. At the point of impact, then, the two interest rates rise by the same amount; the rate of inflation and the level of output both rise. *By assumption*, the expected rate of inflation remains constant.

This is not the end of the story. Since the price level is now rising at a faster rate than π, and since by assumption we have not changed the growth rate of the money supply, it must be that the real money stock is falling. This must further mean that the *LM* curve is shifting to the left. As that happens, interest rates will rise still further, and the economy will slide back up the *IS*′ curve and down the price adjustment curve. As this process moves on, consider first frame (a). The real rate of interest will rise along the line from A′ to A″, and the money rate of interest will rise from B′ to B″. Second, look at frame (b) and notice that inflation and excess demand will gradually fall along the price adjustment curve to the initial inflation rate and full-employment output level. This adjustment path is sketched in frame (c), showing a gradual convergence to the steady state.

If the neoclassical model (as opposed to the basic model) is to be regarded as the relevant model for dealing with what happens in actual economies, it must be that the steady-state effects are regarded as occurring only in the very distant future, and the impact and early adjustment effects are the ones that are dominant and relevant. That being so, the main prediction of the neoclassical model is that the effect of a rightward shift in the *IS* curve is to raise interest rates, output, and inflation and to set up a process in which interest rates continue rising, while inflation and output embark on a path that will eventually, but gradually, return them to their initial equilibrium levels.

You can easily work out the effects of the reverse shock (a leftward shift of the *IS* curve) for yourself.

Change in Growth of Money Supply

Next, consider the effects of a change in the growth rate of the money supply. This is a harder experiment to analyze because more steady-state changes occur. Figure 22.2 will take you through this analysis. As before, there is an initial full-employment equilibrium, with the inflation rate π, real interest rate r, and money interest rate r_m, higher than r by the amount of actual and expected rate of inflation π. The money supply is growing at the same rate as the inflation rate, holding the *LM* curve steady in the position marked *LM*.

Suppose that at time t_0, the point of impact, the money supply growth rate is increased from μ to μ'. This is marked on the time-series graph [frame (c)] as a step increase from μ to μ' and is also shown as a horizontal line in the price adjustment diagram [frame (b)].

Before we begin to try to work out what happens to the economy when it is administered this shock, let us do something that we are fairly familiar with; that is, let us look at the steady state to which this economy is heading. It is always a good idea to try to find out where you are going to end up in an analysis of this kind before you embark upon the adjustment path. This will help to keep directions clear en route. You already know from your analysis in the previous chapter and, indeed, from the analysis of the basic model (for they are both the same in terms of their steady-state effects) that a rise in the growth rate of the money supply will lead to a higher inflation rate and a higher money rate of interest but to an unchanged real rate of interest. The economy will also be at full employment again when it reaches the steady state. The final part of the time-series [frame (c)] shows the economy in its new steady state. The *LM* curve, *LM′* in frame (a), is also the new steady-state *LM* curve. Recall that it gets to the left of the initial *LM* curve because the inflation rate overshoots the money supply growth rate in the adjustment process, thereby lowering real money balances.

Now let us come to the harder task of working out the sort of path that will take us from the initial equilibrium to the new one. What is the path that

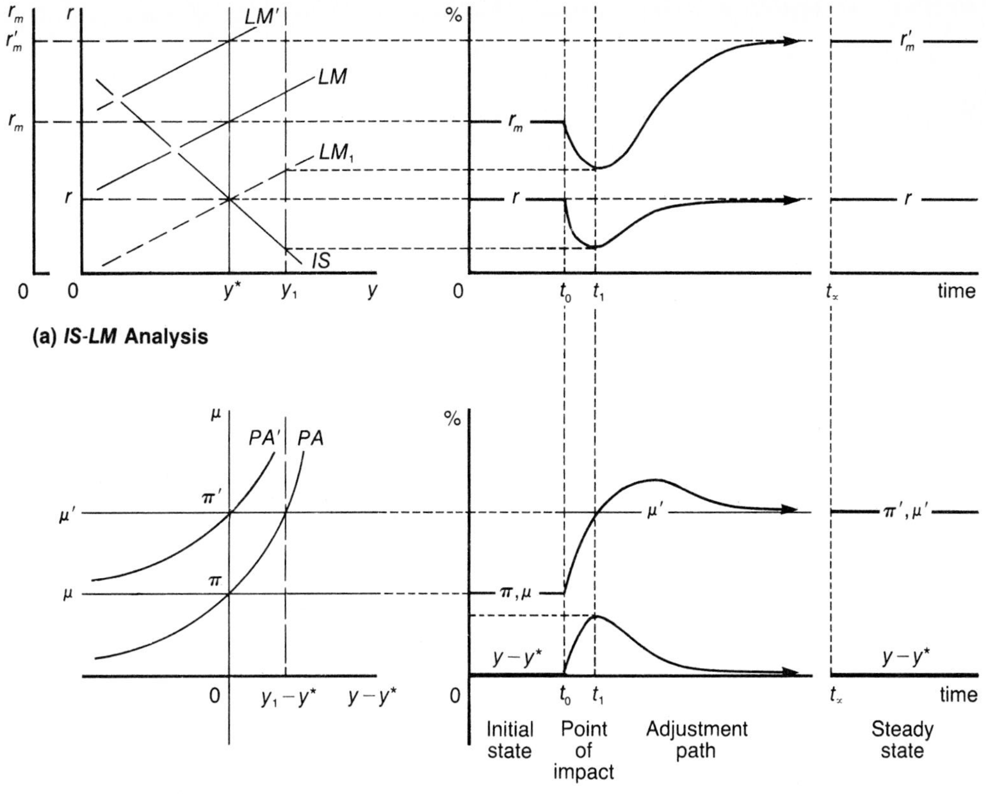

Figure 22.2
The Predicted Effects of a Rise in the Money Supply Growth Rate in the Neoclassical Model

An initial equilibrium exactly the same as that of Figure 22.1 is disturbed by doubling the growth rate of the money supply from μ to μ'. There is no impact effect of this. All the variables gradually adjust from their initial values, with interest rates initially falling and inflation rates and output initially rising. Eventually, interest rates turn upwards and approach their new steady-state values. The inflation rate, having overshot the money supply growth rate, approaches its new steady-state value, and output returns to a steady-state full-employment level.

---

the neoclassical model predicts for the adjustment? The answer, perhaps fairly surprisingly, is that there is no specific prediction contained in the neoclassical model. Why is that? The key to understanding why the neoclassical model does not predict any specific time path in the adjustment process is that it does not have a specific theory about how the expected rate of inflation changes. If the expected rate of inflation was to remain constant at π forever, regardless of the actual growth rate of the money supply and the actual rate of inflation, then the economy would forever experience a state of excess demand, and expectations would be forever wrong. Although it does not say how expectations change, the neoclassical model does insist that, on the average, in the long run, expectations are correct. It therefore predicts that the expected inflation rate will rise from π to π' *at some stage or other*. What it is silent on is precisely how that change will occur.

To see why this is important, consider what would happen if the expected rate of inflation increased from π to π' at the moment t_0, the point of impact of the change in the growth rate of the money supply. In that event, there would be a once-and-for-all jump in the price level, real money balances would fall and the *LM* curve would shift to *LM'*, the money interest rate would rise instantly to its steady-state value, and the inflation rate would immediately thereafter be on the steady-state path. There would, in effect, be a spike in the inflation rate at the moment of impact, and thereafter the inflation rate would be at its steady-state level. There would be no excess demand at any stage in this process. The economy would stay at full employment all the time.

Does the result that you have just obtained seem familiar? It probably does, for it is precisely the result that you obtained when working with the basic model. Recall that in that model we explicitly assumed that the actual and expected rate of inflation were always equal to each other. Whenever there was a change in the growth rate of the money supply in that setup, there was an instantaneous change in both the rate of inflation and market rate of interest, together with an overshooting of the price level to reduce real money balances to their new equilibrium level. There were no effects on output, employment, or unemployment. You have now seen that this result can be generated in the more comprehensive framework of the neoclassical model by making the same assumption as the basic model makes concerning the adjustment of inflationary expectations.

Although the exercise just conducted gives you a better understanding of the connection between the basic model and the neoclassical framework, it does not tell you what the neoclassical model predicts concerning the effects of a change in the growth rate of the money supply. You will get a better feel for that by making the opposite extreme assumption concerning inflation expectations. Specifically, suppose that the expected rate of inflation did not change from π for a very long period of time. While the expected inflation rate remained constant, the path of adjustment of the economy would look like the path from t_0 to t_1 in frame (c). That is, at the moment of impact, when the money supply growth rate increased, the *LM* curve would start to move to the right. It would do this because the money supply growth rate at that moment would be higher than the inflation rate. So long as the *LM* curve is moving to the right, the inflation rate is rising, and real income is also rising. There will come a point at which the *LM* curve will have shifted so far to the right, having generated so much excess demand, that the inflation rate will be equal to the growth rate of the money supply. This happens in frame (a) of Figure 22.2 when the *LM* curve gets to the dotted curve LM_1, with an income level y_1. By construction, this happens on the time diagram [frame (c)] at time t_1. If the expected rate of inflation never changed, the situation in which the economy finds itself at time t_1 would never change. It is a point of rest, given a false expected rate of inflation.

To work out the adjustment path of the economy, it is necessary to specify a path of adjustment for inflation expectations. Since the neoclassical theory is silent on that matter, there is nothing that we can do to provide a detailed picture of the adjustment path. All we know is that the theory predicts that eventually the expected inflation rate will equal the actual rate. That being so, the theory does predict that the steady state, with which you are already familiar, will indeed be arrived at by some means or other. The adjustment path sketched out in frame (c) is the simplest conceivable path that the economy could follow to its steady state. Many other types of paths are possible, including some that cycle around before settling down at the steady state.

Again, recall that the neoclassical model claims to be more useful than the basic model in understanding what is going on in the actual world. It must be, therefore, that the impact and early part of the adjustment path are to be regarded as the relevant set of predictions of this model. To summarize these predictions: A rise in the growth rate of the money supply will at first have the effect of gradually lowering interest rates, raising output, and raising the inflation rate. All of these effects will occur gradually rather than suddenly. Eventually, the money rate of interest will rise above its initial level, but this will not happen in the early phase of the adjustment process.

The analysis that we have just conducted can be regarded as one-half of a cycle of economic activity—the half that takes us from neutral through a boom and back to neutral again. The other half of the cycle could easily be analyzed by examining the effect of a fall in the growth rate of the money supply. These effects can be shown to be exactly the opposite of those analyzed in this section. It will be a useful exercise to work out precisely what those effects are and to satisfy yourself that all the processes set up in the previous example occur in the reverse direction. You can think of the business cycle described in Chapter 6 as being generated by a succession of periods in which the money supply growth rate is increased and then decreased.

The analysis above has all been conducted in terms of movements in inflation, output, and interest rates. An equivalent analysis involving the unemployment rate could have been conducted if we had replaced the price adjustment curve with its Phillips curve equivalent. A further exercise that will be useful for you to carry out is one that reinterprets everything that has gone on in this section in terms of co-movements between inflation and unemployment. To do this you need to refer back to Figures 21.5 and 21.6 and the discussion surrounding those figures and reinterpret the neoclassical price adjustment curve as an expectations-augmented Phillips' curve.

A Supply Side Shock

Let us analyze a shock that many proponents of the neoclassical theory believe to have been important in the 1970s, that of a drop in aggregate supply. Figure 22.3 will illustrate the analysis in this case. As before, the economy is in full-employment equilibrium with an inflation rate π up to time t_0. The *IS* and *LM* curves and the *PA* curve illustrate this equilibrium in frames (a) and (b) of Figure 22.3. At time t_0, the shock that the economy receives is a drop in aggregate supply. Analytically, we can represent this by a leftward shift of the price adjustment curve. In effect, shifting the price adjustment curve to the left

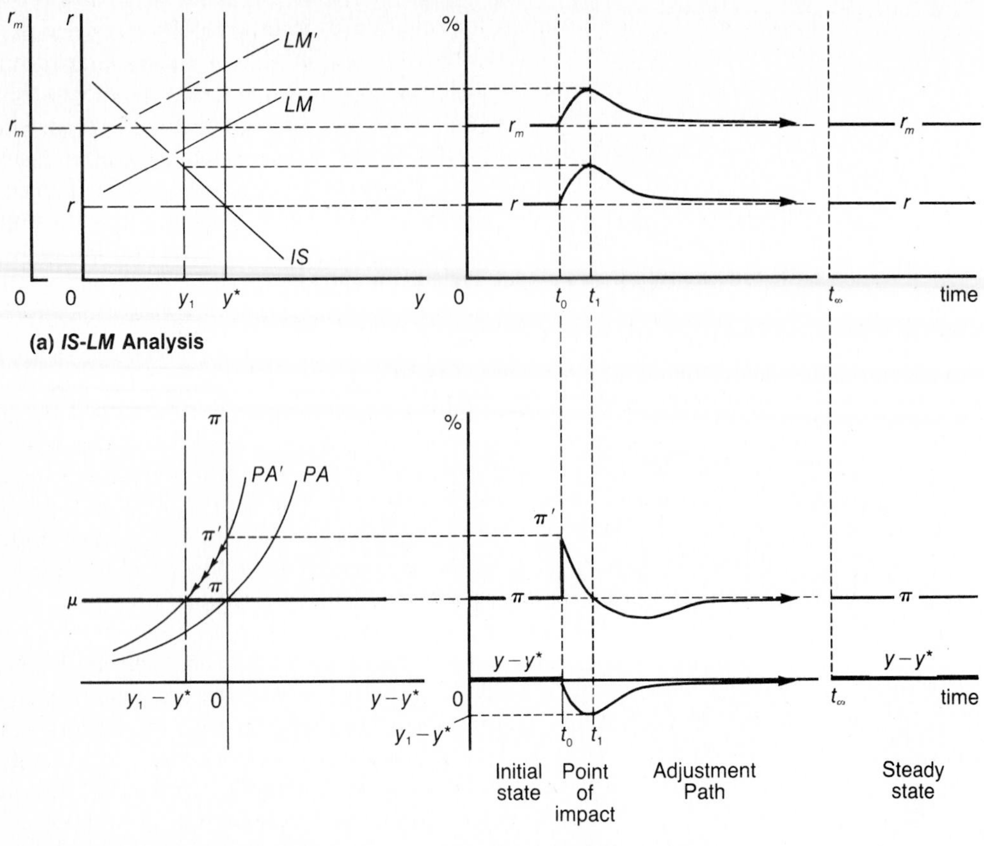

Figure 22.3
The Predicted Effects of a Temporary Fall in Aggregate Supply in the Neoclassical Model

The same initial equilibrium as in Figure 22.1 is disturbed by a temporary drop in aggregate supply. This is depicted as a leftward shift of the price adjustment curve. The impact effect of this is to raise the inflation rate from π to π'. With inflation bigger than money supply growth, real balances fall, and the *LM* curve drifts to the left. This lowers the level of demand (output falls below trend), the inflation rate falls, and interest rates begin to rise. If the shock is temporary, so that the price adjustment curve drifts back from *PA'* to *PA*, then the inflation rate will fall and undershoot its initial value, eventually returning to its original steady state. All the other variables also will return to their initial steady state. If the shock was permanent, the economy would be stuck in a position such as that depicted at time t_1.

---

implies that, at each level of demand, there will now be more excess demand and, therefore, given the price adjustment proposition of the neoclassical model, more inflation. Here the shift in the price adjustment curve from *PA* to *PA'* represents the effect of the drop in aggregate supply.

What are the impacts of this shift in the price adjustment relation? By hypothesis, the *IS* and *LM* curves do not shift. The impact effect must, therefore, simply be to raise inflation to the point at which the price adjustment curve cuts the zero excess demand line. This is shown as the jump in the inflation rate from π to π' in frame (b) and in frame (c). Is this the end of the story? The answer is clearly no. If the initial state was an equilibrium, then the money supply growth rate must have been compatible with the inflation rate π. At an inflation rate π', the money supply growth rate is less than the inflation rate, so real money balances are falling, and the *LM* curve is shifting to the left. As the *LM* curve shifts to the left, the real and money rates of interest rise, as shown in frame (c), and the economy moves into a position of excess supply. That is, the economy starts to travel down the price adjustment curve *PA*′, with falling inflation and falling output. If the supply shock is a permanent one, so that the price adjustment curve is going to be forever at *PA*′, then by the time the economy reached the position t_1, it would be back at a full equilibrium. Output would be at y_1, the inflation rate would be back at π, and interest rates would be higher than initially, but necessarily so, because the full-employment aggregate supply is lower. If, on the other hand, the supply shock is temporary, so that the price adjustment curve gradually moves back to *PA*, then the economy will follow an adjustment path similar to that traced out in frame (c), eventually returning to the initial equilibrium.

Again, since the emphasis in the neoclassical model is on impact effects and early phases of the adjustment path, the presumed relevant predictions of the model concerning the effects of a supply shock are that if aggregate supply is reduced, there will be an impact rise in the inflation rate, a gradual rise in interest rates, and a gradual depression of output below trend. In the early phases of the adjustment process, interest rates will continue to drift upwards, the inflation rate will moderate, but output performance will deteriorate.

As before, it will be a useful exercise to work out the effects of a rise in aggregate supply. You should be able to convince yourself that the process set up is the exact mirror image of that analyzed in Figure 22.3.

Let us now turn to the final exercise in summarizing the predictions of the neoclassical theory—that of analyzing the effects of a change in the expected rate of inflation.

A Rise in the Expected Rate of Inflation

Figure 22.4 illustrates a rise in the expected rate of inflation. As in the previous three cases, the economy starts out in a full-employment equilibrium with an inflation rate equal to π, a market rate of interest r_m, a real rate of interest of r, and output at its full-employment level, y^*. The shock this time is that the expected inflation rate jumps to π'. This shifts the price adjustment curve upwards to the curve *PA*′.

To work out where the economy moves at the moment of impact of this rise in the expected inflation rate, you have to remember that the gap between the market rate of interest, r_m, and the real interest, r, is the expected rate of inflation. Equilibrium in the money market occurs when the economy is on the *LM* curve, and in the goods market when the economy is on the *IS* curve. The only place that that can happen is at the income level y_1. How do we know this? We know this because the vertical gap between the *LM* and *IS* curves at

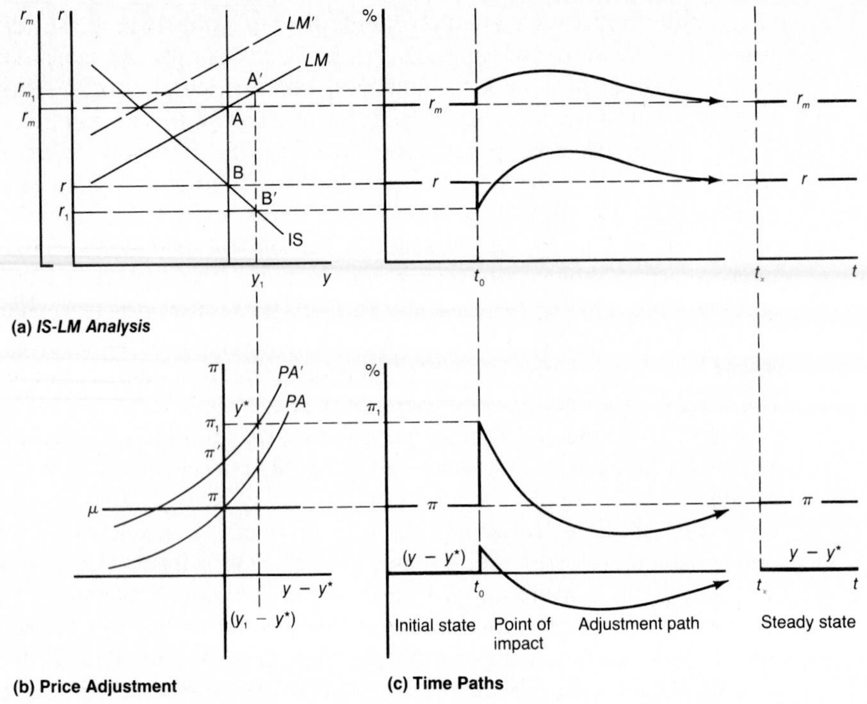

Figure 22.4
The Predicted Effects of a Rise in Inflation Expectations in the Neoclassical Model

The same initial equilibrium as in Figure 22.1 is disturbed by a temporary rise in inflationary expectations from π to π'. With higher inflationary expectations, people try to rid themselves of excess money and bond holdings and acquire additional real assets. As they do this, the economy slides up the *LM* curve and down the *IS* curve until it reaches a point at which the vertical gap between those curves equals the new higher expected rate of inflation (π' equals the distance A′B′). The impact effect is to raise income to y_1, raise the money rate of interest to r_{m_1}, and lower the real rate to r_1. The inflation rate rises to π_1. With inflation higher than money supply growth, the *LM* curve now starts to drift to the left, raising the money rate of interest still higher, and raising real rates as well, but lowering inflation and output. If inflation expectations drift back to their initial level, *PA′* drops back to *PA*, and the economy returns to its initial equilibrium. In so doing, the inflation rate must undershoot the steady state so as to replenish real money balances to their original level. With inflation below its steady-state level, output will be below full employment and real interest rates above their steady-state level.

that income level, the distance A′B′, is equal to the expected inflation rate, π'. The initial expected inflation rate, π, was equal to the vertical distance AB on the same *IS* and *LM* curves. The process that occurs to move the economy from point A on the *LM* curve and from point B on the *IS* curve to points A′ and B′ on those same two curves is one that involves people trying to lower their holdings of financial assets such as money and bonds and to increase their holdings of real assets—real goods.

If, starting from the initial situation, people now believe that the rate of inflation is going to be higher than they previously thought, they will try to sell bonds and also get rid of money balances, buying inventories of goods (capital and consumer durables as well, perhaps, as inventories of other consumer goods). The attempt to sell off bonds will lower the prices of bonds, raising their rates of return. The attempt to acquire bigger volumes of capital goods and consumer durables, as well as inventories of consumption goods, will be associated with a lowering of the marginal productivity of those additional inventories and, therefore, with a lowering of the real rate of interest. As people attempt to rid themselves of unwanted excess money balances and bonds, and acquire additional real goods, the economy will slide up its *LM* curve and down its *IS* curve. The process will continue until they are satisfied that the rates of return that they are making on all assets in real terms are equal. This will happen when the rate of return on bonds, r_m, is higher than the real rate of interest by an amount that reflects the new higher expected rate of inflation.

The upshot of the above discussion is that the economy will move on impact to the income level y_1 and inflation rate π_1, with the money rate of interest r_{m_1}, and real rate of interest r_1. These impact effects are shown in frame (c) of Figure 22.4 as a higher money rate of interest, lower real rate of interest, and higher inflation and output rates.

This, of course, is not the end of the story, since the rate of inflation π_1 now exceeds the rate of growth of the money supply, which, by assumption, has remained constant at its initial level of μ. This being so, the *LM* curve will be drifting to the left, to a position perhaps like that shown as *LM'*. As this process goes on, the market rate of interest and the real rate of interest will rise (maintaining the vertical gap between the *IS* and *LM* curves at the new expected rate of inflation). During this same process, the inflation rate will fall (the economy will slide back down *PA'*), and output will fall. If the expected rate of inflation drifts back to its initial level, so that the price adjustment curve drifts back to *PA*, the economy will eventually return to its initial equilibrium state. As it does so, however, the rate of inflation will necessarily have to go below its original level for a period, and output will have to fall below its full-employment level. We know that this will have to happen because, in the initial part of the adjustment path immediately after t_0, the rate of inflation exceeded the growth rate of the money supply, and real balances therefore fell.

If the economy is to return to its initial equilibrium, real balances will have to rise en route to that equilibrium. They can only do so if the rate of inflation is below the growth rate of the money supply by a sufficient amount, and for long enough, to return real balances to their initial level. The path illustrated in frame (c) is a possible path for the inflation rate and the level of output. In this simplest of cases shown in frame (c), the market rate of interest will eventually turn downwards and approach its new steady-state level from above. The real rate of interest, however, will overshoot its steady state, rising above its initial and long-run equilibrium level at the same time as the inflation rate and output are below their steady-state levels.

As in the previous three cases, the effects of a sudden fall in the expected rate of inflation are exactly the opposite of those analyzed here, and again, it would be a useful exercise for you to determine precisely what the impacts and paths of adjustment look like in that case.

Now that we have examined the predictions of the neoclassical synthesis concerning the effects of the four major types of shocks to which the economy may be subjected within that framework, let us turn to the task of examining some important episodes in U.S. macroeconomic history, and discover the extent to which those episodes conform to the predictions of the neoclassical model as set out above.

B. A Neoclassical Interpretation of the Great Depression

Let us see if we can gain deeper insights into how the neoclassical model works by using it to try to understand the most traumatic macroeconomic event of this century—the Great Depression—and its aftermath. In performing this exercise, you should be aware that the interpretation that you are about to work through is just one of several possible ones. Volumes have been written on this topic, and I do not want to mislead you into thinking that the treatment given here is in any sense definitive. There continues to be considerable controversy concerning these matters and many scholars, some of whom have spent a near lifetime studying the problem, would tell the story in a different way.[3]

Let us begin our interpretation of the Great Depression and its aftermath by recalling the key facts about that period.

The Facts

You are already familiar with some of the facts of the Great Depression from your study of Chapters 2 and 6. The time-series charts in Chapter 2 provide a picture of the course of inflation, unemployment, real income, and interest rates through that period. Table 22.1 repeats some of that information for convenience but also provides you with other pertinent facts concerning the Great Depression and the period immediately following it. In that table, data have been set out from 1929 to 1937. The beginning year, 1929, is chosen because that was the year in which the Great Depression began. It was a year of stable prices and full employment. The ending year, 1937, is chosen because in that year, real income had returned to its 1929 level, so that at least as measured from the perspective of real national income we had gone full cycle. We were still, of course, not back at full employment because population and capital stock had grown in the intervening years, so that the capacity of the economy by 1937 was substantially higher than it had been in 1929. Other events began to dominate the economy in 1938, however, and I do not want to extend the analysis of this chapter to deal with them.

Study the data in Table 22.1 carefully. Notice that real income falls every

[3]If you want to pursue this matter in greater depth, you could do no better than begin by studying two works that will give you different perspectives on the Great Depression. They are Milton Friedman and Anna J. Schwartz, "The Great Contraction, 1929–33," *A Monetary History of the United States 1867–1960* (Princeton: Princeton University Press, 1963), chap. 7; and Peter Temin, *Did Monetary Forces Cause the Great Depression*? (New York: W. W. Norton & Co., Inc., 1976).

TABLE 22.1
The Great Depression and Recovery: 1929–1937

	NATIONAL INCOME AND PRODUCT ACCOUNTS				MONEY, INTEREST, AND PRICES				EMPLOYMENT, UNEMPLOYMENT, AND WAGES				
YEAR	*y*	*c*	*i*	*g*	*M*	*M/P*	*r*	*π*	*ℓf*	*n*	*u*	*W*	*W/P*
1929	203.6	139.6	40.4	22.0	26.6	52.5	5.9	0.0	40.4	39.1	3.2	0.49	0.97
1930	183.5	130.4	27.4	24.3	25.8	52.4	3.6	−2.5	40.5	37.0	8.7	0.48	0.97
1931	169.3	126.1	16.8	25.4	24.1	53.8	2.6	−9.3	40.6	34.2	15.9	0.44	0.99
1932	144.2	114.8	4.7	24.2	21.1	52.4	2.7	−10.8	40.9	31.2	23.6	0.38	0.94
1933	141.5	112.8	5.3	23.3	19.9	50.6	1.7	−5.3	41.0	30.9	24.9	0.37	0.95
1934	154.3	118.1	9.4	26.6	21.9	51.9	1.0	3.3	41.3	32.4	21.7	0.45	1.07
1935	169.5	125.5	18.0	27.0	25.9	60.8	0.8	2.5	41.6	33.2	20.1	0.47	1.10
1936	193.0	138.4	24.0	31.8	29.5	69.0	0.8	1.0	41.7	34.7	16.9	0.47	1.11
1937	203.2	143.1	29.9	30.8	30.9	69.4	0.9	3.5	41.9	35.9	14.3	0.54	1.21

Notes: *y*, *c*, *i*, and *g* are real GNP, consumption, investment, and government expenditure on goods and services, respectively, $billions, 1958 prices. *M* is M1, $billions, *M/P* is M1 deflated by GNP deflator, 1958 = 1, *r* is percent per annum rate on 4–6 month commercial bills, *π* is percent per annum rate of change of CPI, *ℓf* is the labor force, percent of population, *n* is employment, percent of population, *u* is unemployment, percent of labor force, *W* is money wage rate, $ per hour, *W/P* is *W* deflated by GNP deflator, 1958 = 1.

year from 1929 down to 1933 and then begins to rise again. Consumption follows exactly the same pattern as real income. Investment also follows that same pattern but with much greater emphasis, falling to only a little more than one-tenth of its 1929 level by the trough years of 1932–1933. Government expenditure, in contrast, remains fairly steady through the depression and begins to rise as real income rises after 1933. The money supply collapses from 1929 down to 1933. It then begins to grow again after that date. The real money supply remains virtually constant from 1929 to 1932, then falls rather sharply in 1933, and after that begins to rise, at first slowly, but by 1936 at a fairly rapid rate. Interest rates (it is the short-term interest rate that is shown in the table) fall up to 1935 (with a small pause in 1932) and thereafter stay flat. Inflation becomes severely negative, reaching a trough in 1932, and after that it rises to become positive by the middle 1930s. The labor force is growing throughout the depression years at a steady rate. Employment, however, collapses, and unemployment rises so that barely 30 percent of the population has work by 1933, and 25 percent of the labor force is unemployed. Money wages fall from an average of 50¢ an hour down to 37¢ an hour by 1933 and then climb back to 50¢ an hour. Real wages rise at first (to 1931), then fall for two years in the depths of the depression, but after that climb fairly strongly.

These then are the raw facts about the years of the Great Depression and the post depression recovery. How can we explain these facts?

Explanations

The simplest, but in some respects insufficiently deep, explanation is to be seen by considering only the first four columns of Table 22.1—the National Income and Product Accounts. You will recognize these variables as the ones analyzed in the simplest version of Keynesian macroeconomics—the Keynesian cross model of Chapter 16. Let us see how that model explains the Great Depression and the recovery.

Figure 22.5
The Consumption Function and Keynesian Cross Model

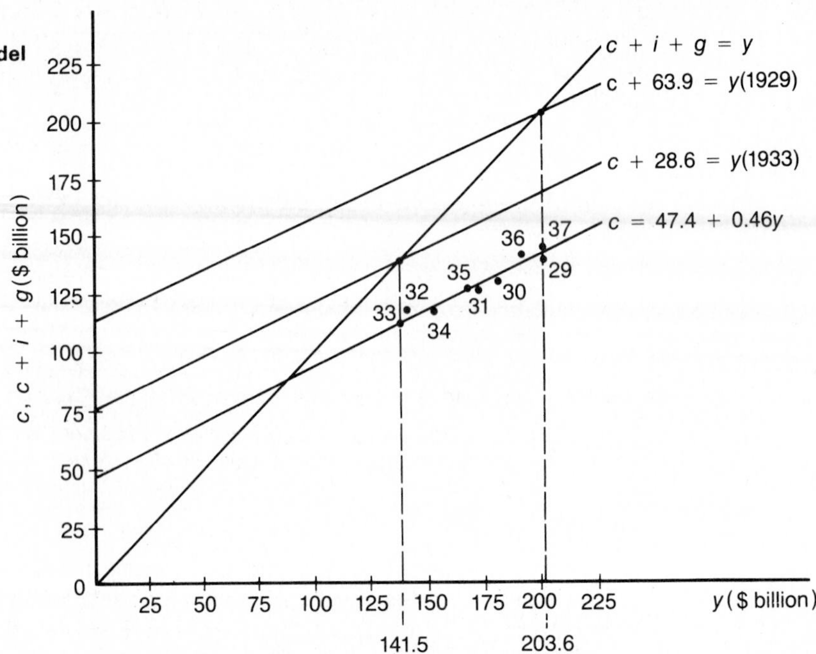

The relationship between consumption and income through the Great Depression years fits the Keynesian consumption function hypothesis closely. Adding investment and government purchases of goods and services to consumption gives the total level of planned expenditures [$c + 63.9 = y(1929)$] and determines equilibrium income in 1929 as $203.6 billion. A drop in investment (with smaller drops in government spending and net exports) shifts the total planned spending line down by 1933 to $c + 28.6 = y(1933)$. This determines a new equilibrium in 1933 at 141.5.
SOURCE: Table 22.1.

The Keynesian Cross Model and the Great Depression The Keynesian cross model (Figure 16.4) is shown in Figure 22.5, but instead of being shown in purely hypothetical terms as it was in Chapter 16, it appears here with the actual numbers generated by the U.S. economy through the period 1929 to 1937. Each heavy point in the diagram represents the value of consumption read off from the vertical axis and the value of real income read off from the horizontal axis in each of the nine years, the year being indicated by the small number set against each point. If we pass a line through these points, we can characterize the U.S. consumption function during these years. Such a line is shown as that labelled

$$c = 47.5 + 0.46y$$

It says that if income was zero, consumption would be $47.5 billion, and for each extra dollar by which income rises, consumption rises by 46¢. The marginal propensity to consume through this period was, thus, 0.46.

In 1929 the value of investment (i) plus government expenditure (g) was \$62.4 billion (see Table 22.1). There was also a small amount of net exports adding to a total of investment-plus-government spending plus net exports of \$63.9 billion. If we add that amount vertically to the consumption function, we obtain the line labelled

$$c + 63.9 = y \text{ (1929)}$$

This line represents total planned expenditure at each level of income. Where this line cuts the 45° line, the equilibrium level of real income and expenditure is determined. That equilibrium in 1929 is \$203.6 billion (again see Table 22.1). If you are not sure what is going on here, refresh your memory by looking again at Chapter 16, Section E.

By 1933, the depths of the Great Depression, investment-plus-government expenditure had fallen to \$28.6 billion (and net exports were zero). This drop in investment-plus-government spending can be represented in Figure 22.5 as a downward shift of the total expenditure line. Such a line is shown as that labelled

$$c + 28.6 = y \text{ (1933)}$$

The vertical distance between that line and the consumption function is \$28.6 billion. Where that line cuts the 45° line determines the equilibrium in 1933. That equilibrium income level is \$141.5 billion (again see Table 22.1).

Now that you know how to read Figure 22.5, let us see what it is telling us about the Great Depression. First, it tells us that the Keynesian theory of the consumption function fits the facts of the Great Depression years very accurately. In other words, variations in income can account for the variations in consumption almost exactly. What happened to produce the recession was that investment fell. The drop in investment expenditure led, because of the multiplier effect, to a larger drop in income. From the peak to the trough, investment-plus-government spending fell by \$35.3 billion. Since the marginal propensity to consume is 0.46, you can work out the Keynesian multiplier to be:

$$\frac{1}{1 - 0.46} = 1.85$$

If the drop in investment-and-government spending (\$35.5 billion) is multiplied by 1.85, then we get a drop in income of \$65.4 billion. The drop in actual income was \$62.1 billion, very close to that predicted by this model. (More precise ways of estimating the marginal propensity to consume than the crude method that I have used here would yield an even closer correspondence between this model and the facts.)

What you have just discovered is that the Keynesian cross model predicts the movements in real income during the Great Depression with remarkable accuracy. The explanation is not, however, a very deep one. Most of the interesting questions are left unanswered by this explanation. The chief of these is the question: Why did investment fall? This question is not answered by the Keynesian cross model for the simple reason that investment is treated as exogenous in that model. In effect, all that the Keynesian cross model is

Figure 22.6
The Facts of the Great Depression Years in *IS*, *LM*, and *PA* Space

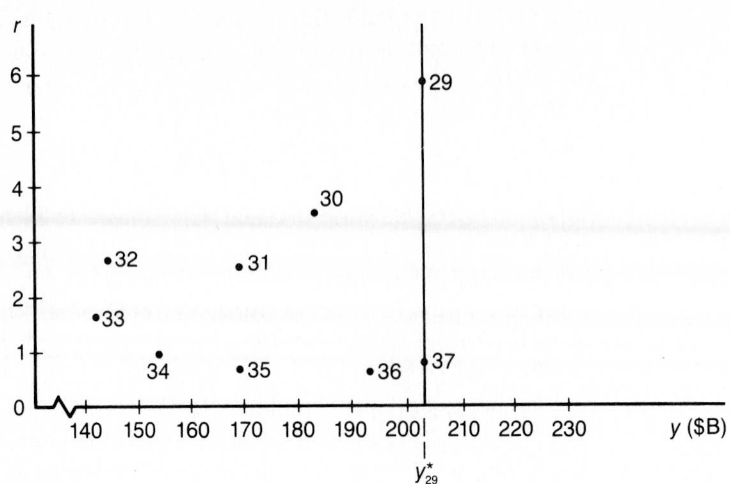

(a) *IS-LM*

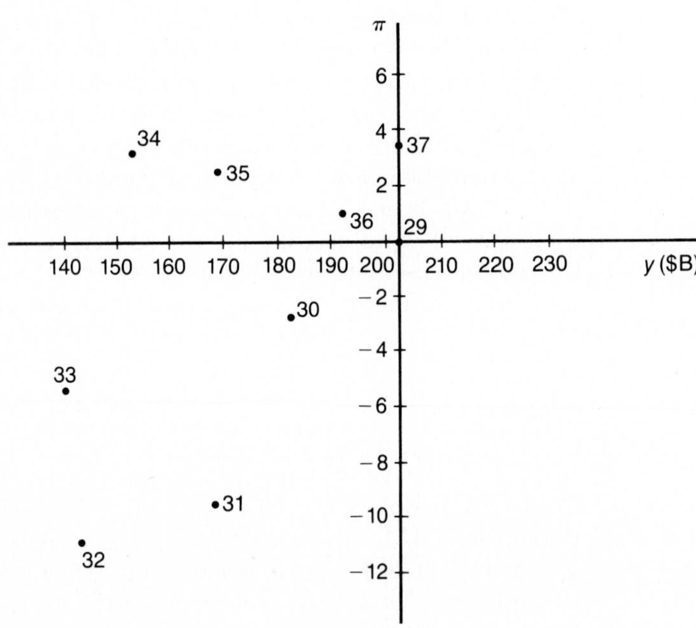

(b) Price Adjustment

Each point in frame (a) shows the short-term rate of interest and level of real GNP in the years from 1929 to 1937. Each point in frame (b) shows the relationship between the rate of inflation (of consumer prices) and the level of real income in those same years. None of the points appears to lie on any identifiable *IS*, *LM*, or *PA* curves.
SOURCE: Table 22.1.

telling us is that the consumption function was fairly stable through the Great Depression years. To obtain a deeper explanation we need to go to a deeper theory. The neoclassical synthesis is such a theory. It provides some additional insights into why investment fell and also provides us with an account of not only movements in income and employment but also movements in the rate of interest and the price level. Let us now see how it accounts for the facts.

The Neoclassical Synthesis Let us begin our investigation of a neoclassical explanation of the Great Depression by looking again at some of the facts set out in Table 22.1 but organized in a way that is suggested by the neoclassical theory. Figure 22.6 does this. The facts are reviewed both in *IS-LM* space [frame (a)] and price adjustment (*PA*) space [frame (b)]. Each heavy point in this two-part diagram represents a year between 1929 and 1937 as indicated by the small numbers. Thus, in frame (a) you can read off the level of real income as $203.6 billion in 1929 [horizontal axis of frame (a)] and the interest rate at 5.9 percent [vertical axis of frame (a)]. Each year is also shown in frame (b), but this time the inflation rate is plotted against the level of real income. For example, 1929 appears at zero inflation with real income again at $203.6 billion.

You have become familiar with diagrams that measure the rate of interest on the vertical axis and real income on the horizontal axis in which appear two curves—an *IS* and an *LM* curve. You have also used a diagram like frame (b) to show the relationship between the rate of inflation and real income with a price adjustment curve (or, more properly speaking, as a series of price adjustment curves, one drawn for each expected rate of inflation). You know that when the price level is constant, the intersection of the *IS* and *LM* curves determines the level of income and the rate of interest. You also know, however, that if the price level is not constant, or being more careful, if the price level is *expected* to change, then the real and nominal rates of interest will be different from each other, and the point of intersection of *IS* and *LM* does *not* determine anything. Rather, in that case, the vertical gap between the *IS* curve and *LM* curve will be the expected rate of inflation, and real income will be determined where that vertical gap is equal to the expected rate of inflation. The market rate of interest will be read off from the *LM* curve at that level of income. Given that level of income, the inflation rate will be read off from the relevant price adjustment curve.

You may by now be thinking that this is all very well except that there are no curves in Figure 22.6—only points! Can we, however, *interpret* the points in Figure 22.6 using the *IS, LM,* and *PA* curves of neoclassical theory? At first look, it does not appear to be very promising. Certainly there are no obvious curves passing through these points. Let us dig a little more deeply though and see how well we can do.

Figure 22.7 provides one possible account of these nine years, based on the neoclassical synthesis. This figure is arranged in chronological order starting with 1929 in frame (a) and ending in 1937 in frame (d). Frame (a) also shows the move to the trough of the depression, and frame (d) shows the recovery from the trough. The turning point years 1932 and 1933 are examined in greater detail in frames (b) and (c).

Take your time working through these figures with the accompanying text and what looks at first glance as a mess will become intelligible to you.

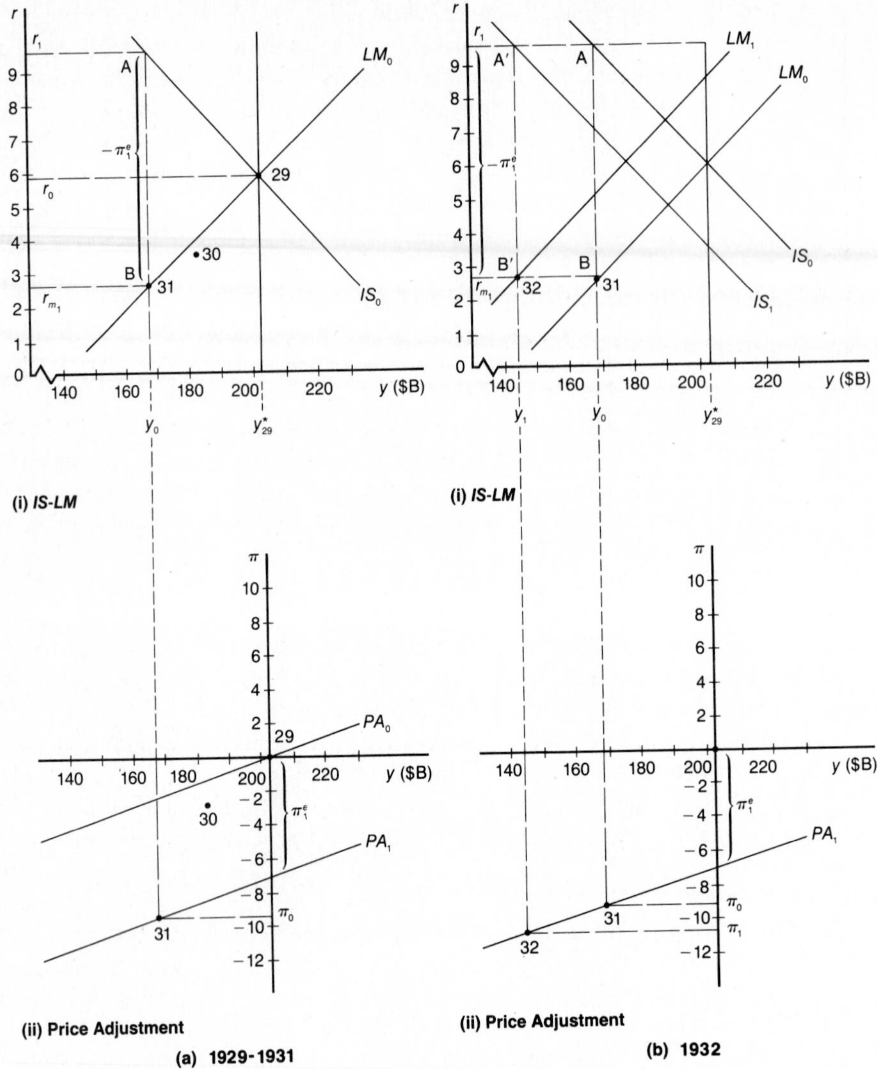

Figure 22.7
The Great Depression: An Interpretation Based on the Neoclassical Model

Frame (a) depicts the economy in 1929 at the intersection of LM_0 and IS_0 curves and on the price adjustment curve PA_0. The onset of the Great Depression was associated with two things—a drop in inflation expectations, shifting the *PA* curve to PA_1, and a drop in the money supply, which was matched by a drop in the price level so that real money balances remained constant. The 1931 equilibrium appears in frame (a). Frame (b) shows the move from 1931 to 1932. The *IS* and *LM* curves shift to the left, but the *PA* curve does not move. Income and inflation fall, but interest rates stay constant. Frame (c) shows the move to 1933. The *IS* curve shifts even further to the left; the *LM* curve moves slightly to the right; and the *PA* curve rises, reflecting a rise in inflation expectations. Frame (d) shows the recovery. Inflation expectations rise still further, the *IS* curve starts to move gently to the right, and the *LM* curve moves strongly to the right as the money supply begins to grow much faster than prices are rising.
SOURCE: Table 22.1.

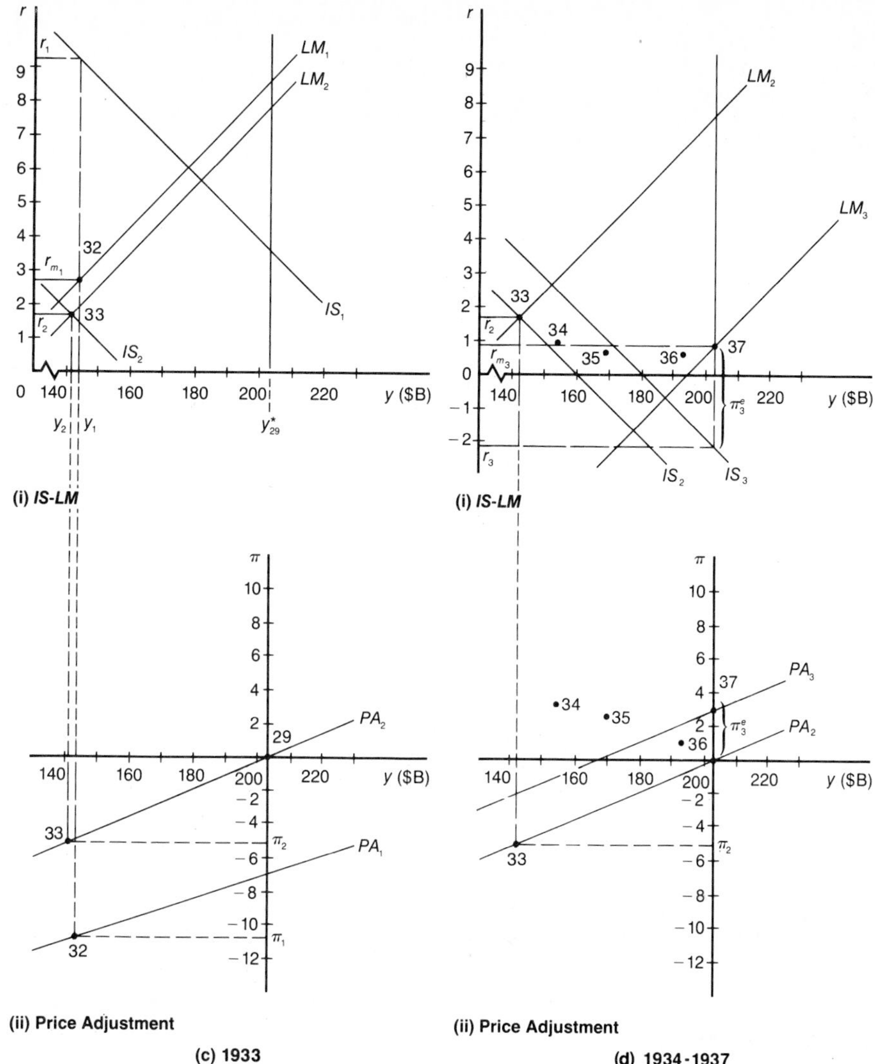

Focus first on frame (a) and within frame (a) on the curves labelled with the subscript zero. The curve LM_0 cuts the curve IS_0 at r_0 and y^*. Also PA_0 passes through a zero rate of inflation. The economy may be characterized in 1929 as being on these three curves. Real income of $203.6 billion is being treated as y^*, the interest rate r_0 is equal to 5.9 percent, and the inflation rate is zero.

From this starting point a process is set up which we look at again in 1931 (1930 is like a temporary resting point and has all the same characteristics as 1931). This process is one in which two things happen, only one of which is directly visible in the diagram. First—visible in the diagram—inflation expectations fall. By 1931 they have become negative and are shown as being minus 7 percent per annum [vertical axis of frame (a), part ii]. Thus, the price adjustment curve has shifted downwards from the curve PA_0 to PA_1. At the same time, not visible in the diagram but vital to make the explanation work, the money supply has been reduced by a percentage amount approximately equal to the percentage fall in prices. This means that the quantity of real money balances has not changed. (Actually real money balances increased by 1.3 billion dollars, but this is only 2 percent of the money supply, and I am going to treat it as zero.)

You already know that if the real money supply does not change, then the *LM* curve does not shift. That is why I have described the second thing that is happening to the economy as something that does not show up in the pictures. It does not show up because two offsetting forces—falling prices and a falling money supply—are keeping the quantity of real money constant and, therefore, are keeping the *LM* curve in its initial position. Thus, by 1931 the *IS* and *LM* curves are shown as having remained in their initial positions, but the price adjustment curve is shown as having dropped by seven percentage points.

What does this do to the equilibrium in 1931? (Answering this question is like reversing the exercise that you conducted above when analyzing the effects of a *rise* in the expected rate of inflation.) To find the equilibrium we need to find a vertical gap between the *IS* and *LM* curves that is equal to minus 7 percent—the expected rate of inflation. Such a gap is found at the income level \$169.3 billion. There you will notice that the vertical distance AB measures 7 percent and is the difference between the real rate of interest, 9.6 percent, and the market rate of interest, 2.6 percent. The real rate is *above* the market rate, so that the gap is *minus* 7 percent. At income level \$169.3 billion, we can read off from the price adjustment curve PA_1 the actual rate of inflation in 1931 as minus 9.3 percent. (Verify that the actual values of these variables marked on the axes agree with the figures in Table 22.1.)

Thus, the opening phase of the Great Depression is seen as being the consequence of a fall in inflation expectations combined with a fall in the money supply that matches the fall in the actual price level. The real rate of interest rises, and the economy slides up its *IS* curve, with investment falling. Market interest rates fall, but they do not fall by as much as inflationary expectations fell because the real rate of interest has risen.

Now turn to 1932. Frame (b) in Figure 22.7 illustrates the move from 1931 to 1932. The 1931 equilibrium is reproduced in frame (b), and you should begin by identifying that equilibrium and verifying that it agrees with the equilibrium that we have just determined in frame (a). The move from 1931 to 1932 involves a slight drop in the rate of inflation (bigger negative inflation), a substantial further drop in real income, and virtually no change in the market rate of interest. How did this happen? The possibility shown here is that the *LM* curve shifted from LM_0 to LM_1 and the *IS* curve shifted from IS_0 to IS_1 with inflation expectations held constant. The vertical gap between the new *IS* and *LM* curves (A′B′) measures the same minus 7 percent expected inflation rate as the vertical gap between the initial *IS* and *LM* curves (AB). The income level associated with the new *IS-LM* equilibrium is \$144.2 billion. The inflation rate falls slightly to minus 10.8 percent as the economy slides further down the curve PA_1.

What produced the shifts in the *IS* and *LM* curves? The *LM* curve shifted as a result of a drop in the quantity of real money balances—that is, the nominal money stock fell by a bigger percentage than did the price level. The *IS* curve probably shifted to the left as a result of increased uncertainty making firms more cautious about their capital replacement and expansion plans. Notice that this contrasts with what was happening between 1929 and 1931. In that phase the real rate of interest was seen as being too high. Firms had not been hit by a loss of confidence in that first phase. Rather they were rationally responding to a very high real rate of interest carrying with it the implication of a high rental rate on capital. By 1932, however, over and above the effects of high real rates of interest, firms were scaling down their investment plans as a result of other factors such as the state of confidence and uncertainty concerning the future.

Next look at frame (c) in Figure 22.7. It reproduces the 1932 equilibrium, and again you should verify that it agrees with the equilibrium for 1932 that you have just studied in frame (b). Two key things happened between 1932 and 1933. First, inflation expectations clearly increased. There is no other way that we could account for the jump in the rate of inflation from minus 10.8 percent up to minus 5.3 percent. Second, investor confidence collapsed even more than in 1932, shifting the *IS* curve even further to the left. The curve labelled IS_2 reflects this further shift in the *IS* curve, and the price adjustment curve, PA_2, reflects the rise in inflation expectations. I have drawn that curve to coincide approximately with PA_0 (the original price adjustment curve), implying zero inflation expectations by 1933.

There was also a minor adjustment in the *LM* curve. Although this is only a minor shift, it involves some mystery, for we know (see Table 22.1) that the real money stock fell by almost $2 billion between 1932 and 1933. On its own this should have shifted the *LM* curve to the *left*. The fact that the *LM* curve shifted to the *right* (as it must have done to pass through the appropriate point, given the slopes that I am assuming) shows that something must have happened to the demand for money. In fact, the demand for money must have fallen between 1932 and 1933 by slightly more than the supply of real money fell. Making these assumptions you can now read off the new equilibrium for 1933. With zero inflation expectations, it is the intersection point of the *IS* and *LM* curves (IS_2 and LM_2) that determines the 1933 equilibrium, with the real and money interest rates equal to each other at 1.7 percent. Real income is now at its lowest level ($141.5 billion), and the inflation rate is minus 5.3 percent.

The recovery phase is illustrated in frame (d) of Figure 22.7. The starting point is to verify that you can find in frame (d) the equilibrium for 1933. The recovery process was one in which three things happened. First, inflation expectations began to rise; second, the money supply began to grow at a faster rate than prices were rising, so that the *LM* curve began to move to the right; and third, investor confidence began to recover, so that the *IS* curve started moving back to the right.

The intermediate steps in the recovery process are not shown, but the state of the economy in 1937 is shown. The price adjustment curve in 1937 is shown as that labelled PA_3 with an expected rate of inflation of 3 percent. The market rate of interest is read off from the *LM* curve; and the *IS* curve must be located such that the real rate of interest, read off from the *IS* curve, is three percentage points below the market rate of interest. Since the market rate of interest is only 0.9 percent in 1937, the real rate of interest must be minus 2.1 percent. Thus, the *IS* curve by 1937 is shown as passing through the point at which the real rate of interest is minus 2.1 percent and real income is $203.2 billion.

A key feature of the neoclassical explanation of the Great Depression, as presented above, has involved changes in inflation expectations. There is no way in which the neoclassical theory could have accounted for the facts of these nine years without such changes. The particular changes that I have assumed could be questioned, and alternative numbers that might be equally plausible could be inferred from the data. What is quite impossible, however, is the advancing of an explanation for the Great Depression and its recovery based on the neoclassical synthesis and based further on the proposition that inflation expectations remained constant. When we looked at the explanation for the Great Depression offered by the Keynesian cross model, we came to the conclusion that although it was accurate in predicting the course of events, its explanation was too shallow to be satisfying. It relied on unexplained exogenous changes in investment expenditure.

The neoclassical synthesis that we have just been through does better than that. It explains where many of the investment changes come from (although not all of them). It also fills out the account by explaining what happened not only to real income and consumption but also to interest rates and inflation as well. Like the Keynesian cross model, however, it has an unsatisfactory shallowness. A key variable that seems to trigger and dominate the explanation—movements in the expected rate of inflation—is itself not explained. This variable is treated as being exogenous in the neoclassical framework. Notice that even if we adopted the so-called adaptive expectations hypothesis, we would still be in deep trouble in understanding the movements in inflation, particularly during 1933 and 1934 when the inflation rate increased some 15 percentage points and at a time when the economy was in severe depression and the actual rate of inflation was, according to the theory of the price adjustment curve, below the expected rate. Thus, although the neoclassical synthesis does a lot more for us than does the Keynesian cross model, it does not do enough.

The Labor Market In the above account of the Great Depression, the labor market has been ignored. This seems odd since one of the central reasons why people regard the Great Depression as so serious is because of its labor market consequences. Also, problems in the labor market lie at the heart of Keynesian macroeconomics. Therefore, let us round off our look at the Great Depression by examining more closely what was going on in the labor market.

Figure 22.8 shows the key features of the labor market in terms of a diagram similar to those that we used when studying unemployment in Chapter 11 and the Keynesian theory of aggregate supply in Chapter 15. The horizontal axis measures employment and the labor force (expressed as a percentage of the population to avoid continuous growth in those variables), and the vertical axis measures the real wage. The heavy points show the relationship between the labor force and the real wage, and the open points show the relationship between the quantity of labor employed and the real wage. Evidently the labor force is almost constant regardless of the level of the

Figure 22.8
The Labor Market in the Great Depression

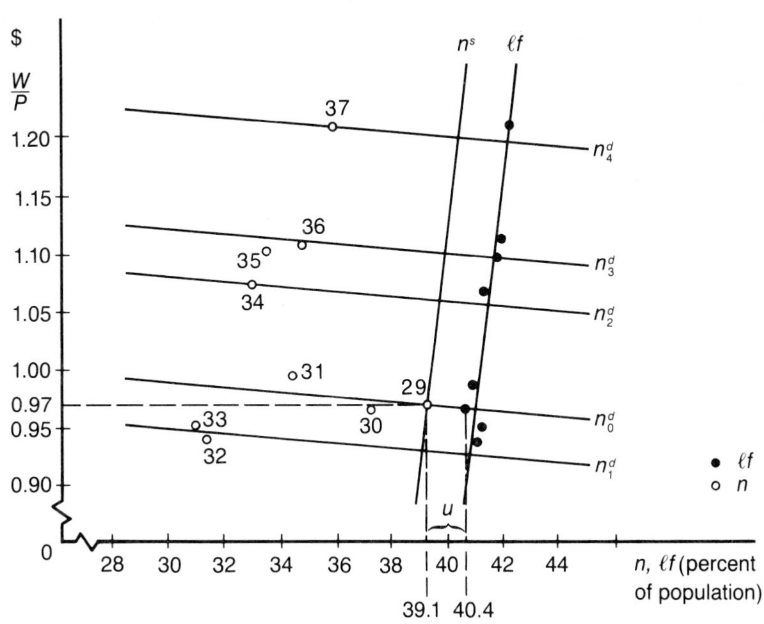

The heavy points trace out the labor force curve and the open points, the relationship between real wages and the level of employment. The year 1929 is shown as an equilibrium where the supply of labor equals the demand for labor. The demand for labor (marginal product) fell in 1932–1933, but thereafter it began to rise. The level of employment is read off from the demand curve, and unemployment is the gap between the amount demanded and the labor force at each real wage rate.
SOURCE: Table 22.1.

real wage. I have put in a line labelled ℓf, which you can think of as the labor force line introduced into the analysis of Chapter 11 (Figure 11.5). If we think of 1929 as a full-employment equilibrium, there will be a supply of labor and demand for labor curve passing through the 1929 employment point. I have shown such curves as those labelled n^s and n_0^d. In that year, the real wage was 97 cents and the level of employment was 39.1 percent of the population as determined by the point of intersection of the demand and supply curves. Unemployment was the amount indicated by *u* in the figure.

Now, according to the Keynesian model and neoclassical synthesis, the level of employment is not necessarily determined at the point of intersection of the supply and demand curves. It is, however, always determined on the demand curve. If the real wage gets too high, then the quantity of labor employed will be the quantity demanded, and the quantity of labor supplied will be irrelevant except for determining the level of *un*employment.

There are various ways in which the points shown in Figure 22.8 can be made to fit the neoclassical labor market analysis. What perhaps makes the most sense is to suppose that the demand for labor curve at any given point in time is fairly flat. This would amount to assuming that the marginal product of labor does not vary very much as the quantity of labor employed varies but does change substantially over time. (Recall that the marginal product of labor is equal to the real wage when firms are maximizing their profits, so that the marginal product curve and the demand curve for labor are one and the same.) It does not seem unreasonable to imagine that the marginal product of labor is fairly constant over the range of variation of employment observed. Nor does it seem unreasonable to imagine that there would be factors shifting the marginal product curve (changing the productivity of labor).

The story concerning the Great Depression that these considerations tell is as follows: First, as the depression began from 1929 to 1931, the economy slid along a fairly flat marginal product of labor (demand for labor) curve such as the one labelled n_0^d. By the depths of the Great Depression (1932–1933), however, there had been two years of virtually zero capital accumulation, so that the capital stock would have become badly deficient. Since the productivity of labor has a great deal to do with the quality of the capital equipment that the labor uses in its work, it is likely that the marginal product of labor declined in that situation. Thus, the demand for labor curve shifted downwards—shown as the curve n_1^d. As the recovery began to get underway, in 1934, the output of capital goods increased dramatically (almost doubled between 1933 and 1934), and so labor productivity began to rise. According to the interpretation in Figure 22.8, it rose each and every year after 1933 and very strongly between 1933 and 1934 and again between 1936 and 1937. This is seen in the demand for labor curves, which are shown as increasing each year, starting in 1934.

The amount of unemployment in the economy can be read off as the horizontal distance between the labor force curve (ℓf) and the demand curve at the relevant real wage rates. Equivalently, the horizontal distances between the heavy spots and the open spots measure unemployment (as a percentage of the population rather than as a percentage of the labor force as usually measured).

Now that you have seen how the neoclassical synthesis copes with the facts of the Great Depression, let us turn our attention to some more recent episodes and see how the same theory deals with the facts of the 1960s and 1970s.

C. The Neoclassical Decade: 1958–1967

The decade that ran from 1958 to 1967 was a period in which the neoclassical model was held in high esteem by practically all economists. There was very little fundamental disagreement concerning the appropriate framework for macroeconomic analysis. It was also a decade in which the neoclassical model fitted the facts almost exactly.

Let us review that period and see just why it was one in which the neoclassical framework had so much appeal. Figure 22.9 summarizes the key facts about interest rates, inflation, and deviations of real income from its full-employment level. Frame (a) shows the facts in *IS-LM* space, and frame (b) shows the facts in price adjustment (*PA*) space. Ignoring, for the moment, the lines and shaded areas and looking only at the points plotted in each of those diagrams, it is evident that in both cases there is a tendency for each of the variables measured on the vertical axes (interest rates and inflation) to rise

Figure 22.9
The Neoclassical Model in a Neoclassical Decade: 1958–1967

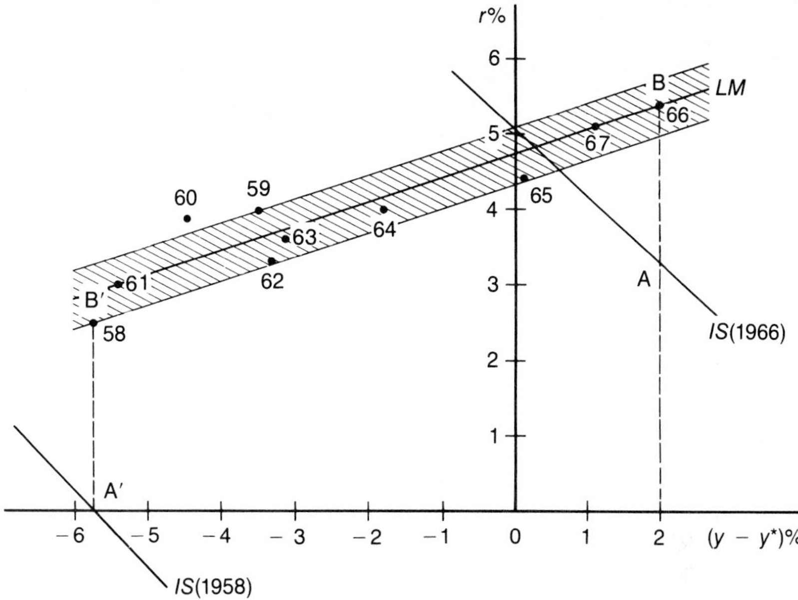

(a) *IS-LM*

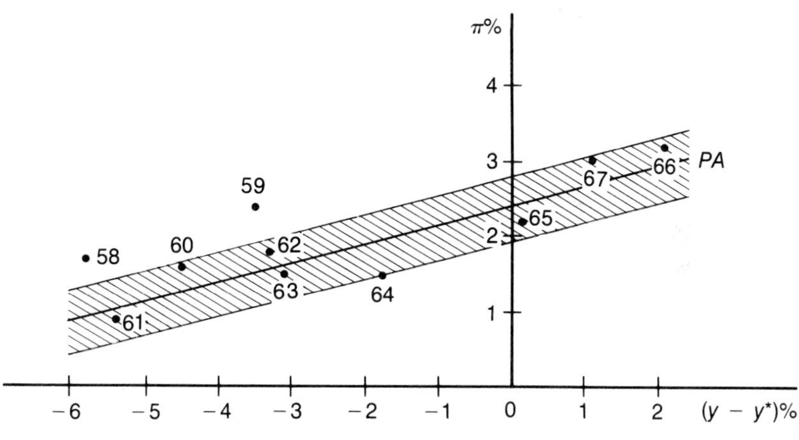

(b) Price Adjustment

The neoclassical decade is well-described by supposing that there was a given *LM* curve (real balances relative to the full-employment demand for real balances being constant) and a fixed price adjustment curve (inflation expectations being constant). Fluctuations in output, interest rates, and inflation were generated by swings in the *IS* curve.
SOURCE: $(y - y^*)\%$: *Economic Report of the President, 1978*, 84. Inflation and the interest rate: Appendix to Chapter 2.

as output rises relative to its full-employment level. In fact, the points in frame (b) can reasonably be regarded as lying on a price adjustment curve such as that shown in the figure and labelled *PA*. If we take a band running half a percentage point on either side of the line labelled *PA*, then we take in almost every observation in that decade. In other words, although the line labelled PA does not exactly describe the data, a band of 1 percent width centered on the line PA is a good description of the data. The line labelled PA may be described by the following equation:

$$\pi = 2.5 + 0.25(y - y^*)$$

This equation and frame (b) of Figure 22.9 indicate that there was a constant expected rate of inflation of 2.5 percent, and actual inflation fluctuated around the expected inflation rate by an amount that varied with the level of output relative to its full-employment level. A one percentage point movement in output would bring about a quarter of a percentage point in the rate of inflation.

The points in frame (b) seem to be clearly explained by the neoclassical theory of price adjustment. What is the neoclassical model's rationalization for the points in frame (a)? As a matter of fact, the points are quite well-described by imagining that they lie on a single LM curve such as the line labelled LM in frame (a). Again, although the points do not lie exactly on the line, if we draw in a band stretching half a percent above and half a percent below the LM curve, we take in all the points except one.

However, it is important to recall that the LM curve will shift each time the real money supply changes. Thus, when we describe the points in frame (a) as lying on a single LM curve, we must be reasonably confident that the real money supply was constant through this period. As a matter of fact, over this period, the real money supply grew by about 1.5 percent per annum. This would have caused the LM curve as we have normally drawn it, to shift to the right.

The LM curve plotted in frame (a) of Figure 22.9 is not, however, quite the same as the LM curve that you have met before. The LM curve that we have been using in our analysis in previous chapters, and indeed the one that we examined in the previous section of this chapter when looking at the Great Depression, is a curve that relates the rate of interest on the vertical axis to the level of real income on the horizontal axis. Frame (a) of Figure 22.9 plots the rate of interest against deviations of real income from its full-employment level. What will cause the LM curve to shift in this diagram, therefore, is a change in real money balances relative to the demand for money at full-employment real income. It turns out that the real money supply relative to the amount of money demanded at full-employment real income was virtually constant through this period, so we are safe in supposing that the LM curve did not shift, or at least if it did, not by much.

The picture of the neoclassical decade is completed with the IS curve. The neoclassical story would be that the actual values of the rate of interest, rate of inflation, and level of real income were determined by the way in which the IS curve shifted and interacted with the LM curve shown in frame (a) of Figure 22.9.

To see how this works out, we need first to recall that the equilibrium is determined not where the IS and LM curves intersect, but at an output level such that the vertical gap between the IS curve and LM curve equals the expected rate of inflation. We have already determined that the expected rate of inflation throughout this period was roughly constant at 2.5 percent. Thus, real income would be determined at a point where the *IS* curve was 2.5 percent below the *LM* curve. The year 1966, in which real income was at its highest relative to trend, could thus be described by the fixed *LM* curve, the fixed *PA* curve, and the *IS* curve labelled *IS* (1966) in frame (a).

The vertical gap marked AB between the *IS* and *LM* curves in 1966 is equal to the expected rate of inflation. This is also read off from the vertical axis of frame (b) as the point at which the *PA* curve cuts that axis at a zero level of deviations of real income from full employment. The year 1958, when real income was below its full-employment level by the largest amount, can be described by the fixed *LM* and *PA* curves and the *IS* curve labelled *IS* (1958) in frame (a). The distance A′B′ is equal to the distance AB and again equal to the assumed constant expected rate of inflation.

The intermediate points occurring in the other eight years would be determined by *IS* curves lying at intermediate positions between the two extreme curves shown in the figure. Thus, swings in the *IS* curve around a fixed *LM* curve would generate movement in real income and in the rate of interest, with the movements in real income relative to trend generating movements in the actual rate of inflation relative to the expected rate of inflation.

In contrast to the years of the Great Depression that needed the simultaneous analysis of many shocks, we see that this period that I have called the *neoclassical decade* is one that can be accounted for with a single type of shock—a shifting *IS* curve. The sources of the shifts in the *IS* curve itself can be identified as arising from changes in government expenditure, taxes, investment expenditure, consumer durable expenditure, and inventories, although a detailed evaluation of the precise reasons for these changes would take us beyond the scope of this book.

D. The 1970s

The period since 1968 stands in sharp contrast to the neoclassical decade that preceded it. This period—the 1970s—saw the evolution of macroeconomic events that are not well explained by the neoclassical model. These facts, in a diagram comparable to that just used, are set out in Figure 22.10. Notice that the points have been joined with lines and arrows indicating the time sequence of the unfolding of this history. In both the *IS-LM* space and *PA* space, these time sequences of relationships amongst the variables appear as counterclockwise spirals. However, the spirals move in a northwesterly direction—that is, interest rates get higher and output deviates more below trend [frame (a)], and inflation gets higher [frame (b)].

With some effort it is possible to tell a story that makes the *IS* and *LM* curves pass through the appropriate points in frame (a). That effort is not, however, sufficiently illuminating for it to be one that we shall indulge in here. It is also possible with some effort to make price adjustment curves pass through the appropriate points in frame (b). It will be clear, however, that those price adjustment curves have to do a fairly considerable amount of jumping around to fit the points shown in frame (b). The major jump between

Figure 22.10
The 1970s

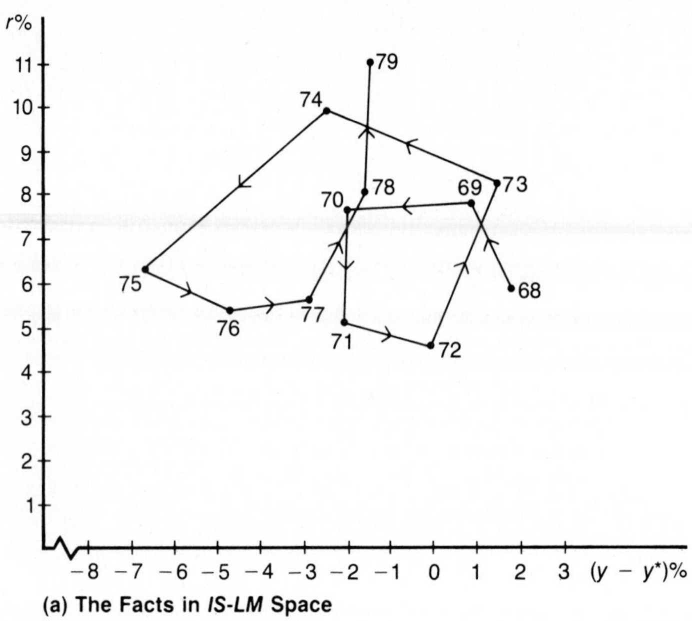

(a) The Facts in *IS-LM* Space

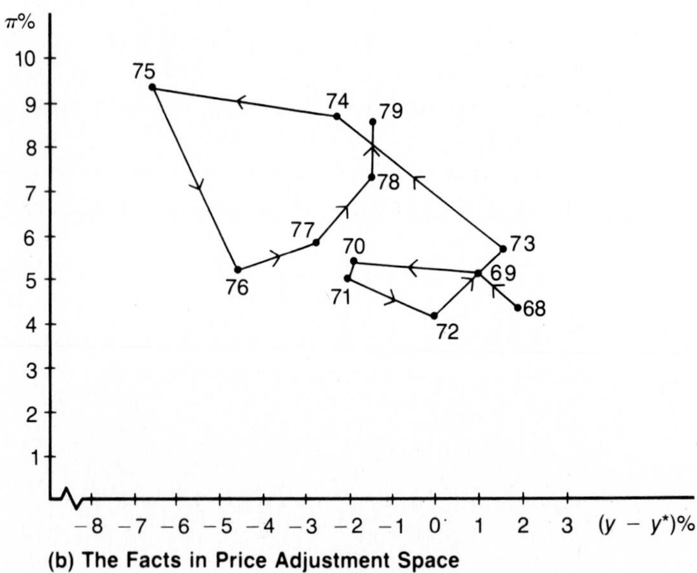

(b) The Facts in Price Adjustment Space

Both the relationships between interest rates and real income and between inflation and real income followed a counterclockwise spiral pattern moving to the northwest (rising inflation and interest rates and falling real income relative to trend). Most of the movements in the inflation rate have to be treated as arising from changes in inflationary expectations. No simple *IS*, *LM*, *PA* story fits the facts of the 1970s.

SOURCE: $(y - y^*)\%$: *Economic Report of the President, 1978*, 84. Inflation and the interest rate: Appendix to Chapter 2.

1973 and 1974 is reasonably well accounted for by the world oil price shock that occurred in the final part of 1973.

The continued rise in inflation and drop in output that occurred in 1975 is harder, however, to explain by that route. Also, the strong rise in inflation in 1978 at a time when the economy was still fairly severely depressed defies simple explanation in this neoclassical framework. After all, in 1977, according to the neoclassical theory, the actual rate of inflation was substantially below the expected rate. Why, therefore, did the expected inflation rate rise, as indeed it must have done between 1977 and 1978 to take the actual inflation rate up by so much? This question gains even greater strength as we move forward into 1979 and 1980. It is the facts shown in frame (b) of Figure 22.10 that constitute the biggest single devastation of the neoclassical theory.

The Great Depression and the 1970s—A Similarity?

The 1930s and the 1970s, in most respects, look very different from each other. The 1930s was a period of falling prices and depression, whereas the 1970s was a period of rising inflation and stagnation—which came to be called "stagflation." Viewed from the perspective of neoclassical macroeconomic theory, there is, however, an interesting similarity between the two periods. It is, in order to account for the facts as they occurred, that the neoclassical theory has to presume that there were exogenous changes in inflationary expectations. During the Great Depression years, those exogenous changes were in a downward direction. The expected rate of inflation fell, and inflation actually fell but by more than people had anticipated it would. During the 1970s, expectations of inflation rose, but inflation did not actually rise as quickly as had been expected. In both cases, prices inflated less quickly than they were expected to. In both cases, the only way in which we can account for the movements in the inflation rate and co-movements between inflation and output is to suppose that most of the action was coming from exogenous (i.e., unexplained) changes in inflation expectations.

E. Strengths and Weaknesses of the Neoclassical Model

The main strength of the neoclassical model is that it provides us with an explanation for the procyclical co-movements of prices and output at times when inflation expectations are relatively constant. It also provides us with a framework within which we can think about and can make some (although limited) sense of the Great Depression.

The major weakness of the neoclassical model lies in the fact that much of our macroeconomic history seems to have been dominated by changes in inflation expectations—changes that are not themselves explicable in terms of the neoclassical framework.

In brief, the neoclassical framework provides us with a useful account of the facts when inflation expectations are fixed. It also provides us with a framework within which we can analyze the effects of changes in inflation expectations. It does not, however, provide us with a way of determining those inflation expectations or understanding any interactions that there might be between the actual evolution of the economy and people's expectations of inflation.

There is a deeper inadequacy in the model that arises from the appearance of irrationality on the part of the suppliers of labor. After all, the only way in which this model can get away from the full-employment equilibrium of the basic model is as a result of supposing that workers, for some reason, are willing to be "off" their supply of labor curves. Mutually gainful trades of labor between firms and households are simply assumed not to happen. This seeming irrationality is of concern because it stands in conflict with the assumptions that we make concerning all other aspects of human behavior. As regards the demand for money, consumption demand, investment demand, and the demand for labor, people are treated as being rational pursuers of maximum profits and maximum utility. Conversely, in this one, and only one area—the supply of labor—people are treated as having different objectives. This seeming schizophrenia makes the neoclassical theory untidy in terms of its internal logic. That need not matter terribly if the theory works. However, the fact that the theory does not work and that it has this internal untidiness leads us to a good deal of dissatisfaction with it.

There is another related irrationality in the neoclassical framework concerning inflation expectations themselves. As we have seen, it is necessary to regard these expectations as exogenous, perhaps evolving slowly in response to actual inflationary experience. Evidently, this makes the neoclassical theory a poor predictor of inflation, for one of the key determinants of inflation is the expected rate of inflation that itself is not explained by the theory! Not only is the theory a weak predictor of inflation, however. It also incorporates a presumption of irrational behavior on the part of individuals. People see inflation around them, have some knowledge and understanding of what causes it, and yet for some reason, they do not use that information to figure out what to expect the inflation rate to be in the current period or immediate future. Rather, they behave like "clockwork mice." You wind them up, and they run their course, repeatedly bumping into the wall and never learning from their experiences. These irrationalities, as well as poor predictive power, are deep shortcomings of the neoclassical model.

Summary

A. Predictions of the Neoclassical Model

The neoclassical model predicts that a shock that shifts the *IS* curve (expansionary fiscal policy or a rise in investment spending) will raise interest rates, inflation, and output. After the impact, interest rates will continue to rise, but inflation and output will drift downwards toward their previous values. A rise in the growth rate of the money supply will have no impact effects. It will set up a process, however, of initially falling interest rates, rising inflation, and rising output. Eventually interest rates will also rise to reflect fully the higher inflation. The impact effect of a negative supply shock will be to raise inflation. The adjustment process will involve rising interest rates, falling inflation, and falling output. The impact effect of a rise in the expected rate of inflation will be to raise inflation, raise output, raise the nominal rate of interest, but cut the real rate of interest. The adjustment process will involve falling inflation and output and rising real and nominal rates of interest. If the rise in inflation expectations was temporary, the economy would eventually return to its initial equilibrium, but inflation and output would undershoot their steady-state values and the real rate of interest would overshoot in the process.

B. A Neoclassical Interpretation of the Great Depression

The onset of the Great Depression is accounted for by the neoclassical model as the result of two simultaneous shocks—a drop in inflation expectations and a cut in the growth rate of the money supply. No shifts in the *IS* or *LM* curves necessarily occurred in the first two years. At the depth of the recession, the *IS* curve shifted to the left as confidence declined, and the *LM* curve shifted to the left as the real money supply was cut by even tighter monetary policies. At the depth of the depression there was a sharp rise in inflation expectations. The recovery was associated with a restoration of investor confidence, shifting the *IS* curve to the right, and a strong increase in the money supply, raising real money balances and shifting the *LM* curve to the right.

C. The Neoclassical Decade: 1958–1967

The neoclassical decade was a period in which inflation expectations appear to have been roughly constant at 2.5 percent per annum, so that the economy was on a single *PA* curve. Most of the movements in real income, interest rates, and the actual rate of inflation can be well accounted for by the notion of an *IS* curve that swung to and fro, generating the cycle in real activity with procyclical co-movements in interest rates and inflation.

D. The 1970s

The major movements in the economy in the 1970s can only be made sense of by supposing that there were sizable shifts (mainly upward) in inflation expectations. No simple neoclassical account for the facts of the 1970s is possible.

E. Strengths and Weaknesses of the Neoclassical Model

The main strengths of the neoclassical model are: (1) its capacity to account for the facts when inflation expectations are constant, and (2) its capacity to provide a framework for analyzing the consequences of changes in inflation expectations.

The main weaknesses of the model are its failure to explain why inflation expectations change and the seeming irrationality in labor supply behavior and in the exogeneity of inflation expectations.

Review Questions

1. Using an analysis and diagrams similar to those set out in Figures 22.1, 22.2, and 22.3, analyze the effects of the following shocks. Be careful to distinguish between impact effects, adjustment paths, and steady states.
   (a) A cut in real government purchases of goods and services.
   (b) A once-and-for-all rise in the money supply (not a continuing ongoing rate of growth of the money supply) of 10 percent.
   (c) A sudden drop in inflationary expectations.
2. Review the neoclassical explanation of the Great Depression given in this chapter. Can you think of other plausible explanations for the same events using the same neoclassical theory? In particular, is there any way in which you could rationalize the Great Depression years that does *not* involve a change in inflation expectations?
3. What is the explanation for the fluctuations in real national income and the procyclical co-movements of inflation and interest rates that occurred during the neoclassical decade provided by the neoclassical model?
4. Using the predictions of the neoclassical model concerning the impact effects and early adjustment paths set up by the four shocks analyzed in this chapter, try to figure out a combination of shocks capable of completely explaining the movements of interest rates, real income, and inflation during the 1970s. Is it always necessary to "fiddle" by letting exogenous changes in inflationary expectations adjust in order to validate the theory ex post?
5. What is wrong with letting inflationary expectations adjust in whatever way is necessary to make the neoclassical theory fit the facts?

23

Introduction to the Rational Expectations Theories of Income, Employment, and the Price Level

You have now reviewed the basic and Keynesian models and have discovered that although there is much in U.S. economic history that these models can explain, there are also important facts of which neither gives an entirely satisfactory account. These facts are the co-movements between real economic activity (output, employment, and unemployment) and inflation. The basic model predicts that movements in prices (and in inflation) will be independent of movements in real variables. That model *does* explain the main trends in inflation, but it is incapable of accounting for the procyclical co-movements in prices and inflation that often occur. The Keynesian model, on the other hand, as extended in the form of the neoclassical synthesis, can, when inflation expectations are constant, account for the procyclical co-movements of prices. There are major episodes, however, for which it cannot account without supposing that there were exogenous changes in inflation expectations. One such episode is the Great Depression, and another is the strong burst of inflation that occurred in the 1970s at a time when unemployment was high and output was below trend.

This and the following six chapters are going to introduce you to some of the recent innovations in macroeconomic theory that seek to overcome these shortcomings of the earlier models.[1]

---

[1]Of the several excellent survey articles on the new theories of macroeconomics, the two that are most readable are those by William Poole, "Rational Expectations in the Macro Model," *Brookings Papers on Economic Activity*, 2 (1976), 463–505; and Robert E. Lucas, Jr., "Methods and Problems in Business Cycle Theory," *Journal of Money, Credit and Banking*, 12, no. 4, pt. 2 (November 1980), 696–715. Another excellent, even entertaining, piece is Rodney Maddock and Michael Carter, "A Child's Guide to Rational Expectations," *Journal of Economic Literature*, 20, no. 1 (March 1982), 39–51. Two other first-rate surveys are Herschel I. Grossman, "Rational Expectations, Business Cycles, and Government Behavior," in *Rational Expectations and Economic Policy*, ed. Stanley Fischer (Chicago: University of Chicago Press, 1980); and Bennett T. McCallum, "Rational Expectations and Macroeconomic Stabilization Policy," *Journal of Money, Credit and Banking*, 12, no. 4, pt. 2 (November 1980), 716–46. Two very fine critical appraisals of the new theories are Robert J. Gordon, "Recent Developments in the Theory of Inflation and Unemployment," *Journal of*

You just have one task in this chapter, which is to:

Know the main components of the rational expectations theories of income, employment, and the price level.

Main Components

The innovations in macroeconomic analysis begun by Keynes were a response to the need for a theory of how the economy operated when there was a substantial amount of excess capacity and unemployment. Keynes characterized the economy as operating on a horizontal section of the aggregate supply curve, so that output and employment were determined by the position of the aggregate demand curve alone. This made it necessary to be rather careful to develop an adequate theory of aggregate demand. This is precisely what Keynes and his followers did, and the theory embodied in the *IS-LM* analysis stands as a component part of the rational expectations theories of the determination of output, employment, and prices.

As we have seen, the major shortcoming of the Keynesian and neoclassical analyses is their inability to explain the facts about inflation and output. It is as if the Keynesian theory, being a careful theory of aggregate demand, has been too cavalier in its treatment of the aggregate supply side of the economy. Just as it became necessary to be very careful about the theory of demand when the economy was operating in a region of considerable excess capacity, so it becomes equally important to be careful about the theory of aggregate supply when the economy is operating at or in the neighborhood of its full-employment output point.

It is on the aggregate supply side that the new theories of macroeconomics make their major contribution. The starting point of the innovations in the theory of aggregate supply have, in effect, already been accepted by, and incorporated into, the body of analysis presented earlier as the neoclassical synthesis. The theoretical innovations of Milton Friedman and Edmund Phelps have already been briefly introduced.[2] In order for you to have a thorough understanding of the nature of their innovations, one of the major tasks in this part of the book is to examine the theory of aggregate supply implied by the analyses of these two scholars. Their central innovation was the analysis of the role of expectations in the labor market and its modification of the theory of aggregate supply of the basic model. They develop what we shall call the *expectations-augmented aggregate supply curve.*

Once expectations become a key part of any model, it is crucial to develop a theory of how expectations are formed and changed. The innovation

---

Monetary Economics, 2 (April 1976), 185–220; and James Tobin, "Are New Classical Models Plausible Enough to Guide Policy?" *Journal of Money, Credit and Banking*, 12, no. 4, pt. 2 (November 1980), 788–99.

You will notice that I have referred you to three articles from the same issue of the *Journal of Money, Credit and Banking*. That issue contains the proceedings of a conference on "Rational Expectations" and includes several other very good pieces.

[2]See Section C on the neoclassical theory of price adjustment in Chapter 21.

in this area—the rational expectations hypothesis—was first introduced by John Muth in 1961.[3] The implications of rational expectations for macroeconomics and for an understanding of economic fluctuations were not seen until the seminal contributions of Robert E. Lucas, Jr. in the early 1970s.[4] Lucas showed us how we could develop a theory that was capable of explaining both the procyclical co-movements in inflation and at the same time explain why, from time to time, inflation would surge ahead or fall independently of the state of excess demand. His theory is based on the idea that individuals supply and demand labor and supply and demand goods, acting upon expectations that are formed rationally and are based on all the information that is available to them.

This rational expectations approach, although still controversial, has a great deal of economic appeal because it assumes that people are indeed rational, do not waste information, and behave in the most efficient and economical manner that they can. It would be too costly for them to acquire full or perfect information and to renegotiate contracts every instant in the light of new information; hence, people commit themselves to actions based on incomplete information, and they sometimes make mistakes. It is the consequence of these mistakes that leads to the observed procyclical co-movements in prices.

Making sense of this and understanding the full implications of the previous paragraphs will be the subject of the next six chapters. As a preview of those chapters, the following "story" may be helpful. The notion of a story, by the way, is a useful one in this context. Just as a fairy story vividly illustrates particular phobias, fears, or moral attitudes, so it is possible to tell a story about the economy that emphasizes particular features of the world. The abstractions used in the story are intended to be useful in making predictions about the world.

A Story about the Economy

Our story about the economy begins with rational individuals. Households maximize their utility, and firms maximize their profits. This means that the lower the real wage, the more labor will be demanded; and the higher the real wage, the more labor will be supplied. It also means that for a given level of the variables that determine aggregate demand (the money supply, government spending, and taxes), the lower the price level, the more goods will be demanded. Individuals do not have full information. They have to do the best they can in the face of limited information. In particular, people have to form expectations about the general price level at which they will be able to buy consumer goods.

There are two variants of the story concerning the way in which people do business with each other: One called *new classical* and the other *new Keynesian.* In the new classical version of the story, individuals do business

---

[3]John F. Muth, "Rational Expectations and the Theory of Price Movements," *Econometrica*, 29, (July 1961), 315–35.

[4]Robert E. Lucas, Jr., "Some International Evidence on Output-Inflation Trade-offs," *The American Economic Review*, 63, (Sept. 1973), 326–34.

with each other in markets that are sufficiently efficient to achieve equilibrium quickly. It is as if there is an effective auctioneer finding the prices at which people can trade with each other, and in so doing, they exploit all the potential gains from trading activities. From a scientific point of view, building a theory on the notion that markets equilibrate quickly is not very different from primitive ideas about gravity. Without really knowing why, man observed that apples tended to fall to the ground rather than to fly around the orchard. Thus, a theoretical physics could be constructed to explain many observations by assuming the existence of gravity. It is much the same with market equilibrium.

In the new Keynesian version of the story, markets do not achieve equilibrium at each and every instant. They do, however, achieve equilibrium *on the average*. Labor is traded not on a market that behaves like an auction but on contracts. A money wage is fixed to achieve an expected equilibrium between supply and demand, and in exchange for a fixed money wage, households agree to supply whatever labor firms demand over the duration of the contract.

Standing alongside the incompletely informed, rational, utility- and profit-maximizing individuals and firms, trading with each other in markets that are in equilibrium (either always or on the average), there is a government (and central bank) that undertakes a certain volume of spending, raises a certain volume of taxes, and creates a certain quantity of money. If the level of aggregate demand so generated is such that it determines a price level that is the same as the expected price level, then the economy settles down at a full-employment equilibrium. If aggregate demand exceeds that quantity, the economy moves to a higher level of prices, employment, and output. If aggregate demand is less than that quantity, the economy moves to a lower level of output, employment, and prices. These movements occur as the rational profit-maximizing and utility-maximizing responses of individuals. Everybody does the best they can for themselves, and positions of employment above or below the full-employment level have many of the characteristics of an equilibrium at full employment. They are all positions at which, given the state of information, no one finds it worthwhile to make any adjustment in their output or employment. The next six chapters will fill out the details of this story.

Throughout this and the next part of the book, both of which deal with the predictions and policy implications of rational expectations models, the analysis will be conducted for an economy whose trend inflation rate is zero. This is a convenient simplification that makes it possible to conduct all the analysis in diagrammatic terms. It is not a limitation of the analysis. The theories that are to be reviewed are equally applicable at *any* trend rate of inflation. You may, therefore, conveniently regard the analysis presented as representing deviations from the trend rate of inflation. Thus, when we talk about a rise in the price level or a fall in the price level, you may—provided you are careful to remember what is going on—interpret this as a temporary rise in the inflation rate above its trend or a temporary fall in inflation below its trend. In making this interpretation you need to be constantly on guard to maintain the sharp analytical distinction introduced earlier concerning the difference between inflation and a once-and-for-all change in prices.

The new models of macroeconomics make predictions about trend inflation that are in most respects identical to those of the basic model with which you are already familiar.

Summary

The rational expectations theories of income, employment, and the price level seek to explain the procyclical co-movements of prices and, at the same time, to account for the important independent movements that occasionally occur between output and prices. They achieve this by radically modifying the neoclassical theory of aggregate supply, although accepting the neoclassical theory of aggregate demand. The new theory of aggregate supply generalizes that of the basic model by introducing the expectations-augmented aggregate supply curve. These theories also incorporate the notion of rational expectations which assumes that people form their expectations on the basis of all the information available to them. That is, they assume that people are rational, do not waste information, and behave in the most efficient and economical manner that they can.

24

Information, Expectations, and the New Classical Theory of Aggregate Supply

This chapter develops what I shall call the *new classical* theory of aggregate supply[1] and the expectations-augmented aggregate supply curve. There are a variety of alternative particular "stories" that lead to the same conclusions as those reached in this chapter. The "story" used here is, in my view, the simplest one. (It will not be until Chapters 28 and 29, however, that the full story will emerge.) This chapter deals with the first building block of the new theories. Subsequent chapters will show how this theory of aggregate supply, when combined with the rational expectations hypothesis and the *IS-LM* model of aggregate demand, is capable of providing an explanation of the facts about output and prices. In order to get you moving toward that objective, this chapter has four tasks, which are to:

(a) Understand how incomplete information affects the supply of and demand for labor.
(b) Understand how the money wage and level of employment (and unemployment) are affected by wrong expectations.
(c) Know the definition of the expectations-augmented aggregate supply curve.
(d) Know how to derive the expectations-augmented aggregate supply curve.

---

[1]The theory of aggregate supply presented in this chapter had its origins in Milton Friedman, "The Role of Monetary Policy," *The American Economic Review*, 58 (March 1968), 1–17. It is also similar to that developed by Robert E. Lucas, Jr. in "Some International Evidence on Output-Inflation Tradeoffs," *The American Economic Review*, 63, no. 3 (1973), 326–34.

A. Incomplete Information and the Labor Market

In the basic model of the labor market, the demand for labor, the supply of labor, and the market equilibrating process paid no attention to any special characteristics of labor. We could have been talking about stocks and shares, wheat, futures contracts in gold, or just about any competitive market for any commodity at all. There are, however, some features of labor that make it unlike many other commodities. One important feature concerns the scale of the costs that individuals (both suppliers and demanders of labor) have to incur in order to find someone with whom to do business. From the household side, there is a heavy search cost—the cost of finding a job that is attractive enough, well paid enough, and satisfactory in other dimensions. From the point of view of the firm demanding labor, there are recruiting costs—the costs of finding potential employees with the required skills and personal attributes.

The fact that there are heavy search and recruiting costs in the labor market implies that labor will typically be traded in a way that is very different from the way in which stocks and commodities are traded. Instead of being traded on a market that works like a continuous auction, labor generally is traded in markets dominated by medium-term contracts. Individuals enter into arrangements with each other for a specified period of time, often for a year or more ahead.

The contracts that govern labor-trading arrangements could, in principle, be very complex documents that incorporate hundreds (perhaps thousands) of contingency clauses specifying the wages and other employment conditions contingent on a variety of potential future events. The costs of negotiating, writing, monitoring, and enforcing such contracts would, however, be very high. To avoid these costs, most labor market contracts are relatively simple. They specify a *money wage* (and other nonwage terms) that will be paid for a certain type of labor over a specified future period. If the contract is to run for more than a year, it will also typically specify an adjustment in the money wage, either in money terms or as some pre-agreed fraction of the change in the cost of living as measured by the Consumer Price Index.

The typical labor market contract is one in which the worker and the employer agree to trade labor services for a certain *money wage*, for a certain period of time into the future, but they make no commitments concerning the quantity of employment. The employer will typically *not* undertake to guarantee employment at the agreed wage and will be free to vary the number of workers hired. Individual workers will also be free to quit their jobs if they can find better ones with other firms.

How will firms decide how much labor to hire, and how will households decide how much labor to supply? Recall that a firm will hire labor up to the point at which the marginal product of that labor equals the real wage paid. In order to calculate the real wage, the firm simply has to divide the money wage by the *price of the firm's own output*. The firm will then hire labor up to the point at which its marginal product equals the firm-specific real wage. On the other side of the labor market, the amount of labor that a household will want to supply at any particular point in time will depend *not* on the real wage as calculated by the firm for the purpose of figuring out how much labor to demand but rather on the real basket of goods and services that the household can consume with its wage. It will depend on the money wage divided by a general index of prices such as the Consumer Price Index. Thus, there is an asymmetry in the labor market concerning the price level that is relevant for calculating the real wage on the two sides of the market. As far as the firm is concerned, what matters is the ratio of the money wage to the price of the output produced by that firm. What matters on the supply side is the ratio of the money wage to an index of prices of all the goods and services from which households will choose their consumption. This asymmetry is the basis of the new theories of aggregate supply.

Let us consider the information that firms and households will need in order to make decisions about how much labor to demand and supply. Firms will need to know the money wage rate and the price of their own output. Households will need to know the money wage rate and the prices of all the goods and services from which they will choose their consumption bundle. A moment's reflection will lead you to a very important conclusion concerning these variables. Nobody has any difficulty in knowing the money wage rate (this will be specified when workers and firms are contemplating doing business together). Further, there will be very little problem in figuring out the price of the output of the firm. For some multiproduct firms, this might not be a totally straightforward matter, but it may be presumed that the firm's own accounting procedures are capable of generating accurate up-to-date information on the prices of the firm's output and that that information is readily available both to the firm and its workers.

However, in contrast to these two bits of information, knowledge of the prices of all the goods and services from which individuals will choose their consumption bundle will be very imperfect and incomplete. It is true that Consumer Price Indexes and the like are calculated and published. It is also a fact, however, that they are published with a time lag; that is, they refer to the past, not to the present or the immediate future. Furthermore, they refer to a basket of goods that the mythical average household consumes and that no particular household consumes. From the perspective of any one individual household, what matters is the average level of prices of all the goods and services from which the final consumption bundle will be chosen. To actually know these prices would involve a process of searching and observing prices, a process that is so expensive that by the time the individual had amassed all the relevant information, there would be no time left either for work or consumption!

The implication of all this is that households cannot know everything that they would need to know if they were to make their labor supply decisions on the basis of the ratio of the money wage to the general level of prices. Put more directly, the notion that the supply of labor depends on the real wage cannot be given operational content since no one can know the relevant real wage at the time that a labor supply decision is being made. Thus, in the absence of information about the general level of prices, it becomes necessary for households to make their supply decision on the basis of some other criterion. The most natural such criterion is the expected real wage. Since there is no difficulty about knowing the money wage component of the real wage, the only problem remaining is to figure out an expectation of the level of prices.

We can summarize the discussion so far in the following way: Firms will decide how much labor to demand by figuring out the real wage on the basis of two known bits of information—the money wage and the price of the firm's own output. Households will decide how much labor to supply by calculating the expected real wage based on the known money wage rate and their expectation of the average level of prices prevailing in the markets for all the goods and services from which they will choose their consumption bundle. It is worth emphasizing that the price expectation that households will have to form in order to make a labor supply decision refers not to past prices but to current and future prices. Any labor supply decision made at a given moment in time, even if it was made on the basis of complete information about prices prevailing at that moment, would still have to be made on the basis of expectations of prices that will prevail at some future point in time when the proceeds from the work are eventually spent.

You may be thinking that it ought to be possible for people to figure out what the general level of prices is simply from knowing the prices in the sector of the economy in which they work, and perhaps knowing the prices of a few goods and services that they are consuming on a regular, almost daily basis. A moment's reflection will convince you, however, that although there is *some* information to be had from such sources, it is not sufficient. The economy is constantly undergoing change that results in constantly changing relative prices. Some relative price changes are, of course, predictable, but many, perhaps most, are not. They are in the nature of random events that arise from a multitude of forces. That being so, it will be very hard for people to figure out what is happening to the overall general level of prices simply from knowing the prices of one or two things. Therefore, in what we shall do in the rest of this chapter, we shall make the extreme (and obviously slightly wrong) assumption that people get no help at all in figuring out the general level of prices from knowing the price of the output in their own sector of the economy. This extreme assumption could be modified, but the result of doing so would be to make our analysis a good deal more complicated without producing any change of substance in the conclusions that we should reach. We shall return to this matter in the next section.

The final thing to notice is that the asymmetry that has been discussed above is not an asymmetry between firms and households concerning the amount of information that each has. Firms are not being supposed, in some sense, to be smarter than households. Rather, the asymmetry arises from the fact that firms sell a small number of goods, so they and their workers are specialized in information concerning the prices of those goods. In contrast, households buy a large number of goods and services and are not specialized in information concerning the prices in all those markets. It is this asymmetry, and not an asymmetry in the amount of information that households and firms have, that provides the basis for a modified theory of aggregate supply that is capable of explaining the observed relationship between output (employment and unemployment) and inflation.

The starting point for developing this theory is an extended analysis of the labor market that builds on the above remarks.

B. Wrong Expectations and the Labor Market

The Labor Market and Money Wages

Recall the basic model of the labor market as shown below in frame (a) of Figure 24.1. This figure shows a competitive labor market in equilibrium at a real wage of $(W/P)^*$ and an employment level n^*. The demand for labor increases as the real wage falls because of profit-maximizing labor demand decisions by firms (marginal product = real wage); the supply of labor increases as real wages rise since more households will enter the labor force, the higher is the real bundle of goods that they can buy in exchange for their work.

Suppose for a moment that the price level is equal to one; i.e., $P_0 = 1$. With the price level equal to one, we may simply rename the vertical axis of Figure 24.1 to measure the money wage. If the price level is fixed at one, and we plot the demand and supply curves against the money wage, this is exactly the same as plotting them against the real wage. Frame (b) reproduces the demand and supply curves, n^d and n^s, and shows the same employment equilibrium, n^*, and the equilibrium money wage, W^*.

Next, notice that the equilibrium real wage $(W/P_0)^*$ [shown in frame (a)] could be attained at *any* money wage. All that is necessary is that the money wage and price level stand in the appropriate relationship to each other: If the price level doubled, the money wage would have to double; if the price level rose by x percent, the money wage would have to rise by x percent. In frame (a) where we draw the demand and supply curves against the real wage,

Figure 24.1
The Labor Market and the Money Wage

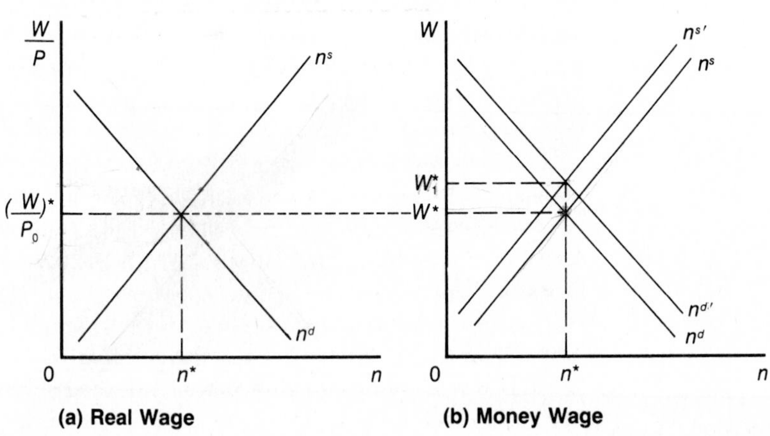

The supply and demand curves in the labor market that are drawn against the real wage [frame (a)] may equivalently be drawn against the money wage [frame (b)]. In that case, there is a separate supply and demand curve for each price level. Both curves move vertically one-for-one as the price level varies.

changes in the price level are not visible. The equilibrium determined in frame (a) is a real equilibrium and is independent of the price level.

Is the same true of the equilibrium in frame (b)? Is the equilibrium depicted in this figure independent of the price level? The answer is that the *real* equilibrium—real wage and employment level—is independent of the price level, but the money wage, measured on the vertical axis of frame (b), is not. Since in frame (b), the money wage is measured on the vertical axis, it is necessary to be aware that the demand and supply curves can only be drawn for a *given* level of prices. The supply and demand curves, illustrated as n^d and n^s, are drawn for a price level equal to one.

Suppose the price level was to increase to P_1, which is higher than P_0 by x percent; i.e.,

$$P_1 = (1 + x)P_0$$

You may find some numbers helpful: If $x = 5$ percent, i.e., 5/100, then the equation $P_1 = (1 + x)P_0$ is $P_1 = (1 + 5/100)P_0$ or $P_1 = (1.05)1 = 1.05$. If the price level rose by x percent, how would the demand and supply curves in frame (b) move? It is clear that the money wages that firms would now be willing to pay for each quantity of labor would be higher by the same x percent as the price level has increased by. Since the firm is only interested in the real wage, and x percent rise in the price level means that at a money wage x percent higher, the firm would be willing to hire the same number of workers as it would be at the lower price level and lower money wage. Thus, the demand for labor curve will shift upwards by the same x percent as the price level has risen by. This is shown as the curve $n^{d'}$ in frame (b) of Figure 24.1.

What happens on the supply side? Precisely the same as on the demand side: The quantity of labor that households are willing to supply depends on the real wage. Therefore, if the price level rises by x percent, the money wage will have to rise by x percent if the quantity of labor supplied is to remain unchanged. Thus, the curve $n^{s'}$ shows the supply of labor at the price level P_1. That is, the supply curve moves upwards by x percent in exactly the same way as the demand curve does.

It is now a simple matter to see that since the two curves have both moved upwards by the same percentage amounts, they must cut at the same employment level as before and at a money wage that is x percent higher than before. This new equilibrium *money wage* is shown in frame (b) as W_1^* and is equal to $(1 + x)W^*$. The equilibrium level of employment remains unchanged at n^*.

So far, nothing new has been introduced other than the idea that the labor market can be analyzed so as to determine the equilibrium wage and employment in the basic model, with the money wage on the vertical axis of the supply-demand diagram instead of the real wage. With the money wage on the vertical axis, the demand and supply curves shift when the price level changes. With the real wage on the vertical axis, the curves are fixed independently of the price level.

How the labor market works with incomplete information will now be analyzed.

First, recall the information assumptions that we have made. Firms and households are presumed to know the price at which the firm will be able to sell its output, but neither firms nor households are presumed to have complete knowledge of the prices of all the goods and services from which households will choose their consumption bundles. Labor supply decisions will be made on the basis of the best available estimate or expectation of those prices. Call the price level that consumers expect to have to pay to buy their basket of consumer goods the *expected price level*, and denote it as P^e.

Next, recall the above discussion about the demand for labor by an individual firm. Each firm will demand labor up to the point at which the real wage that it faces equals the marginal product of labor. The real wage facing any individual firm will be the money wage divided by the price of the individual firm's output. If we add up all the demands of all the individual firms and take an average of the real wages faced by each firm, we would obtain the aggregate or economy-wide demand for labor curve. This aggregate demand for labor would depend on the *actual* economy average real wage, W/P.

This may seem puzzling because we have assumed that nobody knows the average price level. A moment's reflection will reveal, however, that nobody needs to know the actual price level for the economy aggregate demand for labor to depend on the actual real wage. The aggregate demand curve itself is simply arrived at by adding up the individual demands of all the individual firms. Not only does nobody know the average price level, but nobody knows the aggregate demand for labor, and nobody needs to. All that each individual firm needs to know is the price of its own output and its own demand for labor. The aggregate demand for labor and the aggregate price level are constructs of our theory and are not things that are in the minds of the individual firms whose behavior we are analyzing and studying.

The supply of labor by each individual household depends, as we have seen, on the expected real wage, that is, on W/P^e. We can obtain the economy-wide aggregate supply of labor by adding all the supply curves of all the households together. Since the supply of each household depends on the expected real wage, so the aggregate supply of labor will also depend on the expected real wage. There is, thus, a crucial difference between the demand and supply curves once we take account of the information that households and firms have concerning price information.

The final thing that we need to do before we can figure out the implications of our assumptions is to make some proposition about the interaction between households and firms in the labor market. We have already noted that, as a descriptive matter, most labor markets work on the basis of there being a precommitment to a particular money wage, with households and firms then making decisions about how much labor to supply and demand at that money wage, given actual selling prices of output and expectations of the purchase prices of consumer goods. This seems to suggest that we ought to assume, as did Keynes, that money wages are rigid and that labor markets do not necessarily achieve equilibrium. However, we will not make this assumption here, at least not in this chapter. Instead, we shall assume that there is sufficient flexibility in the money wage rate for the average money wage rate to continuously adjust to maintain labor market equilibrium. This is a crucial assumption of the *new classical* analysis, which distinguishes it from the *new Keynesian* analysis that you will look at in the next chapter.

Although most firms and households do business with each other on the basis of pre-agreed wage schedules, there are in fact may ways in which you could think of the effective real wage adjusting so as to continuously maintain labor market equilibrium. One possibility is that the contracted wages themselves build in some automatic variation in the average hourly wage rate as a result of overtime schedules. Another possibility is that the intensity of work could be varied so as to vary the wage rate per unit of effort supplied as opposed to per hour supplied. (You probably know from your own labor market experience, and certainly from your experience as a student, that some hours of work are more intense than others. They range all the way from pure leisure to unadulterated drudgery!)

A further source of flexibility in the average wage paid arises from the heterogeneity of labor and the existence of different wages for different types of labor. This makes it possible for firms to change the quality mix of their labor force, perhaps using a higher proportion of higher paid and more highly skilled labor in times of high demand than in times of low demand. This would lead to an automatic variation in the average rates of wages paid, even though the pre-agreed wage schedules remain unchanged.

The key point to take from these "stories" is not that wages *do in fact* always adjust to achieve labor market equilibrium. Rather, it is that the *assumption* that labor markets always achieve equilibrium is not absurd, and is not contradicted by the commonly observed fact that labor is traded on contracts that specify a money wage rate.

Let me summarize the three assumptions that we have made:

1. The demand for labor depends on the *actual* real wage.
2. The supply of labor depends on the *expected* real wage.
3. The *average* money wage rate adjusts continuously to achieve labor market equilibrium.

Let us now see what these assumptions imply.

Figure 24.2 will be the main vehicle for following the analysis. The vertical axis measures the money wage, and the horizontal axis measures the level of employment. The curve $n^d(P_0)$ is the demand curve for labor when the price level is fixed at P_0. The supply curve of labor is plotted for a given *expected* level of prices. The supply curve, marked $n^s(P^e = P_0)$, is for a level of expected prices that equals the actual price level P_0. Thus, the supply curve $n^s(P^e = P_0)$ and the demand curve $n^d(P_0)$ can be thought of as representing the original curves, n^d and n^s, in frame (b) of Figure 24.1. They determine an equilibrium money wage W^* and an employment level n^*, which will now be called the *full-employment values.* The full-employment values of employment and the real wage are identical to those determined in the basic model.

Now consider what would happen if the price level was higher than P_0, while the expected price level remained at $P^e = P_0$. In particular, consider what would happen if the actual price level increased by x percent to P_1,

Figure 24.2
Expectations Equilibria in the Labor Market

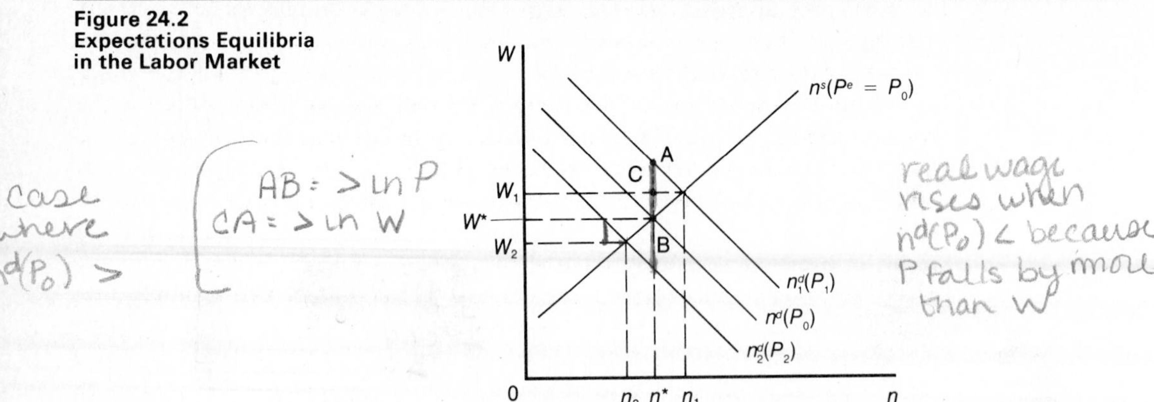

The demand for labor by each firm depends on the firm's own output price. This means that the aggregate demand for labor depends on the actual price level. The supply of labor depends on the expected price level. The equilibrium wage rate and employment level will be different at each different price level. At price level P_0 there is full-employment equilibrium; at price level P_1 there is over-full employment (wages W_1, employment n_1); and at price level P_2 there is unemployment (wage rate W_2, employment level n_2).

where P_1 equals $(1 + x)P_0$. Each firm, knowing that its own selling price had risen by x percent, would now be willing to pay a higher money wage for its labor. That is, the demand for labor curve would shift upwards. The new demand curve that would result is shown as $n_1^d(P_1)$.

Recall that we are conducting a conceptual experiment in which the general price level *expected* by households does not change. Since the *expected* price level has not changed, the supply curve is not affected by the change in the actual price level and remains in its original position.[2]

The labor market will now attain an equilibrium at the money wage W_1 and the employment level n_1. That is, with the actual price level higher than the expected price level, the money wage will be higher than its full-employment value, and the level of employment will be higher than its full-employment value. The real wage, however, will be lower than its full-employment value. This can be seen in Figure 24.2. The price level increase is measured by the full vertical shift of the labor demand curve, for

---

[2]Strictly speaking, there is an inconsistency in the treatment here. Everybody knows the price in the market for the commodity that they are concerned with the production of, and yet they do not seem to take this information into account in forming an expectation of the general price level. This is wasteful of information. A more complete, but more difficult, treatment would extract information from the known price of a particular commodity to obtain a better inference about the general price level. The essence of the new classical theory of aggregate supply is not affected, however, by ignoring this piece of information. For the reader able to follow statistical analysis, the paper by Robert E. Lucas, Jr., "Some International Evidence on Output-Inflation Tradeoffs," *The American Economic Review*, 63, no. 3 (1973), 326–34, and the appendix to Chapter 27 deal with this problem. This Lucas paper is probably the most important, accessible, original presentation of the new classical theory of aggregate supply.

example, the distance AB. The money wage, however, rises by a smaller distance, CD. You see, therefore, that the price level rise is greater than the money wage rise, and therefore the real wage has fallen. This fall in the real wage has induced firms to hire more labor and has generated the increase in employment from n^* to n_1. Households expect the price level to be P_0, and therefore as the money wage rises, households expect the real wage to be (W_1/P_0). This encourages households to supply the extra amount of labor n^* to n_1.

In this situation and while they are doing business with each other, households and firms are in equilibrium. Both households and firms are happy, and there is nothing that either could do to improve their situation. However, as they look backwards to a previous period, households will realize that they have made a mistake. They will realize that they did too much work and at too low a real wage. Of course, bygones are bygones, and there will be nothing that can be done about that. All that households can do the next time around is again to use all the information that is available to them and make the best deal that they can. The situation just analyzed is called one of *over-full employment*.

Next, consider the opposite experiment, of a fall in the price level below P_0, while the expected price level remains constant at $P^e = P_0$. In particular, let us suppose that the price level falls by x percent from P_0 to P_2, but that the expected price level remains at P_0. The demand for labor curve will now shift downwards and is illustrated by the new demand curve, $n_2^d(P_2)$. The supply curve does not shift because the expected price level has not changed. What happens in this event? Again, the answer is clear and is contained in the diagram (Figure 24.2). This time the labor market will come to what is called an *unemployment equilibrium*. The equilibrium wage rate will be W_2 and the employment level n_2. Thus, with a lower price level than that expected, employment and the money wage will fall below their full-employment levels. The real wage, in this case, will rise above its full-employment level. The real wage rises because the price level falls by more than the fall in the money wage. The demand curve falls by the full percentage amount of the fall in the price level; but, as you can see, the money wage falls by only a fraction of that. It is the higher real wage that creates the fall in employment, inducing firms to hire fewer workers. The expected real wage falls, however, because households do not expect the fall in the price level; and when they see a fall in the money wage, they read this as being a fall in the real wage.

There is, therefore, no inconsistency between the behavior of households and the firms concerning the drop in employment and the change in the money wage. Households willingly reduce their employment to n_2 in the face of an expected fall in the real wage, while firms willingly cut their hiring to n_2 since they are expecting a higher real wage.

While households and firms are trading labor, everyone is happy; both firms and households are doing the best they can for themselves. The workers $n^* - n_2$ will choose not to be employed, and their decision to be unemployed is correct in the light of their expectation of a low real wage. They expect a low real wage because, although the money wage has fallen, their expectation is that the price level will remain constant. Each firm, on the other hand, knowing its own output price, regards the drop in the money wage as insufficient to compensate for the drop in its own price, and so the resulting higher actual real wage induces them to hire less labor.

You see, then, that if the price level that is expected actually comes about, the economy will settle down at an equilibrium that is the same as the equilibrium in the basic model. That equilibrium is called *full employment.* If the price level is higher than expected, the labor market will equilibrate at a higher level of employment and a lower level of the real wage than the full-employment levels. In this case there will be *over-full employment.* If the price level turns out to be lower than that which is expected, then there will be a cut in the employment level and a higher real wage—there will be *unemployment.*

In the institutional setting of the United States, such a cut in employment will usually be recorded as a rise in unemployment since the individuals involved will be "available for" and "able and willing to" work. They are not, however, willing to work at the wage that is available. The unemployment survey does not ask questions in sufficient detail to establish that fact. It does not distinguish between people who are willing to work at the wage levels currently prevailing but cannot find such work and those who are unwilling to work at the prevailing wage rates but would like to work for a higher wage than is available.

Once expectations are introduced, there is no single unique equilibrium in the labor market. The equilibrium level of employment and the real wage will be influenced by the actual price level relative to its expected level. The higher the actual price level relative to its expected level, the higher will be the level of employment and the money wage, and the lower will be the level of unemployment and the real wage.

C. Definition of the Expectations-Augmented Aggregate Supply Curve

The expectations-augmented aggregate supply curve shows the maximum amount of output that the economy will supply at each different price level but with a fixed expected price level.

This is an extension of the concept of the aggregate supply curve that was introduced earlier in the basic model. The aggregate supply curve of the basic model can be thought of as showing the maximum amount of output that the economy will supply when there is no difference between the actual and the expected price levels. That is, the aggregate supply curve of the basic model is the same as the expectations-augmented aggregate supply curve when everyone has full information and everyone knows the actual price level.

D. Derivation of the Expectations-Augmented Aggregate Supply Curve

It is a straightforward matter to derive the expectations-augmented aggregate supply curve from the analysis that you have already conducted. Figure 24.3 illustrates how this is done. Frame (a) simply reproduces Figure 24.2. If you have understood Figure 24.2, you will understand frame (a) because it contains nothing new. The demand for labor curve n_1^d is drawn for the price level P_1,

Figure 24.3
Derivation of the Expectations-Augmented Aggregate Supply Curve

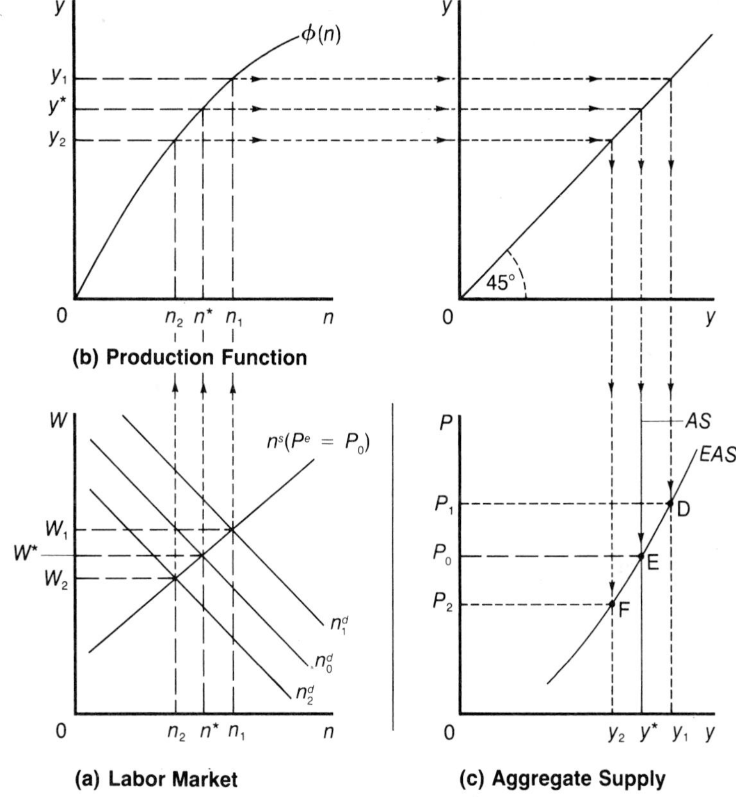

Frame (a) is the same as Figure 24.2. At each different price level there is a different labor market equilibrium. The employment levels associated with these different equilibria translate into different output levels [frame (b)]. By associating the initially assumed different price levels with the output levels generated [frame (c)] the expectations-augmented aggregate supply curve is derived. Position E is the same as full-employment equilibrium in the basic model. The expectations-augmented aggregate supply curve cuts the basic model aggregate supply curve at the expected price level.

the curve n_0^d for the price level P_0, and the curve n_2^d for the price level P_2. The supply curve is drawn for a fixed expected price level P^e equal to P_0.

Figure 24.3 is used to do something with which you are already familiar. It is used to derive the aggregate supply curve of the basic model. This is done by reading off the equilibrium level of output for which the expected price level equals the actual price level. In this case, everyone has full information—no one is fooled. The equilibrium in the labor market is where the demand curve n_0^d cuts the supply curve $n^s(P^e = P_0)$. At this point, employment is n^* and the money wage is W^*.

Transferring this employment level up to frame (b), you can read off from the production function the equilibrium level of output that will be supplied at full-employment equilibrium. This is y^*. Translate that level of output (following the dotted line) round to frame (c), and plot the level of output that will be produced in full-employment equilibrium against the price level P_0, point E. Now, as the price level is varied, *and* provided we also vary the expected price level—so that actual and expected prices are always equal to each other [recall frame (b) of Figure 24.1]—nothing would happen to the equilibrium level of employment or the real wage. The money wage would change proportionately with the price level, and the real equilibrium in the labor market would be undisturbed. This is essentially the exercise we performed when deriving the aggregate supply curve in the basic model: As the price level is varied and as the expected price level is varied so as to always equal the actual price level, the equilibrium level of employment remains constant, and from frame (b), the equilibrium level of output also remains constant. This traces out the aggregate supply curve of the basic model, *AS*, in frame (c).

Next consider what happens when the expected price level is held constant, but the actual price level changes. First, suppose the actual price level rises from P_0 to P_1, while the expected price level stays at P_0. This higher price level is shown on the vertical axis of frame (c) as P_1, which is equal to $P_0(1 + x)$. What is the level of output that profit-maximizing producers would want to supply at that price level? The answer is obtained by starting in the labor market. You know that the demand for labor curve will shift upwards to n_1^d. You also know that the supply curve of labor will not move because its position depends on the expected price level, and this has not changed. The labor market will clear at a higher money wage W_1 and a higher level of employment n_1. At this higher level of employment, firms will produce a higher level of output y_1, which is read off from the production function in frame (b). If we translate this level of output (by following the dotted line) to frame (c), we generate the new point D in frame (c). Point D shows the output level y_1, which profit-maximizing firms are willing to supply if the price level is P_1 and the expected price level is P_0.

Next, consider what would happen if the price level fell to x percent below P_0. Such a price level is shown on the vertical axis of frame (c) as P_2, which equals $P_0(1 - x)$. What is the profit-maximizing supply of output in this case? The answer is again obtained by starting in the labor market. You know that the demand for labor curve falls to n_2^d, so that the equilibrium level of employment and money wage will now move to n_2 and W_2, respectively. At this lower level of employment, firms will produce the lower level of output y_2, read off from frame (b). Now transferring this output level y_2 (following the dotted line) to frame (c) shows that profit-maximizing firms will supply the level of output y_2 at the price level P_2. That is, the economy would operate at point F. Point F says that if the price level is P_2 but the expected price level is P_0, firms will choose to supply y_2 as their profit-maximizing output.

If we join together the points D, E, and F and all other points in between and beyond these, we will generate the expectations-augmented aggregate supply curve, labelled *EAS*.

The expectations-augmented aggregate supply curve shows how the profit-maximizing and utility-maximizing quantity of supply varies as the price level varies—when the expected price level is fixed. Notice that the expectations-augmented aggregate supply curve (*EAS*) cuts the aggregate supply curve (*AS*) at the point at which the actual price level is equal to the expected price level. In the example in frame (c), this is at the price level P_0.

This is not a coincidence. It happens because only when expectations turn out to be correct do we get the same aggregate supply as we would if everyone always had complete information.

This new aggregate supply analysis will be combined with the theory of aggregate demand in Chapter 26 to reexamine the effects of a change in aggregate demand on the level of output and prices.

Summary

A. Incomplete Information and the Labor Market

Because it is costly for workers to find suitable jobs and because it is costly for firms to find suitable employees, labor is not traded as if in a continuous auction market. Rather, contracts are entered into that run for a year or more. Because contracts last for a sizable length of time and because it is expensive to write complicated contracts with detailed contingency clauses, it is typically the case that firms and households fix the price at which they will buy and sell labor in money units—i.e., they fix a money wage. However, because their decisions to buy and sell labor are influenced by the real wage, it is necessary for both households and firms to form an expectation about the price level that will prevail over a wage contract period.

Firms and households can do a better job of forming a reliable expectation about the prices in their own sector of the economy than they can about prices in general. Firms typically sell a small number of commodities and have a large amount of information about the markets in which they operate. In contrast, households buy a very large range of commodities and are not typically well informed about future prices in those markets. As a first approximation, everyone knows the prices at which they will be selling their output over the future wage contract period; however, no one knows *all* the prices that they will be facing when buying, so it is necessary to form an expectation of those prices based on incomplete information.

B. Wrong Expectations and the Labor Market

For a given expectation of prices, a rise in the money wage will be read by households as a rise in the real wage, and they will increase their supply of labor. A cut in the money wage will be read as a cut in the real wage, and they will decrease their supply of labor. However, each firm, knowing the prices of its own limited range of commodities, will not be misinformed about the real wage it is paying, and the demand for labor will depend on the *actual* real wage. The higher the actual price level relative to the expected price level, the lower will be the real wage, the greater will be the amount of labor that firms hire, the higher will be the expected real wage, and the greater will be the amount of labor that households supply. There are many equilibrium levels of the real wage and employment. The only equilibrium that corresponds to that in the basic model is the one in which the expected price level is equal to the actual price level. This occurs when everyone's expectation is correct.

C. Definition of the Expectations-Augmented Aggregate Supply Curve

The expectations-augmented aggregate supply curve traces out the quantities of aggregate output that firms will be willing to supply as the price level varies, at a given expected price level.

D. Derivation of the Expectations-Augmented Aggregate Supply Curve

The derivation is done in Figure 24.3. You should review Figure 24.3 as many times as necessary until you are thoroughly familiar with the derivation of the expectations-augmented aggregate supply curve.

Review Questions

1. What are the key assumptions of the new classical theory of the labor market?
2. What is the asymmetry in the labor market on which the new classical theory of aggregate supply is based? Does it imply that workers are more ignorant than their employers about prices?
3. What are the ways in which firms can vary the wage rate, independently of negotiating a new contract?
4. Why does the aggregate demand for labor in the new classical model depend on the *actual* real wage? How can it do so, when, by the assumptions of the model, no one knows the actual real wage?
5. Why, despite the fact there is never any involuntary unemployment in the new classical model, might there be concern about unemployment even in the context of that model?
6. What markets are in equilibrium along the new classical *EAS* curve? Is there any involuntary unemployment?
7. What determines the slope of the new classical expectations-augmented aggregate supply curve? Show how the slope of the *EAS* curve changes as the supply of the labor curve becomes more elastic.

25

The New Keynesian Theory of Aggregate Supply

There has recently emerged a new Keynesian theory of aggregate supply that differs in subtle but important ways from the new classical theory. The principal architects of the new Keynesian theory are Stanley Fischer of the Massachusetts Institute of Technology, Edmund Phelps of Columbia University, and John Taylor of Princeton University.[1] The approach had its origins, however, in an interesting paper dealing not with the theory of aggregate supply but with a related matter—the linking of wages to the cost of living—by Jo Anna Gray.[2] The treatment of the new Keynesian theory that will be presented in this chapter is in some respects closer to that of Jo Anna Gray than to those of Fischer, Phelps, and Taylor. The work of these three scholars, in fact, have some interesting differences among themselves, some of which will be noted later.

The point of departure of the new Keynesian theory is the description of the institutional arrangements in the labor market presented in the first section of the previous chapter. A key aspect of that institutional description is the general prevalence in labor markets of contracts that specify an agreed and, for a predetermined period, fixed money wage rate. The new classical theory assumes that there remains sufficient flexibility in the labor market for the average money wage to be in a state of continuous adjustment so as to achieve continuous labor market clearing. It is this assumption of the new classical theory that the new Keynesian theory replaces.

The new Keynesian theory regards the contractual fixing of money wages

---

[1]The main contributions to what I am calling the *new Keynesian theory* of aggregate supply are Stanley Fischer, "Long-Term Contracts, Rational Expectations and the Optimal Money Supply Rule," *Journal of Political Economy*, 85 (February 1977), 191–206; Edmund S. Phelps and John B. Taylor, "Stabilizing Powers of Monetary Policy under Rational Expectations," *Journal of Political Economy*, 85 (February 1977), 163–90; and John B. Taylor, "Staggered Wage Setting in a Macro Model," *The American Economic Review, Papers and Proceedings*, May 1979, pp. 108–13. The first two papers cited deal with a much broader range of issues than this chapter and extend into the policy questions that are dealt with in Chapters 33 and 34.

[2]Jo Anna Gray, "Wage Indexation: A Macroeconomic Approach," *Journal of Monetary Economics*, 2, no. 2 (April 1976), 221–35.

as being such a crucial feature of the labor market that it must figure prominently in any theory of how the labor market works. According to the new Keynesian theory, labor markets do not act like markets that are in a state of continuous auction, with prices (wages) being frequently adjusted to achieve an ongoing equality between supply and demand. Rather supply equals demand only on the average. At any particular moment in time, demand may exceed or fall short of supply. Taking explicit account of the institutional fact of contractually fixed money wages has important implications for the specification of the aggregate supply curve. This chapter explores these implications. Four specific tasks will help you in that objective. They are to:

(a) Know the key assumptions of the new Keynesian analysis.
(b) Understand how money wages are determined in the new Keynesian theory of aggregate supply.
(c) Understand the implications of the new Keynesian theory of wage determination for the expectations-augmented aggregate supply curve.
(d) Understand the implications of overlapping labor market contracts.

A. Assumptions of the New Keynesian Analysis

There are four key assumptions in the new Keynesian theory of aggregate supply. The first of these is that wages are set in money terms for a fixed contractual period before the quantity of labor supplied and demanded is known. Wages are not continuously adjusted so as to equate the *actual* supply of labor with the *actual* demand for labor. No explicit theory of maximizing behavior on the part of labor suppliers and demanders is set out that rationalizes this, although the developers of the new Keynesian theories do have in mind some underlying optimization by individuals that involve trading off the costs of collecting information and negotiating changes in wages against the losses that arise when wages fail to adjust continuously to achieve market clearing. It is asserted that, for whatever reason, the real world so obviously is characterized by such arrangements in labor markets that it is inappropriate to develop an analysis of the labor market that ignores the contractual fixity of money wages.

The second key assumption of the new Keynesian analysis is that the actual quantity of labor traded is equal to the quantity demanded. After wages are set, the actual supply and demand conditions become known. Once those conditions are known, both suppliers and demanders in the labor market are tied into a labor contract. There has to be some rule for determining the quantity that will be traded. This rule could be that the short side of the market dominates. What this means is that if demand is less than supply, the quantity traded is the quantity demanded; but if demand exceeds supply, the quantity traded is the quantity supplied. However, this is *not* the assumption employed in the new Keynesian analysis. Instead, it is assumed that the demand side always dominates. The suppliers of labor are assumed to stand ready to supply whatever labor is demanded in exchange for the certainty of a fixed money wage over the duration of the existing contract.

The third assumption of the new Keynesian theory concerns the objectives that govern the setting of the money wage rate at the beginning of a contract. Here, the different scholars who have contributed to this approach each make their own special assumptions. Phelps and Taylor follow an approach that is very similar to that reviewed in Chapter 21—the neoclassical theory of price adjustment. Telling the story in terms of an individual group of workers, Phelps and Taylor propose that wages will be set at the level that takes account of:

1. Any wage changes that have occurred amongst other groups in the period since the previous wage contract date
2. Any expected wage and price changes that are going to take place over the interval for which wages are now being agreed
3. The state of excess demand (or supply)

Stanley Fischer makes a simpler assumption that ignores the effect of excess demand on the level of wages. He proposes wages will be set so as to achieve a *fixed* real wage rate. This assumption makes a great deal of sense for a world in which there are never any changes in technology that would shift the demand for labor curve and change the equilibrium real wage. If, however, technology does keep changing, and equilibrium real wages change as a result, then any wage-setting behavior that seeks to fix the real wage will inject into the labor market a barrier that prevents the supply of labor from ever equalling the demand for labor even on the average. It is very hard to see why people would want to be parties to contracts that had such a feature. Furthermore, we know from simple observation of the behavior of real wages that, in fact, they do, from time to time, vary. This assumption then of Fischer's, although a useful one for his purposes, is too restrictive.

It seems more appropriate to adopt the Phelps and Taylor approach and assume that money wages not only respond to expectations of changes in the wages of others and prices but also respond to the state of supply and demand in the labor market. One way of allowing for the effects of supply and demand on wages that can be viewed as a special case of the Phelps and Taylor assumption is that money wages are set so as to achieve an equality between the expected supply and expected demand for labor over the duration of the labor contract. This, in fact, is the assumption employed by Jo Anna Gray (referred to above), and it is the assumption that I shall use in order to derive a new Keynesian theory of aggregate supply.

Before going on to do that, however, let us be sure that we understand exactly what this assumption is and how it relates to but also differs from the assumptions made by Phelps and Taylor and Fischer. We are going to assume that the money wage rate is set at the beginning of a contract and is held constant throughout the contract period so as to achieve an equality between the *expected supply* and *expected demand* for labor. It will be immediately clear that if there are no expected changes in supply and demand in the labor market, then the expected real wage will be constant, and the money wage will be set so as to achieve this expected constant real wage. Thus, provided there are no expected labor market shocks, the assumption that we are making is equivalent to that made by Stanley Fischer. If, however, there are expected changes in supply and demand in the labor market, there will be an expected change in the real wage, and the money wage will be set to reflect that expectation. To this extent the assumption that we are making is more general than that made by Fischer.

Next compare our assumption with that of Phelps and Taylor. They propose that when there is an excess demand for labor, money wages will rise faster than they otherwise would do. Our assumption agrees with that. If there is an excess demand for labor (which is expected to continue into the future), then money wages will increase by more than they otherwise would have done but by a very specific amount—the amount that produces an expected equality between supply and demand for labor. Phelps and Taylor are not quite as precise as that. They simply say that if there is an excess demand, money wages will rise faster than they otherwise would do. Money wages will not necessarily rise by an amount that will completely close the gap between supply and demand in a given contract period. To this extent the assumption that we are making is slightly more restrictive than that of Phelps and Taylor.

The fourth key assumption of the new Keynesian theory of aggregate supply is that labor market contracts last for a longer term than the frequency with which the economy is being bombarded by various kinds of random and policy shocks. This means that workers and their employers often become aware of the fact that the contractually agreed-upon wage, based on information that was available at the time the agreement was drawn up, may now be in some sense inappropriate for the new conditions. Nevertheless, being tied into an agreement, both sides of the market have to live with the precommitted money wage until the next review date. Taken on its own, this would imply that any shocks occurring after a wage contract has been written will have effects that could persist to some future date on which the longest-term existing contract is to be reviewed.

There is, however, a further consideration that generates even more persistence in the effects of shocks than that. It arises from the fact that not all labor market contracts are signed on the same day to run for the same duration. Rather, they are signed on different dates for different durations (although the differences in durations are not so important as the differences in the dates on which the contracts are signed). The fact that contracts overlap or are "staggered" rather than bunched to the same date and time interval has important implications that will be discussed later in this chapter. The next two sections will not take account of the overlapping nature of labor market contracts, but for simplicity will proceed as if all contracts are signed on the same day and run for the same duration.

B. Determination of Money Wages

The process whereby the money wage rate is determined in the new Keynesian theory is illustrated in Figure 25.1; it is analogous to the diagram used in Figure 24.2. The level of employment is measured on the horizontal axis, and the money wage rate is measured on the vertical axis. The supply curve of

Figure 25.1
The Labor Market in the New Keynesian Model

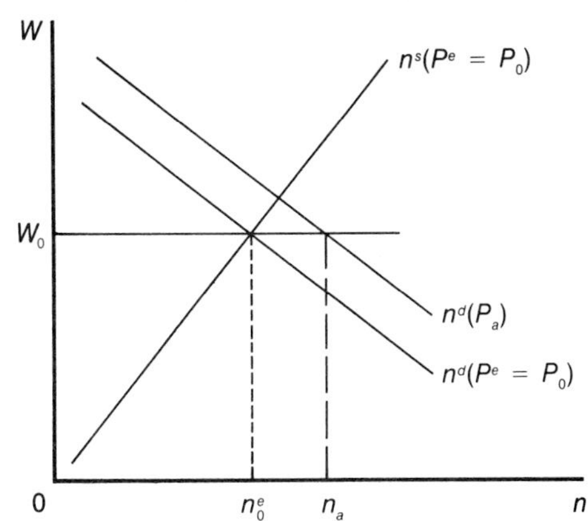

The labor market meets and a money wage is set before the actual price level is known. That wage rate, W_0, is set to achieve an equilibrium in the labor market based on the expected price level (P_0). When the actual price level (P_a) is revealed, the quantity of labor traded will equal the quantity demanded (n_a).

labor $n^s(P^e = P_0)$ is drawn for a fixed expected price level equal to P_0. It is assumed that the labor market convenes and negotiations take place and that the money wage contract is signed prior to the commencement of the period for which the labor will be supplied and demanded. The price level at which the demanders of labor will sell their output is therefore unknown at the time that the labor market contract is signed.

The demand for labor that is relevant for the determination of the wage contract is that based on the expected price level. Such a demand function is drawn in Figure 25.1 as the curve labelled $n^d(P^e = \mathrm{P}_0)$. This is the expected demand for labor curve, given the expected price level equal to P_0. Where the expected demand curve cuts the expected supply curve determines the expected labor market equilibrium. The level of employment n_0^e is the expected equilibrium level of employment, and the wage rate W_0 is the expected market-clearing money wage rate.

The contractually determined money wage rate will be set equal to this expected market-clearing money wage. Once the money wage is determined, nothing is allowed to change it until the next bargaining date at some time in the future. In the meantime, the actual level of employment will be determined at the contracted money wage by the *actual* demand for labor curve. Suppose that the actual price level turns out to be P_a, so that the actual demand for labor curve is $n^d(P_a)$. In this case, the quantity of labor employed will be n_a, and the wage rate, of course, will remain at W_0. The real wage will fall because the price level P_a is higher than the expected price level P_0, on which the fixed money wage rate W_0 is based.

C. The New Keynesian Expectations-Augmented Aggregate Supply Curve

The new Keynesian theory of aggregate supply implied by the theory of wage determination just presented is very similar, in qualitative terms, to the new classical theory. The derivation of the new Keynesian expectations-augmented aggregate supply curve is presented in Figure 25.2. It will be recognized that this figure is almost identical to Figure 24.3, which was used to derive the new classical expectations-augmented aggregate supply curve. The labor market analysis presented above in Figure 25.1 is repeated in frame (a). The production function appears in frame (b), and the aggregate supply curve is generated in frame (c).

As described above, the money wage is determined at W_0, which is the money wage that achieves an expected equilibrium in the labor market. That is, it achieves an equality between the expected supply of labor and the ex-

Figure 25.2
Derivation of the Expectations-Augmented Aggregate Supply Curve in the New Keynesian Model

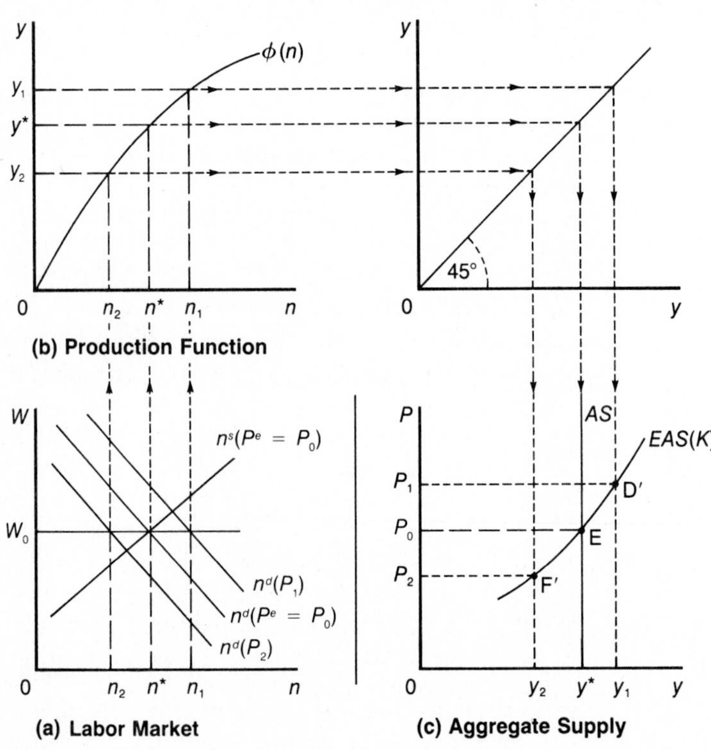

The development in this diagram parallels that of Figure 24.3. In frame (a), the labor market sets a money wage at W_0 based on the expected price level P_0. Full-employment equilibrium would be at n^*. Different actual price levels (P_0, P_1, P_2) generate different demand curves. The quantity traded is read off from the demand curve (n_1 at price level P_1 and n_2 at price level P_2). The output produced by these different labor inputs are read off from the production function in frame (b). The resulting new Keynesian expectations-augmented aggregate supply curve is traced out as F′ED′. The aggregate supply curve based on correct information is that of the basic model labelled *AS*.

pected demand for labor with the expected price level P_0. If the actual price level turned out to be P_1, so that the demand for labor curve was in fact $n^d(P_1)$, then the quantity of labor demanded would be n_1. The quantity of labor n_1 would, through the production function, generate a level of output equal to y_1. This output level y_1 could be traced around through the 45° quadrant to the aggregate supply diagram in frame (c), being the output level y_1 on the horizontal axis of frame (c). The output level y_1 is, of course, associated with the price level P_1, so that point D′ is a point on the expectations-augmented aggregate supply curve of the new Keynesian analysis.

If, conversely, the price level was lower than P_0 at, say, P_2, so that the demand for labor curve dropped to the curve $n^d(P_2)$, then the quantity of labor demanded would become the quantity n_2 on the horizontal axis of frame (a). This level of employment would generate an output level y_2 read off from the vertical axis of frame (b). Transferring the output level y_2 through the 45° quadrant to the aggregate supply diagram shows that the output level y_2 is associated with the price level P_2 at point F′. If the price level turned out to be that which was expected, namely, P_0, then the quantity of labor employed would, of course, be n^*, and the output level would be y^*, generating a point on the aggregate supply curve, point E. Joining together points F′, E, and D′ and extrapolating beyond these points traces out the new Keynesian expectations-augmented aggregate supply curve, labelled $EAS(K)$ in frame (c).

So that you can see clearly the relationship between the new Keynesian expectations-augmented aggregate supply curve and the new classical aggregate supply curve, Figure 25.3 superimposes the two analyses on top of each other. You can easily verify that Figure 25.3 contains everything that is in Figure 25.2 that generates the curve $EAS(K)$ (the new Keynesian aggregate supply curve) and also everything that is in Figure 24.3 that generates the new classical aggregate supply curve, the curve $EAS(C)$. Notice that the new Keynesian aggregate supply curve is flatter than the new classical curve. In a sense, this says that the new Keynesian analysis gives rise to more pessimistic predictions than the new classical analysis about the effects on prices of a cut in aggregate demand, but it also gives more optimistic predictions concerning the inflationary consequences of stimulating aggregate demand.

Aside from the slopes of the two curves, the two theories as presented so far look very similar. There is, however, a crucial difference between the two that has not yet been revealed as fully as it needs to be, and that arises from the fact that the contractually determined wages are not all set on the same date but rather overlap each other. Let us now turn to an examination of the implications of this factor.

D. Overlapping Wage Contracts

The new Keynesian theory of aggregate supply developed above is based on the idea that at the beginning of each period of time, workers and employers sit down together, form an expectation of what the price level will be over the coming period (say a year), agree on a money wage rate that will achieve an expected equilibrium in the labor market, and then agree to trade at that wage

Figure 25.3
A Comparison of the New Keynesian and New Classical Aggregate Supply Curves

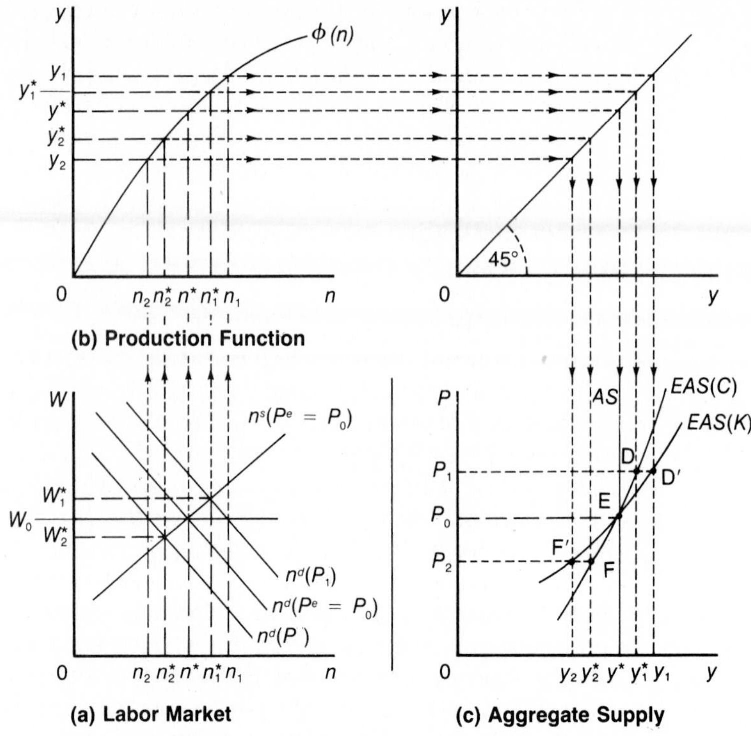

This diagram superimposes Figure 25.2 upon Figure 24.2. The key differences between the new Keynesian and new classical models are seen in frames (a) and (c). In the new Keynesian model, the money wage is fixed at W_0, so that as the price level varies between P_1 and P_2, the quantity of labor traded varies between n_1 and n_2, and output varies between y_1 and y_2. In the new classical analysis, as the price level varies between P_1 and P_2, shifting the demand curve between $n^d(P_1)$ and $n^d(P_2)$, the money wage rate fluctuates between W_1^* and W_2^*. These fluctuations in the wage rate damp off fluctuations in the quantity of labor demanded, so that employment and output fluctuate between n_1^* and n_2^* and output fluctuates between y_1^* and y_2^*. The two expectations-augmented supply curves cut the basic model aggregate supply curve at the expected price level, point E. The new classical curve is steeper than the new Keynesian curve.

for the coming year. The amount of labor that they trade will be determined by the actual demand for labor once the general price level is revealed.

The assumption that all contracts start and end at the same time as each other is obviously a fiction used purely to simplify the diagrammatic analysis. Let us now get rid of that assumption. Suppose, instead, that one-half of the labor force sits down at the beginning of January each year and negotiates a wage that is to prevail, not for one year but for two years. The other half of the labor force will negotiate a wage on the alternate January, again for a period of two years. The analysis contained in Figures 25.1 and 25.2 still applies, but now it only applies to one-half of the labor force. The other half of the labor force has already performed that same exercise one year earlier and will be performing it one year later. Thus the actual wage rate that is observed at any one point in time in the economy will be an average of the wages that have been set at various dates in the past on contracts that are still current. In the example, if one-half of the labor force sets its wages in January of one year and the other one-half in January of the alternate year, then the wage that prevails in any one year will be equal to one-half of the wage determined at the beginning of January of the year in question plus one-half of the wage determined at the beginning of the preceding January. This wage will be based on expectations of the general price level that were formed at two different dates in the past.

This being so, the expectations augmented-aggregate supply curve will depend not only on current expectations of the current price level but also on older (and perhaps by now known to be wrong) expectations of the current price level. Once agents are locked into a money wage decision based on an old, and perhaps falsified, expectation of the price level, there is, by the hypothesis embodied in the new Keynesian analysis, nothing they can do about it until the next wage review date comes along.

It would be incorrect, however, to jump to the conclusion that the effects of expectations that are now known to be wrong would be eliminated once a new contract was written. The fact that contracts overlap means also that they influence each other in a persistent manner. To see this, consider a group of workers setting their wage in the current period. One of the things that they will want to do in determining the money wage is to take a view of the expected behavior of prices over their own contract period. Another thing that will influence them, is the levels of wages that have already been set by other workers. To move their own wages too far out of line with those earlier wages could cause employers to find ways of substituting amongst different types of labor. Thus, the money wage being negotiated today is not going to be entirely independent of money wages that have been negotiated in the past. A forecasting error made by those who set wages in the previous period will influence the wages that are going to be set in the current period, and these effects will persist (although in diminishing form) into the indefinite future.

The fact that labor market contracts are long-term and overlapping has very important implications for the analysis of economic policy as you will see in subsequent chapters in this book.

This new Keynesian analysis is a way of rationalizing "sticky money wages." Money wages are sticky not because of some mysterious downward rigidity as in Keynes's analysis but because contractual commitments prevent people from adjusting money wages in the light of new information. In effect, workers and firms have said to each other, "These are the terms on which we are willing to do business *come what may* until the next time we sit down two years from now."

There is a lively debate in the current literature concerning the efficiency of the labor market contracts that the new Keynesian economists use in their theory of aggregate supply. New classical economists such as Robert Barro insist that such contracts are inefficient and cannot be rationalized as the kinds of contracts that rational profit-maximizing and utility-maximizing agents would enter into.[3] The new Keynesians agree that it is hard to think of convincing reasons why people would enter into contracts such as these. They insist, however, that we do observe such contracts as commonplace, and in the absence of a firm understanding as to why, they argue that we have no alternative but to incorporate them into our macroeconomic models.

The new Keynesian analysis can be viewed as having replaced the traditional Keynesian assumption of a fixed money wage with the assumption of a fixed timing structure for the changes in money wages, that arise in a rather rigid contractual setting.

Summary

A. Assumptions of the New Keynesian Analysis

There are four key assumptions of the new Keynesian analysis:

1. Money wages are set for an agreed period and do not continuously adjust.
2. The actual quantity of labor traded is determined by the quantity demanded.
3. Money wages are set so as to achieve equality between the expected supply and expected demand for labor.
4. Wage contracts last for a longer term than the frequency with which the economy is hit by shocks and overlap in time.

B. Determination of Money Wages

Money wages are determined in the new Keynesian theory of aggregate supply by equating the supply of labor that is expected on the basis of the expected price level with the demand for labor that is expected on the basis of the expected price level. Figure 25.1 illustrates this relationship and should be thoroughly understood.

C. The New Keynesian Expectations-Augmented Aggregate Supply Curve

The new Keynesian theory of wage determination implies that the expectations-augmented aggregate supply curve will have the same basic shape as the new classical expectations-augmented aggregate supply curve. The new Keynesian aggregate supply curve will, however, be flatter than the new classical curve. This arises because, when the demand for labor function shifts because of changes in the actual price level, there are no partially compensating adjustments in the money wage rate to dampen off some of the effects of the shift in demand function on the quantity demanded. The quantity of labor demanded adjusts fully to reflect shifts in the demand function at the fixed money wage rate, and the level of output therefore fluctuates by a larger amount than otherwise would be the case.

[3] Robert J. Barro, "Long-term Contracting, Sticky Prices, and Monetary Policy," *Journal of Monetary Economics*, 3, (July 1977), 305–16.

D. Overlapping Wage Contracts

The fact that not all labor market contracts are signed on the same date, but overlap each other, has fundamental implications for the aggregate supply curve. Instead of the position of the aggregate supply curve depending only on *current* expectations of the price level, it will also depend on *previous* expectations of the current period's price level. Expectations formed in the past and now known to be wrong will be embodied in the position of the Keynesian expectations-augmented aggregate supply curve.

Review Questions

1. What are the four key assumptions of the new Keynesian theory of the labor market?

2. Why is the new Keynesian expectations-augmented aggregate supply curve flatter than the new classical curve?

3. Why do the new Keynesian, new classical, and basic model aggregate supply curves all intersect at full-employment output and the expected price level?

4. The new Keynesian theory of the labor market assumes that households can be "off" their supply curves. How might firms induce households to behave in such a way? Could households be induced to be permanently "off" their supply curves?

5. What are the implications of overlapping labor market contracts?

6. Compare the new Keynesian with the old Keynesian theory of the labor market. What are the main differences? Why do you think the new Keynesian theory is so-called?

7. (a) An economy is described by the following equations: The marginal product of labor curve is described by the equation

$$MPL = 5 - 5n$$

The supply of labor is given by

$$n^s = W/P$$

What is the equilibrium level of employment and the real wage, given complete information? That is, what would the equilibrium of the basic model be?

(b) If the production function is $y = 5n - 2.5n^2$, calculate and plot an equation for the new classical expectations-augmented aggregate supply curve, assuming that the expected price level remains constant at unity.

(c) Calculate and plot an equation for the new Keynesian expectations-augmented aggregate supply curve assuming that the expected price level is fixed at unity. (*Hint*: Try actual price levels of $\frac{1}{2}$, 1, and 2 for the purpose of this exercise.)

26

Equilibrium Income, Employment, and the Price Level with Fixed Expectations

You have now begun to modify the basic model of aggregate supply to allow for incomplete information on the part of market participants. In particular, in Chapters 24 and 25 you were introduced to two theories leading to the expectations-augmented aggregate supply curve. This chapter employs the expectations-augmented aggregate supply curve and analyzes what happens when aggregate demand changes but the expected price level is fixed. However, before embarking on that analysis, there are two preliminary tasks that need attention. Overall, then, you have three tasks in this chapter, which are to:

(a) Know the definition of *full-employment equilibrium*.
(b) Know how to characterize full-employment equilibrium in a simple diagram.
(c) Understand how output, employment, the real wage, the price level, and the money wage are affected by a rise or fall in aggregate demand when the expected price level is fixed.
(d) Understand how output, employment, the real wage, the price level, and the money wage are affected by a rise or fall in the expected price level when aggregate demand is fixed.

A. Full-Employment Equilibrium

Full-employment equilibrium is a situation in which the actual price level is equal to the expected price level. The full-employment equilibrium levels of output, employment, and the real wage are the levels of those variables that occur when the actual price level is equal to the expected price level.

Although the name *full-employment equilibrium* is used to describe a situation in which the price level is equal to the expected price level, this does not mean that there is no unemployment in full-employment equilibrium. This may seem like a contradiction of terms, but it really is nothing more than a convenient use of language. You will remember, from your analysis of the basic model of aggregate output and employment determination, that you were able to generate unemployment even in that model. Recall that there are no wrong expectations in that model. Minimum wages that raise the economy average real wage above the equilibrium real wage, or an economy-wide labor union that raises the real wage above the equilibrium wage, or a rise in unemployment insurance benefits, or a rise in employment or income taxes—all were seen as factors that could produce a level of employment of labor below the labor supply. This amount of unemployment is sometimes named *natural unemployment.*

At full-employment equilibrium, the unemployment rate is equal to the natural unemployment rate. This will be obvious to you if you recall that in developing the basic model, no distinction was made between the expected and the actual price level. Workers were presumed to supply their labor in accordance with full knowledge of the actual price level. So the basic model always depicts a full-employment equilibrium. As a matter of definition, then, when the unemployment rate is equal to the natural unemployment rate, the term *full employment* is used to describe the condition of the labor market.

In what follows in the rest of this chapter and in subsequent chapters, the analysis abstracts from the natural rate of unemployment. That does not mean that the natural rate of unemployment is ignored or assumed not to exist. Rather, the analysis will be thought of as determining the level of unemployment relative to the natural rate of unemployment. In the formal analysis, the natural rate of unemployment will be treated as if it was zero. This is only an analytical convenience. The reason for making this abstraction is that the natural unemployment rate itself is not affected by the factors that are being considered. Conversely, the natural unemployment rate does not affect the factors that will be considered. It is possible, therefore, to analyze fluctuations of unemployment around the natural rate independently of what the natural rate of unemployment is.

To summarize: Full-employment equilibrium values of real income, employment, and the real wage occur when the price level is equal to its expected level. There will be some unemployment in that situation, determined by the real factors (discussed in Chapters 11 and 13) that determine the natural rate of unemployment.

B. A Simple Diagram to Characterize Full-Employment Equilibrium

It is important to characterize full-employment equilibrium before moving on to analyzing the effects of a change in the money supply on the levels of output, employment, and prices. Figure 26.1 illustrates a full-employment equilibrium, and the text in this section guides you through that figure.

Notice that the diagram is similar to Figures 10.2 and 24.3. Frame (a) shows the labor market with the money wage on the vertical axis and employment on the horizontal axis. Frame (b) shows the production function—the relationship between the maximum amount of output that can be supplied and the level of employment. Frame (c) shows the aggregate goods market with aggregate demand and aggregate supply for goods plotted against the price level.

Figure 26.1
Full-Employment Equilibrium

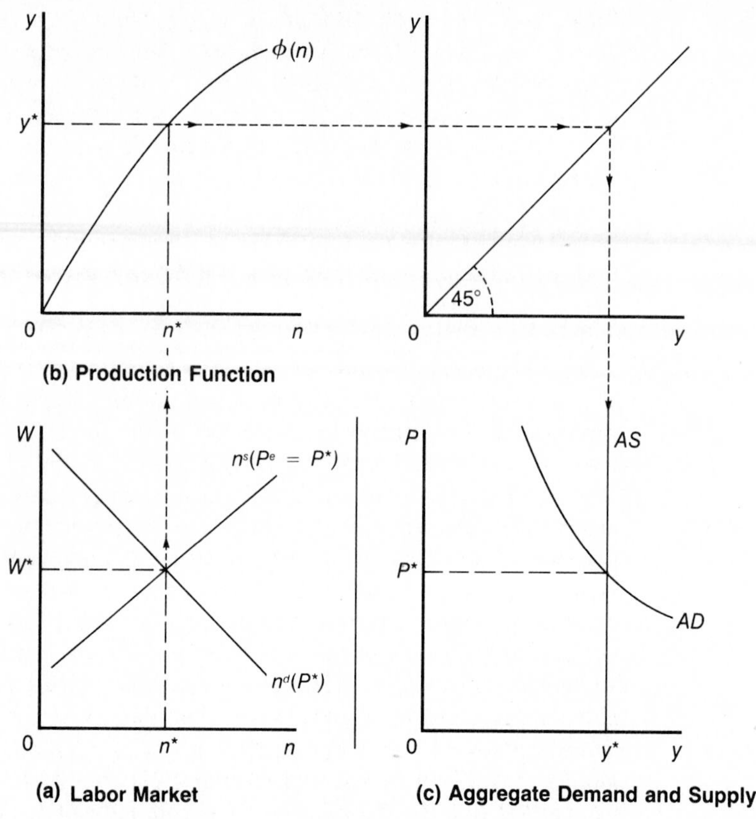

Where the aggregate demand curve cuts the basic model aggregate supply curve [frame (c)] determines the full-employment equilibrium price level P^*. When the supply of labor and demand for labor curves are plotted in frame (a) against the money wage rate but given an actual and expected price level fixed at P^*, they intersect at n^* and determine the money wage rate W^*.

First, pretend that there are no curves in frame (a) at all. Instead of using frame (a), recall the diagram for the labor market that was employed in the basic model of real income and employment [frame (a) of Figure 10.2]. You will recall that in that frame, we plotted the level of employment against the *real* wage. Where the supply of labor curve cuts the demand for labor curve, the equilibrium real wage and the level of employment are determined. Let us suppose that the level of employment determined in that frame is the value n^* plotted on the horizontal axis of frame (a) of Figure 26.1. That is, we have determined n^* from the basic model of Chapter 10.

You can now determine the level of output that will be produced with the level of employment n^*. Following the dotted line from frame (a) to frame (b), you see that the level of output associated with n^* is equal to y^*. Transferring that level of output (following the dotted line) to the aggregate supply and demand diagram [frame (c)] generates the aggregate supply curve shown as the vertical line labelled *AS*.

From either the simple monetary theory of aggregate demand or, more satisfactorily, from the Keynesian *IS-LM* theory of aggregate demand (recall Chapter 20), we may obtain the aggregate demand curve. This is shown in frame (c) as the curve labelled *AD*. Where the aggregate demand and aggregate supply curves intersect determines the equilibrium price level P^*.

Now that the equilibrium price level P^* has been determined, it is possible to work backwards and determine the money wage. This could not have been done before determining the equilibrium price level because you would not have known where in frame (a) to plot the labor supply and demand curves. Recall that although these curves are fixed when graphed against the real wage, they shift with the price level when plotted against the money wage. The demand for labor curve depends on the actual price level, and we can draw this as the curve labelled $n^d(P^*)$. This is the demand for labor curve plotted against the money wage rate when the price level is equal to the equilibrium price level P^*. The supply of labor curve is plotted against the expected price level.

Since the diagram is characterizing full-employment equilibrium, the supply of labor curve is drawn for an expected price level equal to the actual price level, which in turn is equal to P^*. The supply curve is shown as the curve labelled $n^s(P^e = P^*)$. This supply curve cuts the demand curve at the level of employment n^*. This follows directly from the fact that the demand and supply curves are fixed when plotted against the real wage and shift proportionately to each other as the price level varies when plotted against the money wage. It follows, then, that if the supply and demand curves are plotted against the money wage, and for the same given price level, then these curves must cut at the full-employment level of employment n^*.

You can now read off, finally, the money wage that is associated with an equilibrium in the labor market at the given actual and expected price level P^*. This money wage is denoted in frame (a) as W^*.

This completes the characterization of full-employment equilibrium. It is worth emphasizing that there is no difficulty in representing, in this diagram, a positive value for the natural rate of unemployment. You could, for example, supplement frame (a) with a minimum wage rate, thereby shifting the regulated equilibrium level of employment and the aggregate supply curve; or you could modify frame (a) along the lines suggested in the earlier analysis of the effects of unemployment insurance benefits, again generating an equilibrium level of unemployment. All that these things do is to raise the equilibrium money wage and lower the level of employment relative to that shown in frame (a).

C. Effects of a Change in Aggregate Demand with a Fixed Expected Price Level

Suppose that the expected price level P^e is equal to P^* and is fixed at that value. Later (in the next chapter) we shall inquire what determines the expected price level and how it might change. It will be clearer, however, if we proceed in steps, and the first step is to examine what happens to the levels of output, employment and unemployment, the real wage, and the price level when the economy experiences a change in aggregate demand but the expected price level does not change.

The Expectations-Augmented Aggregate Supply Curve

The starting point for the analysis is the expectations-augmented aggregate supply curve discussed at length in the previous two chapters. Either the new Keynesian or the new classical version of the *EAS* curve could be employed. The treatment here uses the new classical version. You may find it a useful exercise to carry out a parallel exercise using the new Keynesian version. Figure 26.2 summarizes the derivation of the new classical aggregate supply curve. You will recall that the supply of labor curve shown in frame (a) depends on the expected price level. Since the expected price level is being held constant, the supply of labor curve is also held constant. You will also recall

Figure 26.2
The Expectations-Augmented Aggregate Supply Curve

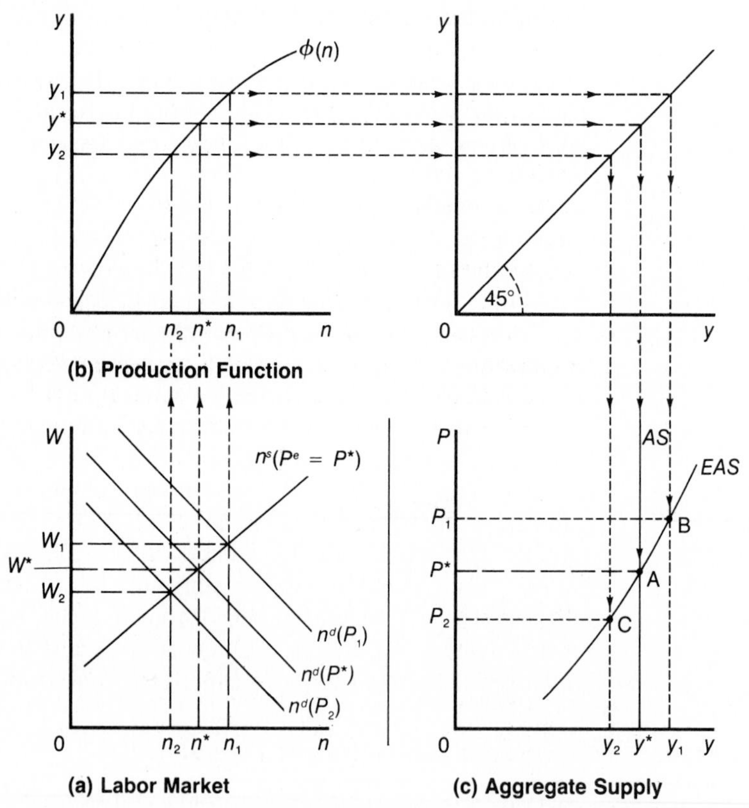

As the actual price level varies between P_1 and P_2 [frame (c)], the demand for labor curve shifts between $n^d(P_1)$ and $n^d(P_2)$ [frame (a)]. With the expected price level fixed at P^*, the supply of labor curve does not shift. Labor market equilibrium employment and wages vary between n_1 and n_2 and W_1 and W_2, generating output fluctuations between y_1 and y_2. Thus, as the price level moves from P_1 to P_2, output moves from y_1 to y_2 along the curve *EAS*.

that the demand for labor curve depends on the *actual* value of the price level. The demand curve labelled $n^d(P^*)$ is drawn for a level of prices equal to P^*. Where that curve intersects the supply of labor curve determines the full-employment equilibrium money wage W^* and employment level n^*.

The production function in frame (b) shows that the employment level n^* will produce a level of output equal to y^*. Following the dotted line from frame (b) to frame (c), you arrive at point A, which represents the full-employment equilibrium point where P^*, the actual price level, is equal to the expected price level.

If the price level being considered is at a higher value than P^*, say P_1, as shown on the vertical axis of frame (c), then you have to replot the demand for labor curve, showing it to have shifted upwards. This is shown as $n^d(P_1)$ in frame (a). This determines a new higher money wage and employment level (W_1 and n_1) and, through frame (b), a higher level of output y_1. If this output level is transferred (following the dotted line) to frame (c), we see that at the price level P_1, the output level will be y_1 and the economy will operate at the point marked B.

Now consider the price level as being less than P^*, say, at P_2, as marked on the vertical axis of frame (c). In this case, the labor demand curve has to be shifted downwards. This is shown as $n^d(P_2)$ in frame (a). This labor demand curve intersects the fixed labor supply curve to determine the lower money wage and employment levels W_2 and n_2. At the employment level n_2, the economy will produce an output level of y_2. Transferring the output level y_2 (following the dotted line) to frame (c) shows us that the economy will produce at the point marked C where the price level is P_2 and the output level is y_2. Joining up all the points C, A, and B generates the expectations-augmented aggregate supply curve marked *EAS*.

Now that your knowledge of the expectations-augmented aggregate supply curve has been reviewed, it is a very simple matter to see how changes in aggregate demand affect output, employment, the real wage, and the price level. First of all, the effects on prices and output will be considered and then subsequently the effects on the labor market.

The Effects of a Change in Aggregate Demand on the Levels of Output and Prices

Figure 26.3 summarizes the effects of a change in aggregate demand on prices and output. The starting point, A, is a full-employment equilibrium. Here the price level, P^*, and output level, y^*, are determined by the intersection of the aggregate demand curve, AD^*, and the aggregate supply curve, *AS*, as well as by the intersection of the expectations-augmented aggregate supply curve, *EAS*. The point A is the full-employment equilibrium as defined above, in the sense that the actual price level P^* is equal to the expected price level that underlies the *EAS* curve.

Hold the expected price level constant at P^* and ask what happens if the level of aggregate demand changes. You can think of aggregate demand changing because the money supply rises, government spending rises, taxes are cut, or there is a shift in the demand for investment goods. (Depending on which of these shocks occur, the rate of interest that is simultaneously deter-

Figure 26.3
The Effects of a Rise or Fall in Aggregate Demand with Fixed Price Level Expectations

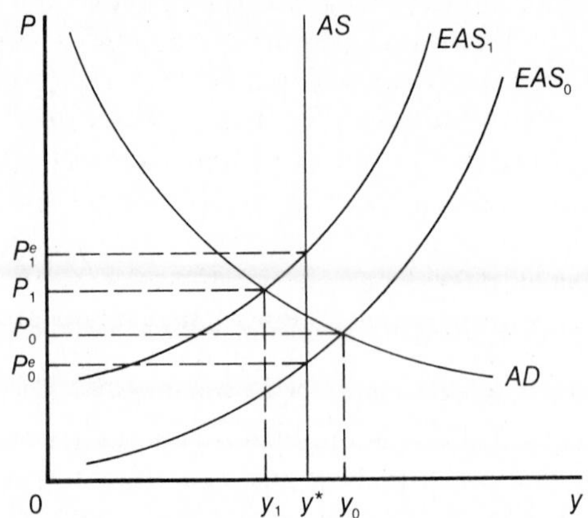

If the expected price level is fixed at P*, the *EAS* curve does not move. When aggregate demand is *AD**, the actual price level is *P**, and the economy is at full employment. If aggregate demand was AD_1, the equilibrium would be at point B with a higher price level and output level (P_1, y_1). If aggregate demand fell to AD_2, then the price level and output would fall to P_2 and y_2 at point C. Fluctuations in aggregate demand when the expected price level is constant produce procyclical movements in output and prices.

mined with the variables being considered here will either rise or fall. It is a fairly straightforward matter to work out the implications for the rate of interest by going back to the *IS-LM* analysis of Chapter 20. In the development here and in the rest of the book, with the exception of a brief section of Chapter 29, movements in interest rates, while occurring, will not be emphasized.) Suppose that for whatever of the above reasons the aggregate demand curve shifts from *AD** to AD_1. It is clear that with this new higher level of aggregate demand, there is only one point where the economy can come to an equilibrium, and that is the point marked B. At point B, output is y_1, and the price level is P_1.

How does this new equilibrium point B come about? Suppose the economy started out in the full-employment equilibrium at point A. Suppose then that aggregate demand suddenly increased from *AD** to AD_1. At the new higher level of aggregate demand, but with the price level remaining at *P**, there would be an excess demand for goods equivalent to the distance *AD* in Figure 26.3. This excess demand would generate rising prices, as people who sought to raise their expenditure would find it necessary to offer higher prices in order to acquire the goods that they were demanding. As the price level was forced upwards, the quantity of goods demanded would decline. This is shown in the diagram (Figure 26.3) as the arrows moving up the aggregate demand curve.

There would also be a response on the supply side of the economy. As the prices of some goods began to increase, firms, being well informed about the markets in which they operate and observing the rising price of their output, would start to increase their demand for labor. Their demand for labor curves would begin to shift upwards, as shown in frame (a) of Figure 26.2. This would produce a rise in the money wage but a fall in the real wage, and therefore, a rise in employment and a rise in the aggregate supply of goods. Households would be willing to supply additional labor in this situation because, although they see a rising money wage rate (and rising prices for the goods that are being sold by their own employers), they do not see the rise in the general price level and so continue to maintain given expectations about the general level of prices. As a result, they believe the real wage to have increased and willingly supply additional labor. There would, therefore, on the supply side, be a tendency for the economy to slide up its aggregate supply curve from A to B, as shown by the arrows in Figure 26.3. As the price level increased, the excess of demand over supply would be choked off, and the economy would come to rest at point B, with firms satisfied that they were supplying the profit-maximizing quantity and households satisfied that they were supplying the right quantity of labor and buying the right quantity of goods.

Next, consider what would happen if aggregate demand was to fall. Specifically, suppose aggregate demand fell from AD^* to AD_2. This aggregate demand curve cuts the expectations-augmented aggregate supply curve at C. This is the new equilibrium point, with the price level P_2 and y_2. To see how this equilibrium comes about, perform a conceptual experiment similar to that which you have just performed in the case of a rise in aggregate demand. Suppose that the price level is initially at P^* and there has just been a fall in aggregate demand to AD_2. In such a case, there will be a cutback in demand, and there will be an excess of supply over demand equal to the distance AE in Figure 26.3. This excess supply will cause prices to fall. As prices begin to fall, firms' demand for labor curves [frame (a) of Figure 26.2] will be shifting downwards. The supply of labor curve would not shift, however, because households continue to expect the price level to remain at its initial level. Thus, the amount of labor employed and the amount of output supplied will fall. The actual real wage will rise since, although the money wage rate falls, it does so by a smaller proportion than does the price level. The expected real wage rate, however, will fall since the money wage rate falls while the expected price level remains constant. As a result of these actions the economy will travel downwards along its expectations-augmented aggregate supply curve from A to C, as shown by the arrows. Households will move along their demand curves, resulting in a movement along the aggregate demand curve from E to C. At point C there is a balance between supply and demand, and there is no further tendency for the price level or the level of output to change.

Although the analysis that has just been performed has been done explicitly within the framework of the new classical theory of aggregate supply, the same broad predictions would have been generated if the new Keynesian theory had been used. In that case, however, the output movements would have been greater and the price movements less than in the new classical case. You can easily verify this by checking back to the comparison of the new Keynesian and new classical expectations-augmented aggregate supply curves. Since the Keynesian curve is flatter than the classical curve, swings in aggregate demand have bigger output and smaller price effects in the Keynesian case than in the classical case.

Key Assumption of Equilibrium Analysis

We assume that the equilibrating processes just described that move the economy from position A to position B when aggregate demand rises and from position A to position C when aggregate demand falls occur quickly enough for points A, B, and C to be the only points observed.

Summary of Effects of Change in Aggregate Demand on Output and Price Level

We can now summarize the effects of a rise or fall in aggregate demand on the level of output and prices:

1. If the expected price level is constant and aggregate demand rises, then output and the price level will both rise.
2. If the expected price level is constant and aggregate demand falls, then output and the price level will both fall.

Effects of a Change in Aggregate Demand on Employment and Wages

The effects on the level of employment, money wages, and the real wage will now be analyzed. Because of the way in which the aggregate demand experiment has been set up, these effects can immediately be read off by referring back to Figure 26.2.

First, consider the case of a rise in aggregate demand. This moves the economy, as you saw in Figure 26.3, to position B. Position B is also shown in Figure 26.2, so that you can easily see the effects on the labor market. At the price level P_1, which is the consequence of a rise in aggregate demand to AD_1, the demand for labor curve will shift to the right and be in the position shown as $n^d(P_1)$. This produces a higher money wage, W_1, and a higher employment level, n_1. It also produces a lower real wage. The real wage falls because the money wage rises by less than the rise in the price level. (Refer back to Chapter 24, Figure 24.1, and the associated discussion if you cannot see that this is true.) Indeed, it is the fall in the real wage that induces a higher level of employment. Firms, seeing that the real wage has fallen, find it profitable to hire additional workers. Households, on the other hand, having a fixed expectation of the price level, think that the real wage has increased and therefore are willing to supply more labor.

Next, consider the case of a cut in aggregate demand. If aggregate demand is cut to the curve AD_2, it will intersect the expectations-augmented aggregate supply curve at point C in Figure 26.3. Point C is also shown in frame (c) of Figure 26.2. You can see that at that price level, the demand for labor curve is shown as $n^d(P_2)$, and the equilibrium levels of wages and employment are W_2 and n_2. Thus a cut in aggregate demand leads to a cut in the money wage and in the level of employment. In this situation, *real wages* will have increased. This occurs because the price level will have fallen by more than the money wage has fallen. Firms, knowing this, will cut back on their demand for labor. Households will not resist this cutback in the demand for labor because, as far as they are concerned, the real wage that they have been offered has fallen. This arises because the money wage has fallen, while the expected price level has remained constant.

Although the above effects have been stated in terms of the new classical theory, similar effects would occur in the new Keynesian case. The key difference between the two would be that in the new Keynesian case, households would be knocked off the supply of labor curve. When aggregate demand increased to AD_1, the money wage rate would remain constant, the price level would rise, and the real wage would fall. This would induce an increase in the demand for labor that would not be matched by an increase in the supply of labor. Nevertheless, workers, because of the assumed nature of the contract they have with their employers, would be required to supply the extra labor even though this was in excess of their labor supply.

In the reverse case, when aggregate demand falls to AD_2, workers are knocked off their supply curves in the opposite direction. In this case, the price level falls, so that with a fixed money wage rate, the real wage rises, thereby lowering the demand for labor. Firms now hire less labor than would like to work. In this case, there will be unemployment over and above any natural unemployment in the economy, and it will have the appearance of being involuntary, in the sense that if they could have signed different contracts, workers would have done so.

Summary of the Effects of a Change in Aggregate Demand with a Constant Expected Price Level

To summarize, the effects of a rise in aggregate demand with a fixed expected price level are as follows:

1. With a fixed expected price level, a rise in aggregate demand will raise output, raise the price level, raise the level of employment, and lower the real wage. Unemployment will fall below the natural rate of unemployment.
2. With a fixed expected price level, a cut in aggregate demand will lower the level of output, lower the price level, lower the level of employment, and raise real wages. It will also create unemployment in excess of the natural rate of unemployment.

This completes the formal analysis of the effects of a change in aggregate demand on the levels of output, employment, the real wage, and the price level—when price expectations are fixed.

You may find it useful, to ensure that you have understood the analysis that lies behind the movement of the economy from position A to position B (Figure 26.3) in the face of a rise in aggregate demand and from position A to position C (Figure 26.3) in the face of a fall in aggregate demand, to check that these movements are consistent with people's rational maximizing choices as described in the story set out at the end of Chapter 23.

Although positions B and C (Figure 26.3) in this economy are equilibrium positions, they differ from equilibrium A in a fundamental respect. That is, they cannot be sustained forever, whereas position A can. To see why they cannot be sustained forever takes us into a discussion of how expectations are formed and changed, and this will be the subject of the next chapter. Before turning to that, however, let us deal with the final task of this chapter.

D. Effects of a Change in the Expected Price Level with Constant Aggregate Demand

Although the title of this chapter is "Equilibrium Income, Employment, and the Price Level with Fixed Expectations," it will be useful if we analyze what happens if the expected price level changes. Let us start the economy out at full-employment equilibrium such as that depicted by P^* for the price level and y^* for real income, in Figure 26.4. These points lie at the intersection of the aggregate demand curve, *AD*, and the expectations-augmented aggregate supply curve, *EAS*, and are also on the aggregate supply curve, *AS*. The expected price level evidently will be P^*, the same as the actual price level.

Hold the level of aggregate demand constant at *AD*, but now imagine that the expected price level for some reason rises to P_1^e. What are the effects of such a change? You already know that lying behind the *EAS* curve is a supply of labor curve that itself depends on the expected price level. A rise in the expected price level will shift the supply of labor curve upwards and by the same percentage amount as the rise in the expected price level. This in turn will shift the *EAS* curve upwards to become the curve labelled EAS_1 in Figure 26.4. We know this because we know that the *EAS* curve cuts the *AS* curve at the expected price level. The new *EAS* curve intersects the fixed *AD* curve at the price level P_1 and the income level, y_1. This position will be the equilibrium when the expected price level is P_1^e and aggregate demand is given by the curve *AD*. In this situation, the economy will be producing less than its full-employment output level. The actual price level will be below the expected

Figure 26.4
The Effects of a Rise or Fall in the Expected Price Level When Aggregate Demand Is Constant

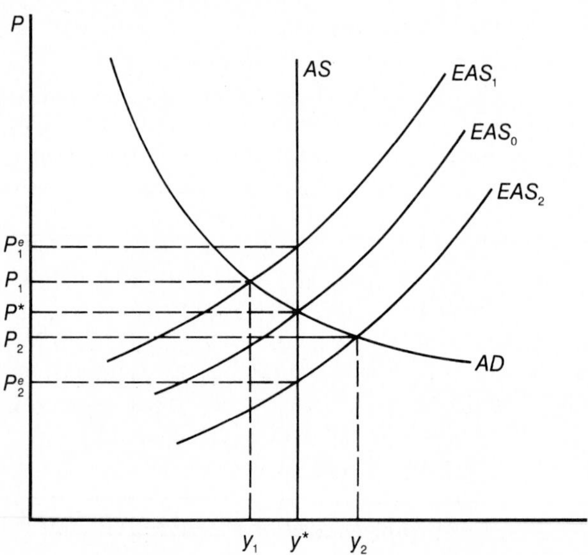

If aggregate demand is fixed, then the *AD* curve does not move. When the expected price level rises, the *EAS* curve moves to EAS_1, so that the price level rises to P_1, and output falls to y_1. If the expected price level falls to P_2^e, the actual price level falls to P_2, and income rises to y_2. Changes in the expected price level with constant aggregate demand lead to countercyclical movements in output and prices.

price level. Notice that this situation (P_1, y_1) in Figure 26.4 is comparable to point C in Figure 26.3.

Returning to Figure 26.4, let us next suppose that the expected price level was to fall from P^* to P_2^e. In this case, the *EAS* curve would shift downwards to become the curve labelled EAS_2. Again, we know this because the *EAS* curve cuts the *AS* curve at the expected price level. As before, we shall hold the level of aggregate demand constant at *AD*. The new *EAS* curve cuts the *AD* curve at the price level P_2 and income level y_2. In this situation there will be a higher than full-employment level of output, and the price level will have fallen relative to P^* but will now be above its expected level. This equilibrium (P_2, y_2 in Figure 26.4) is comparable to position B in Figure 26.3.

You will now be able to see some clear similarities in, but also some important differences between, the effects of a change in aggregate demand when the expected price level is constant and the effects of a change in the expected price level when aggregate demand is constant. The similarities are these: Only when the expected price level and actual price level are equal to each other is the economy at full employment. If the actual price level is below the expected price level, then output is below its full-employment level. This can come about either because of a rise in the expected price level with constant aggregate demand or because of a drop in aggregate demand with a constant expected price level. In the opposite case, if the actual price level is greater than the expected price level, then output will be above its full-employment level. This can arise either because of a rise in aggregate demand with a constant expected price level, or because of a fall in the expected price level with a constant level of aggregate demand.

The differences between the two experiments in the preceding section and this one are the following: A rise in aggregate demand with a fixed expected price level raises both output and the price level, and a fall in aggregate demand lowers both output and the price level, so that output and prices move in the same direction as each other. A change in the expected price level with a constant level of aggregate demand leads to changes in output and in the price level that move in opposite directions to each other.

Aside from these differences in the directions of movement of output and prices between the two cases, all other properties of the equilibria analyzed are the same. The detailed story told concerning how the economy moves from one position to another in the previous section applies with equal force here.

The analysis of the effects of a change in inflation expectations on real wages and on the labor market are easy to figure out. You know that anything that lowers output below its equilibrium level must also lower employment. You also know that anything that lowers employment must also raise the real wage. From this you can immediately figure out that a rise in the expected price level must lead to a rise in the money wage that exceeds the rise in the price level, and a drop in the expected price level must cut the money wage rate by more than the cut in the price level.

We also know, however, if the labor market is to be in equilibrium (continuing to operate with the new classical model), that anything that lowers the equilibrium level of output and employment must lower the expected real wage. Conversely, anything that raises output above its full-employment level must raise the expected real wage. From this we can immediately figure out that a rise in the expected price level must raise the money wage rate by more than it raises the actual price level, but by less than it raises the expected price level. The effect of this is to raise the actual real wage but lower the expected real wage. Conversely, a cut in the expected price level must lower the money wage by more than it lowers the price level, but by less than the amount by which the expected price level has fallen. In this case, the actual real wage will have fallen, but the expected real wage will have risen.

You have now seen how changes in aggregate demand affect output and prices when the expected price level is constant and, also, how changes in the expected price level affect the *actual* price level as well as the level of output. Evidently, expectations of the price level are of crucial importance in influencing the behavior both of the actual price level and other real variables in the economy. It is the task of the next chapter to investigate more thoroughly how expectations of the price level are themselves formed and what factors lead to changes in those expectations.

Summary

A. Full-Employment Equilibrium

Full-employment equilibrium values of output, employment, unemployment, and the real wage occur when the price level is equal to the expected price level. The unemployment present at full-employment equilibrium is called the *natural rate of unemployment.*

B. A Simple Diagram to Characterize Full-Employment Equilibrium

Figure 26.1 is a diagram of full-employment equilibrium, and you should be thoroughly familiar with it. You should also understand that it is identical to the equilibrium in the basic model that we examined in Chapter 10.

C. Effects of a Change in Aggregate Demand with a Fixed Expected Price Level

If the expected price level is fixed, a rise in aggregate demand will raise the level of output, employment, and the price level. It will also lower the real wage and will make unemployment fall below its natural rate.

When the expected price level is fixed and aggregate demand falls, there will be a fall in output, in employment, and in the price level. The real wage will rise, and unemployment will rise above its natural rate.

D. Effects of a Change in the Expected Price Level with Constant Aggregate Demand

If aggregate demand is fixed, a rise in the expected price level will raise the actual price level but by less than the expected price level has increased, and it will lower output. Real wages and unemployment will rise, and employment will fall. Money wages will rise by more than the price level but by less than the expected price level. When aggregate demand is fixed and the expected price level falls, the actual price level will fall, and output will rise. The fall in the actual price level will be less than the fall in the expected price level. Real wages will fall, but expected real wages will rise. Unemployment will also fall below its natural rate.

Review Questions

1. Define *full-employment equilibrium.*

2. Explain why there will be some unemployment at full-employment equilibrium.

3. Define the *natural unemployment rate.* Is the natural unemployment rate affected by the price level? Why or why not? Explain.

4. (a) Characterize full-employment equilibrium in a set of diagrams like those shown in Figure 26.1.

(b) Now introduce a minimum-wage law that fixes the *money wage* above the equilibrium and work out the new equilibrium level of output, employment, and prices. (This is a tricky question.)

5. Consider Figure 26.2. Suppose the expected price level was to rise to P_1. What would happen to the *EAS* curve? Draw a new curve to illustrate your answer.

6. Why does the *EAS* curve slope upwards?

7. What happens to the levels of: (a) output, (b) employment, (c) unemployment, (d) the money wage, (e) the real wage, and (f) the price level if the money supply rises but the expected price level remains constant?

8. What happens to all the variables listed in (a) to (f) of Question 7 if the expected price level falls, while the money supply remains constant?

9. What happens to all the variables listed in (a) to (f) of Question 7 if both the expected price level and aggregate demand rise by the *same* percentage amount?

10. Review the following terms or concepts: *rational maximizing behavior* and *equilibrium.*

27

Price Level Expectations

We saw, when we dealt with the neoclassical synthesis, that a major shortcoming of that body of analysis is its lack of a theory of how inflation expectations are formed and what causes them to change. In the new theories of aggregate supply developed in Chapters 24 and 25, the expected price level has been seen to be a crucial variable that influences the economy. So far, however, we have made no attempt to explain where the expected price level comes from or what causes it to change. It is certain that both the expected price level and the expected rate of inflation do change. We saw that we were unable to make any sense at all of the Great Depression or the 1970s within the neoclassical framework without explicit allowance for "exogenous" changes in inflation expectations.

Not only do the *expected* inflation rate and *expected* price level play important roles in our theories of macroeconomics, they also are featured in much of the more popular (if imprecise) discussions on inflation. We often hear, for example, that there is an "inflation psychology" that is considered to be one of the major causes of inflation.

Thus, both in our theories and in popular discussion, the role played by expectations is central. The time has come to examine the determination of expectations more closely, and to move beyond the assumption that they are exogenous. The two central questions that this chapter deals with are: What determines the expected price level and expected inflation rate? What factors lead to changes in the expected price level and expected inflation rate? You are going to discover that, paradoxical though it may seem, there is no rational basis for a view that inflation can be *caused* by an "inflation psychology"—by inflation expectations. Rather, the very things that generate inflation also generate inflation expectations.

The chapter is organized around six tasks, which are to:

(a) Understand the relationship between the expected price level and the expected rate of inflation.

(b) Understand the distinction between a subjective expectation and a conditional mathematical expectation.

(c) Understand why wrong expectations are costly.

(d) Understand the concept of a rational expectation.
(e) Understand the concept of the rational expectation of the price level.
(f) Know how to work out the rational expectation of the price level.

A. The Expected Price Level and Expected Rate of Inflation

You are already familiar with the distinction between inflation and the price level. You know that inflation is the percentage rate of change in the price level. You also know that in the analysis that we are doing in this part of the book, we are abstracting from inflation. That is, we are conducting an analysis that presumes that the average rate of inflation is zero. This means that the price level is fluctuating around some constant value. Nevertheless, even though we are abstracting from inflation, it is important that you know the connection between the expected rate of inflation and the expected price level. This connection follows directly from the definition of actual inflation and its relation to the actual price level. Equation 27.1 defines the rate of inflation (π) at a particular point in time (t) as:

$$\pi_t = \left(\frac{P_t - P_{t-1}}{P_{t-1}}\right) \times 100 \qquad \textbf{(27.1)}$$

Here, P_t is the price level at date t, and P_{t-1} is the price level at day $t - 1$. The rate of inflation at t is the change in prices from $t - 1$ to t, expressed as a percentage of the prices that prevailed at the previous point in time. For example, if the previous price level was 95 and the current price level is 100, the rate of inflation will be given by

$$\pi_t = \left(\frac{100 - 95}{95}\right) \times 100$$
$$= 5.2\%$$

The expected rate of inflation and the expected price level are related to each other by an equation similar to the above; that is,

$$\pi_t^e = \left(\frac{P_t^e - P_{t-1}}{P_{t-1}}\right) \times 100 \qquad \textbf{(27.2)}$$

This says that the expected rate of inflation is equal to the expected price level minus the previous period's price level, expressed as a percentage of the previous period's price level. As before, suppose the previous period's price level was 95, but the expected price level is 99. Then,

$$\pi_t^e = \left(\frac{99 - 95}{95}\right) \times 100$$
$$= 4.2\%$$

Notice that the expected rate of inflation is the expected percentage change in the price level and not the percentage change in the expected price level. In fact, the change in the expected price level is not a very interesting concept. You could calculate the change in the expected price level if you wished. It would be this period's expected price level minus the previous period's expected price level, expressed as a percentage of that previous period's expected price level.

It is clear from the above that there is a close connection between the expected inflation rate and the expected price level. For the analysis that we are going to be doing in the rest of this part of the book, the distinction between the expected price level and the expected rate of inflation will not be important since we are doing all our analysis on the presumption that, on the average, inflation is zero. (For many purposes, however, the distinction is important.) The key thing to note for current purposes is that, in order to calculate the expected inflation rate, you need to calculate the expected price level. It is expectations about the price level that we shall focus on in the rest of this chapter. We are going to get to that, however, by a slightly roundabout route and shall not reach a good understanding of how the expected price level is determined until later in this chapter.

Let us now begin the first of three preliminary tasks that will lead us to an understanding of how price level expectations are formed.

B. The Distinction Between a Subjective Expectation and a Conditional Mathematical Expectation

Subjective Expectation

The term *expectation* has two distinct meanings. In ordinary speech it is used to describe a more or less *vague feeling* about some future event. This is a subjective expectation. For example, we might be planning to travel by car along a congested highway and expect that it will take an hour to complete our journey; or we might be planning to travel by bus and expect the bus to be running 10 minutes behind schedule because of bad weather. Another example concerns the expectations of a skilled pool player. Such a person might have an expectation as to what will happen when the cue is aligned in a particular direction and applied to the cue ball with a particular direction of spin and force. That expectation may be, for example, that the second ball is dispatched to the center-right pocket and that the cue ball comes to rest lined up for an easy next shot.

Typically, we do not explicitly analyze the reasons why we hold the expectations that we do. We have subjective feelings, which, on the average, seem to be right, and we do not consciously examine the sources of these feelings. The pool player, for example, does not ask himself from where his expectation comes. He simply knows how to play the game and uses a well-developed instinct and skill to achieve the appropriate movements of the balls.

A subjective expectation, then, is simply a feeling that an individual has about the likely consequences of some particular action or as to the likely outcome of some particular event.

Conditional Mathematical Expectation

There is a more precise usage of the term expectation—a conditional mathematical expectation. A mathematical expectation is nothing other than an *average*. An example will make it easy to understand this. Suppose we have 3000 cards: 1000 of them are printed with the number 4 on one side, another 1000 with the number 5, and another 1000 with the number 6. These cards are put into a bag and are shaken up so that they are thoroughly mixed. Then, 300 cards are drawn from the bag at random. You are asked to predict what the average of the numbers drawn will be. You know that there are three kinds of cards in the bag, and that one-third of them have the number 4, one-third have the number 5, and one-third the number 6. Since the cards have been shuffled very thoroughly and have been drawn at random, you will predict that, on the average, out of 300 cards drawn, 100 will have the number 4, 100 the number 5, and 100 the number 6. You calculate the average of this and you arrive at a prediction that the average of all the cards drawn will be 5. You have just calculated a mathematical expectation.

A conditional mathematical expectation is a mathematical expectation calculated when some information is already given. For example, suppose in the numbered card game described above, you were told that of the 300 cards drawn, 200 were numbered 6. (This would be an improbable, although possible, outcome.) You are now asked to predict the average value of all 300 cards drawn. You know that there are as many 4's as 5's in the bag, so you will expect that, of the remaining cards, 50 will be 4's and 50 will be 5's. The average that you will calculate from 200 6's, 50 4's, and 50 5's is

$$\left(\frac{200}{600}\right) \times 6 + \left(\frac{50}{100}\right) \times 4 + \left(\frac{50}{300}\right) \times 5 = 5.5$$

You have now calculated a conditional mathematical expectation or, more simply, a conditional expectation. You have calculated the expected average value (expected value) of the cards, *given* that two-thirds of them are 6's.

Let us go back to those earlier examples of subjective expectations and see whether we can think of a mathematical expectation interpretation of them.

Consider first of all your car journey along a congested highway. Many factors will determine the number of minutes that it will take for you to arrive at your destination. It will depend on the number of cars on the road ahead of you, whether there are any road works that have closed one or more of the lanes, whether or not there are any accidents blocking the road, and perhaps a thousand other difficult to enumerate things. Suppose, however, that you have travelled this particular part of this highway many times in the past. You have a stock of experience from those previous journeys concerning the length of time that it takes. If you had actually kept a written record of the number of minutes it took each time you went on this particular journey, then you could calculate the average journey time. That calculation would be a mathematical expectation.

You may, however, be able to do better than that. It may be that you know that in certain circumstances the journey is quicker than others. Perhaps you know that if you begin your journey between 8:00 A.M. and 9:00 A.M. or between 5:00 P.M. and 6:00 P.M. it takes longer than if you set out at other times of the day. You might also know that the journey typically takes less time on Tuesdays, Wednesdays, and Thursdays than it does on Mondays and Fridays, or that it takes longer in rainy or icy weather than on a sunny day. Given all this extra information, you could calculate the average number of minutes it takes you to complete this particular journey at different times of the day, different days of the week, in different weather conditions, and allowing for other factors that you have noticed affect the outcome. These averages would be conditional expectations. They would be conditional on the information concerning the time of the day, day of the week, state of the weather, and so on.

We could tell an identical story concerning the number of minutes that you expect to have to wait for a bus.

In the case of the pool player example, if the pool player could solve complicated geometrical problems in a very short span of time in his head and program himself to carry out the instructions implied by those solutions, he could make the cue ball follow exactly the trajectory and with exactly the force required to achieve his objective. This would be a rather complicated mathematical expectation calculation; it would be the calculation of a mathematical expectation of the paths of (at least) two balls. Of course, just as in the case of the numbered cards in the bag, there will be no certainty as to the outcome in any of these examples. Unless we were to pull all 3000 cards from the bag, we would not be able to predict for sure the average value of the cards drawn. Likewise, going back to the car journey example, unless we knew absolutely everything about the conditions of the road ahead of us, we would not be able to make an exact prediction concerning the time that it would take to arrive at our destination. We would, nevertheless, be able to calculate a mathematical expectation. That is, we would be able to calculate the expected value of the relevant variable conditional on all the information available.

C. Why Wrong Expectations are Costly

Although expectations are sometimes formed purely for fun, so that wrong expectations have very little consequence other than generating mild displeasure or surprise, you will be able to think of many examples, especially those that impinge on economic behavior, where forming a wrong expectation will lead an individual to incur costs that would be better avoided. The costs arising from wrong expectations come in a variety of sizes and forms.

Consider the examples that were introduced in the previous section when we looked at the distinction between subjective and mathematical expectations. Forming an inaccurate assessment of how long a particular journey would take could have a variety of consequences. Suppose that you expected a journey to take one hour, but in fact it turned out to take an hour and a half. It may be that this is of very little consequence, causing you perhaps simply to have a half an hour less time for shopping, sitting on the beach, or doing whatever it is that you are planning to do at the end of your journey. At the other extreme, it could be very costly indeed. It could cause you to miss the departure time of an airplane on which you have a nonrefundable ticket, or to miss the beginning of a play or concert. Of course, the more serious the consequences of misestimating the length of the journey, the more time you are likely to allow yourself. Even that, however, is not costless. It might involve forcing yourself out of bed at an earlier hour than seems to you ideal, or missing out on some other pleasurable or profitable opportunity.

Next, consider the numbered card game example that we used in the previous section. This is a simplified version of many games that form the backbone of the economy of Las Vegas. Suppose that you are running a casino in that town, and that in the operation of your roulette wheel, you offer the same odds on red as on black. You do this because on most roulette wheels the number of red spots and number of black spots are equal, so that there is an equal chance that a ball will land in one color or the other. Further suppose though that someone has tampered with your roulette wheel and, in fact, 55 percent of the spots are black and 45 percent are red. Let us further suppose that you did not bother to inspect the wheel too carefully and are operating on the *expectation* that the wheel is a standard one with half the spots red and half the spots black. It will not be long before astute investors are putting money on the black spots, thereby turning a nice profit and leaving you rushing for a lawyer and seeking to declare bankruptcy.

This is an example that illustrates rather nicely a further important distinction. It is the distinction between being wrong about an *individual event* and being wrong *on the average*. There is no way in which a casino operator can be right about every single event. Sometimes a client gets lucky and wins an enormous amount of money. Events that have a low probability do happen sometimes. It is possible, nevertheless, to avoid being wrong on the average. That is, it is possible to form expectations such that if we took the average of all our expectations over a period of time and compared them with the average of the events that occurred over that same period of time, although each individual event would not have been correctly predicted, on the average, the outcome and the prediction would agree. In the case of the casino operator, on the average, black was coming up 55 percent of the time and red was coming up 45 percent of the time. The roulette wheel operator was working on the presumption that the two colors would come up 50 percent of the time each, which meant he was wrong on the average.

There is, of course, nothing we can do about being wrong in the case of individual events. We simply have to take random things as they come. What we can do, however, is to try to avoid being wrong on the average. By so doing we will minimize the errors that we make in particular cases. We will not eliminate the errors, but we will be reducing their consequences to the smallest possible level.

All the examples of costs that have been discussed above have been in areas other than those with which macroeconomics is centrally concerned. Let us now consider some macroeconomic examples. Expectations have arisen in our model because of their effects on the supply of labor. Suppose a household has formed an expectation of the price level and makes a labor supply decision on the basis of it, and then discovers that the expectation was wrong. If too high a price level was expected, then too low a real wage would have been calculated, and too little work will have been done. The household will wind up having consumed more leisure than is now regarded as ideal and will have a lower income to spend on consumption goods than is regarded as ideal. Conversely, if the expectation of the price level was too low, then the calculated real wage would be too high, and the household would wind up doing more work and having a larger income and more consumption goods but less leisure than seems, from the perspective of the individual, ideal.

More important economic examples in terms of costliness of errors arise in the area of capital investment decisions. Firms making multimillion- or even billion-dollar investment decisions have to form expectations about the future demand for particular products, the costs of labor, and other inputs. Errors made in such expectations can have enormous costs.

Notice that in the labor supply example (and if I had developed it more fully, the same would apply to the capital investment examples) costs of wrong expectations are symmetric. Expecting a higher price than occurs is just as bad as expecting a lower one. Also notice that the economic example is like the casino example—one in which it is quite impossible for expectations to be always correct but one in which expectations could be correct on the average.

If wrong expectations inflict costs on individuals, it seems reasonable to suppose that they will try to avoid those costs. Of course, the bigger the costs, the harder people will try to avoid making mistakes. We could summarize this by saying they will try to form their expectations rationally.

Let us now go on to apply the ideas of a subjective expectation—a vague feeling about some likely event—and a mathematical expectation—a precise calculation of the expectation of some outcome based on all the information that is relevant and available—and make more precise the concept of a rational expectation.

D. Rational Expectation

Definition

The definition of a rational expectation is as follows.[1] An expectation is said to be rational when the subjective expectation coincides with the conditional mathematical expectation based on all available information. Notice that the definition says that *when* a mathematical and a subjective expectation coincide, *then* the expectation is rational. It does not say that a rational expectation is arrived at by performing all the complicated calculations that it would be necessary to perform in order to arrive at the appropriate conditional mathematical expectation. As in the example given above, an expectation about the length of time it would take to complete a particular journey would

[1]The concept of rational expectations presented here is that of John F. Muth, "Rational Expectations and the Theory of Price Movements," *Econometrica*, 29 (July 1961), 315–35. This concept was first introduced into macroeconomics by Robert E. Lucas, Jr., in "Some International Evidence on the Output–Inflation Tradeoff," *The American Economic Review*, 63, (September 1973), 326–34.

be rational if the expectation arrived at by instinct, intuition, or judgment, based on casual observation, turned out to coincide with the expectation based on a careful and systematic recording of all previous experience and on the calculation of a conditional expectation from those data.

An alternative way of thinking about a rational expectation is to regard it as implying the absence of *systematic* error. If people formed expectations that repeatedly and systematically led them astray in an avoidable way, then those expectations would not be rational.

Some Further Intuition on the Meaning of Rational Expectations

In order to get a better feel for what a rational expectation is, it might be helpful to consider expectations of a particular variable in which man has always been interested, namely, the future state of the weather. There are many ways in which we can arrive at an expectation of the future state of the weather. One would be to turn on the appropriate TV channel and read the latest forecasts being put out by the weather bureau. Another would be to watch the squirrels and observe how many nuts they are stockpiling. Yet a further method would be to recall the various traditional sayings, such as the proposition about the remaining length of winter and the behavior of groundhogs, or the proposition about March beginning like a lion and ending like a lamb, or vice versa. All of these would be methods of forming a view about some future state of the weather.

At the present time and in the present state of knowledge, it is clear that the rational expectation of the future state of the weather is obtained by employing the first of these devices—the forecasts of the weather bureau. Expectations based on the other procedures, unless they are based on well-established empirical regularities, would not be rational. It may be, of course, that the squirrel actually does have some antennae that enable it to know what the likely future winter length is going to be and to react accordingly by stockpiling the appropriate quantity of nuts. In that event, it would be rational to base an expectation of the likely future winter length on the basis of that observed behavior. This simply says that a rational expectation can be based on any information, provided that information can be demonstrated to be *relevant* to the forecasting of the future value of the variable of interest.

Although, in the current state of knowledge, forming a rational expectation of the weather involves the taking of meteorological observations followed by the use of meteorological theory to generate inferences concerning the implications of those observations for the future course of the weather, such predictions are not exact. This inexactness arises from the fact that meteorological information collection is far from total. It would cost an infinite or close to an infinite amount of resources to collect enough information to make predictions about the state and movement of every last molecule of air. Rather than do that, we invest a smaller amount of resources in sampling the atmosphere at various levels and in various places and make inferences concerning the behavior between those points. Further, we do not evaluate intricate, complicated meteorological models involving millions and millions of differential equations. Rather, the meteorologists rely on simpler theories, which, on the average, work out all right, although they do not work out in every case. So, in the area of weather, a rational expectation is an expectation that is based on all the information that is available, even though that information is far from the total set of information that one could imagine being available. This means that a rational expectation will not always be right. It will only be right *on the average*.

Notice, that in this meteorological example, we do not require that each and every individual be an expert meteorologist and be able to work out the weather forecast for himself. All that is necessary is that there be a body of science, and a systematic observation process to inform that body of science, to enable the scientific community to make the relevant predictions. The rest of us can then consume the fruits of that scientific activity.

E. Rational Expectation of the Price Level

The Concept of Rational Expectation Applied to the Price Level

A rational expectation of the price level follows very directly from the examples that have been introduced so far. The rational expectation of the price level is the price level that is predicted on the basis of all the available information at the time at which the expectation is formed. Such information might include all the past history of the key economic variables, such as the price level itself, output, the real wage, the money wage, the money supply, and many other economic variables.

Expectations (forecasts) concerning economic variables are typically made available to the general public by the economics profession in much the same way as weather forecasts are made available by the meteorological profession. Such journals as *The Wall Street Journal*, *Business Week*, and *The Economist* bring together and appraise forecasts of diverse groups of economic analysts. Of course, economic science is less settled than is meteorology. There are, as you were made aware of in Chapter 1, a variety of schools of thought concerning the way the economy works. In the present state of economic knowledge it is necessary, therefore, for each individual, in forming a rational expectation, to weigh the "economic weather forecasts" that are put out by the economics profession against his or her own personal knowledge, information, and experience. Each individual's expectation will be arrived at using a large variety of inputs. This expectation will be a rational expectation if it coincides with the conditional expectation based on all the information that is available.

A More Precise Definition of the Rational Expectation of the Price Level

We can make the definition of the rational expectation of the price level (or the inflation rate) more precise in a way that utilizes the brilliant insights of John F. Muth.[2] The ideas advanced by Muth are fairly deep and apparently difficult to grasp. Let us proceed with some care. First, let us remind ourselves (and keep on reminding ourselves) that a rational expectation is just an

[2] Ibid.

average. Second, consider the question (which seems at first thought totally irrelevant to what we have just been discussing) "What is theory?" Theory is, of course, a set of propositions designed to make predictions about the behavior of some variable or variables. A theory of the price level (or the inflation rate), for example, is designed to make predictions about prices. Now no theory, of course, is exact. The best that we can expect of any theory is that it will be right on the average. This can be put more directly: All theories are designed to make predictions about the average behavior of the phenomena that they address. Realizing that theories are designed to make predictions about averages, and also realizing that a rational expectation is nothing other than an average, led John Muth to a neat and powerful operational definition of a rational expectation. That definition states that *a rational expectation is the same thing as the prediction of the relevant theory.* Thus, the rational expectation of the price level is the same thing as the prediction of the relevant theory for determining the price level.

This is not, of course, to say that the rational expectation of the price level is the prediction of *any* theory of the price level. Theories that are clearly wrong would not yield predictions that coincided with the rational expectation. Only a theory that is not wrong would do so.

Now, of course, in the current state of knowledge, we do not know, at least not with any certainty, what the relevant theory for predicting prices is. We are still in that stage of scientific inquiry of advancing alternative hypotheses and determining which if any of these alternatives is compatible with the facts. Although we do not know for sure that any particular theory is the correct theory, each time we advance a theory we do so in the hope that it will turn out to be the right one. Where that theory contains as part of its structure people's expectations of magnitudes predicted by the theory, the only internally consistent assumption that we can make concerning the way in which those expectations are formed is to postulate that they are formed in the same way as that particular theory says the variable is determined. In so doing, we have a very powerful technique for developing, testing, and usually, although hopefully not always, rejecting a succession of alternative hypotheses concerning the determination of the macroeconomic variables.

You may be suspecting that to assume that people form their expectations in the same way that a particular theory says the variables in question are determined somehow stacks the cards in favor of the theory by making the predictions self-fulfilling. Nothing could in fact be further from the truth. It is harder to get theories to pass the test of prediction when they incorporate rational expectations than when they adopt some more mechanical ad hoc expectations hypotheses such as that embodied in the neoclassical model. A moment's reflection will convince you of the reason for this. We saw, when examining the co-movements of inflation and deviations of output from trend both in the Great Depression years and over the last decade (in Chapter 22), that provided we were willing to make ad hoc assumptions about how the expected inflation rate changed each year, we would be able to account for the facts using the neoclassical model. Clearly if we restricted ourselves by insisting that the expectations of inflation should not be allowed to conveniently change so as to "fit the facts" but evolve only to coincide with the predictions of the theory, then we would be giving ourselves no additional "degrees of freedom" with which to explain the facts. By insisting that expectations be formed in such a way that they coincide with the predictions of the model places greater demands on the model and forces us to work harder to find the right one.

In the next section we shall go on to employ these ideas to calculate the rational expectation of the price level. Specifically, we shall use the theory developed in the previous three chapters that makes predictions about the price level, and we shall assume that people's expectations of the price level coincides with the prediction of that theory.

F. How to Work Out the Rational Expectation of the Price Level

The Boot-Laces Problem!

There is a preliminary problem that needs some discussion, arising from a key difference between the rational expectation of the price level and the rational expectation of something like how hot the summer will be or the amount of rain that is going to fall tomorrow. Tomorrow's weather is not going to be affected, at least as far as we know on the basis of existing information, by our expectations of what it will be.

From the work already done in Chapter 26, however, you know that this is *not* true of the price level. The actual price level next year, according to our theory, will depend on our expectation of the price level next year. To see this more clearly, consider Figure 27.1. It shows the goods market as described by the theory developed in Chapter 26. The vertical axis measures the price level, and the horizontal axis measures the level of output. The curve *AD* is the

Figure 27.1
The Effect of the Expected Price Level on the Actual Price Level

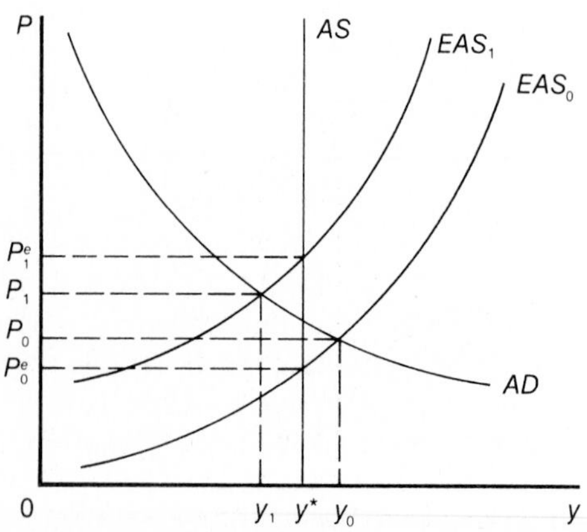

Aggregate demand is held constant at the curve *AD*. If the expected price level is P^e_0, then the expectations-augmented aggregate supply curve is EAS_0, and the actual price level is P_0 (and income is y_0). If the expected price level is P^e_1, then the *EAS* curve is EAS_1, and the actual price level is P_1 (and income is y_1). Thus holding everything else constant, the higher the expected price level, the higher will be the actual price level.

aggregate demand curve, and AS is the aggregate supply curve derived from the labor market equilibrium conditions and the production function. The curve EAS_0 is the expectations-augmented aggregate supply curve drawn for an expected price level equal to P_0^e. Notice that the curve EAS_0 cuts the aggregate supply curve AS at the price level P_0^e. If the expected price level is P_0^e, so that we are on EAS_0, and if aggregate demand is AD, then the intersection of EAS_0 and AD will determine the actual price level as P_0 and the level of output as y_0. If, however, the expected price level was higher than P_0^e at, say, P_1^e, then the expectations-augmented aggregate supply curve would become the curve shown as EAS_1, which cuts the aggregate supply curve AS at P_1^e. In this case, with the aggregate demand curve held constant, the actual price level will be determined as P_1 and the level of output as y_1.

From this exercise you see that the actual price level is not independent of the expected price level. All that has been done in Figure 27.1 is to consider two alternative expectations for the price level, with everything else the same. Reading off the equilibrium solutions shows that there is a direct relationship between the expected and actual price levels. The higher the expected price level, the higher will be the actual price level, given a constant money supply.

How then can economic theory be used to determine the expected price level when the actual price level depends on the expected price level? It is rather like asking the question, How can we lift ourselves off the ground by pulling at our own boot laces? We can pull as hard as we like, but no matter how hard we pull, we shall stay put on the ground and make no progress. It looks a little bit as if the same is true concerning the use of economic theory to generate a prediction about the expected price level. If the expectation of the price level is necessary for forecasting the actual price level, how can the predictions of economic theory be used to form an expectation about the price level? How can we get off the ground?

Working Out the Rational Expectation of the Price Level

It turns out that we can solve this problem. The way in which it is solved is illustrated in Figure 27.2. Remember that what we want to do is to form an expectation of the price level that will prevail in a *future* period, and we want that expectation to be the prediction of the theory of the actual price level that will prevail in that future period.

The starting point has to be to form an expectation of the position of the aggregate demand curve. Suppose that we have done this and that the aggregate demand curve that we expect in the following period is shown as AD^e. What this means, of course, is that we have formed an expectation of the value of the money supply, government expenditure, and taxes in the next period and have figured out what they imply for the position of the aggregate demand curve in the next period. Let us also put in the diagram the aggregate supply curve, the vertical line labelled AS, with the full-employment output level y^*.

Now let us perform a purely conceptual experiment. Let us suppose that we start out with an entirely arbitrary expectation of the price level for the next period equal to P_0^e, as shown on the vertical axis of Figure 27.2. This means that we can now locate an expectations-augmented aggregate supply

Figure 27.2
Calculating the Rational Expectation of the Price Level

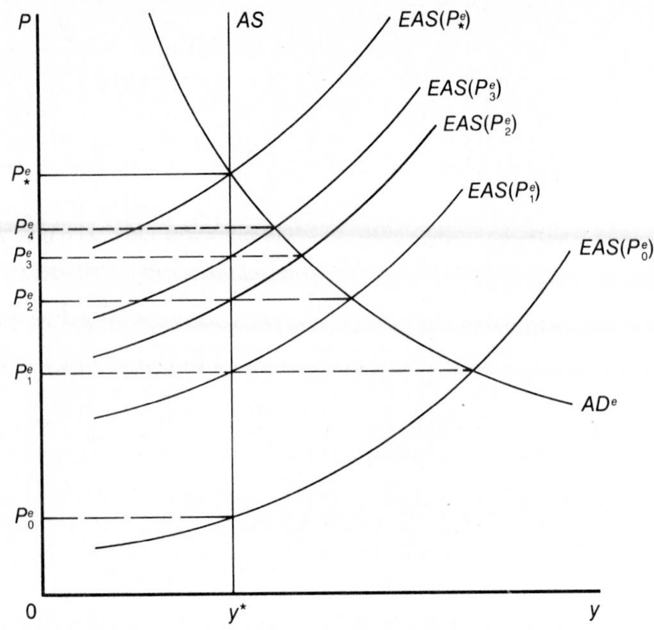

The starting point for the calculation of the rational expectation of the price level is the formation of an expectation of aggregate demand. This requires that an expectation be formed of the values of the variables that determine aggregate demand as well as their influence upon demand. The curve AD^e denotes the expected aggregate demand curve. The rational expectation of the price level can be calculated by performing a conceptual experiment. Try P_0^e as the expected price level. This cannot be the rational expectation because the predicted price level is different from that initial trial value. It is P_1^e. The expected price level P_1^e in turn predicts P_2^e as the actual price level. Then P_2^e in turn predicts P_3^e, and so on. Only the *expected* price level P_*^e predicts an *actual* price level equal to P_*^e. This is the rational expectation of the price level. It is the price level at which the expected aggregate demand curve (AD^e) cuts the full-employment aggregate supply curve (AS).

curve based on that expected price level. This is shown as $EAS(P_0^e)$. If P_0^e is the expected price level, then we see, given our expectation of the position of the aggregate demand curve for the next period, that we would be forecasting a price level higher than the expected price level P_0^e. In fact, we would be forecasting a price level equal to P_1^e. It is clear that we have a conflict. We started with a purely arbitrary expectation of P_0^e, and we see that if P_0^e is our expectation our theory does not lead to a prediction that the price level will in fact be the value that we are expecting. Therefore, the expectation P_0^e is not a rational expectation. It is not the conditional expectation of the price level that is generated by our theory.

Suppose, continuing to perform the conceptual experiment, we now try a different expected price level. In particular, let us try P_1^e as the expected price level. This is the price level predicted by the first experiment conducted. With this higher expected price level, we now have a different expectations-augmented aggregate supply curve, namely, $EAS(P_1^e)$. (Recall that EAS cuts AS

at the price level equal to the expected price level.) This higher expected price level, P_1^e, generates, as we see, a forecast for the price level next period of P_2^e. This is the price level at which the expectation of the aggregate demand curve cuts the expectations-augmented aggregate supply curve EAS_1. Again, we have a conflict. The forecast of our theory is different from the expectation P_1^e, which we arbitrarily assumed. Also, the prediction of the theory is higher than the assumed expectation.

Still continuing with the conceptual experiment, let us now try a yet higher expected price level, namely, P_2^e. With this expected price level, the expectations-augmented aggregate supply curve becomes $EAS(P_2^e)$. This curve cuts the expected aggregate demand curve at the price level P_3^e. Yet again there is a conflict.

You can now see what is happening. Each time we use a trial value for the expected price level, we are generating a prediction for the actual price level that is higher than the expected price level. However, you will notice that the gap between the initially assumed expected price level and the conditional prediction of the price level is becoming smaller. Can we bring this process to an end? The answer is that we can, and we do this by predicting that the price level will be equal to that value generated by the point at which the expected aggregate demand curve cuts the aggregate supply curve AS at P_*^e.

Suppose we started out with that expectation for the price level. The expectations-augmented aggregate supply curve that passes through the AS curve at that point is $EAS(P_*^e)$. This is the expectations-augmented aggregate supply curve based on an expected price level of P_*^e. The theory now predicts that the price level in the next period will also be P_*^e. Notice that we are not saying that the price level next period will actually turn out to be P_*^e. Rather, we are saying that the prediction of our theory concerning the price level is that it will be P_*^e, given that our expectation is that the aggregate demand will be AD^e.

This leads to a very important proposition. The rational expectation is that the price level will be equal to its expected full-employment value. This is the only expectation of the price level that is consistent with the prediction of our theory concerning what the price level will be. You should not confuse this with the statement that "everyone expects full employment always to prevail." People know that random shocks will be hitting the economy and that we may *never* have full employment. They do the best they can, however, before the event, to form an expectation about the price level that, should that expectation turn out to be correct, will ensure full employment.

You now know how to determine the rational expectation of the price level in the context of the new theories of aggregate supply and the Keynesian *IS-LM* theory of aggregate demand.

Individual Thought Experiments

The hypothesis about individual economic agents is that they will behave on the basis of a subjective expectation of the price level that coincides with a conditional mathematical expectation of the price level, given the available information. That is, they behave on the basis of a rational expectation of the price level. That is not to say that everybody knows the same piece of economic theory that you know and that they are capable of calculating the rational expectation from this model or any other particular model. Rather, it is to say that people form their expectations of the price level in much the same way as the pool player forms his expectation of the trajectories of the balls. Just as the pool player follows instinctive and subjective calculations of the appropriate angles and forces and degrees of spin, so economic agents form their price expectations on the basis of ill-articulated thought processes. Of course, not everyone is a good pool player and not everyone is good at forming expectations of future levels of prices. Those who are good pool players, however, typically play a lot and are paid for their skills. Likewise, those who are good at making price level expectations (and who approximate to making rational expectations) typically make the expectations upon which the rest of us base our behavior. They also get paid for their special skills!

Summary

A. The Expected Price Level and Expected Rate of Inflation

The expected rate of inflation is equal to the expected price level minus the previous price level expressed as a percentage of the previous price level. It is not the percentage change in the expected price level but rather the expected percentage change in the price level.

B. The Distinction Between a Subjective Expectation and a Conditional Mathematical Expectation

A subjective expectation is a vague intuitive feeling about the likely value or outcome of some future event. A conditional mathematical expectation is the true average value of the outcome of a future event conditional on (i.e., given) whatever are the known actual values of all the relevant variables.

C. Why Wrong Expectations Are Costly

Actions are based on expectations, and wrong expectations lead to actions that may turn out to be inappropriate. If the price turns out to be higher than was expected, real wages will turn out to be lower than was expected, and people will have ended up doing more work and consuming less leisure than they would have liked to have done had they known the correct real wage rate ahead of time. A symmetric cost applies to an error in the opposite direction. It is important to distinguish between being right every time (which in general is impossible) and being right on the average. The casino example in the text illustrates this distinction.

D. Rational Expectation

A rational expectation of a variable is a subjective expectation that *coincides* with the conditional mathematical expectation of that variable, given the available information.

E. Rational Expectation of the Price Level

The rational expectation of the price level is the prediction of the price level that is based on all the available information at the time at which the expectation is formed. This information includes the body of economic theory relevant for predicting the price level.

F. How to Work Out the Rational Expectation of the Price Level

The rational expectation of the price level in the context of the new theories is the price level at which the expected aggregate demand curve cuts the aggregate supply curve. (The conceptual experiment whereby this expectation is worked out is discussed in the section on rational expectation and illustrated in Figure 27.2 and should be thoroughly understood.)

Review Questions

1. What is the connection between the expected price level and the expected rate of inflation?
2. Define a *subjective expectation.*
3. Define a *conditional mathematical expectation.*
4. Give some examples of the costs of wrong expectations.
5. Give the definition of a *rational expectation* and explain the relationship between a rational, a conditional mathematical, and a subjective expectation.
6. What are the key distinguishing features of a rational expectation?
7. What basic postulate concerning economic behavior suggests that individuals would form expectations rationally?
8. Give some examples of economic agents (firms, individuals, etc.) who are "in the business" of providing forecasts and selling other informational services. How do individuals benefit from these services?
9. What factors govern the degree to which the expectation of the price level affects aggregate supply? Under what circumstances will an increase, for example, in the expected price level have the greatest effect on aggregate supply?
10. What factors would you expect to determine the expected price level? How responsive might the expected price level be to observations on past prices?
11. Illustrate diagrammatically the derivation of the expected price level.
12. What relationship does the rational expectation of the price level bear to the full-employment price level?

Appendix to Chapter 27

The Signal Extraction Problem

In Chapter 24 when we derived the new classical expectations-augmented aggregate supply curve, we assumed that people formed expectations about the average price level, ignoring the knowledge that is readily available to them concerning the price of the output of their own industry. In this chapter, we have calculated the rational expectation of the price level using only an expectation of the level of aggregate demand. We have again ignored any current information that might be available concerning the prices of some limited range of goods and services.

This appendix extends the analysis to the case in which people do use currently available information concerning the price in their own sector of the economy.[3] The level of analysis in this appendix is more demanding than that in the text. To follow everything in this appendix you need to know a small amount of statistics and calculus. You will probably, however, be able to obtain a good feel for what is going on even if you do not have that background.

The starting point is to imagine that the economy comprises many "islands" of information. Individuals (firms and their employees) know the prices on their own island, but they do not know the prices on any other. Imagine that the individual firms and workers on a given island that we shall call island i observe their price to be P_i. Then let us suppose that everyone knows that the price on island i deviates from the economy average price, P, by a random amount, R_i, which itself is not observed. In other words, everyone knows that

$$P_i = P + R_i \tag{27A.1}$$

The price P_i on the left-hand side of Equation (27A.1) is observed, but the general price level, P, and the deviation of the individual price from the general price, R_i, are not observed.

Rational people would like to use the information that they have on P_i to make the best inference possible concerning P and R_i. Let us suppose that people know that on the average, $R_i = 0$. Let us also suppose that people know that the relative price on island i deviates from the average price by a random amount that is drawn from a normal distribution that has a fixed amount of dispersion, which we will measure by its "variance." Let us denote the variance of the distribution of R_i by τ^2. A small value of τ^2 would mean that the relative price deviated very little from the average economy price (such as the distribution labelled A in Figure 27A.1). A large value of τ^2 would mean that the relative price was drawn from a distribution that varied widely around the economy average price (such as the curve labelled B in Figure 27A.1).

Next, let us suppose that people have formed an expectation of the economy average price just prior to observing the price in their own island. Call that expectation P_0^e. You can imagine that P_0^e has been calculated in exactly the same way as was done in the body of this chapter.

Suppose that everyone knows from past experience that the actual economy average price deviates from the prior expectation by some random amount that we will call U (for unexpected price fluctuations), so that the

[3]The analysis presented in this appendix is a simplified version of that developed by Robert E. Lucas, Jr. in "Some International Evidence on the Output–Inflation Tradeoff," *The American Economic Review*, 63, (September 1973), 326–34.

Figure 27A.1
The Dispersion of Prices

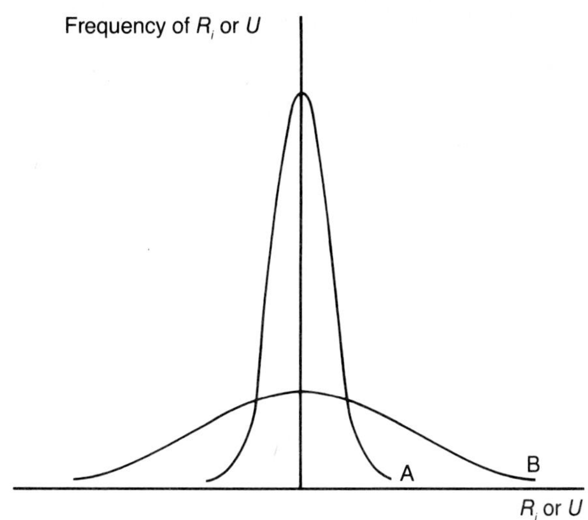

An economy that has low variability of prices will have a small variance to the unexpected component of prices (like the distribution labelled A), and an economy that has very volatile or noisy prices will have a large variance to the unexpected component of prices (like the distribution labelled B).

actual price level is equal to the sum of the expected price level and the unanticipated component. That is,

$$P = P_0^e + U \tag{27A.2}$$

This equation contains no variables that people observe, although P_0^e is known to them because it is their prior expectation. Let us suppose that U, the unexpected portion of prices, has an average value of zero, but it too is drawn from a normal distribution and has a dispersion measured by its variance, which we shall call σ^2.

An economy that has little variability of prices will have a small variance and the unexpected component of prices will look like the distribution labelled A in Figure 27A.1. An economy that has very volatile or noisy prices will be one in which people's expectations frequently deviate substantially from the actual level, so that the distribution of U will be like that labelled B in Figure 27A.1.

Now it is possible to combine Equations (27A.1) and (27A.2) by noticing that we can replace P in Equation (27A.1) with the right-hand side of Equation (27A.2). This gives

$$P_i = P_0^e + U + R_i \tag{27A.3}$$

If we subtract P_0^e from both sides of Equation (27A.3), we obtain

$$P_i - P_0^e = U + R_i \tag{27A.4}$$

Notice that what is on the left-hand side of this equation is something that is known to everyone on island i. It is the difference between the price that they have just observed on their own island and the price level that, prior to that observation, they expected would prevail on the average in the economy as a whole. They also know that $P_i - P_0^e$ is equal to the sum of two random variables—their error in forecasting correctly the economy-wide price level, U, and the random price on their own island relative to the economy average price, R_i.

Their task is to decompose the observed sum of these two variables into their separate components so that a better expectation of the economy-wide average price level may be calculated. It is important to notice that prior to observing the price on their own island, they expected that both U and R_i would be zero. Now that they know the sum of these two random variables, unless that sum happens to be zero (which is a possibility, although not a very likely one), they will now want to revise their estimate of the values of these variables.

We could say the same thing slightly differently. That is, the people on island i had a prior expectation about the economy-wide price level, P_0^e; they have now observed a new piece of information, the price on their own island; and they now want to use the new information to revise their expectation about the economy average price.

To do this they can use the so-called law of recursive projection. The law is easily stated and intuitively appealing. In order to state the law, we need one small piece of notation. Let us agree that the expectation of a random variable (x) given the piece of information (I) will be called $E(x \mid I)$. We can use this notation to express the expectation of the price level that the people on island i originally had before observing the price on that island as

$$P_0^e = E(P \mid I_0)$$

Here, I_0 stands for all the information originally available before observing the price. What the people on island i are going to calculate is the expectation of the price level in the economy as a whole, given that initial information, I_0, and the observation of the price on island i. That is, they are going to calculate

$$E(P \mid I_0, P_i)$$

To perform this calculation, they are going to use the law of recursive projection, which is as follows:

$$E(P \mid I_0, P_i) = E(P \mid I_0) + E([P - E(P \mid I_0)] \mid [P_i - E(P_i \mid I_0)]) \qquad \textbf{(27A.5)}$$

This looks much more formidable than it is. The left-hand side is simply the output that the agents want, namely, their expectation of the economy average price level, given all the information that they now have available to them. The starting point for the calculation is given by the first term on the right-hand side of Equation (27A.5) and is nothing other than their original expectation. The second term on the right-hand side is the adjustment that is going to be made to the original expectation. It too is an expectation. It is the expectation of the error made in originally predicting the general price level,

$$P - E(P \mid I_0)$$

That expectation itself is going to be calculated, given the information

$$P_i - E(P_i \mid I_0)$$

What is this information? Evidently it is the difference between the actual price observed on island i and the expectation of what that price would be given the initial information. In other words, it is the error in forecasting the price on island i.

You can now interpret Equation (27A.5) in the following way. It says that the expectation of the general price level, given the original information and the new information about island i's price, will be equal to the original expectation made prior to knowing island i's price plus the expectation of the error made in forecasting the general price level, given knowledge of the error that has been made in forecasting the island's own price. If you inspect Equation (27A.2), you will see that

$$P - E(P \mid I_0) = U$$

Therefore we can replace $P - E(P \mid I_0)$ with U in Equation (27A.5). Also, by examining equation (27A.3), you will see that the expectation of the price on island i prior to observing that price must have been that it would be the same as the price in the economy as a whole, P_0^e, since the expectation of the random variables U and R_i are both zero. Thus, the difference between P_i now observed and its prior expectation must be the sum of the two random variables, $U + R_i$. We can use that sum therefore to replace $P_i - E(P_i)$ in Equation (27A.5). Making these adjustments gives

$$E(P \mid I_0, P_i) = P_0^e + E(U \mid U + R_i) \qquad \textbf{(27A.6)}$$

What the people on island i need to do then, according to Equation (27A.6), is to figure out as best they can the likely value of U, given that they know $U + R_i$.

A natural way to do this is to imagine that some fraction of the sum of U and R_i is to be treated as being generated by U and the remaining fraction by R_i. Of course, if a particular fraction of $U + R_i$ is assigned to U, in general, an error will be made. Call the fraction in question a. Then the following equation can be defined to be true:

$$U = a(U + R_i) + Error \qquad \textbf{(27A.7)}$$

What this says is that the random variable U that people would like to observe but have not observed is equal to some fraction a of the random variable $U + R_i$ that they have observed plus some error. Equivalently, we could say that the error that they will make in estimating the value of U as a fraction a of $U + R_i$ is given by

$$Error = U - a(U + R_i)$$

How can a value for a be chosen to make this into an operational estimation procedure? Clearly, the *expected* error is equal to zero since the expectation of U and R_i is equal to zero. Any value of a would deliver an expected error of zero. What people care about presumably is not just having an expected error of zero but in some sense making the smallest possible errors. Since positive errors and negative errors will cancel out, a useful way of giving weight to the errors is to consider the square of the error made. This renders all the errors positive and gives symmetric weights to both positive and negative errors. Let us square the error and see what we get. Evidently, squaring the error gives

$$Error^2 = U^2 + a^2(U^2 + R_i^2) - 2aU^2 - 2aUR_i$$

Of course, no one knows the actual error at any point in time. It is possible, nevertheless, to calculate the *expected* squared error. Calculating the expectation of the squared error gives

$$E(Error^2) = E(U^2) + a^2E(U^2 + R_i^2) - 2aE(U^2) - 2aE(UR_i)$$

The expectation $E(U^2)$ is the variance of the distribution of U, which we are calling σ^2, and the expectation $E(R_i^2)$ is the variance of the distribution of R_i that we are calling τ^2. The expectation of the product of U and R_i is, by assumption, zero. That is, we are supposing that the random shocks hitting the individual island's relative price are independent of the random shocks that hit the economy average price level. With that assumption, it is evident that

$$E(Error)^2 = \sigma^2 + a^2(\sigma^2 + \tau^2) - 2a\,\sigma^2 \qquad \textbf{(27A.8)}$$

What the people on island i would like to do is find a value for a that minimizes this expected squared error. In so doing they will reduce to a minimum the costs of having wrong expectations. They can do this by differentiating Equation (27A.8) with respect to a and setting the result equal to zero, and then finding the value of a that satisfies that equation. Evidently, the required value for a is

$$a = \frac{\sigma^2}{\sigma^2 + \tau^2}$$

This can now be used to calculate the expectation of U, given an observation of $U + R_i$. This expectation is

$$E(U \mid U + R_i) = a(U + R_i)$$

But, we know from Equation (27A.2) that $U = P - P_0^e$ and from Equation (27A.3) that

$$(U + R_i) = (P_i - P_0^e)$$

Using these two equations enables us to write the expectation of the economy-wide price level on island i as

$$E(P \mid I_0, P_i) = P_0^e + a(P_i - P_0^e)$$

or, equivalently,

$$E(P \mid I_0, P_i) = aP_i + (1 - a)\, P_0^e \qquad \textbf{(27A.9)}$$

You can now perhaps see more clearly why the calculation just performed is called the law of recursive projection. A projection is made, P_0^e; new information arrives, P_i; the old projection and the new information are then combined to arrive at a new projection. The weights attached to the original belief $(1 - a)$ and the new information (a) depend on the quality of the new information.

Let me try to make the notion of the "quality of the new information" a bit more precise. You know that

$$a = \frac{\sigma^2}{\sigma^2 + \tau^2} \qquad \textbf{(27A.10)}$$

and therefore that

$$1 - a = \frac{\tau^2}{\sigma^2 + \tau^2}$$

You can think of σ^2 as measuring the amount of aggregate noise in the economy. A large value of σ^2 signifies a very noisy economy, that is, an economy whose price level is very hard to forecast. You can think of a large value of τ^2 as indicating considerable randomness in relative prices, that is; an economy in which relative prices are hard to forecast. Evidently, the bigger is σ^2, the bigger will be the value of a; and the bigger is τ^2, the smaller will be the value of a. Since a is the weight that we attach to the new information, we could equivalently say that the noisier is the aggregate price level, the bigger the weight we attach to the new piece of information; and the noisier are relative prices, the smaller the weight we attach to the new piece of information. This seems to be natural enough.

If the economy is subject to very large random fluctuations in the general level of prices, then an observation on one price that is very different from what was previously expected will be interpreted as indicating that what was previously expected was wrong and is in need of major revision. Thus, the weight attached to the new piece of information will be large. Conversely, if relative prices are exceedingly random, then observing the price on an individual island is not going to be giving very much information concerning movements in the average price level. Hence, a small weight would attach to the current piece of information in that case. The precise way in which aggregate noise and relative price noise are combined are given by Equation (27A.10) that defines a.

So far we have only talked about one island, island i. Let us suppose that the economy is made up of many such islands. Furthermore, suppose that all the islands are similar in the sense that they all are bombarded by random shocks to their own relative price that come from the same distribution as the one that we have just analyzed. Different islands get different values of the random shock, R_i, at each moment in time, but they all come from the same distribution with the same amount of dispersion τ^2 around a zero mean. In this case, the expectations of the economy-wide price level on each island are going to be determined by an equation like (27A.9).

We may aggregate these price expectations over all the islands to arrive at the economy average beliefs about the price level. Those economy average beliefs are given by

$$P_t^e = aP_t + (1 - a)P_0^e \quad \textbf{(27A.11)}$$

I am calling P_t^e the economy average expected price level at time t. It will be a weighted average of the actual price level, P_t, and the prior belief about the expected price level, P_0^e. The weights will be the same as the weights attaching to each individual island's price expectations. It is important to remind yourself that no individual knows the economy-wide average price, P_t, and no individual knows the economy average of the expectations of the price level, P_t^e. On each island there is a different expected price level as described by Equation (27A.9). Equation (27A.11) is something that the economist analyzing this economy can construct, but it is not something that people in the economy observe at the time at which the events that we are analyzing are occurring.

Let us now see how these considerations affect the labor market and the *EAS* curve. Figure 27A.2 is the vehicle for our analysis. First identify, in Figure 27A.2, Figure 24.2. Notice that the upward-sloping curve $n^s(P^e = P_0, a = 0)$ is the same curve as that shown in Figure 24.2 and the three demand curves are the same as those in Figure 24.2. The supply curve is drawn for a value of a equal to zero. In other words, everyone ignores the information contained in their own price and sticks to their prior expectation of the economy-wide average price regardless of what they observe.

Let us go to the opposite extreme. Imagine that $a = 1$. We will examine below precisely what that would mean. For the moment simply assume that a is 1. This means that in observing their own island price level, P_i, people assume that the entire movement in their own price level reflects a movement in the economy average price, and they revise their expectations accordingly. Thus, if the economy average price was P_1, moving the demand curve for labor to n_1^d, and if everyone on seeing their own island's price revises their expectation in accordance with their observed own price, the average expectation in the economy as a whole would move in exactly the same way as the actual price level had moved.

Figure 27A.2
Signal Extraction and the Labor Market

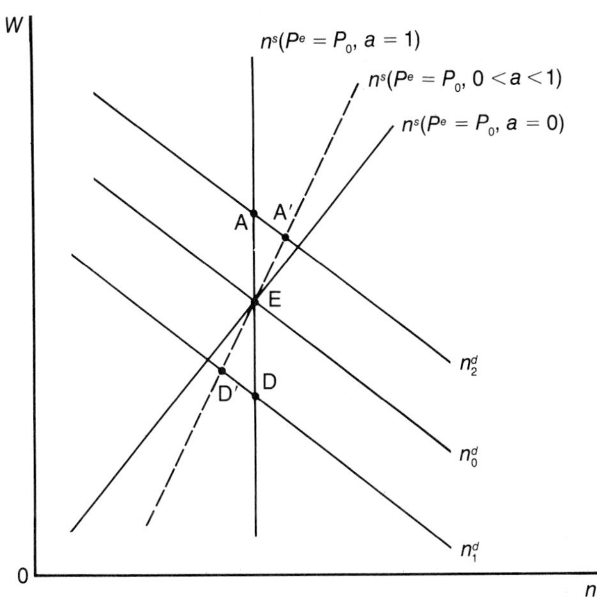

Consider what happens when the actual price level fluctuates between a low level of P_1 and an upper level of P_2. The demand for labor curve will fluctuate between n_1^d and n_2^d. Individual prices will fluctuate, and the amount of information extracted from those individual prices concerning the general price level will affect the supply of labor. If individual prices fluctuate so widely around the average price level that they give no information, then the supply of labor curve will remain fixed at $n^s(P^e = P_0, a = 0)$. If individual prices never deviated from the average price level, so that the observation of an individual price gives complete information about the aggregate price level, then the supply of labor curve would become $n^s(P^e = P_0, a = 1)$. In general, observations of individual prices will contain *some*, although incomplete, information about the average price level. In this case, the labor supply curve will be one such as that labelled $n^s(P^e = P_0, 0 < a < 1)$. The more information that individual prices contain, the smaller will be the fluctuations in employment and output, and the larger will be the fluctuations in money wages and prices.

You know from the analysis lying behind Figure 24.1 that a change in the actual price level that is fully expected will move the supply and demand curves for labor in exactly the same way. The supply of labor curve, instead of staying at $n^s(P^e = P_0,\ a = 0)$, would now move up parallel to itself to pass through the point marked A. Conversely, if the price level was to fall to P_2, so that the demand for labor curve fell to n_2^d, and again if everyone seeing their own prices inferred that the economy average price had changed in exactly the same way as their own price had, the supply curve of labor would shift down parallel to itself to pass through the point D. In effect, the locus AED represents the effective supply curve of labor when a weight of one is placed upon current price information that is observed. That vertical line is therefore labelled $n^s(P^e = P_0,\ a = 1)$. It is not really a labor supply curve, although it is the equilibrium supply locus that is obtained as a result of allowing price expectations to react to current actual prices with a coefficient of one.

It is easy to see that if a was something greater than zero but less than one, the labor supply curve would slope upwards and would lie somewhere between the original curve (for $a = 0$) and the vertical line (for $a = 1$). Passing through a point like A′, there would be a supply of labor curve parallel to the curve $n^s(P^e = P_0, a = 0)$. That curve would have shifted upwards as a result of the revised price level expectations but not by as much as the actual price level had increased. Likewise, there would be a supply curve passing through the point D′ that would represent a downward revision of price level expectations resulting from an actual price level of P_2.

You can see then that the slope of the effective labor supply curve will depend on the extent to which people revise their current price level expectations in the light of their current observation of the particular price level in their own sector of the economy. The more those price expectations are revised, the closer is a to unity, and the steeper will be the labor supply locus. The special case discussed in Chapter 24 is for $a = 0$.

Evidently, by tracing through the implications of this analysis in Figure 24.3, the slope of the *EAS* curve will also depend on the value of a. The curve shown in Figure 24.3 is for $a = 0$. If $a = 1$, evidently the *EAS* curve would become the same curve as *AS*. It too would become vertical. For intermediate values of a, the *EAS* curve will lie somewhere between the *AS* and *EAS* curves shown in Figure 24.3—being closer to the *AS* curve, the closer is a to one; and being closer to the *EAS* curve, the closer is a to zero.

We have seen that the value of a will in fact depend on how "noisy" the economy is at the aggregate level and how big the relative price shocks are that hit the individual "islands." An economy that is subject to a large volume of aggregate noise (large σ^2) will be one that has a high value of a. This means that such an economy will have a steep *EAS* curve compared with an economy that has a small amount of aggregate noise.

Relative price "noise" works the other way. The bigger the source of "noise" (the larger is the value of τ^2), the smaller is a. Thus, an economy with highly variable relative prices will have a flat *EAS* curve compared with an economy that has a small amount of relative price noise.

The key conclusion of the analysis that we have just conducted is that the slope of the *EAS* curve is not independent of the amount and sources of noise in the economy.

28

Equilibrium Income, Employment, and the Price Level with Rational Expectations

This chapter takes the next step in completing the rational expectations theory of the determination of the price level and real economic activity. From what you have learned so far concerning the rational expectations theory, you will almost be able to guess what this chapter has to deal with. You now know that the expected price level is determined by expected aggregate demand. You also know from your analysis of the determination of output and prices with a fixed price level expectation that the actual price and output level are determined where the actual demand curve cuts the expectations-augmented aggregate supply curve. All that needs to be done, therefore, to complete our analysis is to explore the full implications of the distinction between expected (or anticipated) and unexpected (or unanticipated) changes in aggregate demand. Three tasks in this chapter will achieve that. They are to:

(a) Understand the distinction between an anticipated and unanticipated change in aggregate demand.
(b) Understand how output, employment, unemployment, the real wage, the money wage, and the price level are affected by an *anticipated* change in aggregate demand.
(c) Understand how output, employment, unemployment, the real wage, the money wage, and the price level are affected by an *unanticipated* change in aggregate demand.

A. Anticipated and Unanticipated Change in Aggregate Demand

Definition of Anticipated and Unanticipated Changes in Aggregate Demand

The level of aggregate demand in any particular year (say, year t) may be thought of as being equal to aggregate demand in the previous year (year $t-1$) plus the change in demand over the year (Δy^d). That is,

$$y_t^d = y_{t-1} + \Delta y_t^d \tag{28.1}$$

Notice that since actual output is always equilibrium output, actual output at $t - 1$, y_{t-1}, is equal to y^d_{t-1} (aggregate demand at time $t - 1$). As soon as time $t - 1$ is past, the value of output at that date becomes known. (Actually it's a little bit strong to say that this becomes known *as soon as* the time is past. It takes a short while for the data to be accumulated.) The level of aggregate demand for time t, however, will not be known. Since rational economic agents need to form an expectation of the price level, and since the price level will depend on the level of aggregate demand, it is necessary, in order to form a rational expectation of the price level, to form a rational expectation of the level of aggregate demand. It is necessary, therefore, to forecast the change in aggregate demand so that its future value may be predicted.

The predicted component of the change in aggregate demand is referred to as the *anticipated change* in aggregate demand, and the unpredicted component is known as the *unanticipated change* in aggregate demand.

The actual change in aggregate demand is made up of these two components. That is,

$$\Delta y^d_t = \Delta y^{de}_t + \Delta y^{du}_t \qquad \textbf{(28.2)}$$

The superscript ^{e} denotes the expected or anticipated part of the change in aggregate demand, and the superscript ^{u}, the unanticipated or unexpected part. There is not, in general, any reason why the expected and unexpected components of the change in aggregate demand should be of the same sign. They may be, in which case they will each be a fraction of the actual change. It is possible, nevertheless, for the anticipated change to be greater than the actual change, so that the unexpected change is negative.

Four examples give the range of possibilities. They are set out in Table 28.1. The first example is of a correctly anticipated change in aggregate demand. The actual change is 100, and the expected change is 100. The second example is one in which the change in aggregate demand is entirely unanticipated. The expected change is 0, but the actual change is 100. The third example is one in which the actual change in aggregate demand is divided between an anticipated and unanticipated component. This example may be thought of as the most likely case. In this example, the division is 50/50, although in general, of course, it would not be so evenly split. The fourth and final example is one in which the actual change is less than the anticipated change, so that there is a negative unexpected component. (Of course, these are all examples of a rise in aggregate demand. Aggregate demand could actually fall and be expected to fall.)

TABLE 28.1
Examples of Divisions of the Actual Change in Aggregate Demand between Anticipated and Unanticipated Changes

EXAMPLE	Δy^d_t	=	Δy^{de}_t	+	Δy^{du}_t
1	100	=	100	+	0
2	100	=	0	+	100
3	100	=	50	+	50
4	100	=	200	–	100

In order to actually measure the anticipated and unanticipated changes in aggregate demand, it is necessary to divide the changes in the variables that determine aggregate demand into their anticipated and unanticipated components. One such variable is the change in the money supply.

What determines the division of the actual change in the money supply between its anticipated and unanticipated components? This is not a settled matter. Robert Barro of the University of Chicago has conducted the pioneering studies on this question, using U.S. money supply data.[1] He has attempted to decompose the actual money supply growth into its anticipated and unanticipated components. However, his work is by no means uncontroversial, and matters are not yet settled.

The way in which he proceeded was to search for statistical regularities in the past history of money supply growth and then to suppose that rational agents would exploit those statistical regularities in forming a rational expectation of money supply growth. Specifically, he discovered that the money supply growth rate tends to be faster:

1. The faster the money supply growth has been in the preceding two years.
2. The bigger the level of federal government expenditure is relative to its trend.
3. The higher the level of unemployment was in the previous year.

These findings are more than statistical patterns. They also make good intuitive sense. The proposition that money supply growth will be faster, the faster the previous two years' money supply growth has been, reflects the fact that the Fed[2] exhibits some inertia in its decision making. It does not change course suddenly and rapidly in a zigzag fashion; rather, it changes course gradually. This means that the behavior of the Fed can, on the average, be described by a version of the formula that says that tomorrow will be very much like today.

The proposition that money supply growth increases when federal government expenditure is below its trend level is a natural consequence of the fact that money printing is a form of taxation. When there is a burst of government expenditure or a sharp drop in government expenditure, it is much easier to vary the rate at which money is printed than it is to vary such things as, for example, the sales tax, income tax, or capital gains tax. Hence, the efficient financing of government expenditure will entail varying the growth rate of the money supply to cover unusually large changes in expenditure.

The responsiveness of the money supply to the previous year's unemployment or output growth reflects a widespread belief on the part of governments that they can manipulate the economy by activist monetary policies. The

---

[1]The most comprehensive account of Barro's work is Robert J. Barro and Mark Rush, "Unanticipated Money and Economic Activity," chap. 2 in Stanley Fischer, ed., *Rational Expectations and Economic Policy*, National Bureau of Economic Research Conference Report (Chicago and London: University of Chicago Press, 1980).

[2]Short for Federal Reserve System.

Keynesian idea that stimulating demand in times of depression and holding demand back in times of boom will moderate the business cycle lies behind this kind of monetary policy action.

The propositions just discussed can be given a precise numerical form by the use of statistical techniques that lie outside the scope of this book. From those statistical exercises it is possible to make a forecast of what the money supply will be in the subsequent year (or in distant future years for that matter) conditional on information about the previous two years' money supply growth, the behavior of government expenditure, and the recent history of unemployment. Such a forecast becomes the anticipated change in the money supply. A movement in the actual money supply that is different from the calculated anticipated change becomes the calculated value of the unanticipated change in the money supply.

The above discussion concerning the decomposition of changes in the money supply into anticipated and unanticipated components applies in principle to changes in government expenditure, taxes, or any other variables that influence aggregate demand.

Now that the distinction between anticipated and unanticipated changes in aggregate demand is understood, and we have seen how in practice it is possible to distinguish between them, it will be useful to go on to analyze the way in which these two components of the change in aggregate demand influence the key macroeconomic variables.

B. Effects of an Anticipated Change in the Aggregate Demand

The effects of an anticipated change in aggregate demand are analyzed first. This is an extreme case, but it is the clearest and simplest case with which to begin.

The analysis will be illustrated using Figure 28.1. You will recognize this as the diagrammatic summary of the theory of the determination of output (real income) and the price level. Suppose that you are looking at an economy at a particular time, called period 0. At that time the money supply is equal to M_0. The aggregate demand curve is the curve labelled AD_0. Suppose that period 0 is one of full-employment equilibrium. This is simply a convenient reference point. With period 0 being one of full-employment equilibrium, you know that the expectations-augmented aggregate supply curve, the aggregate supply curve, and the aggregate demand curve all intersect at the same point. (If you do not understand why this is so, review Chapter 24.) Thus, the actual price level and the expected price level equal each other at P_0 and P_0^e.

Now imagine that you are looking forward one year and are trying to form a view about the price level in that period. Suppose that you expect aggregate demand to rise, so that the aggregate demand curve is expected to be the curve labelled AD_1^e. This is where you expect the aggregate demand curve to be next year. You can now calculate the rational expectation of the price level, which is equal to P_1^e. (If you are not sure as to the reason for that, check back with Chapter 27, Figure 27.2) The expected price level P_1^e is the only expected price level that is consistent with the prediction of this model,

Figure 28.1
The Effect of an Anticipated Change in Aggregate Demand on the Price Level and the Level of Output

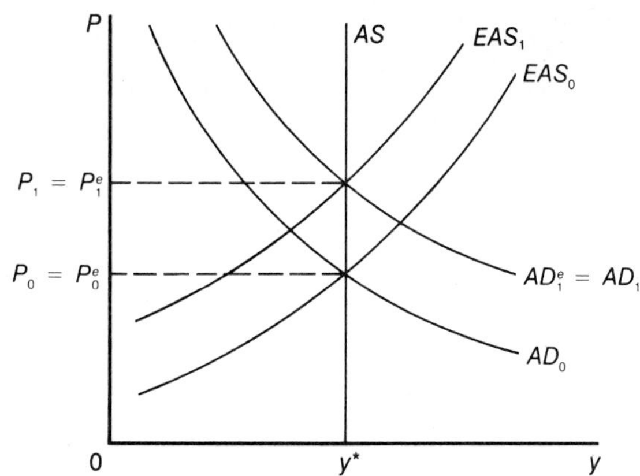

The economy is initially at full-employment equilibrium where AD_0 intersects EAS_0 at output y^* and price level P_0. Aggregate demand increases in an anticipated way from AD_0 to $AD_1 = AD_1^e$. The expectations-augmented aggregate supply curve shifts to become EAS_1 with the expected price level P_1^e. The actual price level is determined at P_1 and output at y^*. An anticipated rise in aggregate demand raises the price level but leaves output unaffected.

given that the expected aggregate demand is AD_1^e. This means that the expectations-augmented aggregate supply curve for period one will be located as shown by the curve EAS_1.

Next, suppose that aggregate demand actually increases by exactly the amount expected, so that the aggregate demand change is anticipated. This means that the *actual* aggregate demand curve will be the same as the *expected* aggregate demand curve. To remind you of this, the aggregate demand curve has been labelled as $AD_1 = AD_1^e$. This is to emphasize that the actual aggregate demand curve is the same as the expected aggregate demand curve.

What is the new equilibrium level of output and prices in this economy? Recall that equilibrium occurs at the point at which the aggregate demand curve cuts the expectations-augmented aggregate supply curve. The expectations-augmented aggregate supply curve is EAS_1—the aggregate supply curve when the expected price level is P_1^e, based on the expected aggregate demand curve AD_1^e.

You can now read off the new equilibrium. The aggregate demand curve AD_1 cuts the aggregate supply curve EAS_1 at the full-employment output level y^* and at the price level P_1. Thus the price level rises, and the level of output remains unchanged.

This is the first proposition concerning the effect of an anticipated change in aggregate demand. An anticipated rise in aggregate demand raises the price level and leaves output unchanged.

What happens to the remaining variables in the economy? Specifically, what happens to employment, unemployment, the real wage, and the money wage?

You will recall that the diagram displayed in Figure 28.1 was derived originally (in Chapter 26) from an analysis of the labor market and the production function. It is convenient now to recall Figure 26.2. (Refresh your memory by turning back to it.) Starting from the fact that output has not changed, you can travel back (reversing the arrows in Figure 26.2) through the production function and immediately establish that the level of employment has not changed. If the level of employment has not changed, then firms must willingly be hiring the same quantity of labor as they were hiring before. This immediately implies that the real wage has not changed. Furthermore, if the level of employment has not changed, the level of unemployment is also unchanged—it remains at the natural unemployment rate. Finally, since the real wage has not changed, but the price level has risen, it follows that the money wage rate must also have risen and by the same percentage amount as the price level has risen.

It is now possible to summarize all the consequences of an anticipated change in the aggregate demand: An anticipated change in aggregate demand changes the price level and the money wage by the same percentage amount as each other. It has no effects on any of the real variables in the economy, i.e., on output, employment, unemployment, and the real wage.

It is not difficult to understand the reason for these results. An anticipated changed in aggregate demand has the same effects as a change in aggregate demand had in the basic model.

Let us now go on to analyze the opposite extreme.

C. Effects of an Unanticipated Change in Aggregate Demand

Figure 28.2 will be used to illustrate the effects on the price level and output of an unanticipated change in aggregate demand. Suppose that the economy is initially in exactly the same situation as that depicted in Figure 28.1 for period 0. That is, the aggregate demand curve is AD_0, and the expectations-augmented aggregate supply curve is EAS_0. These curves intersect at a price level of P_0, which is also the expected price level P_0^e. Output is at the full-employment level, y^*.

Unlike the previous example, suppose that everyone expects that in period 1 aggregate demand will remain at AD_0. This aggregate demand curve is marked $AD_0 = AD_1^e$ to remind you that aggregate demand expected in period 1 is the same as actual aggregate demand in period 0. From this, the rational expectation of the price level in period 1, P_1^e, remains at P_0^e. The expectations-augmented aggregate supply curve for period 1 is the same as EAS_0, and this curve is marked EAS_1 to remind you of that.

Now suppose that instead of remaining constant at AD_0, aggregate demand actually rises in period 1 to become AD_1. You can read off the equilibrium price and output levels in period 1, given that the expected price level P_1^e is constant but that actual aggregate demand has increased above the level that was expected. Equilibrium will now be at the point at which the expectations-augmented aggregate supply curve EAS_1 cuts the *actual* aggregate demand curve AD_1. The price level and output level determined by this intersection point are P_1 and y_1, respectively.

Figure 28.2
The Effect of an Unanticipated Change in Aggregate Demand on the Price Level and the Level of Output

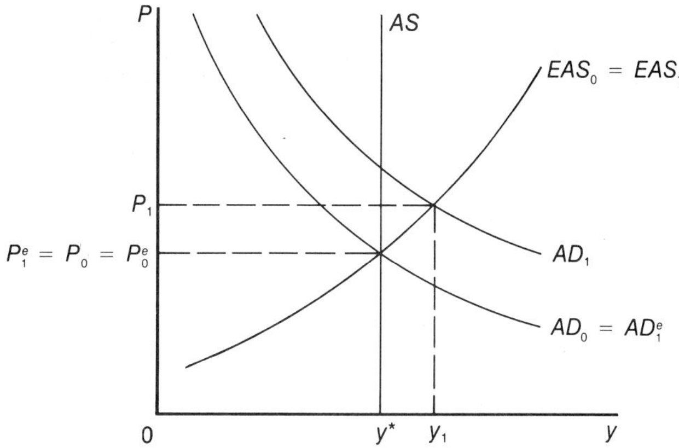

An initial equilibrium at P_0 and y^* (exactly as in Figure 28.1) is disturbed by an unanticipated shift in aggregate demand to AD_1. The expectations-augmented aggregate supply curve remains fixed at EAS_0. The new equilibrium price and output are where the new aggregate demand curve cuts the original *EAS* curve at P_1, y_1. An unanticipated rise in aggregate demand raises output and prices but raises prices less than proportionately to the rise in aggregate demand.

Notice that in this experiment we have an *unanticipated rise* in aggregate demand. Anticipated aggregate demand remains constant, but actual aggregate demand rises, so the unanticipated rise in aggregate demand is exactly equal to the actual rise in aggregate demand.

The effects of this unanticipated rise in aggregate demand are as follows: The price level is above its expected level, and output is above full-employment output. The percentage by which the price level rises above its expected level is less than the percentage unanticipated rise in aggregate demand. This occurs because part of the unanticipated rise in aggregate demand raises real income, and part of it raises the price level. Any given percentage unanticipated rise in aggregate demand will result in the combination of a rise in real income and a rise in the price level, which, in percentage terms, sums to the percentage change in aggregate demand. How much of the unanticipated aggregate demand rise goes into output and how much into the price level depends on the steepness of the *EAS* curve. A very steep *EAS* curve will result in a large price level and small output rise. A flat *EAS* curve will produce the reverse allocation of the effects of the unanticipated demand increase with a large output rise and a small price rise.

What are the effects on the other variables in the economy? (Again recall Figure 26.2.) Since you know from Figure 28.2 that output has risen, you also know that it must be the case that employment has also risen. How does this come about? For employment to have increased there must have been a rise in the demand for labor. You can easily verify that this indeed will have happened. The unanticipated rise in the price level will have produced an upward shift in the demand for labor curve, but since the expected price level is constant, there will have been no rise in the position of the supply of labor curve. As a result, the money wage will have increased. Its increase, however, will be less than the percentage rise in prices, so that the real wage has fallen, and firms are therefore demanding more labor. With a rise in the money wage but no change in the expected price level, the expected real wage has increased, and thus households will slide along their labor supply curve and willingly supply the additional labor demanded.

It is now possible to summarize the effects of an unanticipated change in aggregate demand: An unanticipated rise in aggregate demand will raise the price level, but by a smaller percentage amount than the unanticipated rise in aggregate demand. It will also produce a rise in the money wage, but by an even smaller percentage than the percentage rise in the price level. It will cause a fall in the real wage and a fall in unemployment below the natural rate. It will also produce a higher level of employment and output than the full-employment levels. The above can be readily restated for an unanticipated fall in the money supply.

Summary

A. Anticipated and Unanticipated Change in Aggregate Demand

The change in aggregate demand may be decomposed into its anticipated or expected component and its unanticipated or unexpected component. The anticipated change in aggregate demand may be greater or smaller than the actual change. When the anticipated change is exactly the same as the actual change, we speak of a fully anticipated change in aggregate demand. The unanticipated change in aggregate demand is simply the difference between the actual and anticipated changes. Since the change in actual aggregate demand is determined by changes in the money supply, government spending, and taxes, decomposing the change in aggregate demand into its expected and unexpected components involves decomposing the changes in these determinants of aggregate demand into their anticipated and unanticipated components.

B. Effects of an Anticipated Change in Aggregate Demand

An anticipated change in aggregate demand has the effect of changing the price level and the money wage by exactly the same percentage amount and by the same percentage as the rise in aggregate demand. It has no effects on any of the real variables. Specifically, it has no effect on output, employment, unemployment, or the real wage.

C. Effects of an Unanticipated Change in Aggregate Demand

An unanticipated change in aggregate demand has both real and nominal effects. It will raise the price level, but by a smaller percentage amount than the unanticipated rise in aggregate demand, and it will raise the money wage by an even smaller percentage amount than it raises the price level. It thus will lower the real wage, raise the level of employment, raise the level of output, and lower the level of unemployment.

Review Questions

1. What is the distinction between anticipated and unanticipated changes in aggregate demand?
2. What factors determine anticipated changes in aggregate demand?
3. What factors determine unanticipated changes in aggregate demand?
4. In what ways do the effects of anticipated changes in the money supply differ from the effects of unanticipated changes in the money supply?
5. Illustrate diagrammatically the effects of:
   (a) An anticipated increase in the money stock.
   (b) An unanticipated increase in the money stock.
   (c) An increase in the money supply—part of which was anticipated and part of which was unanticipated.
   (d) An anticipated rise in the money stock that turns out to be the opposite of the actual change.

6. "Whereas an unanticipated increase in the money supply lowers the real wage rate paid by firms, it increases the perceived real wage rate received by employees." Is this statement true or false? Explain.
7. "Only anticipated increases in the price level have output effects, since in order for producers to increase production during times of high prices, such increases must be anticipated." Within the context of the model we have developed, explain what is wrong with this statement.

Appendix to Chapter 28

The Algebra of Rational Expectations Equilibrium

This appendix sets out the simple algebra of a rational expectations equilibrium model. It presents the simplest example of a rational expectations equilibrium so that you may see the connection between the solution to this model and the solution of the fixed price *IS-LM* model of aggregate demand. There is nothing of substance in this appendix that does not appear in the preceding chapters. As with the other algebraic appendices, if you feel comfortable with this kind of treatment, you will probably find this a convenient, compact summary of the material presented in words and diagrams in the text of the chapter.

The starting point is the *IS-LM* theory of aggregate demand. Recall, or check back if necessary to Equation (20A.11) from the appendix to Chapter 20, that the level of real income as determined in the *IS-LM* model is

$$y = \frac{(a + i_0 + g - bt) + \dfrac{h}{l}\left(\dfrac{M}{P_0} - m_0\right)}{1 - b + (kh/l)} \qquad \textbf{(28A.1)}$$

This will be the level of real income (y) if the price level is *fixed* at P_0. You may think of Equation (28A.1) as determining *aggregate demand* by allowing the price level to *vary*. The level of income at each price level (P) is the level of aggregate demand (y^d). To emphasize this, Equation (28A.1) is modified as follows:

$$y^d = \frac{(a + i_0 + g - bt) + \frac{h}{l}\left(\frac{M}{P} - m_0\right)}{1 - b + (kh/l)} \qquad \textbf{(28A.2)}$$

Notice that the difference between Equations (28A.1) and (28A.2) is that Equation (28A.1) tells us the actual level of y for a given level of P (that is, P_0), whereas Equation (28A.2) tells us what the level of aggregate demand (y^d) will be as the price level (P) varies.

We can rewrite Equation (28A.2) with a different emphasis as

$$y^d = \left[\frac{(a + i_0 + g - bt) - \frac{h}{l}(m_0)}{1 - b + (kh/l)}\right] + \left[\frac{\frac{h}{l}}{1 - b + (kh/l)}\right]\left(\frac{M}{P}\right) \qquad \textbf{(28A.3)}$$

Calling m the logarithm of M and p the logarithm of P, we may write an approximation to the above as

$$y_t^d = \alpha_t + \beta(m_t - p_t), \qquad \beta > 0 \qquad \textbf{(28A.4)}$$

In Equation (28A.4), α represents the first term in brackets in Equation (28A.3), and $\beta(m_t - p_t)$ is a logarithmic approximation to the second term. The subscript t is added to each variable in Equation (28A.4) to remind us that these magnitudes vary over time. Thus, t represents a given point in time. Evidently, α stands for all the things that cause aggregate demand to vary, other than the real money supply. It incorporates, therefore, government expenditure, taxes, and any shifts in the investment function or the demand for money function. The money supply (m) and the price level (p) are expressed as logarithms, so that $m - p$ is the same as log M/P. (This formulation, which is linear in the logarithm of real money balances rather than the level of real money balances, makes the explicit calculation of expectations more straightforward.) The parameter β is the multiplier effect of a change in the logarithm of real money balances on aggregate demand.

We can represent the expectations-augmented aggregate supply curve in equation form as

$$y_t^s = y^* + \gamma(p_t - p_t^e), \qquad \gamma > 0 \qquad \textbf{(28A.5)}$$

where y^* represents full-employment output and p and p^e are the logarithms of the actual and expected price level, respectively. This is just a convenient translation into equation form of what you already know. To convince yourself of this, notice first that if the price level was equal to its expected value ($p = p^e$), then aggregate supply would be equal to full-employment aggregate supply y^*. As the actual price level exceeds the expected price level, so output rises above y^*. The positive parameter γ captures this. The only difference (in this simple treatment) between the new classical and new Keynesian approaches to the aggregate supply curve is that the value of γ would be different in the two theories because the new Keynesian γ would be bigger than that for the new classical. Both, however, would have the parameter positive.

Next, equilibrium prevails, in the sense that aggregate supply equals aggregate demand, and actual output y is also equal to demand and supply. We can write this as two equations. That is,

$$y_t = y_t^d = y_t^s \qquad \textbf{(28A.6)}$$

The first step in finding the rational expectations equilibrium of this model is to calculate the expected values of output and prices, *given* the expected values of α and m. (A full treatment would also have an explicit theory for the determination of α and m. We shall not make that extension here.) Calculating the expected values of y and p, given the expected values of α and m, simply involves taking the expectations of Equations (28A.4) and (28A.5) and using the fact that actual output is the same as aggregate demand and supply. Letting the superscript ^{e} stand for the expected value of a variable, you can immediately see that this implies

$$y_t^e = \alpha_t^e + \beta(m_t^e - p_t^e) \qquad \textbf{(28A.7)}$$

and

$$y_t^e = y^* \qquad \textbf{(28A.8)}$$

Equation (28A.7) follows directly from Equation (28A.4). If Equation (28A.4) describes what determines the actual level of aggregate output demanded and if demand equals actual output, then expected output must be equal to the expected value of α plus β times the expected value of real balances. That is all that Equation (28A.7) says. Equation (28A.8) follows directly from Equation (28A.5). It says what you already know, namely, that expected output will be equal to full-employment output since the expected price level is the rational expectation. That is, p_t^e is the same thing as the expectation of p_t, and so the second term in Equation (28A.5) is expected to be zero.

You can now solve Equations (28A.7) and (28A.8) for the price level. Substitute Equation (28A.8) into Equation (28A.7) and rearrange to give

$$p_t^e = m_t^e - \frac{1}{\beta}(y^* - \alpha_t^e) \qquad \textbf{(28A.9)}$$

Recall that p and m are logarithms, so this says that the expected price level is proportional to the expected money supply.

To calculate the actual levels of output and prices, first of all, subtract Equation (28A.7) from Equation (28A.4) and Equation (28A.8) from Equation (28.5). The results are

$$y_t^d - y^* = (\alpha_t - \alpha_t^e) + \beta(m_t - m_t^e) - \beta(p_t - p_t^e) \qquad \textbf{(28A.10)}$$

and

$$y_t^s - y^* = \gamma(p_t - p_t^e) \tag{28A.11}$$

Equation (28A.10) says that aggregate demand will deviate from its full employment level by the amount that α deviates from its expected level, plus the amount that the money stock deviates from its expected level, multiplied by the parameter β minus the amount by which the price level deviates from its expected level, multiplied by the same parameter β. It is, in terms of the concepts discussed in the chapter, the unexpected component of aggregate demand. Equation (28A.11), in effect, is simply a rearrangement of Equation (28A.5). It says that deviations of aggregate supply from its full employment level will be proportional to deviations of the price level from its expectation.

We may now solve these two Equations (28A.10) and (28A.11) for the *actual* levels of output and prices. Using Equations (28A.10) and (28A.11) with (28A.6), these solutions are

$$y_t = y^* + \frac{\gamma}{\gamma + \beta}[\alpha_t - \alpha_t^e + \beta(m_t - m_t^e)] \tag{28A.12}$$

and

$$p_t = m_t^e - \frac{1}{\beta}(y^* - \alpha_t^e) + \frac{1}{\gamma + \beta}[\alpha_t - \alpha_t^e + \beta(m_t - m_t^e)] \tag{28A.13}$$

The output equation says that output will deviate from its full-employment level by an amount that depends on the unexpected components of α and the money supply. The price level will deviate from its expected level—the first two terms in Equation (28A.13)—by an amount that depends on the deviations of α and the money supply from their expected levels.

Thus, you can see that it is only unanticipated shifts in aggregate demand that affect output, and it is the fully anticipated and unanticipated shifts in aggregate demand that affect prices. The multipliers of the *IS-LM* analysis tell us about the distance of the horizontal shift of the aggregate demand curve. Equations (28A.12) and (28A.13) tell us that, to the extent that the horizontal shift is fully anticipated, it will do nothing but raise the price level. To the extent that it is unanticipated, it will raise both output and prices and will distribute its effects between output and prices in accordance with the slope parameter γ, the slope of the *EAS* curve. You can see, as a matter of interest, that if γ was infinitely big, the effect of an unanticipated shift in aggregate demand would be exactly the same as the *IS-LM* model says, and it would have no effect on prices. You can see this immediately for the price level in Equation (28A.13). For output, divide the top and bottom of $\gamma/(\gamma + \beta)$ by γ to give $1/[1 + (\beta/\gamma)]$. You now see that as γ approaches ∞, so $1/[1 + (\beta/\gamma)]$ approaches 1, and Equation (28A.12) becomes the *IS-LM* solution for income.

29

Explaining the Facts

After we had completed our review of the basic model of income, employment, and the price level, we examined the ability of the model to explain the facts. In Chapter 13 we discovered that the broad trends in inflation and some of the movements in unemployment are reasonably well accounted for by this model. The model is not capable, however, of explaining the procyclical co-movements of prices and output. Furthermore, the cyclical movements in real GNP and unemployment cannot be explained by the basic model.

Then, after examining the Keynesian model and the post-Keynesian neo-classical synthesis, in Chapter 22, we discovered that this model *is* capable of explaining one of the main things not explained by the basic model—the procyclical co-movements of prices. However, the major difficulty of the neo-classical model is its inability to account for surges in the rate of inflation that are not accompanied by low unemployment or, equivalently, by positive deviations of output from trend.

Now that we have completed our review of the rational expectations theories of income, employment, and prices, it is possible to examine how well these new macroeconomic models cope with the facts.

There is a marked contrast between the rational expectations theories and the mainstream neoclassical theory that arises purely from the length of time that each of them has been around. As was indicated in the introduction to Chapter 22, the post-Keynesian neoclassical synthesis has been the main-stream macroeconomic model for a whole generation, and so a vast amount of work has been done comparing the predictions of that model with the facts. In contrast, the new theories have been around for less than a decade and, in many cases, are still being digested. Not nearly so much work has been done on these models[1] as on the mainstream neoclassical synthesis. It is not yet

[1]The main contributions have been Robert E. Lucas, Jr., "Some International Evidence on Output-Inflation Tradeoffs," *The American Economic Review*, 63, (September 1973) 326–34, Robert J. Barro and Mark Rush, "Unanticipated Money and Economic Activity," Chap. 2 in Stanley Fischer, ed., *Rational Expectations and Economic Policy*, (Chicago and London: University of Chicago Press, 1980), Thomas J. Sargent, "A Classical Macroeconomic Model for the United States," *Journal of Political Economy*, 84 (June 1976), 207–37 and John B. Taylor, "Estimation and Control of a Macro-

clear, therefore, to what extent these new theories are going to be successful in explaining the facts. They look very promising at this stage, and this chapter will indicate to you why that is so.

For at least two reasons, it would be surprising if the rational expectations theories do not do as at least as good a job of explaining the facts as the basic model and the neoclassical synthesis do. First, the new theories have been devised with the benefit of hindsight; we know what is wrong with the basic and neoclassical models and can design new theories to take account of the anomalies or failures of prediction of those earlier models. Second, as we have seen, there are some areas in which the basic model predicts well and others in which the neoclassical model predicts well. It so happens that the areas where one of those two models predicts badly are exactly the areas where the other does well.

We cannot, at least not if we are going to obey some pretty basic rules of logic, simultaneously maintain the neoclassical model and the basic model as explaining the facts. They are mutually inconsistent. The basic model assumes that prices adjust quickly to achieve continuous equilibrium in all markets, whereas the neoclassical model denies this and assumes instead that price adjustment and wage adjustment are slow and, furthermore, asymmetric in the sense that prices and wages rise more easily than they fall.

What the new theories do, in effect, is to provide us with a trick that enables us to have the best of both models, while, as a matter of logic, denying that either of them is correct. The basic model is seen as the special case when the shocks are not fully anticipated. The Keynesian model (in its strict sense) applies when the shocks are entirely unanticipated.

Of course, this identification of the basic and Keynesian models as two special cases and the neoclassical synthesis as a set of intermediate cases of the rational expectations theories does not, in and of itself, tell us that the rational expectations theories are going to turn out to be correct. We cannot simply define the shocks that have hit the economy as being anticipated or unanticipated or some combination of the two so as to ensure that the theory fits the facts. It is necessary to establish a priori how changes in policy instruments and other exogenous variables have been perceived–the extent to which they have actually been anticipated and unanticipated—so as to test the rational expectations theories.

That task is well beyond anything that can be done in this chapter (or indeed in this book) and is going to be the subject matter of a great deal of research activity in macroeconomics in the coming years. What we can do, nevertheless, is to see how, in principle at least, the new theories are capable of explaining the facts and what is the nature of the research task ahead. In pursuit of that objective, this chapter takes you through six tasks, which are to:

(a) Understand how unanticipated changes in aggregate demand generate procyclical co-movements in prices.

---

economic Model with Rational Expectations," *Econometrica*, 47 (September 1979), 1267–86. These last two papers are technically *much* more demanding than the first two and all of them more demanding than the presentation given here.

(b) Understand how a combination of unanticipated and anticipated changes in aggregate demand generates surges in inflation that are independent of output and also generates procyclical co-movements in prices.

(c) Know how the rational expectations theories explain the autocorrelation of output and employment.

(d) Understand the implications of the rational expectations theories for interest rate behavior.

(e) Understand how the rational expectations theories explain the business cycle.

(f) Understand the nature of the hypothesis testing problem posed by the rational expectations theories.

A. Procyclical Co-Movements in Prices

You have seen in Chapter 28 how an anticipated change in aggregate demand affects only the nominal variables of the economy, and how an unanticipated change in aggregate demand has both nominal and real effects. It is now possible to use this analysis to understand how the swings in economic activity that are characterized by procyclical co-movements in prices occur.

For illustrative purposes it is going to be easiest to assume that the expected aggregate demand curve does not change. Equivalently, this implies that the expected money supply and expected government expenditure and taxes are constant. (It would be possible to assume that the expected *growth rate* of the money supply was constant, so that the expected level of the money supply was increasing by a constant percentage amount each period. In that case, the aggregate demand curve would be shifting upwards at a constant percentage rate, and there would be a trend rate of inflation. We would then analyze variations in aggregate demand around its rising trend position. However, such an exercise would complicate the analysis without adding any insights and will not be pursued here.)

In order to fix our ideas, let us suppose that the level of aggregate demand that actually occurs differs from that which is expected because the actual money supply is randomly fluctuating around its anticipated level. Sometimes it is above and sometimes it is below its anticipated level. Figures 29.1 and 29.2 will illustrate what is going on. Figure 29.1 shows a hypothetical random path for the money supply. (These illustrative numbers are random drawings from a normal distribution with a mean of 100 and a standard deviation of 2.) The average value of the money supply is 100; therefore, the rational expectation of the money supply is also 100. The maximum value of the money supply in this example, 104, occurs in period 5 and is marked A. The minimum value, 95.8, occurs in period 9 and is marked B.

Figure 29.2 shows the aggregate demand and aggregate supply curves. The curve $AD(M = 100)$ is the aggregate demand curve drawn for the expected value of the money supply. The expectations-augmented aggregate supply curve, EAS_0, is drawn for an expected price level equal to its rational expectation, P^e_0. The vertical curve, AS, is the full-employment aggregate supply curve.

Figure 29.1
Hypothetical Money Supply Path

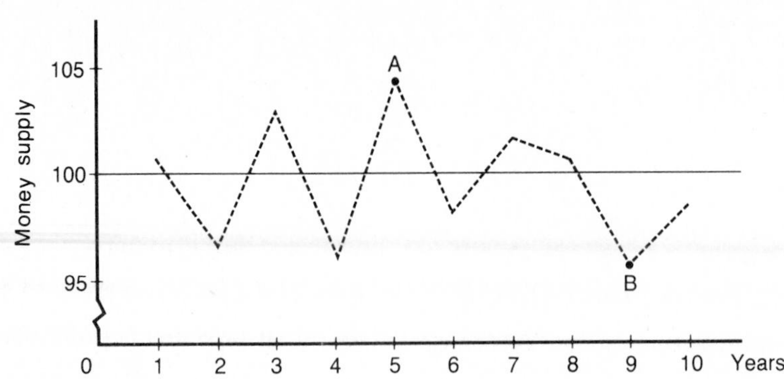

A hypothetical path for the money supply is generated by drawing random numbers from a normal distribution that has an average value of 100 and a standard deviation of 2. The path plotted was generated by taking ten drawings from such a distribution.

If the money supply behaves as shown in Figure 29.1, then the economy will, on the average, be at the price level P_0^e and, on the average, will have a full-employment output level of y^*. There will, however, be fluctuations around these points. When the money supply is at A, its maximum value in this example, the aggregate demand curve will be the curve shown as $AD(M = 104)$. This determines output as y_a and the price level as P_a. When the money supply is at B, its minimum value in this example, the aggregate demand curve will be at the position shown as $AD(M = 95.8)$. In this case, output will be y_b, and the price level will be P_b. For intermediate values of the money supply (periods 1 to 4, 6 to 8, and 10), output and the price level will be determined at points in between these two extremes and along the EAS_0 curve. The thickened portion of the curve traces out the range of values of y and P generated by this hypothetical money supply path.

Although random variations in the money supply about the anticipated level have been stylized as random variations around a *constant* anticipated money supply, as noted above, it would not be difficult to generalize this analysis. If the anticipated money supply was growing, then the expected aggregate demand curve and, therefore, the expectations-augmented aggregate supply curve would also drift upwards. The actual variations in the money supply, however, would fluctuate around the rising trend, so that the actual aggregate demand curve would fluctuate around the expected curve. We would, therefore, still generate procyclical co-movements of prices, although the amplitude of the price movements would be accentuated, and those of the output movements would be smaller than those illustrated.

The predicted procyclical co-movements of prices shown in Figure 29.2 can easily be translated into a predicted negative relationship between inflation and unemployment. When output is above its full-employment level, unemployment will be below its natural rate, and vice versa. When the price level is higher than expected, the inflation rate will also be higher than expected. Therefore, procyclical co-movements of prices automatically imply a

Figure 29.2
The Procyclical Co-Movements of Prices

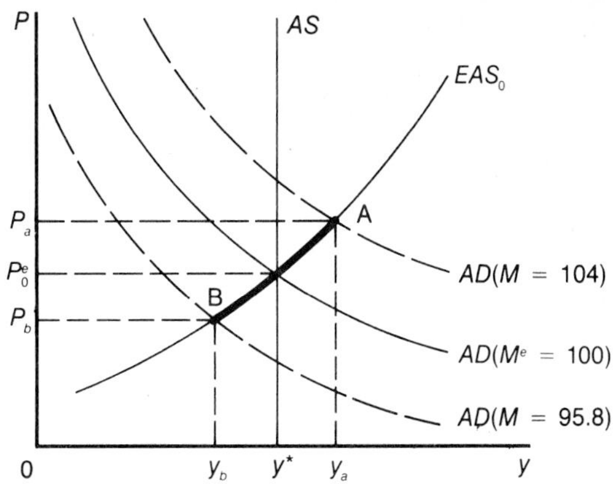

If the money supply was equal to its average value (and rationally expected value) of 100, the aggregate demand curve would be the solid line $AD\,(M^e = 100)$, output would be y^*, and the price level P^e_0. Actual movements in the money supply will shift the demand function as shown between the limits $AD\,(M = 104)$ and $AD\,(M = 95.8)$. With a constant expected price level, the expectations-augmented aggregate supply curve remains at EAS_0, and the actual levels of output and prices are generated along the thick line AB. This thickened line traces out the generally procyclical price movement.

negative correlation between inflation and unemployment—the Phillips curve.

You have now seen how the rational expectations theories generate one aspect of the facts that need to be explained—the sometimes observed, systematic, procyclical co-movements of prices. This is a phenomenon that the neoclassical synthesis could also cope with, but one that the basic model failed to predict. Let us now move on to consider how the rational expectations theories cope with some other facts.

B. Independent Movements in Output and Prices

There is not much to be said that has not already been said in previous chapters about the effects of an anticipated change in aggregate demand. This was explored in Chapter 28, and you saw there that the effects of such a change are identical to the predictions of the basic model. The entire analysis presented in Part III of this book, therefore, stands as the prediction of the rational expectations theories concerning the effects of a fully anticipated change in aggregate demand.

It is particularly worthy of emphasis that the basic model makes the same predictions as does the rational expectations theories concerning the effects of an anticipated change in the growth rate of the money supply. Specifically, the basic model predicts that a change in the growth rate of the money supply will lead to a change in the rate of inflation that will, on the path toward the new steady state, overshoot the growth rate of the money supply. This carries over, without modification, to the rational expectations theories as the predicted effect of an anticipated change in the money supply growth rate. Since, in the basic model, changes in the inflation rate occurred *independently* of the level of output, you will recognize as a strength of the rational expectations theories their ability to explain what the Keynesian theory was not able to explain, namely, sudden surges in the rate of inflation that are independent of the level of output.

To see how the rational expectations theories are capable of accounting, in principle, for all the patterns that we observe in the co-movements of output and prices, let us consider separately the effects of anticipated, unanticipated, and combined monetary shocks to the economy.

Suppose first, as described in detail in the previous section, that there is a rise in the money supply that raises aggregate demand in an unanticipated fashion. We know that this will raise the price level (and the inflation rate) and will raise output. There will thus, from this source of shock, be a procyclical co-movement in prices. Suppose, at the opposite extreme, that there is a rise in the money supply that is anticipated. This will lead to a rise in the price level (inflation rate) with no corresponding movement of output. Now combine these two effects. There are two interesting cases. One is where the money supply increases by an amount that is partly anticipated and partly not. In this case, there will be a rise in both output and prices, but the rise in prices will be greater than if the rise in the money supply was unanticipated. Let us translate this into a prediction about inflation and unemployment rather than about prices and output.

In the experiment just reviewed, a higher output level will be associated with a lower unemployment rate, and a higher price level will be associated with a higher observed rate of inflation. This would mean that a rise in the money supply that was partly anticipated and partly not would generate a rise in inflation and a drop in unemployment. The amount by which prices rise would depend on the anticipated and unanticipated components of the rise in the money supply. The amount by which unemployment falls would depend only on the unanticipated change in the money supply. What this implies is that the slope of the Phillips curve (the pattern of points linking inflation to unemployment) will not be constant and will, in general, depend on the decomposition of the change in the money supply between its anticipated and unanticipated components.

We can see this in a more extreme case by considering a second example. Suppose that the money supply *is anticipated* to grow at a high rate. In this situation, suppose further that the money supply actually increases at a slow rate. This is a situation in which there is high anticipated money growth but negative unanticipated money growth. In such a situation, output will fall, and unemployment will rise. The inflation rate may either rise or fall, depending on the strength of the two offsetting effects upon it. The effect of a high anticipated growth of the money supply will be to keep inflation high, whereas the effect of a negative unanticipated change in the money supply will be to lower inflation. We cannot say, a priori, which of these two effects will dominate. It is possible, however, for the first to dominate, thereby producing a higher rate of inflation with a higher unemployment rate and an output rate that is below trend. This would be the case observed on several occasions in the 1970s when there was a tendency for both inflation and unemployment to rise together.

The behavior of U.S. unemployment and inflation in the 1970s may potentially be accounted for by this line of reasoning.

The crucial thing to emphasize and reiterate is that the way in which a change in aggregate demand is divided between a change in output and a change in prices depends on the extent to which that change in aggregate demand is anticipated. On the average, output and prices will move in the same direction as each other, since swings in actual aggregate demand are likely to have greater amplitude than swings in expected aggregate demand. From time to time, however, there may be large shifts in anticipated aggregate demand, usually less than, but occasionally greater than, the change in actual aggregate demand. These occasional strong changes in expected aggregate demand will produce co-movements that are opposite to those normally observed, and when they occur, they will be associated with the appearance of badly deteriorating (or, although it has not happened in the 1970s, of miraculously improving) macroeconomic performance.

The discussion in this section and in the preceding one has focused on the way in which the price and output co-movements might be understood. There is one further feature of the behavior of output, however, on which that discussion has not touched and to which we now turn.

C. Autocorrelation of Output and Employment

There are two distinct, although not mutually exclusive, explanations for autocorrelation of output and employment. One is based on costs of adjustment of labor and is employed in the new classical analysis. The other is based on overlapping contracts and is used in the new Keynesian theory. Let us look at each of them in turn.

Adjustment Costs

The theory of profit-maximizing firms' demand for labor and supply of output, as developed in Chapter 8, which underlies all the models—the basic, Keynesian, and rational expectations—implicitly assumes that firms can vary their output and labor inputs instantly and costlessly. This is a reasonable assumption to make for the purpose of getting some theoretical principles straight. It is probably not a good assumption, however, if we want to explain the facts as they appear in actual economies. It is costly to hire and fire labor, and in the event of a change in demand, firms will only gradually adjust their labor inputs and outputs to meet the new demand conditions. Therefore, when the price level rises, instead of the demand for labor curve instantly shifting to reflect the new higher price level, it will move only gradually. Thus, if the economy experienced an unanticipated (say) rise in the money supply, then, although the response to that rise will be a higher price level and higher levels of output and employment, it will take firms some time to raise their output and employment levels by the amounts suggested by the theories developed in this book. Instead of the demand for labor curve suddenly shifting, it will gradually move to the right, thereby leading to a gradual change in employment and output rather than a sudden jump.

To make things clearer, suppose that after a period in which there had been an unanticipated rise in the money supply, there was a subsequent unanticipated fall. Firms will already have hired additional labor and be producing additional output, having moved some way toward satisfying the demand associated with the previously unanticipated rise in the money supply. Now that they are confronted with an unexpected fall in the money supply (and therefore an unexpected fall in the price level), they will not suddenly jump to the new lower employment and output position. Rather, they will, *starting from where they are*, gradually move toward the new lower output and employment position. This is not to say that firms are irrational and are not maximizing profits. On the contrary, it is precisely because they are maximizing profits that their adjustments will be gradual. They have to take account not only of the cost of labor and capital and the price of output in their profit-maximizing decisions but also of the costs of *changing* their output and employment. Thus, the costs of hiring and firing labor make the demand for labor curves move slowly, and this imparts gradual adjustment to output and employment.

Gradual adjustment may be described as *autocorrelation.* If output and employment adjust gradually, then where they will move to in the current period depends on where they started out from in the previous period, and where they will go to in the next period depends on where they are now. This can be described by saying that the values of output and employment in period t depend in part on the values of those variables in period $t - 1$.

The explanation for autocorrelation just presented is the one that is incorporated in the new classical theory of aggregate supply. A second way in which autocorrelation of output and employment can arise is emphasized in the new Keynesian theory and comes from the fact that contracts in the labor market are long and overlapping. Let us now look more closely at this explanation of autocorrelation.

Overlapping Contracts

It is not the case that everyone negotiates a labor contract on the same day of each year for the coming year. Some labor market contracts run for less than a year, some for a year, some for more than a year. The fact that labor market contracts overlap has important implications for the amount by which wages will change.

These implications are most easily seen in a simplified framework in which we imagine that contracts run for two years and that one-half of them are renegotiated each year. Figure 29.3 illustrates this setup. There are two groups: Group 1 negotiates contracts in odd-numbered years and group 2 in even-numbered years. In 1979, group 2's wages were W_0 (fixed in 1978), and group 1 negotiated a wage of W_1 to run for 1979 and 1980. In 1980, group 1's wages were predetermined at W_1 and group 2 set its wages at W_2 to run for 1980 and 1981. The pattern repeats forever. Now when group 1 is deciding on the appropriate level of wages in 1979, it will have to take some account of the wages that group 2 is receiving, W_0. How much influence group 2's wage will have on group 1's decision will depend on how substitutable the labor is

Figure 29.3
Overlapping Contracts

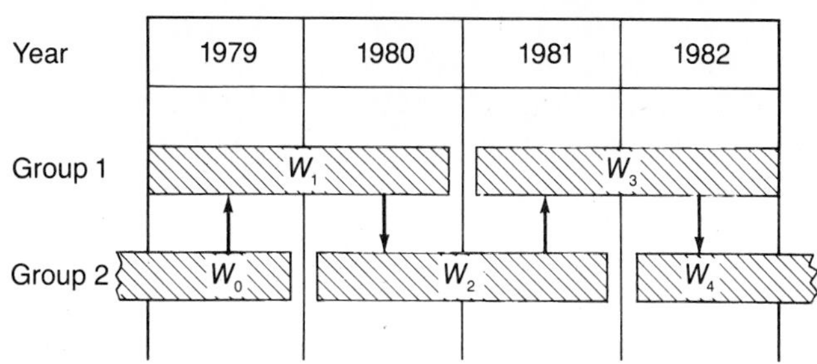

Wages set in 1979 (W_1) are influenced by wages already determined (W_0) and in turn influence wages that will be set in 1980 (W_2). The pattern repeats, so that wages set in 1982 (W_4) are indirectly influenced by all earlier set wages.

between the two groups. If it is not very substitutable, then the wages of one group will not be a major factor influencing the wages of the other. If on the other hand, the two groups are very close substitutes for each other, then the wages of one will have a major influence on the wage level of the other. Why is this?

Recall that the basic assumption of the new Keynesian analysis is that money wages are set to achieve an expected equilibrium in the labor market. When just one group of workers are negotiating wages in their own sector, they have to take account of the fact that the demand for their services will depend both on their own wages and on the wages of alternative substitute labor. There is also substitutability on the supply side. The higher the wages of one group relative to another, the more people would want to supply their services to the activities of that group. We see then, that the expected equilibrium wage for one group depends on the wage level of the other group. The closer substitutes that the two groups are for each other, the more sensitive will the equilibrium wage of one group be to the wage of the other group.

In terms of Figure 29.3, the wages set in 1979, W_1, will be influenced by the wages that already prevail in that year, W_0. The arrow indicates the line of influence going from W_0 to W_1. Likewise, in 1980 when group 2 sets its wages, it would be influenced by the wages that have been set by W_1. Again, the arrow illustrates this line of influence. The same pattern repeats in 1981 and 1982 and so on. This means that the wages that are being set at any particular date will be influenced directly by the wages that already prevail at that date, and they will be influenced indirectly by all the wages that have been set at all previous dates. Thus, the wages at any particular point in time will be influenced by wages at all past points in time.

EXPLAINING THE FACTS

Wages will adjust more gradually as a result of overlapping contracts than they would if all contracts were renegotiated on the same day. This is because, even though demand conditions might have changed, the movement of one wage too far out of line with other wages in competing activities would not be compatible with an expected full-employment equilibrium in the relevant labor market.

The fact that wages set at any particular point in time depend on the wages set at all previous points in time means that when setting a wage today, it is known by the parties agreeing to the wage that the decision being made will itself have an influence on decisions that are going to be made in the future.

Since future wages will be influenced in part by wages that are being fixed today, it is important in fixing today's wages to take account of likely future demand conditions. This means that rational wage setters in an economy in which contracts overlap will want to look as far into the future as they can in assessing the likely future course of aggregate demand and demand in their own particular sector. They will seek to form rational expectations not just about the immediate future period but about all future periods.

There is a second important implication of overlapping contracts. It is that contracts in existence in any particular year, having been negotiated at different dates in the past, will incorporate expectations that were formed in the past, and therefore are based on old information—information available at the past dates on which wages currently enforced were set. Thus, what was unanticipated when one set of contracts was written, some time in the past, might already have occurred and therefore be part of the information on the basis of which some other, more recent contracts were written. This means that a monetary (or other aggregate demand) shock that occurs after a contract has been written, and which was unanticipated when the contract was written, will continue to have effects on output and employment until that particular contract is replaced with a new one. Furthermore, those effects will persist long beyond the date on which all existing contracts have been replaced with new ones.

To see this, you simply have to recall that wages currently being set are influenced by wages already in place. This means that if the wages set last year (to run for two years) were set at a level that is now known to have been inappropriate in the light of changes that have occurred in aggregate demand, the fact that those wages are going to remain in place for another year means that wages being set this year, while taking some account of the new information about the change in aggregate demand, also have to be set such that they do not get so far away from the wages already set that they create an excess supply or demand in the part of the market whose wages are currently being determined. Also, when the wages set last year are reset next year, they will be influenced by the wages that have been set this year, and therefore they too will not fully incorporate all the new knowledge about current demand conditions but will continue to be influenced in part at least by their own previous value.

Thus, random shocks that bombard the economy will have effects that persist from period to period over the indefinite future. Their effects will die away gradually but not instantly.

You will recognize fairly readily that the behavior of wages in an economy with overlapping contracts may be described as displaying autocorrelation—that is, wages today depend on wages in some previous period. What we are seeking to understand, however, is not autocorrelated wages but autocorrelated output and employment. It is, however, only a short step from the behavior of wages to the behavior of employment and output. If wages are autocorrelated, so will employment and output be. To see this, you simply have to recall that the level of employment depends on the level of wages (real wages). The gradual adjustment of money wages takes account of the expected price level and is, in effect, an attempt to gradually adjust expected real wages. A gradual adjustment of real wages would automatically imply a gradual adjustment of the profit-maximizing level of employment and, therefore, of the level of output. Thus, overlapping labor market contracts lead not only to autocorrelated wages but to autocorrelated output and employment as well.

An Analogy The idea that costly labor input adjustments and overlapping long-term contracts can generate autocorrelation in output, employment, and prices has a vivid physical analogy that perhaps will make things clearer. Suppose one was to hit a rocking chair at random.[2] The chair is sometimes hit frequently and sometimes infrequently, sometimes with a hard knock and sometimes with a gentle one. Within wide limits, the chair will rock in a very systematic and persistent fashion regardless of how hard or often it is hit. It will swing to and fro much more systematically than the shocks that are being imparted to it by the person who is rocking it. It is much the same with the economy. The adjustment costs in labor markets and the negotiation costs in setting up new contracts mean that when unexpected events occur, there is sufficient inertia in the economy to ensure that it does not radically alter its course as a result of the random shock. Rather, its course is much more systematic and smooth than the path of the shocks themselves.

D. Interest Rate Behavior

Although, in the presentation of the rational expectations theories in Chapters 24 to 28, we have not explicitly analyzed the determination of the rate of interest, there are strong implications for interest rate determination in the rational expectations theories. To explore those implications fully and completely would require more time and space than is available here and, in some respects, would take us into a level of analysis that is substantially more demanding than would be appropriate. Nevertheless, it is possible to obtain a good understanding of the general implications for interest rate determination in the rational expectations theories. This brief section will pursue that task.

You already know that the market rate of interest deviates from the real rate of interest because of expected inflation. Let us recall why this is so. People borrow and lend for future periods of different lengths. That being so, the real rate of return that they will obtain at the end of a loan term will be

---

[2]The rocking analogy was first suggested as long ago as 1907 by the brilliant Swedish economist Knut Wicksell and was elaborated upon in 1933 by Ragnar Frisch: "If you hit a wooden rocking horse with a club, the movement of the horse will be very different to that of the club." Quoted from Ragnar Frisch, "Propagation Problems and Impulse Problems in Dynamic Economics," *Economic Essays in Honour of Gustave Cassell* (New York: Augustus M. Kelley, 1967), p. 158; this was originally published in 1933.

equal to the market rate of interest on the loan minus the actual rate of inflation that emerges over the term of the loan.

At the time at which a loan is contracted, the actual rate of inflation is unknown. The only substitute for the actual rate of inflation that both borrowers and lenders can use is their anticipation of the inflation that will occur over the term of the loan. Lenders will demand a premium on the interest rate to compensate for their anticipation of the inflation that is going to occur over the term of the loan, and borrowers will willingly pay a premium equal to their anticipation of inflation. Since both borrowers and lenders occupy the same economic environment and form their expectations in the same rational manner, there should be a consensus as to what the anticipated rate of inflation is. This amounts to saying that the market rate of interest that we should observe will equal the equilibrium real rate of interest (itself a variable), plus the rational expectation of the rate of inflation *over the term of the loan in question.* Thus, for three-month loans, this will mean that the anticipated three-month rate of inflation will be added to the real rate of interest; similarly, for 15-to-20-year loans, the rate of inflation expected over the long term, on the average, will be added to the real rate of interest.

The anticipated rate of inflation (the rational expectation of the future price level expressed as a percentage change over the current known price level and converted to an annual rate of change) will be determined by the expectations of those things that determine the actual rate of inflation. Since the actual rate of inflation is determined by the growth rate of the money supply and the trend growth rate of output, the expected rate of inflation will depend on the expected growth rate of the money supply and the expected output growth. In general, we would expect the actual growth rate of the money supply (and actual growth rate of aggregate demand) to be more volatile than movements in the expected growth rate of the money supply and expected growth of aggregate demand. This is precisely the consideration that led to the prediction of procyclical co-movements in prices as discussed above.

Further, in general, we would expect fluctuations in the expected long-term average growth rate of the money supply to be much smaller than fluctuations in expectations of, say, the next three-months' growth rate of the money supply or the next twelve-months' growth rate. Recall that the rate at which prices change depends on *both* the anticipated and unanticipated changes in the money supply. Movements in the interest rate, however, will depend only on the anticipated inflation rate and therefore only on the anticipated movements of the money supply. This implies that fluctuations in prices (inflation) will have greater amplitude and be more erratic than fluctuations in interest rates. Further, because fluctuations in the expected long-term average money supply growth rate will be smaller than fluctuations in the expected money supply growth rate over the short term, fluctuations in short-term interest rates will have greater amplitude than fluctuations in long-term interest rates.

It is an implication of the rational expectations theories that, like prices, interest rates will display procyclical co-movements. Interest rates, however, will have fluctuations of smaller amplitude than prices, and the longer the term of the interest rate, the smaller will be the amplitude of the fluctuation. You will recognize these predictions as being in accord with the facts if you recall the information on U.S. interest rates presented in Chapters 2 and 6 of this book.

E. The Business Cycle

This section does little more than bring together and consolidate what has already been said above.[3] The first feature of the business cycle that was identified in Chapter 6 was the description of the movements of real economic activity (as measured by output) as a low-order stochastically disturbed difference equation. Specifically, we saw that it was possible to describe real GNP by an equation that says that deviations from trend in real GNP in year t is equal to 0.84 of its value in the previous year plus a random component. You can now see how the rational expectations theories explain that simple description of the evolution of real GNP. The autocorrelation component (the persistence effect) is rationalized either in terms of costly adjustment of inputs of labor or in terms of overlapping wage and employment contracts. The sources of randomness that hit the economy are identified as the unanticipated components of monetary and fiscal changes as well as, of course implicitly, randomness in decisions concerning private expenditure and money holding.

The second feature of the business cycle described in Chapter 6 and identified as being present in the United States is the procyclical co-movement of prices and interest rates. We have seen in this chapter how the normally observed procyclical co-movements of prices are to be explained as the consequence of fluctuations in actual aggregate demand having greater amplitude than the fluctuations in anticipated aggregate demand. We have also seen that the procyclical co-movements of interest rates, smaller in amplitude than the fluctuations in prices and of even smaller amplitude in the case of long-term interest rates, are all explicable in these same terms. Basically, fluctuations in expected values of variables are (usually) less marked than fluctuations in actual values, and the longer the period over which an average expectation is being formed, the smaller will be the amplitude of the fluctuations in that expectation.

The key ingenuity of the rational expectations theories lies in their ability to account for the autocorrelated movements of output and the procyclical co-movements of prices and interest rates, while at the same time being able to account for the infrequent but, when they occur, important independent movements of inflation and output. You have seen in this chapter how that explanation is achieved. The final task of this chapter is to set out a few problems that arise in the area of testing the explanation just advanced.

---

[3]For a much fuller treatment of this topic and more—indeed with the entire subject matter of this book—you will want to read two brilliant papers by Robert E. Lucas, Jr., "Understanding Business Cycles," *Journal of Monetary Economics*, vol. 5, supp. 1977, Carnegie-Rochester Conference Series on Public Policy; and "Methods and Problems in Business Cycle Theory," *Journal of Money, Credit and Banking*, 12, pt. 2 (November 1980), 696–715. For a thoughtful critique, you will also want to read James Tobin's discussion of the second cited Lucas paper, on pp. 795–99 of the same journal.

F. The Hypothesis Testing Problem Posed by the Rational Expectations Theories

This chapter has tried to show you how the rational expectations theories of income, employment, and prices are capable, *in principle*, of explaining the facts. This exercise should not be confused with one of actually explaining the facts—a task that is much more difficult and requires careful, indeed, painstaking measurement and statistical inference.[4] Testing the explanations advanced in this chapter is something that is only in its infancy and is going to occupy a great deal of time and energy in the coming years.[5] This section merely reviews some of the highlights of the problems that arise for that activity.

The first problem that has to be solved is that of finding a plausible, a priori defendable, and, ideally, noncontroversial way of decomposing changes in money, government spending, taxes (and perhaps other exogenous variables) into their anticipated and unanticipated components. This involves studying the *processes* that describe the evolution of these variables and finding ways of forecasting them that mimic reasonably well the ways in which agents in the real world might go about that task. In the example of the money supply, referred to in Chapter 28, the money supply process was described as a low-order autoregression that reacts to unusually large fluctuations in government spending and to unemployment. This seems like a promising hypothesis for explaining how anticipations of monetary growth are formed.

The second major problem arises in discriminating between the new Keynesian and new classical theories. As you saw, these two theories are very similar, but they differ in three respects. First, they imply different slopes for the expectations-augmented aggregate supply curve, and second, one theory implies that households will always be "on" their labor supply curve, whereas the other implies that they may at some stages be "off" that curve. From an observational point of view it is very difficult to discriminate between these two differences, since we do not know, a priori, what the slope of the expectations-augmented aggregate supply curve is; nor would it be very easy, a priori, to identify whether or not individuals were "on" or "off" their labor supply curves.

The third source of difference does provide a potential way of discriminating, but it will not be easy to exploit. It is the difference between the two theories arising from the overlapping nature of labor market contracts emphasized by the new Keynesian theory. The difference in question is the way in

---

[4]A useful overview and survey of this topic may be found in Stanley Fischer, ed., *Rational Expectations and Economic Policy*, National Bureau of Economic Research Conference Report (Chicago and London: University of Chicago Press, 1980), esp. pp. 49–70.

[5]Three good examples of such work, though much more demanding than the level of this book, are Robert J. Barro and Mark Rush, "Unanticipated Money and Economic Activity," in Stanley Fischer, ed., (see note 4 above), 23–54; Thomas J. Sargent, "A Classical Macroeconometric Model for the United States," *Journal of Political Economy*, 84, (June 1976), 207–37; and John B. Taylor, "Estimation and Control of a Macroeconomic Model with Rational Expectations," *Econometrica*, 47, (September 1979), 1267–86. The work of Barro and Sargent is "neoclassical," and that of Taylor is new Keynesian.

which the random shocks combine to affect the current value of output, employment, and prices. According to the new classical theory, the current random shock combined with the previous actual value of output is all that is required to explain what is happening in the current period, whereas for the new Keynesian approach, the shocks from previous periods explicitly have to be combined with the current period shock to generate the current period output, employment, and price level.

There is a third problem known as "observational equivalence."[6] Although not a precise statement of this problem, you can still get a feel for it if you contemplate the task of attempting to discriminate between the neoclassical synthesis of Chapter 22 and the rational expectations models being discussed here. The neoclassical synthesis places no restrictions on the factors that lead (effectively) to exogenous changes in inflation expectations. It is possible, therefore, to set out an infinite number of alternative neoclassical models which incorporate any imaginable alternative hypothesis about those factors and the time lags in their influence. There will always exist (at least) one such model that "fits the facts" with identical precision to the "fit" of any given rational expectations model.

It is always possible, as a matter of logic, to construct such an observationally equivalent theory. What this implies is that the ultimate test of a theory is its ability to predict the future rather than the past!

Summary

A. Procyclical Co-Movements in Prices

Generally, the swings in the actual values of variables that determine aggregate demand (for example, the money supply) are bigger than the swings in the anticipated values of these variables. This means that the aggregate demand curve fluctuates with greater amplitude than the expectations-augmented aggregate supply curve. The consequence of this is procyclical co-movements of prices in general.

B. Independent Movements in Output and Prices

Anticipated changes in aggregate demand will move the price level but leave output undisturbed, whereas unanticipated changes in aggregate demand will move with the price level and output. By combining anticipated and unanticipated movements in aggregate demand (generated by anticipated and unanticipated movements in monetary and fiscal policy variables), we are able, in principle, to account for the facts about output and prices (or, equivalently, unemployment and inflation). As a general rule, prices are procyclical (inflation and unemployment are negatively related) for the reasons summarized above. Occasionally there will be a surge in inflation that is independent of, or

[6]This problem is explained in Thomas J. Sargent, "The Observational Equivalence of Natural and Unnatural Rate Theories of Macroeconomics," *Journal of Political Economy*, 84 (June 1976), 631–40.

even sometimes goes in the same direction as, the unemployment rate. This will arise because the anticipated rise in the money supply is high, whereas the unanticipated change in the money supply is negative.

C. Autocorrelation of Output and Employment

Output is autocorrelated even though the shocks that hit the economy are purely random because the costs of changing labor inputs and overlapping labor contracts impart inertia into firms' adjustments of employment and output.

D. Interest Rate Behavior

Money rates of interest will exceed real rates of interest by an amount equal to the anticipated rate of inflation. The term over which inflation has to be anticipated is the same as the term over which a loan is made. For three-month loans, the relevant anticipated inflation rate is that over the next three months. For twenty-year loans, the average anticipation of average inflation over the next twenty years is required. Anticipated inflation depends only on anticipated money growth, whereas actual inflation depends on both anticipated and unanticipated money growth. Interest rates will fluctuate in a generally procyclical manner but with less amplitude than prices because the anticipated money supply growth rate will fluctuate with a smaller amplitude than the actual money supply growth rate. Longer-term interest rates will have an even smaller amplitude of fluctuation because fluctuations in the anticipated long-term average money supply growth rate will have smaller amplitude than those of short-term anticipations.

E. The Business Cycle

The first feature of the business cycle, the autocorrelation of output, is explained by the costs of adjusting labor input and the costs of overlapping labor market contracts. The procyclical co-movements of prices and interest rates are explained by the tendency for the actual variables that generate aggregate demand (monetary and fiscal policy variables) to fluctuate with bigger amplitude than their expected values. The nonuniversality of the procyclical co-movements of prices arises from the occasional jump in the anticipated money supply growth rate (sometimes in excess of that which actually occurs).

F. The Hypothesis Testing Problem Posed by the Rational Expectations Theories

The major problem is that of finding a convincing and noncontroversial way of decomposing changes in the actual values of exogenous variables into their anticipated and unanticipated components. Discriminating between the new Keynesian and new classical theories will be difficult because they are almost equivalent from an observational point of view. Further, discriminating the rational expectations theories from traditional theory purely on the basis of the past will be difficult since it is always possible to patch up the traditional theory with an appropriately general theory of the time lags involved in the adjustment of expectations for the two theories to yield identical predictions. The ultimate test of any theory will lie in its ability to predict the future rather than the past.

Review Questions

1. Explain how, in general, procyclical co-movements in prices and output are explained by the rational expectations theories.
2. Show how the rational expectations theories explain the fact that, on occasion, there is a strong rise in inflation accompanied by low output and high unemployment.
3. Do the new Keynesian and new classical theories differ as regards their explanation of the phenomenon described in Question 2? If so, how?
4. What is the explanation offered by the new classical theory of auto-correlation in output and employment?
5. What is the explanation offered by the new Keynesian theory of the auto-correlation in output and employment?
6. What is the explanation given by the rational expectations theories of interest rate behavior? Why do long-term interest rates fluctuate with smaller amplitude than short-term rates, and why do short-term rates fluctuate with smaller amplitude than inflation?
7. Review the explanation offered by the rational expectations theories of the business cycle. How do they differ from the neoclassical explanation?
8. Assess the assertion that the rational expectations theories are non-scientific because they can never be falsified.
9. (Similar to 8!) Assess the assertion that since we can decompose the changes in monetary and fiscal variables into anticipated and unanticipated components so as to make the rational expectations theories fit the facts, any such theory will suffer from the ultimate weakness of being capable of explaining everything and predicting nothing.
10. State succinctly why the assertions in Questions 8 and 9 are wrong.

Appendix to Chapter 29

A Methodological Postscript

I have an aversion to methodological discussions in the abstract—no doubt arising from the fact that I am an economist and not a philosopher of science. It is possible, however, that extra insights will be obtained into the theories that have been presented in the last 22 chapters if we stand back a little from the detail and think about what we have been doing in more general abstract terms. This methodological postscript discusses two interrelated matters. The first has to do with the distinction between *ex post* or realized values of variables and *ex ante* or planned values, as well as the closely related distinction between accounting identities and equilibrium conditions. The second matter to be discussed is the distinction between equilibrium and disequilibrium methods of modelling economic activity.

Economic Variables and the Relations Amongst Them

We have, in the last 22 chapters, developed models that purport to make predictions about actual events in the world. These are predictions about the behavior of such variables as income, output, employment, unemployment, prices, and interest rates. The models seek to make predictions about the *actual* values of variables. These actual values are called *ex post* or *realized values. Ex post* or realized variables are linked together with *accounting identities.* That is, certain realized values of certain variables are defined to be equal to certain sums of other variables. Some of the most obvious of such accounting identities are those that say that one variable is identically equal to another. The equality between national income, expenditure, and output is an example of this. In general, purchases always equal sales. Certain stocks are related to each other in a similar way; for example, the stock of money issued by the central bank is equal to the stocks of money held by the commercial banks and private individuals.

In explaining—in generating predictions about—these actual variables, we have developed theories that make statements about the plans of economic agents. We have postulated that rational agents maximize utility or profit and as a result of these maximization experiments come through with plans for consumption or labor supply or output supply or labor demand. Aggregating these plans over all agents leads to aggregate plans such as aggregate demand, the aggregate demand for money, investment, consumption, and the like. These are not actual quantities. They are not even a single quantity. They are *conditional* quantities; that is, aggregate demand will be so much if the price level is some particular value. If the price level is a lower value, then aggregate demand will be a higher value. These planned magnitudes are called *ex ante* or, more directly, *planned variables.*

It is possible to imagine a situation in which the plans of different individuals are not necessarily compatible with each other. A situation in which plans are compatible is called an *equilibrium.* A situation in which plans are not compatible is called a *disequilibrium.* The statement that one *ex ante* (planned) magnitude is equal to some other relevant *ex ante* (planned) magnitude is known as an *equilibrium condition.* For example, supply equals demand is such a condition. Equilibrium conditions and accounting identities look very similar to each other. For example, purchases equals sales is an accounting identity and supply equals demand an equilibrium condition. Although they look very similar, the meaning of these two statements is fundamentally different. An accounting identity is always true from the definition of the variables. An equilibrium condition is a statement about the compatibility of plans.

The above discussion of equilibrium and disequilibrium invites us to go further and examine these two concepts as ways of developing economic models.

Equilibrium and Disequilibrium Methods in Economic Modelling

There are two distinct ways in which it is possible to develop an economic model—the equilibrium method and the disequilibrium method. In the equilibrium method, "the concepts of excess demands and supplies play no observational role and are identified with no observed magnitudes."[7] All observed quantities and prices are at the intersection points of supply and demand curves. That is, they are points in which plans of individual agents are compatible with each other. Movements in prices and quantities are the results of movements in supply and/or demand curves.

Disequilibrium models, in contrast to equilibrium models, are ones in which (to negate the above quotation) excess demands and supplies play an observational role and are indeed identified with observed quantities. In the context of macroeconomics, unemployment is a phenomenon identified with the concept of the excess supply of labor, and inflation is a magnitude identified with the excess demand for goods. In the disequilibrium method, observed quantities are, in general, disequilibrium quantities. Movements in prices and quantities are responses to disequilibrium.

Choosing between these two alternative ways of building an economic model is *not an empirical matter*. It is a *matter of axiomatic principle*. When one model fits the facts and another one doesn't, choosing between them is a relatively straightforward matter. If two models fit the facts equally well but differ in the assumptions they make about matters that are essentially nonobservable, choosing between them is a more delicate matter. Criteria such as the number of assumptions required and even such aesthetic matters as the elegance of the model become relevant considerations. There is an ongoing debate in economics (in macroeconomics in particular) as to which of these two methods is the most appropriate one to use.[8]

The following brief diagrammatic analysis will explain to you why it is possible to model the same phenomenon either as a disequilibrium or an equilibrium process. Figure 29A.1 illustrates a market for a single quantity q (it could be labor or goods, an aggregate market or an individual commodity or factor market), the initial quantity traded of which is q^* and the initial price of which is p^*. To keep the picture very simple, imagine that supply is completely inelastic and is illustrated by the vertical line s in both frame (a) and frame (b). Initially, demand is given by the curve d, which is shown in both frames (a) and (b). Imagine that at a particular point in time, the price began to rise above p^*, but the quantity remained constant at q^*. Thus the economy goes through a process in which the price level gradually rises from p^* to $p^{*\prime}$ but with a constant quantity. How could this process be explained using the two alternative methodologies?

First, consider the disequilibrium approach [frame (a)]. According to this theory, the demand function has shifted to d', generating excess demand of $q' - q^*$. With excess demand, prices begin to rise—as shown by the price adjustment curve in the lower part of frame (a). As prices rise, excess demand falls, and eventually when prices have risen all the way to $p^{*\prime}$, there is no excess demand left, and the economy is back at an equilibrium. Throughout

[7]Robert E. Lucas, Jr., "Methods and Problems in Business Cycle Theory, "*Journal of Money, Credit and Banking,*" 12, no. 4, pt. 2 (November 1980), 709.

[8]The entire paper by Lucas cited in the previous footnote is an excellent statement of the case for an equilibrium methodology. Also see, by the same author, "Tobin and Monetarism: A Review Article," *The Journal of Economic Literature*, 19, no. 2, (June 1981), 558–85.

Figure 29A.1
Equilibrium-Disequilibrium Price Adjustment Processes

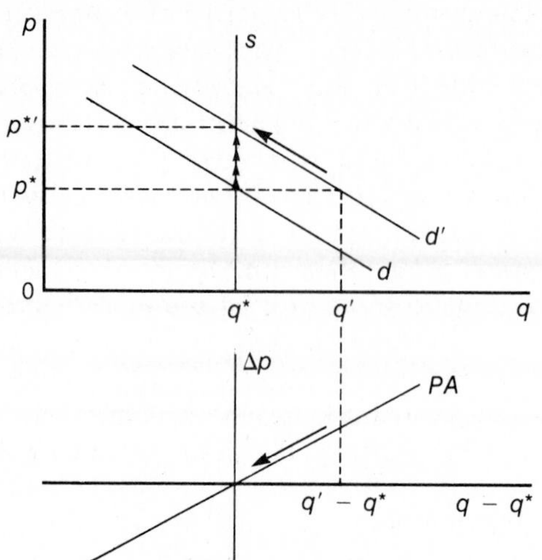

(a) Disequilibrium Price Adjustment Process

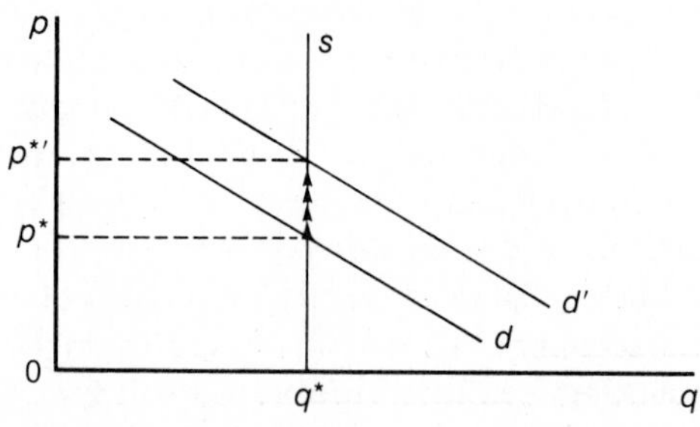

(b) Equilibrium Price Adjustment Process

The same facts, a gradual rise in the price with a constant quantity, is explained by two alternative theoretical methods. Frame (a) describes the event as a disequilibrium process. The demand curve shifts to d', creating an excess demand. Excess demand leads to rising prices, so that the economy slides up d' and down PA to the new equilibrium price $p^{*\prime}$. Frame (b) illustrates an equilibrium representation of the same process. Demand conditions change, but at the moment of impact, the demand curve does not move. The equilibrium price and quantity remain constant, therefore, at p^*, q^*. Gradually the demand curve moves upwards, and as it does so, it intersects the supply curve at higher and higher prices. Eventually, the demand curve moves all the way to d' (the same curve as that postulated to have arisen instantaneously in the case of the disequilibrium approach), and the price level has risen to $p^{*\prime}$.

the process of moving from p^* to $p^{*\prime}$, the economy has been in disequilibrium. The quantity demanded has exceeded the quantity supplied throughout that process.

The alternative methodology—the equilibrium methodology—would explain the same events in the following way. In the very short run, demand does not change but remains at the level shown by the demand curve labelled d.

Something has happened, however, to change demand conditions, and so demand gradually increases. This will take the form of the demand curve gradually shifting upwards from d to d'. As it does so, it will intersect the supply curve at higher and higher prices, and eventually the demand curve will have moved to d' (the postulated instantaneous shift in the disequilibrium approach). Throughout the process of adjustment in frame (b), the economy has been in equilibrium. The quantity demanded has been equal to the quantity supplied.

The same facts occur in both situations and are clearly amenable to explanation by the two alternative methods.

If two equilibria are compared, the analysis being undertaken is known as *comparative statics*. According to the equilibrium method, comparative statics is an empirically relevant exercise. It involves comparing two situations, which, according to the method being employed, are situations that are relevant to the actual economy and not simply relevant to the theoretical construct—the model economy. According to the disequilibrium method, comparative statics is interesting in that it tells us where the economy is headed for but uninteresting as a general description of where the economy was initially and will move to following some exogenous shock.

The process whereby the economy moves from one stationary position (such as p^*, q^*) to another (such as $p^{*\prime}$, $q^{*\prime}$) is called a *dynamic process*, and the analysis of such a process is called *dynamics*. From what has been said above, it will be clear to you that dynamics is *not* synonymous with disequilibrium. There are both equilibrium and disequilibrium theories of dynamic processes.

You may find it helpful, in the light of the methodological discussion presented in this postscript, to review again the material presented in Part II concerning the measurement of economic variables. In that part, all the variables presented as *ex post* or realized and all the relations amongst them are accounting identities. Additionally, you may find it helpful to review again the alternative theories of macroeconomics. The basic model as well as the new classical model use the equilibrium method, whereas the Keynesian model and the neoclassical synthesis use the disequilibrium method. The new Keynesian model is always in an expected equilibrium but never in an actual equilibrium (except of course in the event that the random shocks are zero).

30

Introduction to Macroeconomic Policy

You have completed your study of macroeconomic theory—the problem of explaining macroeconomic phenomena—and are ready to examine the implications of that theory for the formation and conduct of macroeconomic policy. There has been a good deal of policy discussion implicit in the presentation of the theory itself, but it is now time to address the policy issues more directly and systematically. This brief introductory chapter will enable you to start on that process by doing three things. It will enable you to:

(a) Know what macroeconomic policies seek to achieve.
(b) Know the highlights in the evolution of the policy debate.
(c) Understand the idea that policy is a process and not an event.

A. What Macroeconomic Policies Seek to Achieve

There is little disagreement among economists concerning what an ideal macroeconomic performance would look like. There might be some arguments of detail, but these are insignificant compared with the broad agreement on two matters. First, it would be ideal if unemployment, except for that associated with job searching and normal labor turnover, could be entirely eliminated. That is, it would be ideal if unemployment could be kept at its "natural" rate. Equivalently, it would be ideal if output could be maintained at its full-employment equilibrium value on a continuous basis. Second, it would be ideal if inflation could be held at a steady, constant, low (perhaps, ideally, zero) rate. Associated with this would be the ideal that the market rate of interest would be equal to the real rate of interest. Recognizing that perfection is impossible, the objective could be expressed slightly more generally as that of minimizing the deviations of: (1) unemployment from its natural rate, (2) output from its full-employment rate, (3) inflation from zero, and (4) market interest rates from real interest rates.

It is worth emphasizing that the specification of the unemployment objective is that of keeping unemployment as close to its natural rate as possible and *not* that of lowering the natural rate to as low a level as possible. It is important to understand that too little unemployment can have serious consequences for the economic welfare of all, even for those who are from time to time unemployed. Job search and job changing are productive activities. Further, even if it is judged that the natural rate of unemployment is, in fact, too high, then the only policy measures that can be taken to influence that rate are *microeconomic* (relative price) policies. It would be necessary to change the unemployment insurance arrangements, methods of taxing income from employment, or some other similar matter such as was discussed in Chapter 11. In other words, the natural rate of unemployment is not itself a variable that can be influenced by the macroeconomic policy instruments of aggregate government spending, taxes, or monetary growth.

The *objectives of macroeconomic policy*, then, are to minimize the variability of unemployment and output about their natural rates and to minimize the variability of inflation around some low, possibly zero, value.

B. Highlights in the Evolution of the Policy Debate

In the pre-Keynesian era, the general feeling was that the fluctuations in economic activity that characterized the business cycle were natural phenomena that simply had to be put up with. They were in the same class as storms, floods, and tempests. They buffeted human societies in a serious and sometimes devastating way but simply had to be accepted as one of the harsh facts of life. The Keynesian revolution, which began in the middle 1930s, but didn't achieve its full influence until the 1950s and 1960s, radically changed that view. The business cycle was seen as entirely controllable. It was widely believed that monetary and fiscal policy could and should be used to manipulate aggregate demand to ensure the achievement of full employment and stable prices. Some believed that monetary and fiscal policies could achieve the objective of high employment and output but not that of price stability: they were nevertheless undaunted in their pursuit of both objectives and regarded the implementation of direct controls on wages and prices or, more euphemistically, "incomes policies," as the appropriate additional instrument for achieving price stability.[1]

As we moved into the 1970s, it became increasingly apparent that macroeconomic policy was not delivering the promised stability. Inflation rates accelerated, and this despite the fact that unemployment rates were historically high and output growth sagging. Coinciding with this dismal macroeconomic policy performance, there emerged a radically new view of how economic fluctuations are generated and what might be done to moderate them. The centerpiece of the new view is the hypothesis that expectations are formed rationally.[2] This hypothesis not only leads to a radical transformation in the

[1]For a superb account of this view, see Franco Modigliani, "The Monetarist Controversy or, Should We Forsake Stabilization Policies?" *American Economic Review*, 67 (March 1977), 1–19.

[2]A very good presentation of this view, which does not explicitly introduce the rationality of expectations, but which is clearly groping in that direction, is Milton Friedman, "The Role of Monetary Policy," *American Economic Review*, 58 (March 1968), 1–17. The best discussion in the context of an explicit rational framework is Thomas J. Sargent and Neil Wallace, "Rational Expectations and the Theory of Economic Policy," *Journal of Monetary Economics*, 2 (April 1976), 169–84.

explanation of the phenomenon of the business cycle but also leads to a radically different view of policy.

The business cycle is viewed as the outcome of shocks to the economy that are either not correctly foreseen or not fully perceived. Policy influences the cycle in that the *unanticipated* variations in policy instruments lead to variations in output and prices. According to this view, policy is a process that has to be decomposed into an anticipated and unanticipated component. By minimizing the unanticipated variations in policy, the business cycle will be smoothed as much as is possible. There may be a case for having a pre-announced, countercyclical policy response, but there will never be a case for random, haphazard "discretionary" policy intervention. The cycle will not go away, and it may sometimes be quite severe. But ad hoc, previously unexpected attempts to intervene and boost aggregate demand can only be more destabilizing on the average than doing nothing other than pursuing a previously announced policy strategy.

It is this new view of policy that you will be introduced to in the remaining chapters of this part of the book. Before moving on to that, it will be worthwhile spending a moment or two on the final topic of this chapter.

C. The Idea That Policy is a Process and Not an Event

The old-fashioned way of analyzing macroeconomic policy was to ask questions like, What will happen if the level of government spending is raised by 10 percent or if the money supply growth rate is cut from 7 percent to 4 percent? What will happen if taxes and spending are cut by the same amount? Questions of this kind are questions that treat policy as an *event* in the sense that a certain well-defined policy action occurs. The idea, then, is to trace out the effects of this policy shock on output, prices, interest rates, employment, etc. You now understand that accepting the hypothesis that expectations are formed rationally implies that such exercises are meaningless.

It is simply not possible to analyze the effect of a single-event policy change without knowing whether or not that change was anticipated or unanticipated. Once this is known, it is possible to analyze the effects on output, prices, and the other variables in the economy. *It is not possible, however, to know whether or not a particular policy event was anticipated or unanticipated by considering that event in isolation.* It is necessary to have a model of the evolution of the policy instruments that enables the policy instruments at any particular time to be decomposed into their anticipated and unanticipated components. It is unavoidable that the entire policy process be analyzed so that a particular policy event may be identified as anticipated, unanticipated, or partly one and partly the other.

It is also necessary to examine the broader institutional and political setting within which policies are being made, for it is the entire policy process that influences the quality of macroeconomic performance. Work of this kind is only in its infancy. It will, however, become a major part of the next generation of research in understanding and improving macroeconomic policy.

The remaining chapters in this part of the book are first of all going to examine the links between monetary and fiscal policy. This will show you that when viewing the entire monetary and fiscal policy processes, these two sets of policies are inextricably linked together. Next, we shall examine the way in which the Fed conducts its policies for achieving a particular path for the money supply. After these two preliminary chapters we shall move to the substance of the policy debate and analyze the key reasons for the differences in policy views that were set out in Chapter 1 of this book.

Summary

A. What Macroeconomic Policies Seek to Achieve

Macroeconomic policies seek to minimize fluctuations of unemployment and output about their natural rates and to minimize the variability of inflation around some low, possibly zero, value. Other objectives, such as lowering the natural rate of unemployment, are not, strictly speaking, *macroeconomic* policies. They involve *microeconomic* intervention to change relative prices.

B. Highlights in the Evolution of the Policy Debate

The pre-Keynesian view of macroeconomic policy was that nothing could be done. Fluctuations simply had to be lived with in the same way as other natural disorders. The Keynesian revolution led to the optimistic view that by manipulating monetary and fiscal policy, aggregate demand could be controlled in such a way as to achieve full employment and price stability. The new view is that because expectations are formed rationally, the best that policy can do is to avoid injecting uncertainty into the economy. Fully predictable policy is therefore required. It may be possible to achieve the best outcome with a pre-announced policy-feedback rule, but it will not be possible to do better with ad hoc discretionary intervention.

C. The Idea that Policy is a Process and Not an Event

If expectations are formed rationally, analyzing the implications of a policy change requires that it be decomposed into an anticipated and unanticipated component. Only by analyzing the entire process of policy is it possible to say whether a particular event was anticipated or unanticipated.

Review Questions

1. What are the objectives of macroeconomic policy?

2. Review your understanding of the three main stages in the evolution of ideas on the proper role of macroeconomic policy.

3. What does it mean to say that "policy is a process and not an event"?

31

The Constraints on Monetary and Fiscal Policy

Although governments are sovereign (within the limits of the constitution), even they must obey certain economic laws. The most fundamental of these laws, to which even governments are subject, is the law of opportunity cost or, equivalently, the principle that "there is no such thing as a free lunch."

A government cannot command use over real resources without taking them from private individuals and firms. Like private individuals and firms, the government has a budget that must be balanced, in the sense that, in the short run, the government must either tax or borrow to cover its spending. In the long run, its loans have to be repaid, so that in some fundamental sense, the government must raise taxes in an amount sufficient to cover its expenditure. This places some important limitations on the conduct of fiscal and monetary policy and introduces some important linkages between these two areas of policy.

Let us go on to explore these linkages and examine the constraints on government by pursuing three tasks, which are to:

(a) Understand the nature of the government budget constraint.
(b) Understand the implications of the government budget constraint for the conduct of monetary and fiscal policy.
(c) Understand the implications of the government budget constraint for the formation of rational expectations.

A. Government Budget Constraint

Let us begin by examining the main items in the government's budget. Table 31.1 summarizes the government's payments and receipts. The first payment listed is government expenditure on goods and services. This is the variable that appears in the national income accounts as one of the aggregate expenditure items; it also features prominently in the theory of aggregate demand developed in Part IV of this book. The second item is transfer payments. These are the direct payments by the government to households and firms under various income-support programs. The third item is the interest

TABLE 31.1
The Government's Payments and Receipts

	ITEM
	Payments
	Government expenditure on goods and services
plus	Transfer payments
plus	Debt interest payments
equals	Total payments
	Receipts
	Legislated taxes
plus	Net issues of debt
plus	Net issue of currency
equals	Total receipts

that the government has to pay on outstanding debt. These three items added together constitute the total payments made by the government. They must be matched by government receipts.

The first item listed under receipts is legislated taxes. The prefix "legislated" is there to alert you to the idea that there are some receipts by the government that are in the nature of taxes but are not explicitly legislated. (More of this in a moment.) The legislated taxes are those on incomes, expenditure, wealth, foreign trade, and a variety of specific activities. The second receipt item is net issues of debt. Like any large organization, the government is constantly borrowing and repaying debt previously contracted. The net issue of debt constitutes the excess of newly issued debt over loans repaid. The final receipt is the net issue of currency. In a sense, this is not really a receipt. In effect, the government mints new currency simply by stamping the appropriate images on the appropriate bits of metal. Nevertheless, in terms of the government's accounts, this has to be reckoned as a receipt, since, from the point of view of the government, it is one of the things the government can use to cover its expenditure.

The debt issued by the government is not all bought by the general public. Some of it is bought by the Fed. Although the Fed is an independent agency, its profits, nevertheless, are paid to the federal government. This being so, it is of some importance to consider separately what happens in the Fed when new debt issues of the government are purchased by the Bank rather than by the general public. Equally important is to examine what happens inside the Fed when it buys existing debt from the public. We can examine these Fed transactions very straightforwardly by considering the changes in the Fed's balance sheet that occur in any period of time. Table 31.2 summarizes these changes.

Table 31.2 is very closely related to Table 4.2, which you studied in Chapter 4. In effect, it is the change in any given period in the items in the fourth column (the Fed's balance sheet) shown in that table. The first item is the change in government security holdings by the Fed. This represents the change in the Fed's assets. The second two items—change in commercial bank deposits with the Fed, and net issue of new Federal Reserve bank notes—

TABLE 31.2
Changes in the Fed's Balance Sheet

	Change in government securities
less	Change in commercial bank deposits with the Fed
less	Net issue of new Federal Reserve bank notes
equals	Fed's profit

constitute changes in the Fed's liabilities. The difference between the change in its assets and liabilities constitutes the Fed's profit, or the change in the Fed's net worth. You can see by checking back to the fourth column of Table 4.2 (Chapter 4) that these balance sheet changes agree with the balance sheet levels set out in that table. (This abstracts from any changes in foreign exchange holdings by the Fed, which in this treatment are being assumed to be zero.) The importance of changes in government security holdings by the Fed (minus Fed profits) is that they are equivalent to changes in the two components of the economy's monetary base—the commercial bank deposits with the Fed, and the Federal Reserve bank notes.

We gain important insights if we consolidate the government's receipts and payments with the changes in the Fed's balance sheet. This is done in Table 31.3. The first two items in Table 31.3 are exactly the same as in Table 31.1—government expenditure on goods and services, and transfer payments. The next two items appeared in Table 31.1 as a single item. Debt interest paid by the government has now been divided into two items, that paid to the public and that paid to the Fed. Total payments, then, in Table 31.3 are exactly the same as those in Table 31.1, but with debt interest payments separated into those paid to the Fed and those paid to the general public.

The receipts shown in Table 31.3 are more detailed than those in Table 31.1. The first item, legislated taxes, is exactly the same as before. The next item shown in Table 31.1 has been split into two parts; net issue of debt to the public and net issue of debt to the Fed. The first of these appears as the second receipt in Table 31.3. The net issue of debt to the Fed may be expressed more conveniently by using Table 31.2. Notice that the net issue of debt to the Fed (called "change in government securities" in Table 31.2) is equal to the Fed's profit, plus the change in commercial bank deposits with the Fed plus the net issue of new Federal Reserve bank notes. These three items appear in Table 31.3 to represent the net issue of government debt to the Fed. The final item, net issue of currency, is exactly the same as that in Table 31.1.

Now focus on the column on the right-hand side of Table 31.3. It provides a summary of the payments and receipts by the consolidated government-central bank sector. Government expenditure are called G, transfer payments TR, and debt interest paid to the public DI. Debt interest paid to the Fed is not given a symbolic name, nor are profits received from the Fed. Assuming that Fed operating costs are small relative to the total interest payments received by the Bank, these two items may be regarded as approximately offsetting each other because there is a receipt and a payment that are of approximate equal magnitude. On the receipts side of the account, legislated taxes are labelled TAX, and the net issue of debt to the public is labelled ΔD. The final three items—the change in commercial bank deposits with the

TABLE 31.3
Consolidation of Government and the Fed

	ITEM	$
	Payments	
	Government expenditure on goods and services	G
plus	Transfer payments	TR
plus	Debt interest paid to public	DI
plus	Debt interest paid to the Fed	
equals	Total payments	
	Receipts	
	Legislated taxes	TAX
plus	Net issue of debt to the public	ΔD
plus	Profits from the Fed	
plus	Change in commercial bank deposits with the Fed	ΔMB (Change in commercial bank deposits with the Fed, Net issue of bank notes, Net issue of currency)
plus	Net issue of bank notes	
plus	Net issue of currency	
equals	Total receipts	

Fed, the net issue of bank notes, and net issue of currency—are lumped together as a single item. You will recognize that item (referring back if necessary to Chapter 4) as the change in the monetary base, ΔMB.

The sum of the receipts by the government must exactly equal the sum of the payments made by the government. This is the government budget constraint:

$$G + DI + TR - TAX - \Delta D - \Delta MB = 0 \tag{31.1}$$

This says that the government must raise taxes or borrow or create money on a scale exactly equal to the volume of its purchases of goods and services and its payments of debt interest and transfer payments. Let us now move on to consider some of the implications of this government budget constraint.

B. Government Budget Constraint and the Conduct of Monetary and Fiscal Policy

The government's budget constraint with which we ended the last section may be rewritten in the following form:

$$\Delta MB + \Delta D = G + DI + TR - TAX \tag{31.2}$$

This emphasizes that the expansion of the stock of monetary base and of government debt will necessarily be equal to the difference between the government's total spending and its legislated tax receipts. This immediately places a link between monetary policy and fiscal policy. You can think of monetary policy as the rate at which the money stock grows. You can think of fiscal policy as the scale of government spending and the scale of taxes. The government budget constraint says that there is a connection between these two. It also says, however, that so long as the government is able or willing to issue debt (ΔD) and pay interest on it (DI), there is no hard-and-fast link between the two branches of macroeconomic policy. In any given short-term period (a year or two, or perhaps even five years or so), the government may issue debt to loosen the link between monetary and fiscal policy. You are now going to discover, however, that on the average and over the long run, this cannot be so.

To get a feel for why this is, imagine what would happen if you spent more than your income. For the first year you could perhaps go to the bank and get a loan to cover the deficit. You might even be able to do that for two years, or if you had a very indulgent bank manager, perhaps for a third year. At some stage, however, the day of reckoning would arrive. It would be necessary to pull in your horns, lower consumption, and start to pay off the loans that had accumulated. Although the details differ, exactly the same constraints necessarily apply to the government. To see why this is so, it is necessary to understand that when the government issues debt, it is doing nothing other than deferring taxes.

The government issues all kinds of debt. Some of it is long-term debt, with 25 or more years to run to the date at which the government will redeem it. Some debt is medium-term, with 10 to 15 years to run to the redemption date; and some is short-term debt, with up to 5 years to run to the redemption date. In addition, the government issues very short-term debt in the form of three-month treasury bills. Further, some government debt is nonmarketable and takes the form of savings bonds. This type of debt is redeemable on demand, but at a penalty to the holder.

Although the government issues many different kinds of debt, it is sensible to think of government debt as if it was a *perpetuity*. A perpetuity is a bond that will never be redeemed by the issuer. The British government issued such bonds in the eighteenth and nineteenth centuries. They are called *consols*. Although the U.S. government does not issue such bonds, it is nevertheless sensible to think of all U.S. government debt as perpetual debt. The reason why this is so is that although the particular bonds issued by the government will be redeemed, when they are redeemed, they will be replaced by new bonds. Thus, the debt is continuously turned over, with new bonds being issued to replace the old bonds that are retired. We can therefore think of government debt as perpetual debt rather than as debt that will be repaid.

A perpetuity is a bond that promises to pay a certain sum of money each year forever. Call that amount $\$c$. The bond will never be redeemed, so that it has no redemption price. However, it can be sold to someone else, and the new owner will receive the $\$c$ per annum while in possession of the bond. How much would a person be willing to pay for a bond that promised to pay $\$c$ per annum in perpetuity? Let us call the price that a person would be willing to pay $\$V$. If you invested $\$V$ in the best alternative asset, say a corporate bond or some physical capital or a private business, you would make a rate of return of, let us say, r percent per annum. Clearly, you would not be interested in buying a government bond that promised to pay $\$c$ per annum unless the rate of return on that bond was at least as great as the r percent per annum that you could obtain from some other activity.

Expressed as an equation—with the price of the bond $\$V$ and the payment by the government \$$c$ per annum—the rate of return on the bond is as follows:

$$\text{Rate of return} = \frac{\$c}{\$V} \cdot 100$$

If

$$\frac{\$c}{\$V} \cdot 100 > r\%$$

then you would be interested in buying government bonds. But if

$$\frac{\$c}{\$V} \cdot 100 < r\%$$

then you would want to sell government bonds.

Since what you would want to do everyone else would want to do too, in the first situation everyone would be buying government bonds and in the second situation they would be selling them. With everyone buying government bonds their price would rise and with everyone selling government bonds their price would fall. Thus, government bonds will have an equilibrium price when

$$\frac{\$c}{\$V} \cdot 100 = r\%$$

From this, it is clear that the price of the government bond will be

$$\$V = \frac{\$c}{r\%} \cdot 100$$

For example, if a bond promised to pay \$5 per annum, and if the rate of interest was 5 percent per annum, then the price of the bond would be \$100. The price of a government bond could be written equivalently as

$$\$V = \frac{\$c}{r}$$

where r is the rate of interest expressed as a proportion of 1 (i.e., $r\% \div 100$).

Now suppose the government issues a bond and receives \$$V$. So that you can see the value of this to the government, let us isolate the bond sale and subsequent interest payments on the bond from the other receipts and expenditure of the government. To do this we must assume that the government is not going to change its expenditure on goods and services or transfers, nor change the taxes that it legislates, nor create any new money. It is simply going to issue its bond and allow the bond to be completely self-financing. You can think of this as meaning that when the government receives the proceeds from its bond sale, \$$V$, it has to set aside a fund that will generate sufficient interest

TABLE 31.4
The Funds Needed to Pay Interest on a Perpetuity

To pay \$c in one year, you need	$\$a_1$ now such that $\$a_1\ (1+r) = \$c$
To pay \$c in two years, you need	$\$a_2$ now such that $\$a_2\ (1+r)^2 = \$c$
To pay \$c in three years, you need	$\$a_3$ now such that $\$a_3\ (1+r)^3 = \$c$
To pay \$c in *i* years, you need	$\$a_i$ now such that $\$a_i\ (1+r)^i = \$c$

income to enable it to meet the interest payments on the bond of \$*c* per annum in perpetuity.

Let us suppose, then, that the government has sold a bond for \$*V* (which is equal to \$*c*/*r*, where \$*c* is the number of dollars per annum that the government will pay out on the bond). How much must the government set aside to be able to meet these interest payments? At the end of the first year the government will need \$*c* from its fund. If it set aside a sum of money $\$a_1$ such that $\$a_1$ plus the interest received on $\$a_1$, namely $r\$a_1$, was equal to $\$c_1$, then it would have enough money to pay out \$*c* at the end of the first year.

For example, if the rate of interest is 5 percent and the government is committed to paying \$5 on the bond at the end of one year, it will need to set aside approximately \$4.76 at the beginning of the year. The \$4.76 invested at 5 percent would yield a 24¢ interest income, which, when added to the \$4.76 investment, would give the government the \$5 that it needs to meet its bond-interest payment. To meet its bond-interest payments in two years' time, it needs to set aside a sum of money such that the interest on the sum plus the interest on the first year's interest would add up to a sufficient sum to pay the bond interest. Call this sum of money $\$a_2$. It would be a sum such that $\$a_2(1+r)^2 = \$c$. In general, then, in order to meet *all* its interest payments out into the future, the government would need to set aside sums of money as shown in Table 31.4. Thus, if the government is going to have enough funds to meet the interest payments on its bond over the infinite life of the bond, it will need a fund equal to $\$a_1 + \$a_2 + \$a_3 + \cdots + \$a_i \cdots$. (The dots "···" stand for all the terms not written explicitly.) We can work out the value of each $\$a_i$ from Table 31.4: If you divide \$*c* by $(1 + r)$, then you get $\$a_1$; if you divide \$*c* by $(1+r)^2$, then you get $\$a_2$; if you divide \$*c* by $(1+r)^i$, then you get $\$a_i$.

Thus, the amount that the government will have to set aside (*S*) to meet *all* the future interest payments on its bonds is

$$S = \frac{\$c}{1+r} + \frac{\$c}{(1+r)^2} + \cdots + \frac{\$c}{(1+r)^i} + \cdots$$

or, equivalently,

$$S = \left[\frac{1}{1+r} + \frac{1}{(1+r)^2} + \cdots + \frac{1}{(1+r)^i} + \cdots\right]\$c \qquad \textbf{(31.3)}$$

To figure out how much this is, we need to add up the infinite sum inside the brackets in Equation (31.3) above. To do this, multiply both sides of Equation (31.3) by $1/(1+r)$. This will give

$$\left(\frac{1}{1+r}\right)S = \left[\frac{1}{(1+r)^2} + \frac{1}{(1+r)^3} + \cdots + \frac{1}{(1+r)^i} + \cdots\right]\$c \qquad \textbf{(31.4)}$$

All the missing terms in Equation (31.3) represented by the dots will be identical to the missing terms in Equation (31.4), except for the last term in Equation (31.4). That last term in Equation (31.4) will equal the last term in Equation (31.3) multiplied by $1/(1 + r)$. However, as you go further and further into the future, the terms $1/(1 + r)^i$ become very very small and can be ignored. So, ignoring the last term in Equation (31.4), you can subtract Equation (31.4) from Equation (31.3) to obtain

$$S - \left(\frac{1}{1+r}\right)S = \left(\frac{1}{1+r}\right)\$c \tag{31.5}$$

Then multiply both sides of Equation (31.5) by $(1 + r)$ to give

$$S(1 + r) - S = \$c \tag{31.6}$$

or

$$S + rS - S = \$c \tag{31.7}$$

Or, more simply,

$$S = \frac{\$c}{r} \tag{31.8}$$

So, S, the sum that the government would need to set aside in order to meet the interest payments on its bond, is equal to $\$c/r$. But this is exactly the sum the government receives when it sells the bond. *It is necessary, therefore, if the government is to make its bond self-financing, to set aside all the receipts from the bond to meet future interest payments.* Thus, when proper accounting is made for the future interest payments that a bond will generate, the government gets precisely nothing when it sells a bond. You can think of selling a bond as simply putting off the evil day of raising taxes. It is possible for the government to increase its revenue in any one year by selling more bonds, but it cannot increase its revenue indefinitely by selling bonds since it immediately commits itself to an interest stream that exactly offsets the receipts that it obtains from its bond sales. The implication of this for the government's budget constraint is very important. It means that *the government cannot regard bond financing as anything other than deferred taxes.*

It may have occurred to you that there is a possibility of the government avoiding eventually having to raise taxes to pay for its current bond financing by always selling bonds to pay the future interest commitment on its current bonds. In effect, the government could put off the evil day forever by always borrowing more. A moment's reflection will lead you to the conclusion that if the government did pursue this course, and if—aside from borrowing to cover debt interest—the government had a balanced budget, the stock of government bonds outstanding would grow at a rate equal to the rate of interest on bonds.

You can see this directly by considering a situation in which the government initially had a stock of bonds outstanding of, say, \$100, and on which the rate of interest was, say, 10 percent per annum. In year 2 the government would sell $10 worth of bonds to pay the interest on the initial $100 worth. Its outstanding stock of bonds would then be $110. The next year the government would issue $11 worth of bonds to pay the $10 interest on the original $100 worth plus the $1 interest on the $10 bond issued in year 2. This process would continue forever with the stock of bonds outstanding growing at 10 percent per annum. Of course, since the rate of interest on bonds represents in part the real rate of interest and in part an inflation component, the real stock of government bonds outstanding would not be growing at that same rate of interest. The real stock would in fact grow at a rate equal to the real rate of interest. Provided the economy is growing—the population, the stock of capital equipment, and wealth in general—the government can get away with this device of always borrowing to pay interest on its debt but only to the extent that it permits its stock of bonds outstanding to grow at the same rate as the economy as a whole.

Now consider what would happen if the government tried to issue new bonds to pay interest on its old bonds, but at a rate that involved the stock of government bonds growing faster than the growth rate of total wealth in the economy. In such a situation the fraction of government bonds held in the portfolios of households and firms would be continuously rising. There would come a point at which the total amount of private sector assets consisted of nothing other than government bonds. There would be no space in people's balance sheets to hold physical capital and corporate debt. Government debt would be the only debt in existence.

Of course real capital generates a real rate of return and is itself the source of economic growth. In contrast, government debt does not generate any real return for the economy as a whole. The interest payments on government debt simply constitute a transfer of wealth from taxpayers to bondholders. Thus, an economy in which the government had attempted to increase its outstanding debt to pay interest on old debt at too fast a rate would be one in which the stock of capital had declined and general economic decline had set in.

It is clear from these considerations that the maximum long-run sustainable growth rate of government debt is equal to the growth rate of the overall stock of real wealth in the economy. In what follows I shall abstract from such long-term growth considerations. You should be careful to note, therefore, that the analysis that follows would need to be modified slightly to allow for the case where the economy was growing at some positive steady rate. In effect, you would need to add to the government's revenue sources the possibility of obtaining revenue in perpetuity by allowing the stock of its bonds outstanding to grow at the same rate as the economy as a whole. Let us now return to the case where there is no ongoing growth and the government cannot regard its bond financing as a permanent source of revenue but rather as deferred taxes.

We can use the result that we obtained above to condense the government budget constraint into a more fundamental statement. First, let us consolidate taxes, TAX, and transfers, TR, into a single item—$NET\ TAX$ is equal to TAX less TR. Second, since the receipts from bond sales less the debt interest paid on outstanding bonds generates a future tax liability, let us also combine those items with *NET TAX* to obtain a single item $\bar{T}$ equal to *NET TAX* plus ΔD less DI. Be careful to notice that this is an unconventional definition of taxes. It includes all *current* taxes minus all *current* transfers plus the *future* taxes that are implied by the *current* difference between bond sales and interest payments. The government budget constraint may now be collapsed into the simpler statement, namely,

$$G - \bar{T} = \Delta MB \tag{31.9}$$

In the next chapter, the connection between the monetary base and the money supply itself will be explored. For the rest of this chapter, let us agree to take on trust the proposition that, on the average, the growth rate of the monetary base and the growth rate of the money supply will be the same. Equivalently, we could say that the change in the monetary base will be some fraction of the change in the money supply. Let us call that fraction q. In this case,

$$\Delta MB = q\Delta M \tag{31.10}$$

We could now use Equation (31.10) to replace the change in monetary base with the fraction q of the change in the total money supply to obtain

$$G - \bar{T} = q\Delta M$$

However, it may be more instructive to view this government budget constraint in *real terms*—the real government budget constraint. We can do this by dividing through the budget constraint by the price level. Let us divide the above equation by the GNP deflator P to obtain

$$\frac{G}{P} - \frac{\bar{T}}{P} = \frac{q\Delta M}{P}$$

Now define $G/P = g$ and $\bar{T}/P = \bar{t}$. This means that

$$g - \bar{t} = q\left(\frac{\Delta M}{P}\right) \tag{31.11}$$

Next multiply and divide the right-hand side of this equation by M; i.e.,

$$q\left(\frac{\Delta M}{P}\right) = q\left(\frac{\Delta M}{P} \cdot \frac{M}{M}\right)$$

This, of course, leaves the value of the equation undisturbed. However, you can now see, changing the order of the variables, that

$$q\left(\frac{\Delta M}{P}\right) = q\left(\frac{M}{P} \cdot \frac{\Delta M}{M}\right)$$

Also, you will recall that $\Delta M/M = \mu$, the growth rate of the money supply. Therefore,

$$q\left(\frac{\Delta M}{P}\right) = q\left(\frac{M}{P} \cdot \mu\right)$$

Using this equation to replace the right-hand side of Equation (31.11) gives

$$q - \bar{t} = q\left(\frac{M}{P}\right)\mu \qquad \textbf{(31.12)}$$

This is the *fundamental government budget constraint equation.* This equation cannot be violated. It tells us that whenever the government changes its expenditure, it must change at least one other variable. It must either change taxes or change the growth rate of the money supply.

Another instructive way of looking at the government's fundamental budget constraint equation is one that emphasizes the nature of money creation as a tax. When the government creates new money (monetary base) it is able to use that money to acquire goods and services, or make transfer payments, in exactly the same way as it does when it spends the revenue collected in legislated taxes. Thus, money creation is like a tax. Part of the money creation tax is available purely as a consequence of real economic growth. As real incomes grow so also the demand for money grows and the government can obtain resources by spending the new money that is created merely to meet the growing demand for money. This part of the tax from money creation is known as the growth tax.

If the government creates money at a rate in excess of that needed to meet the demands of a growing economy it is still able to use that additional money to acquire goods and services. As a consequence, however, inflation will ensue. The part of the tax from money creation over and above that needed to meet the demands of a growing economy is called the inflation tax.

The rate of economic growth tends to be rather constant so the growth tax is not highly variable. Rather, variations in the tax from money creation are primarily reflected in variations in the inflation tax.

To summarize: the government must raise taxes to cover its spending. There are two sources of tax—legislated taxes, $\bar{t}$, and the money creation tax, $\mu q M/P$. The latter comprises the growth tax (which does not vary much) and the inflation tax. There is no restriction on the government as to the extent to which it uses either of these sources of revenue. The restriction is that it must raise a large enough total from both of them, taken together, to cover its expenditure.

C. Government Budget Constraint and Formation of Rational Expectations

The government budget constraint has dramatic implications for the formation of rational expectations. It will not be rational to expect a monetary and fiscal policy that violates the government's budget constraint. To expect a violation of that constraint is to expect something that cannot happen. Such an expectation would not be rational. This means that if at some time a government is running a large current deficit and issuing a larger quantity of bonds, then the rational expectation will be that at some future date, government expenditure is going to be cut, or legislated taxes are going to be increased, or the rate of money printing, and therefore of inflation, is going to be increased. Based on the best analysis available of the constraints operating upon the government and its likely course in the future, individuals will rationally assign weights to these alternative future changes in government actions. A government, or more generally, a political system, that has a long-run track record of repeatedly inflating its way out of short-run financial problems will rationally be expected to pursue such policies again in the future. A government that has heavily constrained itself from using the inflation tax by, for example, setting up a highly independent central bank with extensive powers to control the growth rate of the money supply independently of the short-term wishes of the government will be one that will rationally be expected to correct any short-term deficit by either raising legislated taxes or cutting spending rather than by increasing the inflation tax.

There will be no hard-and-fast, simple-to-state rule that will enable individuals to make the correct inferences concerning future monetary and fiscal policy. The hard fact of the government budget constraint must, however, be taken into account in forming a rational expectation as to likely future changes in the direction of policy. Only if the government is currently running a deficit that is being financed by its current rate of money printing is it pursuing a policy that can be pursued on the average over the long term. The pursuit of such a policy will simplify the task faced by individuals in forming rational expectations, but it will by no means eliminate the problem.

Summary

A. Government Budget Constraint

The government budget constraint states that total government expenditure on goods and services, transfers to individuals, and debt interest must equal receipts from legislated taxes, the sales of new debt, and the creation of new money.

B. Government Budget Constraint and the Conduct of Monetary and Fiscal Policy

Although the government can issue debt, thereby weakening the link between monetary and fiscal policy in the short run, on the average over the long term, debt interest has to be paid that exactly offsets the receipts from debt sales. This means that, in effect, issuing debt is the same thing as deferring taxes. The long-term average government budget constraint does not give the government the option of raising debt. There is, therefore, on the average, a fundamental connection between fiscal policy and monetary policy. Conventionally, legislated taxes together with the creation of new money must raise sufficient funds to cover the government's expenditure. Monetary policy and fiscal policy, on the average, are interdependent.

C. Government Budget Constraint and Formation of Rational Expectations

It will not be rational to form an expectation of long-term money growth and inflation that is based on a violation of the government's budget constraint. In a situation in which the government is currently running a deficit or surplus and issuing (or retiring) large volumes of debt, individuals will have to form a rational expectation concerning which of the variables in the government's budget constraint will be varied in order to satisfy the long-term average budget constraint. In some situations it will be rational to expect a future burst of inflation, whereas in others it will be rational to expect continued mild inflation and adjustments of legislated taxes or expenditure.

Review Questions

1. Review the items that appear in the government's budget constraint.

2. Sort the following items into the three items in the government's budget constraint (i.e., expenditure on goods and services, taxes, and money creation):

(a) Welfare payments.
(b) The purchase of a typewriter financed by printing $100.
(c) The purchase of a foreign security (be careful here).
(d) Social security payments and receipts.
(e) National defense expenditure.

3. Why are "legislated" taxes so-called?

4. Explain why transfer payments may (as a first appproximation) be treated as negative taxes.

5. Review the links between the government and central bank and explain how the "change in the monetary base" gets into the government's budget constraint?

6. What is the relationship between the price that someone will pay for a bond and the stream-of-interest payments on that bond?

7. Calculate the equilibrium market price of a perpetuity that promises to pay $1 per annum, given that interest rates on alternative available assets are currently 8 percent.

8. "The present value of a bond is always zero." Explain.

9. If the price for which a bond can be sold is exactly the same as the present value of the future stream-of-interest payments, why would anyone issue bonds?

10. Explain why bond sales are deferred taxes.

11. If the government can issue money on which it does not have to pay interest, why do you suppose we observe governments issuing debt on which they do have to pay interest?

12. Explain why, on the average, the government must finance its expenditure with either legislated taxes or the inflation tax.

13. Review your understanding of why it would be irrational to expect the government to be able to issue debt on an increasing scale indefinitely.

14. Looking at U.S. monetary policy and fiscal policy in the 1970s, what conclusions do you reach concerning a rational expectation about future monetary and fiscal policy changes in the United States?

32

Control of the Money Supply

The quantity of money in existence—the money supply—features prominently in all macroeconomic models, from the basic model through the Keynesian, and from the neoclassical synthesis to the new theories. Therefore, the final thing that we need to do before getting on with the substance of analyzing macroeconomic policy is to examine how the money supply is determined and controlled. In the last chapter I asked you to take on trust the proposition that, on the average, the monetary base and the total money supply stand in some constant relationship to each other. This chapter will explain why this is a reasonable proposition. It will also look at the detailed linkages between the money supply and the monetary base, and at the way in which the Fed conducts monetary policy with a view to achieving its target growth path for the monetary aggregate M1. The chapter will *not* present a comprehensive description of Fed operations, however. In particular, it will sidestep the important, but for present purposes noncentral, foreign exchange market operations of the Fed.

The chapter contains two tasks, which are to:

(a) Understand the links between the monetary base and the money supply.
(b) Understand how the Fed operates to achieve its target growth path for the money supply.

A. The Links Between the Monetary Base and the Money Supply

The starting point for understanding the links between the monetary base and the money supply is two definitions. Both definitions are implied in the economy balance sheet structure that you studied in Chapter 4. The first is the definition of the money supply. It is convenient when analyzing the determinants of the money supply to decompose it into two parts—the monetary base held by the public and the bank deposits held by the public. (Which bank deposits we would count would depend on which monetary aggregate we were dealing with. I am going to deal with M1 in this chapter, although I shall use the symbol M to denote this aggregate.) Let us write the definition of the money supply as follows:

$$M = MB_p + D \tag{32.1}$$

In this definition, M stands for the money supply, MB_p for the notes and coins held by the public, and D for bank deposits.

The next definition concerns the monetary base itself. The monetary base consists of the notes and coins held by the public (MB_p), which is already in the above definition, and the notes and coins together with deposits at the Fed held by the commercial banks, which we will call MB_b. The monetary base, then, is allocated across the two holders—the public and the banks—so that

$$MB = MB_p + MB_b \tag{32.2}$$

These are just definitions, of course, and they don't tell us anything about what determines either the money supply or the monetary base.

The first behavioral hypothesis that we need is one concerning the general public's allocation of money between notes and coin and deposits. The general idea is that in conducting our everyday transactions, there is a fairly stable fraction of those transactions that we would customarily undertake with notes and coin. This means that we would want to hold a fairly stable fraction of our total money holdings in the form of currency. Let us call that fraction v. This means that we could say that

$$MB_p = vM \qquad 0 < v < 1 \tag{32.3}$$

This simply says that v is some fraction, and the amount of monetary base (notes and coin) that people on the average hold is equal to that fraction v of their total money holdings. Of course, there is an equivalent proposition, which is that bank deposits are equal to one minus the fraction v times total money. That is,

$$D = (1 - v)M \tag{32.4}$$

Although this is a pretty mechanical proposition about how people allocate their money between currency and bank deposits, provided the bank deposits are noninterest bearing, it seems to be a reasonable hypothesis and one that adequately describes the facts.

The next thing that we need to consider is how the banks decide how much monetary base to hold. That is, what is the demand for monetary base by the banks? This question is a lot like the question, What determines the demand for money by households and firms? Why do the banks hold monetary base? That is, why do they hold notes and coin and deposits with the Fed? The answer is, of course, that they hold notes and coin in order to be able to meet demands for currency on the part of their customers. They also hold deposits at the Fed so that they can make payments to other banks. They need to do this when the total value of all the checks paid by their customers in any one trading period exceeds the value of checks paid to their customers during that same period. As a general rule, it will be obvious that the bigger the volume of bank deposits that a bank has accepted, the bigger the size of currency reserves and Fed deposits the bank will need to keep on hand. The volume of bank deposits, then, is the first determinant of the demand for monetary base by the commercial banks.

When studying the demand for money by individuals, we discovered that, at high rates of interest (and high rates of inflation), there is a bigger incentive for people to try to economize on their holdings of money than when interest rates and inflation are low. Interest and inflation are seen as the opportunity cost of holding money. Similar considerations apply to the decision by a commercial bank on how much of its deposits to hold in the form of monetary base reserves. Deposits placed with a bank can be used by that bank for two kinds of purposes. One is to hold monetary base. The other is to acquire interest-earning assets of various kinds, including making loans to households and firms. Clearly, the bank makes no money on its holdings of monetary base. Profits for a bank are obtained by making loans and buying interest-earning securities. Just as households economize on their holdings at high interest rates, so also will banks. The higher the rate of interest on loans and securities, the more will banks economize on their holdings of monetary base, and the smaller will be the fraction of their deposits held as reserves and the larger the fraction that will be lent.

There are two factors, then, that determine the bank's demand for monetary base. One is the total volume of deposits that the bank has accepted. The larger the volume of deposits, the bigger the amount of monetary base required. The other is the level of interest rates. The higher the interest rate, the more will the bank seek to economize on its monetary base, and therefore the lower will be its holdings of monetary base.

We can summarize all this in a very simple equation that looks a lot like the demand for money function of households and firms. This equation says that

$$MB_b = zD + mb_0 - l_b r_m \qquad 0 < z < 1;\ mb_0,\ l_b > 0 \qquad \textbf{(32.5)}$$

What this equation says is that, other things being equal (for a given market rate of interest), the higher the level of bank deposits, the more monetary base the banks will hold. For a \$1 million rise in deposits, they would hold a fraction z of a \$1 million in extra monetary base.

The fraction of total deposits z that the banks will want to hold in the form of monetary base represents two kinds of influences: one imposed on the bank, and the other, part of its voluntary behavior. Imposed on the bank is a minimum required reserve holding below which the bank is not permitted to let its monetary base holdings fall. Over and above this, on the average, the bank will find it prudent to hold a certain level of reserves in excess of the required reserves. The fraction z represents the sum of both of these influences.

In addition to the effect of deposits on monetary base holdings of the bank, there is the influence of interest rates. Let us suppose that the term $mb_0 - l_b r_m$, on the average, is equal to zero. That is, if interest rates are at their long-run average level, the demand for monetary base by the banks would be completely described by the fraction z of total deposits. If, however, interest rates go above their average level, then the banks will seek to economize on monetary base holdings; and if interest rates go below their average level, then the banks will be less eager to make loans and will economize on their monetary base. This is what the second two terms in the above equation are saying.

In order to derive the supply of money in the economy, all that is necessary is to examine the equilibrium in the market for the monetary base itself. The supply of money function is not like an ordinary supply function. Like the aggregate supply function, it is an equilibrium locus. The market that is in equilibrium on the money supply function is the market for monetary base. By setting the supply of monetary base equal to the demand for monetary base, we can find the quantity of money that will be supplied. To do this, we need the following equation:

$$MB = vM + z(1 - v)M + mb_0 - l_b r_m \qquad \textbf{(32.6)}$$

The left-hand side of this equation is the supply of monetary base. The right-hand side is the demand for monetary base by the public and by the banks. The term (vM) is the demand for monetary base by the public (fraction v of the total money supply). The remaining terms represent the demand for monetary base by the banks. The first of these is z times bank deposits. Bank deposits are represented as $(1 - v)M$; we know this from Equation (32.4) above. The final two terms represent the interest-sensitive component of the demand for monetary base by the banks, which, on the average, we are taking to be zero. You can now collect together the first two terms that multiply M and obtain

$$MB = [v + z(1 - v)]M + mb_0 - l_b r_m$$

Then divide both sides of this equation by $[v + z(1 - v)]$, to give

$$M = \frac{1}{v + z(1 - v)}(MB - mb_0 + l_b r_m) \qquad \textbf{(32.7)}$$

What this says is that the money supply will be some multiple of the monetary base—the multiple being $1/[v + z(1 - v)]$ on the average—but it will deviate from that in the same direction as variations in the interest rate. The higher the market rate of interest, other things given, the higher would be the money supply.

You are now in a position to summarize the links between the monetary base and the money supply. When the demand for monetary base equals the supply of monetary base, there is a direct relationship between the supply of money and the supply of monetary base. Other things being equal, a $1 million rise in the monetary base will produce a rise in the money supply of $1/[v + z(1 - v)]$ million dollars. For a given monetary base, the higher the market rate of interest, the greater will be the money supply. This arises because banks will seek to economize on their use of monetary base at higher interest rates.

We can link the above discussion with that in the previous chapter by noting that, on the average, the money supply and money base will be linked by the simpler relation

$$M = \frac{1}{v + z(1 - v)}(MB) \tag{32.8}$$

or, more compactly, defining $v + z(1 - v) = q$, we have

$$M = \frac{1}{q}(MB) \tag{32.9}$$

The fraction q in this equation is exactly the same fraction as q introduced in the previous chapter.

The link that we have established between the monetary base, interest rates, and the money supply is not to be confused for a statement that says the money supply is determined by the monetary base and the rate of interest. It could well be that the monetary base itself responds to interest rates and the money supply in such a way that the actual path of the money supply is determined by some exogenous policy decision, and the monetary base and interest rates are the variables that do the adjusting to make that path possible. To emphasize this possibility, consider the above relationship between the money supply and the monetary base written in the following way:

$$MB = qM$$

(This is, of course, exactly the same as Equation (32.9) except that both sides have been multiplied by q and the two sides of the equation have been reversed.) If the money supply itself was determined by the factors that influence the demand for money, then the monetary base would be indirectly determined by the demand for money. Thus,

$$MB = qM^d$$

This alternative way of looking at the link between the money supply and the monetary base is, in fact, one that better describes the way in which the money supply and monetary base have been determined by the policy actions of the Fed. This is what we are now going to examine.

B. Fed's Control of the Money Supply

There are two broad methods whereby a central bank may control the money supply.[1] One method controls the money supply by directly influencing the

---

[1]This section contains the briefest possible account of the techniques for controlling the money supply. A good description of this process viewed from the perspective of the Fed may be found in Stephen H. Axilrod, "Monetary Policy, Money Supply, and the Federal Reserve's Operating Procedures," *Federal Reserve Bulletin*, 68, no. 1 (January 1982), 13–24. (Stephen Axilrod is the director for monetary and financial policy at

monetary base, and the other method controls the money supply by directly manipulating the level of interest rates. On October 6, 1979, the Fed changed its operating procedures from an approach that was based on the manipulation of interest rates to one that was based on manipulating the monetary base.

Control of Money Supply via the Monetary Base

Let us first consider how the monetary base may be used in order to control the money supply. In effect, the Fed works with the relationship expressed as Equation (32.7) above, or the simpler representation, Equation (32.9). If the Fed wants to achieve a particular level of the money supply, then it will supply a volume of monetary base consistent with its desired money stock, taking account of the multiplier $(1/q)$ that links the monetary base to the money supply.

In order to influence the size of the monetary base, all that the Fed has to do is to buy or sell government securities. Buying government securities involves a rise in the assets of the Fed and a corresponding rise in its liabilities. You can think of this as happening automatically as a result of the fact that when the Fed buys securities from households and firms, it will pay for those securities with newly created money (newly created monetary base) that will show up as a rise in the bank deposit holdings of the individuals from whom the Fed has bought its government securities. It will also show up as a rise in the reserves of the banks whose customers have sold government securities to the Fed.

The reverse will occur in the event of the Fed selling securities. In that case, as people paid the Fed for securities sold from its portfolio, their own bank deposits would fall and so would the reserves of the commercial banks whose customers they are. Since the Fed has day-to-day, even hour-by-hour and minute-by-minute, control over the size of its own holdings of government securities, it can, by conducting operations in the securities markets, known as *open market operations,* continuously manipulate the size of the monetary base with a view to achieving any particular target for the money supply.

There are many detailed technical issues relating to the precision with which the Fed can exploit the relationship between the money supply and the monetary base. Fluctuations in bank holdings of reserves, for example, and, indeed, fluctuations in the ratio of currency to deposits in the hands of the public will make the multiplier $(1/q)$ fluctuate and sometimes in a manner that induces unwanted and perhaps hard-to-control fluctuations in the money stock.

---

the Fed.) A highly detailed description of the procedures adopted by the Fed after the changes of October 6, 1979, may be found in the Federal Reserve Staff Study, *New Monetary Control Procedures* (Washington, D.C.: Board of Governors of the Federal Reserve System, February 1981), vols. 1 and 2.

There are many excellent textbooks on money and banking that also give a detailed account of money supply control. One that I like particularly is Chapter 11 of *The Essentials of Money and Banking* by Leonardo Auernheimer and Robert B. Ekelund, Jr. (New York: John Wiley & Sons, Inc., 1982).

Also, there are some technical details arising from the way in which the Fed regulates the banks' required reserve holdings that make the relationship less predictable than it could be. The arrangements in question concern the way in which required reserves are calculated. Until 1983, the banks' required reserves were calculated on the basis of what is known as *lagged* reserve accounting, which means that the banks' required reserves on some date, t, were calculated on the basis of a required fraction of their deposit levels at some previous date. This induced fluctuations in the commercial banks' demand for monetary base, that further reduced the predictability of the money supply multiplier. In 1983, a form of contemporaneous reserve accounting was introduced.

Notwithstanding these problems, it does appear to be possible for the Fed, by continuously monitoring and manipulating the monetary base, to achieve its desired level of (or rate of growth of) the money supply.

Control via Interest Rates

Prior to October 6, 1979, the Fed manipulated the money supply by operating not on the market for monetary base but by attempting to slide up and down the demand for money function. The following is a stylized description of this earlier technique of monetary control.

The first input into this money supply control mechanism is the demand for money function itself. Recall that the demand for money function says that the demand for money depends on real income and the market rate of interest. That is, writing the demand for money function as we did in Chapter 19,

$$\frac{M^d}{P} = ky + m_0 - lr_m$$

In effect, the way the Fed proceeds is to estimate, using statistical techniques, the values of the parameters of the demand for money function (k, m_0, l). It then selects its target for the money supply—we shall call that monetary target M^*. Next it forecasts the price level and the income level that it thinks will prevail, on the average, over the coming few months. Let us call the Fed's forecasted values of the price level and real income, respectively, P^f and y^f. The Fed then "solves" the demand for money function for the market rate of interest that would be required in order to make the amount of money demanded equal the money supply target, given the forecast of prices and income.

You can obtain this solution simply by rearranging the demand for money function in the following way. First of all, set the demand for money M^d equal to the target money supply M^*, and set the levels of income and prices equal to their forecasted values y^f and P^f. That is,

$$\frac{M^*}{P^f} = ky^f + m_0 - lr_m$$

Now rearrange this equation to "solve" for the market rate of interest. That is,

$$r_m = \frac{1}{l}\left[(ky^f + m_0) - \left(\frac{M^*}{P^f}\right)\right]$$

This equation tells us the market rate of interest, which, if the Fed achieves it and if the Fed's forecasts of income and prices are correct, will on the average make the money supply equal to M^*, the target money supply.

The way in which the Fed actually gets the interest rate to move up or down to the desired level is by tightening or loosening its hold over the monetary base. If the Fed wants to make interest rates rise, it sells government securities from its own portfolio to the general public. As people pay for these securities, the monetary base falls, and the banks find themselves short of reserves. To replenish their reserves, the banks start to sell their short-term securities, thereby putting further upward pressure on market rates of interest. The Fed will hold conditions tight in the credit markets until the market rate of interest has risen to the level the Fed wishes to achieve in accordance with the above equation, a level that it is hoped will achieve the monetary target.

If the Fed wants to lower the rate of interest, then it would go into the market and buy government securities, paying for them, in effect, with newly created monetary base. In this event, the banks would find themselves with surplus reserves, would seek to lend those reserves, and in the process, would put downward pressure on interest rates. Again, the Fed would keep credit market conditions loose until interest rates had fallen to the level that it felt appropriate for the achievement of its monetary target.

This technique of monetary control that was employed by the Fed until October 1979 is, of course, far from perfect. The Fed could be considerably wrong in its forecasts of prices and income, and to the extent that it was wrong, it would miss its money supply target. You can see this very easily if you perform the following exercise. Use the equation that we solved above for the Fed's chosen rate of interest and substitute that back into the demand for money function. You will then obtain the following equation:

$$\frac{M^d}{P} = ky + m_0 - \frac{l}{l}\left[(ky^f + m_0) - \left(\frac{M^*}{P^f}\right)\right]$$

Notice that this equation simplifies considerably to the following:

$$\frac{M^d}{P} = \frac{M^*}{P^f} + k(y - y^f)$$

which may be further rearranged by multiplying through by the price level to give

$$M^d = M^*\left(\frac{P}{P^f}\right) + k(y - y^f)P \qquad \textbf{(32.10)}$$

Let us pause and see what this equation is telling us. Under this technique of control of the money supply, it is the demand for money that will determine how much money is in existence. The left-hand side of the equation therefore tells us what the quantity of money will be. It will be the same as M^d. How will that relate to the money supply target M^*? The answer is that, in general, it will deviate from the target. In order to be bang on target, the Fed would have to forecast the price level correctly. That is, the actual price level P would have to equal the forecasted price level P^f. Furthermore, the forecast of income would have to be equal to actual income. If the actual price level turns out to be bigger than the forecasted price level, then, with a correct income forecast, the money supply will exceed the desired money supply by the same percentage as the price level exceeds the forecasted price level. If the level of income turns out to be higher than the forecasted level of income, then the money supply will exceed its target by an amount equal to the excess of actual income over forecasted income multiplied by the price level and by the parameter k. In effect, the money supply simply adjusts to accommodate the unforecasted changes in the price level and the money supply.

Implications

The implication of the foregoing description of two techniques of monetary control is that we may regard the money supply as a controllable instrument of macroeconomic policy and may go on to analyze the effects of alternative *strategies* for varying its quantity.

Summary

A. The Links Between the Monetary Base and the Money Supply

The money supply function is, like the aggregate supply function, an equilibrium locus. The market that is in equilibrium along the money supply function is the market for monetary base. The demand for monetary base by the public (the demand for currency) may be presumed to be a fairly stable fraction of the demand for money in total. The demand for monetary base by banks will depend partly on the level of deposits and partly on the market rate of interest. The greater the level of deposits, the more monetary base demanded by the banks; the higher the market rate of interest, the smaller the monetary base demanded by banks.

Other things being equal, the higher the monetary base, the higher the money supply; and the higher the market rate of interest, the higher the money supply. On the average, the money supply will be a fairly stable multiple of the monetary base, although over shorter periods there will be independent fluctuations in the two variables associated with movements in market rates of interest.

B. Fed's Control of the Money Supply

The Fed seeks to control the money supply by using open market operations to vary the size of the monetary base, thereby inducing changes in the quantity of money.

An alternative technique of monetary control, employed by the Fed until 1979, was to operate on the demand side of the money market. Under that method, the Fed "solved" the demand for money function to determine the level of interest rates that would induce the amount of money demanded to equal the target value of the money supply, given the Fed's own forecasts of the price level and the level of real income. This technique of control is imperfect in the sense that deviations of prices or income from their forecasted values will lead to deviations of the money supply from target.

Review Questions

1. What is the monetary base? Who issues it (whose liability is it) and who holds it (whose asset is it)?
2. What determines the demand for currency by households and firms?
3. What determines the demand for monetary base by the commercial banks?
4. What is the money supply function?
5. What markets are in equilibrium when the economy is "on" the money supply function?
6. What would lead to a shift in the money supply function?
7. Does the money supply function imply that the monetary base determines the money supply?
8. Does the Fed exploit the money supply function to control the U.S. money supply, or does it ignore it?
9. How does the Fed manipulate the monetary base in order to change the supply of money?
10. How did the Fed use the demand for money function in its old method of controlling the supply of money?
11. What are the main potential sources of error, or looseness, in the Fed's old method of monetary control?
12. What are the main potential sources of error, or looseness, in the Fed's current monetary control procedures?

33

Monetary Policy I: Aggregate Demand Shocks

You are now in a position to ask the central macroeconomic policy question, namely, What can and should monetary policy do to offset the business cycle? This is a controversial question. There are two broad views concerning its answer, and this chapter, along with the next, is designed to help you understand the nature of the controversy. The material presented in these two chapters will take you right to the frontiers of the current debate in economics.[1] However, nothing that will be dealt with in these chapters is inherently more difficult than the material that you have handled so far.

The chapter will help you with five tasks. They are to:

(a) Know the key difference between the monetary policy advice given by monetarists and that given by Keynesians.
(b) Know what aggregate demand shocks are and how they affect the aggregate demand curve.
(c) Understand the consequences of following monetarist monetary policy advice in the face of aggregate demand shocks.
(d) Understand the consequences of following Keynesian monetary policy advice in the face of aggregate demand shocks.
(e) Understand why monetarists and Keynesians offer conflicting monetary policy advice.

---

[1]The leading articles on this topic are much more demanding than the simplified presentation given in this and the next two chapters. On the monetarist side, the leading pieces are: Thomas J. Sargent and Neil Wallace, "Rational Expectations and the Theory of Economic Policy," *Journal of Monetary Economics*, 2 (April 1976), 169–84; and Robert E. Lucas, Jr., "Rules, Discretion and the Role of the Economic Advisor," in Stanley Fischer, ed., *Rational Expectations and Economic Policy*, National Bureau of Economic Research (Chicago and London: University of Chicago Press, 1980), 199–210. On the Keynesian side, the best pieces are: Edmund Phelps and John B. Taylor, "Stabilizing Powers of Monetary Policy under Rational Expectations," *Journal of Political Economy*, 85 (February 1977), 163–89; and Stanley Fischer, "Long-Term Contracts, Rational Expectations, and the Optimal Money Supply Rule," *Journal of Political Economy*, 85 (February 1977), 191–206.

A. Monetarist and Keynesian Monetary Policy Advice

For present purposes, monetary policy will mean manipulating the money supply. The procedures whereby the Fed achieves its monetary policy objectives, described in the previous chapter, are understood to be capable of delivering whatever supply of money the Fed chooses. This chapter will be concerned with the effects of the Fed achieving alternative targets for the money supply rather than with the ways in which these targets are achieved.

The monetary policy advice given by Keynesians is:

1. Raise the money supply to a higher level than it otherwise would have been if output is (or is forecast to be) below its full-employment level.
2. Lower the money supply below what it otherwise would have been if output is (or is forecast to be) above its full-employment level.

The precise amount by which the money supply should be moved in order to achieve the desired level of output is a technically complex matter, but one that Keynesians believe they can handle with the help of large-scale econometric models.

The monetarist policy advice contrasts very sharply with the Keynesian advice which is as follows:

> If output is below its full-employment level so that there is a recession, monetarists advise holding the money supply on a steady course that is known and predictable, rather than raising the rate of growth of the money supply above that known and predictable path. Conversely, when the economy is in a boom, with output above its full-employment level, the monetarist advice is again to hold the money supply growing at a steady and predictable rate rather than to reduce its growth rate.

Thus, Keynesian advice is to manipulate the money supply growth rate, raising it in a depression and lowering it in a boom; the monetarist policy advice is to keep the money supply growth rate steady, regardless of whether the economy is in a boom or a slump.

To see *why* each group of economists gives the advice that it does and to see precisely why there is a disagreement, it is necessary to analyze how the economy reacts to shocks that do not themselves stem from the actions of monetary policy. It is then necessary to ask how monetary policy can (and should) be used to counter the effects of these shocks. There are two broad sources of shocks—one on the aggregate demand side and the other on the aggregate supply side of the economy. The aggregate demand shocks are considered in this chapter, and the aggregate supply shocks in the next one.

B. Aggregate Demand Shocks and the Aggregate Demand Curve

The *IS-LM* model of aggregate demand, developed in Part IV, did not explicitly contain aggregate demand shocks. It was presented as if the level of output, employment, unemployment, the real wage, the money wage, and the price level are determined *exactly* once the value of the money supply and the fiscal policy variables were set. This was an oversimplification, and one that it is now necessary to relax. In this chapter, we relax this simplification on the demand side of the economy.

You will recall that the theory of aggregate demand was developed from a theory of consumption, investment, and the demand for money. A moment's reflection will tell you that if the money supply and fiscal policy variables are constant, the position of the aggregate demand curve will be fixed and fully predictable only if the consumption function, the investment function, and the demand for money function are fixed and fully predictable. If a significant group of individuals decided in one particular year that they would manage with a smaller ratio of money balances to income than normal, then in that particular year there would be a surge of expenditures. This would happen as this group of individuals put into action their decisions to lower their money balances below their normal level in relation to their incomes. Conversely, if a significant group of individuals decided in a particular year that they wanted a higher ratio of money balances to income than normal, they would cut back on their expenditures as they put their decisions into effect.

There are many factors that could lead individuals to vary, over time, their consumption, investment, and demand for money. On the average, such factors would cancel out and, for most of the time, when aggregated over all the individuals in the economy, would not be very important. From time to time, however, such factors could be important and might knock the economy significantly away from its *normal* equilibrium position.

Perhaps some examples will be helpful. Suppose it is widely believed that there is going to be a major drought. This might lead people to invest in a stockpile of food and to lower their average money holdings for a period. While this stockpiling was going on, there would be an increase in the level of aggregate demand as people attempted to put through their increased expenditure plans. In the opposite direction, suppose that it was widely believed that there was going to be a major technical innovation in, say, automobiles, such that the current year's model would be quickly superseded by a vastly superior technology. In such a case, the sales of cars in the year in question would be unusually low, and people would hold on to their money balances in readiness for a subsequent increase in expenditures. In this case, there would be a retiming of expenditures, with sales in one year being unusually low, and sales in some subsequent year, or years, being unusually high.

These are simply examples; you can probably think of many more. Most of the examples that you will think of will turn out to involve *randomness in the timing of people's expenditures in acquiring either durable goods, capital goods, or other goods to store. Random fluctuations in the composition of people's assets—between money holdings on the one hand and real asset holdings on the other hand—lead to random fluctuations in aggregate demand.*

You can think of the aggregate demand curve that we have been working with in the earlier parts of this book as being the level of the aggregate demand curve *on the average*. This curve is reproduced in Figure 33.1 as the solid line labelled $AD(M_0, g, t)$. It is labelled in this way to remind you that the position of the AD curve depends on the money supply, M, government spending, g, and taxes, t. The subscript on M is there to denote the initial value of the money supply, M_0. Later we shall analyze what happens when we change M, holding everything else constant.

Figure 33.1
Aggregate Demand Shocks

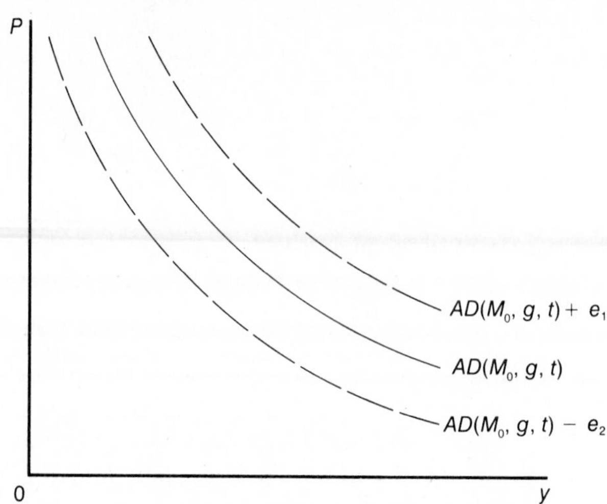

Random fluctuations in consumption, investment, and the demand for money summarized as the shock e shifts the aggregate demand curve around its average position, even though monetary and fiscal policy variables are fixed. On the average, the shocks will be zero. The shock e_1 is an example of a positive shock and minus e_2 is a negative shock.

Now allow also for random shocks arising from the considerations just described to affect the position of the aggregate demand curve. Sometimes the aggregate demand will be higher than its average value, and sometimes lower than its average value. We can capture such random shocks as an addition to or subtraction from the average position of the aggregate demand curve. Let us call the aggregate of all the random shocks to demand e. On the average, e is equal to zero. It will, however, take on large positive or negative values. If e took on a positive value, say, e_1, then the aggregate demand curve would move to the right, such as that shown as the broken line $AD(M_0, g, t) + e_1$. If there was a negative random shock, say, *minus* e_2, then the aggregate demand curve would move to the left, such as that shown as the broken line labelled $AD(M_0, g, t) - e_2$. At any particular point in time the aggregate demand curve might lie anywhere inside the range of the two broken-line curves. On the average, the aggregate demand curve would be located in the middle of this range at $AD(M_0, g, t)$.

Thus, for any given level of the money supply you can think of there being a whole set of possible aggregate demand curves. The *actual* position of the aggregate demand curve depends on the size of the random shock, e, and on the money supply.

C. Consequences of Monetarist Policy

Let us now analyze what happens when there is an aggregate demand shock and when the monetary policy pursued is that advocated by monetarists. Figure 33.2 illustrates the analysis. Let us suppose that the anticipated money supply is M_0. Recall that the monetarist policy involves making the money

Figure 33.2
The Consequences of Following Monetarist Policy Advice

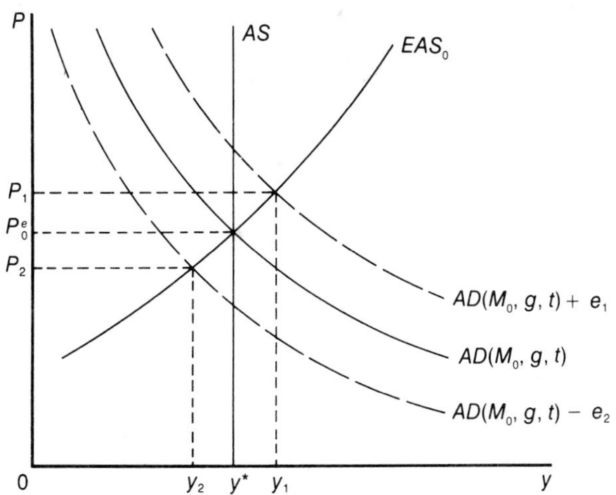

Monetarist policy holds the money stock constant. Expected aggregate demand is $AD(M_0, g, t)$, and the rational expectation of the price level is P^e_0. Actual random fluctuations in aggregate demand will generate fluctuations in output with procyclical co-movements in prices.

supply follow a totally predictable path under all circumstances. Specifically, assume the actual money supply is held constant at M_0. It will now be obvious that the actual money supply will equal the anticipated money supply. In other words, if the monetarist policy rule is followed, there will be no unanticipated changes in the money supply.

Since, on the average, the aggregate demand shock e will be zero, it will be rational to expect a zero aggregate demand shock. Thus the rational expectation of the price level P^e_0 is found where the expected aggregate demand curve $AD(M_0, g, t)$ cuts the aggregate supply curve AS. This aggregate demand curve is the expected aggregate demand curve *in the double sense that it is drawn for an expected value of the aggregate demand shock equal to zero and for the money supply equal to its anticipated level of* M_0. Passing through the point P^e_0 and y^* is the relevant expectations-augmented aggregate supply curve. This is the expectations-augmented aggregate supply curve drawn for the rational expectation of the price level of P^e_0.

Now suppose that there is a random increase in aggregate demand by an amount e_1 such that the demand curve *actually* moves rightwards to $AD(M_0, g, t) + e_1$. If the monetary policy advice of the monetarists is followed and the money supply is held at M_0, its anticipated level, the result of this random shock to aggregate demand will be a rise in the price level to P_1 and a rise in output to y_1.

Next consider the oppposite case. Suppose there is a negative random shock to aggregate demand—a random fall in aggregare demand—so that the aggregate demand curve shifts leftwards to $AD(M_0, g, t) - e_2$. Again, following the monetarist policy advice, the actual money supply is held steady at its anticipated level M_0. There is therefore a drop in the price level to P_2 and a drop in output to y_2.

You can see that the consequences of following the monetarist policy advice are that the economy will experience random deviations of output from its full-employment level and random deviations of the price level from its expected level as the economy is continuously "bombarded" with random aggregate demand shocks. These shocks are not offset by changes in the money supply. There will also be fluctuations in employment, unemployment, the real wage, and the money wage. You can work out the directions in which these variables will move from Chapter 28. Further, for the reasons discussed in Chapter 29, there will be only a gradual return to full employment following a shock.

Let us now examine the consequences of following Keynesian policy advice.

D. Consequences of Keynesian Policy

Let us begin with exactly the same setup as before. The anticipated money supply is M_0, and the expected aggregate demand curve drawn for an expected zero aggregate demand shock is the curve $AD(M_0, g, t)$. (For the moment ignore the other labels on that curve in Figure 33.3.) The rational expectation of the price level is P_0^e, and the relevant expectations-augmented aggregate supply curve is EAS_0.

Now suppose that there is a positive random shock to aggregate demand (e_1) taking the aggregate demand curve to the higher curve $AD(M_0, g, t) + e_1$. The Keynesian policy advice in this situation is to cut the money supply. If the money supply is cut by exactly the right amount, it is possible to offset the positive aggregate demand shock, thereby making the actual aggregate demand curve the same as the curve $AD(M_0, g, t)$. Suppose that the money supply that exactly achieves that effect is M_1. Then the aggregate demand curve would be the same as $AD(M_0, g, t)$. I have given that aggregate demand curve a second label, $AD(M_1, g, t) + e_1$. This is to indicate to you that *the same aggregate demand curve can arise from different combinations of the money supply and the random aggregate demand shock.* If the aggregate demand shock was zero and the money supply was M_0, the aggregate demand curve would be the same as in a situation in which the money supply was M_1 (smaller than M_0) and the aggregate demand shock was e_1 (a positive value). Following this Keynesian policy rule of changing the money supply to offset the aggregate demand shock gives the prediction that the level of output will stay constant at y^* and the price level will stay at its rational expectation level P_0^e.

The same conclusion would arise if the consequences of a negative aggregate demand shock were examined. If aggregate demand fell by a random amount, e_2, with a fixed money supply M_0, the aggregate demand curve would move to $AD(M_0, g, t) - e_2$. If this random shock was offset by a rise in the money supply to (say) M_2—a value big enough to raise the aggregate demand curve back to its original level—then the aggregate demand curve would again become the same as $AD(M_0, g, t)$. The curve $AD(M_0, g, t)$ has been labelled yet a third time as equal to $AD(M_2, g, t) - e_2$ to remind you that

Figure 33.3
The Consequences of Following Keynesian Monetary Policy Advice

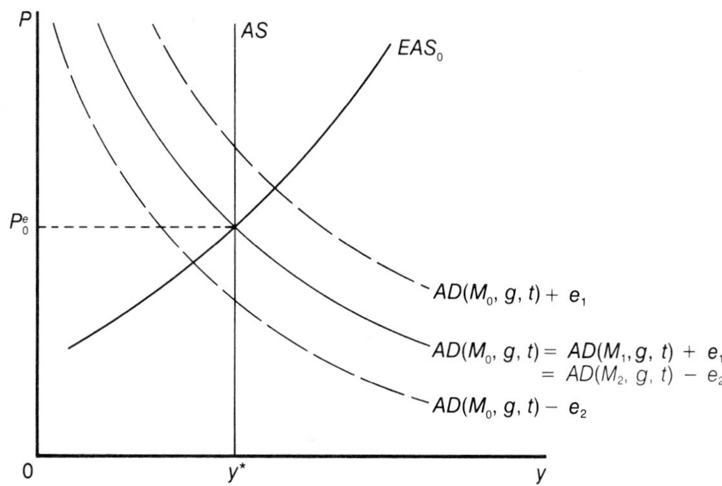

If a random shock hits the economy, thereby shifting the aggregate demand curve (with the money stock constant), Keynesian policy would change the money stock so as to offset the random demand shift. The actual aggregate demand curve would remain constant as the continuous line in the figure. Output would be stabilized at full employment and the price level at its expected level.

with a higher money supply (M_2) and a negative value of the aggregate demand shock (e_2), it is possible to place the aggregate demand curve in the same place as it would have been with a lower value for the money supply (M_0) and a zero random shock to aggregate demand.

Again, following Keynesian policy advice, the economy stays at the price level P_0^e and the full-employment output level y^* where the aggregate demand curve labelled $AD(M_2, g, t) - e_2$ cuts the expectations-augmented aggregate supply curve EAS_0.

You see then that the consequences of following Keynesian stabilization policy are to remove all the fluctuations from output and to keep the price level at its rationally expected level.

E. Why Monetarists and Keynesians Offer Conflicting Advice

Comparison: Keynesian Policy Seems to Be Better than Monetarist Policy

From the above presentation of the effects of following a monetarist policy rule versus Keynesian policy intervention, it is apparent that monetarist policy leaves the economy contaminated by the effects of random shocks to aggregate demand, whereas Keynesian policy completely insulates the economy from these shocks by exactly offsetting their effects. It would appear, then, that monetary policy can be used to keep the economy free from random fluctuations in output and the price level, and assuming that to be a desirable end, Keynesian monetary policy should so be used. Put more directly, it would appear that Keynesian policy is better than monetarist policy.

Naturally, since there is a debate about the matter, things are not quite as simple as they have been presented in the above two sections. Let us now try to find out why Keynesians and monetarists disagree with each other.

Informational Advantages

In the two monetary policy experiments that we have conducted and compared in the preceding sections, we have not made the same assumptions concerning the information available to the Fed and to private economic agents.

When conducting the monetarist policy analysis, it was assumed implicitly—and it is now time to be explicit about the matter—that the Fed and private economic agents all had the same information. No one knew what value e would take in the coming time period. Everyone, including the Fed, expected that it would be zero.

When conducting the Keynesian policy analysis, however, it was assumed implicitly—and again it is now time to be explicit—that no private agent was able to forecast the value of the random shock e, but that the Fed knew the value of e exactly and was able to move the money supply so as to precisely offset its effects on aggregate demand. In other words, it was assumed that the Fed knew more than private economic agents concerning the position of the aggregate demand curve.

Instead of assuming that the Fed has such an informational advantage, let us analyze what would happen if the Fed had to operate a Keynesian policy with a time lag such that it could only change the money supply when it knew that there had been an aggregate demand shock that it was able to observe. Also, however, let us recognize that what can be observed by the Fed can also be observed by anybody else. If the Fed knows that the economy is experiencing a positive (or negative) aggregate demand shock, then it seems reasonable to suppose that everyone else knows that too.

In order to make things as clear as possible, let us look at two periods of time (years). We will analyze what would happen if there was a positive aggregate demand shock (e_1) in the first period and then no aggregate demand shock in the second period. Suppose that the Fed reacts to an aggregate demand shock with a one-period lag. That is, if there has been a positive aggregated demand shock in period one, the Fed cuts back on the money supply in the second period in an attempt to offset the effects of the observed, first-period aggregate demand shock. Further, let us suppose that everyone knows as much as the Fed knows about the aggregate demand shock. *Further, let us suppose that everyone knows that the Fed is pursuing a Keynesian policy and will react with a one-period lag by changing the money stock.* Let us now work out what will happen as a result of this monetary policy response.

Figure 33.4 illustrates the analysis. The economy is initially expected to be on the demand curve $AD(M_0, g, t)$, at a price level P_0^e and an output level y^*. The relevant expectations-augmented aggregate supply curve is EAS_0. Let this be the point at which the economy starts out. Then, in period one, let there be a positive aggregate demand shock e_1. No one can predict the aggregate demand shock before it happens, and therefore, no one reacts to it until

Figure 33.4
The Consequences of Following Keynesian Monetary Policy Advice with an Information Lag

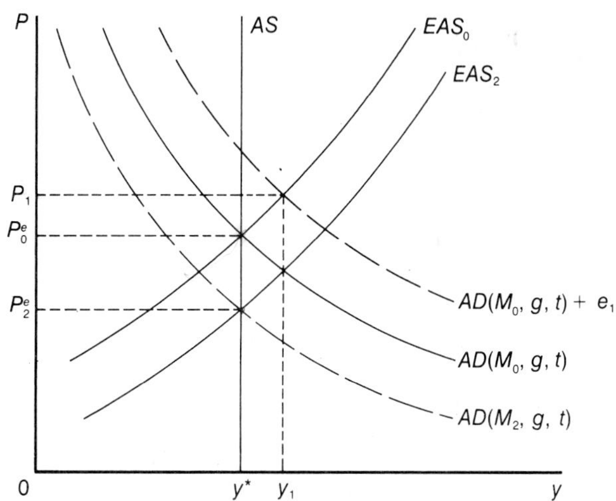

An economy initially at full-employment equilibrium (y^*, P_0^e) is disturbed by a random shock to aggregate demand (e_1). Output and prices rise to y_1, P_1, the same as they would if the monetarist rule was being pursued. The higher output level induces a monetary contraction under the Keynesian rule (lowering the aggregate demand curve to $AD(M_2, g, t)$. Since everyone knows the government is using the Keynesian rule, the aggregate demand curve (in the absence of random shocks) will be the same as the expected curve. The economy will return to full employment but with a lower price level. Pursuing a Keynesian rule with a one-period lag leaves output on the same path as in the case of the monetarist rule but makes prices more volatile.

period two. However, the shock affects the actual behavior of the economy in period one, and the price level and output level settle down at P_1 and y_1, respectively. These are the values of the price level and output at which the new aggregate demand curve $AD(M_0, g, t) + e_1$ cuts the expectations-augmented aggregate supply curve EAS_0.

Now, in the next period (period two), everyone has observed that there has been a positive aggregate demand shock. Furthermore, everyone can work out the size of the shock from knowing what the actual price and output levels turned out to be. The Fed reacts to this aggregate demand shock by cutting the money supply in period two to a value of (say) M_2. Assuming that there is no aggregate demand shock in this second period, the new aggregate demand curve will be below the original curve $AD(M_0, g, t)$ since the money supply has been cut below M_0. In particular, the aggregate demand curve will be $AD(M_2, g, t)$. Private agents will expect the aggregate demand curve to be $AD(M_2, g, t)$ because they will expect the monetary authorities to cut the money stock as a reaction to the previous period's aggregate demand shock e_1. They will form a rational expectation of the price level of P_2^e, and the expectations-augmented aggregate supply curve will become EAS_2. If (as we are assuming) there is no aggregate demand shock in period two, the economy will settle at its full-employment output level of y^* and the price level of P_2^e.

Thus, following a Keynesian policy rule, but with a one-period information lag, implying that the Fed has no better information than the private sector has, leads to a movement in output that is exactly the same as that which occurs when the monetarist policy rule is followed. However, there is a difference between the two policies in the behavior of the price level. The price level fluctuates more when Keynesian policy advice is followed than it does with the monetarist rule. Output behaves exactly the same under either policy, but the price level is more variable with Keynesian policy than with monetarist policy.

We see, then, that following Keynesian policy advice, which has a one-period lag on information and with no informational advantage for the Fed, is exactly the same as following monetarist policy advice in its effect on output. However, Keynesian policy leads to bigger fluctuations in the price level than does monetarist policy.

The Essence of the Dispute Between Keynesians and Monetarists

The essence of the dispute between Keynesians and monetarists concerning the effects of monetary policy turns on the question of information and the use that may be made of new information. The monetarist asserts that the Fed has no informational advantage over private agents and that it can do nothing that private agents cannot do for themselves. Any attempts by the Fed to fine tune or stabilize the economy by making the money supply react to previous shocks, known to everybody, will make the level of output behave no better than it otherwise would have done and will make the price level more variable.

Keynesians assert that there is an effective informational advantage to the Fed. They agree that individuals will form their expectations rationally, using all the information that is available to them. But they go on to assert that individuals get locked into contracts based on an expected price level that, after the fact of an aggregate demand shock, turns out to be wrong. *The Fed can act after private agents have tied themselves into contractual arrangements based on a false price level expectation* to compensate for and offset the effects of those random shocks. Figure 33.3 can be reinterpreted as showing what happens if the private sector is tied into contracts based on a wrong expected price level. In that case, if both the Fed and private agents *observe* an aggregate demand shock of (say) e_1, but if private agents are tied into contracts based on the expected price level P_0^e, *and if* the Fed can change the money supply quickly enough, then the Keynesian policy outcome shown in Figure 33.3 can be achieved.

The essence of the debate, then, concerns the flexibility of private sector responses vis-à-vis the flexibility of Fed responses to random shocks that hit the economy. If everyone can act as quickly and as effortlessly as everyone else, there is no advantage from pursuing Keynesian policy, and indeed, there are disadvantages because the price level will be more variable. If, however, the Fed can act more quickly than the private sector, there may be a gain in the form of reduced variability of both output and the price level from pursuing Keynesian policy.

There is no easy way of deciding which of these two views better describes the world, and further scientific research is required before the matter will be settled.

One thing that can be said, however, is that because it is difficult to know exactly what random shocks are hitting the economy, attempts to pursue Keynesian policy will make the money supply more random and less predictable than would monetarist policy. You have seen (Chapters 28 and 29) that an unpredictable monetary policy gives rise to cycles in economic activity arising from the money supply movements themselves. Thus, Keynesian policy will necessarily impart some cyclical movements into the economy as a consequence of the fact that the money supply itself is less predictable under Keynesian policy than under a monetarist policy rule. Monetarist policy will (as far as possible) remove any fluctuations from aggregate demand that arise from the money supply itself. The only things that can lead to business cycles under a monetarist policy rule are the random fluctuations arising from private aggregate demand (or aggregate supply) shocks. The random shocks emanating from the behavior of the Fed are eliminated.

Whether random shocks that arise from the private sector are the dominant shocks is another matter of dispute. Here, however, there seems to be less room for disagreement. It is fairly well established that one of the major sources of fluctuations in economic activity in modern industrial economies is instability in monetary policy itself. Unanticipated variations in the money supply seem to account for *most* of the variations that we observe in the level of economic activity. However, they certainly do not account for all the observed fluctuations. The Great Depression of 1929 through 1934 has not yet been satisfactorily explained by *any* theory. We must therefore remain cautious and display a certain amount of humility. This does not, however, bode well for the Keynesian policy recommendation, which, in order that it may improve matters, must be based on the presumption that we know rather a lot about the way in which the economy behaves.

The bottom line defense for the monetarist policy recommendation is that we are simply too ignorant about the workings of the economy to be able to do any better than to remove at least those sources of fluctuation in economic activity that we *can* control, namely, those that stem from instability in the money supply. If such fluctuations were removed, the economy would behave in a more stable manner than it has in the past. Of course, it would not be perfect. Perfection, however, requires a great deal more information than we currently have available to us.

Summary

A. Monetarist and Keynesian Monetary Policy Advice

Monetarists recommend the adoption of a steady and predictable money supply growth rule. The money supply growth rate should be kept constant no matter what the current state of the economy.

Keynesians recommend the use of active variations in the money supply to offset aggregate demand shocks. They recommend raising the money supply when output is below its full-employment level and lowering the money supply when output is above its full-employment level.

B. Aggregate Demand Shocks and the Aggregate Demand Curve

Aggregate demand shocks are random variations in the level of aggregate demand that arise from random movements in the timing of expenditures and from random fluctuations in desired holdings of real assets and financial assets. If people try to hold more real assets and fewer financial assets, there will be a rise in the demand for goods—a rise in aggregate demand.

Aggregate demand shocks shift the aggregate demand curve. For any given price level, the level of aggregate demand will vary around its most likely value, depending on the size of the aggregate demand shock.

C. Consequences of Monetarist Policy

Adopting a monetarist policy permits fluctuations in output, employment, unemployment, the price level, the money wage, and the real wage. For example, in the case of a positive aggregate demand shock, output, employment, the price level, and the money wage will rise, and the real wage and unemployment will fall.

D. Consequences of Keynesian Policy

Keynesian policy is designed to isolate the economy from a random shock and to eliminate fluctuations in output and the price level. In the case of a positive aggregate demand shock, Keynesian monetary policy advice is to lower the money supply so as to leave aggregate demand (and thus the position of the aggregate demand curve) unchanged. This would lead to no adjustment in the rational expectation of the price level, so that the level of output, employment, unemployment, the price level, and the real and money wage would remain constant.

E. Why Monetarists and Keynesians Offer Conflicting Advice

The dispute between monetarists and Keynesians rests on whether the Fed has an informational advantage over private agents in the economy. Monetarists argue that the Fed has no more information than do private agents. Any attempt by the Fed to offset *previous* random aggregate demand shocks (now known to all agents in the economy) by varying the money supply will not reduce the fluctuations in output, whereas it will increase those in the price level.

Keynesians assert that the Fed has an *effective* informal advantage over private agents because private agents get locked into contracts that cannot be revised quickly as new information becomes available. Private agents are locked into contracts based on the wrong expected price level, whereas the Fed can respond quickly to the new information (the aggregate demand shock) and can change the money supply quickly enough so that output, employment, and the price level remain steady.

The successful application of Keynesian policy would require a vast amount of information on the part of the Fed and government, and there is a presumption that, in the present state of knowledge, they do not have sufficient information. Attempts at pursuing Keynesian policy will be likely to generate bigger fluctuations in both output and prices than would the adoption of a monetarist rule.

Review Questions

1. Summarize and contrast the monetary policy positions of Keynesians and monetarists.
2. Give some examples of factors that might cause aggregate demand shocks.
3. Work out, using the appropriate diagrams, the consequences of pursuing monetarist policy in the face of random fluctuations in aggregate demand.
4. Explain the rationale that monetarists use for permitting random aggregate demand shocks to influence aggregate output and prices.
5. Work out, using the appropriate diagrams, the Keynesian monetary policy required to stabilize the economy in the face of a positive shock.
6. Work out, using the appropriate diagrams, the effects of pursuing Keynesian policy, but with the monetary authorities reacting with a one-period lag to aggregate demand shocks.
7. Set out the major differences in the predicted consequences of pursuing monetarist and Keynesian policies in the face of random aggregate demand shocks.
8. What is the primary source of disagreement between Keynesians and monetarists that causes each group of economists to give the advice that it does?

34

Monetary Policy II: Aggregate Supply Shocks

In September 1973, the members of the Oil-Producing Exporting Countries (OPEC) announced a fourfold increase in the price of crude oil. At the same time they announced an embargo on the shipment of oil to certain countries and a decision to cut back their production levels. In a single afternoon, the OPEC decision delivered a *supply shock* to the Western world that has only been matched by the events of major wars. The consequences of the OPEC oil price rise have been widespread and long drawn out. They also triggered a fierce debate as to what constituted the appropriate macroeconomic policy response.[1]

This chapter is going to help you to understand some of the main macroeconomic effects of the OPEC oil shock and also help you to evaluate alternative policy recommendations for dealing with supply shocks of this kind. You have six tasks, which are to:

(a) Understand how a supply shock affects: the production function, the real wage and levels of employment and unemployment, and the aggregate supply curve.
(b) Understand the distinction between the expectations-augmented aggregate supply curve and the expectation of the aggregate supply curve.
(c) Understand the consequences of following monetarist policy advice in the event of an aggregate supply shock.
(d) Understand the consequences of following Keynesian policy advice in the event of an aggregate supply shock.
(e) Understand the consequences of following a Keynesian policy with an information lag.
(f) Understand the essence of the dispute and why there is a further presumption in favor of monetarism.

---

[1]An excellent presentation of a Keynesian view on this is Robert M. Solow, "What to Do (Macroeconomically) When OPEC Comes," in Stanley Fischer, ed., *Rational Expectations and Economic Policy*, National Bureau of Economic Research (Chicago and London: University of Chicago Press, 1980), 249–64. Also see Neil Wallace's comment on Solow on pp. 264–67 of the same volume.

Figure 34.1
How an Aggregate Supply Shock Shifts the Short-Run Production Function

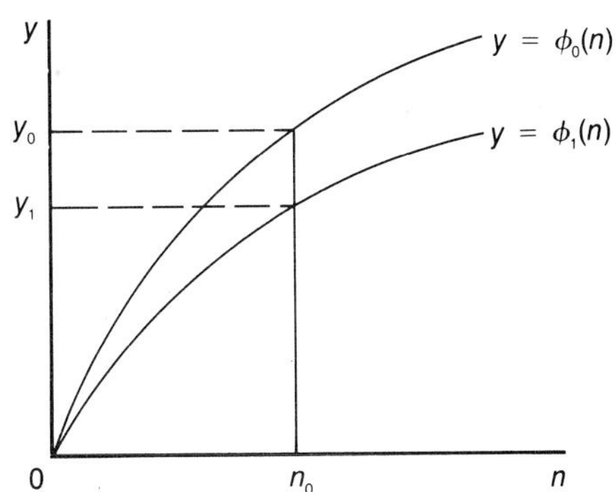

An aggregate supply shock lowers the output that can be produced at each level of labor input. It also lowers the marginal product of labor. For example, a labor input of n_0 would only be able to produce y_1 after a shock, whereas it could have produced y_0 before the shock.

A. Effects of Supply Shocks

The Production Function

You will recall that the theory of aggregate supply developed in Chapter 8 started from the concept of the short-run production function. The production function tells us the maximum output that can be produced using given inputs. The short-run production function tells us how the maximum output level varies as the labor input alone is varied, holding capital, land inputs, and the state of technology constant. An aggregate supply shock such as the cutback of oil supplies and the quadrupling of the price of oil can be thought of as shifting the short-run production function. Figure 34.1 illustrates such a shift. The short-run production function $\phi_0(n)$ may be thought of as that relating to the presupply shock situation, and $\phi_1(n)$ to the postshock situation. At the employment level n_0, more could be produced before the shock, y_0, than after the shock, y_1.

There are thousands upon thousands of individual actions that lead to the shift in the production function. For example, following a supply shock like the oil shock, many extra resources would be diverted into the search for alternative sources of lower-cost energy, thereby lowering the volume of output that would result from a given level of employment. Also, much labor and capital would be diverted to finding ways of using less fuel, again lowering the available supply of goods produced at a given level of employment. A concrete example of such a diversion of resources is in the car industry. As a result of the higher price of oil, there has been a switch to more fuel-efficient cars. Large quantites of labor (and capital) had to be employed in designing, testing, and building these cars. The actual output of cars produced by this labor could have been much higher if the more traditional engines and sizes had not been discarded in favor of the new types. This example is just one of thousands in all areas of industrial activity and transportation.

Figure 34.2
How an Aggregate Supply Shock Affects the Labor Market

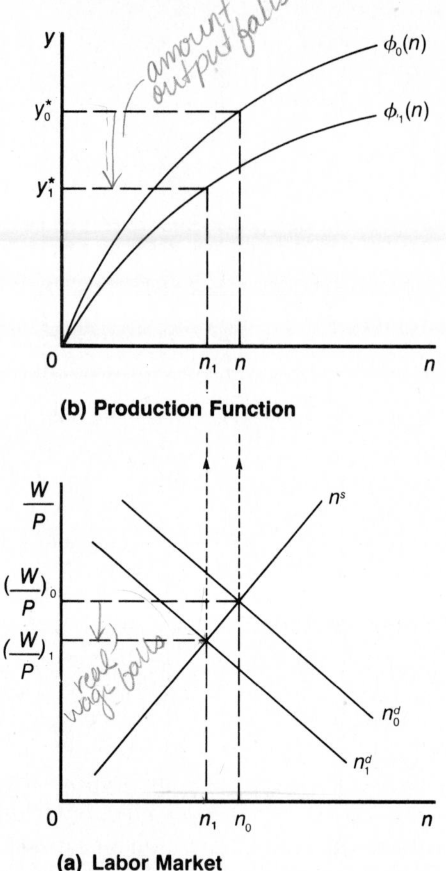

A drop in the production function that lowers the marginal product of labor shifts the demand for labor curve downwards. Employment and the real wage fall from n_0 to n_1 and from $(W/P)_0$ to $(W/P)_1$. Real output falls from y_0 to y_1.

The Real Wage and Levels of Employment and Unemployment

An aggregate supply shock not only shifts the production function, it has an effect in the labor market as well. It shifts the demand for labor function downwards. Another way of saying the same thing is to say that the marginal productivity of labor declines. The reason why marginal productivity declines is the same as the reasons given above for the shift in the production function. Following a shock like the oil price rise, much labor gets absorbed in activities designed to minimize the adverse effects of the price rise rather than in the direct production of goods for final consumption and investment.

The car industry example may be used again to illustrate the point. Suppose that as a result of higher oil prices, a production line for larger cars is scrapped long before it normally would have been and is replaced by a new line to make smaller cars. Suppose also that the small car is to be powered with a new engine, completely redesigned for fuel-efficient operation and with

Figure 34.3
The Effects of an Aggregate Supply Shock on the Aggregate Supply Curve

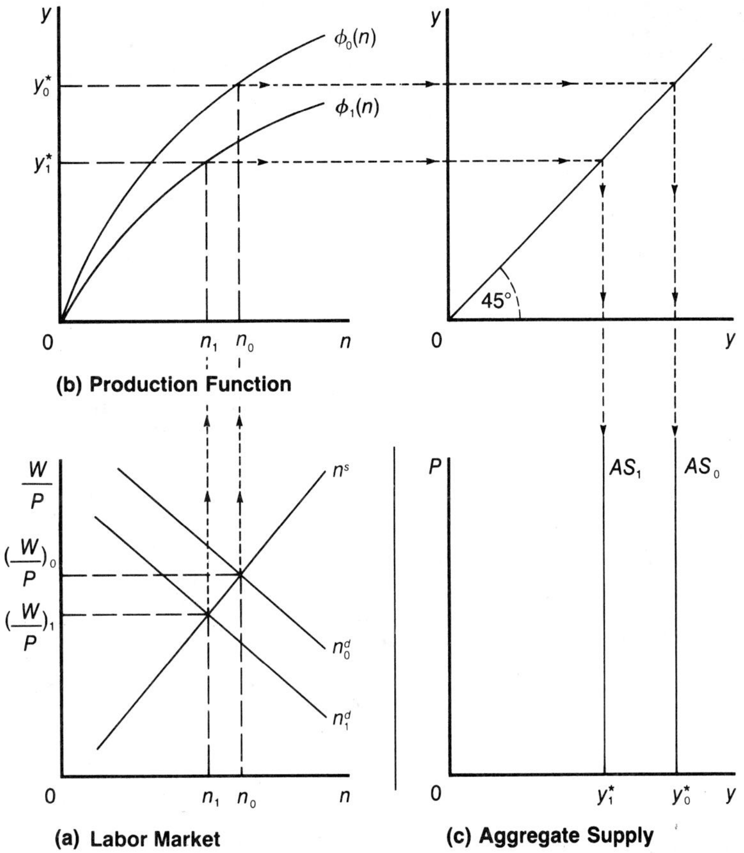

The aggregate supply curve shifts to the left in the face of a negative aggregate supply shock. The leftward shift is bigger then the drop in output for a given level of employment. Employment falls because the real wage falls. Thus, aggregate supply falls for two reasons: a drop in the production function, and a reduction of work effort.

an electronic fuel- and pressure-monitoring system. The amount of labor required to produce a given quantity of the new type of car will be substantially larger than that required for the traditional design and technology. Further, the extra output (marginal product) that could be produced by raising the labor force by a given amount will be less than would have been the case with the older-technology car.

The shift in the production function and the associated shift in the demand for labor function are shown in Figure 34.2. The economy was originally producing y_0^* with a labor force of n_0, and the real wage was $(W/P)_0$. After the supply shock, the production function shifts to $\phi_1(n)$, and the demand for labor function shifts to n_1. The labor market equilibrium now is achieved at a *lower* level of employment, n_1^d, and a lower real wage, $(W/P)_1$. The difference between n_0 and n_1 will be the drop in employment resulting from the supply shock. Initially, at least, these workers may remain in the labor force and will be recorded as unemployed as they search for new jobs. Eventually, if the supply shock is permanent, they will leave the labor force as they realize that the real wage has permanently fallen.

The Aggregate Supply Curve

The effect of an aggregate supply shock on the aggregate supply curve is shown in Figure 34.3. Frames (a) and (b) are the same as Figure 34.2. The amount of output produced initially was y_0^*, and the aggregate supply curve was AS_0. After the supply shock, the level of employment drops to n_1, and the level of output drops to y_1^*, with the aggregate supply curve shifting to AS_1. Notice that the drop in aggregate supply from y_0^* to y_1^* results from two factors—first, the shift in the production function from $\phi_0(n)$ to $\phi_1(n)$, and second, the cut in employment induced by the drop in the marginal productivity of labor, which reduces the demand for labor.

B. Expectations-Augmented Aggregate Supply Curve and the Expectation of the Aggregate Supply Curve

Before going further in the analysis of aggregate supply shocks, I want to draw your attention to an important distinction that you need to be clear about. The word *expectation* is going to be attached to the aggregated supply curve in two very different ways. First, there is the expectations-augmented aggregate supply curve, *EAS*. This is what it always has been, namely, a curve showing the level of aggregate supply for a given expected price level. Second, the concept of the expectation of the aggregate supply curve will be used. This is a new concept that has not been used before. The aggregate supply curve is the vertical aggregate supply curve *AS*—which shows the level of aggregate supply when the expected and actual price levels are equal to each other. If there are no aggregate supply shocks, the position of this curve is determined uniquely by the production function and the condition of equilibrium in the labor market. However, when random shocks affect the production function, they also affect the position of the aggregate supply function. The size and direction of random shocks to the production function cannot be known before they occur, and on the average, these shocks cancel out—are zero. Thus the aggregate supply curve based on a zero aggregate supply shock—the expected or average aggregate supply shock—will be called the *expectation of the aggregate supply curve.*

Keeping this distinction clear, and as a prelude to analyzing the effects of alternative policies toward aggregate supply shocks, let us see how each of these aggregate supply curves shifts in response to such a shock.

Figure 34.4 shows the effects of an aggregate supply shock on the aggregate supply and expectations-augmented aggregate supply curves. Suppose that initially the economy was on the curve AS_0 and the aggregate demand curve $AD(M_0, g, t)$, at a full-employment equilibrium y_0^* and P_0^e. The expectations-augmented aggregate supply curve has both a superscript and a subscript. The subscript refers to the value of the money supply, and the superscript refers to the value of the aggregate supply curve. Thus, EAS_0^0 is at the point of intersection of AS_0 and $AD(M_0, g, t)$.

Figure 34.4
An Aggregate Supply Shock and the Aggregate Supply Curves

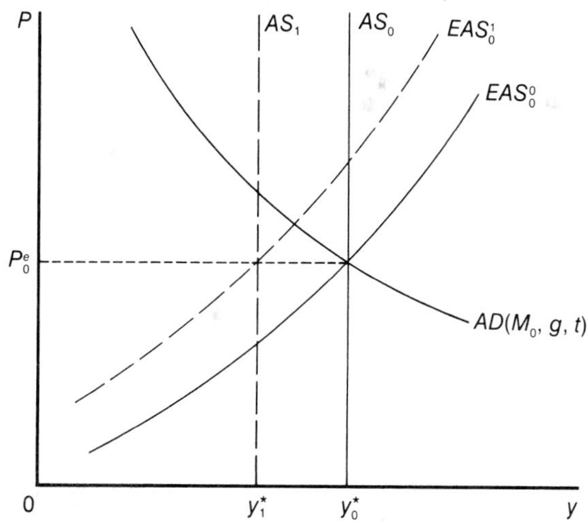

An unexpected aggregate supply shock shifts the aggregate supply for example from AS_0 to AS_1. The expectations-augmented aggregate supply curve is dragged along horizontally with the AS curve. EAS_0^0 is the expectations-augmented aggregate supply curve for the expected price level P_0^e (expected money stock M_0) and an expected aggregate supply curve of AS_0. The curve EAS_0^1 refers to the same expected price level and money stock but to the lower level of aggregate supply.

Now suppose that there is a random shock in aggregate supply that cuts aggregate supply at each level of employment. This will shift the aggregate supply curve to (say) AS_1. Suppose further that the expected value of the money supply remains at M_0, so that the aggregate demand curve $AD(M_0, g, t)$ is expected to remain unchanged. Also, suppose the aggregate supply shock is unanticipated, so that the expectation of the aggregate supply curve is that it remains at AS_0. In this case, the rational expectation of the price level will remain at P_0^e. The aggregate supply curve shift is easy to work out. It simply shifts leftwards by the amount of the drop in output that results from the aggregate supply shock.

What happens to the expectations-augmented aggregate supply curve? This is not as straightforward to figure out. However, a moment's reflection will tell you that that curve must also shift horizontally by the same amount as the aggregate supply curve has shifted. The expectations-augmented aggregate supply curve always cuts the *actual* aggregate supply curve at the expected price level. Since the aggregate supply shock is (by assumption) unanticipated, there is no prior knowledge about it. The aggregate supply curve has shifted, at random, from its expected position AS_0 to an unexpected position AS_1. The expectations-augmented aggregate supply curve will have been dragged along with the aggregate supply curve so as to intersect it at the expected price level P_0^e. Given the aggregate supply shock, there will now be a lower level of output available at all price levels. Nothing has happened to change the expected price level, which remains at P_0^e. That is, nothing has happened to yield new information to economic agents that would lead them to revise their price level expectation.

Thus, the effect on the aggregate supply curves of an aggregate supply shock is to shift both the aggregate supply curve and the expectations-augmented aggregate supply curve horizontally by the amount of the shock. The curve EAS_0^1 is the expectations-augmented aggregate supply curve when the expectation of aggregate demand is $AD(M_0, g, t)$ and when aggregate supply has unexpectedly dropped to AS_1.

You are now in a position to go on to compare the effects of alternative policies.

C. Consequences of Monetarist Policy

Figure 34.5 illustrates the consequences of following monetarist policy in the event of an aggregate supply shock. Suppose that there is a random drop in aggregate supply from AS_0 to AS_1 and that a monetarist policy rule of fixing the money stock at M_0 is followed, so that the aggregate demand curve remains as $AD(M_0, g, t)$. The initial equilibrium in the economy is point A, where output is y_0^* and the price level is P_0^e. When the supply shock occurs, the aggregate supply curve shifts to AS_1, and the expectations-augmented aggregate supply curve shifts with it to EAS_0^1. There is no monetary policy reaction, and the economy settles at point B, with a price level of P_1 and an output level of y_1.

If, in the next period, the aggregate supply shock disappears, so that the economy reverts to its normal position on the aggregate supply curve AS_0, with the expectations-augmented aggregate supply curve EAS_0^0, the economy will return to the full-employment point A from which it started. Thus, following monetarist policy in the face of an aggregate supply shock leads to movements in output and in the price level in opposite directions to each other.

Figure 34.5
The Consequences of Following Monetarist Policy Advice in the Event of a Supply Shock—Stagflation

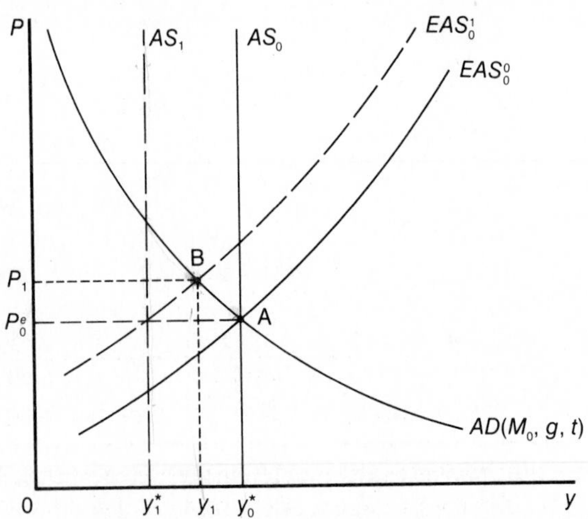

An economy initially at full-employment equilibrium (y_0^*, P_0^e) is disturbed by a negative aggregate supply shock that unexpectedly takes the aggregate supply curve to AS_1 and the EAS curve to EAS_0^1. The impact equilibrium is at y_1, P_1. Prices rise and output falls: The economy experiences stagflation.

This is the phenomenon sometimes called *stagflation.* That is, the economy stagnates and inflates at the same time. It is to avoid stagflation in the face of an aggregate supply shock that some economists advocate adjusting the money supply to accommodate the supply shock. Let us now see what would happen if we follow this Keynesian policy.

D. Consequences of Keynesian Policy

Figure 34.6 illustrates the analysis. Again, suppose the economy starts out at point A at the intersection of the aggregate demand curve $AD(M_0, g, t)$, the aggregate supply curve AS_0, and the expectations-augmented aggregate supply curve EAS_0^0. As before, let there be a shock to aggregate supply that moves the aggregate supply curve to AS_1 and the expectations-augmented aggregate supply curve to EAS_0^1. Keynesian policy would counter this drop in aggregate supply with a stimulation to the money supply. The Keynesian response would be to raise the money supply to (say) M_1, such that the aggregate demand curve shifts to the curve labelled $AD(M_1, g, t)$. The new equilibrium would then be at point C, with the output level at y_0^* as originally, but with the price level at P_1.

If, in the next period, the aggregate supply shock disappeared and the economy reverted to its normal aggregate supply curve AS_0, then one of *four* possibilities arise. First, if the money supply is returned to its original level, M_0, and if everyone expects that to happen, the economy will return to the

Figure 34.6
The Consequences of Following Keynesian Monetary Policy Advice in the Event of a Supply Shock—Avoiding Stagflation

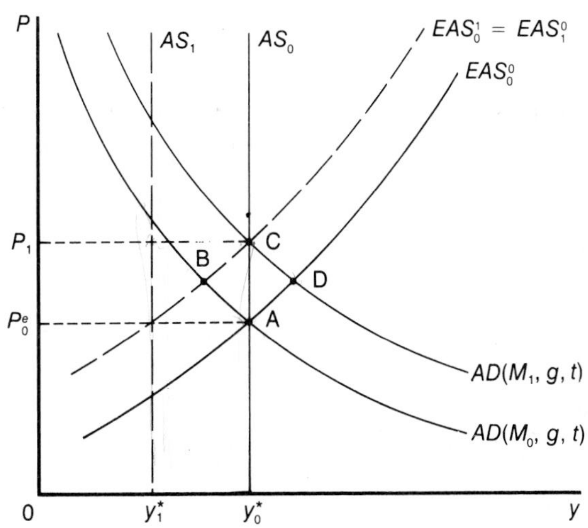

In the same situation as analyzed in Figure 34.5, the Keynesian advice is to raise the money supply, thereby raising aggregate demand from $AD(M_0, g, t)$ to $AD(M_1, g, t)$. This would move the economy to point C (full employment with a price level P_1). What happens in the next period depends on what the government does and what it is expected to do. A fully anticipated return of the money stock to its initial level will return the economy to its initial position A. A fully anticipated maintenance of the money stock at its new level will keep the economy at point C. If the money stock is expected to fall back to the original position but actually stays at the new position, the economy will go to D, and finally the money stock is lowered to its original level, but unexpectedly so, the economy will go to B.

original position A. Second, if the money supply is kept at its higher level M_1 and, again, if everyone anticipates that that will happen, the economy will stay at point C, but the expectations-augmented aggregate supply curve EAS_0^1 will become EAS_1^0, being the expectations-augmented aggregate supply curve drawn for a value of the money stock equal to M_1, with the aggregate supply curve at AS_0. Third, and fourth, if there is confusion in the minds of economic agents as to whether the monetary authorities will revert to the original money supply or stay with the new money supply, then the expectations-augmented aggregate supply curve will be located somewhere in between positions A and C on the AS_0 curve, and the economy will experience an output boom if the money supply stays at M_1, or an output slump if the money supply is returned to M_0. The price level will be between P_0^e and P_1. At the extremes, if the money supply was expected to revert to M_0, but in fact remained at M_1, the economy would move to point D; and if the money supply was expected to remain at M_1, but in fact reverted to M_0, the economy would move to point B.

Which of the above four possibilities would in fact arise would depend on the monetary policy *process* being followed by the Fed. If the Fed had a history of responding to supply shocks with a one-period loosening of monetary policy and a subsequent reverting back to the original level of the money supply, then the first possibility analyzed above would in fact arise. If the Fed had a history of expanding the money stock in response to a supply shock and then keeping the money supply at its new level, then the second possibility would arise. Possibilities three and four would only arise if the Fed had generated confusion in the minds of economic agents as a result of its own previous random behavior.

We may now summarize the consequences of following a Keynesian policy in the face of an aggregate supply shock as follows: Such a policy leads to inflation initially, but with no drop in output and employment. In the next period, whether inflation falls and/or output falls, rises, or stays at its full-employment level depends on what the expected and actual money supplies are. Notice that the Keynesian policy of adjusting the money supply so as to accommodate the supply shock avoids the reduction in output generated by following the monetarist's policy, but only at the expense of higher inflation.

E. Consequences of Keynesian Policy with an Information Lag

Next, consider what would happen in the case of following a Keynesian policy with an information lag. Suppose a Keynesian policy is adopted with a one-period reaction lag to the aggregate supply shock. Figure 34.7 illustrates this case. Again, let the economy begin at position A on the aggregate demand curve $AD(M_0, g, t)$, the expectations-augmented aggregate supply curve EAS_0^0, and the aggregate supply curve AS_0. Then let there be an aggregate supply shock shifting the aggregate supply curve to AS_1 and the expectations-augmented aggregate supply curve to EAS_0^1. Since this is a random shock that no one has been able to predict, the economy will move to position B, with an output level of y_1 and a price level of P_2. *This is exactly the response resulting from following the monetarist policy rule.*

Figure 34.7
The Consequences of Following Keynesian Monetary Policy Advice in the Event of a Supply Shock with an Information Lag

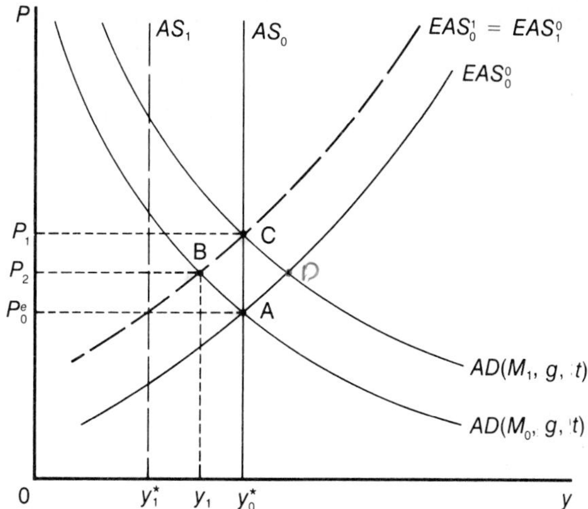

The economy is subjected to exactly the same shock as in the previous figures. Since there is a one-period policy response lag, in the first period of the shock the economy behaves in the same way as it would under a monetarist rule. It moves from A to B. If the monetary authority now stimulates demand, but the people know that a Keynesian policy is being pursued and therefore expect this policy response, the price level will rise to P_1 and output returns to y_0^* in the next period. Thus, the behavior of output is identical in the Keynesian case to the monetarist case, but the price level is more variable under a Keynesian rule.

Next, suppose that in the following period, the Fed reacts to this cut in aggregate output by raising the money supply to M_1. Provided that everyone correctly anticipates this monetary policy reaction, this will put the economy back at the full-employment output level, but at the higher price level P_1, at position C. To help you see more clearly what is going on at the equilibrium marked C, the expectations-augmented aggregate supply curve has been given a second label—EAS_1^0. This tells you that this particular EAS curve describes two situations: one in which the expected money supply is M_0 and the actual aggregate supply curve is AS_1; and a second situation in which the expected money supply is M_1 and the actual aggregate supply curve is at the position AS_0. Thus, with a one-period information lag, a Keynesian stabilization policy in the face of an aggregate supply shock leads to exactly the same path for output as occurs under the monetarist policy, but the price level has a different behavior. With the monetarist policy, the price level returns to its original level; but with the Keynesian policy, the price level rises to P_1.

F. The Essence of the Dispute and Why There Is a Further Presumption in Favor of Monetarism

Exactly the same considerations are relevant in judging the appropriateness of Keynesian and monetarist policy responses to an aggregate supply shock as were relevant in the case of an aggregate demand shock. There is now, however, an additional reason for suspecting that a Keynesian policy will be difficult to carry out. You have already seen in the previous chapter that a Keynesian policy requires a great deal of information. It requires information about the magnitude of the aggregate demand shocks. You now see that to pursue appropriate aggregate supply corrections, it is necessary to have good information about aggregate supply shocks as well. It will be apparent that if *both* of these types of shocks occur simultaneously, it will be necesary for the monetary authorites to have the ability to disentangle the separate shocks that are affecting the economy and to offset both of them in the appropriate way and with greater speed than the private sector can react to them.[2]

Further, if the private sector learns that the public sector is going to react to aggregate supply shocks and if the private sector has as much information as the Fed does concerning those shocks, then the Fed's reaction will always be built into the private sector's expectations, and the Fed's actions themselves will result in price level variability.

Thus, *the monetarists' key objection to Keynesian policy is that it does not improve the performance of the economy as regards the behavior of output, and they unambiguously make the price level less stable and predictable than would a monetarist policy.*

Summary

A. Effects of Supply Shocks

A negative aggregate supply shock lowers the amount of output that can be produced at each level of labor input. It also lowers the marginal productivity of labor and shifts the demand for labor curve downwards. The new equilibrium in the labor market following a negative aggregate supply shock is one with a lower real wage and a lower level of employment. There may be a temporary rise in the measured unemployment rate as people who were previously in employment seek alternative occupations. The aggregate supply curve shifts leftwards, partly as a result of the production function shift and partly as a result of the reduced equilibrium level of employment.

B. Expectations-Augmented Aggregate Supply Curve and the Expectation of the Aggregate Supply Curve

The expectations-augmented aggregate supply curve traces the amount of aggregate supply as the price level varies for a given expected price level. The expectation of the aggregate supply curve refers to the vertical aggregate supply curve, which traces the quantity that will be supplied at each price level when that price level is fully expected. The expectation of that vertical aggregate supply curve refers to its position in normal or usual periods, when aggregate supply shocks are zero.

---

[2]A thorough (although demanding) analysis of precisely this topic is presented by Gary C. Fethke and Andrew J. Policano in "Co-operative Responses by Public and Private Agents to Aggregate Demand and Supply Disturbances," *Economica*, 48 (May 1981), 155–72.

C. Consequences of Monetarist Policy

A random negative shock to aggregate supply with a fixed money supply will lower the level of output and raise the price level in the period in which the aggregate supply shock occurs. The level of employment will fall. The economy will experience stagflation.

D. Consequences of Keynesian Policy

Keynesian policy in the face of a negative aggregate supply shock would be to stimulate demand by raising the money supply. Perfectly conducted, this would have the effect of leaving output and employment unchanged, but raising the price level.

E. Consequences of Keynesian Policy with an Information Lag

If a Keynesian policy is followed but with a one-period lag in the receipt of information concerning the aggregate supply shock, the economy would respond in exactly the same way under Keynesian policy as it would have done under monetarist policy in the period in which the shock occurs. If, using Keynesian policy, the monetary authorities stimulate demand with a one-period lag and if everyone correctly anticipates this, there will be a rise in the price level but no output effect in the second period.

F. The Essence of the Dispute and Why There Is a Further Presumption in Favor of Monetarism

The essence of the dispute between Keynesians and monetarists concerning the appropriate response to aggregate supply shocks is exactly the same as that discussed in the previous chapter concerning aggregate demand shocks. The issue turns on who gets information fastest and who can react fastest to new information. If the Fed has no superior information, then the use of Keynesian policy to correct aggregate supply shocks will leave the behavior of output unaffected and will produce a greater degree of price level variability than will the pursuit of a monetarist policy.

Review Questions

1. Explain why an aggregate supply shock shifts the short-run aggregate production function.
2. Trace the effects of an aggregate supply shock on the labor market and on the aggregate supply curve.
3. What is the distinction between the expectations-augmented aggregate supply curve and the expectation of the aggregate supply curve?
4. How does the expectations-augmented aggregate supply curve shift in the event of a negative aggregate supply shock?
5. Work out, using appropriate diagrams, the effects of pursuing a monetarist policy in the face of a temporary (one period only), but unpredictable, drop in aggregate supply.

6. For the same shock as in Question 5, work out the effects of pursuing a Keynesian policy.

7. Contrast the output and price-level paths in your answers to Questions 5 and 6.

8. If there was a previously unpredictable but, once occurred, known to be *permanent* shock to aggregate supply, what would happen to output and the price level:

(a) With a monetarist policy?

(b) With a Keynesian policy?

9. If a negative aggregate supply shock was always responded to with a rise in the money supply, and a positive aggregate supply shock was responded to with an unchanged money supply, what would the path of the inflation rate be like? (This is a tougher question than the others.)

35

Fiscal Policy

This chapter examines how fiscal policy affects the level of output, employment, unemployment, the real wage, the money wage, and the price level. You will be aware that there is a great deal of popular discussion concerning the desirability of alternative government spending and tax policy changes. This chapter is designed to help you to understand and evaluate this discussion. Your tasks are to:

(a) Understand the key differences between the Keynesian and monetarist policy recommendations concerning fiscal policy.
(b) Understand the distinction between anticipated and unanticipated fiscal policy.
(c) Know how output, employment, unemployment, the real wage, the money wage, and the price level are affected by an anticipated change in government expenditure.
(d) Know how output, employment, unemployment, the real wage, the money wage, and the price level are affected by an unanticpated change in government expenditure.

A. Keynesian and Monetarist Fiscal Policy Advice

The Keynesian and monetarist disagreement concerning the appropriate use of fiscal policy is much like their disagreement over monetary policy.

Keynesian Fiscal Policy Advice

Keynesians recommend that:

1. When output is *below* its full-employment level, either (a) raise government expenditure, or (b) cut taxes, or (c) raise government expenditure and cut taxes together.
2. When output is *above* its full-employment level, either (a) cut government expenditure, or (b) raise taxes, or (c) cut government expenditure and raise taxes together.

Keynesians also tend to favor a political constitution that gives centralized fiscal control so as to facilitate active fiscal policy changes.

Monetarist Fiscal Policy Advice

Monetarists disagree profoundly with the Keynesian fiscal policy advice. They say that government expenditure should be set at a level that is determined with reference to the requirements of economic efficiency rather than with reference to macroeconomic stability.

Government Expenditures Monetarists recommend that government expenditure be set at a level such that the marginal utility derived from public expenditures per dollar spent is equal to the marginal utility derived from private expenditure per dollar spent. (Recall your microeconomic analysis of the optimum allocation of a consumer's budget. Monetarists assert that the same considerations that apply to an individual's budget allocation are relevant for the allocation of resources between the public and private sector.) If the marginal utility per dollar spent on private goods is less than the marginal utility per dollar spent on government goods, then government expenditure is too low and private expenditure is too high, and there is a need to reallocate resources away from the private sector and toward the government sector—to increase public expenditure. Conversely, if the marginal utility per dollar spent on private expenditure is greater than the marginal utility per dollar spent by the government, then the government sector is too big, and there is a need to reduce government spending so that private spending may be increased.

Monetarists would therefore begin by looking at the marginal utility per dollar spent on such items as national defence, law and order, education, health services, and all the other things purchased directly by the government and would compare these with the marginal utility per dollar of private expenditure. Monetarists assert that government expenditure should be set with reference to this economic efficiency criterion alone.

Monetarists—or at least some of them—go on to point out that there is a problem arising from an imperfection in the political marketplace. They point out that there appears to be a tendency for the interaction of politicians, the bureaucracy, and the electorate to generate a level of government expenditure that exceeds the efficient level. That is, there is a tendency for government expenditure to rise, relative to private expenditure, to a level such that the marginal utility per dollar spent on goods bought by the government is below that in the private sector. They therefore advocate a constitutional limitation on the fraction of aggregate output that may be spent by the government.

Further, monetarists tend to favor political constitutions that have decentralized federal and local fiscal authorities, so that those who levy and spend taxes on public consumption are not too distant from the people who they represent, and also so as to encourage competition between jurisdictions.

To summarize: Monetarists advocate setting the level of government expenditure on considerations of economic efficiency and independently of the state of the aggregate level of output, employment, unemployment, or prices. There is a presumption that government expenditure should be held to a steady fraction of aggregate output.

Taxes Monetarists recommend that taxes be set at a level that enables the government to buy the utility-maximizing volume of public goods and services and to maintain a constant money supply growth rate.

This policy recommendation follows directly from the monetarist view about the appropriate government spending policy and money supply policy. Recall that the government is constrained by the budget equation:

$$g - \bar{t} = q\left(\frac{M}{P}\right)\mu$$

Also recall from Chapter 33 that the monetarists' advice on the money supply growth rate, μ, is that it be set at a constant and steady value. One possible value would be zero, but usually monetarists recommend that μ be set equal to the rate of growth of output, so that the level of prices (recalling the fundamental inflation equation) is constant. Since monetarists recommend that government expenditure be set equal to their utility-maximizing level (independently of the state of the macroeconomy) and that the money supply should grow at a steady rate (independently of the state of the macroeconomy), it follows that they want to see the level of legislated taxes set such that these other two objectives may be met.

In other words, for monetarists, taxes and government expenditure go together. Both need to be set at levels such that an efficient allocation of resources between the government and private sector is achieved and, further, so that the money supply growth rate stays at a constant zero-inflation rate.

You see, then, as in the case of monetary policy, that Keynesians advocate that fiscal policy be used in an active manner to raise output if it is below its full-employment level and to lower it if it is above its full-employment level, whereas monetarists recommend that policy be set steady, independently of fluctuations in the level of output and the other macroeconomic variables.

B. Anticipated and Unanticipated Fiscal Policy

The distinction between anticipated and unanticipated fiscal policy is directly analogous to the distinction between anticipated and unanticipated changes in the money supply. The level of government expenditure, g_t, in any year t is equal to the value in the previous year g_{t-1}, plus the change between the previous year and the current year Δg. That is,

$$g_t = g_{t-1} + \Delta g$$

The change in government expenditure Δg can be decomposed into the change that was anticipated Δg^a and the component that was unanticipated Δg^u. That is,

$$\Delta g = \Delta g^a + \Delta g^u$$

The same distinction applies to taxes as well.

C. The Effects of an Anticipated Change in Government Expenditure

The Effects on Output and the Price Level

The effects of an anticipated change in government expenditure will be analyzed by working out, first of all, its effects on output and the price level. After that, the implications of these effects for changes in the labor market variables (employment, unemployment, and the real and money wages) will be worked out. Figure 35.1 will be used to illustrate the analysis.

Suppose that the money supply is fixed at M_0 and the level of government expenditure is initially at g_0 and taxes at t_0. This means that the aggregate demand curve will be the solid curve labelled $AD(M_0, g_0, t_0)$. The rational expectation of the price level, given this aggregate demand level, will be P_0^e. This is the price level where the aggregate demand curve cuts the aggregate supply curve. The expectations-augmented aggregate supply curve EAS_0 cuts the aggregate supply curve at the same point. The economy will initially be at full-employment equilibrium, so that the actual price level is equal to the expected price level P_0^e, and the actual level of output is y^*.

Now suppose there is an anticipated rise in government expenditure. Further, suppose that there is a matching anticipated rise in taxes, so that there is a balanced budget multiplier shift in the aggregate demand curve. (If you are not sure about this, check back to Chapter 20.) If government spending was to rise without a rise in taxes, then it would be necessary to raise the rate of money supply growth, and this would generate inflation. (It would not be impossible to analyze this case, but the balanced budget fiscal policy is easier to analyze.)

Suppose that the balanced budget increases in government expenditure and taxes are such as to shift the aggregate demand curve to the broken line

Figure 35.1
The Effects of an Anticipated Change in Government Expenditure and Taxes on the Level of Output and Prices

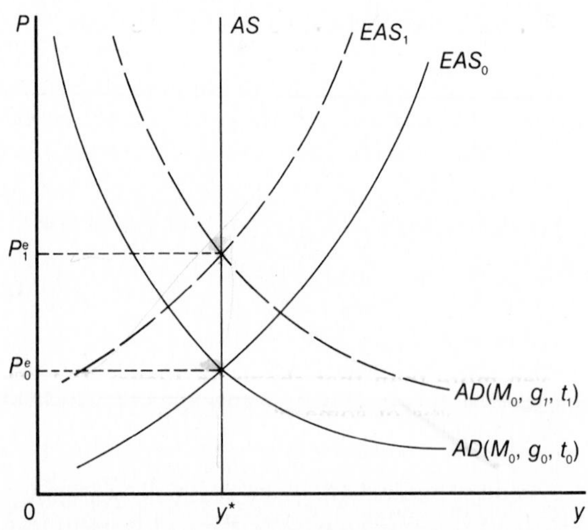

An anticipated rise in government spending and taxes with a constant money stock will raise the price level and leave output undisturbed.

labelled $AD(M_0, g_1, t_1)$. With the money supply being held constant at M_0, but with government expenditure and taxes raised to g_1 and t_1, respectively, the aggregate demand curve has shifted rightwards.

Also, recall that the rise in government expenditure to g_1 is assumed to be anticipated. This means that all economic agents will be aware that government expenditure has increased to g_1. Everyone will be aware, therefore, that the price level is going to rise because the new aggregate demand curve is to the right of the original one. The new rational expectation of the price level will be calculated as P_1^e. This is the price level where the new aggregate demand curve cuts the aggregate supply curve. A new expectations-augmented aggregate supply curve (the broken line labelled EAS_1) will be located so that it goes through the point where the new aggregate demand curve cuts the aggregate supply curve.

You can now read off directly the effects of an anticipated rise in government expenditure on output and the price level. If the level of government expenditure and taxes *actually* rises to g_1 and t_1, so that the actual aggregate supply curve becomes the same broken curve $AD(M_0, g_1, t_1)$, then the level of prices will be equal to the rational expectation of the price level, namely, P_1^e, and output will remain at its full-employment level y^*.

You can see then that an anticipated rise in government expenditure (matched by an anticipated rise in taxes) will raise the price level and leave the level of output unchanged.

The Effects on the Labor Market

It is a trivial matter to work out the effects of an anticipated rise in government spending (matched by a tax rise) on the labor market variables. Since output has not changed, neither will employment, unemployment, nor the real wage have changed. Since the price level has gone up, so must the money wage rate have risen. The money wage rate will rise by the same percentage amount as the rise in the price level, thereby leaving the real wage unchanged. This is all there is to the effects of an anticipated rise in government expenditure.

There is, however, a very important caveat. You should be aware that the analysis that has just been performed is based on the assumption that the extra taxes raised in the experiment are nondistorting. That is, that they are of a form that does not affect the supply of, or demand for, labor. If there were changes in such taxes as income or payroll taxes, there would be further important effects on employment and on the real wage to take into account. These in turn would lead to a different response of output to that worked out above. In fact, if higher taxes shifted the labor supply curve to the left, the levels of output and employment would *fall*, and the price level would rise by even more than that shown in Figure 35.1. This is the essence of the supply-side analysis of some of the economists and other supporters of the Reagan economic program. They argue that by *cutting* taxes and government spending, in a predictable, i.e., anticipated way, the supply of labor will rise, output and employment will rise, and the inflation rate (the price level in the analysis here) will fall. You will be taken through an analysis of this view in Part VII of this book.

The Effects on Interest Rates

You can work out the effects of an anticipated rise in government spending and taxes on interest rates by using the analysis developed in Chapters 18 and 21. From that analysis you know that a balanced budget rise in government spending (rise in spending matched by tax rise) will shift the *IS* curve to the right by the amount of the spending rise. This means that, at full employment, the rate of interest increases. You will recall that this occurs as part of the equilibrating mechanism whereby room is made for the extra government spending as a result of private investment decisions being cut back. This is sometimes stated as the phenomenon of a rise in government spending "crowding out" private spending.

Random Shocks and Policy Responses

If there were any random shocks to aggregate demand or to aggregate supply such as those discussed in Chapters 33 and 34, it would not be possible to offset these shocks with an anticipated change in government expenditure. Any anticipated fiscal policy action would be allowed for by private economic agents in forming their own rational expectations and would leave the level of output undisturbed. Therefore, anticipated fiscal policy changes cannot be used to stabilize the level of output, employment, and unemployment in the face of random shocks. They only have price level effects.

Let us now go on to analyze the effects of an unanticipated change in government expenditure.

D. The Effects of Unanticipated Change in Government Expenditure

The Effects on Output and the Price Level

To analyze the effects of an unanticipated change in government expenditure, let us again begin by working out the effects on the level of output and the price level. Figure 35.2 will illustrate the analysis. The economy initially has a money supply M_0 and government spending level g_0 and taxes t_0, so that the aggregate demand curve is the continuous line $AD(M_0, g_0, t_0)$. The aggregate supply curve is *AS*, and equilibrium is at the full-employment output level y^* and the actual and rationally expected price level of P_0^e. Also, suppose that all economic agents anticipate that government expenditure, taxes, and the money supply will be maintained at their initial levels of g_0, t_0, and M_0, respectively. Suppose, however, that instead of doing the expected, the government unexpectedly increases its expenditure and taxes by equal amounts to g_1 and t_1, respectively. With equal unexpected rises in government expenditure and taxes, the Fed will maintain the money supply constant at the initial level of M_0. The unanticipated rise in government expenditure and the equal unanticipated rise in taxes will shift the aggregate demand curve outwards to the curve $AD(M_0, g_1, t_1)$. Since this shift is unanticipated, the expectations-augmented aggregated supply curve remains the curve EAS_0. The new equilib-

Figure 35.2
The Effects of an Unanticipated Change in Government Expenditure and Taxes on the Level of Output and Prices

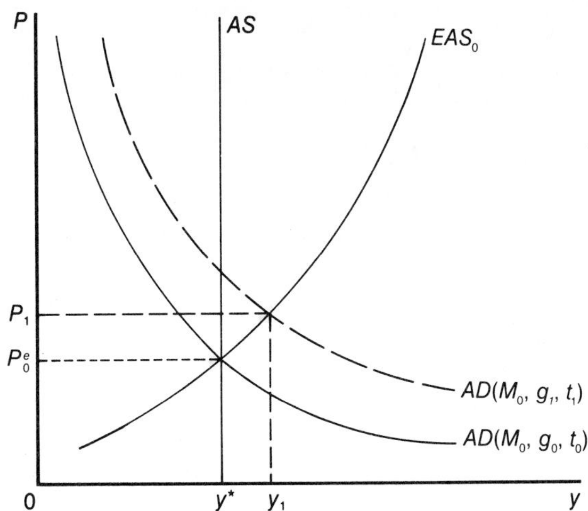

An unanticipated rise in government spending and taxes with a constant money supply will raise both output and prices.

rium is obtained at the point at which the new aggregate demand curve $AD(M_0, g_1, t_1)$ cuts the expectations-augmented aggregate supply curve EAS_0. You can read off this new solution as the price level P_1 and the output level y_1 in Figure 35.2.

You can now easily see the effects of an unanticipated rise in government expenditure (matched by an equal tax rise). An unanticipated rise in government expenditure (matched by an unanticipated tax rise to maintain a balanced budget) will raise the level of output and raise the price level.

We could easily reverse the above experiment and consider an unanticipated cut in government expenditure (matched by a tax cut to maintain a balanced budget), and, of course, this would lead to a fall in both output and the price level.

The Effects on the Labor Market

It is now possible to work out the effects of these unanticipated changes in government expenditure on the labor market variables. Let us consider for illustrative purposes an unanticipated *rise* in government expenditure. (You can work out the effects of an unanticipated *fall* for yourself.)

Since an unanticipated rise in government spending raises output, it follows immediately that it must also raise the level of employment. You can read this off by considering Figure 26.2 in Chapter 26. Further, since the level of employment rises, the level of unemployment falls below its natural level. In order to induce a rise in employment, firms must willingly hire the additional labor and still be maximizing profits. This implies that the real wage must fall. However, the real wage falls only if the money wage rises by less than the rise in the price level. This therefore is a further implication of the analysis concerning the effects of an unanticipated change in government spending.

real wage bit

To summarize the effects of an unanticipated rise in government spending on the labor market variables: An unanticipated rise in government expenditure (matched by an unanticipated tax rise) will raise the level of employment, lower the level of unemployment, lower the real wage, and lead to a rise in the money wage but by a smaller percentage amount than the rise in the price level.

Random Shocks and Policy Responses

You see, then, that an unanticipated change in government expenditure is capable of moving the level of aggregate output and employment around. It is possible to stimulate demand and raise output with an unanticipated rise in government spending and to cut back on output with an unanticipated cut in government spending.

It follows, therefore, that an unanticipated change in fiscal policy could be used to offset a random shock to either aggregate demand or aggregate supply. However, exactly the same considerations that were discussed in Chapters 33 and 34 concerning monetary policy apply here. If the government can change its expenditure (and taxes) quickly enough to offset shocks that private agents know have occurred, but which they are contractually unable to respond to, then it would be possible to use fiscal policy along the lines suggested by the Keynesians to reduce the amount of variability in economic activity. However, if government expenditure and tax changes can only be engineered slowly and no more quickly than private contracts can be renegotiated, then there is no scope for government expenditure and tax variations to do anything other than lead to price level variability. Because of the legislative and bureaucratic lags in the enactment and implementation of fiscal policy changes, many Keynesians are now coming to the view that fiscal policy is not a useful stabilization weapon and are placing more emphasis on active variations in the money supply as the appropriate way of stabilizing the economy.

There is a further reason for concern over the use of fiscal policy as a stabilizing device. This concerns its inflationary consequences. Throughout the exercises conducted in this chapter, it has been supposed that the inflation rate was being held at zero, with the money supply growth rate held at the output growth rate (in the case of this model, both zero). If, starting from an initial situation of zero inflation, there was to be a permanent rise in government expenditure, with a permanent commitment not to change taxes, then we know that the money supply would eventually have to start growing at a faster rate. This means that the aggregate demand curve would begin to shift upwards continuously. Also, the expectations-augmented aggregate supply curve would shift upwards continuously as rational agents would continuously revise their price level expectations upwards. Provided the money supply growth was anticipated, these two curves would move up at the same pace as each other, with inflation ensuing. With an anticipated inflation, the economy would stay at full employment. It is unlikely, however, that the money supply growth rate would be precisely anticipated. The money supply growth rate could be either above or below its anticipated level. This being the case, there could either be an output boom or an output slump (stagflation) as the inflation rate increased. Either of these effects is possible, depending on whether the money supply growth accompanying a fiscal policy change is under- or overanticipated.

Summary

A. Keynesian and Monetarist Fiscal Policy Advice

Keynesians recommend the active use of variations in government spending and taxes to raise demand when output is below its full-employment level and to lower demand when output is above its full-employment level.

Monetarists urge the maintaining of a steady fiscal policy that is dictated by resource-allocation considerations between the public and private sector, and not by economic-stabilization considerations. They advocate a level of government spending consistent with an optimal division of resources between the government and private sector, and a level of taxes such that the money supply growth target that they advocate may be achieved.

B. Anticipated and Unanticipated Fiscal Policy

Just as in the case of monetary policy, a change in government expenditure or taxes may be decomposed into the part that was anticipated and the part that was unanticipated. The unanticipated change in government spending and taxes is simply the actual change minus the change that was anticipated. When there is no unanticipated change, fiscal policy is anticipated.

C. The Effects of Anticipated Change in Government Expenditure

An anticipated rise in government expenditure matched by an equal anticipated tax rise will raise the price level and raise the money wage by the same percentage amount. It will leave the level of output, employment, unemployment, and the real wage unchanged. These predictions assume *neutral* tax changes.

D. The Effects of Unanticipated Change in Government Expenditure

An unanticipated rise in government expenditure matched by an equal unanticipated tax rise will raise the level of output and the price level. It will also raise the level of employment and the money wage. However, the money wage will not rise by as much as the price level, and the real wage will fall. There will also be a fall in the unemployment rate.

Exactly the same considerations apply to evaluating the appropriateness of alternative fiscal policies as were discussed in Chapters 33 and 34 concerning monetary policies. That material should be studied carefully and its relevance to the fiscal policy debate understood.

Review Questions

1. Outline the key disagreements between Keynesians and monetarists regarding fiscal policy.

2. What criterion does the monetarist use for determining whether or not additional government spending is recommended? What criterion does the typical Keynesian policy advisor use?

3. Why is it that some monetarists feel there should be a constitutional limitation on the fraction of GNP that may be spent by the government?

4. What are the implications, in terms of the government's budget deficit, of following a monetarist rule of setting the rate of growth of the money supply equal to the rate of growth of output?

5. Suppose there is a random shock to aggregate demand. Work out, using the appropriate diagrams:

(a) The consequences for real income, the price level, and the levels of employment, unemployment, and real wages of a monetarist fiscal policy.

(b) The consequences for real income, the price level, and the levels of employment, unemployment, and real wages of Keynesian fiscal policy.

(c) The consequences for real income, the price level, and the levels of employment, unemployment, and real wages of a Keynesian policy with a one-period lag in changing government spending and/or taxes.

6. Suppose there is an anticipated rise in government expenditure not matched by a tax rise. Suppose further that initially the inflation rate is zero. Trace out the future time path of the inflation rate following this policy change.

7. Suppose there is a rise in government expenditure, not matched by a tax rise, that at first is unanticipated, but then is maintained and subsequently becomes anticipated. Trace out the time path that will be followed by the rate of inflation, output, and unemployment.

36

Wage and Price Controls

The emergence of rapid inflation combined with politically unacceptable unemployment rates has led, in the postwar years, to a search for new anti-inflation policies.

You already know from your understanding of the new theories of output and the price level that it is possible to reduce the rate of inflation by reducing the growth rate of the money supply. You also know that provided the reduction in the growth rate of the money supply is anticipated, inflation will fall without causing a recession—without causing a drop in output and a rise in unemployment. However, it is practically impossible for the Fed to engineer a cut in the money supply growth rate that is anticipated. Simply to announce a cut is not sufficient. People have to see before they believe. This means that while the Fed is convincing people of its intentions to lower the money supply growth rate, there will be a tendency for the actual money supply growth rate to be below the anticipated growth rate. In other words, the money supply will be below its anticipated level. As you know, the consequence of this is that the actual price level will be below the expected price level, and the actual level of output will be below the full-employment level.

It is to avoid this problem that new policies have been searched for. The major alternative "new" policy that has been widely advocated and used throughout the postwar years is that of wage and price controls—sometimes alternatively and more euphemistically called "prices and incomes policy."

The United Kingdom and other Western European countries were among the first to embark upon such policies after World War II. In the United Kingdom there have been eleven episodes of wage and price controls. The United States has had three such policies in the postwar years—the Kennedy "guideposts," the Nixon controls, and the Carter "price and pay standards."

Although viewed by their supporters as sophisticated "new" weapons, wage and price controls are perhaps better to be described as "blunt old instruments."

One of the earliest recorded episodes of wage and price controls was in A.D. 301, when the Roman emperor Diocletian, in his famous Edict, sought to control the prices on 900 commodities, 130 different classes of labor, and a large number of freight rates. Penalities for the violation of Diocletian's controls ran all the way to death. Controls have been used on and off ever since that time (and possibly in earlier times as well).

It is clear, then, that the controls are certainly an old and not a new idea. The view that they are a blunt instrument rather than a sophisticated weapon will take the rest of this chapter to develop. However, as a prelude to this and so as to leave you in no doubt about my own view of controls, let me summarize my view in the following way:

> The so-called "new" policies are the oldest and crudest, best likened to medieval medicine based on ignorance and misundertanding of the fundamental processes at work and more likely to kill the patient than to cure him.
>
> It was not until relatively recently in the long sweep of human history, in the seventeenth and eighteenth centuries, that the principles governing the determination of the general level of prices were made clear. The insights of Bodin and Hume and the refinements which have followed through the work and writings of Irving Fisher, Wicksell, Keynes and modern monetary theorists, such as Milton Friedman, are critical for understanding and influencing the monetary forces which determine the general level of prices [and] the rate of inflation.[1]

The new policies for controlling inflation, then, are monetary policies. There has been no essential technical advance in this field since the eighteenth century. There have been some refinements, but the fundamental ideas developed by Bodin and Hume remain the theoretical underpinnings of any successful anti-inflationary policy. The rest of this chapter is designed to help you understand and appreciate this.

You have five tasks. They are to:

(a) Know the main features of the content of a wage and price control program.
(b) Understand the distinction between a posted price and an actual price.
(c) Understand why wage and price controls do not affect the expected price level.
(d) Understand why wage and price controls do not affect the actual price level.
(e) Understand why wage and price controls can only make matters worse.

A. Content of a Wage and Price Control Program

A wage and price control program typically has three sets of features:

1. A set of rules about wages, prices, and, sometimes, profits.
2. A set of penalties for a violation of the rules.
3. A monitoring agency.

---

[1]From Michael Parkin, *The Illusion of Wage and Price Controls* (Vancouver: The Fraser Institute, 1976), pp. 101–2.

Rules

The rules concerning wages center on the specification of a maximum normally allowable rate of increase of wages. Thus, for example, the policy may specify that the maximum rate of increase in wages shall not normally exceed some given percentage amount over a given specified period. There are almost always exception clauses built into such rules. Often, these permit higher than "normal" increases in the cases of the lowest paid workers.

The price rule sometimes takes a similar form to the wage rule. That is, a maximum allowed rate of price increase over a particular period is specified. More often, however, the price rule is couched in terms of a restriction allowing prices to rise only by an amount sufficient to cover the increased costs that arise from labor cost increases allowable under the wage rule.

Profit rules are more complex, both to state and to administer, and often are absent. When explicit profit rules are used, they are typically couched in terms of some maximum percentage of a previous period's average profits. For example, it could be that profit margins are required to be held to not more than 95 percent of the margins obtained, on the average, in the five years preceding the controls.

Penalties

Penalties for violation of the rules vary enormously. In the case of Diocletian's controls, the penalties ran all the way to death. In modern times they typically involve fines and *roll-backs*—a requirement that the wage or price be rolled back to the level that it would have been had the rules been obeyed.

Monitoring Agency

Monitoring agencies also vary enormously. Sometimes a special monitoring agency is set up. This was done, for example, in the case of the Nixon controls in 1971. In other cases, existing government departments are used to provide the policing and monitoring, and the ordinary courts are used to carry out enforcement.

B. Posted Price and Actual Price

There are many dimensions to a transaction. These can be conveniently summarized under three headings: (1) a price dimension, (2) a quantity dimension, and (3) a quality dimension.

When you decide to buy something, you are buying a certain quantity of a commodity of a presumed quality for a certain price. This is true not only for commodities; it also applies to labor services. For example, you might hire a certain quality of plumber for a certain number of hours for a certain price (i.e., wage).

A wage and price control program seeks to control directly one dimension of a transaction, namely, the price. In principle, of course, what it is trying to control is the price at which a specific quantity and quality of product or labor service is traded. It is extremely difficult, however, to monitor quantity and quality. Some examples will perhaps help to make this clear.

Suppose that the price dimension of a transaction is policed completely effectively. A good example of this would be the policing of the price of a university professor working for a U.S. university. Suppose the wage of the university professor is controlled by a wage control program and is effectively controlled to be below the market equilibrium wage. What will the professor do in this situation? It is clear that he will seek to maximize his utility by changing either the quality or the quantity of the labor that he supplies. If the wage rate being offered is below the market equilibrium wage rate, then he will lower the quantity and/or quality of work below the market equilibrium quantity/quality. Specifically, he will either take more leisure or indulge in more nonteaching, nonresearch, income-earning activities. The effective price of a unit of professorial services will not have been controlled. The posted price will have been controlled fully, but the actual price—the price for a specific quality and quantity—will have remained at exactly the same level as it would have been in the absence of the controls.

As another example, suppose that to perform some industrial job a certain grade of electrician is required (call it a grade-three electrician). Suppose that although a grade-three electrician is required to do this particular job, the wages of grade-three electricians have been controlled below the equilibrium wage, and a particular firm cannot hire enough of this type of labor. Clearly, what the firm will do is to hire the next, more-expensive grade of electrician (call it grade two), and, if necessary, the firm will upgrade people to that grade in order to get the job done and maximize profits. Again, the posted price—the price of a grade-three electrician—will have been effectively controlled. However, the actual price paid to a particular individual supplier of effort will not have been controlled. People who otherwise would have been grade-three electricians have now become grade-two electricians, and their wages rise in exactly the same way as they would have done in the absence of controls.

Consider a commodity market. The sticker price of a car is a posted price. However, as you know, the actual price at which a car gets traded is typically different from the sticker price, because it includes a discount. Precisely what discount is offered is very hard to monitor and police. It is true that a discount is a reduction of the actual price below the posted price. However, if the posted price was controlled below its equilibrium level, then by reducing the size of the discount, the actual price could increase to achieve and maintain market equilibrium. Thus, when posted prices are controlled, the gap between posted prices and actual prices—if actual prices are at a discount—will narrow.

The distinction between posted and actual prices should now be clear from the above examples. The posted price is the visible price but not necessarily the price at which trades actually take place. It is, of course, the actual price and the average of all actual prices that constitute the general price level and not the fictitious numbers that are stuck on car windshields or attached to jobs of specific grades.

Let us now move on to examine the effects of wage and price controls on actual prices. As a prelude to this, however, it is necessary to analyze the effects of controls on *expected* prices.

C. Wage and Price Controls and the Expected Price Level

The most sophisticated advocates of wage and price controls base their belief in the potency of these measures on a view that controls can effectively lower inflationary expectations and, as a result, lower the actual rate of inflation without generating a recession. You already know that if inflationary expectations indeed can be lowered, then it is possible to lower the inflation rate and even have an output boom while the inflation rate is falling. (Go back to Chapter 26 and study the analysis shown in Figure 26.4. If the expectations-augmented aggregate supply curve can be lowered while the aggregate demand curve is held constant, then you see that the equilibrium price level falls and equilibrium output rises.)

Let us begin our analysis of the effects of wage and price controls, then, by working out what their effects on the expected price level are. *Do wage and price controls lower the expected price level and lower the expectations-augmented aggregate supply curve?*

To analyze this, consider Figure 36.1. The curve $AD(M_0, g_0, t_0)$ is the aggregate demand curve. To focus our attention exclusively on controls, let us hold the level of the money supply, government expenditure, and taxes constant at the levels M_0, g_0, and t_0 and, furthermore, let us suppose that they are anticipated. You will recall that this implies that the actual position of the aggregate demand curve and its expected position are one and the same. This assumption enables us to isolate the effects of the controls.

The curve AS is the aggregate supply curve generated from equilibrium in the labor market. The expectd price level P_0^e is determined by the intersection of the aggregate demand curve and the aggregate supply curve. Through this

Figure 36.1
Why Controls Do Not Lower the Expected Price Level

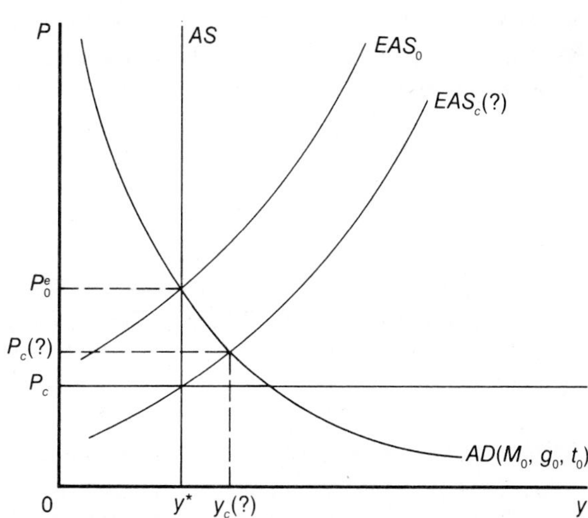

If the full-employment equilibrium is y^*, P_0^e, and a price control program seeks to maintain the price level at no higher than P_c, the expected price level will remain at P_0^e. To see this, notice that if the expected price level was equal to the controlled price level the EAS curve would be $EAS_c(?)$. This would generate a price level of $P_c(?)$. The only expected price level that is rational (that predicts itself) is P_0^e. Thus controls do not lower the expected price level.

same point at which the aggregate demand curve cuts the AS curve passes the expectations-augmented aggregate supply curve EAS_0. This is the aggregate supply curve drawn for an expected price level of P_0^e, which, in turn, is the rational expectation given a money supply of M_0 and a government spending level of g_0. Let us suppose that the economy is in equilibrium, with the actual price level at P_0^e and the output level at full-employment y^*.

Now suppose the government introduces price and wage controls. Mark on the vertical axis of Figure 36.1 the price level P_c that the government is seeking to achieve with its controls. It is the price level that would emerge if the rules that specify the allowable behavior of wages and prices in the economy were effectively enforced. Thus the horizontal line at P_c represents the ceiling that the government would like to enforce on the price level.

It is important to recognize that there is a major difference between the government attempting to impose a price ceiling on the general price level and the imposition of a price ceiling on some specific commodity such as, say, apartment rents or house rents. It is imaginable that sufficient resources could be devoted to monitoring and enforcing rent control regulations. This, however, is a far cry from being able to control the general price level. There are literally trillions of individual prices that make up a modern economy. To monitor, police, and effectively control the actual prices—the *actual* as opposed to the *posted* prices—on all the trillions of different kinds of commodities and factor services would require more resources than the entire gross national product.

Private individuals, maximizing their utilities and profits, will do the best that they can for themselves, subject to the constraints that they face. If, by adjusting the quality dimension of transactions, they can evade without detection the effects of a control on posted prices, then they will find it profitable to do so and, indeed, will do so. There is no presumption, therefore, that the actual price level in the economy will be equal to the price level that would emerge if all the rules that specified the allowable behavior of wages and prices were followed. Such rules will not be followed, and the price level will be different from the level implied by the exact adherence to those rules.

With this in mind, we now want to return to the question, What will be the effects of controls on the expected price level? Specifically, will the target price level P_c become the expected price level? Let us conduct a conceptual experiment exactly like the one we conducted in Chapter 27 when discussing the determination of the rational expectation of the price level.

Let us first suppose that the expected price level is indeed the controlled price level P_c. Would this be a rational expectation? If P_c was the expected price level, then the expectations-augmented aggregate supply curve would become the curve EAS_c(?). I have put a (?) after this expectations-augmented aggregate supply curve to remind you that we are conducting a conceptual experiment and are asking the question, Could this be the relevant expectations-augmented aggregate supply curve once the controls are imposed? You can see immediately that if the expectations-augmented aggregate supply curve is EAS_c(?), and if the aggregate demand curve remains unchanged (which by assumption it does), then the price level and output level will be determined at y_c(?) and P_c(?). Again, I have put a (?) after these quantities to remind you that they are conceptual experimental values that we are considering and not necessarily actual values that the economy will achieve.

Now, recall the concept of a rational expectation. It is the prediction implied by the relevant theory, conditional on all the information available at the time the prediction is made. If the prediction of the theory is that the price level will be $P_c(?)$, it is clear that we cannot have P_c as the rational expectation of the price level. Further, therefore, $EAS_c(?)$ cannot be the relevant expectations-augmented aggregate supply curve. If you follow through the analysis in Section D of Chapter 27 on the determination of the rational expectation of the price level, and apply that analysis to this case, you will see that there is only one price level that will be rationally expected. That price level is P_0^e. In other words, only the expected price level P_0^e leads to the prediction that the actual price level will be equal to the expected price level; and hence, only the price level P_0^e is the rational expectation. It follows, therefore, that the expectations-augmented aggregate supply curve will not move as a consequence of introducing controls and will remain at EAS_0.

Another way of thinking about the above analysis is as follows: Rational economic agents will expect the price level to be determined by the forces that in fact determine the price level, namely, aggregate supply and aggregate demand. Wage and price controls (as a first approximation, to be modified in the final section) will not be expected to have much effect on aggregate supply. Further (again as a first approximation, to be modified in the final section), controls will not affect the money supply or the level of government expenditure and taxes, so aggregate demand will be unaffected. Holding all these things constant, nothing that the controls have introduced would lead any rational person to expect that the actual price level would change as a result of the imposition of the controls. Hence, the rational person will expect the price level to be exactly the same with controls in place as without them.

The above remarks are to be interpreted as applying only if there is indeed no expectation that aggregate supply AS, the money supply, government spending, or taxes are going to be changed *as a consequence* of the introduction of controls. The possible effects of controls on these variables will be analyzed in the final section of this chapter.

D. Wage and Price Controls and the Actual Price Level

You have now seen that the theory of output and the price level predicts that the introduction of wage and price controls will have no effect on the expected price level and no effect on the position of the expectations-augmented aggregate supply curve. It is now a simple matter to analyze the effects of controls on the *actual* price level.

Figure 36.2 illustrates the analysis. The curves AS, $AD(M_0, g_0, t_0)$, and EAS_0 are the relevant aggregate supply, aggregate demand, and expectations-augmented aggregate supply curve, respectively, in the immediate precontrol situation. The economy is at full-employment output y^*, with the actual and expected price level at P_0^e. Now suppose that wage and price controls are imposed, which would imply, if they were fully observed, a price level of P_c, as shown on the vertical axis of Figure 36.2. What happens to the actual price level in this situation?

Figure 36.2
Why Controls Do Not Lower the Price Level (or the Inflation Rate)

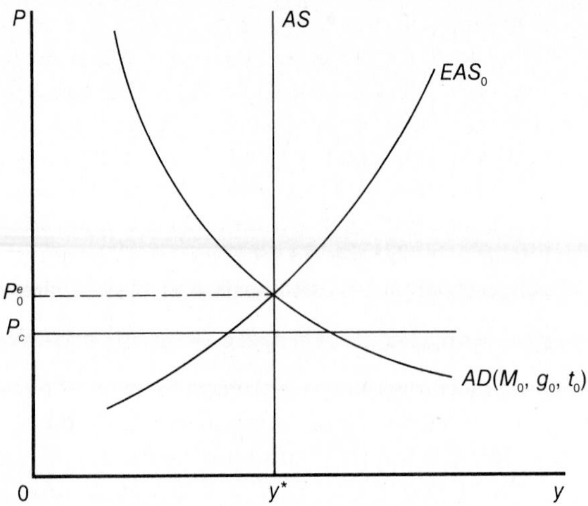

The imposition of controls does not affect either the *EAS* curve or the *AD* curve. The equilibrium price level is determined at the intersection of those curves and therefore will be independent of the control price level.

Recall that the actual price level is determined at the point of intersection between the expectations-augmented aggregate supply curve and the aggregate demand curve. By the analysis of the preceding section, the controls will not move the expected price level and will not, therefore, move the expectations-augmented aggregate supply curve. The expectations-augmented aggregate supply curve remains at EAS_0.

Wage and price controls are not monetary policy and are not fiscal policy. As a first approximation, there will be no change in the money supply and no change in government expenditure and taxes when the controls are imposed (we will modify this in the next section). Therefore, nothing happens to the aggregate demand curve when we impose controls.

Since nothing happens to the expectations-augmented aggregate supply curve, nor to the aggregate demand curve, it is clear that the point at which these curves intersect remains unchanged. The price level remains at P_0^e, and the output level remains at y^*. Thus, as a first approximation, controls have no effect on the actual price level. They may well control posted prices, and an index of posted prices may not rise by as much as actual prices. Indeed, an index of posted prices may well approximate to P_c for a period. However, the actual price level in the economy will be unaffected, and if the price index is constructed from accurate price sampling, the recorded overall price index will show a price level of P_0^e rather than the controlled price level of P_c.

It is often suggested that the use of wage and price controls in conjunction with appropriate monetary and fiscal (aggregate demand) policies can lower inflation at a more acceptable price than by pursuing demand policies on their own. The analysis that you have just been through explains to you why that line of reasoning is incorrect. You know from your analysis of the effects of monetary and fiscal policy in the three preceding chapters that a reduction in aggregate demand will have both output and price level effects. The closer the demand change comes to being anticipated, the more will those effects be on the price level and the less on real output. An ideal anti-inflation policy, therefore, would be one that lowered the rate of growth of aggregate demand and in an anticipated way.

You have further seen in the analysis in this chapter that introducing wage and price controls does nothing *over and above* what is being achieved by aggregate demand policy to influence the expected price level. It follows that what is required in order to make anti-inflation policies more successful and less painful is not wage and price controls but greater credibility concerning the ongoing pursuit of anti-inflationary aggregate demand policies. There are, unfortunately, good reasons for supposing that wage and price controls will actually work against the achievement of such credibility because they introduce additional problems of their own. Let us now examine these problems.

E. Wage and Price Controls Make Matters Worse

The conclusion of the preceding section is that wage and price controls have no effects. However, there are many reasons for supposing that they will have some effect on the economy. It is best to regard the conclusion of the previous section as a first approximation rather than as the whole story. Let us now examine some of the possible effects.

First of all, controls divert real resources from other productive activities. The army of bureaucrats, accountants, lawyers (and even economists!) hired directly and indirectly by the wage-price monitoring agency could be employed in other productive activities. To the extent that there is a diversion of labor resources from producing goods and services (from producing y), there will be a shift in the aggregate supply available for private and government consumption. You can think of this as a shift in the aggregate supply curve (as illustrated in Figure 36.3) from AS_0 to AS_1. Of course, in asserting that the aggregate supply curve has shifted to the left, we are asserting that the value of the output of the army of bureaucrats, accountants, lawyers, and economists employed in administering the control program is zero.

Just as the price level may very well be incorrectly measured during a period of wage and price controls, so may the value of national income. The national income statisticians would certainly impute a value of output to those employed in administering the wage and price control program equal to the factor incomes paid to them. In suggesting that income would fall in the event of the diversion of real resources away from productive activities to administering the program, I am saying that the national income accounts are incorrectly calculated and that the wages of those employed in administering the program should be regarded as a transfer payment from productive people to those who are unproductive. In this respect, it is no different from other forms of government transfer payments. (Although the remarks made here arise in connection with a discussion of wage and price controls, you may reflect on their more general applicability!)

Second, a wage and price control program typically involves additional

Figure 36.3
Why Controls Can Only Make Things Worse

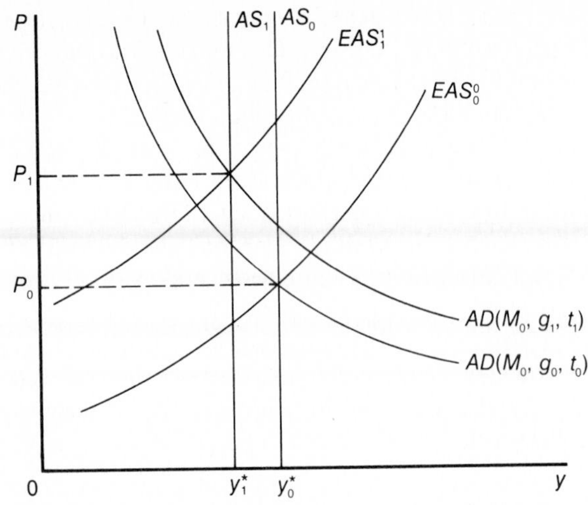

Controls divert resources from productive activity, thereby lowering aggregate supply. They also involve additional government expenditures and taxes to administer the control program. This raises the aggregate demand curve. The consequence is a higher price level and lower output. These effects are probably not large, but they are certainly in the wrong direction.

government expenditure, both on the bureaucratic side and on professional labor hired on a short-term contract basis. Such a rise in government expenditure and taxes needed to pay for this expenditure would lead to a shift in the aggregate demand curve, as illustrated in Figure 36.3, from $AD(M_0, g_0, t_0)$ to $AD(M_0, g_1, t_1)$.

It is clear that the combination of diverting resources from private activities, which lowers the output supplied, and raising government expenditure and taxes, which shifts the aggregate demand curve, exerts separate but reinforcing effects on the price level. The rightward shift of the aggregate demand curve and the leftward shift of the aggregate supply curve will both tend to make the price level higher than it otherwise would have been (and the inflation rate higher than it otherwise would have been). Also, output will be lower than it otherwise would have been.

It would be wrong to suggest that these effects are likely to be of a large magnitude. However, they are certainly going to be present in the *directions* indicated in Figure 36.3, and there have been episodes in history when such effects may have been large.

There is a third possible factor to be taken into account. This is the effect of wage and price controls on monetary policy. With a wage and price control program in place to control the inflation rate, it is possible that the Fed and the federal government will both become less concerned with maintaining anti-inflationary monetary policy. There also may be a temptation to use monetary policy in an attempt to stimulate aggregate demand, while using wage and price controls to keep inflation in check. If the money supply rises more quickly while the controls are in place, there will be a tendency for the

Figure 36.4
How an Effective Price Control Causes a Loss of Welfare

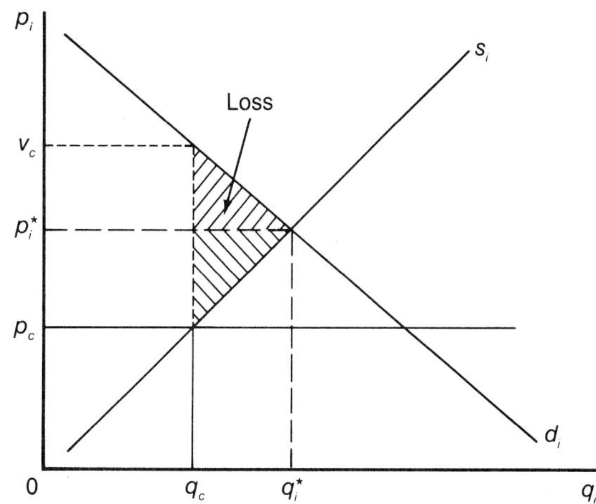

If a price control on some particular commodity or group of commodities is effective in holding the price below the equilibrium level, the value placed on the commodity at the margin by the consumer (v_c) exceeds the real cost of production (p_c). A loss of producer and consumer surplus (the shaded area) results.

inflation rate to rise even further than it would have done had there been no control program.

A fourth and major consideration concerning the effects of the controls arises from the fact that some prices are in fact controlled effectively, whereas others are not. The overall average effect of controls on the general price level of zero can be seen as hiding some effective control in some particular areas, with a tendency for demand to spill over into less controlled areas, where prices will rise to even higher levels than they would have in the absence of controls. If this happens (and there is good reason to suppose that it does because of the excessive attention paid by the wage and price monitoring board to specific sensitive sectors), then there will be some further serious economic losses inflicted.

Figure 36.4 illustrates the market for some particular good. It could be steel plate or any other highly visible commodity that the monitoring agency can effectively and fully control. The price on the vertical axis is the *relative* price of the good in question. This is equal to the money price of the good divided by the price level; that is, $p_i = P_i/P$. The horizontal axis in Figure 36.4 measures the quantity of the good. The curves d_i and s_i are the demand and supply curves (which you studied in your microeconomic theory course), and p_i^* and q_i^* are the competitive equilibrium price and quantity, respectively. Now suppose that an *effective* price control of p_c is imposed on this particular commodity. Assume that effective policing of quantity and quality ensures that p_c is the actual price and not just the posted price. It is clear that the quantity supplied will be reduced from q_i^* to q_c as the firms that produce this commodity seek to avoid the heavy losses that would be incurred if they maintained their output at q_i^*. The consumer places a value on the marginal quantity consumed of v_c. That is, the marginal utility of the last unit consumed exceeds the price by the distance $v_c - p_c$. The shaded triangle represents the total loss that results from the imposition of an effective price control of p_c. You can think of the shaded triangle as measuring the total difference between the value placed on consumption of this commodity and the marginal cost of producing it as we move from the competitive equilibrium position of q_i^* to the controlled position of q_c. There will, in general, be a large number of losses of this kind arising from the unevenness with which wage and price controls are imposed on the economy.

Overall, then, the effects of wage and price controls that we can detect are all in the direction of either raising prices or lowering output, or lowering economic welfare.

Summary

A. Content of a Wage and Price Control Program

A wage and price control program has three features:

1. Rules about wages, prices, and profits.
2. Sanctions and penalties.
3. A monitoring agency.

B. Posted Price and Actual Price

A posted price is the published or announced price; an actual price is the price at which a trade actually takes place for a given quantity and quality of product (or factor service).

C. Wage and Price Controls and the Expected Price Level

Since wage and price controls do not (as a first approximation) affect the level of the money supply or the level of government spending, they do not affect the level of aggregate demand. Also, as a first approximation, they do not affect aggregate supply. Since they do not therefore affect anything that determines the actual price level, it would be irrational to expect the actual price level to be affected by controls.

D. Wage and Price Controls and the Actual Price Level

The actual price level is determined at the intersection of the aggregate demand curve and expectations-augmented aggregate supply curve. Wage and price controls do not shift either of these curves and do not therefore affect the actual price level.

E. Wage and Price Controls Make Matters Worse

To the extent that wage and price controls divert resources from the private sector, they lower output and raise the price level. To the extent that they generate a bigger government spending level to finance the program, they raise the price level. To the extent that they encourage slack monetary policies, they raise the inflation rate. To the extent that wage and price controls are applied unevenly and made to stick in some sectors, they generate relative distortions and produce losses of economic welfare from a misallocation of resources.

Review Questions

1. What are the three features of a wage and price control program? Give an example of each of these features.
2. Distinguish between the actual price and the posted price level in terms of the three dimensions of a trade outlined in this chapter.
3. Explain why wage and price controls may be used to control posted prices but not actual prices.
4. List some products and the way in which each product's actual price can be adjusted in response to controls on its posted price.
5. Explain why wage and price controls cannot influence the rational expectation of the price level.
6. Work out, using the appropriate diagrams, the effects of expansionary monetary policy during a period of price controls.
7. Explain what is meant by the statement that "wage and price controls can only make matters worse."
8. In terms of ordinary demand and supply curves, illustrate the welfare loss associated with price controls.
9. Who benefits from wage and price controls? Why do you think they are so popular?

37

U.S. Macroeconomic Policy

You have now completed your examination of the *theory* of macroeconomic policy. The previous chapters in this part of the book have taken you through an analysis of what happens to aggregate output and the price level when alternative policy strategies are pursued. This chapter is going to examine the macroeconomic policies that have been pursued in the United States in the postwar years. There exist many useful surveys of this topic.[1] None of them, however, examines policy from the perspective suggested by the analysis that you have just completed. The viewpoint adopted by most available surveys of U.S. macroeconomic policy is that of the neoclassical model. Consequently, policy actions are described, and the likely effects of each policy change are calculated, using the types of policy multipliers that you studied in Part IV of this book.

As we have seen, although the neoclassical framework for understanding macroeconomic phenomena was remarkably successful for a period during the late 1950s and 1960s, it became, in other respects, a fairly spectacular failure during the 1970s.

The new theories of macroeconomics predict that the effects of policies will depend on whether variations in policy instruments are anticipated or not. This fact requires that we take a broader view of the policy process in order to evaluate policy and to understand the role that it has played in influencing the economy. Since the new theories of macroeconomics are indeed new, it is not possible to give a detailed, definitive, solidly researched account of how policy has in fact influenced the economy. Much more basic research will have to be done before that is possible.

What we can do, however, is to take a broader look at the monetary and fiscal policy processes that have been at work in the United States and form a picture as to what the major directions of policy have been. We may also attempt to reach some judgments as to whether or not the major changes in

---

[1]One such survey is Robert J. Gordon, "Post-War Macroeconomics: The Evolution of Events and Ideas," in Martin Feldstein, ed., *The American Economy in Transition*, National Bureau of Economic Research (Chicago and London: University of Chicago Press, 1980), pp. 101–62.

the thrust of policy were anticipated or not. On the basis of such an assessment, we may reach some tentative conclusions concerning the influence of policy on output, unemployment, and inflation.

Some specific questions are suggested by the analysis that has been conducted in the previous chapters. For example, Has U.S. macroeconomic policy been Keynesian or monetarist in nature? What have been the effects of monetary, fiscal, and wage price policies pursued by successive administrations? More specifically, have different administrations pursued policies that were importantly different in strategy? For example, do Democratic administrations tend to be Keynesian and Republican administrations monetarist or visa versa, or are they all more or less the same?

This chapter will address these questions, focusing on the period that begins with the election of President Truman at the end of 1948, then running through the successive administrations of Presidents Eisenhower, Kennedy, Johnson, Nixon, Ford, and Carter, and ending at the middle of the current term of President Reagan. This chapter will pursue four tasks, which are to:

(a) Review the content of monetary policy.
(b) Review the content of fiscal policy.
(c) Review the content of the wage and price control programs.
(d) Understand how each of the policies has contributed to the performance of inflation, unemployment, and output.
(e) Compare and evaluate the economic policies and performance of each administration from Truman to Reagan.

A. Monetary Policy

Background

There have been four distinct eras of monetary policy making in the United States since World War II. The first era, and the longest, ended on August 15, 1971. On that day, President Richard Nixon announced the suspension of the convertibility of the U.S. dollar into gold at a fixed price of $35 an ounce—he "closed the gold window." Up to that date, the United States had stood ready to buy or sell gold at $35 an ounce *on demand*. This meant that 35 U.S. dollars and one ounce of gold were equally valuable. The dollar, to use a well-known phrase, was "as good as gold." Over the years there were *some* restrictions on *who* could demand gold in exchange for dollars, and that right has not been extended to citizens of the United States at any time during the postwar period—U.S. citizens were even prohibited from holding gold bullion until the mid–1970s. By the time of the suspension of convertibility into gold in 1971, the right to demand gold in exchange for dollars only extended to other central banks. Nevertheless, the arrangement kept gold and the U.S. dollar in a fixed relation to each other and provided the centerpiece of a world monetary system based on fixed exchange rates.[2] That system, set up as a result of

[2]These matters are explained in the final part of this book, which deals with the United States in the world economy.

negotiations at Bretton Woods, New Hampshire, in 1944, prevailed throughout the 1950s and 1960s.

The second phase of monetary policy ran from the suspension of the convertibility into gold to 1975. This was a period in which U.S. monetary policy was operating in a vacuum. The commitment to convert dollars into gold at a fixed price had been abandoned, but nothing had been put in its place. There were no pre-announced constraints of any kind on monetary policy.

The third phase began in 1975 and ran to October 6, 1979. This was a period of monetary targeting with interest rate control. *Targeting* is a procedure of monetary control whereby the Fed declares its monetary policy objectives in terms of desired (or target) growth rates for particular monetary aggregates.[3] These targets are stated and published in advance. The basic idea is that if the targets are treated seriously by the Fed they may be used both as a guide to the Fed's likely future policy actions and as a basis for judging the Fed's performance. During the first period of targeting, the Fed sought to hit its targets using interest rate control.

The fourth phase began on October 6, 1979, and was a continuation of monetary targeting, but using open market operations to influence the size of the monetary base.[4]

Money Supply Growth

In our study of monetary policy, we have focused on the *money supply* as the central variable of importance. It seems natural, therefore, in describing monetary policy, to examine the course of that variable over the relevant years. Figure 37.1 does this and also shows the four different eras of monetary policy that have just been described. From 1949 up to the vertical line marked G, the United States was operating on a gold-exchange standard; the years from G to T represent the hiatus between the end of the gold-exchange system and the beginning of monetary targeting; the years from T to B are the period of monetary targeting with interest rate control; and beyond B is the period of monetary targeting with direct management of the monetary base. The money supply growth targets for M1, established from 1975 onwards, are also shown in the figure. Let us first, however, focus on the course of the actual money supply.

The patterns of monetary growth in the United States over this more than 30-year period are strikingly simple and clear. First, after a surge of rapid monetary expansion in the early 1950s, there was a clear tendency for the growth rate of the money supply to fall systematically to a low of close to zero in 1960. Since that date, the money supply growth rate has been on a distinctly rising trend, reaching an all-time high in 1978. Superimposed on these two distinct trends are some clear cycles. Measured from peak to peak, the cycles

---

[3]These procedures are described in Chapter 32.

[4]Targets were established for various aggregates. In the treatment here, however, only M1 is used. Some scholars prefer to use the broader M2. There are important issues involved in choosing amongst alternative definitions of money, but to pursue those matters here would take us too far away from our central purpose.

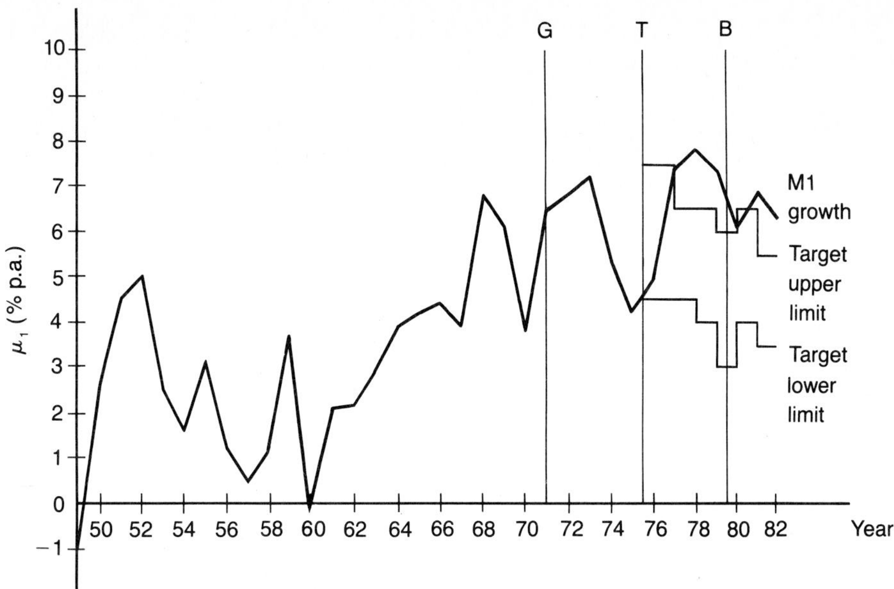

Figure 37.1
Money Supply Growth, 1949–1982

Money supply growth in the United States was on a falling trend to 1960 and a rising trend after that date. Distinct cycles are visible, with an average duration of four years, but ranging from two to seven years in length. The volatility of monetary growth does not appear to change with the changing regimes.

SOURCES: M1 growth: The money supply growth rate is $[\log(M_t) - \log(M_{t-1})]100$, where M_t is the annual average of monthly observations of M1. For the period 1949 to 1976 the data are from Robert J. Barro, "Unanticipated Money, Output and the Price Level in the United States," *Journal of Political Economy*, 86, August 1978, pp 549–80, and are the old definition of M1. For 1977–1982 the data are the new definition of M1 taken from the *Federal Reserve Bulletin* and incorporating revisions up to April 1983. The growth rate of M1 on the old and new definitions is virtually identical before 1976 and the old definition is used here so that Barro's findings may be presented later in this Chapter. For full details of the old and new definitions of the money supply and for a comparison of the behavior of the two definitions see, "The Redefined Monetary Aggregates," *Federal Reserve Bulletin*, 66(2), February 1980, 97–114. Target Limits: *Economic Report of the President*, 1981, p. 53, and *Federal Reserve Bulletin*, April 1982, pp. 233–34.

range from as short as two years (1966–1968) to as long as seven years (1959–1966). Measured from trough to trough, they range from three years (the three cycles beginning 1954, 1957, and 1967) to seven years (1960–1967). The average cycle length, whether measured from peak to peak or trough to trough, was just over four years.

It is of some interest to examine how the money supply growth rate has behaved in the four policy eras. During the gold-exchange standard period (up to 1971), monetary growth displayed substantial fluctuations and went through a period of falling growth (1952–1960) and one of accelerating growth (1960–1971). In the period of targeting since 1975, monetary growth has continued to fluctuate, with no noticeable change in amplitude compared with the late 1960s and early 1970s. Also, there is no indication that the acceleration in the growth rate that began in the 1960s and early 1970s was arrested by the targets. Indeed, the peak money supply growth rate in 1978 was above the peaks achieved in each of the two preceding cycles. Furthermore, M1 growth has systematically exceeded its targets.

It is not possible to see any clear modification in the overall trends of monetary growth following the introduction of base control in 1979, at least from the data presented in Figure 37.1. In the interim period between the abandonment of the gold-exchange arrangements and the introduction of monetary targeting, it is clear that monetary growth was exceedingly volatile but not noticeably more so than under the other regimes.

Summary

To summarize: The patterns of money supply growth in the United States over the past 30 or so years are: (1) a falling trend to 1960 and a rising trend since then, (2) a marked cycle with an average duration of about four years but with some cycles as short as two to three years and one as long as seven years, (3) extreme volatility with no apparent differences in the amplitude of fluctuations from one regime to the next.

Before attempting to establish how these patterns of money supply growth may have influenced the economy, let us go on to describe the other aspects of macroeconomic policy, turning next to fiscal policy.

B. Fiscal Policy

From the perspective of macroeconomics, the aspects of fiscal policy that are interesting are the total levels of government spending and taxes and the difference between the two—the surplus (or deficit).

Federal Spending and the Surplus

Figure 37.2 summarizes the main features of fiscal policy since 1949. It shows the level of federal government spending and the federal budget surplus, each expressed as a fraction of GNP (the dashed line). The level of federal receipts is not shown separately but can easily be worked out since the deficit represents the difference between spending and revenues. Just as there were some simple striking patterns in the monetary policy that we examined in the previous section, so there are some equally simple and striking patterns in fiscal policy apparent in Figure 37.2.

First, the level of federal spending expressed as a fraction of GNP has persistently increased during this period. At the same time, the surplus has also persistently decreased. That is, there is a clear upward trend to the spending graph and a downward trend to the surplus graph. Indeed, by the 1970s the surplus became negative—a deficit. Like monetary policy, these trends are disturbed by a very pronounced cycle. The cycle in spending, as well as in the surplus, whether measured from peak to peak or trough to trough, has an average duration of very close to five years.

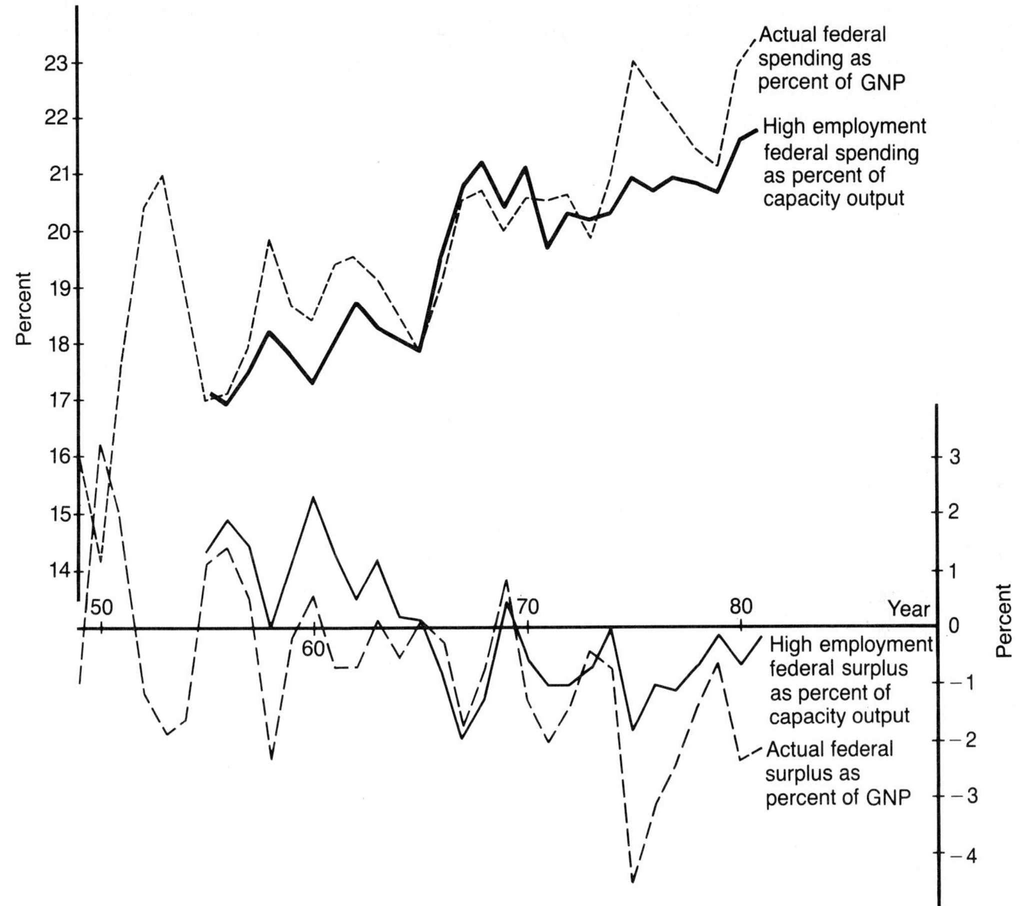

Figure 37.2
Fiscal Policy, 1949–1981

Federal spending has represented a rising fraction of GNP and has risen faster than taxes, so the surplus (as a fraction of GNP) has declined. The surplus became negative (a deficit) in the 1970s. The dominant influence in the 1950s was a fall in military spending after the Korean War. There are distinct cycles (averaging five years in length) in spending and the surplus. "High-employment" spending and surplus levels (continuous lines) are less volatile but have a similar trend to that of the "actual" levels (dashed lines).
SOURCE: Actual federal spending and actual federal surplus: See Table 37.4. High employment federal spending: *Survey of Current Business*, Table 3, April 1982, 62, no. 4, p. 26.

To some extent, the cycle in federal spending and the cycle in the federal surplus are induced by the cycle in the economy itself. As the economy goes into a recession, spending rises as a result of increased spending on welfare programs, and revenues fall as less taxes are paid on smaller income. Thus, there is a tendency for spending to rise and the surplus to fall as a fraction of GNP as the economy goes into recession. At the other extreme, as the economy goes into a boom, spending falls with welfare programs attracting less expenditure, and revenues rise as higher taxes are paid on higher incomes. Thus, the level of spending falls and the surplus rises as the economy goes into boom.

High Employment Spending and the Surplus

The fluctuations in federal spending and the surplus that are induced by the cycle in economic activity can be adjusted for by calculating what is called the *high-employment* levels of federal spending and the surplus and by expressing those high-employment levels, not as fractions of actual GNP but of the full-employment level of GNP—known as capacity GNP. The continuous lines in Figure 37.2 display the adjusted calculations.[5] What these serve to show is that the cycles in fiscal policy are less pronounced than the cycles in the actual levels of spending and the surplus. The difference between the continuous and dashed lines can be thought of as changes in spending and the surplus that are initiated not by policy changes but rather represent the automatic response to the economy itself. Thus, the continuous line provides a better indication of the effects of active policy decisions than the dashed line. What is strikingly apparent, however, is that the story told by both of these lines is remarkably similar. In both cases the trend increase in spending and the trend decrease in the surplus are equally apparent in the case of the high-employment figures as they are in the case of the actual figures. Also, the cycle is still present, although in less accentuated form.

There is one feature of the description of federal fiscal policy contained in Figure 37.2 that seems different when the high-employment data are used, and that concerns the strength of the upward trend in federal spending. This upward trend seems, on the high-employment figures, to have been particularly strong during the 1960s and is almost absent in the 1970s, with spending having been held at between 20.5 and 21.4 percent of GNP.

Wars and Fiscal Policy

It is apparent that some of the biggest swings in federal spending are associated with military activity. The strong burst of spending in the early 1950s and its subsequent decline were a direct consequence of the Korean War, and the (less pronounced) surge in the late 1960s was, in part, a consequence of the Vietnam War. These swings in spending are not, of course, designed with the needs of macroeconomic policy in mind. They do, however, have macroeconomic consequences.

It is noteworthy that the rise in military spending associated with the Korean War and its subsequent decline were so strong that they completely offset any trends in nonmilitary expenditures and gave aggregate federal spending a slightly downward trend during the 1950s as a whole.

[5]The "high-employment" figures run from 1956 only because that year was the beginning year of the latest available Department of Commerce revisions of these data.

Summary

The key characteristics of fiscal policy may be summarized as follows: Both spending and the surplus (measured in actual and high-employment terms) have shown clear trends—spending upwards and the surplus downwards—in the period since 1949. Each has been subject to a pronounced cycle with an average duration of close to five years. The dominant feature of fiscal policy in the 1950s was the decline in spending after the Korean War. This swamped any upward trend in nonmilitary spending. The upward trend in federal spending became strong in the 1960s, although it steadied in the 1970s when measured in high-employment terms. The trend in the surplus has been downward no matter on which of the two bases it is measured.

Let us now turn to an examination of the third aspect of policy—direct controls of wages and prices.

C. Wage and Price Controls

The only thoroughgoing wage and price controls employed in the United States in the postwar era were those initiated by President Nixon on August 15, 1971. During the Kennedy period, wage and price "guideposts," as they were called, had been established. These, however, were more in the nature of voluntary arrangements designed to be what Professor Robert Solow (of M.I.T.), a supporter of these policies, called "a step in the education process."[6] A similar program of "Price and Pay Standards" was implemented by the Carter administration. Neither of these programs, however, compared in thoroughness and severity with the Nixon program.

On August 15, 1971, Richard Nixon announced his Economic Stabilization Program (ESP).[7] Its main initial feature was a 90-day freeze on prices, rents, and wages. At the same time, a cabinet-level agency was created known as the Cost of Living Council (CLC), whose task was to administer the 90-day freeze and to provide advice on further stabilization policies. On October 7, 1971, the President announced phase II of the ESP to begin on November 15. The goal of phase II of the program was to reduce inflation to between 2 and 3 percent by the end of 1972. Two agencies, a Price Commission and a Pay Board, were established to administer this phase of the program. A pay standard of 5.5 percent was established, as were rules limiting price increases. The biggest companies were required to prenotify the Price Commission or Pay Board concerning price and wage increases, and medium-size firms had to report, but not prenotify, their price and wage changes. The Pay Board and Price Commission had powers to ensure that wage and price increases were within the guidelines established. Phase II ran until January 11, 1973, when

[6]Robert M. Solow, "The Case Against the Case Against the Guideposts," in George P. Shultz and Robert Z. Aliber, eds., *Guidelines, Informal Controls and the Market Place* (Chicago: University of Chicago Press, 1966), pp. 41–54.

[7]The ESP is most fully described in Chapter 2 of the "Annual Report of the Council of Economic Advisors," published in the *Economic Report of the President*, (Washington, D.C.: U.S. Government Printing Office, 1972, 1973, and 1974).

TABLE 37.1
Economic Stabilization Program, 1971–1974

PERIOD	PHASE	WAGES	PRICES	PROFITS	PRIOR NOTIFICATION
Aug. 1971	I	0	0	—	—
Nov. 1971	II	5.5	"In relation to costs"	Margins limited	Yes if sales > $100 million (for prices). Yes if employment > 5000 (for wages)
Jan. 1973	III	5.5	"In relation to costs"	Margins limited	No
Jun. 1973	IV(a)	5.5	0	—	No
Aug. 1973	IV(b)	5.5	"In relation to costs"	Dollar amount limit per unit	Same as Phase II for prices. No for wages.
Apr. 1974	—			Controls abandoned	

SOURCE: *Economic Report of the President*, 1974, p. 91.

phase III took over. In this phase there was a relaxation of prenotification, but most of the reporting requirements to the Pay Board and Price Commission were maintained. Phase IV began with a brief second price (but not wage) freeze in June 1973, which lasted just two months. Phase IV and the ESP ended in April 1974. Thus, from August 1971 to April 1974, the United States had mandatory wage and price controls. The targets and key features of that program are summarized in Table 37.1.

As Table 37.1 indicates, for three months from August to November 1971, wages and prices were frozen. There were no restrictions on profit margins and no prior notification requirements. An outright freeze makes such matters redundant. Profits would be whatever emerged from frozen wages and prices, and since no prices or wages could be changed, prior notification was unnecessary. The program proper started with phase II when wages were required to rise by no more than 5.5 percent. Profit margins (the percentage rate of profit per unit of output) were restricted, and prices were only allowed to rise in relation to costs. Prenotification of price changes was imposed on corporations with sales of more than $100 million for prices and with a labor force of more than 5000 for wages. Phase III was exactly like phase II except that prenotification was relaxed. Phase IV began with the freeze on prices but with no change in the rules for wages. Profit margin rules were abolished since having frozen prices and having a rule for wages implies that profits will have to be the residual. No prenotification was required in this case. Prenotification was reintroduced for prices but not for wages in the final part of phase IV, and the profit restriction was replaced as a dollar limit per unit of sales rather than a percentage limit per unit of sales.

Overall, this program was designed to hold wage increases to around 5.5 percent per annum, and price increases to a rate consistent with that wage target and with the presumption that productivity would grow at about 3 percent per annum, implying price increases of around 2.5 percent per annum.

This completes our brief description of policy in the three areas of monetary, fiscal, and wage and price controls, and we are now ready to go on to attempt to evaluate the effects of these policies.

D. Policy and Performance

You already know from your study of U.S. macroeconomic history (Chapter 2 and Chapter 6) how the U.S. economy has performed. You also know from the preceding sections of this chapter the key features of macroeconomic policy in the United States in the postwar years. The question that we now want to tackle is, How has policy affected the performance of the U.S. economy? As I remarked in the introduction to this chapter and as I shall now repeat for emphasis, in the present state of knowledge there can be no hard, definitive answer offered to a question of this type. What we are going to do in this section is to see how the new theories of macroeconomics would answer this question.

The central thing that the new theories tell us is that we need to distinguish between anticipated and unanticipated changes in aggregate demand. Anticipated changes in aggregate demand affect the price level, whereas unanticipated changes affect both the price level and real variables such as deviations of GNP from trend and unemployment. In thinking about how policies have been perceived—whether they have been anticipated or unanticipated—we have to examine the political process within which policy is made. As regards fiscal policy, we know that it is made by a legislative process that involves a good deal of prior debate and discussion before any policy change may be enacted. Both Houses of Congress must debate proposals before the President signs any new provisions into law. During that process, a great deal of lobbying and public airing of the pros and cons of a particular measure goes on. By the time Congress comes to vote on a measure, there is very rarely any doubt as to which way the vote will go. This line of reasoning suggests that most of the changes in fiscal policy in the United States will, by the time they occur, take few people by surprise. Thus, from the perspective of the new theories of macroeconomics, it seems reasonable to suppose that most fiscal policy changes are anticipated ones.

Monetary policy contrasts sharply with this. It is made by the Federal Reserve Board. Most of the policy discussion that leads to the detailed day-by-day monetary policy operations takes place in a committee of the Federal Reserve Board, known as the Federal Open Market Committee (FOMC). This committee publishes its minutes, but only *after* the event. Thus, in contrast to the making of fiscal policy, monetary policy is a much less public affair. It seems reasonable to suppose, therefore, that in contrast to fiscal policy, to some extent monetary policy is anticipated but to some extent it is not. Let us now examine how monetary policy may be decomposed into its anticipated and unanticipated components.

Anticipated and Unanticipated Monetary Supply Growth

The major study of this topic is one that has already been referred to in Chapter 28 and is that by Robert Barro.[8] Barro examined the growth rate of M1 in the United States from 1941 to 1976. In this examination he searched

---

[8]See Robert J. Barro and Mark Rush, "Unanticipated Money and Economic Activity." Chapter 2 in Stanley Fischer, ed., *Rational Expectations and Economic Policy*, (Chicago and London, 1980), University of Chicago Press and Robert J. Barro "Unan-

TABLE 37.2
Predicting M1 Growth

Annual Percentage Growth Rate of M1			
Equals	−2.3		
plus	0.4	of	M1 growth in previous year
plus	0.2	of	M1 growth two years ago
plus	0.07	of	percentage by which federal government expenditures are above their "trend"
plus	0.6	of	unemployment rate in previous year

Note: This is a linear approximation to Barro's equation that contains a nonlinearity in the unemployment rate. See text for an explanation on how to interpret this table.
SOURCE: Robert J. Barro, "Unanticipated Money, Output and the Price Level in the United States," *Journal of Political Economy*, 86, no. 4, August 1978, 549–80.

for patterns that might have been useful, had people known of them, for predicting what M1 growth would be in the coming year. In his search Barro did not find it necessary to distinguish between monetary policy regimes as political regimes. He found a stable pattern in the money supply growth process that was independent of these considerations. The main characteristics of patterns found (already briefly described in Chapter 28) are summarized in Table 37.2.

The way to read this table is as follows: First, if everything else was zero, the money supply would actually fall at an annual rate of 2.3 percent (line 1 of Table 37.2). Of course, everything else is not zero. Most particularly, money supply growth responds to unemployment (see line 5). On the average, a one percentage point rise in the unemployment rate in a given year will generate a rise in the money supply growth rate of about six-tenths of one percentage point in the following year.

Also, there is inertia in monetary policy. This is captured in lines 2 and 3. Line 2 says that a one percentage point rise in M1 growth in the previous year will, on the average, lead to a four-tenths of a percentage point rise in M1 growth in the current year. Line 3 says that a one percentage point rise in M1 growth two years previously will, on the average, lead to a two-tenths of a percentage point rise in M1 growth in the current year. In other words, monetary policy reacts to its own previous performance, with a gradual adjustment.

Finally, line 4, monetary policy, responds to federal government spending. By calculating a path for what Barro calls "normal" federal government expenditure (which is something like a trend, but not one that grows at a constant rate), Barro was able to calculate the percentage by which federal government expenditure deviated from its "normal" level. He discovered that 7 percent (.07) of a given percentage deviation of federal government spending from its "trend" will be financed by additional money creation.[9]

ticipated Money, Output and the Price Level in the United States," *Journal of Political Economy*, 86, no. 4 (August 1978), 549–80. The particular numbers used in this section have been taken from this source, including my calculations in Table 37.3.

[9] Ibid

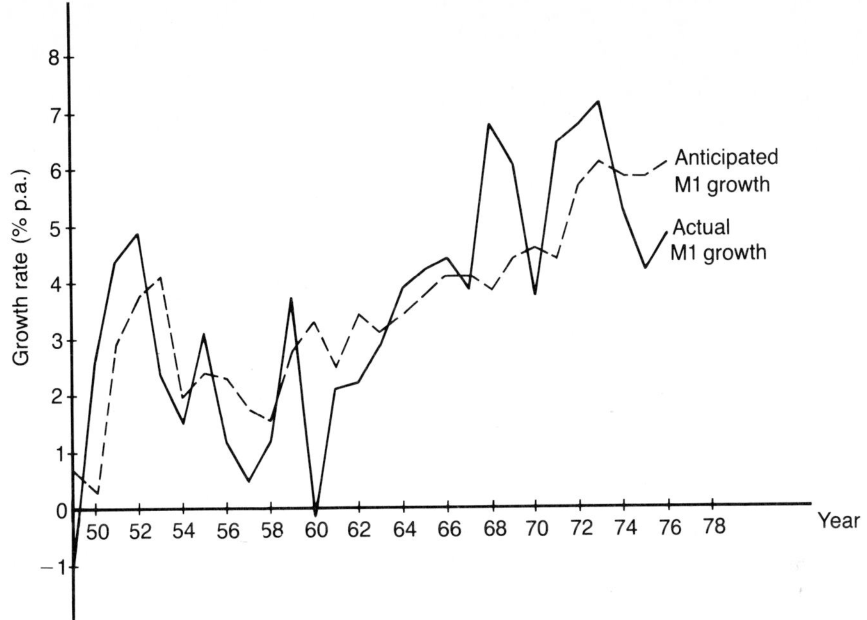

Figure 37.3
Actual and Anticipated M1 Growth, 1949–1976

Anticipated M1 growth—anticipated on the basis of the two previous years' M1 growth, the previous year's unemployment rate, and the current year's level of federal government spending relative to its "trend"—is shown as the dashed line. The broad trend of anticipated M1 growth is the same as the actual, but it fluctuates much less markedly. The major swings in actual money growth are missed by anticipated money growth and show up partly as unanticipated.
SOURCE: Robert J. Barro, "Unanticipated Money, Output and the Price Level," *Journal of Political Economy*, 86, August 1978, pp. 549–80, Table 1, p. 552.

Thus, these three factors—a response to unemployment, inertia, and a partial financing of federal government expenditures—are those that, on the average, generate movements in the money supply growth rate. If people had used an equation like that shown in Table 37.2 (implicitly rather than explicitly, of course) to form their expectations of money supply growth, they would have calculated for their one-year-ahead forecast the path shown as the dashed line in Figure 37.3. The money supply actually grew in accordance with the continuous line in Figure 37.3. Notice that the anticipated growth path does not fluctuate as much as the actual growth path. This is exactly in line with the hypothetical example that you examined in Table 29.1 and Figure 29.2 when discovering how the rational expectations theories account for procyclical co-movements in prices.

Look first at the trends in anticipated money growth shown in Figure 37.3. Notice that from 1953 down to 1958, the trend is downwards and then begins to rise. There are gentle cycles in anticipated M1 growth, but its main features are its gentle downward trend in the 1950s and persistent upward trend after 1958.

The trend movements in anticipated money growth were determined by two other trends with which you are already familiar. The first of these is the trend in unemployment that occurred through the decade of the 1960s. As unemployment trended upwards, the money supply growth accelerated in response. This presumably was the consequence of the Fed stimulating demand in an attempt to lower unemployment. The second trend that has influenced money growth is the trend in federal government expenditure. You have seen that trend in Figure 37.2 above. In the 1950s, the decline of military expenditure after the Korean War was the dominant influence on total federal spending and led to a fall in the growth rate of the money supply. In the 1960s, the strongly rising trend in federal spending added to the effects of the trend rise in unemployment to accelerate M1 growth. Of course, as is clear from Table 37.2, the weight of federal government expenditure (0.07) is not as big as that on unemployment (0.6) in influencing the growth rate of the money supply, although it does have some effect.

The deviations of actual money growth from anticipated money growth are not graphed separately in Figure 37.3. You may see them, nevertheless, as the vertical distances between the dashed and continuous lines in that figure. Thus, for example, money growth was substantially below its anticipated levels in 1956–1958, and again in 1960–1963. It was substantially above its anticipated levels in 1968–1969, and again in 1971–1973. After 1973, actual money growth has been substantially below its expected level.

How have these variations in anticipated and unanticipated money growth affected the U.S. economy? Let us now turn to an examination of that question.

Effects of Anticipated Money Growth

The main effects of anticipated money growth are, of course, on inflation. Indeed, theory predicts that in a steady state, the rate of inflation will equal the anticipated growth rate of the money supply (minus an adjustment for output growth). Changes in the anticipated growth rate of the money supply would lead to changes in the rate of inflation, changes that would overshoot the anticipated money supply growth rate as a consequence of the induced change in the demand for money that occurs when the inflation rate changes.

It is evident, by inspecting the broad trends of inflation (Chapter 2), that the movements in anticipated money growth line up remarkably well with movements in the inflation rate. The burst of inflation in the early 1950s resulted from the rise in the anticipated money supply growth rate at that time. The trend decline in inflation through the 1950s resulted from the trend decline in anticipated money growth that occurred from 1953 to 1958. Again, the trend rise in inflation through the 1960s and 1970s resulted from the trend rise in anticipated money growth that occurred in that period. There was a particularly strong rise in the anticipated money supply growth rate between 1971 and 1973, which may be assumed to have had the effect of raising the inflation rate by even more than the rise in the anticipated growth rate of the money supply—the overshooting phenomenon. This too, indeed, occurred almost precisely as is predicted by the theory. Thus, there is little difficulty in accounting for the broad patterns in inflation in the U.S. economy in the period since the end of World War II using this theory.

Steady-State Inflation

It is possible to discover, from the information contained in Table 37.2, the steady-state rate of inflation. You can think of that table as an equation that predicts the growth rate of the money supply. That equation can be solved for the rate of growth of the money supply that would occur if money growth was constant (if it was the same each year), if federal government expenditure was constant relative to its "normal" level, and if the unemployment rate was constant. Performing such a calculation and supposing federal government expenditure to be at its "normal" level (so that we can ignore it), we can discover the steady-state relationship between the rate of unemployment and the rate of growth of the money supply.

Solving the equation in Table 37.2 gives the long-term average relationship between money growth and unemployment set out in Table 37.3. Unemployment rates ranging between 4 and 6 percent are very close to what the United States experienced in the late 1950s and early 1960s. That was at a time when very little inflation was experienced. Thus, low inflation and low unemployment went together in the sense that the Fed's reaction to unemployment, itself low, did not trigger rapid inflationary money growth. If unemployment settled down in the range from 7 to 9 percent, money growth would settle down in the steady state at between 4 and 6 percent. This is the range in which unemployment seems to have been stuck in the United States in the late 1970s. At these higher unemployment rates, the Fed on the average creates more money and, as a consequence, ends up generating more inflation.

We may use the above description to account for the rising rate of inflation in the 1960s and 1970s. The story begins with the sources of the rise in unemployment. We identified, in Chapter 13, a possible source of the trend

TABLE 37.3
Steady-State Money Growth and Unemployment

STEADY-STATE GROWTH RATE OF MONEY M1 (Percent Per Annum)	UNEMPLOYMENT RATE (Percent)
0	4.0
1.5	5.0
2.8	6.0
4.0	7.0
5.1	8.0
6.0	9.0
6.8	10.0

Note: The calculations are based on Barro's equation that contains a nonlinear unemployment variable. The numbers set out in Table 37.2 give approximately the same relationship as shown here, but the approximation error rises sharply at unemployment rates in excess of 7 percent.
SOURCE: Barro, "Unanticipated Money, Output and the Price Level." (My calculations.)

rise in unemployment as a rise in job-search unemployment resulting from the spread of unemployment insurance benefits to a wider population of workers. There undoubtedly were, and are, other factors at work that we did not identify in Chapter 13. Nevertheless, the starting point is a trend rise in unemployment originating from "real" sources—a rise in the natural rate of unemployment.

The second step in the story concerns the Fed's reactions to the state of the economy. Other things being equal, the Fed will raise the growth rate of the money supply by 0.6 percent for every 1 percent of unemployment (see Table 37.2). Thus, with a rising trend unemployment rate, a rising trend rate of growth of the money supply has been induced. To some degree, this rising money supply growth has been anticipated and, therefore, has lead to a rise in the rate of inflation one-for-one with the rise in anticipated money growth. Further, on occasion, the predicted tendency for inflation to overshoot the anticipated growth rate of the money supply has been observed. One notable such occasion was in 1971–1973, when there was a substantial rise in the anticipated money supply growth rate.

Notice that this explanation for rising inflation makes the "exogenous" source of that inflation those factors that have raised the natural rate of unemployment. Everything else is endogenous. Let us now turn to examine the effects of unanticipated money growth.

Effects of Unanticipated Money Growth

It is very easy to discover that unanticipated money growth in any given year does *not* provide a good explanation for the deviations of real income from trend in that same year. We do know, however, both from the description of the business cycle given in Chapter 6 and from our investigation of the sources of inertia in Chapter 29, that any random shocks hitting the economy should not have *all* their effects in the year in which they occur. Rather, they are predicted to have effects that are spread out over time.

To see how those shocks spread out over time, consider what would happen if there was a 1 percent unanticipated rise in the money supply. According to Barro's numbers,[10] this would have the effect of raising output above trend by 1 percent in the year in which it occurred. In the following year, it would raise output above trend by even more than that, by about 1.2 percent. It would have a small effect stretching over to a third year (about 0.4 of 1 percent) and then an even smaller effect lasting to a fourth year (about 0.25 of 1 percent). Thereafter, the effects would be negligible.

This could be put differently by saying that the deviation of income from trend in any given year is equal to the unanticipated money growth for that year, plus 1.2 times the unanticipated money growth for the previous year, plus 0.4 of the unanticipated money growth from the year before that, and finally, plus 0.25 of unanticipated money growth from three years earlier.

If the unanticipated money growth calculated from Figure 37.3 is used with this formula to predict the deviations of real GNP from trend, the figures shown as the dashed line in Figure 37.4 are calculated. The actual deviations

[10]Ibid

Figure 37.4
Actual and Predicted Deviations of GNP from Trend

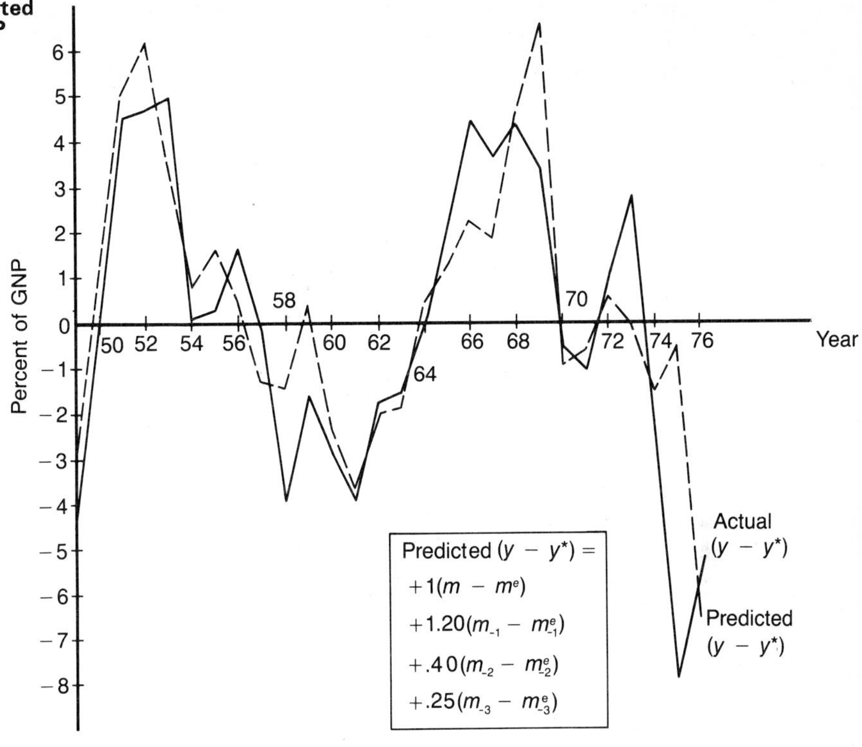

Actual deviations of GNP from trend are shown as the continuous line. The values that are predicted on the basis of the current and three previous years' anticipated money growth are shown as the dashed line. Evidently, most of the swings of GNP about trend can be accounted for by unanticipated money growth in this way. Between 1958 and 1961, however, real GNP was further below trend than predicted and between 1965 and 1968, it was further above trend than predicted.

SOURCE: Robert J. Barro, "Unanticipated Money, Output and the Price Level," *Journal of Political Economy*, 86, August 1978, pp. 549–80, Table 1, p. 552.

of real income from trend are shown as the continuous line in that figure. Evidently, unanticipated money growth from the current and three previous years, combined in this way, provides a remarkably close account of the path followed by deviations of real GNP from trend. There are some periods when there are sizable unexplained variations, but the broad pattern that occurred seems to be well explained by movements in unanticipated money growth in the current and previous three years, with the weights attaching to the current and previous year being the dominant ones.

What is Figure 37.4 telling us? First, it is clearly telling us that the hypothesis that states that unanticipated money growth generates fluctuations in real economic activity is one that is consistent with the facts. However, it is *not* telling us that this is the *only* hypothesis consistent with the facts. There may be others. Furthermore, and this is of considerable importance for the new macroeconomic theories, the facts summarized in Figure 37.4 in no way enable us to discriminate between the new classical and new Keynesian versions of the theory. Both theories predict that there will be inertia in the economy, leading to the spreading out over time of the effects of unanticipated changes in aggregate demand. We cannot, therefore, on the basis of the research that is being described here, make any firm inferences or draw any sharp conclusions concerning which of those two theories is more in accord with the facts.

The Effects of Fiscal Policy

So far in our unravelling of the role that policy has played in influencing the course of the economy, we have downplayed the effects of fiscal policy. We have not ignored these effects, however. Fiscal policy has been seen as one of the factors influencing the growth rate of the money supply, and to that extent, we have taken account of it. Further, the trend in fiscal policy has been one of the key factors leading to the trend rise in monetary growth in the 1970s, which, in turn, has been one of the key factors lying behind the trend rise in inflation. Thus, fiscal policy clearly has played a major role in generating what is still the major macroeconomic problem of the United States in the 1980s—inflation. The question arises, however, as to whether or not fluctuations in fiscal policy might have accounted for some of the fluctuations in real GNP about its trend.

There are two particular periods of three to four years identifiable in Figure 37.4 when variations in GNP around its trend were not well predicted by unanticipated money growth. One such period is 1958–1961, during which time real GNP deviated below trend by more than would have been predicted on the basis of monetary policy alone. The second is the period from 1965–1968 when the reverse occurred, and real GNP was above trend by more than would have been predicted on the basis of monetary policy alone. Are these periods when fiscal policy was doing anything unusual? The answer may be seen by going back to Figure 37.2. Evidently, the answer is yes. Between 1959 and 1960, the high-employment surplus increased to almost 2.5 percent of capacity GNP and stayed high through 1963. This increase in the surplus occurred partly as a result of a cut in high-employment spending, but also as a result in high-employment taxes. It seems inconceivable that this fiscal contraction was not in part responsible for the drop in GNP relative to trend in 1958–1959. In the second period, 1965–1968, you can see, again by inspecting Figure 37.2, that there is a massive rise in the high-employment level of federal spending. There was some accompanying rise in taxes because the deficit was not enlarged by the same amount as spending rose. Nevertheless, this was clearly a period of strong fiscal policy expansion. Again, it seems likely that this expansion was also associated with that strong rise in income above trend in those same years.

Of course, for this interpretation to be correct in the context of the new theories, it must be that to some degree, the contraction in fiscal policy in 1959 through 1962 and the expansion in 1965 through 1968 were unanticipated. Since fiscal policy is made by a slow, public, deliberative process, it is hard to sustain this conclusion. It is clear, however, that the particular changes that have been identified in these two episodes were unusually large, and it is not inconceivable, therefore, that their magnitude was to a degree unanticipated. The fiscal contraction of 1959–1962 and the fiscal expansion of 1965–1968 might even have been partly unanticipated by the legislators themselves, who did not realize the full quantitative consequences of the legislative changes being implemented.

Monetary and Fiscal Policy: Summary

We have now seen from our examination of monetary and fiscal policy that we can explain the broad trends in inflation in the United States in the postwar years and can also account for most of the cycles in real economic activity. The key input in determining the trends has been the expansion of various government programs, resulting in a strong rise in federal government expenditure, together with extensions of the coverage of unemployment insurance and other programs, as well as other unidentified factors, that have increased the natural rate of unemployment. Because the Fed's monetary policy reacts to federal government spending and unemployment, the trend rise in unemployment has led to a trend rise in the growth rate of the money supply beginning in the late 1950s. During the early 1950s, these trends in government spending, unemployment, and inflation were, for a brief period, moving in the reverse direction.

Superimposed on its trend, money growth has shown erratic and unpredictable fluctuations. The unanticipated component of money growth has been a dominant influence on deviations of real income from trend. Over and above that there were two occasions on which very large, and possibly not entirely anticipated, fiscal policy changes occurred that further added to the deviations of real GNP from trend—in 1959–1962 in a negative direction and in 1965–1968 in a positive direction.

Wage and Price Controls

Let us now turn our attention to the wage and price control program (the Economic Stabilization Program, ESP) of 1971–1974.[11] What were its effects? Is it possible that such a program could be a useful additional weapon in the economic policy armory?

The 1971–1974 controls have been studied extensively, and the consensus conclusion is that they had virtually no effect on wages, and at most held down price rises by 1.5 percent a year for the two years to mid-1973. I say "at most" because some scholars have argued that the *measured* effects are illusory and that, in fact, the controls had no effect on either wages or prices.

Let us begin our assessment of the ESP by recalling the performance of inflation during those three years. As you may verify by examining the data given in the Appendix to Chapter 2, inflation fell by one percentage point

---

[11]An excellent volume on the topic of this section is Karl Brunner and Allan H. Meltzer, eds., *The Economics of Wage and Price Controls*, Carnegie-Rochester Conference Series, vol. 2. (Amsterdam: North-Holland Publishing Co., 1976), For an easier but still very worthwhile treatment, see Michael Walker, ed., *The Illusion of Wage and Price Control* (Vancouver, B.C.: The Fraser Institute, 1976).

between 1971 and 1972, and then, in 1973, it rose by almost two percentage points. Thus, inflation fell slightly during the first year of the ESP and increased in its second year. In neither year did inflation come close to the target range of 2 to 2.5 percent. Indeed, by 1973 it was running in the neighborhood of 6 percent.

Of course, we cannot simply examine the performance of inflation during a period of controls and conclude on the basis of that examination that the controls were ineffective. To isolate the effects of the controls on inflation, we first of all must try to predict what the inflation rate would have been in the absence of controls. The actual rate of inflation may then be compared with the prediction, and the difference, if any, may be regarded as being the effect of the controls.

Several studies that followed such a procedure concluded that the controls did manage to lower the rate of inflation compared with what it otherwise would have been. Typical of these are the work of Robert J. Gordon of Northwestern University.[12] Gordon's method was to make predictions of U.S. inflation by looking at the relationship between inflation and unemployment from looking at the Phillips curve. His idea was that since variations in inflation are known to be systematically related to variations in the unemployment rate, the state of unemployment should be taken into account when figuring out whether or not the controls had any effect. If, for example, the inflation rate fell (as it did during the first year of the controls), but the unemployment rate rose, then it may be that what was happening was simply the normal response to unexpectedly tight monetary policies. To attempt to remove from the figures potential influences of this type, Gordon looked at the U.S. Phillips curve during the years before the controls and then asked whether the rate of inflation during the controls lay on, above, or below the Phillips curve. He found that the inflation rate was below the Phillips curve by an average of about 1.5 percent a year.

Several studies have proceeded in a different way and have concluded that these same controls had no significant effect on U.S. inflation. Typical of these is a study by Michael Darby (of U.C.L.A.).[13] Darby began by suggesting that there is good reason for suspecting that the conventionally measured price indexes are biased during a period of controls. He tells the story this way:

> Suppose that we are interested in measuring the rate of increase in the price of hot chocolate mixes from 1973 to 1974. Suppose that we knew the total number of boxes sold in 1973 and the dollar amount spent on chocolate mixes; by dividing total dollars spent by the total number of boxes sold, we could get the average price of a box of hot chocolate mix. Assuming that the information was available, we could perform the same calculation for 1974 and then calculate the percentage increase.

---

[12] "The Response of Wages and Prices to the First Two Years of Controls," *Brookings Papers on Economic Activity*, no. 3 (1973), 765–79.

[13] Michael R. Darby, "The U.S. Economic Stabilization Program of 1971–1974," in Michael Walker, ed., *The Illusion of Wage and Price Control* (Vancouver, B.C.: The Fraser Institute, 1976), pp. 135–59. The passage quoted is from pp. 147–48.

> The situation would be made more complicated if we had reason to believe that the quality of the mix had changed from one year to the next. Suppose for example, we found that 1.5 teaspoons of the 1974 vintage were required to brew an excellent cup, whereas only 1 teaspoon of the 1973 mix was required—the difference caused by the percentage of cocoa in the mix. We would have to conclude that the quality of the mix had fallen. As a result, our price calculation would have to be adjusted to reflect the decline in quality.

What Darby is suggesting is that quality changes make measured price changes biased indicators of true price changes. Thus, for example, if the measured price of hot chocolate mix had increased 2 percent between 1973 and 1974, but if the quality had changed in the way in which Darby tells the story above, then the quality-corrected price of hot chocolate mixes would have increased by 53 percent in that year! Now, of course, a change as dramatic as that would be noticed and would cause the maker of hot chocolate mixes in question to go out of business. Suppose, however, that things were not quite so dramatic. Suppose that the 1973 vintage required 1 *level* teaspoon and that the 1974 vintage needed a slightly heaped, but only very slightly heaped, teaspoon. In particular, suppose that 1 percent more mix was needed in 1974 than 1973 to brew the same excellent cup. In that case, the 2 percent rise in the price per packet would translate to a 3 percent quality-corrected rise. If you are accustomed to making your hot chocolate in a laboratory, measuring the last gram of mix used in the process, then you would be likely to detect this deterioration in quality. But if you are more casual about the way in which you make your hot chocolate, it is very unlikely that you would have noticed the deterioration in quality, and therefore the true price rise may well have gone undetected even by a consumer of the product. How much harder, therefore, would it be for the true price changes to be detected by the Price Board set up under the ESP. Furthermore, it will not be easy for the econometrician attempting to assess the effects of the controls to allow for these matters.

Darby suggested an ingenious way of tackling the problem. He suggested that if undetected quality changes occurred during the control period, the result of this would be a mismeasurement of the true prices of output, and therefore, as a consequence, would result in a mismeasurement of the true value of real GNP.[14] If real GNP is mismeasured, we might stand some chance of detecting that fact, said Darby, by looking not at the Phillips curve, but at another statistical regularity, the relationship between real GNP and the unemployment rate. Darby discovered that there was a shift in that relationship during the period of controls that could be interpreted as implying that real GNP had been overmeasured during phase II and at the beginning phase III, and undermeasured during the later part of the control period. Using the normal relationship between unemployment and real GNP to recalculate true real GNP and using the result to recalculate a true or quality-adjusted price index, Darby showed that, on the basis of his particular quality adjustment, the controls had no effect on the rate of inflation. He reached this conclusion by conducting an analysis similar in method to Gordon's but using

[14]Ibid.

his own "quality-corrected" price indexes in place of the officially calculated indexes used by Gordon.

In attempting to choose between these two results, it is important to recall the discussion in Chapter 36 on the distinction between a "posted" price and an actual price. Darby's study takes that distinction seriously and tries to allow for it. Gordon's does not. Whether or not Darby's method of correcting for quality is the best or the right one, the need to correct for quality is certainly clear, so that Gordon's procedure has almost surely overestimated the disinflationary effects of the Nixon control program. Since his estimate is that, at most, the controls clipped 1.5 percent off the rate of inflation for each of two years, it seems safe to conclude that the controls had either marginal or no effect on U.S. inflation.

E. Comparison of Administrations—Truman to Reagan

Let us round off our study of macroeconomic policy in the postwar period by looking at the economic performance and policy summarized across six political regimes. Table 37.4 provides a snapshot view. From 1949 to 1952 the administration was essentially the same democratic administration that had been in power throughout World War II. The economic problems of that period were dominated by the devastation of Europe and Japan, the growing "cold war," and the emergence of war in Korea. It was a period during which U.S. inflation began to accelerate and, briefly in 1951, it looked potentially serious. It was also a period of falling unemployment. Money supply growth accelerated during those years, and the federal spending level (as a fraction of GNP) grew sharply, mainly as a result of military spending in connection with the Korean War. The deficit remained fairly static at around 1 percent of GNP.

In 1952, a conservative Republican president—Dwight Eisenhower—was elected to office. He remained in power for two full terms. On the average, during the Eisenhower regime, inflation was remarkably moderate (1.7 percent), and unemployment averaged below 5 percent. Monetary policy was in line with this low-inflation performance, and the federal budget was basically in balance. The Eisenhower years were not without their problems. Unemployment was generally regarded as being unsatisfactorally high, especially toward the end of the period.

The Kennedy administration was the first explicity to identify itself as embracing Keynesian policies. When John F. Kennedy became president at the beginning of 1961, it was generally and firmly believed that active Keynesian policies could "fine-tune" the economy near the neighborhood of full employment, and that, if necessary, other measures—wage and price guidelines or controls—could be used to contain inflation. In President Kennedy's first year of office, the inflation rate was a mere 1 percent, but unemployment was, by the standards of that time, extremely high (6.7 percent). During the Kennedy years, fiscal and monetary policy was really quite moderate but pointed cautiously in the direction of stimulation in order to lower the unacceptably high rate of unemployment inherited from the Eisenhower period.

Following the assassination of President Kennedy in November 1963,

TABLE 37.4
Economic Performance and Policy in Six Political Regimes

REGIME	INFLATION	UNEMPLOY-MENT	MONEY SUPPLY GROWTH	FEDERAL SPENDING PERCENT GNP	FEDERAL SURPLUS(+) OR DEFICIT(−) PERCENT GNP	WAGE AND PRICE CONTROLS
Truman 1949–1952						
First year	−1.0	5.9	−1.0	16.0	−1.0	
Last year	2.2	3.0	4.9	20.4	−1.1	—
Average	2.1	4.4	2.7	17.0	+0.8	
Eisenhower 1952–1960						
First year	0.8	2.9	2.5	21.0	−1.9	
Last year	1.6	5.5	−0.1	18.4	+0.6	—
Average	1.4	4.9	1.6	18.6	+1.0	
Kennedy-Johnson 1961–1968						
First year	1.0	6.7	2.0	19.4	−0.7	Guide-
Last year	4.2	3.6	6.8	20.7	−0.7	posts
Average	2.0	4.9	3.8	19.3	−0.5	
Nixon-Ford 1969–1976						
First year	5.4	3.5	5.8	20.0	+0.9	Controls
Last year	5.8	7.7	5.5	22.4	−3.1	1971–1974
Average	5.7	5.8	5.6	21.0	−1.6	
Carter 1977–1980						
First year	6.5	7.0	7.4	22.0	−2.4	Price-Pay
Last year	13.5	7.1	6.1	22.9	−2.4	Standards
Average	9.7	6.5	7.2	21.9	−1.7	
Reagan 1981–1982						
First year	9.9	7.6	6.9	23.5	−2.1	—
Second year	6.0	9.7	6.3	23.8	−3.6	—

SOURCES: Inflation: Appendix to Chapter 2. Unemployment: Appendix to Chapter 2. Money supply growth: See Figure 13.4. Federal spending: *Economic Report of the President*, 1982, Tables B-72, B-73, pp. 316–19. GNP: Appendix to Chapter 2. Federal surplus or deficit: *Economic Report of the President*, 1982, Tables B-72, B-73, pp. 316–19. Wage and price controls: *Economic Report of the President*, 1974, p. 91; 1980, p. 7; 1967, pp. 99–134.

Vice President Lyndon Johnson became president and was to remain in office until 1968. It was during the Johnson years that there was a particularly strong expansion of government expenditure and of monetary growth. A rise in both federal spending and money supply growth was in part associated with the costs of the Vietnam War, but also in part was associated with the expansion of social programs—the so-called Great Society program. On the average, the performance of inflation and employment under the Kennedy-Johnson policies was almost identical to what it had been in the previous Eisenhower years. However, there were some distinctly different trends emerging. By the end of the Kennedy-Johnson period, inflation had quadrupled, and unemployment had been reduced to almost one-half of the level experienced in the first of their years. Money supply growth had doubled on the average between the two regimes, however, and, by the end of the Kennedy-Johnson years, was running at almost 8 percent. Federal government spending had increased by more than one percentage point of GNP between the two regimes. Also, a near balance in the federal budget had been turned into an average deficit of 0.5 percent of GNP.

The administrations of Richard Nixon and Gerald Ford came next. They managed to hold the line on inflation but at a much higher level than had been experienced in previous years. They also presided over a rise in unemployment (more than doubling) and a substantial rise both in money supply growth and in federal government spending. What had been a modest deficit during the Kennedy-Johnson years was now turned into a sizable one by the end of the Ford administration.

The Carter years saw the inflation rate more than double and unemployment stay high at close to 7 percent. The deficit remained steady (close to 2.5 percent of GNP), and government spending rose yet further to almost 23 percent of GNP. Money supply growth averaged 6 percent, although it declined between the first and last of the Carter years.

During the first two Reagan years, inflation fell from the peak of the last Carter year, but unemployment rose substantially. There was a yet further rise in federal government spending as a fraction of GNP, and the deficit increased to an all-time post-war high. Money supply growth was higher than in the last Carter year.

The trends that we have seen in the performance of the U.S. economy and in monetary and fiscal policy can be seen very clearly in this administration-by-administration summary and in Table 37.4.

In terms of one of the questions posed at the beginning, there is certainly no clear tendency for there to be an identifiable difference in the way that policy is conducted based on political parties. Both Republican and Democratic regimes have presided over accelerating inflation. Only a Republican administration has used mandatory controls on wages and prices. Regardless of the administration, monetary policy seems to have been following much the same course and has become increasingly inflationary over the decades of the 1960s and 1970s.

Judged by macroeconomic performance, the highest marks presumably would have to go to the Eisenhower administration for maintaining inflation at less than 2 percent, and unemployment on the average at less than 5 percent. Many would want to argue, however, that during those years there were too many social problems not being adequately addressed by the federal government. They would point to the trend increases in federal government spending that occurred, regardless of the administration in office, all the way through the 1960s and 1970s as being vital to address those problems. Whether or not that is so goes well beyond the scope of macroeconomics, and I do not want to sidetrack you into a broader political, social, and economic debate on the merits and demerits of federal government spending. However, from a technically narrow macroeconomic perspective, it does seem hard to deny the proposition that the trend rise in federal government spending with some associated increases in state programs has been associated with a rising trend rate of unemployment, and the combination of those two facts has been the key source of increasingly inflationary monetary growth.

Viewed in this light, there is no easily identified villain responsible for the macroeconomic plight of the United States at the present time. Doing things that, right or wrong, were judged desirable at the time had consequences that were perhaps predicted by a few but certainly were not foreseen by most. Understanding the processes at work and then taking steps to redesign social and political institutions so that they are capable of delivering a different macroeconomic performance remains high on the agenda of unsolved problems.

Summary

A. Monetary Policy

U.S. monetary policy may be summarized by examining the growth rate of the money supply. After a strong burst of monetary growth in the early 1950s, there was a general downward trend in its rate that persisted to 1960. Since then, the money supply has grown increasingly quickly on the average. There have been clear cycles in the growth rate of the money supply, ranging from two to seven years, and averaging four years. The money supply growth rate has been volatile, and there is no appearance of reduced volatility in its rate in the years since monetary targeting was introduced in 1975.

B. Fiscal Policy

Whether measured in "actual" or "high-employment" terms, the federal government has been taking an increasing fraction of GNP in the postwar years, although the decline in military spending following the Korean War was the dominant influence on fiscal policy in the 1950s. Taxes have not increased as quickly as expenditure, however, and the deficit has gradually grown. There have been clear cycles in fiscal policy averaging five years in duration. Fiscal policy was particularly tight (or contractionary) during 1958–1960 and loose (or expansionary) during 1965–1968.

C. Wage and Price Controls

"Guideposts" were employed in the Kennedy years and "Price and Pay Standards" during the Carter years. The only full-blown mandatory wage and price control program was the Economic Stabilization Program of Richard Nixon, which ran from 1971 to 1974. The program had four phases, the first of which was an outright freeze and the remaining phases of which were designed to hold wage increases to 5.5 percent and price increases to 2.5 percent.

D. Policy and Performance

Decomposing the growth rate of the money supply into its anticipated and unanticipated components makes it possible to look at the extent to which these two separate parts of monetary policy have influenced the economy. Trends in the anticipated growth rate of the money supply, themselves generated by trends in fiscal policy and in unemployment, seem clearly capable of accounting for the trends in inflation. Unanticipated variations in money supply growth appear to account for the fluctuations of real GNP about its trend. Some of the fluctuations, however, that actually occurred, are more extreme than can be explained on the basis of only unanticipated money growth. These occurred in 1958 to 1961 (below trend) and 1965 to 1968 (above trend). Major swings in fiscal policy seem to be able to make some contribution to understanding these movements of real GNP.

Wage and price controls probably had very little effect either on wages or prices, after induced changes in quality and mismeasurement of the normal aggregate price indexes are allowed for.

E. Comparison of Administrations—Truman to Reagan

In narrow macroeconomic terms—as judged by inflation and unemployment—the Eisenhower administration turned in the best performance in the postwar years. All administrations since then have presided over rising inflation and (with the exception of Kennedy-Johnson) rising unemployment. Regardless of the political party forming the administration, both government spending and the deficit have trended upwards. There does not appear to be any significant difference between political parties concerning the way in which they manage the economy. With only two years of evidence in so far, it is too early to judge whether that statement will be applicable to the Reagan administration. On current showing it appears that it will.

Review Questions

1. Review the main facts about money supply growth in the United States in the postwar years.

2. What difference, if any, did the abandonment of the gold-exchange standard make to the growth rate of the money supply in the United States?

3. What have been the main trends in fiscal policy in the United States since the early 1950s?

4. What exactly do we mean by the high-employment level of government spending and the high-employment surplus? How have the high-employment levels compared with the actual levels?

5. Describe the content of the Nixon Economic Stabilization Program, initiated on August 15, 1971.

6. Why do we need to decompose the money supply growth into its anticipated and unanticipated components?

7. Review the main trends in anticipated money supply growth outlined in this chapter and compare them with the trends in inflation shown in the Appendix to Chapter 2. Can variations in the anticipated growth rate of the money supply account for variations in the rate of inflation?

8. Can we choose between the new Keynesian and new classical theories of macroeconomics on the basis of the discoveries of Robert Barro, concerning the way in which unanticipated money supply growth affects deviations of real GNP from trend? Explain why or why not in some detail.

9. How do the trends in fiscal policy and unemployment affect U.S. inflation?

10. How would you go about assessing the effects of a wage and price control program on the rate of inflation? Is there any reason why you would have to be particularly careful in your use of conventional price indexes?
11. Compare the macroeconomic performance of the United States under the different political administrations as shown in Table 37.4. Are Republicans monetarist and Democrats Keynesian on the basis of this examination?

38

Long-Term Trend in Output

We saw in Chapter 2 that the most dominant feature of the path of output is its long-term growth trend. Average output in the United States since 1900 has grown at 3.1 percent per annum. Population has grown during that same time period at 1.2 percent per annum, so that per capita income has grown at 1.9 percent per annum. This is equivalent to a doubling of per capita income every 37 years. Most of the material that you have studied in this book has abstracted from these long-term trends and has been concerned with understanding the fluctuations around the trend. Understanding what determines the trend itself will be the subject of this chapter.

The subject of this chapter is an enormous one. To do full justice to it would require another book at least as long as this one. Economists have been interested in the questions concerning long-term growth for as long as there has been a subject of economics. The founder of economics as we know it today, Adam Smith, wrote at length on the subject in his famous *On the Nature and Causes of the Wealth of Nations* published in 1776. In the period since then, the topic has exercised the talents of the giants in our discipline such as Thomas Malthus and David Ricardo and, in more recent years, James Meade of Cambridge University, Trevor Swan of the Australian National University, Robert Solow of M.I.T., and James Tobin of Yale University.[1] These scholars have made their major contributions to the abstract analysis of the determinants of economic growth. In addition, many scholars have undertaken careful measurement and empirical investigation, the most notable of these being Edward F. Denison, of the U.S. Department of Commerce and Brookings Institution.[2]

---

[1]Some of the seminal contributions to this topic are: James Meade, *A Neoclassical Theory of Economic Growth* (London: George Allen and Unwin, 1960); Trevor Swan, "Economic Growth and Capital Accumulation," *The Economic Record*, 32 (November 1956), 334–61; Robert M. Solow, "A Contribution to the Theory of Economic Growth," *Quarterly Journal of Economics*, 70 (February 1956), 65–94, and James Tobin, "A Dynamic Aggregative Model," *Journal of Political Economy*, 63 (April 1955), 103–15.

[2]Edward F. Dennison, *Accounting for United States Economic Growth 1929–1969* (Washington, D.C.: The Brookings Institution, 1974).

In view of the enormous volume of literature on the topic of economic growth, this chapter cannot pretend to do any more than provide an account of the highlights of the subject.[3] In this process you will be taken through five principal tasks, which are to:

(a) Understand the concept of the per capita production function.
(b) Know how to represent per capita output and savings in a simple diagram.
(c) Understand the concept of the steady-state investment rate.
(d) Know how to find the equilibrium values of per capita output, capital, consumption, savings, and investment.
(e) Understand what determines the trend rate of growth of output.

A. The Per Capita Production Function

You are already familiar with the concept of the production function. You met it in Chapter 8 when dealing with aggregate supply and the labor market. As you discovered there, a production function is simply a statement about the maximum output that can be produced with a given list of inputs and, more than that, a statement of how that maximum level of output will vary as the inputs themselves are varied. The maximum output of some particular good that can be produced will depend on the amount of capital employed, the state of technology, the amount of land resources used, and the number and skill of the workers employed. In Chapter 8, where we were concerned only with the short run, we supposed that all of the inputs into the production process, with the exception of the number of workers employed, were fixed. In this chapter, however, we want to focus on the process of growth itself and to allow for variations in inputs other than labor.

It will be a useful approximation to imagine that total land resources are fixed and that, over the long run, what may be varied in order to vary output are the amounts of labor and capital employed and the state of technology that is utilized. The larger the number of people employed or the larger the stock of capital equipment used, the greater will be the volume of output. As labor and capital inputs are increased, output will increase, but by diminishing amounts—the law of diminishing returns will apply both to labor and capital. However, as technology advances, over time, the amount of output that will be attainable from any given amount of labor and capital will increase.

Since the focus of our attention in this chapter is going to be on long-term trends in output, it turns out to be useful to consider the *per capita* (per

---

[3]There are many excellent, although advanced, treatments of this topic that cover the subject in a comprehensive way. Perhaps the best introductory collection of readings of some of the major contributions to this topic is *The Modern Theory of Economic Growth*, edited by Joseph E. Stiglitz and Hirofumi Uzawa (Cambridge, Mass.: M.I.T. Press, 1969). In addition to presenting the original contributions on which this chapter is based by James Meade, Robert M. Solow, and Trevor Swan, this book also contains a seminal contribution that integrates monetary and growth theory by James Tobin, as well as much other material. The level of difficulty of the essays in this work is, however, substantially higher than the presentation given in this chapter.

head) production function rather than the aggregate production function. The previous paragraph has talked about the relationship between aggregate output and the amount of labor and capital employed in the production process. The per capita production function is a statement about how output per head varies as we vary the inputs per head as well as the state of technology. It turns out to be extremely convenient to assume that output per head varies as capital per head is varied and in a similar way to the way in which total output varies as the capital input is changed. Thus, as capital per head is increased, output per head increases but in successively diminishing amounts—the law of diminishing returns again.

In general, it is possible that output per head will depend both on capital per head and on the number of people employed—the scale of output. By assuming that output per head depends *only* on capital per head, we are assuming that there are constant returns to scale. This is an important, although probably not violent, simplification. There is a great deal of evidence to the effect that the real-world production functions are characterized by constant returns to scale.

B. Per Capita Output and Savings

The per capita production function can be represented in a diagram to look much like the short-run production function with which you are already familiar (Figure 8.2). Figure 38.1 illustrates this same type of relationship but in per capita terms. As you see, we measure the amount of capital per head (k/n) in

Figure 38.1
Per Capita Production and Savings Function

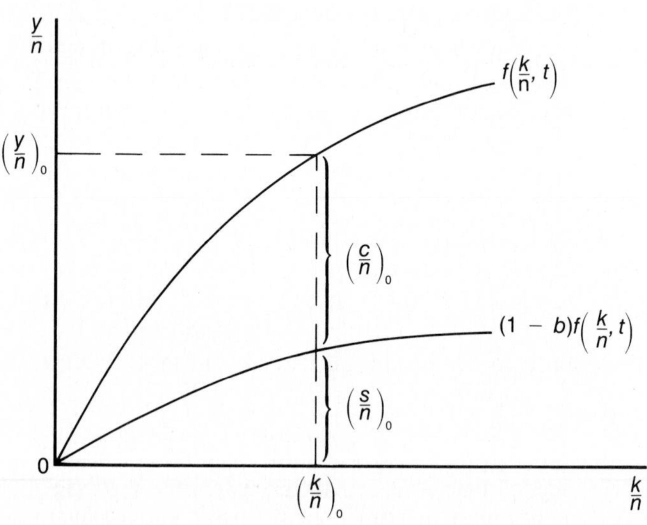

Per capita output will be an increasing function of the capital-labor ratio and will be subject to diminishing marginal productivity of capital—the curve labelled $f(k/n, t)$. Per capita savings will be a fraction of per capita output—the curve labelled $(1 - b)f(k/n, t)$. At the capital-labor ratio $(k/n)_0$, output per head is $(y/n)_0$, consumption per head is $(c/n)_0$, and savings per head is $(s/n)_0$.

Figure 38.1, whereas in Figure 8.2 we measured n. On the vertical axis in Figure 38.1 we measure output per head (y/n), whereas, in contrast, in Figure 8.2 we measured aggregate output. The production function is the line labelled $f(k/n, t)$. This line shows that, as capital per head is increased, so output per head increases. The curvature of the function shows that as capital per head is increased, output per head increases but by decreasing amounts.

The curve is labelled $f(k/n, t)$ to remind you that there are two things that affect output per head. The first of these is capital per head, and we measure the effect of it on output per head as movements along the per capita production function. The second variable that affects output per head is the state of technology represented by the letter t. At any given point in time there will be a given state of technology and a given per capita production function. However, as time progresses and technology changes, in general, the per capita production function will shift upwards indicating that, at a given level of capital per head, output per head will increase.

The term *capital per head* is a slightly clumsy one and is replaced by the equivalent term, the *capital-labor ratio.*

As you already know both from the discussion of flows and stocks in Chapter 3 and from our analysis of investment demand in Chapter 17, there are some important linkages between investment, savings, and the stock of capital. The capital stock changes as a result of investment activity. In our analysis of fluctuations of economic activity around its trend, we found it convenient to ignore the ongoing effects of investment on capital accumulation and proceeded on the simplifying assumption (although a strictly untenable assumption) that the capital stock was constant. Now that we are analyzing the determinants of the long-term trends in output, we need to explicitly focus on the effects of ongoing savings and investment on the rate of capital accumulation.

In the most basic terms, you can think of the rate at which capital is being accumulated as the difference between the rate at which goods are being produced and consumed. You need to be careful to include in your definition of consumption the consumption of capital goods through their wear and tear and depreciation—what is called *capital consumption.* Provided that consumption is measured to include capital consumption it will be clear to you that the change in the capital stock is identical to income minus consumption. You know, however, (ignoring government and international economic activity for simplicity) that income minus consumption is savings. You also know that a reasonable proposition about savings is that, in the long run, it is equal to some constant fraction of income. Let us, as we did in Chapter 16, call the fraction of income consumed b, so that the fraction of income saved is $1 - b$.

We can represent the amount of income saved in the same diagram as our per capita production function (Figure 38.1). This is the lower line labelled $(1 - b)f(k/n, t)$. It is simply the production function scaled down by the fraction $1 - b$, so that it shows the amount of per capita income that is not consumed—in other words, income that is saved—at each capital-labor ratio. For example, if the capital-labor ratio was $(k/n)_0$, then per capita income would be $(y/n)_0$, as indicated on the vertical axis of the figure, and that income would be divided between per capita consumption of $(c/n)_0$ and per capita capital accumulation—savings—of $(s/n)_0$.

What Figure 38.1 now shows us are the amounts of output per head and savings per head—capital accumulation per head—that will be achieved at each possible capital-labor ratio. The diagram has an interesting feature that has not been met before in this book. It is that one of the variables that is being measured on the vertical axis represents the amount by which the variable on the horizontal axis is *changing*. That is, if we were to pick a particular capital-labor ratio again, say, $(k/n)_0$, then a certain amount of output would be produced, a certain fraction of that output would be consumed, and the rest would be added to the stock of capital. Thus, the stock of capital would be changing. If the labor force is also growing (if n is rising), then the capital-labor ratio will either rise, fall, or stay constant depending on whether the rise in the labor force exceeds, falls short of, or happens to just equal the growth of the capital stock.

The next section will analyze the process whereby the actual rates of savings, investment, and output are determined.

C. Steady-State Investment Rate

There is one and only one rate of investment that is compatible with the economy being in a steady state. By *steady state* we mean nothing other than a situation in which the relevent variables are constant over time. The relevent variables for the present are per capita output and capital stock and the rates of consumption, savings, and investment. To figure out what the steady-state rate of investment is we want to work out the rate of investment that maintains the capital-labor ratio at some given constant level. To work this out, let us begin with the obvious proposition that the rate of savings (s) is equal to the change in the stock of capital or investment; that is,

$$s = \Delta k \tag{38.1}$$

We can divide savings and the change in the capital stock by the population to give per capita savings that are equal to per capita capital accumulation; that is,

$$\frac{s}{n} = \frac{\Delta k}{n} \tag{38.2}$$

Let us do something that at first seems pointless but which turns out in fact to be very useful. That is, let us multiply and divide the right-hand side of Equation (38.2) by the capital stock. This, of course, multiplies the right-hand side of the equation by one, leaving it unchanged. If we do this, we obtain

$$\frac{s}{n} = \frac{\Delta k}{k}\left(\frac{k}{n}\right) \tag{38.3}$$

This is still nothing other than a definition. It tells us that per capita savings are equal to the growth rate of the capital stock ($\Delta k/k$) multiplied by the capital-labor ratio (k/n).

Figure 38.2
Steady-State Investment Line

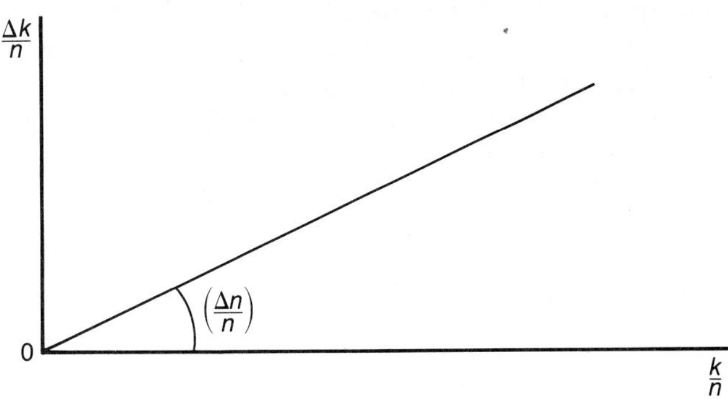

The rate of per capita capital accumulation that will maintain the capital-labor ratio intact is shown as the line having a slope equal to the growth rate of the population.

Now, in order that the economy be in a steady state, the capital-labor ratio (k/n) must be a constant. This can only occur when the stock of capital is growing at the same rate as the labor force is growing. If, for example, neither was growing at all, then the capital-labor ratio would be constant. Equally, the capital-labor ratio would be constant provided each was growing at the same rate. Thus, the condition for the steady state is that

$$\frac{\Delta k}{k} = \frac{\Delta n}{n} \tag{38.4}$$

Equation (38.3) above is simply a definition, and Equation (38.4) is the condition that, if satisfied, gives rise to a steady state. We can combine these two propositions to give

$$\frac{s}{n} = \frac{\Delta n}{n}\left(\frac{k}{n}\right) \tag{38.5}$$

What this says is that in the steady state, per capita savings will be equal to the growth rate of the population multiplied by the capital-labor ratio. The growth rate of the population is treated as being exogenous—that is, it does not vary as a consequence of variations in any of the variables whose values we are determining in the analysis. (This assumption of neoclassical growth theory contrasts with that of the classical economists such as Malthus and Ricardo who viewed the population growth rate as one of the factors that adjusted to the underlying economic conditions.)

We can represent the steady-state rate of capital accumulation in a simple diagram such as Figure 38.2. This figure, like Figure 38.1, measures the capital-labor ratio on the horizontal axis and measures the rate of savings (capital accumulation) per head on the vertical axis. The slope of the line, as is readily seen from Equation (38.5), is equal to the (exogenous) population growth rate, $\Delta n/n$. Figure 38.2, like Figure 38.1, has the interesting property that the value of the variable measured on the vertical axis is the change in the variable on the horizontal axis for a given value of n. The line plotted in Figure 38.2, however, traces all those values of s/n that deliver a constant k/n. If the economy was above that line with s/n greater than the steady-state value, the capital stock would be growing faster than the population, and k/n would be rising. At points below the line in Figure 38.2, the rate of capital accumulation would be less than the rate of population growth, and the capital-labor ratio would be falling. The points on the line are those at which the capital stock and labor force are growing at the same rate and therefore deliver a constant capital-labor ratio.

D. Equilibrium Per Capita Output, Capital, Consumption, Savings, and Investment

It is now a relatively simple matter to bring together the analyses of the two preceding sections and determine the equilibrium levels of per capita output, consumption, savings, investment, and capital. This is done in Figure 38.3. A preliminary examination of this figure will reveal that it is nothing other than a combination of Figures 38.1 and 38.2. The curve labelled $f(k/n, t)$ is the per capita production function. That labelled $(1 - b)f(k/n, t)$ is the savings rate as a function of the capital-labor ratio, and the line having the slope $\Delta n/n$ is the steady-state investment line.

To get a feel for how the figure works and how it determines the equilib-

Figure 38.3 Equilibrium per Capita Output, Capital, Consumption, Savings, and Investment

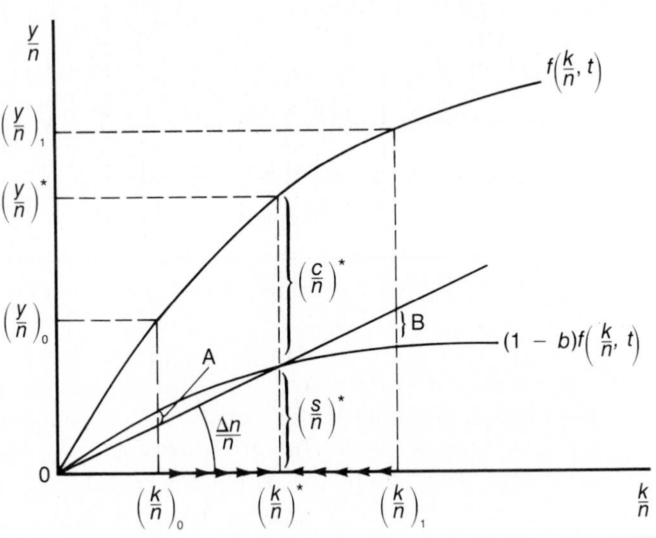

The per capita production and savings functions are combined with the steady-state investment line to determine the steady-state capital-labor ratio and output per head. In a situation like $(k/n)_0$, capital grows at a faster rate than the steady-state requirement, so that the capital-labor ratio rises. In a situation like $(k/n)_1$, the captial stock grows at a slower rate than that required for the steady state, so that the capital-labor ratio falls. At $(k/n)^*$, the savings rate equals the steady-state investment rate, and the capital-labor ratio remains constant.

rium, let us imagine initially that the economy has a capital-labor ratio of $(k/n)_0$ as marked on the horizontal axis of Figure 38.3. The level of output per head is immediately determined as $(y/n)_0$. How much capital accumulation is taking place in this situation? Is it more or less than that required to maintain the capital-labor ratio at its constant $(k/n)_0$ level? You know that the amount of actual capital accumulation is that read off from the savings line $(1 - b)f(k/n, t)$. You also know that the amount of capital accumulation required to maintain the capital-labor ratio at a constant is read off from the steady-state investment line. At the capital-labor ratio of $(k/n)_0$, there is evidently a gap between these two amounts—labelled A in the figure. Evidently, at the capital-labor ratio $(k/n)_0$, actual capital accumulation exceeds that required to maintain a constant capital-labor ratio by the amount A. This means that the capital-labor ratio will not remain constant at $(k/n)_0$. Instead it will be rising.

Next consider what will be happening if the economy had a capital-labor ratio $(k/n)_1$ on the horizontal axis of Figure 38.3. In this case, output per head would be $(y/n)_1$. Conducting exactly the same type of exercise as that above, you can now see that there is a gap between the amount of capital that will be accumulated and the steady-state investment line of the amount labelled B in the diagram. This time, however, there is less capital being accumulated than that required to maintain a constant capital-labor ratio. That is, the steady-state investment line lies above the savings function. This means that the capital-labor ratio $(k/n)_1$ is not a steady state because if the economy started out in that position, capital would be growing at a slower rate than the labor force, so that the capital-labor ratio would be falling. You can now immediately see that there is one, and only one, capital-labor ratio that is consistent with a steady state, and it is that labelled $(k/n)^*$.

This capital-labor ratio generates an output rate of $(y/n)^*$ and a savings rate equal to the steady-state rate of capital accumulation. That is, at $(k/n)^*$, the savings function intersects the steady-state investment line. There is no gap between the rate at which capital is in fact being accumulated and the rate at which it needs to be accumulated in order to maintain a constant capital-labor ratio. Thus, $(k/n)^*$ and $(y/n)^*$ represent the equilibrium capital-labor ratio and output per head in the economy. The output is divided between consumption and savings (capital accumulation), with $(c/n)^*$ being consumed and $(s/n)^*$ being saved and added to the stock of capital. In this economy, the long-term trend in output will have the same growth rate as that of the population $(\Delta n/n)$.

E. Determinants of the Trend Rate of Growth of Output

In the analysis of the preceding section, you have seen that the trend growth rate of output will be equal to the population growth rate, since there is a built-in equilibrating mechanism that ensures that the capital-labor ratio approaches its steady-state rate, thereby producing a fixed output per head. The diagrams used in order to characterize the solution in the previous section use a per capita production function that itself does not move. If, however, as a result of technical change, the production function is continuously shifting

Figure 38.4
The Effect of a Change in the Savings Rate

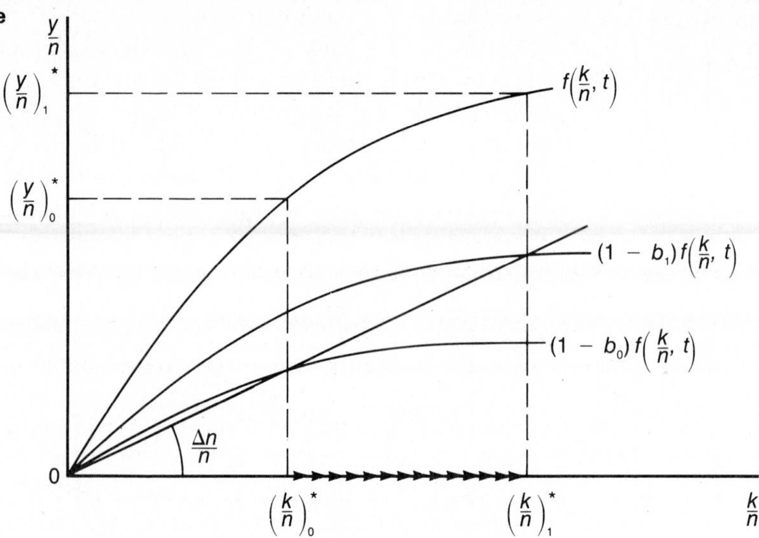

If the savings rate rises from $(1 - b_0)$ to $(1 - b_1)$, the savings function shifts upwards. At $(k/n)_0^*$, the rate of capital accumulation exceeds that necessary to hold the capital-labor ratio constant. Thus the capital-labor ratio rises and continues to do so up to $(k/n)_1^*$, when a new steady state is reached.

upwards, then output per head will grow at a rate over and above the population growth rate. This growth rate, however, will depend only on the rate at which the production function is shifting upwards and will have to be added to the basic growth rate of output—the growth rate of the population.

What this says is that the trend growth rate of output is determined by the trend growth rate in the population and the trend growth in output per head made possible by changes in technology. Specifically, the growth rate of output does not depend on the rate of saving. A change in the rate of saving would affect the level of output per head and the capital-labor ratio but would not affect the growth trend.

You can see this very clearly by considering the analysis in Figure 38.4, which, again, abstracts from changing technology and analyzes the situation for a given production function at a given moment in time. The initial equilibrium depicted in Figure 38.3 is reproduced as the equilibrium labelled $(k/n)_0^*$ and $(y/n)_0^*$. This is an equilibrium associated with a given population growth rate $(\Delta n/n)$ and a savings rate equal to $1 - b_0$. Now imagine that the savings rate was to increase to $1 - b_1$. This would result in an upward shift in the savings function as shown in Figure 38.4. Starting out at $(k/n)_0^*$, the savings rate will now be higher than that required to maintain a constant capital-labor ratio. As a consequence, the capital-labor ratio will rise, and as it does so, output per head will also rise. The higher the capital-labor ratio, the higher will be the rate of savings needed to maintain a given constant capital-labor ratio (we move along the steady-state investment line).

Eventually, we reach the capital-labor ratio $(k/n)_1^*$, which produces the

Figure 38.5
The Effects of a Change in the Population Growth Rate

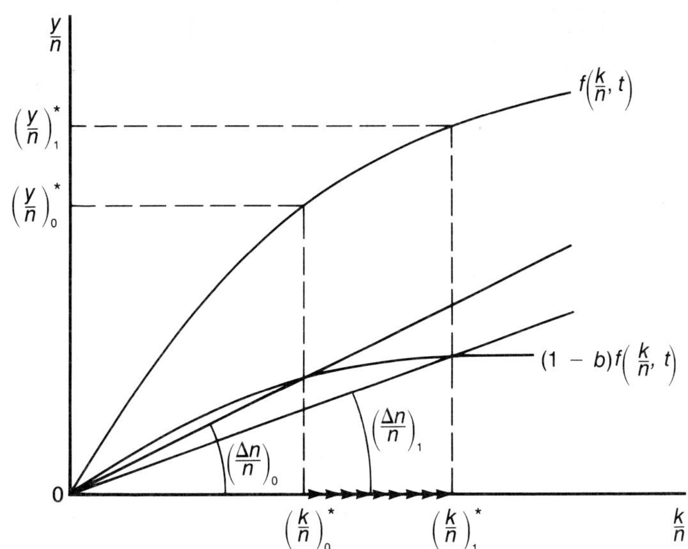

The population growth rate decreases from $(\Delta n/n)_0$ to $(\Delta n/n)_1$. At the initial equilibrium $(k/n)^*_0$, the savings rate is bigger than that required to maintain the capital-labor ratio constant. The capital-labor ratio therefore increases and continues to do so until it reaches $(k/n)^*_1$, its new steady state.

income level $(y/n)^*_1$ that is a steady state. At this capital-labor ratio, the steady-state investment ray intersects the savings function, so that the capital-labor ratio remains constant. During the transition from the initial to the new capital-labor ratio, the growth rate of output will have exceeded the growth rate of the population. This is obvious because the ratio (y/n) has increased, so that y must have been growing faster than n. However, once the new steady state is reached, the rate of growth of output will again equal the rate of population growth.

Thus, except for the process of adjustment from one steady state to another, the growth rate of output is independent of the savings rate. A different way of putting this would be to say that the growth rate of output does not depend on the savings rate but does depend on *changes in* the savings rate.

Although the savings rate does not affect the growth rate of output, it does affect the level of output per head. You can see immediately from Figure 38.4 that the higher the rate of savings, the greater will be the levels of capital and output per head.

Although the savings rate does not affect the growth rate of output, the population growth rate does. It also influences the level of output per head in a way that you can readily see. Figure 38.5 will illustrate the analysis this time. Again, the initial equilibrium as depicted in Figure 38.3 is reproduced in Figure 38.5 as $(k/n)^*_0$ with per capita output at $(y/n)^*_0$. This is the equilibrium associated with the population growth rate of $(\Delta n/n)_0$. Now imagine that the population growth rate declines to $(\Delta n/n)_1$. This will have the effect of rotating the steady-state investment line downwards as shown in Figure 38.5. At the initial capital-labor ratio $(k/n)_0^*$, there will now be a level of savings and capital accumulation that exceeds the steady-state investment requirement. This means that the capital-labor ratio will rise. It will do so until it reaches $(k/n)_1^*$, at which point the new steady-state investment line intersects the savings function. During the process, the capital-labor ratio will have increased from $(k/n)_0^*$ to $(k/n)_1^*$, and per capita output will have grown from $(y/n)_0^*$ to $(y/n)_1^*$. In the new steady state, the growth rate of total output will have declined by exactly the same amount as the growth rate of the population. In the transition to the new steady state, output will have grown at a faster rate than the population growth rate.

You have now seen that the *level* of output per head depends on both the population growth rate and the savings rate. The lower the population growth rate or the higher the savings rate, the higher will be output per head, and the higher will be the capital-labor ratio. The growth rate of output, however, except for transitions arising from changes in the savings rate or the population growth rate, depends only on the population growth rate and the rate of technical change.

We have focused on the effects of the population growth rate and the savings rate on per capita output and the capital-labor ratio. It is now of some interest to examine how the rate of per capita consumption is influenced by these factors. Let us examine the possible steady-state per capita consumption levels. Figure 38.6 shows these possibilities. The figure contains the production function and the steady-state investment line. The gap between these two lines (shaded area) indicates the steady-state consumption possibilities. Of course, to realize any one of these possibilities, the actual savings behavior of the population would have to be appropriate.

Let us suspend consideration of what that savings behavior needs to be for a moment and simply look at the amounts of consumption per capita that are available in different steady states. Visual inspection of Figure 38.6 reveals that as the capital-labor ratio increases from zero, at first, per capita consumption also increases. A point is reached, however, at which per capita consumption is at a maximum. This is at the capital-labor ratio marked in Figure 38.6 as $(k/n)^*$. At capital-labor ratios greater than $(k/n)^*$, consumption per capita declines as the capital-labor ratio increases. You can see, as a result of the line labelled AA in Figure 38.6, that the slope of the production function at the point of maximum per capita consumption is equal to the slope of the steady-state investment line. That slope you know to be the growth rate of population.

What does the slope of the per capita production function measure? A moment's reflection will convince you that it measures the marginal product of capital. Think of increasing capital per head by a small amount and ask how much extra output per head do we get; the answer is that it depends on the slope of the per capita production function. At very low capital-labor ratios, we get a large amount of extra output; whereas at very high capital-labor ratios, we get very little. The slope of the per capita production function thus measures the (diminishing) marginal productivity of capital. The slope of the

Figure 38.6
Per Capita Consumption and the Golden Rule

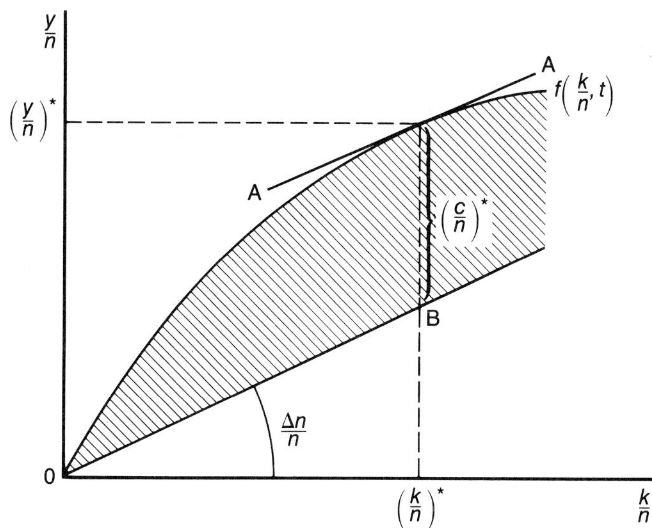

Possible steady-state values of consumption are shown by the shaded part of the figure. Evidently, consumption per capita is at a maximum at $(k/n)^*$. At that capital-labor ratio, the marginal product of capital, that is the slope of the line AA, is equal to the population growth rate. This is the "golden rule." If the savings function passes through B, then per capita consumption will in fact be maximized. Savings may be either too great or too small to maximize per capital consumption.

line AA measures the marginal product of capital at the point of maximum per capita consumption.

You have just discovered what is known as the "golden rule." The golden rule states that per capita consumption is maximized when the marginal product of capital is equal to the growth rate of population.

Of course to achieve the golden rule it would be necessary that the savings fraction be such as to pass the savings function through the point marked B in Figure 38.6. Savings rates larger than that would imply a higher capital-labor ratio than $(k/n)^*$, a higher output level than $(y/n)^*$, but a smaller consumption rate than $(c/n)^*$. Savings rates lower than that necessary to pass the savings function through B would be associated with lower output per head, lower capital per head, and lower consumption per head.

You have now seen that the growth rate of output depends on the growth rate of population and on the rate of technical change. You have also seen that the level of output per head and the capital-labor ratio depend on both the population growth rate and the savings rate. You have seen, however, that the ultimate objective of economic activity, consumption, at any given point in time in a given state of technology, has a well-defined maximum. There is thus a unique per capita consumption-maximizing rate of saving, which, if achieved, would deliver not the maximum possible output per head and capital stock per head but the optimum values of those variables.

Over time, of course, output per head and consumption per head will increase if technical change is shifting the production function upwards. There is no "free lunch" in this direction, however, because more rapid technical change would require devoting more resources to research and development and less resources to consumption. Just as there is a per capita consumption-maximizing rate of saving, so also there will be an optimum rate at which to devote resources to research and development. Like all other economic activities, that too is subject to the law of diminishing returns.

Summary

A. The Per Capita Production Function

The per capita production function shows the maximum amount of per capita production obtainable as the capital-labor ratio is increased. The per capita production function will shift over time as a result of technical change.

B. Per Capita Output and Savings

Per capita savings (which is the same thing as per capita capital accumulation) will be some fraction of per capita output. Thus, the rate of per capita capital accumulation depends on the level of capital per head.

C. Steady-State Investment Rate

Because the per capita rate of capital accumulation depends on the capital-labor ratio, it follows that, in general, at any given capital-labor ratio, there will be a tendency for the capital-labor ratio to either rise or fall. The steady-state investment rate is the rate of investment (of capital accumulation) that maintains the capital-labor ratio constant. The investment rate that maintains the capital-labor ratio constant is the capital-labor ratio multiplied by the population growth rate.

D. Equilibrium Per Capita Output, Capital, Consumption, Savings, and Investment

The equilibrium value of the capital-labor ratio is determined as the capital-labor ratio that generates a volume of savings per head equal to the steady-state rate of investment per head. When savings per head equal steady-state investment per head, the capital-labor ratio, output per head, consumption per head, and savings per head are all constant.

E. Determinants of the Trend Rate of Growth of Output

The trend rate of growth of output is determined by the population growth rate and the rate of technical change. It does not depend on the savings rate. If the savings rate changes, however, there is a transition from one level of output per head to another that involves a change in the growth rate. Specifically, a rise in the savings rate raises the capital-labor ratio and output per head. A fall in the population growth rate also has these same effects. Per capita consumption is maximized when the marginal product of capital equals the population growth rate. This is known as the "golden rule." There is a unique saving rate that will deliver the golden rule. Too much savings relative to the golden rule will produce a higher output per head but a lower consumption per head than the golden rule value.

Review Questions

1. What is a per capita production function? How does it differ from an ordinary aggregate production function? Does it still possess the property of diminishing returns?

2. What happens to the per capita production function if there is technical progress? Illustrate in a diagram.

3. How does savings per head vary as output per head varies?

4. You are given the following information:

k/n	0	1	2	3	4	5	6	7	8	9	10
y/n	0	2.0	3.7	5.0	6.2	7.2	8.0	8.6	9.1	9.5	9.8

Plot the per capita production function. If the fraction of income consumed is 0.8, plot the relationship between capital per head and savings per head.

5. What is the meaning of the concept the steady-state rate of investment?

6. What determines the steady-state rate of investment?

7. Show in a diagram how the equilibrium values of output per head, consumption per head, savings per head, and investment per head are determined. Analyze the forces that would act on these variables if they were not at their equilibrium values.

8. Review what happens to the four variables referred to in the previous question if there is a rise in the production function generated by technical progress.

9. Analyze the effects on the four variables in Question 7 in the event of a rise in the growth rate of population.

10. Does capital accumulation cause a growth in the standard of living? If not, what does?

39

The "Supply Side"

In recent years, and especially in the period since the Reagan/Carter election campaign, a great deal has been heard about "supply-side" macroeconomics. This is presented as some "new" magic that, in contrast to the old Keynesian policies, can cure all the ills of inflation, unemployment, and sagging productivity. As a matter of fact, the analysis that provides the basis for the propositions of the "supply-siders," as they are known, is not new at all. It is *pre*-Keynesian. This does not mean that it is wrong. It does mean, however, that the way in which it is presented, especially by the media, is misleading. This chapter is designed to help you evaluate the claims of the supply-siders. To that end you will pursue eight tasks, which are to:

(a) Understand why governments are productive.
(b) Understand how productive government activity affects the production function and the demand for labor.
(c) Understand how paying for government (taxation) affects the supply of labor.
(d) Understand how efficient government raises output and employment.
(e) Understand how overgrown government lowers output and employment.
(f) Know the effects of supply-side policies on the price level.
(g) Understand how the supply-side analysis can be extended to apply to savings and capital accumulation.
(h) Appraise (briefly) the supply-side policies of the Reagan administration.

A. Why Governments are Productive

The easiest way to convince yourself that governments are productive is to conduct a thought experience. Imagine a world in which there is no government. What are the most basic services provided by government that such a world would lack?

Perhaps the most fundamental service provided by government is the establishment of property rights and the enforcement of contracts. Thus government can be thought of as an economic agent that has a monopoly in the legitimate use of coercion. Governments use that monopoly power to require the rest of us to behave in certain well-defined ways. If we enter into contracts with each other, then we are required to fulfill our part of the bargain. Failure to do so may result in the injured party seeking a satisfactory settlement by appealing to the courts. Our persons and our physical property are also protected by criminal laws that automatically come into action if our rights are violated. The punishment of those convicted of crimes is the government's way of imposing a price penalty that is designed to deter such criminal activity. The provision of national defense can be thought of as a natural extension of such activity whereby the government seeks to guard the personal and physical property of its citizens against damage or theft by foreigners.

Try to imagine a world in which these services are not provided by monopoly government. How are they provided? The answer is that individuals and groups will seek to provide for their own security by carrying arms themselves or by hiring others to protect them. More of human history has been characterized by such arrangements than by those with which we are familiar in the modern world. In such a world, a large volume of human and physical resources would be devoted to the provision of personal and collective security. These resources, if released from such activities, could be put to other productive use. In the absence of a government, however, private individuals are not going to see it as being in their interest to divert resources from the provision of personal security to the production of other goods and services. They will use their scarce resources in the most productive way and that will involve protecting what they have acquired rather than producing additional goods and services.

The emergence of a government with a monopoly in the use of coercion that uses that monopoly to establish and enforce property rights by operating a criminal and civil legal system confronts rational individuals with a different set of constraints. Instead of seeing it as being in their best interests to protect what they have, individuals will benefit from the collective (or shared) provision of such protection services and will enjoy a greater measure of freedom that may be employed in other productive activities.

A second activity that would not be present in a world without government is the provision of public health services. By *public* health services I mean such things as the provision of clean drinking water, sewage services, inoculation programs against easily communicated diseases, and the like. These should be distinguished from *private* health services, which deal with the prevention and treatment of conditions specific to a given individual. It is the nature of public health services (but not of private health services) that their fruits may be consumed by all regardless of individual contributions. It is likely therefore that unless the government directly organizes and provides public health services, no one will see it as being in his or her own interest to expend such resources to provide an appropriate level of such a service. As a consequence, disease will reduce the effective productivity of the population.

Governments provide many things other than a basic legal system and public health services. Some of these activities are productive, although it is a controversial matter as to whether they may be more productively provided by government than by the private sector. Still other activities of government are not productive at all. They involve, in effect, the replacement of private violations of property rights with public violation.

Examples of productive activities are the provision of a road system, schools and universities, and various kinds of insurance. There is no easy way of knowing whether the government provision of these activities is more or less efficient than would a private provision of the same services. Certainly there are large variations across jurisdictions in this regard. Some countries (for example, Switzerland) seek to provide almost everything they can privately, whereas others (for example, the Soviet Union) have sought to shrink the private sector to provide only a narrow range of consumer goods. Although it is controversial and impossible to settle in any definitive way whether private or public provision other than in the area of a basic legal and security system and the provision of public health is the more productive, it does seem reasonable to suppose that the more things government provides, the more likely it is that it will start encroaching on areas where it is less able to produce efficiently than the private sector would be.

Examples of activities indulged in by modern governments that appear to have no productivity at all involve the massive income and wealth redistributions that take place. Macroeconomics is not the subject that deals in detail with this topic. We may note, however, that if it is desired to redistribute income and wealth in an efficient way, there exist well-defined so-called negative income tax schemes that could achieve this with vast reductions in the volume of bureaucracy required as compared with the schemes that most modern governments, including that in the United States, pursue at the present time. It is also transparently obvious that most of the transfers that take place do not go from the rich to the poor, but go from the rich and the poor to the politically powerful middle. Thus, the political process itself may be seen as, to some degree, performing the same function as is performed by a less formal system and indeed more primitive system of property expropriations.

It is easy to summarize the above: Some things that governments do they do better than any other agent conceivably could. A monopoly provider of law and order and national security together with public health is almost certainly the most efficient such provider. A government monopoly in most other activities is probably about equally efficient with private provision. However, as an agent that transfers wealth amongst individuals, government is fairly definitely inefficient.

B. How Productive Government Activity Affects the Production Function and the Demand for Labor

In order to go beyond the description of government activity in the previous section and develop an analysis of how government affects aggregate economic activity, it is necessary to see how productive government activity affects the basic model that we have developed in Part III.

The first effect that we shall identify is perhaps the obvious one—this is the influence of productive government activity on the short-run production function and on the demand for labor. This is illustrated in Figure 39.1. Frame

Figure 39.1
How Prodctive Government Affects the Production Function and Demand for Labor

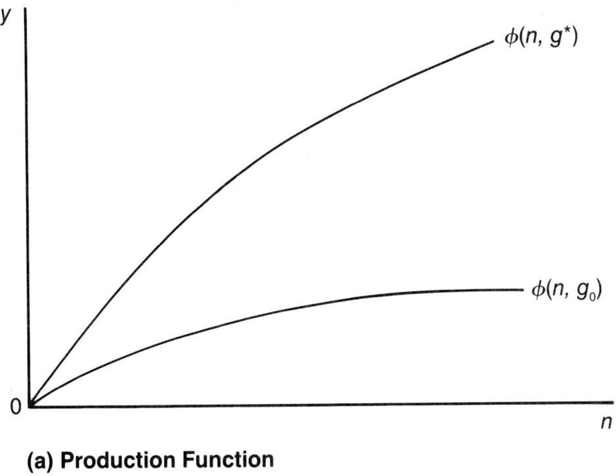

(a) Production Function

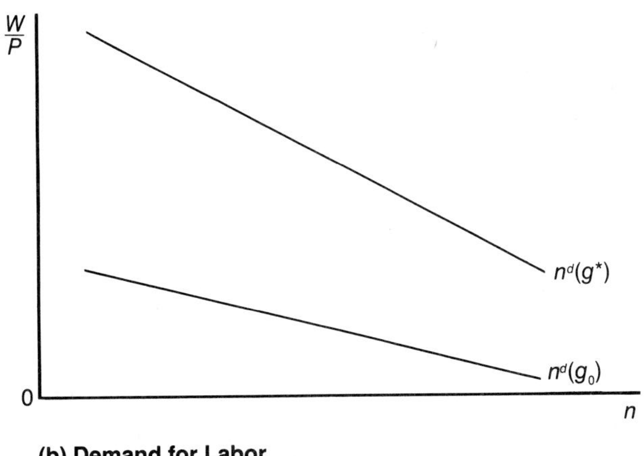

(b) Demand for Labor

An economy with no government has a production function $\phi(n, g_0,$ [frame (a)] and a demand for labor curve, $n^d(g_0)$ [frame (b)]. If the government provides productive services that enable individuals to pay less attention to the needs of their own security and also provides for basic public health, the production function and labor demand function will shift upwards to the curves labelled $\phi(n, g^*)$ and $n^d(g^*)$.

(a) shows the production function for two economies. One economy has no government provision of productive services such as those described above, and its production function is the one labelled $\phi(n, g_0)$. The other is an economy in which the government is providing a level of activity that supports a legal system, national defense, and public health services that raise the productive efficiency of the population and enable them at each level of employment to produce more output than they could in the absence of these government services. The production function that relates to that economy is the one labelled $\phi(n, g^*)$, as representing the maximum output that can be achieved no matter what services the government provides. In other words, think of g^* as a level of government activity that maximizes the economy's productive potential.

We do not need to become bogged down here in controversies as to precisely what government services are involved in the production function. Certainly included are the provision of law and order, defense, and public health, in addition to some other activities provided by modern governments.

Just as the provision of productive goods and services by the government shifts the production function, so it also shifts the labor demand curve. Recall from the discussion in Chapter 8 that the demand for labor curve is nothing other than the marginal product of labor curve. In the no-government economy of frame (a), the marginal product of labor is very low. Thus, the demand for labor curve in such an economy would be a curve such as that shown in frame (b) and labelled $n^d(g_0)$. In contrast, in the economy that has a government providing the output-maximizing volume of public goods and services, the marginal product of labor is much higher. This would be depicted in frame (b) as the curve $n^d(g^*)$.

Recall that the slope of the production function measures the marginal product of labor. The slope of the production function with no government is much lower than that of the production function with productive government activity. These differences in the slopes of the production function are reflected in the levels of the demand for labor curves.

C. How Taxes Affect the Supply of Labor

Government services are paid for by taxes. Governments levy taxes on all kinds of activities, but to keep the analysis simple, we shall suppose that all taxes are levied on labor income. What do taxes on labor income do to the

Figure 39.2 How Taxes Affect the Supply of Labor

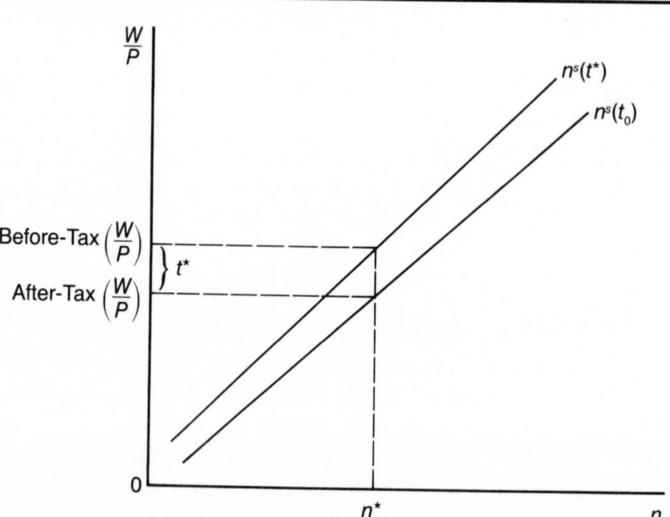

The supply of labor depends on after-tax real wages. Higher after-tax real wages induce a bigger labor supply. The higher the taxes, the higher before-tax real wages will have to be to induce any given labor supply. Thus a tax of t^* at an employment level n^* would shift the supply of labor curve from $n^s(t_0)$ to $n^s(t^*)$.

supply of labor? Although there are qualifications to any answer (which you will probably study in a course on public finance), the basic answer is that taxes lower the supply of labor. Figure 39.2 illustrates why this is so. In this figure the curve labelled $n^s(t_0)$ is the labor supply curve in an economy that has no taxes. Thus, if the wage rate was the amount labelled "after-tax (W/P)," then the quantity of labor supplied would be the amount labelled n^*.

Suppose now that the government was to levy a tax of an amount labelled t^*. Ask the question, How much would have to be offered in order to induce n^* workers to work in this new situation? The answer presumably is that the after-tax wage would have to be the same as the wage in the no-tax situation. This could only be achieved if the before-tax wage was the amount labelled on the vertical axis as "before-tax (W/P)." Thus, to induce a supply of labor n^*, the real wage would have to be higher, if taxes were t^*, by an amount t^* than they would have to be in a no-tax situation. The same would be true of any level of employment, and so the entire labor supply schedule would be shifted to the left of $n^s(t_0)$ to become the supply curve labelled $n^s(t^*)$. Clearly the higher the taxes, the further will the supply curve shift to the left.

D. How Efficient Government Raises Output and Employment

It is now possible to bring together the analysis of the two preceding sections and see how efficient government leads to a rise in both output and employment and also to a rise in real wages. There are two offsetting effects to be considered. First, the provision of government productive activities shifts the production function and demand for labor curve upwards. Second, the payment for these government activities through taxes has the effect of lowering the supply of labor. There is a strong presumption that the former expansionary activity strongly dominates the latter contractionary activity. Figure 39.3 shows how things work out.

This figure contains two frames just like Figure 39.1 did and frame (a) is identical to that in Figure 39.1. Frame (b) of Figure 39.3 brings together the demand for labor—frame (b) of Figure 39.1—with the supply of labor—Figure 39.2. First let us consider an economy with no government. This will be an economy with a production function $\phi(n, g_0)$ and a demand for labor $n^d(g_0)$. With no government there will be no taxes, and the labor supply curve would therefore be that labelled $n^s(t_0)$. Equilibrium in the labor market in this economy would occur at the employment level n_0 with the real wage $(W/P)_0$. The level of output in this economy would be read off from the production function in frame (a) as the amount y_0.

Contrast this economy with one in which there is a government that provides a level of services that makes it possible to raise output for each level of labor input, as depicted by the production function $\phi(n, g^*)$. In this case, the demand for labor would be $n^d(g^*)$. Assume that the government pays for its productive activities with the minimum possible taxes and that that level of taxes is t^* per worker. This would shift the supply of labor curve to $n^s(t^*)$. The equilibrium in this case occurs where the tax distorted labor supply curve cuts the government productivity-enhanced demand for labor curve at n^* and the

Figure 39.3
Efficient Government

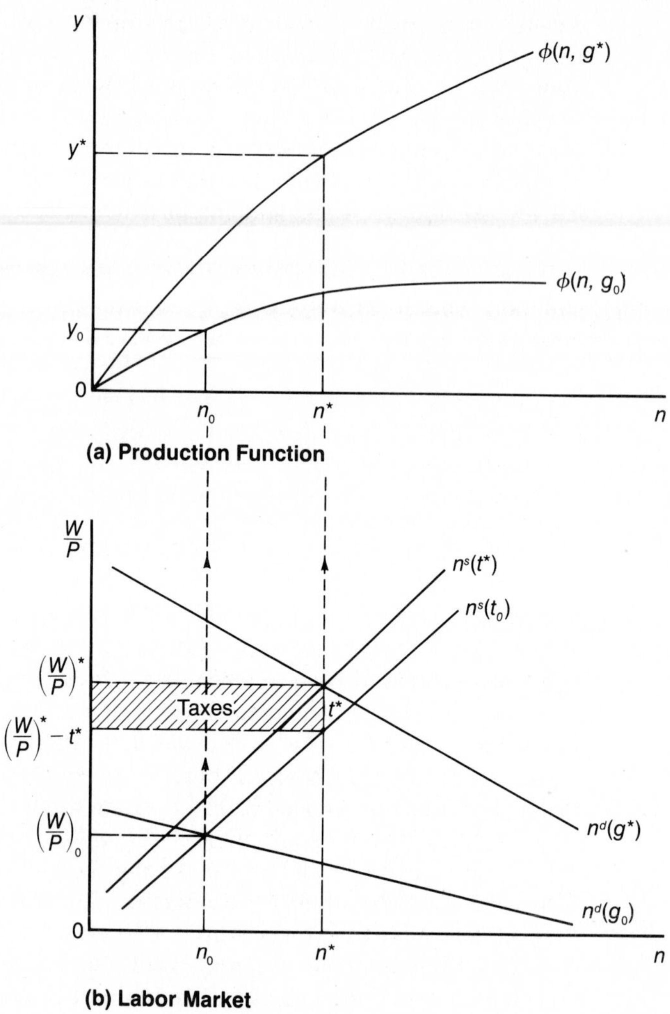

An efficient government will provide productive services that shift the production function up from $\phi(n, g_0)$ to $\phi(n, g^*)$ [frame (a)], with an associated upward shift in the demand for labor curve [frame (b)]. This government activity will be paid for by the minimum possible level of taxes, which will have a modest distorting effect in the labor market shifting the labor supply curve from $n^s(t_0)$ to $n^s(t^*)$. The resulting equilibrium will be one that has higher employment (n^*), output (y^*), and after-tax real wages $(W/P)^* - t^*$ than in the no-government case.

real wage rate $(W/P)^*$. The level of output in this economy is that read off from the higher production function $\phi(n, g^*)$ at y^*. Thus, in this economy, government has the effect of raising employment from n_0 to n^*, raising output from y_0 to y^*, and raising real wages from $(W/P)_0$ to $(W/P)^*$. Of course, the government has to be paid for with taxes, and the tax per worker of t^* multiplied by the number of workers n^* gives a total tax bill as indicated by the shaded area in frame (b). After-tax wages are $(W/P)^* - t^*$.

In terms of real world events, in the no-government economy, a large amount of productive labor over and above n_0 will be expended on self-protection and property protection, but only a small amount of goods and services (y_0) will be produced. People will be in a general state of belligerence and will not be very productive. In the economy with an efficient government, the government will be maintaining law and order (presumably with some equilibrium amount of violation taking place), and people will be freed from the need for self-protection and will be able to engage in productive work.

E. How Overgrown Government Lowers Output and Employment

It will by now be pretty obvious to you that a government that grows too big will actually lower output. This will happen because as government gets bigger and bigger, it contributes nothing extra to the productive capacity of the economy but has a negative effect on production as a result of the fact that higher taxes lower the labor supply.

Figure 39.4 illustrates an economy with an overgrown government. The equilibrium labelled y^*, n^*, $(W/P)^*$ is that for the economy with an efficient government as shown in Figure 39.3. The equilibrium marked y_0, n_0, $(W/P)_0$ is that for an economy with no government and exactly like that in Figure 39.3. Now suppose that government grows bigger than the efficient size shown in Figure 39.3. Specifically, suppose the government raises taxes substantially above the levels necessary to provide a volume of government services that maximizes the productive potential of the economy. It doesn't much matter what the government does with those taxes. The legislators may squander them on self-aggrandizement, they may give them to the poor, or they may use them to provide goods and services that would otherwise have been provided privately. The point is that the taxes are not spent on any activity that can enhance the productive capacity of the economy. Thus, the production function that is relevant remains that labelled $\phi(n, g^*)$. The higher taxes shift the supply of labor curve to the left to a position such as that labelled $n^s(t)_1$. The demand for labor remains at $n^d(g^*)$. Equilibrium occurs at the employment level n_1 and the real wage $(W/P)_1$. The output level associated with that employment level n_1 is y_1. Clearly, by raising taxes above the minimum level necessary to provide the output-maximizing volume of government services, the government has introduced a distortion in the labor market that reduces overall work effort and output. Real wages exceed $(WP)^*$—those that occur in the economy with an efficient government (Figure 39.3). After-tax wages are lower in the economy with the overgrown government because the government takes a bigger tax bite—as shown by the shaded area in frame (b).

THE "SUPPLY SIDE"

Figure 39.4 provides the essence of the supply-side argument. By lowering taxes and lowering the volume of unproductive government services provided with those taxes, it would be possible to raise output, raise employment, and raise after-tax real wages. You can see this directly by comparing the equilibrium y_1, n_1, $(W/P)_1 - t_1$ with the equilibrium y^*, n^*, $(W/P)^* - t^*$. Clearly, if the overgrown government was to reduce its size to the efficient size, output, employment, and after-tax wages would all rise.

Figure 39.4
Overgrown Government

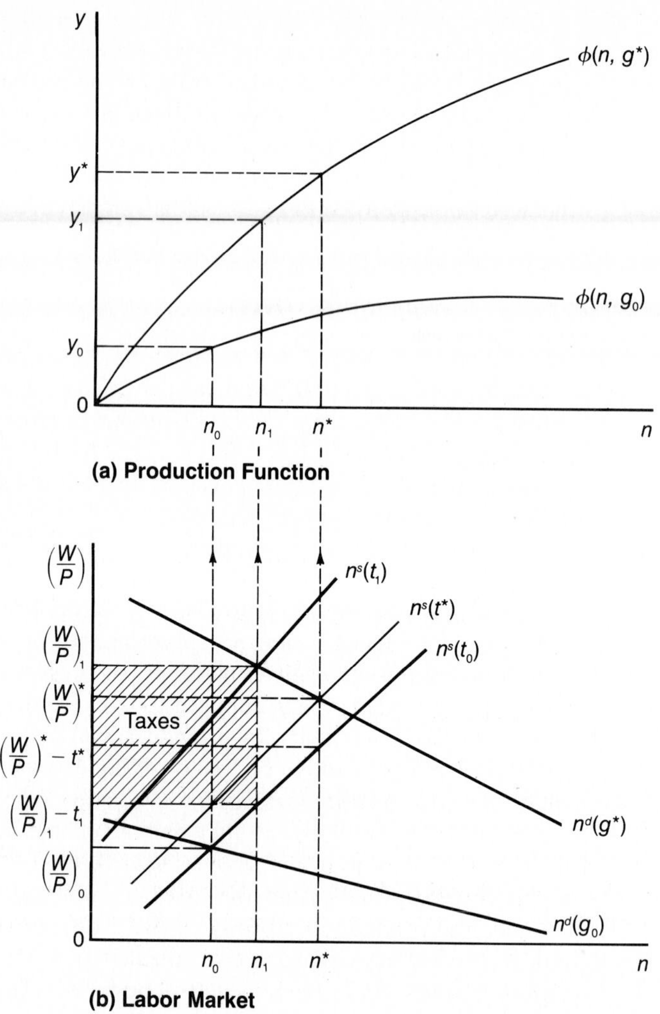

A government that grows too big is one that raises taxes over and above the levels necessary to pay for the efficient scale of government. As this happens, the distorting effect of taxes shifts the supply of labor curve to the left, thereby raising wages (before taxes) and lowering output and employment. After-tax real wages fall.

There is, of course, in any actual real-world situation, disagreement and room for genuine doubt as to which government activities are productive and which unproductive. To a larger degree disagreements between supply-siders and others turn not on the analysis contained in Figure 39.4 but on the empirical judgment concerning the productivity of government services. If reducing taxes involved reducing the provision of productive government services, then as taxes fell the production function would also fall, and the demand for labor curve would shift downwards. Whether or not such a reduction in government would raise or lower output and employment would

Figure 39.5
The Laffer Curve

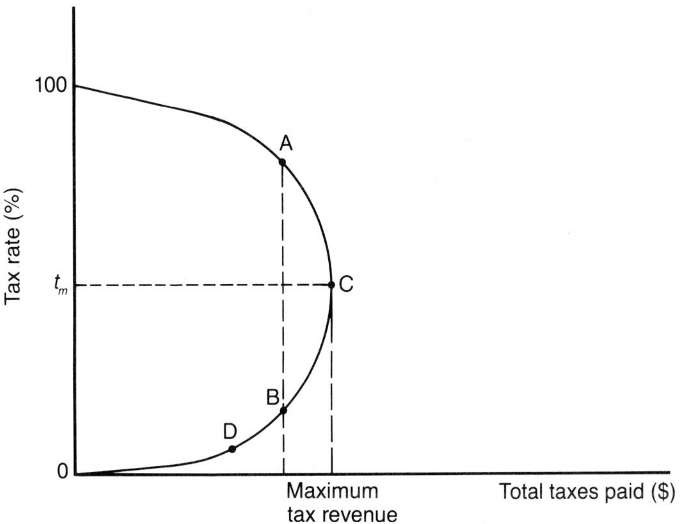

The Laffer curve shows the relationship between taxes paid and the rate of tax. At a zero tax rate no taxes are paid, and at a 100 percent tax rate no one will have any incentive to work (or do whatever other activities are being taxed), and so again no taxes will be paid. The general shape of the curve will be that shown so that at some tax rate (t_m), tax revenues are at a maximum.

depend on which of the two effects was stronger. If, at the margin, government activity is very unproductive and the distorting effects of taxes on labor supply are very severe, then a reduction in government would raise output and employment. If, in contrast, as the marginal government activities are slightly productive and the disincentive effects of taxes on labor supply only slight, then a reduction in government activity could lower output and employment. There is little agreement on which of these two effects dominate and not much in the way of solid empirical evidence that can readily settle the issue.

In the above comparison of an economy with an efficient government and an economy with an overgrown government, we have stumbled into a concept often used in discussion of supply-side matters—the so-called Laffer curve.[1] Figure 39.5 illustrates a Laffer curve. It is a curve that measures the tax rate on the vertical axis and the amount of taxes paid on the horizontal axis. The curve has the shape shown for a reason that, if not immediately obvious, will be obvious in a moment. If the tax rate was zero, fairly clearly no taxes would be paid. Thus, the Laffer curve starts at the origin of the diagram. If the tax rate was a 100 percent, then presumably nobody would do any work (or indulge in whatever other activity that tax is based on). Thus again, no revenue would be generated by the government, and no taxes would be paid. The Laffer curve therefore bends back on itself, starting at the origin when the tax rate is zero and returning to zero taxes raised when the tax rate is 100 percent.

[1]The Laffer curve is so-named because it was popularized by Professor Arthur B. Laffer of the University of Southern California.

For intermediate tax rates there is a range over which, as the tax rate rises, tax revenues also rise. This is the portion of the curve ODBC. For tax rates above that marked t_m, as tax rates are increased, revenues fall. This happens because the activity that is being taxed will decline at a faster percentage rate than the tax rate itself increases. Figure 39.5 has been drawn such that the revenue-maximizing tax rate is 50 percent. There is, however, no presumption that this will be the revenue-maximizing rate. Such a rate would vary and would depend on the slopes of the supply and demand curves in question. The economy with an efficient government shown in Figure 39.3 might be thought of as being at a point such as D on the Laffer curve. The economy with an overgrown government might be in a position such as that depicted by B on the Laffer curve.

A government that was interested in raising taxes to the maximum possible level, presumably to further the interests of bureaucrats and legislators, would levy taxes at the revenue-maximizing rate. It has sometimes been suggested, and some of the current supply-siders in the United States have joined in this suggestion, that taxes in the United States at the present time are so high that the economy is in a position like that shown as position A on the Laffer curve. A moment's reflection will suggest that although this is a possibility, it is unlikely. If the government had raised taxes to such a high level that their revenues were the same as they would be with a much lower rate of taxes, then the government would be denying itself some revenue and at the same time would be inflicting costs on the rest of the economy over and above those that would be inflicted at a maximum revenue situation. In other words, at position A on the Laffer curve, the economy would generate an output level below that being generated at position B on the Laffer curve.[2]

A key point to note is that it is unlikely that the economy is in a position like point A and much more likely that it is in a position like point B. If the economy is in a position like A, then it clearly pays to go to B, since that would involve the same tax revenues but more output and employment. However, if the economy is in a position like B, whether it would be desirable to move to a position like D depends on empirical judgments concerning the strength of the supply-side effects.

F. The Effect of Supply-Side Policies on the Price Level

Not much needs to be added to the analysis that you have already conducted in Chapter 12, Section B. There we analyzed the effects of various labor market shocks on the price level, showing that anything that lowered the level of aggregate supply would raise the price level. Exactly the same considerations apply to the supply-side analysis. Any tax change that raises output will

[2]Professors James Buchanan and Dwight Lee of the Virginia Polytechnic Institute have an ingenious argument that suggests that perhaps it would be possible for a government to get to a position like point A as a result of taking a too myopic view of the consequences of increasing tax rates: see James M. Buchanan and Dwight Lee, "Politics, Time and the Laffer Curve," *Journal of Political Economy*, 90, (August 1982), 816–19.

in effect shift the aggregate supply curve rightwards, thereby lowering the price level. This is why supply-siders believe that their policy recommendations will have advantageous effects on the inflation rate. It is important to notice, however, that even if supply-side policies are successful, they would have a once-and-for-all effect on the price level and no effect on the trend rate of inflation. That effect, as always, will be determined by the rate of growth of the money supply.

G. Extension of Supply-Side Analysis to Savings and Capital Accumulation

The entire analysis that has been conducted in terms of a short-run production function could also be extended to apply to longer-term savings and capital accumulation. Over time, the economy's productive potential grows as a result of technical progress and capital accumulation. The amount of this activity undertaken is determined by an equilibrium process much like the one that determines the level of employment. Other things being equal, the more capital the economy has, the lower will be the marginal product of that capital. The higher the marginal product of capital, the more will people seek to save and acquire capital. Taxes on the income from capital will lower the incentive to save and will lower the incentive to accumulate capital. These taxes will, therefore, act in exactly the same way as taxes on labor. They will reduce the amount of economic activity that is taking place and will lower the output of the economy.

H. Reagan's Supply-Side Policies

This final section will briefly examine the supply-side aspects of the Reagan economic program. It will not, however, go into any detail at all. It will simply help you to relate that program to the analysis that has been conducted in this chapter. For a more detailed description of the program, you should refer to the *Economic Report of the President* for January 1982 and 1983.[3]

The Supply-Side Program in a Nutshell

There are four key features to the Reagan supply-side program. They are:

1. The provision of more national defense.
2. Reductions in domestic programs.
3. Tax cuts.
4. Deregulation.

Supposed Effects (Claims by Supply-Siders)

What are the likely effects of a program having these four features? Let us examine this question not in the journalistic terms with which you are prob-

[3](Washington, D.C.: U.S. Government Printing Office, 1982 and 1983.)

ably familiar but in terms of the analysis that we have conducted in the previous sections of this chapter.

First, a rise in defense expenditure may be thought of as a provision of a larger volume of productive government activity. How much would be contributed by additional defense expenditure depends, of course, on the marginal productivity of the additional defense services provided. Presumably, the idea of the supply-siders would be that by providing more national defense, the government is providing a greater measure of security than would otherwise be available, and that this is either desirable for its own sake (security is a good that people value) or because it will enable (and perhaps induce) a greater measure of confidence in the medium- to long-term future, thereby encouraging a greater volume of savings and investment.

The reduction in domestic programs is presumably viewed as a reduction in either low-productivity or unproductive government activity. Taken together, the rise in defense spending and the cut in other programs would be viewed by a supply-sider as releasing resources for productive use, thereby shifting the aggregate production function upwards.

The tax cuts in the Reagan program are seen as increasing both the supply of labor and the supply of savings, thereby increasing the equilibrium volumes of employment and capital accumulation.

The deregulation aspects of the Reagan supply-side program were not analyzed in the previous sections of this chapter. You may, however, conveniently think of deregulation as being equivalent to the reduction of taxes and the reduction of (unproductive?) government expenditure. If the government imposes a regulation on a private individual or firm, the effect of that is to require that individual agent to undertake actions that would otherwise not be pursued. This causes the individual to divert resources from voluntary to involuntary uses. This aspect of regulation is exactly like the imposition of a tax that also diverts resources from voluntary to involuntary uses—from voluntary consumption and savings activity to the involuntary payment of taxes.

The other aspect of regulation is that it requires government itself to employ large numbers of professional and clerical labor simply to monitor the activities of those being regulated and to enforce the regulations. Thus, regulation imposes additional government expenditure and additional diversion of private resources from voluntary uses. The reduction of regulation seen in these terms would involve a reduction in both taxes and government spending. Its effects, therefore, would be exactly the same as the effects of reducing taxes and reducing government spending on unproductive activities that we have analyzed in earlier sections of this chapter.

In overall terms, the Reagan supply-side program adds up to a net increase in government spending and a net decrease in taxes. This arises because the defense-spending increases are greater than the cuts in spending on domestic programs. This means that the Reagan program has the effect of raising the federal budget deficit. Supporters of the supply-side view argue that this increase in the deficit is purely a short-run or transitory phenomenon. They predict that the supply-side policies will raise income by so much that the increase in overall tax revenues in the medium and longer term will be sufficient to offset the spending increase and put the federal budget in surplus.

These then, are the claims of the supply-siders. Are they justified?

Likely Effects of Supply-Side Programs

In evaluating the effects of supply-side programs such as those pursued by the Reagan administration, it is vital to distinguish between long-run and short-run effects. It seems likely (and is apparently confirmed by most empirical investigations) that, in the short run, the responsiveness of labor supply and the supply of savings to changes in taxes will be small. The key reason for this is that it is costly for people to change their behavior. They will be inclined to change their behavior only gradually in response to new conditions that call forth a different pattern of activity. Further, if there is some uncertainty as to the permanence of a change in policy, there will be even more reluctance to commit oneself to a change in behavior. In terms of the diagrams that we have used in this chapter, you can think of this as saying that in the short run, the supply curve of labor (and the supply curve of savings) is very steep. This means that, although a tax cut would indeed shift the labor supply curve (and the supply of savings curve) to the right, the amount of that rightward shift would be very small in the short run. In addition, the effects of changes in government activity on the overall productivity of the economy are likely to be slight in the short run. These two things taken together imply that the immediate and short-run effects of the Reagan supply-side policies are likely to be very small in terms of what they do to the level of employment and output.

There is an additional short-run consequence of policies such as those currently being pursued that is of considerable importance. It is the essence of the supply-side policies of the Reagan administration that labor (and other) resources be *reallocated*. In other words, certain activities will be decreased and others will be expanded. For example, less urban renewal and more defense would involve a shifting of resources away from building and civil engineering activities and into electronics and high-technology metals. These, of course, are just examples of many millions of reallocations of labor and other resources. Now when labor is reallocated, this does not take place costlessly. Workers leaving one type of job have to find another job. This involves a period of job search such as that analyzed in Chapter 11. When policies are pursued that increase the amount of reallocation going on in the economy, they also increase the amount of job-search activity. This also gives rise to an increase in unemployment.

We have already seen that the advocates of supply-side policies recognize that these policies, at least as being pursued by the Reagan administration, will have the effect of increasing the government's budget deficit in the short run. The analysis that we have just conducted concerning short-run effects agrees with this but would suggest adding an additional burden to the government's budget deficit, namely, the increased expenditures on unemployment compensation that are a necessary accompaniment of the increased amount of resource and labor reallocation taking place.

The long-run effects of consistently pursuing lower taxes and lower levels of unproductive government activity will certainly, in qualitative terms, be the same as those claimed by the supply-siders. Output, employment, and savings will all rise. How important this would be in *quantitative* terms is virtually impossible to say on the basis of what we currently know. Some believe that the effects would be slight; others that they would be enormous. What can be said with reasonable confidence, however, is that the long run may in fact be a very long way off. Notions of short run and long run in economic analysis are not clear statements about how long things take to happen in calendar time. Indeed, if properly understood, "short run" and "long run" are not things that happen after a specified period of time at all. Rather, they are things that happen after certain adjustments have been made. By "short run" we usually mean a situation in which adjustments have taken place in response to a given shock while holding constant all the stocks of the various capital (including human capital) assets in the economy. By "long run" we mean the adjustment that will have taken place when all the capital stocks (physical and human) have adjusted to a given shock. Clearly, adjusting the stock of human capital takes at least as long as the length of time that it takes to replace a generation. Individuals typically acquire their human capital in specific form and just once in a lifetime. Long-run adjustments, therefore, can be presumed to take a very large amount of calendar time. In the intervening period the effects that will be felt will be those that pertain to the short run.

We have already seen that in the short run, it is recognized that the federal deficit will rise as a result of Reagan's supply-side programs. If this deficit increase persists for a substantial amount of time, then it will place inflationary burdens on the economy. You know this from the analysis that we conducted in Chapter 31 where we analyzed the linkages between fiscal and monetary policy. This consideration has to be added to the other predictions coming from the supply-side policies concerning the behavior of the price level. It is true, as we saw earlier in this chapter, that a successful supply-side program that lowers taxes and lowers unproductive government activity will raise the full-employment level of output. With a given money supply this will indeed lower the price level. If, however, the supply-side program adds to the federal deficit for a substantial period of time, then this in itself will put pressure on the monetary authorities to increase the *growth rate* of the money supply, thereby leading to a higher rate of inflation.

There are no easy and ready ways of deciding how successful, over the long run, programs of the type being pursued by the Reagan administration will be. What can be said, however, fairly confidently, is that in the short run, such policies would be much more easily pursued if the federal budget was not badly unbalanced. This would involve seeking to cut out unproductive government spending wherever it may be found, regardless of whether it is in the defense or domestic programs area and finding savings at least equal to the short-run cut in tax revenues. By combining the supply-side programs with an overall federal budget balance, the danger of subsequent inflationary pressures would be avoided and the policies could be pursued with a greater likelihood of success.

Summary

A. Why Governments are Productive

Governments are productive because, by using their monopoly in coercion, they are able to reduce the resources involved in the protection of persons and property and are able to enforce public health standards that raise the productivity of labor. Governments do many other things that are productive, but there is controversy and imprecise knowledge concerning the productivity of these additional government activities as compared with the productivity of equivalent privately provided services. In addition, governments indulge in many activities that have either low or perhaps even negative productivity.

B. How Productive Government Activity Affects the Production Function and the Demand for Labor

Productive government activity can be viewed as shifting the production function upwards, so that higher output levels are attainable at each level of labor input. Similarly, the slope of the production function is increased or, equivalently, the marginal product of labor rises. This means that the demand for labor curve shifts upwards.

C. How Taxes Affect the Supply of Labor

The higher the taxes, the lower will be the supply of labor. The supply of labor will depend on the after-tax real wage. In general, the higher the after-tax real wage, the more labor will be supplied. Thus, a rise in taxes that lowers the after-tax wage rate will cause the labor supply curve to shift to the left.

D. How Efficient Government Raises Output and Employment

Efficient government raises output, employment, and real wages as a result of the operation of two offsetting forces, one of which clearly dominates. The dominant force is the rise in the production function and the rise in the demand for labor that results from the provision of productive government activity. To some degree offsetting this, although only partially so, is the effect of the taxes levied to pay for the government services. These lower the supply of labor. Nevertheless, the two effects combined (Figure 39.3) result in higher output, higher employment, and higher real wages.

E. How Overgrown Government Lowers Output and Employment

Government can grow too big in the sense that taxes continue to be increased and to be spent on activities that do not raise the production function and the marginal product of labor. When this happens, all the effects of increased government size are negative, and the supply of labor curve shifts to the left, thereby producing a lower level of employment, lower output, and a lower after-tax real wage (Figure 39.4).

F. The Effects of Supply-Side Policies on the Price Level

Any action that shifts the aggregate supply curve will, other things given, change the price level in the opposite direction. Thus, a rise in output (shifting aggregate supply to the right), resulting from supply-side policies, lowers the price level. Supply-side policies in and of themselves have no effect on the rate of inflation, which is determined by the growth rate of the money supply.

G. Extension of Supply-Side Analysis to Savings and Capital Accumulation

The supply-side analysis applied in this chapter to the labor market could be applied equally well to the market for capital goods and the supply of savings. Just as higher taxes on labor income are a disincentive to work, so high taxes on capital income are a disincentive to save. Lower savings result in lower capital accumulation and lower output. As an empirical matter, the importance of these effects is in dispute and is badly in need of detailed numerical measurement.

H. Reagan's Supply-Side Policies

The supply-side policies of the Reagan administration involve increasing defense spending, cutting spending on domestic programs, cutting taxes, and deregulating. In terms of the analysis of this chapter, this should be thought of as *attempting* to raise productive government spending and to cut unproductive government spending, thereby shifting the production function upwards. Tax cuts are designed to shift the supply of labor (and supply of savings) curves to the right. Deregulation is like cutting both taxes and government spending simultaneously. The hoped-for effects of these policies is a rise in output and employment. It is recognized that these effects will occur in the long term and that in the short term there will be a rise in the federal budget deficit. However, there are good reasons to believe that the short term may well last for a long time, so that the hoped-for effects may be so long in coming that the short-run budget deficit triggers a renewed burst of inflation in the intervening period. The policies would be more convincingly pursued with more vigorous cutting of unproductive government activity and a balanced federal budget.

Review Questions

1. What productive services do governments provide? List five government activities that you regard as definitely productive (*productive* meaning that the government can provide the services more efficiently than could the private sector); five activities that you think are neutral (meaning that you think that the private sector could provide them about as effectively as the government can); and finally, five activities that you think are definitely wasteful (meaning that you think that the activities either should not be pursued at all or that, if they are to be pursued, they should be pursued by the private sector).
2. How do productive government activities affect the production function?
3. Show the effects of a rise in the provision of some productive government service on the demand for labor.
4. What happens to the supply of labor if taxes increase? Is it always the case that the supply of labor curve shifts in the way presented in this chapter?
5. (This question should be done only by students who have studied the appropriate microeconomic theory of public finance.) Analyze the effects of a change in taxes on the supply of labor and on the demand for consumption

using indifference curve analysis. What do you hav[illegible]
"income effect" in order to ensure that a rise in taxes lo[illegible]
labor?

6. Show in a diagram how a balanced budget cut in taxes and [illegible] unproductive government spending affects the levels of output, employm[illegible] and the real wage.

7. Analyze the effects of the experiment described in the previous question on the price level.

8. Suppose that a tax cut induced an additional amount of savings. What would be the effect of the increased savings rate on the economy? (This is a harder question, and a full answer requires that you refer back to Chapter 38, which analyzed long-term growth.)

9. Set out the key features of the supply-side aspects of the Reagan economic program and review their likely effects.

U.S. Economic Links with the Rest of the World

The U.S. economy has extensive economic links with the rest of the world. In 1981, of every dollar spent in the United States, almost 13 cents represented expenditure on goods imported from other countries. Similarly, of every dollar's worth of goods produced, 12 cents worth was sent abroad as exports. Although when measured as percentages of U.S. GNP, these amounts are not large, in absolute terms they are enormous. The United States is one of the world's most important international trading countries. In the four-year period from 1978–1981, the United States had an overall surplus in its trading and capital transactions with the rest of the world of almost $14 billion. During that same four-year period, the value of the U.S. dollar in terms of other currencies sank and then rose again by almost 12 percent. Movements against some of the stronger currencies such as the German mark and the Japanese yen were even more pronounced.

In these final chapters a broader view of the problems of macroeconomics will be taken so as to enable you to understand why the United States has experienced in recent years a massive balance of payments surplus and why the foreign exchange value of the U.S. dollar has fluctuated so much. It will also show you how shocks emanating in other countries affect the U.S. economy and how those in the United States affect the rest of the world. This brief chapter will get you started on that process by clarifying some basic concepts and definitions.

This chapter pursues two tasks, which are to:

(a) Know the definitions of the current account, the capital account, the official settlements account, and the balance of payments.

(b) Know the definitions of a foreign exchange rate, an effective exchange rate, a fixed exchange rate, a flexible exchange rate, and a managed floating exchange rate.

A. Definitions of the Balance of Payments

The Current Account

The current account of the balance of payments is the account in which the values of the flows of goods and services and other *current* receipts and payments between residents of the United States and residents of the rest of the world are recorded. Specifically, the current account contains the items shown in Table 40.1. (The values of the items for 1980 are indicated to give you a feel for the orders of magnitude involved.)

The receipts from U.S. residents come from merchandise exports, exports of various types of services, income from investments made in the rest of the world by American residents, and from what are known as unilateral transfers from foreigners. The payments made by U.S. residents are those for merchandise imports, imports of other services, the payment of dividends and interest on foreign investments in the United States, and finally, unilateral transfers by Americans to the rest of the world. In the balance of payments current account shown in Table 40.1, some of these items appear in what are called *gross* terms and others in what are called *net* terms. Items recorded in gross terms appear on both sides of the balance of payments account. That is, the total amount received and the total amount paid appear in the account. Items shown in net terms record only the difference between the total amount received and the total amount paid. Thus, for example, merchandise trade appears as merchandise exports minus merchandise imports in lines 1 and 2, with the net of merchandise trade in line 3. In contrast, travel and transportation (line 8) are shown only as the net difference between the total amount spent by foreigners in the United States and the total amount spent by Americans in the rest of the world.

Let us examine the various items appearing in the current account of the balance of payments a little more closely. Clearly, the biggest receipt from the

TABLE 40.1
The Balance of Payments Current Account, 1980

	ITEM	$ MILLION	$ MILLION
	1. Merchandise exports	223,966	
less	2. Merchandise imports	−249,308	
equals	3. Net merchandise trade		−25,342
	4. Investment receipts	75,936	
less	5. Investment payments	−43,174	
equals	6. Net investment income		32,762
	7. Net military transactions		− 2,515
	8. Net travel and transportation		− 798
	9. Other services, net		6,674
	10. Remittances, pensions, and other unilateral transfers		− 7,056
equals	11. Balance on current account		$ 3,723

SOURCE: *Economic Report of the President*. (Washington, D.C.: U.S. Government Printing Office, 1982), p. 346.

rest of the world is that arising from merchandise exports. In 1980 this item was almost a quarter of a trillion dollars. It represents the value of all the physical goods exported from the United States. Some of these exports are food, beverages, tobacco, and unprocessed raw materials, but the vast bulk of U.S. exports is manufactured goods and much of it large-scale capital equipment such as, for example, airplanes made by Boeing, jet engines made by G.E. and Pratt & Whitney, and electronic and communications equipment, as well as a vast variety of smaller capital and consumer goods. Offset against these receipts are the payments that Americans make to foreigners for merchandise imports. This magnitude was greater in 1980 than the amount of merchandise exports. It represents the physical goods shipped to the United States and bought by Americans. It includes, of course, many raw materials and other basic inputs used by American industry. It also includes manufactured goods, particularly such items as cars and small electronic equipment as well as clothing made in the Pacific basin countries of Southeast Asia. Line 3 shows the net difference between the merchandise exports and imports of the United States.

The next three lines in Table 40.1 record the transactions arising from U.S. investments in the rest of the world and foreign investments in the United States. Line 4 shows the payments by foreigners to Americans of dividends and interest on U.S. investments abroad. This includes payments by multinational corporations to their parent companies of any profits remitted from foreign operations. Also included are interest payments by foreign governments to Americans who hold foreign government debt. Investment payments (line 5) are payments by American individuals and corporations to foreigners of dividends and interest on U.S. stocks and securities held abroad. Line 6 shows the net value of these transactions. Evidently, this item is the largest single net receipt of Americans, indicating that Americans own more assets abroad than are owned by foreigners in the United States.

The next three items (lines 7–9) show the net receipts or payments by Americans on various "service" transactions. These are transactions that do not involve the physical movement of goods but rather the rendering of services and the payment for those services. As the major partner in various international alliances such as NATO and SEATO, the United States gives military aid to a variety of countries. The net payments on military services made abroad are shown in line 7. Travel and transportation services are a major feature of international trading activity. They are shown in line 8. These represent the net payments by Americans to the rest of the world on transport facilities connected with the import and export of merchandise as well as international travel expenses for business or vacation paid by individual Americans—minus similar expenditures by foreigners in the United States. In addition to military and travel services there is, of course, a whole variety of other services that may be traded internationally. Prominent among these are banking and insurance services connected with the finance and security of international trade. The net value of these services is shown as line 9.

The final item in the current account of the balance of payments represents what are called *unilateral transfers.* These are payments that do not represent compensation for the direct rendering of a service or the transfer of physical goods. A good example of a unilateral transfer would be the foreign aid given by the U.S. government to a foreign government or gifts by churches in the United States to various underprivileged groups in the rest of the world.

The net of all these items—the net balance on merchandise trade, on investment income, on the various service transactions, and on unilateral transfers—represents the balance on the current account. Thus line 11 is equal to the sum of all the net balances shown in the right-hand column of Table 40.1. (There is a slight rounding error, so that the total on line 11 is not quite equal to the sum of the numbers above it.)

It is useful to think of an individual analogy to the country's current account balance. The merchandise and services of a country can be thought of as being analogous to an individual's labor income. That is, from the viewpoint of the country as a whole, merchandise exports and service exports are similar to the receipt of wages and salaries and other fees for labor services from the viewpoint of an individual. Investment receipts are analogous to income from investments made by an individual. Finally, on the receipts side of the account, unilateral transfers are analogous to gifts. On the outgoing side, merchandise imports and service imports are analogous to an individual's expenditures on consumption and capital goods. Investment payments are analogous to an individual's payment of interest on loans made to him by, for example, banks and mortagage companies; and unilateral transfers are the equivalent of gifts made by the individual to others.

A moment's reflection will reveal that for an individual, the current account balance just described represents the net addition to (surplus) or subtraction from (deficit) his wealth. If an individual has a current account surplus, he is becoming wealthier in the sense that assets are being acquired and/or liabilities are being paid off. It is exactly the same for a country. If a country has a current account surplus, its residents in aggregate have become wealthier in the sense that their assets have increased (and/or their liabilities have decreased). Conversely, if a country has a current account deficit, it has become poorer in the sense that it now has fewer assets or more liabilities than previously.

The Capital Account

The capital account records the receipts from nonresidents and payments made to nonresidents arising from the issuing of new debt or the repayment of old debt. For example, if IBM sells bonds some of which are bought by residents of other countries, the money that IBM receives on the sale of those bonds would appear as an import of capital into the United States. It would therefore be recorded as a receipt in the U.S. capital account. Equivalently, if a resident of Canada buys an apartment in Florida for $50,000, using (say) a Canadian bank deposit, when the apartment is paid for, there will be a capital inflow of $50,000 into the United States, and that too will be recorded in the capital account as a capital import. On the other side of the capital account, if a foreign corporation or government issues new debt, some of which is bought by U.S. residents, then the payments to those foreign corporations and governments will appear as an export of capital from the United States. Also, the purchase of property abroad by Americans using U.S. funds will appear as a capital export.

definition

The difference between capital imports and capital exports represents a country's capital account balance. In 1980, the U.S. capital account balance was a deficit of $37 billion. That is, in 1980, the capital exports of the United States exceeded its capital imports by $37 billion.

Another individual analogy may be helpful. The capital account of an individual is a statement of the receipts of that individual arising from the negotiation of new loans minus the outlays for paying off old loans. Thus, for example, if an individual negotiated a bank loan for $10,000 and a mortgage for $40,000 and repaid a charge card account outstanding of $2,000, that individual would have a capital account surplus of $48,000.

The Offical Settlements Account

The official settlements account records the net receipts and payments of gold and foreign currency that result from the current account and capital account transactions just described. The balance on the official settlements account, known more simply as the *official settlements balance*, is the change in the foreign exchange reserves less the change in official borrowing of the country. It is, if everything is accurately measured, exactly equal to the sum of the current account balance and the capital account balance. By accounting convention, the official settlements balance is defined as the negative of the sum of the current account and capital account balance so that when the balances on all three accounts are added together the resulting sum is always zero.

Another individual analogy might be helpful here. Suppose an individual has a current account deficit of, say, $50,000 in some particular year in which perhaps a house and some furnishings and other durable goods have been bought. That is, in the particular year the individual received, from the sale of labor and in interest and dividends and gifts, $50,000 less than was spent on goods and services. Suppose further that the individual negotiated loans such that there was a net capital account surplus of $40,000. If the individual spent $50,000 in excess of income and received $40,000 from new loans, where did the difference of $10,000 come from? It must be the case that the individual used $10,000 of the cash balances that were previously being held. If this were not so, the individual's expenditure could not have exceeded total receipts by the $10,000 that they did. Thus, the individual analogy of the official settlements balance is simply the change in the individual's cash balances—his bank account and currency holdings.

Although the individual's cash holdings have fallen, in this example, by $10,000, this would be recorded (using the accounting convention noted above) as a positive balance on the individual's equivalent of the official settlements account.

The Balance of Payments

In Chapters 41 to 43 you will study the theory of the balance of payments. It will be convenient, and more natural, when studying this theory, if you think of the balance of payments simply as the sum of the balances on the current and capital accounts and not as the official settlements balance. The magnitude of the balance of payments, so defined, will be the same as the official settlements balance but its algebraic sign will be reversed. Thus, when the sum of the current and capital accounts is positive we shall call that a balance of payments surplus, even though, as measured by the balance of payments accountants, the official settlements balance is negative.

The U.S. Balance of Payments, 1971–1981 The U.S. balance of payments accounts—current account, capital account, and official settlements account—for the years 1971–1981 are set out in Table 40.2. As you can see, the United States has typically experienced a surplus on its current account, although the first two years shown and the years 1977–1979 are an exception to this. The capital account of the United States is always in deficit. This means that Americans are constantly investing more abroad than foreigners are investing in the United States. The magnitude of the capital account deficit fluctuates but typically has been in excess of $10 billion and, in the record year of 1980, reached $37 billion.

The official settlements balance (column 4 of Table 40.2) has to be read carefully. Remember that a positive amount means a deficit on the official settlements account, and a negative amount means a surplus. Evidently the United States has typically been in a deficit in its overall balance of payments. The years 1979 and 1981 are the only exceptions to this. The U.S. deficit on its official settlements account in effect represents the net creation of dollars held as reserves by other countries. With a continuously growing world economy there is a continuous growth in the demand for U.S. dollars, and therefore to some extent an ongoing official settlements balance deficit may be regarded as normal. Over and above this, however, through the 1970s the world has been experiencing substantial inflation, so that, in part, the ongoing official settlements deficit of the United States represents a rise in the world stock of dollars, matched by a rise in world prices.

The theoretical concepts of the current account balance, capital account balance, and official settlements balance add up to zero. In practice, however, there are problems of measuring international transactions. In recent years

TABLE 40.2
The U.S. Balance of Payments, 1971–1981 ($ MILLION)

YEAR	(1) CURRENT ACCOUNT	(2) CAPITAL ACCOUNT	(3) STATISTICAL DISCREPANCY	(4) OFFICIAL SETTLEMENTS BALANCE
1971	−1,433	−16,694	−9,779	25,040
1972	−5,795	−17,963	−1,879	10,289
1973	7,140	− 9,734	−2,654	5,248
1974	2,124	−9,281	−1,620	8,777
1975	18,280	−28,693	5,753	4,660
1976	4,384	−25,259	10,367	10,508
1977	−14,068	−18,508	−2,465	35,041
1978	−14,773	−29,027	11,866	31,934
1979	−446	−10,009	25,212	−14,757
1980	1,520	−37,116	28,870	6,726
1981	4,471	−29,959	25,809	−321

SOURCE: *Survey of Current Business*, June 1982, p. 43.
Notes: Column (1) is line 79; column (3) is line 75; column (4) is the sum of lines 80 and 81; column (2) is the sum of columns (1), (3), and (4) with the sign reversed.

these measurement problems have become very serious. The third column of Table 40.2 shows the extent of the measurement error by recording the statistical discrepancy. This is the discrepancy between the sum of the three accounts as measured by the national accounting statisticians.

The statistical discrepancy is one that arises from the mismeasurement of the current account and private capital account transactions. There is no way of knowing the extent to which this discrepancy should be allocated to each of these two accounts, and so it is left as a separate item. It is somewhat disquieting to note that in the last three years, the statistical discrepancy has been much bigger than either the official settlements balance or the current account balance, and it has been, on the average, of comparable size to the capital account balance itself. It may be inferred from this that there is considerable uncertainty concerning the facts about the U.S. balance of payments. The fourth column, however, the official settlements balance, may be regarded as known with certainty since this represents transactions that go through the official books of the U.S. Treasury, the Fed, and the central banks of other countries. The official settlements balance is, therefore, a firm number.

B. Exchange Rate Definitions

Foreign Exchange Rate

A foreign exchange rate is the relative price of two national monies. It expresses the number of units of one currency that must be paid in order to acquire a unit of some other currency. There are two ways in which a relative price may be defined. It may be expressed as so many units of *a* per unit of *b*, or as so many units of *b* per unit of *a*. For example, the average exchange rate between the U.S. dollar ($U.S.) and the pound sterling (£) in 1980 was $U.S. 2.33 per £. This may be expressed equivalently as 43 pence (UK) per U.S. dollar.

It is always necessary to be precise as to which way the exchange rate is being defined. When the value of a currency *rises* (called *appreciation*), the exchange rate, when expressed as units of domestic currency per unit of foreign currency, *falls*; but when expressed the other way, as units of foreign currency per unit of domestic currency, the exchange rate *rises*. Conversely, when the value of a currency *falls* (called *depreciation*), the exchange rate, when expressed in units of domestic currency per unit of foreign currency, *rises*; but expressed the other way, as units of foreign currency per unit of domestic currency, the exchange rate *falls*. Think carefully about these distinctions and work out one or two simple numerical examples.

An Effective Exchange Rate

There is not, of course, only one foreign exchange rate. Rather, there are as many foreign exchange rates as there are foreign currencies. The more commonly encountered exchange rates are those between the U.S. dollar and the currencies of the major trading partners of the United States such as the Canadian dollar, the British pound, the French franc, the German mark, and the Japanese yen. So as to be able to measure the value of one currency in relation to an average of other currencies the concept of the *effective exchange rate* is used.

The effective exchange rate is an index number—just like the Consumer Price Index, for example. This index number is calculated as a weighted average of the value of one currency in terms of all other currencies where the weights reflect the importance of each currency in the exports and imports of the country in question.

If we denote the effective exchange rate in some period, t, by EER_t, the formula with which EER_t may be calculated is

$$EER_t = \left\{\frac{a_1 E_{1_0} + a_2 E_{2_0} + \cdots + a_n E_{n0}}{a_1 E_{1_t} + a_2 E_{2_t} + \cdots + a_n E_{n_t}}\right\} \cdot 100 \qquad \textbf{(40.1)}$$

In this formula, the a's represent weights—the fraction of U.S. international trade with country 1 is a_1, the fraction with country 2, a_2, and so on. The E's represent exchange rates between the U.S. dollar and each other currency—E_1 being the number of U.S. dollars per unit of the currency of country 1, E_2 being the number of U.S. dollars per unit of the currency of country 2, and so on. The subscript t denotes the current period and the subscript 0 denotes the base period—the period for which the effective exchange rate is, by definition, 100.

The effective exchange rate of the U.S. dollar is calculated by the International Monetary Fund using this type of formula. You should be careful to note that the effective exchange rate will behave in the same way as a measure of a single exchange rate expressed as the number of units of foreign currency per unit of domestic currency. That is, when the effective exchange rate falls in value the domestic currency depreciates. Conversely, when the effective exchange rate rises in value the domestic currency appreciates.

Instead of calculating an effective exchange rate using Equation (40.1)—the type of calculation performed by the International Monetary Fund—we could alternatively calculate an effective exchange rate which represents the number of units of domestic currency per unit of foreign currency. Such a calculation would be performed by using Equation (40.2).

$$E_t = \left\{\frac{a_1 E_{1_t} + a_2 E_{2_t} + \cdots + a_n E_{n_t}}{a_1 E_{1_0} + a_2 E_{2_0} + \cdots + a_n E_{n0}}\right\} \qquad \textbf{(40.2)}$$

As you will see by comparing Equation (40.2) with Equation (40.1) the effective exchange rate E is equal to 100 divided by EER. The effective exchange rate measured by E behaves in the opposite way to EER. When the value of E rises the domestic currency depreciates and when the value of E falls the domestic currency appreciates. When EER is equal to 100, E is equal to 1.

The effective exchange rate expressed as E is a more natural definition to use for the purposes of conducting macroeconomic analysis. If a foreign price index is multiplied by the effective exchange rate E it becomes, in effect, a domestic price index. That is, a price expressed in foreign currency units is converted into a price expressed in domestic currency units by multiplying

TABLE 40.3
The Effective Exchange Rate of the U.S. Dollar, 1970–1982

YEAR	EFFECTIVE EXCHANGE RATE	E
1970	119.2	0.84
1971	116.1	0.86
1972	107.8	0.93
1973	98.8	1.01
1974	101.1	0.99
1975	100.0	1.00
1976	105.2	0.95
1977	104.7	0.96
1978	95.7	1.04
1979	93.7	1.07
1980	93.9	1.06
1981	105.7	0.95
1982	118.1	0.83

SOURCE: 1970–1981: *International Financial Statistics Yearbook*, 1982, pp. 464–65.
1982: *International Financial Statistics*, April 1983, p. 428.

that price by E. It is the definition of the exchange rate based on Equation (40.2) that we shall use in subsequent chapters when analyzing the behavior of an open economy.

The U.S. Effective Exchange Rate, 1972–1982 The effective exchange rate of the U.S. dollar since 1970 (the first year for which the IMF calculates figures) is set out in Table 40.3. Alongside it is the effective exchange rate defined as E. The index is normalized as 100 in 1975 (1 for the E definition). The effective exchange rate has varied between a low of 93.7 in 1979 and a high of 119.2 in 1970. Between 1970 and 1973 there was a near 17% effective depreciation of the U.S. dollar. It then gradually appreciated by about 6% over the next four years. There then followed a depreciation of about 12% in the period between 1976 and 1980. Since 1980 the U.S. dollar has appreciated by more than 25%.

The next three chapters will present an analysis of the forces that influence the course of the exchange rate. Before proceeding with that task, however, three more definitions are needed.

A Fixed Exchange Rate

A fixed exchange rate regime is one in which the Fed declares a central or par value at which it will act to maintain the value of its currency. It also usually involves declaring what is known as an *intervention band.* That is, in declaring a fixed exchange rate, the central bank announces that if the exchange rate rises above the par value by more than a certain percentage amount, then it will intervene in the foreign exchange market to prevent the rate from moving any further away from the par value. Likewise, if the rate falls below the par value by a certain percentage amount, the central bank declares that it will intervene to prevent the rate from falling any further.

In order to maintain a fixed exchange rate, the central bank stands ready to use its stock of foreign exchange reserves to raise or lower the quantity of money outstanding so as to maintain its price relative to the price of some other money.

From 1945 to 1972 the Western world operated on a fixed exchange rate system sometimes called the Bretton Woods system. This name derives from the fact that the plan for the world monetary system, which survived for 30 years after the war, was negotiated at Bretton Woods, near Washington, D.C., by John Maynard Keynes and Harry D. White. This system pegged the world's monetary system to gold. This was achieved by the United States declaring that one fine ounce of gold was worth $35 U.S. Each country then defined its own currency value in terms of the U.S. dollar. Under the Bretton Woods fixed exchange rate system, the United States took no responsibility for maintaining the exchange rates between the U.S. dollar and other currencies. Its job was to maintain the price of gold at $35 U.S. per ounce. Each of the other countries was then left to worry about its own exchange rate against the U.S. dollar. Thus, for example, if the pound sterling began to fall in value to the lower limit or to rise in value to the upper limit of the exchange rate band, the Bank of England (the central bank of the United Kingdom) would intervene in the foreign exchange market, exchanging U.S. dollars from its foreign exchange reserves for pounds, or exchanging pounds for U.S. dollars, in order to keep the value of the pound inside the target band.

A Flexible Exchange Rate

A flexible exchange rate—sometimes called a *floating exchange rate*—is one that is determined by market forces. The central bank declares no target value for the exchange rate and has no direct interest in the value of the exchange rate. The central bank holds a constant stock of foreign exchange reserves—or even a zero stock—and does not intervene in the foreign exchange market to manipulate the price of its currency.

A Managed Floating Exchange Rate

A managed floating exchange rate is one in which the exchange rate is manipulated by the central bank, but the rate is not necessarily being held constant. Usually, a managed floating regime is one in which the central bank announces that it is floating, but the bank does not give any indication to the market concerning the course that it would like to see the exchange rate follow. It does, however, have a view about the appropriate behavior of the exchange rate, and it intervenes in order to achieve its desires. This method of operating the foreign exchange market is one that gives the most difficulty to speculators. They not only have to speculate on what other private individuals on the average will be doing, but they also have to make predictions about central bank intervention behavior.

Summary

A. Definitions of the Balance of Payments

The current account is the account that records the values of current goods and services sold abroad, the purchases of goods and services from abroad, debt interest receipts and payments, and unilateral transfers received from and paid abroad.

The capital account records the receipts and payments between residents and nonresidents arising from the issue of new debt or the retirement of old debt.
The official settlements account records the movements in gold and foreign currency reserves (adjusted by any official borrowing) resulting from the net of the balances on the current and capital accounts. By accounting convention it is measured as the negative of the sum of the current and capital account balances so that the sum of the balances on all three accounts is always zero.
The balance of payments is defined as the sum of the balances on the current and capital accounts or, equivalently, as the negative of the official settlements balance.

B. Exchange Rate Definitions

A foreign exchange rate is the relative price between two currencies.
An effective exchange rate is an index representing the relative price between one national currency and an average of other currencies. The weights on other currencies in the average reflect the importance of each currency in the international trade of the country in question.
A fixed exchange rate is one that takes on a value declared by and maintained by the active intervention of the central bank.
A flexible exchange rate is an exchange rate, the value of which is determined purely by market forces, with no direct central bank intervention.
A managed floating exchange rate is one that is manipulated by the central bank but it is not manipulated according to any preannounced rules.

Review Questions

1. Divide the following items into four categories: those items that belong in (a) the current account, (b) the capital account, (c) the official settlements account, and (d) none of the balance of payments accounts:

1. Your summer vacation expenses in Europe.
2. The government of Quebec's receipts for the sale of bonds to U.S. residents.
3. The Bank of Montreal's purchase of U.S dollar Travelers' Cheques from the American Express Company.
4. The transfer by the Bank of England to the Fed of 1,000 ounces of gold.
5. U.S. imports of Japanese cars.
6. U.S. exports of wheat.
7. The takeover of a Canadian corporation by a U.S. corporation.
8. The payment of interest on its bonds by the U.S. government.
9. The money brought to the United States by newly arrived immigrants.
10. U.S. aid to poor countries.

2. Using the following items and numbers, construct the balance of payments accounts of the hypothetical economy:

ITEM	$MILLION
Capital imports	2000
Debt interest received from abroad	800
Exports of goods and services	1000
Capital exports	1800
Gifts made to foreigners	100
Imports of goods and services	1100
Debt interest paid abroad	700
Rise in gold and foreign exchange reserves	400

(a) What is the statistical discrepancy?
(b) What is the current account balance?
(c) What is the capital account balance?
(d) What is the balance on the official settlements account?
(e) What is the balance of payments?

3. What is a foreign exchange rate?
4. What is an effective exchange rate?
5. What is a fixed exchange rate? How is it kept fixed?
6. What is a flexible exchange rate?
7. What is a managed floating exchange rate? How is it "managed"?

41

The Basic Model of the Balance of Payments and the Exchange Rate

The balance of payments and the exchange rate are frequently in the news, although there is less concern about the balance of payments in the United States than in most other countries. Nevertheless, the state of the U.S. balance of payments is of crucial importance for both the United States and the rest of the world. The bigger the U.S. balance of payments deficit, the more dollars are being piled up in the rest of the world and the more that prices will rise. Rising prices will in turn feed back to affect the U.S. economy.

The importance of the exchange rate for Americans is much more obvious and clear than is the balance of payments. Over the last few years of floating exchange rates, the U.S. dollar has, on the average, depreciated strongly against other currencies, although it has recently regained most of the ground that it had lost. Nevertheless, these gyrations in the foreign exchange value of the U.S. dollar have an important influence not only on vacation travelers to Europe and other parts of the world but also on the U.S. economy as a whole.

This chapter deals with the basic forces that determine the balance of payments and the exchange rate.[1] You are going to discover that there is a great deal of mythology about these matters and that the factors that actually determine the balance of payments and the value of the U.S. dollar have very little to do with the factors that the popular mythology supposes to be relevant. In addition, this chapter continues the analysis of inflation begun in Chapter 12. In particular, it extends the analysis of inflation to an open economy with international trading and investment links with the rest of the world. You will discover how the analysis of that earlier chapter needs modification in order to understand the inflationary process of a fixed exchange rate economy. You will also discover that the analysis of Chapter 12 emerges with

---

[1]The origins of this theory, a theory that has not changed much in more than two hundred years, is David Hume, "Of the Balance of Trade," *Essays: Moral, Political and Literacy* (London: Oxford University Press, 1963), pp. 316–33; first published in 1741. An excellent modern restatement of Hume's theory, in slightly more general terms than that given in this chapter, is Harry G. Johnson, *Further Essays in Monetary Economics* (London: George Allen and Unwin Ltd., 1972), pp. 229–49.

little need for modification in the case of an economy operating on a flexible exchange rate.

You have five tasks in this chapter, which are to:

(a) Understand the connection between the money supply and the foreign exchange reserves.
(b) Understand the "law of one price": (1) purchasing power parity (PPP), and (2) interest rate parity (IRP).
(c) Understand how the balance of payments is determined when the exchange rate is fixed.
(d) Understand how the exchange rate is determined in a flexible exchange rate regime.
(e) Understand how the balance of payments and the exchange rate are linked in a managed floating regime.

A. Money Supply and Foreign Exchange Reserves

The Banking Sector Balance Sheets

As a preliminary to understanding the factors that determine the balance of payments and the exchange rate, it is necessary to understand the connection between the money supply and the country's stock of foreign exchange reserves. This connection is most readily seen by considering the items in the balance sheets of the Fed and the commercial banks (columns 3 and 4 of Table 4.2, Chapter 4) and by examining the balance sheet of what is called the *consolidated banking sector*. The consolidated banking sector is the Fed and the commercial banks viewed as a whole. Table 41.1 sets out the relevant balance sheets. (You might like to refer back to Chapter 4 on aggregate balance sheet accounting to see how these balance sheets fit in with those in the other sectors of the economy.)

First consider the balance sheet of the Fed—the first part of Table 41.1. Its assets are aggregated into two items: gold and foreign exchange reserves, and domestic credit. The gold represents actual gold in the vaults of the Fed. The foreign exchange reserves are either bank accounts that the Fed maintains with other central banks (i.e., central banks of other countries) or highly liquid foreign currency denominated securities. From the point of view of the country as a whole, the stock of gold and foreign exchange reserves serves the same purpose as notes and coins and a checking account do for you as an individual. Denote the stock of gold and foreign exchange reserves as F.

The second item in the Fed's balance sheet is the stock of government securities that the Fed has purchased. You will recall that the Fed creates a monetary base by buying government securities, either from the government directly or from the general public, and makes the purchase with newly created money. The whole collection of securities held by the Fed is called *domestic credit*. Denote the domestic credit of the Fed as DC_c.

Apart from miscellaneous items such as real estate, which may be ignored, these two items—gold and foreign exchange reserves, and domestic credit—constitute the entire stock of assets of the Fed.

TABLE 41.1
Banking System Balance Sheets

FED			
Assets		Liabilities	
Gold and foreign exchange reserves	F	Monetary base	MB
Domestic credit	DC_c		
COMMERCIAL BANKS			
Assets		Liabilities	
Notes and coins plus deposits at the Fed	MB_b	Deposits	D
Domestic credit	DC_b		
CONSOLIDATED BANKING SECTOR			
Assets		Liabilities	
Gold and foreign exchange reserves	F	Notes and coins in circulation with the public $(MB - MB_b)$	MB_p
Domestic credit $(DC_c + DC_b)$	DC	Deposits	D
Money supply	M	Money supply	M

The liability of the Fed is the monetary base. This is the stock of notes and coins that have been issued and are held either by the general public or in the tills of commercial banks, together with the stock of bank deposits maintained by the commercial banks at the Fed. Denote the monetary base as MB.

The Fed's balance sheet balances, so that

$$MB = F + DC_c$$

Next, consider the commercial banks. As in the case of the Fed, it is useful to distinguish between the two sets of assets. First, the commercial banks hold reserves in the form of notes and coins as well as deposits with the Fed. Denote commercial bank reserve assets as MB_b.

Notice that the same letters are being used to denote the commercial banks' reserves as those used to denote the monetary base because they are in fact the same thing. Part of the monetary base, MB, which is a liability to the Fed, is held as an asset by the commercial banks.

The other assets of the commercial banks have all been grouped into a single item—domestic credit of the commercial banks. This item consists of all the securities held by commercial banks, including any loan obligations that private individuals and firms have to the banks. Denote domestic credit of the commercial banks as DC_b.

Apart from some real estate, which may be neglected, these two items—reserve assets and domestic credit—constitute the entire assets of the commercial banks.

The liabilities of the commercial banks consist of the deposits that have been placed with them by households and firms. (You can think of deposits as checking account deposits only, and you can think of domestic credit as being net of savings deposits.) Denote these bank deposits as D.

The balance sheet of the commercial banks balances, so total deposits are equal to the stock of reserves plus the domestic credit. That is,

$$D = MB_b + DC_b$$

Next consider the consolidation of these two balance sheets. A consolidated balance sheet is simply the balance sheet that arises from adding together individual balance sheets and netting out any items that appear as an asset in one balance sheet and as a liability in another. To consolidate the two balance sheets of the Fed and the commercial banks, first notice that gold and foreign exchange reserves appear only once in the Fed's balance sheet and therefore will appear in the consolidated balance sheet. Domestic credit appears twice, as DC_c and DC_b. If these two items are added together, the domestic credit of the economy as a whole is obtained. Denote domestic credit as DC. So that you are absolutely clear what domestic credit is, let me elaborate a little. Domestic credit is the total of all the assets held by the Fed and by the commercial banks—other than the gold and foreign exchange reserves held by the Fed. These assets include holdings of government securities by the Fed and by the commercial banks as well as private securities held by, and loans made by, the commercial banks.

On the liability side of the consolidated balance sheet, notice that the monetary base, MB, is partly held as the reserve asset of the commercial banks, MB_b. In the consolidated balance sheet, the difference between these two items is recorded. This difference is notes and coins in circulation with the public (denoted MB_p).

Bank deposits appear just once, in the commercial banks' balance sheet, and therefore they appear again in the consolidated balance sheet.

The total liabilities of the consolidated banking system now have a familiar look. The total liabilities of the consolidated banking system consist of notes and coins in circulation plus bank deposits. This total, of course, is precisely the definition of the money supply.

Since the two underlying balance sheets balance, so also the consolidated balance sheet will balance. From this fact it will be clear that the money supply can be defined either as notes and coins in circulation plus bank deposits, a definition with which you are already familiar, or alternatively, as gold and foreign exchange reserves plus domestic credit. That is,

$$M = MB_p + D$$

or

$$M = F + DC$$

These, of course, are simply definitions. The second definition, however, is a useful one in helping us to organize our thinking about the determination of the balance of payments and the exchange rate.

The next step is to recognize that the relationship between the money supply and the stock of foreign exchange reserves and domestic credit holds each and every year, and therefore, the change in the money supply from one year to the next will be equal to the change in foreign exchange reserves plus the change in domestic credit. That is (using Δ to denote change),

$$\Delta M = \Delta F + \Delta DC \tag{41.1}$$

This is a very important equation because ΔF is the balance of payments. That is, the change in the stock of foreign exchange reserves is what we mean by the balance of payments. Thus, the balance of payments is related to the change in the money supply and the change in domestic credit.

The change in domestic credit, ΔDC, is usually called *domestic credit expansion.*

It will be convenient for the next step of the story to look at the equation that describes the change in reserves, in the money supply, and in domestic credit in terms of growth rates, or proportionate rates of change, rather than in terms of absolute changes. To convert the above equation into growth rates, first divide both sides of Equation (41.1) by M. This will give

$$\frac{\Delta M}{M} = \frac{\Delta F}{M} + \frac{\Delta DC}{M} \tag{41.2}$$

Terms like $\Delta F/M$ and $\Delta DC/M$ do not have immediately obvious meanings. They become much clearer if the first term is multiplied and divided by F and if the second term is multiplied and divided by DC. This will give

$$\frac{\Delta M}{M} = \left(\frac{F}{M}\right)\frac{\Delta F}{F} + \left(\frac{DC}{M}\right)\frac{\Delta DC}{DC} \tag{41.3}$$

(Be sure that you understand how Equation (41.3) was obtained.)

Equation (41.3) can be interpreted very easily. First notice that the term $\Delta M/M$ is the growth rate of the money supply, which we have been calling μ. Next, define $F/M \equiv \psi$ so that $DC/M \equiv 1 - \psi$. The symbol ψ (the Greek letter psi) is the fraction of the money supply that is held by the banking system in foreign exchange reserves, and $1 - \psi$ is the fraction of the money supply held by the banking system in domestic assets. (*Stop*: Check that $F/M + DC/M$ equals 1 since $F + DC = M$.)

Also define $\Delta F/F \equiv f$ and $\Delta DC/DC \equiv dc$. The letter f is the rate of change of the stock of foreign exchange reserves, and dc is the rate of change of domestic credit.

The somewhat cumbersome Equation (41.3) may, with the new definition, be written as the simpler looking equation

$$\mu = \psi f + (1 - \psi)dc \tag{41.4}$$

This is the fundamental relationship between the rate of growth of the money supply, the rate of change of the stock of foreign exchange reserves, and the rate of growth of domestic credit. It says that the growth rate of the money supply, μ, is a weighted average of the growth rate of the stock of foreign exchange reserves and domestic credit. The weights, which add up to one, are the fraction of the total money supply backed by holdings of foreign exchange reserves, ψ, and the fraction of the total money supply backed by domestic credit, $1 - \psi$.

This relationship may be used in order to understand how, in a fixed exchange rate setting, the balance of payments is determined, and how, in a flexible exchange rate regime, the exchange rate itself is determined. Before we can take these next steps, however, we need to pursue one further preliminary task.

B. The "Law of One Price"

A fundamental law of economics that is of great use in understanding the forces that determine the balance of payments and the exchange rate is the "law of one price."

The law of one price is a proposition concerning the effects of arbitrage. Arbitrage is the buying of a commodity at a low price and simultaneously contracting to sell it for a higher price, thereby making a profit in the process. If it is possible to buy a particular good for some price, say, p_b, and sell the good for a price p_s, then it is possible to make a profit at a rate given by:

$$\text{Arbitrage Profit Rate} = \frac{(p_s - p_b)}{p_b}$$

If such a situation exists, individuals who see the profit opportunity available will increase their demand for the good whose price is p_b. They will also increase their supply of the good at the price p_s. This arbitrage activity of increasing demand at the price p_b and increasing supply at the price p_s will put upward pressure on the buying price—that is, p_b will rise—and downward pressure on the selling price—that is, p_s will fall. Arbitrage will continue to the point at which one price prevails, that is, $p_s = p_b$, until there are no arbitrage profits to be made.

This is the law of one price, namely, that arbitrage will compete away all price differences between identical commodities. Of course, where there are transport costs between two locations, or where there are tariffs and impediments to trade imposed by the government, or where there are costs of acquiring information about the prices of alternative sources of supply, arbitrage will not compete price differentials all the way to zero. It will, however, compete differentials down to the level such that the only remaining price difference reflects underlying real technological- or government-induced barriers to further price gap reductions.

The law of one price has two important implications that are useful for understanding the determination of balance of payments and exchange rates, namely, the purchasing power parity and interest rate parity theorems.

Purchasing Power Parity (PPP)

The purchasing power parity theorem states that the price of a good in one country will be equal to the price of that same good in another country where the prices are expressed in units of local currency and converted at the current exchange rate. (Of course, this has to be modified to allow for any tariffs and transportation costs.)

As an example, if a car in the United States costs $U.S. 5,000, that identical car (trade barriers and transport costs absent) would, at an exchange rate of 80¢ per $Canadian, cost $C 6,250 in Canada. Even allowing for transport costs and tariffs, if these factors were *constant*, then, although the *level* of prices in the United States might be different from the *level* of prices in Canada, the *rate of change of prices* in the two countries would be linked to each other by the relation:

Percentage change in $U.S. price

equals Percentage change in $C price

plus The percentage rate of depreciation of the $U.S. in terms of the $C

To go back to the car example, suppose that car prices in the United States are rising by 5 percent per annum. This will mean that the car that would sell for $5,000 this year will sell for $5,250 next year. Further, suppose that the $U.S. depreciates from $U.S. 0.80 per $C to $U.S. 0.84 per $C—a 5 percent depreciation—then the purchasing power parity theorem states that the price of a car in Canada next year will remain at $C 6,250. That is, car prices in the United States will change by the percentage change of car prices in Canada, adjusted for the percentage change in the value of the $U.S.

Interest Rate Parity (IRP)

The interest rate parity theorem is a close cousin of the purchasing power parity theorem. It arises from arbitrage activities in asset markets. The interest rate parity theorem states that (abstracting from political risk differences) the rate of interest available in one country will be equal to the rate of interest available in another country adjusted for the expected rate of change of the exchange rate between the currencies of the two countries.

Thus, suppose for example, the rate of interest in the United States is 10 percent, and the rate of interest in Canada is 12 percent. Then, if it is expected that the $U.S. is going to appreciate by 2 percent, the rate of interest that would be obtained by an American investing in a Canadian security will be the 12 percent interest on Canadian bonds minus the expected depreciation of the $C of 2 percent, which would equal 10 percent, the same as he could obtain in the United States. Conversely, a Canadian investing in the United States would obtain 10 percent interest on the U.S. security plus a 2 percent gain from the appreciation of the $U.S. vis-à-vis the $C, totalling 12 percent. This would, of course, be equivalent to what could be obtained in Canada.

As another example, if the rate of interest in Canada was greater than 12 percent, the rate of interest in the United States was 10 percent, and the expected rate of depreciation of the \$C was 2 percent, there would be gains to be made from investing in Canada. As investors sought to exploit these gains, they would increase the demand for Canadian securities and lower the demand for U.S. securities. This would raise the price of, and lower the rate of interest on, Canadian securities and would lower the price of, and raise the rate of interest on, U.S. securities.

If there were flexible exchange rates, the flow of funds into Canada would also lead to a rise in the value of the \$C relative to its expected future value. This would mean that the expected rate of future depreciation of the \$C would rise. The combination of a higher U.S. interest rate, a lower Canadian interest rate, and a rise in the expected rate of depreciation of the \$C would restore the interest rate parity relation. That is, the interest rate in Canada would equal the interest rate in the United States plus the expected rate of depreciation of the \$C.

These two propositions may now be used to enable you to understand the basic forces that determine the balance of payments and the exchange rate.

C. Determination of the Balance of Payments Under a Fixed Exchange Rate

The rate of change of the stock of foreign exchange reserves, f, is the balance of payments (expressed as a proportion of the existing stock of reserves). The factors that determine f are therefore exactly the same as the factors that determine the balance of payments. It is tempting to rearrange Equation (41.4), derived above, so that the variable in which we are interested, f, appears on the left-hand side. If you divide Equation (41.4) by ψ and then subtract $[(1-\psi)/\psi]dc$ from both sides of the equation, you obtain

$$f = \frac{1}{\psi}\mu - \left(\frac{1-\psi}{\psi}\right)dc \qquad \textbf{(41.5)}$$

This equation says that the percentage change in the stock of foreign exchange reserves—the balance of payments expressed in percentage terms—depends on the rate of growth of the money supply and the rate of growth of domestic credit. If it is possible to work out what determines these two factors, then we shall have a theory that explains the balance of payments.

Domestic Credit Expansion

Let us deal first with domestic credit expansion, dc. In an open economy with a fixed exchange rate, domestic credit growth is the variable that the monetary authorities can control by their monetary policy actions. If the Fed wants to see the growth of domestic credit increased, then all it has to do is buy bonds from individuals, thereby increasing its own stock of domestic securities. This also makes more reserves available to the commercial banks and encourages them to acquire more domestic securities. Conversely, if the Fed wants to reduce the amount of domestic credit, it can do so by selling government securities, thereby reducing its own holdings of those items. This will also encourage the commercial banks to sell securities since the availability of reserves to those banks will have been lowered.

Thus, *the Fed controls the growth rate of domestic credit.* This is an exogenous variable. Under fixed exchange rates, however, the Fed cannot control the money supply. The very act of pegging the foreign exchange rate means that the Fed must always be willing to buy and sell foreign exchange. That is, the Fed must always be willing to raise or lower its own stock of foreign exchange in order to preserve the fixed value of its currency in terms of foreign currencies. Thus, although the Fed can decide how many domestic assets to buy and hold, it has no control over the gold and foreign exchange reserves that it holds. It follows, therefore, that it cannot control the money supply since the money supply is the sum of domestic credit (which the Fed can control) and foreign exchange reserves (which it cannot control).

Now recall that Equation (41.5) above tells us that the balance of payments depends on both the growth rate of the money supply and the growth rate of domestic credit. Although the growth rate of domestic credit may be treated as being under the control of the Fed, the money supply growth rate may not be regarded as being controlled by the Fed, so it is necessary to enquire what does determine its value.

Growth Rate of Money Supply

When the Fed is pegging the foreign exchange rate and is, as a result, unable to determine the supply of money, the quantity of money in existence will be determined by the amount of money demanded. We have already discovered, in Chapter 9, what determines the demand for money—it depends on the price level, the level of real income, and the rate of interest. The demand for money will change therefore as the price level changes, as real income changes, and as the interest rate changes. In a steady state, when the rate of interest is constant, the growth rate of the money supply will be equal to the rate of inflation plus the rate of growth of output. That is,

$$\mu = \pi + \rho \qquad \textbf{(41.6)}$$

Now recall that the rate of output growth depends on such things as demographic trends, capital accumulation, and technical progress, all of which are being treated as exogenous to, and independent of, the processes that are being analyzed here (and that were analyzed in Chapter 38). The rate of output growth, then, may be taken as given. This still leaves two variables—the rate of inflation and the rate of money supply growth—which have to be determined.

The theory of inflation developed in Chapter 12 (which dealt only with a closed economy) used Equation (41.6) to determine the steady-state rate of inflation. In a closed economy, the Fed was viewed as determining the growth rate of the money supply (μ), and with a given output growth rate, this determines the steady-state rate of inflation. In a fixed exchange rate open economy, however, it is not possible for the Fed to decide what the money supply growth rate will be since it has no control over one of the components of the money supply, namely, the change in the foreign exchange reserves. Equation

(41.6), therefore, cannot be regarded as one that determines the rate of inflation. Rather, given the inflation rate and the growth rate of output, and given a fixed exchange rate, this equation will determine the growth rate of the money supply. Thus, the growth rate of the money supply is determined by the growth rate of the demand for money.

If the growth rate of the money supply is determined by the growth in the demand for money, what determines the rate of inflation in a fixed exchange rate economy? The answer is the law of one price.

The Law of One Price

The next step is to recall the law of one price and its implication—the purchasing power parity proposition. You will recall that the law of one price says that the rate of change of prices in one country (where the prices are expressed in the currency of that country) will be equal to the rate of change of prices in another country (expressed in units of currency of that other country) plus the rate of depreciation of the first country's currency against that of the second country. In other words, calling the rate of inflation in the rest of the world π_f and the rate of depreciation of the currency $\Delta\varepsilon$, we have

$$\pi = \pi_f + \Delta\varepsilon \tag{41.7}$$

This equation may be better understood with an example. Suppose that inflation in the rest of the world was running at 10 percent and that the currency was appreciating at 2 percent per annum. This would imply that the rate of inflation in the domestic economy would be 8 percent. Thus, there is a relationship between inflation rates in different countries and exchange rates arising from arbitrage operations in the markets for goods and services.

Now, recall that the analysis being conducted refers to an economy with a fixed exchange rate. If the exchange rate is fixed, then the rate of change of the exchange rate will be zero. From this it follows that, in a fixed exchange rate economy, the domestic rate of inflation, π, will equal the inflation rate in the rest of the world, π_f. That is,

$$\pi = \pi_f \tag{41.8}$$

This is a fundamental proposition concerning the behavior of the rate of inflation in an open economy operating under a fixed exchange rate. It does not hold exactly because there are other real disturbances going on that change *relative* prices in the world. How useful an approximation to reality it is, we shall see in the final chapter of this book.

You can think of the rate of inflation in the rest of the world as being independent of the behavior of the domestic economy that is being analyzed. It is certainly true that a change in the inflation rate in the United States will have some effect on the inflation rate in other countries, which in turn will feed back to influence the United States. It is a useful first approximation, however, to assume that effect to be zero.

You may think of the world inflation rate as being determined by world aggregate money supply growth in exactly the same way as was analyzed in

Chapter 12. It is as if the whole world has one money, since all monies can be converted into any money at a known fixed exchange rate. The relevant money supply, therefore, is not the national money supply but the sum of all the national money supplies converted into a common unit. Its growth rate is the growth rate that determines world average inflation.

With domestic inflation being determined by world inflation, it is now clear that in a fixed exchange rate economy, the fundamental inflation equation becomes an equation that tells us about the rate of growth of the money supply rather than about the rate of inflation itself. That is, the equation

$$\mu = \pi_f + \rho \tag{41.9}$$

determines μ. The rate of inflation π_f is determined in the rest of the world, and the rate of output growth ρ is determined by long-run forces that are exogenous. What this says is that in a fixed exchange rate open economy, the rate of growth of the money supply will be equal to the rate of growth of the demand for money. More money is demanded if prices become higher, and more money is demanded if output increases. The growth in the demand for money is equal to $\pi_f + \rho$. Money is supplied to meet this demand automatically as a result of the central bank's operations in the foreign exchange market, designed to peg the value of the exchange rate. If, when there was a rise in the demand for money, the central bank did not supply the extra money needed, the currency would tend to rise in value. To prevent this from happening, the central bank would have to take in additional foreign exchange reserves and supply additional domestic money in exchange for the foreign money taken into its reserves.

The Balance of Payments

It is now possible to see what determines the balance of payments. The balance of payments (expressed as a proportion of the stock of foreign exchange reserves) shown in Equation (41.5) is:

$$f = \frac{1}{\psi}(\mu) - \left(\frac{1-\psi}{\psi}\right)dc$$

Also, the money supply growth rate is given in Equation (41.9):

$$\mu = \pi_f + \rho$$

By combining these two propositions, we now have

$$f = \frac{1}{\psi}(\pi_f) + \frac{1}{\psi}(\rho) - \left(\frac{1-\psi}{\psi}\right)dc \tag{41.10}$$

This equation is a fundamental proposition concerning the determination of the balance of payments under fixed exchange rates. It says that if a country has a fixed exchange rate, it may have either a balance of payments surplus or a deficit or an equilibrium, and it is a simple matter to achieve whichever of these outcomes is desired.

The one policy variable that determines the overall balance of payments is the rate of growth of domestic credit. By selling government securities from its portfolio and tightening reserves and forcing commercial banks to sell securities from their portfolios, the central bank can achieve a surplus on the balance of payments. By doing the contrary, that is, buying domestic securities from the general public and giving the commercial banks enough reserves to increase their holdings of domestic securities, the central bank can generate a deficit on the balance of payments.

The balance of payments is fundamentally a monetary phenomenon caused by the monetary policies of the central bank. As a first approximation, the balance of payments is independent of the trade flows and capital flows that underlie it.

Aggregate Demand and Supply

Since the money supply is endogenous and not subject to control, you may be wondering what has become of our theory of aggregate supply and aggregate demand in an open economy with a fixed exchange rate. Figure 41.1 illustrates what is going on. This is a standard aggregate supply, aggregate demand diagram. If the rate of growth of output is zero, then y^*, full-employment output, is constant. Also, if the level of foreign prices is held constant, the inflation rate will be zero. Suppose the foreign price level is P_f, so that the domestic price level implied by that foreign price level is P_f converted into domestic currency at the exchange rate E. This is shown as EP_f on the vertical

Figure 41.1 Output, the Price Level, and Aggregate Demand in a Fixed Exchange Rate Open Economy

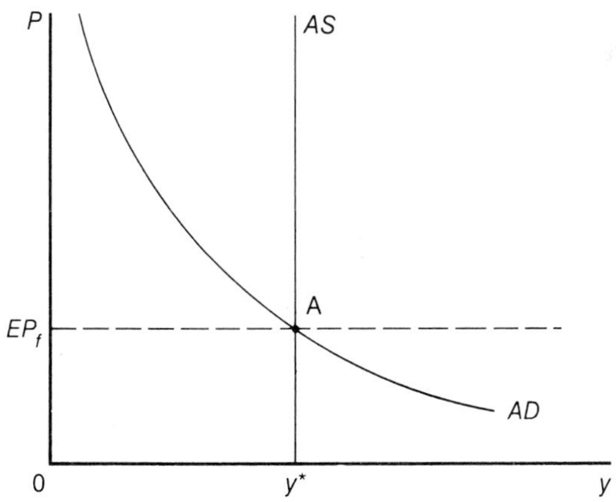

The aggregate supply curve *AS* determines full-employment output, y^*. The foreign price level P_f, when converted to domestic prices by the exchange rate E, determines the domestic price level as EP_f. The position A denotes the equilibrium. Aggregate demand *AD* will automatically pass through this point because the supply of money that influences the position of the aggregate demand curve is determined by the demand for money and therefore by the price level and output level at the point A (rather than being determined exogenously as in the case of the closed economy).

axis. The aggregate supply curve is shown as *AS*. These two curves intersect at point A. This is the equilibrium point for the economy.

You now ask the question, But what if the aggregate demand curve does not pass through the point A? The answer is that the aggregate demand curve cannot avoid passing through the point A because the money supply, which determines the position of the aggregate demand curve, is determined by the demand for money. The demand for money at point A is an amount such that the aggregate demand curve evaluated for that money supply passes exactly through A.

If you conduct a thought experiment, you can see that the economy can only be at point A. Such a thought experiment was conducted in 1741 by David Hume and is still relevant today.

> Suppose four-fifths of all the money in Great Britain to be annihilated in one night, and the nation reduced to the same condition, with regard to specie [money supply] as in the reigns of the Harrys and Edwards, what would be the consequence? Must not the price of all labour and commodities sink in proportion, and every thing be sold as cheap as they were in those ages? What nation could then dispute with us in any foreign market, or pretend to navigate or to sell manufactures at the same price, which to us would afford sufficient profit? In how little time, therefore, must this bring back the money which we had lost, and raise us to the level of all the neighbouring nations? Where, after we have arrived, we immediately lose the advantage of the cheapness of labour and commodities and the farther flowing in of money is stopped by our fulness and repletion.
>
> Again, suppose that all the money of Great Britain were multiplied fivefold in a night, must not the contrary effect follow? Must not all labour and commodities rise to such an exorbitant height, that no neighbouring nations could afford to buy from us—while their commodities, on the other hand, became comparatively so cheap, that, in spite of all the laws which could be formed, they would be run in upon us, and our money flow out—till we fall to a level with foreigners, and lose that great superiority of riches, which had laid us under such disadvantages?
>
> Now it is evident, that the same causes, which would correct these exorbitant inequalities, were they to happen miraculously must prevent their happening in the common course of nature, and must for ever, in all neighbouring nations, preserve money nearly proportionable to the art and industry of each nation. All water, wherever it communicates, remains always at a level. Ask naturalists the reason: they tell you, that, were it to be raised in any one place, the superior gravity of that part not being balanced, must depress it, till it meet a counterpoise; and that the same cause, which redresses the inequality when it happens, must for ever prevent, without some violent external operation.[2]

This completes the basic theory of the balance of payments in a fixed exchange rate economy. Let us now go on to see how, with a flexible exchange rate regime, the exchange rate itself is determined.

[2]Hume, "Of the Balance of Trade," pp. 318–19.

D. Determination of the Exchange Rate under a Flexible Exchange Rate Regime

Fundamental Inflation Equation Again

The starting point in understanding what determines the exchange rate is to recall the factors that determine trend movements in inflation. You will recall from Chapter 12, that provided the rate of money supply growth is steady, the rate of inflation will settle down at a rate equal to the difference between the growth rate of the money supply and the growth rate of full-employment output. That is, the fundamental inflation equation is

$$\pi = \mu - \rho \tag{41.11}$$

Recall why this relationship holds. If the rate of money supply growth (less the growth rate of output) is higher than the rate of inflation, then real money balances will be increasing faster than the demand for money is increasing, and the aggregate demand of goods curve will shift outwards, thereby raising the rate at which prices rise. If the rate of money supply growth (less the growth rate of output) is slower than the rate of inflation, then real money balances will be declining faster than the demand for real money balances is declining. As people attempt to restore their money balances to the desired level, the level of demand for goods will be cut, and this in turn will slow the rate at which prices rise. These forces will always operate when the inflation rate is different from the money supply growth rate (less the growth rate of output).

What Is True for One Country Is True for Another

The fundamental inflation equation used above, Equation (41.11),

$$\pi = \mu - \rho$$

is not a proposition that is true for only one country. It is true for all countries. Consider some other country, called f for foreign. The fundamental inflation equation must also be true for that foreign country. That is,

$$\pi_f = \mu_f - \rho_f \tag{41.12}$$

This simply says that in the foreign country the rate of inflation will be equal to its rate of money supply growth minus its rate of full-employment output growth.

Purchasing Power Parity Again

Next recall the important proposition that arbitrage in goods generates purchasing power parity. You will recall that although tariffs, transport costs, and other impediments to trade may drive a wedge between the level of prices in one country and the level in another, arbitrage will ensure that, for given levels of trade distortions, the rate of change of prices in one country will be brought to equality with the rate of change of prices in the other when adjusted for any change in the exchange rate. This was stated in Equation (41.7) as:

$$\pi = \pi_f + \Delta\varepsilon$$

This says that the rate of inflation in the domestic economy (π) will be equal to the rate of inflation in the foreign economy (π_f), plus the rate at which the currency of the domestic economy is depreciating against the currency of the foreign economy ($\Delta\varepsilon$).

Movements in the Exchange Rate

The above propositions may now be brought together to work out what determines the foreign exchange rate. Combining the domestic forces that make for a domestic inflation with the international arbitrage forces that ensure that purchasing power parity is, on the average, maintained, produces a theory of the trend movements in the exchange rate. To see this, first of all notice that the purchasing power parity relationship, Equation (41.7), may be rewritten using the two fundamental inflation Equations (41.11) and (41.12). Since the domestic inflation rate (π) is equal to the domestic money supply growth rate (μ) minus the rate of output growth (ρ), the left-hand side of Equation (41.7)—π—may be replaced with $\mu - \rho$. The same is true of π_f. Notice that π_f is equal to the rate at which the money supply is growing in the foreign country (μ_f) minus the rate of output growth in that country (ρ_f). Let us therefore replace π_f on the right-hand side of Equation (41.7) by $\mu_f - \rho_f$. Making both of these substitutions results in:

$$\mu - \rho = \mu_f - \rho_f + \Delta\varepsilon \qquad \textbf{(41.13)}$$

This is nothing other than the purchasing power parity proposition (Equation 41.7) combined with the fundamental inflation equation for each country [Equations (41.11) and (41.12)]. This equation may now be rearranged so that it provides an explicit statement as to what is happening to the exchange rate ($\Delta\varepsilon$). That is,

$$\Delta\varepsilon = (\mu - \mu_f) - (\rho - \rho_f) \qquad \textbf{(41.14)}$$

This is the *fundamental exchange rate equation.* It says that

	The rate of change of the foreign exchange rate between the currencies of two countries
equals	The difference between the money supply growth rates in the two countries
minus	The difference between the output growth rates in the two countries

This equation also says that:

1. The faster the money supply growth rate in the domestic economy, the faster will the currency depreciate (the bigger will be $\Delta\varepsilon$).

2. The faster the money supply growth rate in the foreign country, the faster will the domestic currency appreciate in terms of the foreign currency.
3. The faster the growth rate of output in the domestic economy, the stronger will be the domestic currency ($\Delta\varepsilon$ will be smaller).
4. The faster the rate of growth of output in the foreign economy, the weaker will be the domestic currency.

Supply and Demand Yet Again

The factors that determine the exchange rate in the above analysis are nothing other than the forces of supply and demand. The exchange rate is a price like any other price. It is the relative price of two national monies. The exchange rate is determined by the supply of and the demand for domestic money relative to the supply of and demand for foreign money. (Remember that money is a stock, not a flow.)

Look again at the fundamental exchange rate equation—Equation (41.14). The first part of this equation tells us about the growth rate of the relative supplies of two monies ($\mu - \mu_f$). If $\mu - \mu_f$ is positive, the domestic money supply is growing at a faster rate than the foreign money supply because the domestic money supply is rising relative to the foreign money supply. The second part of the equation, $\rho - \rho_f$, tells us about the growth rate in the relative demands for the two monies. If the growth rate in output is greater in the domestic economy than in the foreign economy, then the demand for domestic money will grow at a faster rate than the demand for foreign money.

Now, if the growth in the relative supplies of money ($\mu - \mu_f$) is just equal to the growth in the relative demands for money ($\rho - \rho_f$), the exchange rate will not change, i.e., $\Delta\varepsilon$ will be zero. This means that there is a critical growth rate for the domestic money supply (let us call it μ^c) at which the exchange rate will be steady. To find the growth rate μ^c, simply solve the fundamental exchange rate equation—Equation (41.14)—for the μ that is associated with $\Delta\varepsilon = 0$; i.e.,

$$\Delta\varepsilon = (\mu - \mu_f) - (\rho - \rho_f) = 0 \qquad \textbf{(41.15)}$$

so,

$$\mu^c = \mu_f + (\rho - \rho_f) \qquad \textbf{(41.16)}$$

If the money supply grows at a faster rate than μ^c, the currency will depreciate ($\Delta\varepsilon$ will be positive); and if the money supply grows at a slower rate than μ^c, the currency will appreciate ($\Delta\varepsilon$ will be negative).

Therefore, the key thing that a country can control to influence its exchange rate is its money supply growth rate. Other things being equal, the faster the money supply grows, the faster will the currency depreciate (or the slower will it appreciate). The exchange rate will only be steady if the money supply grows at the critical rate that equals the foreign money supply growth rate plus the difference between the domestic and foreign output growth rates.

Does a Depreciating Currency Cause Inflation?

There is a popular view which says that inflation is caused by a depreciating currency and that a country can be trapped in a vicious circle of inflation and depreciation about which nothing can be done. You now know enough to know that this is not true. A depreciating exchange rate is a symptom of inflation and is caused by the same thing that causes inflation. You know from the fundamental inflation equation that, other things being equal, inflation will be higher, the higher is the money supply growth rate. You also know from the fundamental exchange rate equation that the exchange rate will depreciate faster ($\Delta\varepsilon$ is positive and increasing), the bigger is the growth rate of the money supply (μ). Thus both inflation and a weak currency are caused by too high a growth rate of the money supply.

If a country wants to maintain a steady exchange rate, it is necessary for that country to achieve a money supply growth rate relative to the growth rate of the money supply in the rest of the world that exactly offsets the difference in the growth in demands for domestic and foreign money arising from any differences in output growth rates. This being the case, with a steady exchange rate, the country must accept the inflation rate that is generated in the rest of the world. If, on the other hand, a country wants to achieve a zero rate of inflation, it becomes necessary for the country to make its own money supply grow at the same rate at its own output growth. That is, set μ equal to ρ. This will not ensure a constant value for the exchange rate, however, since the exchange rate will depend on both domestic monetary policy and the monetary policy of the rest of the world. If the rest of the world is inflating, whereas the domestic economy is maintaining stable prices, then the exchange rate will appreciate ($\Delta\varepsilon$ will be negative). If, however, the foreign economy is deflating, that is, has falling prices, while the domestic economy is maintaining steady prices, then the exchange rate will depreciate ($\Delta\varepsilon$ will be positive).

Stable Exchange Rates vs. Stable Prices

The above remarks serve to emphasize that a country cannot choose both its inflation rate and the behavior of its exchange rate simultaneously. A country must make a choice as to whether it wants to achieve stable prices, thereby allowing its exchange rate to adjust from time to time to reflect the difference between domestic and foreign inflation; or whether it wants to achieve a fixed exchange rate with the rest of the world, in which case it will have to allow the foreign inflation rate to be fully reflected in the domestic inflation rate.

You now have an understanding of the factors that determine the long-term movements in exchange rates. You see that there are no effects on the exchange rate in the long run arising from such things as import and export demands and the flow of goods and services across national boundaries. In the long run, the exchange rate is determined by monetary equilibrium. With a fixed exchange rate, the country abdicates control over its money supply. The automatic changes in the stock of foreign exchange reserves ensure that the growth rate of the money supply is exactly equal to the growth rate of the demand for money, the latter being equal to the world rate of inflation plus the domestic output growth rate. In the case of a flexible exchange rate, the domestic monetary authority controls the stock of foreign exchange reserves and the domestic money supply, thereby forcing the adjustment onto the exchange rate itself. It is movements in the exchange rate that ensure that the stock of money that has been determined by the Fed is willingly held by private economic agents.

E. Determination of the Balance of Payments and the Exchange Rate in a Managed Floating Regime

The basic theory of the determination of the exchange rate under a floating regime and of the balance of payments under a fixed exchange rate regime may be combined in a fairly natural and perhaps even obvious way to set out the fundamental constraints upon the actions of a central bank seeking to pursue a managed floating exchange rate policy. To see these constraints, we simply need to combine three bits of information that have already been examined in the previous sections of this chapter. The first is the relationship between the growth of the money supply, the growth of the stock of foreign exchange reserves, and the growth of domestic credit, that is, Equation (41.4), which says that

$$\mu = \psi f + (1 - \psi)dc \qquad \textbf{(41.4)}$$

The second ingredient is the steady-state relation between money growth, inflation, and output growth, Equation (41.6), which says that

$$\mu = \pi + \rho \qquad \textbf{(41.6)}$$

The final ingredient is the purchasing-power parity proposition, Equation (41.7), which says that

$$\pi = \pi_f + \Delta\varepsilon \qquad \textbf{(41.7)}$$

Combining these three propositions—substituting the inflation rate out of Equation (41.6), using Equation (41.7), and substituting the money supply growth rate out of Equation (41.4), using Equation (41.6)—gives

$$\pi_f + \Delta\varepsilon + \rho = \psi f + (1 - \psi)dc$$

If you subtract the foreign inflation rate from both sides of this equation, subtract ρ from both sides and also subtract ψf from both sides, you obtain

$$\Delta\varepsilon - \psi f = (1 - \psi)dc - (\pi_f + \rho) \qquad \textbf{(41.17)}$$

The left-hand side of this equation contains the rate of change of the exchange rate ($\Delta\varepsilon$) minus the rate of change of the stock of foreign exchange reserves (weighted by the fraction of the money stock backed by those reserves, ψ), that is ψf. Let us give a name to the left-hand side of Equation

(41.17): *exchange market pressure*[3]. The right-hand side is simply the growth rate of domestic credit (weighted by the fraction of the money supply backed by domestic credit, $1 - \psi$) minus the sum of the foreign rate of inflation (π_f) and output growth (ρ).

All Equation (41.17) says is that for a given foreign rate of inflation, a given π_f, the greater the rate of domestic credit expansion and the lower the output growth, the stronger will be the exchange market pressure. Exchange market pressure will have to be reflected in either the exchange rate or the stock of reserves. Either the exchange rate will have to rise (the currency will have to depreciate), or reserves will have to fall. Some combination of these two things cannot be avoided. If the central bank wants to manage the exchange rate and keep the exchange rate from falling, then it will have no alternative but to accept a drop in its foreign exchange reserves.

The converse of all this is that the lower the domestic credit growth and the higher the output growth relative to the foreign rate of inflation, the less will be the exchange market pressure. This would imply that the lower the growth rate of domestic credit, the more would the foreign exchange reserves rise, and/or the stronger would be the rate of appreciation of the currency ($\Delta\varepsilon$ negative). In other words, a central bank wishing to pursue tight domestic credit policies (low *dc*) but at the same time prevent the exchange rate from appreciating (prevent a high negative value of $\Delta\varepsilon$) would have to be willing to allow the foreign exchange reserves to rise. Equation (41.17) states the fundamental constraint on the freedom of the central bank to pursue a managed floating policy.

A fixed exchange rate is the special case of Equation (41.17) where the central bank manages the value of $\Delta\varepsilon$ equal to zero, permitting all of the exchange market pressures to come out in the stock of foreign exchange reserves—in the balance of payments.

A flexible exchange rate regime is the other opposite extreme, where f is set equal to zero (reserve changes do not occur), and all exchange market pressures are felt by the exchange rate itself.

A managed float is simply a linear combination of these two extremes determined by the political and other pressures that operate on the conduct of monetary policy.

Summary

A. Money Supply and Foreign Exchange Reserves

The money supply is, by definition, equal to the sum of foreign exchange reserves and domestic credit.

[3]The term was first suggested by Lance Girton and Don Roper in "A Monetary Model of Exchange Market Pressure Applied to the Postwar Canadian Experience," *The American Economic Review*, 67, (December 1977), 537–48.

B. The "Law of One Price"

The law of one price asserts that arbitrage will reduce price differentials to the minimum consistent with transport costs, tariffs, and other physical barriers and impediments to trade.

The purchasing power parity theorem states that the price of a particular good in one country will be the same as the price in another country (when the prices are converted at the current exchange rate). This proposition does not strictly apply to price levels, since tariffs and transportation costs drive a wedge between price levels. However, it does apply to price *changes* expressed in percentage terms. That is, the percentage change in the price of some commodity in the United States will be equal to the percentage change of the price of the same commodity in Canada (say) plus the percentage rate of depreciation of the U.S. dollar in terms of the Canadian dollar.

The interest rate parity theorem is an application of the law of one price to asset markets. It states that the rate of interest in Canada will be equal to the rate of interest in the United States plus the expected rate of depreciation of the $C.

C. Determination of the Balance of Payments under a Fixed Exchange Rate

In an economy with a fixed exchange rate, the balance of payments (as a first approximation) is determined by the domestic credit policies of the central bank. If the central bank creates too much domestic credit, there will be a balance of payments deficit. If the central bank creates too little domestic credit, there will be a balance of payments surplus. The central bank can always achieve a zero balance by permitting exactly the right amount of domestic credit to be created.

D. Determination of the Exchange Rate under a Flexible Exchange Rate Regime

When the exchange rate is flexible, the money supply and its growth rate are controllable by the central bank. Inflation is determined in such a case in exactly the same way as it is in the closed economy, by the growth rate of the money supply. The exchange rate is determined by differences in money supply growth rates and output growth rates between countries. Specifically, the exchange rate, being a price like any other price, is determined by supply and demand. Since the exchange rate is the relative price between two monies, it is determined by the relative supplies (stocks) of the two monies and the relative demands for them. There is a sense in which the exchange rate is unlike any other price in that its value depends directly on the relative monetary policies of the two countries.

E. Determination of the Balance of Payments and the Exchange Rate in a Managed Floating Regime

For a given foreign rate of inflation, the faster the growth rate of domestic credit, the greater will be the amount of exchange market pressure. Exchange market pressure must come out either in a depreciation of the currency or a loss of foreign exchange reserves. The central bank can select a policy that favors smoothing exchange rate adjustments by permitting reserves to take the strain, or it may select a policy that favors a steady stock of foreign reserves by permitting the foreign exchange rate to take the strain. The central bank cannot choose both the exchange rate and the stock of foreign exchange reserves.

Review Questions

1. Explain what the following equation means:

$$\Delta M = \Delta F + \Delta DC$$

2. Illustrate your answer to Question 1 by showing what happens to the U.S. money supply, the stock of foreign exchange reserves, and domestic credit in the event that:

(a) The Fed buys British government bonds with its reserves of £ sterling.
(b) The Fed buys £ sterling with new U.S. dollars.
(c) The Fed buys U.S. federal government bonds with new U.S. dollars.

3. What would be the price of jelly beans in Canada if the U.S. price was \$5 U.S. per kilogram and if there were no tariffs or taxes on jelly beans, and if the Canadian dollar was worth 81¢ U.S.? Suppose, one year later, that jelly beans cost \$5.50 U.S. per kilogram and the Canadian dollar was worth 85¢ U.S. What is the percentage change in the Canadian price? What is the percentage change in the U.S. price? What is the percentage change in the exchange rate? How do these variables relate to each other?

4. You have \$10,000 to invest for one year. If you buy a U.S. government bond, it will give you a sure return after one year of 10 percent. If you convert your \$10,000 into Canadian dollars, you will do so at an exchange rate of 83¢ U.S. per \$C. You can buy a Canadian government bond that will give a sure return after one year of 13 percent.

(a) What would the exchange rate between U.S. and Canadian dollars have to be one year hence for it to be worth buying the U.S. bond?
(b) If you firmly expected the U.S. dollar to be cheaper than your answer to (a), what would you do?
(c) If people generally shared your expectation, what would happen?

5. Work out the effects on the balance of payments when the exchange rate is fixed, of the following:

(a) A rise in the price level.
(b) A rise in interest rates.
(c) A rise in real income.
(d) A rise in domestic credit.
(e) A collapse of U.S. wheat production due to drought.

6. Work out the effects on the exchange rate, in a flexible exchange rate regime, of the shocks listed in Question 5 above.

7. Why can't a country pursue any balance of payments *and* exchange rate objectives it chooses? Draw parallels between a country's exchange rate policy and the price and output policies of a monopolist.

42

The Keynesian Model of the Open Economy

In the last chapter we examined the determinants of the balance of payments and the exchange rate in the full-employment equilibrium flexible price setting of the basic model. This chapter provides a sharp contrast. It examines the determination of output, interest rates, the balance of payments, and the exchange rate in a fixed price level, underemployed, Keynesian economy.[1] Instead of operating at full-employment output, it will be assumed that the economy is operating on the horizontal section of the Keynesian inverse "L" aggregate supply curve (Chapter 15). In that setting we shall examine the effects of domestic monetary and fiscal policy actions on aggregate demand and also analyze the effects of foreign shocks on the domestic economy. We shall do this in the context of both a fixed exchange rate economy, where the shocks affect the balance of payments, and a flexible exchange rate economy, where the exchange rate itself is also going to be influenced by the various shocks that we shall consider.

The chapter pursues its objectives by taking you through six tasks, which are to:

(a) Know how to derive the *IS* curve for an open economy.
(b) Know the definition of the *BP* curve.
(c) Know how to derive the *BP* curve.
(d) Understand what makes the *IS*, *LM*, and *BP* curves shift.
(e) Know how to determine the levels of output, interest rate, and the balance of payments in a fixed exchange rate regime.
(f) Know how to determine the levels of output, interest rate, and the exchange rate in a flexible exchange rate regime.

[1]The material presented in this chapter was developed primarily by Robert Mundell and J. Marcus Fleming. The two most important papers by these two outstanding scholars are: Robert A. Mundell, "The Appropriate Use of Monetary and Fiscal Policy under Fixed Exchange Rates," *IMF Staff Papers*, 9 (March 1962), 70–77; and J. Marcus Fleming, "Domestic Financial Policies under Fixed and Floating Exchange Rates," *IMF Staff Papers*, 9 (March 1962), 369–77. Although Keynesian, the material in this chapter is often called the Mundell-Fleming analysis.

A. Derivation of the *IS* Curve for an Open Economy

You already know the meaning of the *IS* curve for an economy that has balanced trade or, equivalently, a closed economy. It is the relationship between the rate of interest and level of income at which savings-plus-taxes are equal to investment-plus-government expenditure. In the open economy there are two additional expenditure flows to be taken into account in defining and deriving the *IS* curve. These are exports and imports of goods and services. In a closed economy, aggregate demand is the sum of consumption plus investment plus government spending; whereas in an open economy, aggregate demand is equal to the sum of those three items plus net foreign demand or, equivalently, exports minus imports. That is, defining exports as *ex* and imports as *im*, aggregate demand in an open economy is

$$y = c + i + g + ex - im \tag{42.1}$$

Subtracting consumption from both sides of Equation (42.1) gives

$$y - c = i + g + ex - im \tag{42.2}$$

The left-hand side of the above equation $(y - c)$ is, of course, simply savings-plus-taxes. We could equivalently, therefore, write this equation as

$$s + t = i + g + ex - im \tag{42.3}$$

Adding imports to both sides of the above equation gives

$$s + t + im = i + g + ex \tag{42.4}$$

This is the condition that, for the open economy, must be satisfied at all points on the *IS* curve. That is, savings-plus-taxes-plus-imports must equal investment-plus-government spending-plus-exports.

To derive the open economy *IS* curve, we need some propositions about how imports and exports are determined. Let us now proceed to do that.

First, consider exports. Two key variables determine a country's exports. The first of these is the total level of income of the people who are demanding those exports. This income level is, of course, the aggregate income of the rest of the world. It is the sum of the gross domestic products of all the countries in the world other than the country whose economy we are analyzing. The second variable that influences exports is the price of the goods produced in the domestic economy relative to the prices ruling in the rest of the world. This relative price, expressed as an economy-wide average, could be stated precisely as

$$\theta = \frac{EP_f}{P} \tag{42.5}$$

The price of foreign goods is P_f, the domestic price level is P, and the effective exchange rate (as defined in Chapter 40) is E. Thus, θ (the Greek letter theta) may be thought of as the price of foreign goods relative to the price of domestic goods. This ratio is sometimes called the *real exchange rate.* That is, the real exchange rate is the effective exchange rate E multiplied by the ratio of foreign to domestic prices (P_f/P). The bigger the value of θ, the bigger will be the volume of exports. That is, the higher the foreign price level relative to the domestic price level, the bigger will be the rest of the world's demand for domestically produced goods.

We can summarize these propositions about exports as follows: Exports will be higher, the higher is the rest of the world income and the higher is the real exchange rate.

Next, consider the factors that determine imports. Again, there are two key variables that may be isolated as having important effects on imports. The first is the level of domestic income (real GNP). The higher the level of domestic real income, the higher will be imports. The other influence is the same real exchange rate variable that influences exports. This time its effect will be opposite in sign. That is, a rise in the rest of world prices relative to domestic prices—a rise in the real exchange rate—will lead to a reduction in imports. To summarize: Imports will be higher, the higher is real income, and imports will be lower, the higher is the real exchange rate.

We may now proceed to derive the *IS* curve for an open economy. Figure 42.1 illustrates this derivation. The figure is set up with an *IS* curve labelled *IS*(*C*)—*C* standing for closed economy—which is identical to the *IS* curve derived in Figure 18.4. The *IS* curve for the open economy is labelled *IS*(*O*)—*O* standing for open economy. To see the differences between the *IS* curve of the closed economy and that of the open economy, begin by considering frame (c) of Figure 42.1. There, on the horizontal axis, we are measuring investment-plus-government spending-plus-exports. For given values of world real income and the real exchange rate, exports will be constant. We may therefore add exports to investment-plus-government spending by drawing a line parallel to the $i + g$ curve, the new curve representing $i + g + ex$. The horizontally shaded area in frame (c) represents the volume of exports.

The second change occurs in frame (a) of Figure 42.1. There we are measuring savings-plus-taxes-plus-imports on the vertical axis, and investment-plus government spending-plus exports on the horizontal axis. The 45° line defines the open economy equilibrium condition for the *IS* curve.

The third change comes in frame (b). In this frame we measure savings-plus-taxes-plus-imports on the vertical axis. It is necessary, therefore, to add imports to the previously derived savings-plus-taxes schedule. To do this, recall that imports are presumed to depend on the level of domestic real income, and the real exchange rate. As in the case of exports, hold the real exchange rate at some fixed value. That done, the level of imports will depend solely on the level of domestic real income. We can show this in frame (b) by drawing a line above the savings-plus-taxes line that is steeper than that line. The vertical distance between the two lines will then measure the volume of imports—the shaded area in frame (b). To derive the *IS* curve for the open economy, we proceed in the same way as for the closed economy but use the $i + g + ex$ and the $s + t + im$ lines. Following exactly the same procedure as in Chapter 18, you can readily verify that the curve *IS*(*O*)—*O* for open—is the open economy *IS* curve. Notice that it is steeper than that for the closed

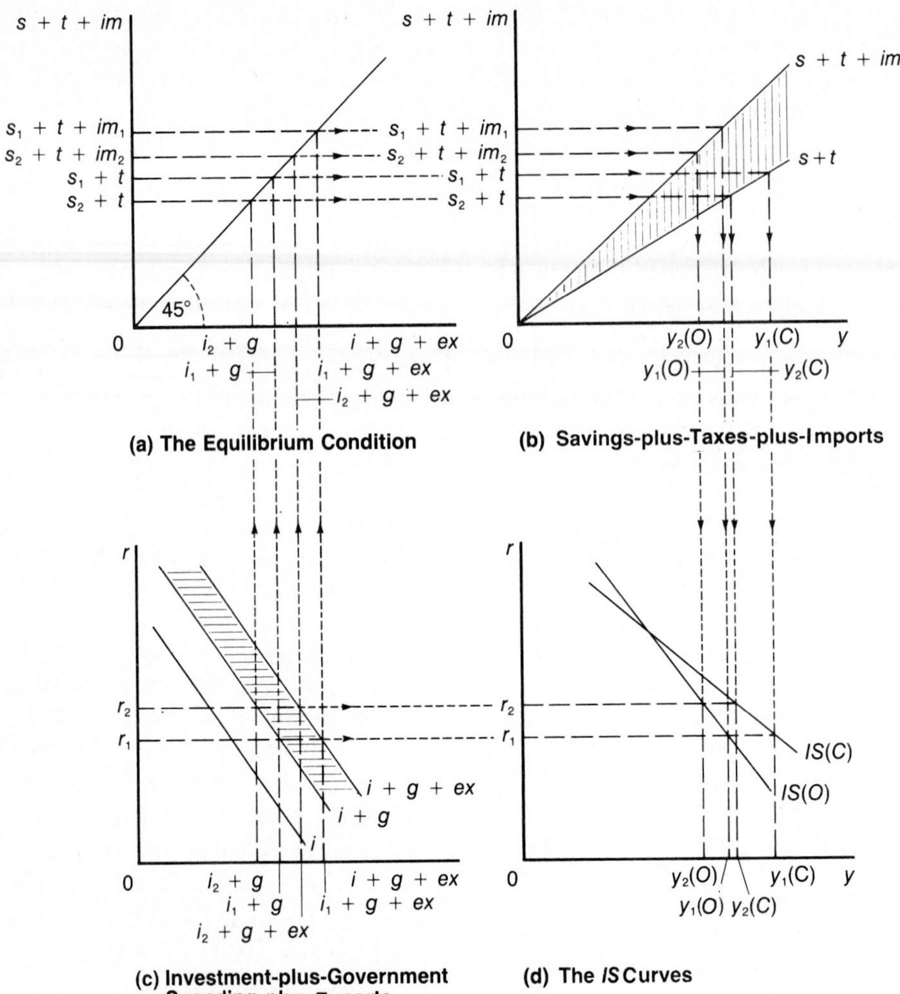

Figure 42.1
The Derivation of the *IS* Curve for an Open Economy

Frame (a) shows the equilibrium condition that defines the *IS* curve in an open economy—the equality of savings-plus-taxes-plus-imports with investment-plus-government spending-plus-exports. In frame (c), exports are added to investment-plus-government spending (the shaded area). In frame (b), imports are added to savings-plus-taxes (the shaded area). In frame (d), the *IS* curve, *IS*(*C*), is for a closed economy (ignoring exports and imports) and that labelled *IS*(*O*) is for the open economy. The two curves intersect at the real income level that generates a volume of imports equal to the fixed volume of exports. A rise in exports shifts the $i + g + ex$ line and the *IS* curve. The relationship between the two shifts depends on the slope of the $s + t + im$ curve. The steeper the slope of $s + t + im$, the smaller will be the shift in the *IS* curve for a given shift in $i + g + ex$.

---

economy. It cuts the closed economy *IS* curve at the level of income that generates a volume of imports exactly equal to the fixed volume of exports.

Since, in deriving the *IS* curve, we hold the real exchange rate fixed, it follows that at each different real exchange rate there will be a different *IS* curve. Precisely how the *IS* curve shifts as the real exchange rate (and other variables) change will be explored below. Before that, let us go on to define and derive a new curve—the *BP* curve.

B. Definition of the *BP* Curve

The *BP* curve is a relationship between the rate of interest and level of income such that at all points on the *BP* curve there is a balance of payments equilibrium. Put differently, at all points on the *BP* curve, the balance of payments is zero, i.e. balanced. Equivalently, there is a capital account surplus that exactly matches the current account deficit (or capital account deficit that exactly matches the current account surplus).

C. Derivation of the *BP* Curve

The starting point for deriving the *BP* curve is the balance of payments equilibrium condition that states that the sum of the current account balance and the capital account balance is zero. The prices at which a country exports and imports goods and services are determined by the world price level P_f, converted into domestic money units at the exchange rate E, so that the current account balance is $EP_f ex - EP_f im$. Dividing this by the domestic price level P, and remembering that EP_f/P equals the real exchange rate θ, gives the real current account balance as $\theta(ex - im)$. Adding the real capital account surplus denoted by *kas* gives the condition for the *BP* curve as

$$\theta(ex - im) + kas = 0 \qquad \textbf{(42.6)}$$

This says that the balance of payments *BP* is equal to the *value* of exports minus the *value* of imports (of goods and services) plus the capital account surplus (denoted as *kas*). We have already discussed the determinants of the *volume* of exports and imports and the real exchange rate θ, and need now only concern ourselves with the things that determine the capital account surplus.

The capital account of the balance of payments depends primarily on rates of return on investments that are available in the domestic economy compared with rates of return available in the rest of the world. As a general proposition, the higher the rates of return available in the domestic economy relative to those available in the rest of the world, the greater will be the tendency for domestic capital to stay at home and for foreign capital to be sucked into the domestic economy. Conversely, the lower the domestic rates of return relative to foreign rates of return, the greater will be the tendency for domestic capital to seek the higher returns available in other countries, and the greater will be the tendency for foreign capital to stay at home.

In order to compare rates of return between two countries, it is necessary to look at the rates of interest that are available in the two countries and also to make an allowance for any change in the value of one money in terms of another (change in the exchange rate). As was discussed in the previous chapter, if there were two securities, identical in all respects except for the currency of denomination, then the rates of interest on those two securities would be related by the interest parity condition; that is,

$$r = r_f + \Delta\varepsilon^e \tag{42.7}$$

Recall that r is the domestic rate of interest, r_f the foreign rate of interest, and $\Delta\varepsilon^e$ the expected rate of depreciation of the domestic currency. Although the interest rate parity condition may be expected to hold exactly under the precise conditions that are used to define it—identical assets—it will not hold when applied to average interest rates across the entire collection of assets issued in one economy and the rest of the world. In general, domestic interest rates will have some room to move higher or lower, on the average, than what is predicted by the interest parity condition. The more that domestic interest rates rise above the interest rate parity level, the more will be the tendency for foreign capital to enter the economy; the lower the domestic interest rates relative to their interest rate parity value, the less will foreign capital flow into the economy.

We are now in a position to derive the *BP* curve. Figure 42.2 illustrates the derivation. First, it will be useful to familiarize yourself with what we are measuring on the axes of the different frames: Frame (d) is going to show the *BP* curve and measures the rate of interest against the level of real income; frame (c) measures the rate of interest against total receipts from the rest of the world—exports-plus-capital account surplus; frame (b) measures imports against the level of real income; and frame (a) measures imports on the vertical axis and exports-plus-capital account surplus on the horizontal axis. The line in frame (a) defines the balance of payments equilibrium condition. It is a 45° line indicating that when imports equal exports-plus-capital account surplus, then there is a zero balance on the balance of payments. In frame (c), the upward sloping line *kas* denotes the capital account surplus. It slopes upwards, indicating that the higher the domestic rate of interest, other things being equal, the larger will be the capital account surplus. In drawing that line, the foreign rate of interest and the expected rate of change of the exchange rate are being held constant. The second, thicker line in frame (c) results from adding the fixed volume of exports (for constant world real income and real exchange rate) to the capital account surplus to denote the total inflow of money from the rest of the world. In deriving the *BP* curve it is convenient to assume that the real exchange rate θ is one. Later in this chapter we shall examine what happens to the *BP* curve when the value of θ changes.

Frame (b) shows the import function—the relationship between imports and real income. In drawing the line in frame (b), as in frame (c), the real exchange rate is being held constant. To derive the *BP* curve, select a rate of interest r_1 and notice that in frame (c), at the interest rate r_1, there is a capital account surplus of kas_1 and a total inflow of money from the rest of the world of $kas_1 + ex$. Tracing up from frame (c) to frame (a), we know that if there is to be a balance of payments equilibrium, the level of imports must equal im_1. Taking that import level across to frame (b), we discover that in order for the import level to equal im_1, it will be necessary for domestic real income to be y_1. Transferring that real income level into frame (d), and transferring the initially assumed rate of interest r_1 across to frame (d) gives a point on the *BP*

Figure 42.2
The Derivation of the *BP* curve

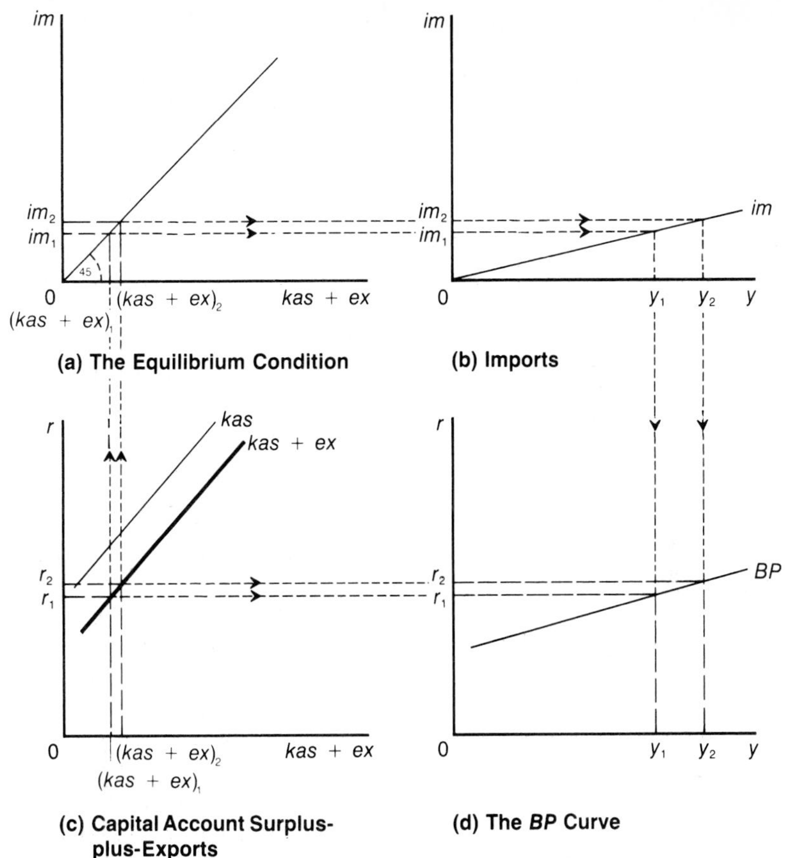

Frame (a) contains the condition that defines the *BP* curve—the equality of imports with exports plus the capital accounts surplus. Frame (c) shows the capital account surplus rising with the rate of interest. Exports are added to the capital account surplus in frame (c). Frame (b) shows imports rising with real income. Frame (d) shows the *BP* curve as the relationship that satisfies the three lines in the other frames. The *BP* curve will shift if there is a rise in exports. The distance of the horizontal shift of the *BP* curve relative to the shift in *kas* + *ex* depends solely on the slope of the import function. The flatter the *im* curve, the greater will be the shift in the *BP* curve for any given change in the *kas* + *ex* curve.

curve. The income level y_1 combined with the interest rate r_1 generates a level of imports and capital account surplus such that there is a zero balance on the balance of payments. By selecting other interest rates, it is possible to derive other real income levels, and by experimenting you will discover that you can generate the entire line labelled *BP*.

The *BP* curve will slope upwards in general, but it could, in a special and important circumstance, be horizontal. That special circumstance would be one of perfect capital mobility. Perfect capital mobility means that any interest differential between the domestic economy and the rest of the world would automatically and instantly bring in, or drive out, funds, so that the domestic interest rate always equals the rate given by the interest parity relation. In that case, the domestic interest rate would always be equal to the foreign rate of interest plus the expected rate of depreciation of the domestic currency and would never deviate from that level. The *BP* curve would be a horizontal line at that rate of interest. As a general matter, the *BP* curve will slope up, as shown in the figure. It may be presumed, however, that it will not be a very steep relationship since modest interest rate differentials seem to be sufficient to induce large international movements of capital. (The perfect capital mobility case will feature prominently in the next chapter.)

Let us now go on to consider the things that make the open economy *IS*, *LM*, and *BP* curves shift.

D. Shifts in the *IS*, *LM*, and *BP* Curves

Recall that when we derived the *IS* curve, we held constant the level of world income, which influences exports, and the real exchange rate, which influences both exports and imports. What happens to the *IS* curve if either of these variables change? If world income rises, exports rise. This has the effect of shifting the *IS* curve to the right. If the real exchange rate rises, this also raises exports and lowers imports. This, too, shifts the *IS* curve to the right. The real exchange rate might rise because of a rise in the exchange rate (depreciation), a rise in the foreign price level, or a fall in the domestic price level.

The *LM* curve in the open economy is exactly the same (at least in the presentation given here) as that of the closed economy. As in the case of the closed economy, the only thing that shifts the *LM* curve is a change in the money supply. There is an important difference between the open and closed economies, however, concerning the sources of variation in the quantity of money. You know from the analysis in Chapter 41 that a change in the quantity of money may be decomposed into two parts—a change in the stock of foreign exchange reserves and a change in domestic credit. The first of these items is the balance of payments. If domestic credit is held constant, which would be the natural way of interpreting a neutral domestic monetary policy, then unless the economy is on the *BP* curve, the quantity of money will be changing. Specifically, at all points above the *BP* curve, the quantity of money will be rising; and at all points below it, the quantity of money will be falling. This means that if the economy is above the *BP* curve, it is experiencing a balance of payments surplus, and the *LM* curve will be shifting to the right. Conversely, if the economy is below the *BP* curve, it is experiencing a balance of payments deficit, and the *LM* curve will be shifting to the left.

An alternative domestic monetary policy would be to stabilize the quantity of money regardless of the state of the balance of payments. This would involve changing domestic credit by an equal but opposite amount to the change in the stock of foreign exchange reserves resulting from the balance of payments deficit or surplus. Such an action is known as *sterilizing* the balance of payments. Such a policy can be undertaken, but only for limited periods of time, since, in general, sterilization actions accentuate the balance of payments problem. Pursuing tighter and tighter domestic monetary policies in the face of the balance of payments surplus tends to make that surplus bigger, and pursuing slacker and slacker monetary policies in the face of the balance of payments deficit tends to make the deficit worse. A situation in which the quantity of money changes by the same amount as the change in the stock of foreign exchange reserves is, therefore, an interesting one to analyze since it represents the only policy action that can be sustained over an indefinite period. Sterilization cannot.

Next, consider the factors that shift the *BP* curve. In drawing the capital account surplus line in Figure 42.2, we held constant the world rate of interest and the expected rate of change of the exchange rate. A rise in either the world rate of interest or the expected rate of depreciation of the domestic currency will shift the *kas* line to the left (or upwards). The factors that determine exports and imports have already been discussed in the above discussion of the factors that shift the *IS* curve. Changes in world real income or the real exchange rate that shift the *IS* curve will also, necessarily, shift the *BP* curve. Anything that raises exports or lowers imports will shift the *BP* curve to the right. Thus, a devaluation of the currency (a higher value of *E*), a rise in foreign prices, a rise in world real income, or a fall in the domestic price level will all have the effect of shifting the *BP* curve to the right.

You have now seen that some factors shift the *IS* curve and the *BP* curve simultaneously. It is of some importance to establish which of these two curves shifts more in the event of a change that shifts them both. There is no ambiguity about this when the factor leading to a shift in both curves is a change in world real income. In this case, both curves will shift in the same direction, but the *BP* curve will shift by more than the *IS* curve. To see this, all that you need do is to examine Figures 42.1 and 42.2 again. Consider the effect of a rise in world real income, which raises exports. In Figure 42.1, this would shift the investment-plus-government spending-plus-exports line to the right and also the *IS* curve to the right. The amount by which the *IS* curve shifts depends solely on the initial change in $i + g + ex$ and on the slope of the savings-plus-taxes-plus-imports line in frame (b). The steeper this line is, the smaller will be the shift in the *IS* curve.

Now consider what happens to the *BP* line. In frame (c) of Figure 42.2, the $kas + ex$ line would shift to the right. Also, the *BP* curve in frame (d) would shift to the right. The amount by which the *BP* curve shifts depends solely on the initial shift in $kas + ex$ and on the slope of the import line in frame (b). The flatter this line is, the bigger will be the shift in the *BP* curve. The initial change in exports recorded in frame (c) of both figures is identical, of course. Since we know that the slope of the savings-plus-taxes-plus-import line is steeper than the slope of the import line (convince yourself of this by simply noting that savings also rise as income rises), we also know that the *BP* curve must shift to the right by more than the *IS* curve shifts.

A change in world real income is not the only factor that leads to shifts in both the *IS* and *BP* curves. A change in the real exchange rate (a change in the exchange rate or the domestic or world price levels) will also shift both curves. In this case, there is a potential ambiguity as to which of the two curves shifts more. The ambiguity arises from the fact—apparent by comparing Equations (42.4) and (42.6) above—that the definition of real expenditure that underlies the *IS* curve is one based on a constant (base period) real exchange rate—refer back to Chapter 3 and Equation (3.6)—whereas the definition of the balance of payments that underlies the *BP* curve is one based on the current real exchange rate. Thus, when analyzing a change in the real exchange rate, it is necessary to work out its effect on the *volume* of exports and imports in order to calculate the *IS* curve shift, and its effect on the real *value* of exports and imports in order to calculate the *BP* curve shift. To avoid a lengthy treatment of all possible cases, we shall *assume* that a change in the real exchange rate has the same type of effect on the *IS* and *BP* curves as the effect of a change in world real income that we have just analyzed. That is, we shall assume that a rise in the real exchange rate (a rise in $\theta = EP_f/P$) will raise both the volume and value of (net) exports and will shift both the *IS* and *BP* curves to the right. The *BP* curve will be assumed to shift further to the right than the *IS* curve.

It will be useful for the subsequent analysis to introduce a further curve that summarizes the shifts of the *IS* and *BP* curves. Let us call that curve the *IS-BP* curve. Figure 42.3 illustrates its derivation. Imagine that the economy starts out on the curves *IS* and *BP* at the interest rate r_1 and income level y_1. There is then some shock that shifts both the *IS* and *BP* curves to *IS'*, *BP'*. The new income level is y_2 and the interest rate is r_2. The line traced by the intersection points of the *IS* and *BP* curves will be called the *IS-BP* curve. It slopes downwards because we know that the *BP* curve shifts by more than the *IS* curve following any shock that shifts both of these curves. The *IS-BP* curve will be useful for analyzing the effects of changes in rest of world variables and in the exchange rate, all of which shift both the *IS* and *BP* curves in the manner illustrated in Figure 42.3.

You now have all the tools that are needed to analyze the determination of output, interest rates, the balance of payments, and the exchange rate and how these variables respond to various policy and other shocks when the price level is constant and output is below full-employment level.

Figure 42.3
The *IS-BP* Locus

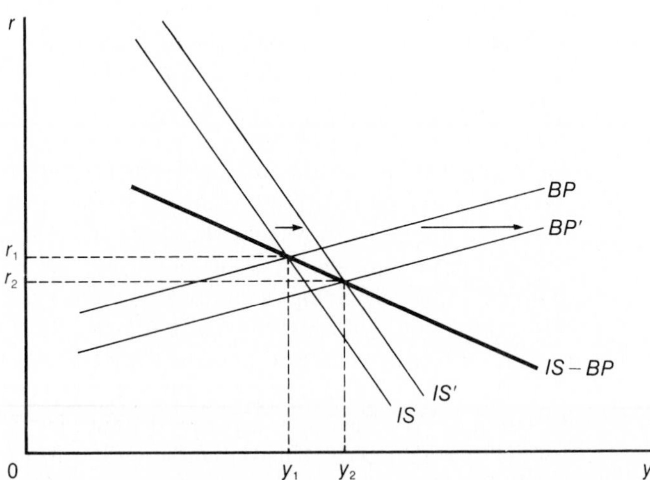

Because a shock that influences both the *IS* and *BP* curves shifts the *BP* curve by more than the *IS* curve, the intersection points of successive *BP* and *IS* curves fall on a downward sloping line *IS-BP*.

Figure 42.4
Equilibrium with Fixed Exchange Rates

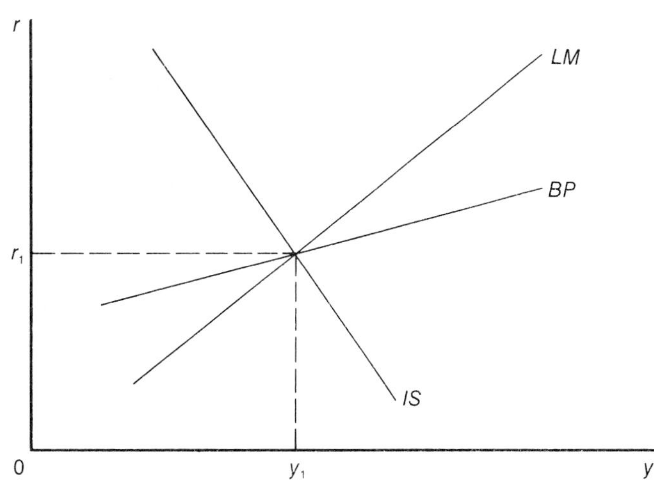

Equilibrium output and interest rates are determined at the point of intersection of the *IS* and *BP* curves. The *LM* curve will also pass through this intersection point because the money supply adjusts to ensure that this happens.

E. Determination of Output, Interest Rate, and the Balance of Payments in a Fixed Exchange Rate Regime

Let us now determine the equilibrium values of output, the interest rate, and the balance of payments when the exchange rate is fixed. We shall do this for given levels of world income, interest rates, and the price level; for the given fixed exchange rate; for fixed levels of government spending and taxes; and for a fixed domestic price level (remembering that throughout we are dealing with the Keynesian situation in which full-employment output exceeds any output level that we are considering). The equilibrium levels of output, the rate of interest, and the balance of payments will be determined at the triple intersection point of the *IS*, *LM*, *BP* curves as shown in Figure 42.4. The *IS* and *BP* curves are exactly the same as those derived in Figures 42.1 and 42.2. The *LM* curve is exactly the same as the curve derived in Chapter 19.

Equilibrium

The way the model works to determine the equilibrium is slightly more complicated than the standard closed economy variant of the *IS-LM* analysis. The idea is that real income and the rate of interest are determined at each instant by the intersection of the *IS* and *LM* curves, as they were before in the closed economy analysis. This is not, however, the end of the story. If the intersection of the *IS* and *LM* curves is above the *BP* curve, then there is a balance of payments surplus, and the money supply will be rising. A rising money supply means that the *LM* curve will be shifting to the right, so that income will be rising and the rate of interest falling (the economy will be sliding down the *IS*

Figure 42.5
The Effects of an Expansionary Fiscal Policy under Fixed Exchange Rates

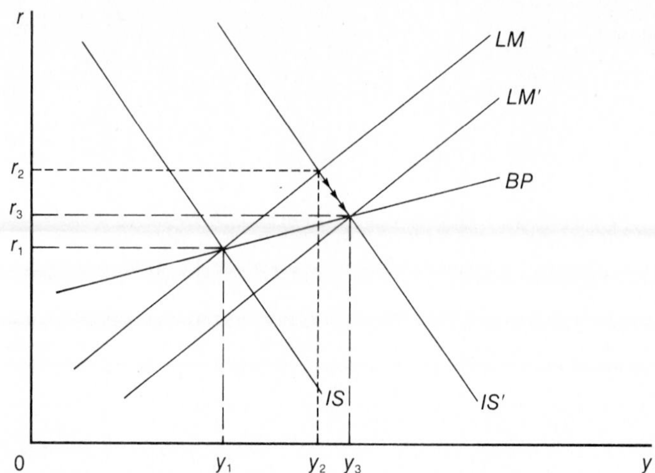

An initial equilibrium y_1, r_1 is disturbed by a rise in government spending or tax cut that shifts the *IS* curve to *IS'*. The impact effect of this is to raise interest rates and real income to r_2 and y_2. In this situation, there is a balance of payments surplus that raises the money supply, thereby shifting the *LM* curve to the right. The final equilibrium is the interest rate r_3 and real income y_3 where the curve *IS'* intersects the *BP* curve. The *LM* curve will by then have become *LM'*. The adjustment process will take the economy down the *IS* curve.

curve). Such a process would continue until the *LM* curve comes to rest where the *IS* curve intersects the *BP* curve. At such a point, the balance of payments will be zero and the money supply constant, so that the *LM* curve will no longer be shifting.

Conversely, if initially the *IS* and *LM* curves cut each other below the *BP* curve, then there will be a balance of payments deficit. The money supply will be falling, and the *LM* curve will be moving to the left. In the process, the level of income will fall, and the interest rate will rise (the economy will slide up the *IS* curve). This process will continue until the *LM* curve intersects the intersection point of the *IS* and *BP* curves. At that point, the balance of payments deficit will have disappeared and the money supply will be constant.

You will probably get a better feeling for what is going on here by working through a series of experiments that result from the economy being shocked by a variety of domestic and foreign disturbances. We shall now turn to such an exercise.

Fiscal Policy

First, consider the effects of an expansionary fiscal policy. Figure 42.5 illustrates the analysis. The economy is at an initial equilibrium exactly like that depicted in Figure 42.4, with the interest rate at r_1 and income at y_1. There is then a rise in government spending or a cut in taxes that shifts the *IS* curve to *IS'*. The impact effect of this fiscal policy action is to raise the rate of interest and the level of income to r_2 and y_2, respectively. The economy would now, however, be experiencing a balance of payments surplus since it is operating at

Figure 42.6
The Effects of a Rise in the Money Supply under Fixed Exchange Rates

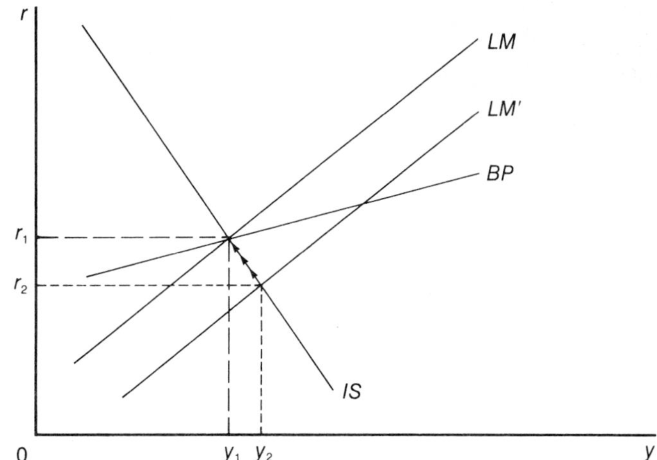

An initial equilibrium at y_1, r_1 is disturbed by a once-and-for-all rise in domestic credit that shifts the *LM* curve to *LM′*. The impact effect of this is to lower the interest rate to r_2 and raise real income to y_2. A balance of payments deficit results, and this leads to an outflow of money. As the money supply falls, the *LM* curve shifts back to the left and settles eventually at the initial equilibrium y_1, r_1.

a point above the *BP* curve. With a balance of payments surplus, the money supply will be rising, so the *LM* curve will shift to the right. As this happens, the succession of *LM* curves intersects *IS′* at lower and lower interest rates but at higher and higher income levels (along the arrowed path). The economy will finally settle down at the interest rate r_3 and income level y_3. The effect, then, of an expansionary fiscal policy in a fixed exchange rate, fixed price level, underemployed economy will be to produce higher interest rates and higher real income levels. A balance of payments surplus will bring an inflow of money that will subsequently lower interest rates, but not to their initial level,[2] and will raise real income still further.[3]

Monetary Policy

Second, consider the effects of an expansionary monetary policy. Again, let the economy start out at the initial equilibrium level r_1, y_1 depicted in Figure 42.4. Figure 42.6 shows the effect of a monetary disturbance. Imagine raising the quantity of money (by raising domestic credit) in a once-and-for-all manner, so

[2]In the special case of perfect capital mobility, the interest rate will return to its initial level.

[3]There is a possible, although most unlikely, case that would arise if the *BP* curve was steeper than the *LM* curve. In this case, the impact effect of the expansionary fiscal policy would be to produce a balance of payments deficit. Money would flow out of the economy, thereby shifting the *LM* curve leftwards, raising the rate of interest, and lowering the level of real income. The new equilibrium would be one in which both interest rates and real income had increased above their initial levels.

that the *LM* curve shifts to *LM′*. Initially, the interest rate drops to r_2 and real income rises to y_2. Clearly, with a higher real income level bringing in more imports and a lower interest rate lowering the capital account surplus, there will be a balance of payments deficit. In this situation, the money supply will fall, and the *LM* curve will move to the left. As it does so, it will intersect the *IS* curve at higher and higher interest rates and lower real income levels (the arrowed path). Eventually, the quantity of money will have returned to its initial level, and the economy will have returned to its initial interest rate and income position. All that will have happened is that the quantity of money will be backed by a higher amount of domestic credit and a smaller amount of foreign exchange reserves in the final situation than initially. This will be the only change between the initial and final situation. Thus, in a fixed exchange rate economy, monetary policy has no permanent effects on aggregate demand.

The analysis that we have just conducted implicitly assumes that the country has a sufficiently large stock of foreign exchange reserves to permit the initially assumed expansion of the domestic money supply. Of course, if the country did not have sufficient foreign exchange reserves, then the experiment could not be conducted. If the country attempted to increase its money supply in a situation in which it had insufficient foreign exchange reserves, it would cease to be a fixed exchange rate country. It would find itself forced off the fixed exchange rate when its foreign exchange reserves fell to such a low level that it was unable to intervene in the foreign exchange market to maintain the value of its currency. One possibility in such a situation would be for the country to devalue its currency. Let us now analyze this case along with the effects of foreign shocks.

Devaluation and Foreign Shocks

Third, consider the effect of a devaluation of the currency. A devaluation is a once-and-for-all rise in the value of the exchange rate *E*. Again, suppose the economy starts out at the real income and interest level y_1, r_1, as depicted in Figure 42.7. Then imagine that there is a once-and-for-all rise in the value of the exchange rate (devaluation). This raises exports and lowers imports, thereby shifting both the *IS* curve and the *BP* curve to the right. The new curves are shown as *IS′* and *BP′* and are drawn to reflect the fact that the *BP* curve shifts rightwards by more than does the *IS* curve. The initial impact of the devaluation will be to take the economy to the equilibrium y_2, r_2, where the original *LM* curve intersects the new *IS* curve. In this situation, there is a balance of payments surplus since the economy is above the new *BP* curve (*BP′*). The balance of payments surplus causes the quantity of money to rise and the *LM* curve to start shifting to the right. As the *LM* curve shifts to the right, it intersects the *IS* curve at lower and lower interest rates and at higher and higher real income levels (along the arrowed adjustment path). Eventually real income rises to y_3 and the interest rate falls to r_3. The final effect of a devaluation, therefore, is to raise real income and lower interest rates. The balance of payments moves into surplus during the adjustment process, but it is in equilibrium at the end of the process.

It should be emphasized that these responses to a devaluation are all

Figure 42.7
The Effect of a Devaluation

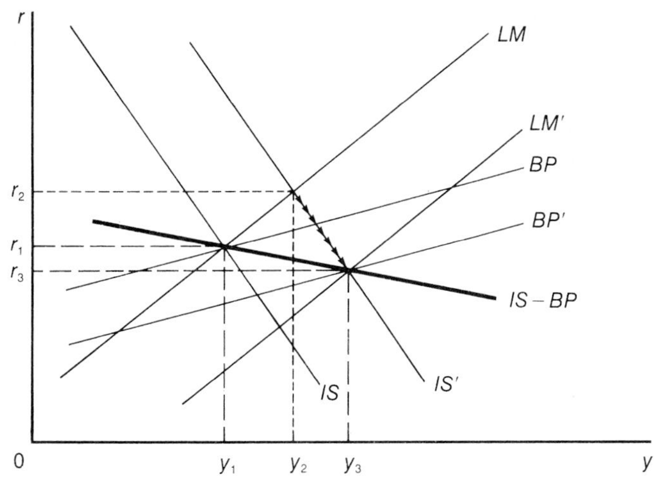

The initial equilibrium y_1, r_1 is disturbed by a devaluation of the currency. This raises exports and lowers imports, shifting the *IS* and *BP* curves to the right. The impact effect of this is to raise the level of real income to y_2 and the interest rate to r_2. There is a balance of payments surplus in this situation that leads to a rising money supply. The *LM* curve shifts to the right, producing a falling rate of interest and a continuing increase in real income. The resting point is where the curve *IS′* intersects the curve *BP′*, at which state the *LM* curve will have become *LM′*. The devaluation then raises real income and initially raises the rate of interest but eventually lowers the rate of interest.

conditional on the price level remaining constant. If the price level was to rise by the same percentage amount as the devaluation, then the real exchange rate would not be affected, and the economy would remain at its initial equilibrium level. Alternatively, if the price level *initially* remained constant, the path described in Figure 42.7 would be set up, and the economy would move from y_1, r_1 to y_2, r_2 and then start to proceed toward y_3, r_3. If, during this process the price level began to rise and eventually rose all the way to full proportionality with the devaluation, then instead of continuing to travel down the curve *IS′*, both the *IS′* and *BP′* curves would shift leftwards, and the economy would gradually move back to y_1, r_1.

Shocks emanating from the rest of the world would have effects similar to a devaluation. A rise in world real income or a rise in the world price level would have exactly the same effects as a devaluation. Conversely, a fall in the world rate of interest, which would shift the *BP* curve but not the *IS* curve, would have no impact effect on real income and the interest rate. It would, however, set up a process in which the balance of payments was in surplus and so would start the *LM* curve moving to the right. Real income would rise, and the interest rate would fall until the point of intersection of the original *IS* curve with the new *BP* curve was reached.

This completes our analysis of the effects of domestic policy and foreign shocks on output, interest rates, and the balance of payments in a fixed exchange rate regime. Let us now turn to examine a flexible exchange rate economy.

F. Determination of Output, Interest Rate, and the Exchange Rate in a Flexible Exchange Rate Regime

Analyzing a flexible exchange rate economy is slightly harder than the fixed exchange rate case. The problem arises because the *IS* and *BP* curves have three variables in them—real income, the rate of interest, and the exchange rate—all of which we want to determine, and it is therefore hard to construct diagrams in two dimensions that have the simplicity of those in the fixed exchange rate case. In order to make the analysis of the flexible exchange rate economy as comparable as possible with that of the fixed exchange rate economy, we shall use a series of diagrams (Figures 42.8–42.10) drawn in interest rate real income space, as we did before when analyzing the fixed exchange rate case. This means that the exchange rate will not appear explicitly on one of the axes of the diagrams. It will be possible, nevertheless, to work out the directions of change of the exchange rate when various shocks are administered to the economy. This is analogous to the way in which the balance of payments was analyzed in the previous section.

Equilibrium

It will be useful, as a starting point, to reinterpret Figure 42.4 as a flexible exchange rate equilibrium rather than as a fixed exchange rate equilibrium. Under flexible exchange rates, the quantity of money (both the stock of foreign exchange reserves and domestic credit) is determined by the central bank. The position of the *LM* curve is therefore bolted down, so to speak, by monetary policy. If the point of intersection of the *IS* and *BP* curves is not on the *LM* curve, something has to adjust. The adjustment that occurs is in the exchange rate. Since domestic and foreign prices are constant, different values of the exchange rate E generate different values of the real exchange rate θ. Different values of θ generate different values of exports and imports and therefore produce different *IS* and *BP* curves.

Since the *IS* curve slopes downwards and the *BP* curve slopes upwards, there is one, and only one, point (a real income level of y_1 and interest rate of r_1) at which they intersect and at the same time fall on the *LM* curve. The value of the exchange rate that underlies the *IS* and *BP* curves when they cut the *LM* curve is the equilibrium exchange rate. Thus, you may interpret Figure 42.4 as a flexible exchange rate equilibrium in the sense that the exchange rate has to be the particular value that causes the *IS* and *BP* curves to intersect each other at a point on the *LM* curve. This contrasts with the fixed exchange rate interpretation of Figure 42.4, which is that the *IS* and *BP* curves are fixed in position, while the *LM* curve takes up the slack—the money supply varying to ensure that the *LM* curve is located at the point of intersection of the fixed *IS* and *BP* curves.

To repeat for emphasis, in a fixed exchange rate world, the *IS* and *BP* curves are fixed in position and determine the steady-state equilibrium, while the quantity of money and, therefore, the *LM* curve are dragged along to that fixed intersection point. In the case of the flexible exchange rate economy, the *LM* curve is fixed in position, while the exchange rate is free to move, thereby shifting the *IS* and *BP* curves to an intersection point on the *LM* curve.

Figure 42.8
The Effects of an Expansionary Fiscal Policy under Flexible Exchange Rates

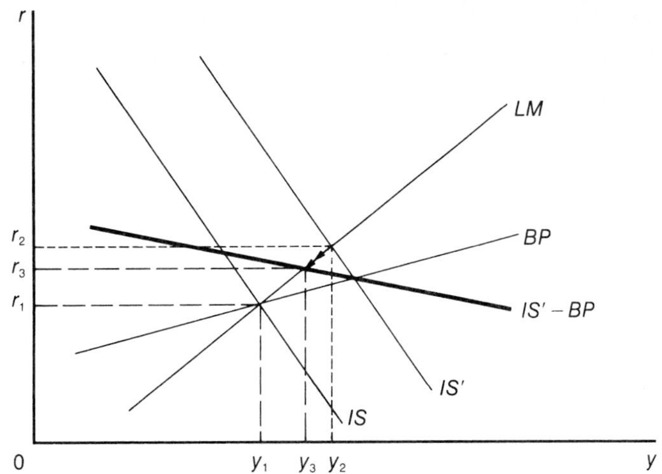

An initial equilibrium y_1, r_1 is disturbed by a rise in government spending or a tax cut that shifts the *IS* curve to *IS'*. If there was no change in the exchange rate, real income would move to y_2 and the interest rate to r_2, thereby producing a balance of payments surplus. With a flexible exchange rate, this does not happen. Instead the exchange rate falls (the currency appreciates), thereby lowering exports and raising imports. Both the curve *IS'* and the *BP* curve shift to the left. The equilibrium will be at the point at which the *IS'-BP* locus intersects the *LM* curve, at the interest rate r_3 and real income y_3. Thus the effect of an expansionary fiscal policy is to raise real income, raise the rate of interest, and appreciate the currency.

Fiscal Policy

Let us now proceed to analyze the effects of the same set of policy and foreign shocks that were analyzed in the preceding section in the flexible exchange rate case. First, consider the effect of an expansionary fiscal policy. The economy is initially in an equilibrium, such as that shown in Figure 42.8, at y_1, r_1. There is then an expansion of government spending or a tax cut that shifts the *IS* curve from *IS* to *IS'*. The impact effect is to raise the real income level to y_2 and the interest rate to r_2. In this situation, if the exchange rate was fixed, there would be a balance of payments surplus. With a flexible exchange rate, however, the balance of payments surplus is not allowed to occur. The central bank simply does not stand ready to take in foreign exchange at a pegged exchange rate. Instead, the exchange rate adjusts. If there is an excess supply of foreign currency, its price falls, or alternatively, the domestic currency appreciates. This lowers the real exchange rate, thereby raising imports and lowering exports. In this process, the *IS* and *BP* curves shift to the left. Since we are assuming that the *BP* curve shifts by more than the *IS* curve, as they move they intersect along the line marked *IS'-BP*. They will eventually come to rest, interesecting the *LM* curve at the interest rate r_3 and real income level y_3. The exchange rate at that point is lower than the initial exchange rate (the currency has appreciated). Thus, the effects of an expansionary fiscal policy in a flexible exchange rate economy are to raise real income and the rate of interest and to appreciate the currency.

Figure 42.9 The Effects of an Expansionary Monetary Policy under Flexible Exchange Rates

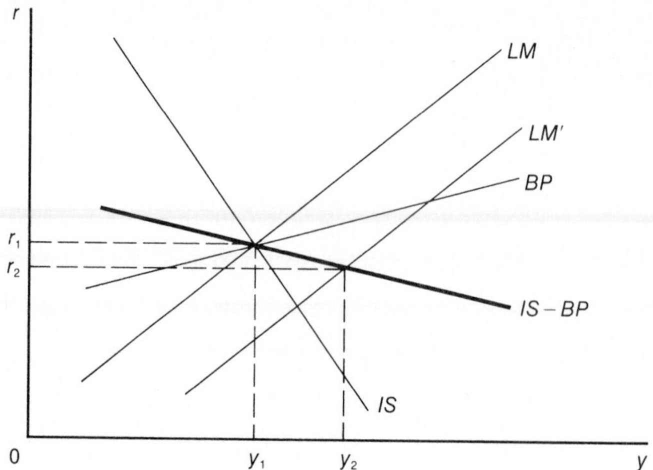

An initial equilibrium at y_1, r_1 is disturbed by a rise in the money stock that shifts the *LM* curve to *LM'*. This leads to a higher exchange rate (devaluation), which shifts the *IS* and *BP* curves along the *IS-BP* locus until they intersect the new *LM* curve at y_2, r_2. Thus, the effect of an expansionary monetary policy under flexible exchange rates is to lower the interest rate, raise real income, and depreciate the currency.

The rural sector of the economy may be hostile toward such an outcome and may complain about the difficulty of doing profitable business in foreign markets. In effect, what is happening is that because the government is spending more, real resources have to be diverted from the rest of the economy to the government, and this is accomplished by making total world demand for domestic goods decline and domestic demands for rest of world goods increase. The appreciation of the currency is the mechanism whereby this happens. It is not the *cause* of problems perceived by domestic farmers and manufacturers.

Monetary Policy

Next, consider the effects of an expansionary monetary policy. Again, start the economy out at the equilibrium (y_1, r_1) shown in Figure 42.9. This is at the triple intersection of *LM*, *IS*, and *BP* curves. Then let there be a rise in the quantity of money that shifts the *LM* curve to *LM'*. The new equilibrium clearly has to be somewhere on the curve *LM'*. At the initial exchange rate, the *IS* and *BP* curves intersect on the old *LM* curve. There is another value of the exchange rate (a higher value) at which the *IS* and *BP* curves intersect on the new *LM* curve, *LM'*. The *IS-BP* curve traces out the intersection points of the *IS* and *BP* curves as the exchange rate changes. The intersection of the *IS-BP* curve and the *LM'* curve determines the new equilibrium level of real income y_2 and the interest rate r_2. We know that the exchange rate is higher than the initial one because we know that it is associated with a higher level of exports and lower level of imports than prevailed initially. Recall that a higher value of the exchange rate implies a depreciation of the currency.

Figure 42.10
The Effects of a Rise in World Income under Flexible Exchange Rates

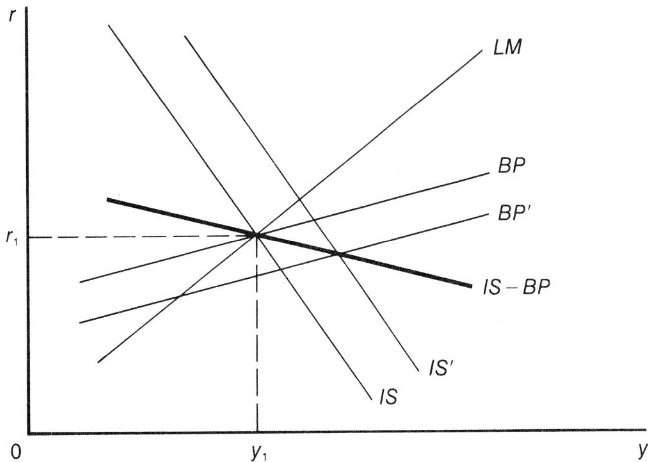

An initial equilibrium y_1, r_1 is disturbed by a rise in world real income that shifts the *IS* and *BP* curves to *IS′* and *BP′*. The currency appreciates to produce an equivalent shift of those curves back to their initial positions, so that the real income level and interest rate are undisturbed. Thus the effect of a world real income rise under flexible exchange rates comes out entirely as a change in the exchange rate.

The effects of an expansionary monetary policy in a fixed price level, underemployed, flexible exchange rate economy may be summarized as follows: A rise in the money supply leads to a lower rate of interest, a higher level of real income, and a depreciation of the currency.

Foreign Shocks

Finally, consider the effects of a change in world real income. Imagine that the economy is at (y_1, r_1) in Figure 42.10 and that then the rise in world real income shifts the *IS* and *BP* curves to *IS′* and *BP′*. These curves necessarily intersect along the line *IS-BP*. Varying the exchange rate changes exports and imports, thereby shifting the *IS* and *BP* curves. Varying foreign real income (the shock that we are considering here) also changes exports and shifts the *IS* and *BP* curves. Since the *LM* curve has not changed (the domestic money supply being held constant), we know that the final equilibrium must be at a point on the *LM* curve. We further know that it has to involve the intersection of the *IS* and *BP* curves. We can see that there is only one such point, and this is the initial equilibrium real income and interest rate level (y_1, r_1). What happens is that the exchange rate has to change (appreciate in this case) so as to return the *IS* and *BP* curves from their shocked positions *IS′*, *BP′* to their initial positions. The initial *IS* and *BP* curves then describe the initial exchange rate and the initial level of world real income and also the new higher level of world real income and lower value of the exchange rate (appreciated currency).

Comparison of Fixed and Flexible Exchange Rate It is of some interest to compare the responses of the economy in the fixed and flexible exchange rate cases. You can do this by comparing Figures 42.5 with 42.8 (fiscal policy), 42.6 with 42.9 (monetary policy), and 42.7 (interpreted as a foreign shock) with 42.10 (for a rise in world real income). An expansionary fiscal policy has a bigger output effect but a smaller interest rate effect under fixed exchange rates than under flexible exchange rates. An expansionary monetary policy raises real income and lowers the interest rate under flexible exchange rates, but it has no effect, in the steady state, under fixed exchange rates. An expansion of world real income raises domestic real income and lowers domestic interest rates under fixed exchange rates, but it has no effect on interest rates and real income, in the steady state, in a flexible exchange rate economy.

Summary

A. Derivation of the *IS* Curve for an Open Economy

The *IS* curve for an open economy shows the relationship between the rate of interest and level of real income at which savings-plus-taxes-plus-imports equals investment-plus-government spending-plus-exports. It is steeper than the *IS* curve for a closed economy and intersects the latter at the real income level and interest rate at which imports equal exports.

B. Definition of the *BP* Curve

The *BP* curve shows the relationship between the rate of interest and level of real income at which the sum of the current account and capital account and thus the balance of payments is zero.

C. Derivation of the *BP* Curve

For a given real exchange rate (i.e. a given level of domestic and foreign prices and nominal exchange rate) and given level of world real income, exports will be fixed. The capital account surplus depends on the domestic rate of interest, and imports depend on domestic income. By finding the level of real income that generates an import volume equal to the exports-plus-capital account surplus generated by a given interest rate, it is possible to trace out the *BP* curve. The curve slopes upwards, except in the case of perfect capital mobility, in which case it is horizontal.

D. Shifts in the *IS*, *LM*, and *BP* Curves

In addition to the factors that shift the *IS* curve in a closed economy, a change in world real income, the exchange rate, or the foreign price level shifts the *IS* curve in an open economy. A rise in world real income, a rise in the world price level, or a depreciation of the domestic currency shifts the *IS* curve to the right. The *LM* curve shifts because of changes in the money supply. In an open economy, when the exchange rate is fixed, this occurs if the balance of payments is other than zero. The balance of payments surplus is associated with a rising money supply, the balance of payments deficit with a falling money supply. Thus, if the economy is off the *BP* curve, the *LM* curve is shifting if the exchange rate is fixed. The *BP* curve shifts as a result of changes in world real income, the exchange rate, the world price level, or the world rate of interest. A rise in world real income, a rise in the world price level, a fall in the world rate of interest, or depreciation of the currency shifts the *BP* curve to the right. A change in world income that shifts both the *IS* and the *BP* curves shifts both curves in the same direction but shifts the *BP* curve by more than it shifts the *IS* curve. A change in the real exchange rate also shifts both the *IS* and *BP* curves, and we assume that the *BP* curve shifts by more than the *IS* curve.

E. Determination of Output, Interest Rate, and the Balance of Payments in a Fixed Exchange Rate Regime

At each instant, the real income level and interest rate are determined at the point of intersection of the *IS* and *LM* curves. If that intersection point is off the *BP* curve, the *LM* curve is shifting. The steady state occurs where the *IS* and *BP* curves intersect. The *LM* curve intersects this point as a result of the money supply adjusting, while the balance of payments is out of equilibrium.

Expansionary fiscal policy raises output and interest rates and leads to a temporary balance of payments surplus. Expansionary monetary policy leads to a temporary balance of payments deficit and no steady-state change in real income or the rate of interest. A devaluation initially raises the rate of interest and real income level, but it eventually lowers the rate of interest below its initial level and raises real income still further. In the process, the balance of payments will have been in surplus. A rise in world real income has a similar effect to that of a devaluation.

F. Determination of Output, Interest Rate, and the Exchange Rate in a Flexible Exchange Rate Regime

Under flexible exchange rates, the *LM* curve is fixed in position. The positions of the *BP* and *IS* curves depend on the value of the exchange rate. As the exchange rate varies, these curves shift to intersect each other along a downward sloping *IS-BP* locus. The equilibrium exchange rate is the exchange rate that locates the *BP* and *IS* curves at an intersection point along the *LM* curve. In a flexible exchange rate economy, an expansionary fiscal policy raises real income and the rate of interest and appreciates the currency. An expansionary monetary policy lowers the rate of interest, raises the level of real income, and depreciates the currency. An expansion in world real income leads to an appreciation of the currency but no change in real income or the rate of interest.

Review Questions

1. What is the equilibrium condition that an open economy satisfies as it moves along its *IS* curve?

2. How does the *IS* curve of an open economy differ from that of a closed economy?

3. What determines the slope of the open economy *IS* curve?
4. What makes the open economy *IS* curve shift, and in what direction?
5. What is the equilibrium condition that is satisfied as the economy moves along its *BP* curve?
6. What determines the slope of the *BP* curve?
7. What makes the *BP* curve shift, and in what direction?
8. Explain how a rise in world real income shifts the *IS* and *BP* curves. Which shifts by most? Why?
9. What happens to the *LM* curve if the economy is (a) above, (b) below, and (c) on its *BP* curve?
10. Work out the effects on all the relevant variables, under fixed exchange rates, of the following shocks:

(a) A rise in government spending.
(b) A rise in domestic credit.
(c) A rise in the exchange rate.
(d) A rise in world real income.
(e) A rise in world prices.
(f) A rise in the world rate of interest.

How do the effects depend on the degree of capital mobility?
11. Work out the effects on all the relevant variables, in a flexible exchange rate regime, of the six shocks listed in Question 10. How do the effects depend on the degree of capital mobility?
12. On the basis of your answers to Questions 10 and 11, how would you choose between the two alternative exchange rate regimes?

43

The Rational Expectations Theory of the Open Economy: A Selective Sketch

This chapter is going to introduce you to some recent developments in the analysis of the macroeconomic problems of the open economy. This material is of a very recent origin, and it is still not fully digested in the professional literature. Although you are only going to be given a selective sketch in this chapter, you will be introduced to some of the central issues involved in dealing with the development of a rational theory of the open economy. There are four tasks that will enable you to achieve this, and they are to:

(a) Understand the need for a rational expectations theory of the open economy.
(b) Understand the implications of the assumption of perfect capital mobility for the determination of aggregate demand.
(c) Understand how output and the price level are determined with perfect capital mobility, rational expectations, and a fixed exchange rate.
(d) Understand how output, the price level, and the exchange rate are determined with perfect capital mobility and rational expectations in a flexible exchange rate regime.

In pursuing these tasks it will be convenient, as in the case of the closed economy analysis of rational expectations models, to abstract from trends in the variables. We shall determine the price level rather than the rate of inflation and the exchange rate rather than the rate of depreciation of the currency. As before, you can think of what we are doing as analyzing movements about trends, but not changing the underlying trends in the variables. The basic model (Chapter 41) analyzed the trends.

Let us proceed immediately with the first task.

A. The Need for a Rational Expectations Theory of the Open Economy

The previous two chapters have taken you through the basic and Keynesian models of the open economy. The basic model of the open economy is an extension of the basic model of the closed economy and analyzes what happens to output, prices, interest rates, the exchange rate, and the balance of payments when the economy is at a continuous full-employment position. The Keynesian model of the open economy is a natural extension of the Keynesian model of the closed economy. It tells us what happens to output, interest rates, the exchange rate, and the balance of payments when the price level is fixed and there is excess capacity. Both models are extremes. We have seen that each is capable of explaining some of the facts, but neither is capable of explaining all the facts. The virtue of the rational expectations analysis is that, in effect, it combines the best of both the basic and Keynesian models. The basic model is seen as generating the consequences of fully anticipated shocks, whereas the Keynesian model gives predictions that are approximately the same as those that arise when the economy is administered unanticipated shocks. Using the notion that actual policy processes involve varying degrees of anticipation and error, in principle at least, enables all the facts to be accommodated by the one theory.

It clearly would be an unsatisfactory state of affairs if we were unable to extend these notions to the open economy. It would be intellectually unsatisfying if we had to live with the basic and Keynesian models as the only models available for handling open economy questions, especially when we know that, in the context of the simpler closed economy, they are in some respects unsatisfactory—hence, the need for an extension of the rational expectations theory of the closed economy to the open economy.

There are some challenging problems in achieving a completely satisfactory rational analysis of the open economy. In the open economy, there are more variables to be determined and more sources of shocks than in the closed economy, and this increases the dimensionality of the problem that we need to solve. It makes it harder to arrive at simple, intuitive, easily grasped models.

In this chapter, I am going to try to give you a feel for how the rational expectations theory can be applied to the problems of the open economy by working with a particular model that employs an extreme assumption. That assumption is that capital is perfectly mobile between the economy that we are analyzing and the rest of the world. My own judgment is that this is only a slightly extreme assumption. It is not quite the way the world is, but it is close. The virtue of making this assumption, aside from the fact that it does not strike me as being wildly at odds with the world, is that it simplifies the analysis considerably. It also makes it possible to gain insights about issues that otherwise would be hard to understand.

There is an alternative extreme assumption that also yields a much simplified analysis, although it yields very different conclusions. It is the opposite extreme to perfect capital mobility—zero capital mobility. This alternative strikes me as being so violently at odds with the world as to be uninteresting and not worthwhile analyzing.

Both perfect capital mobility and zero capital mobility simplify the task of analysis. One of them does it in a way that only mildly violates the facts, whereas the other does it in a way that renders the analysis utterly pointless.

By way of an analogy, assuming perfect capital mobility seems to me to be quite analogous to assuming there to be no atmosphere (a vacuum) for the purpose of calculating the length of time it would take for a 10-pound rock to fall from the top of the Empire State Building and hit the ground. The atmospheric resistance may be presumed to be negligible and, hence, the calculations are simplified considerably by assuming it to be zero. The answer obtained will be wrong, but not misleadingly wrong. The alternative assumption of zero capital mobility strikes me as being analogous to simplifying the calculation of the power required to put a satellite into earth orbit by assuming zero gravity. The assumption would be so wildly at odds with the fact that the rocket would never even leave its launching pad!

Let us proceed then, using the assumption of perfect capital mobility, and see what we can learn about the behavior of an open economy under rational expectations.

B. Aggregate Demand When Capital Is Perfectly Mobile

In order to develop a theory of the open economy comparable to the closed economy theories worked out in the previous chapters, we need to see how expected aggregate demand determines the rational expectation of the price level and how actual aggregate demand, interacting with the expectations-augmented aggregate supply curve, determines the actual levels of output and prices. We further need to work out, under a fixed exchange rate regime, how the balance of payments is determined, and how, under flexible exchange rates, the exchange rate is determined. The key difference between doing this analysis for an open economy and for a closed economy is in the theory of aggregate demand. We need to take on board the extension of the closed economy Keynesian theory of aggregate demand that was set out in Chapter 42. The task of this section is to see how, by assuming perfect capital mobility, we may derive a theory of aggregate demand from the Keynesian model of the open economy that carries over to the rational expectations theory of output and the price level. We shall continue to assume that there are no ongoing trend changes in prices or exchange rates, so that we are, in effect, analyzing movements about trends rather than changes in trends.

The first thing to notice is that if capital is perfectly mobile, the domestic rate of interest r, will be equal to the world rate of interest r_f. The *BP* curve will be horizontal at that rate of interest. The exogeneity of the rate of interest has powerful simplifying implications for the analysis. In the *IS*, *LM*, *BP* framework of Chapter 42, we had to determine the values of three variables—output, the rate of interest, and either the balance of payments (under fixed exchange rates) or the exchange rate (under flexible exchange rates). By assuming perfect capital mobility and, therefore, the exogeneity of the rate of interest, the problem reduces to that of determining two variables, namely, the level of real income and either the balance of payments (under fixed exchange rates) or the exchange rate (under flexible exchange rates).

The Keynesian analysis does, of course, hold the price level constant. This is one of its major drawbacks and one of the things that the rational expectations theory seeks to improve on. Indeed, we want to interpret the Keynesian analysis as determining an aggregate demand function that can interact with the aggregate supply side of the economy. That being so, although we have eliminated from consideration the determination of one variable (the rate of interest), we want to bring into focus the determination of another variable that the Keynesian analysis treats as fixed, namely, the price level. This is a lot easier to do in the case where the interest rate is fixed than where we simultaneously seek to determine the interest rate as well as all the other variables of concern.

Aggregate Demand with a Fixed Exchange Rate

With these preliminary remarks in mind, what we now want to do is to use the Keynesian analysis to develop a theory of aggregate demand for the open economy under fixed and flexible exchange rates. The two exchange rate regimes give rise to different propositions about aggregate demand in a rather interesting way. First, recall what the aggregate demand curve is. It is the relationship between the price level and the quantity of output that will be demanded such that the economy is on the *IS* and *LM* curves. Let us derive the aggregate demand curve for an open economy under both fixed and flexible exchange rates in the case where there is perfect capital mobility.

First, consider the fixed exchange rate economy. Figure 43.1 will illustrate the analysis. Frame (a) contains the *IS*, *LM*, and *BP* curves, and frame (b) is where the aggregate demand curve is generated. The *BP* curve is horizontal at the world rate of interest r_f. Imagine first, that the price level is arbitrarily given as P_0, marked off on the vertical axis of frame (b). With the price level at P_0, the *IS* curve would be the curve labelled $IS(EP_f/P_0)$. We know that under fixed exchange rates, the money supply is endogenous and has to be equal to whatever quantity is demanded at the level of income generated by the intersection of the *IS* and *BP* curves. Thus, the *LM* curve will automatically pass through the intersection of the curves *IS* and *BP* at the world interest rate r_f and the real income level y_0. Call the money supply in that case M_0, so that the *LM* curve is $LM(M_0/P_0)$. The point A in frame (b) at (y_0, P_0) is a point on the aggregate demand curve.

Next, consider raising the price level to P_1. In this case, the *IS* curve becomes $IS(EP_f/P_1)$ to the left of the original *IS* curve. Why does this happen? It happens because world prices have fallen relative to the domestic price level, thereby lowering the net demand for domestic output in the rest of the world and raising domestic demand for world output. This leftward shift of the *IS* curve intersects the *BP* curve at income level y_1. Again, the money supply will adjust through the balance of payments to ensure that the *LM* curve passes through this point. Call the new money supply M_1, so that the *LM* curve is that labelled $LM(M_1/P_1)$. Point B in frame (b) at the real income level y_1 and price level P_1 is another point on the aggregate demand curve.

Consider a still higher price level, P_2. This shifts the *IS* curve further to the left to $IS(EP_f/P_2)$, which determines the real income level y_2. The money stock would fall even further through a balance of payments deficit, so that the *LM* curve becomes $LM(M_2/P_2)$. Point *C* at real income level y_2 and price level P_2 is yet another point on the aggregate demand curve. Joining up the points A, B, C generates the aggregate demand curve.

You will notice from the way in which the aggregate demand curve has been derived that the exogenous variables that determine the position of the aggregate demand curve are entirely in the *BP* and *IS* curves. The *LM* curve is a slack relationship that automatically adjusts (via a balance of payments

Figure 43.1 The Aggregate Demand Curve under Fixed Exchange Rates and Perfect Capital Mobility

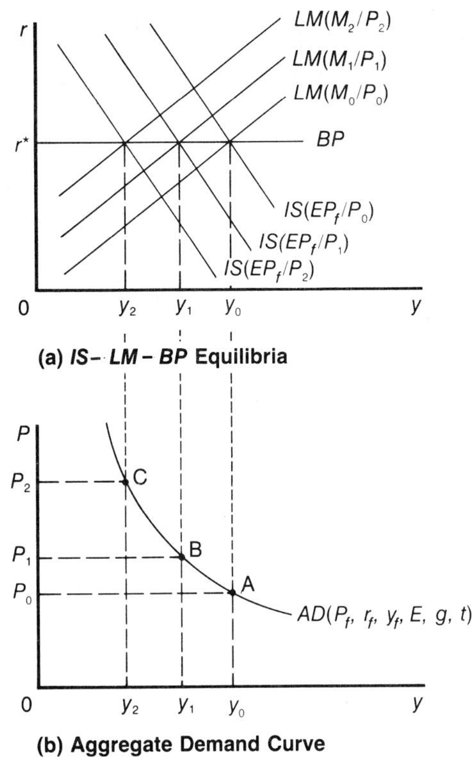

(a) *IS–LM–BP* Equilibria

(b) Aggregate Demand Curve

With perfect capital mobility, the *BP* curve is horizontal [frame (a)]. Where the *IS* curve cuts the *BP* curve determines the level of aggregate demand. As the price level rises, the *IS* curve shifts to the left with aggregate demand falling. The curve ABC traces out such an aggregate demand curve. The *LM* curve shifts as a result of a change in the money supply via the balance of payments to ensure money market equilibrium at each point along the aggregate demand curve. Aggregate demand will depend only on the factors that underlie the *BP* and *IS* curves, that is, the exchange rate, the world price level, the world rate of interest, world real income, government expenditure, and taxes.

adjustment of the money supply) to ensure an equilibrium money stock to support the interest rate, real income, and price level generated by the *IS-BP* intersection. The position of the aggregate demand curve therefore depends only on the things that influence the position of the *IS* and *BP* curves. These variables are the world price level, real income, and rate of interest; government spending and taxes; and the exchange rate. These are shown in parentheses on the label of the aggregate demand curve to remind you that the curve will shift as a result of changes in these variables. The money supply does not in any way determine the position of the aggregate demand curve in the fixed exchange rate, perfect capital mobility, open economy.

To summarize: For a fixed exchange rate open economy with perfect capital mobility, the aggregate demand curve is determined by the intersection of the *IS* and *BP* curves and in no way depends on the *LM* curve. This does not mean that the *LM* curve is irrelevant. Rather, it means that the *LM* curve determines the quantity of money, but not the levels of real income, prices, or interest rate.

Aggregate Demand with a Flexible Exchange Rate

Let us now go on to consider the derivation of the aggregate demand curve in a flexible exchange rate, perfect capital mobility economy. Figure 43.2 will illustrate this. For the moment ignore frame (c) of that figure. Frame (a) contains the *IS*, *LM*, and *BP* curves, and frame (b) derives the aggregate demand curve. Again, the *BP* curve is horizontal at the world rate of interest r_f. Recall that in the flexible exchange rate case, the exchange rate that underlies the position of the *IS* curve is determined in the analysis, whereas the money supply that underlies the position of the *LM* curve is exogenously determined by the monetary policy actions of the central bank.

To derive the aggregate demand curve, again pick a price level (initially P_0) marked on the vertical axis of frame (b). With a fixed money supply M_0 and the price level at P_0, the *LM* curve will be $LM(M_0/P_0)$. The level of aggregate demand y_0 is determined where that curve intersects the *BP* curve. The *IS* curve will pass through the point of intersection of the curves $LM(M_0/P_0)$ and *BP* because the exchange rate will adjust until the change in the real exchange rate generates sufficient domestic demand to ensure that the *IS* curve passes through precisely that point. Indeed, this is how the exchange rate is determined. The output level y_0 determined by the intersection of the *LM* and *BP* curves, along with the price level P_0, marked as point A in frame (b), represents a point on the aggregate demand curve.

Next, consider a higher price level P_1, marked on the vertical axis of frame (b). At this higher price level, while maintaining the money supply at M_0, the *LM* curve will shift to the left to become $LM(M_0/P_1)$. This intersects the *BP* curve at the lower income level y_1. The real income level y_1 with the price level P_1 [marked as point B in frame (b)] represents another point on the aggregate demand curve. The *IS* curve will pass through this point because the exchange rate will adjust to E_1, giving the *IS* curve $IS(E_1P_f/P_1)$.

Finally, suppose the price level was P_2, so that the real money supply was reduced still further, and the *LM* curve shifted yet further to the left to $LM(M_0/P_2)$. This would generate a real income level of y_2, shown as point C in frame (b). Again the *IS* curve would shift to the left with an adjustment in the exchange rate to E_2 to ensure that the real exchange rate moved by exactly the amount required to put the *IS* curve at the point of intersection of *LM* and *BP* curves.

The points A, B, C in frame (b) trace out the aggregate demand curve for the perfect capital mobility economy under flexible exchange rates. Notice that in the derivation of this aggregate demand curve, it was purely the intersection of the *LM* and *BP* curves that determined the level of aggregate demand. This curve is therefore labelled as $AD(M_0, r_f)$ to remind you that it is the variables that underlie the *LM* and *BP* curves, namely, the money stock and the foreign interest rate, that determine the position of the aggregate demand curve in a flexible exchange rate, perfect capital mobility economy.

To summarize: Under flexible exchange rates with perfect capital mobility, aggregate demand is determined by the intersection of the *LM* and *BP*

Figure 43.2
The Aggregate Demand and *RE* Curves in a Flexible Exchange Rate, Perfect Capital Mobility Economy

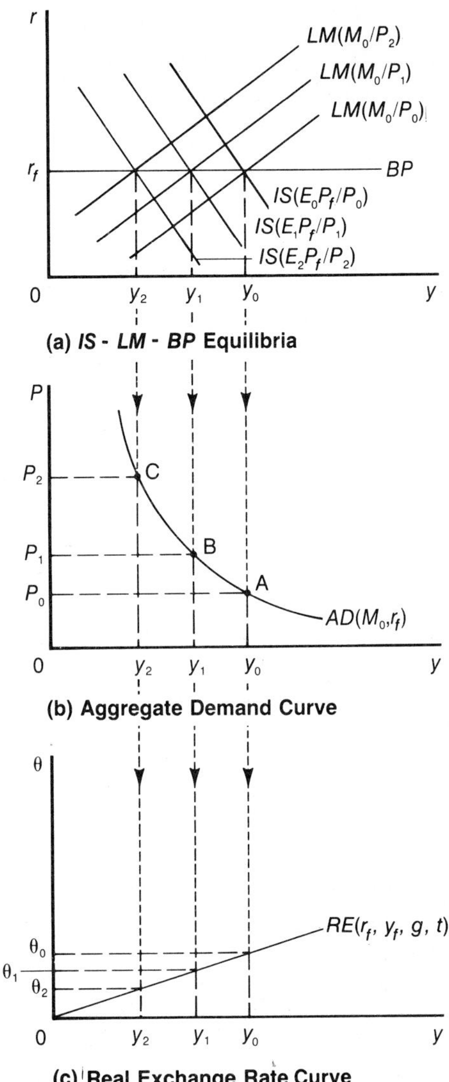

Under flexible exchange rates, the intersection of the *LM* and *BP* curves determines aggregate demand. As the price level rises from P_0 through P_2, real money balances fall and aggregate demand falls along the line ABC. Where the *IS* curve cuts the intersection of the *LM* and *BP* curves is determined the real exchange rate. The lower the level of real income the further to the left must the *IS* curve be, and the lower must be the net demand for domestic goods. The real exchange rate must fall, therefore, as real income falls.

curves, and the position of the aggregate demand curve depends only on the world rate of interest and the domestic money supply. It in no way depends on world real income or prices or domestic fiscal policy. The *IS* curve is not irrelevant in the flexible exchange rate economy; it determines the exchange rate but not output, prices, or the rate of interest.

Aggregate Demand: Summary

Both the fixed and flexible exchange rate aggregate demand curves slope downwards, and both depend on the world rate of interest. A higher world rate of interest would shift the fixed exchange rate aggregate demand curve to the left and the flexible exchange rate aggregate demand curve to the right. You can easily see why this is so. Under fixed exchange rates, it is the *IS-BP* intersection that determines aggregate demand, so that a higher world interest rate would mean a lower level of aggregate demand; whereas under flexible exchange rates, it is the *LM-BP* intersection that determines aggregate demand, so that a higher world interest rate would give a higher domestic velocity of circulation of money and a higher level of aggregate demand for a given money supply. Aside from the world rate of interest, the two aggregate demand curves have no other variables in common. Under fixed exchange rates, it is the exchange rate, the world price level, world real income, and domestic fiscal policy variables that affect domestic aggregate demand; whereas under flexible exchange rates, it is the domestic money stock only that affects aggregate demand.

The Real Exchange Rate

The concept of the *real exchange rate* has already been introduced in Chapter 42. It is, you will recall,

$$\theta = EP_f/P$$

In the following sections of this chapter we are going to analyze the determination of the real exchange rate and the way in which it interacts with the other variables in the model. One of those other variables is, of course, the exchange rate E. Sometimes, for emphasis, or to avoid confusion between θ and E the term *nominal exchange rate* will be used to refer to the exchange rate E. Thus, the term "*real* exchange rate" will always refer to θ and the two alternative terms "exchange rate" or "*nominal* exchange rate" will be used to refer to E. It is convenient to begin by examining how the real exchange rate varies with real income. Frame (c) of Figure 43.2 shows this. It plots the real exchange rate (θ) on the vertical axis and real income (y) on the horizontal axis. This curve will be called the *real exchange rate curve* and will be labelled *RE*. Why does the *RE* curve slope upwards? The answer to that question is found in the properties of the *IS* curve. Indeed, the *RE* curve in effect shows the value of the real exchange rate that ensures that the *IS* curve passes through the intersection point of the *LM* and *BP* curves. As the price level is raised from P_0 to P_1 and P_2, so the nominal exchange rate moves from E_0 to E_1 to E_2 to ensure that the real exchange rate equals θ_0, θ_1, and θ_2, the values that make the level of real income read off from the *IS* curve equal to the level of aggregate demand determined by the *LM-BP* intersection.

The variables that make the *RE* curve shift are the same as those that make the *IS* curve or the *BP* curve shift. They are world real income, world interest rates, and domestic fiscal policy variables. The *RE* curve does not shift as a result of any monetary action. It is, as its name suggests, entirely a real curve. The *RE* relationship will be important in the subsequent analysis of the behavior of a flexible exchange rate economy.

We are now in a position to move on to see how we can use the theory of aggregate demand to determine all the aggregate variables of interest to us.

C. Determination of Output and the Price Level with a Fixed Exchange Rate

First, let us consider the fixed exchange rate case. The theory of aggregate demand generated in Figure 43.1 tells us what determines the *actual* demand for goods and services in the economy. This aggregate demand curve may be used in an analogous way to the closed economy aggregate demand analysis to determine the rational expectation of the price level and, therefore, the position of the expectations-augmented aggregate supply curve. Figure 43.3 will illustrate the analysis. In this figure, the aggregate supply curve of the basic model is shown as *AS* at the output level y^*. The aggregate demand curve drawn for the expected values of the variables that determine its position, $AD^e(P^e_f, y^e_f, r^e_f, E^e, g^e, t^e)$, is the aggregate demand curve that is expected on the basis of expectations of the exogenous variables that influence aggregate demand and given that the economy is operating under fixed exchange rates. The rational expectation of price level P^e is determined where this expected aggregate demand curve intersects the *AS* curve. The expectations-augmented aggregate supply curve (exactly the same curve as that derived in Part V of the book) passes through that point and is the upward-sloping curve *EAS*.

If the actual aggregate demand curve is in exactly the same position as the expected aggregate demand curve, then output and prices will be deter-

Figure 43.3
Equilibrium with Fixed Exchange Rates

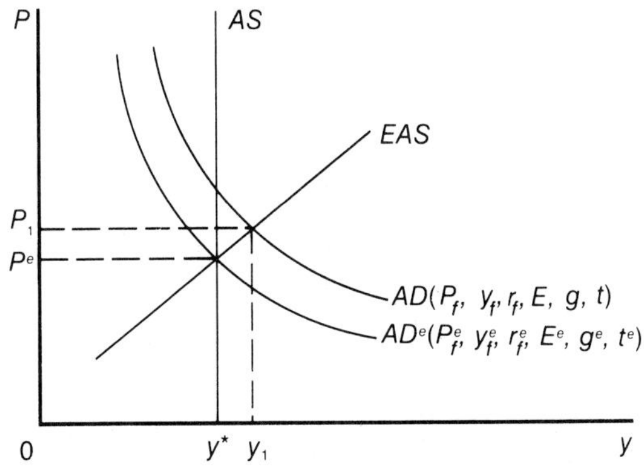

With fixed exchange rates, the expected price level is determined where the expected aggregate demand curve cuts the aggregate supply curve. This position will depend on the expected values of foreign prices, real income, and interest rates and on the exchange rate and fiscal policy variables. Actual output and prices are determined where the actual aggregate demand curve cuts the expectations-augmented aggregate supply curve. An anticipated change in any of the variables that determine aggregate demand will have price level effects only, and an unanticipated change will affect both output and prices.

mined at their full-employment and expected levels, respectively. The balance of payments will be in equilibrium, with perfect capital mobility ensuring a capital account surplus that exactly matches whatever the current account deficit is (or capital account deficit matching the current account surplus).

If, however, the actual values of the variables that determine aggregate demand turn out to be different from their expected value, so that the actual aggregate demand curve is in a different position, say, at $AD(P_f, y_f, r_f, E, g, t)$, then actual output and prices will be determined where that actual demand curve cuts the expectations-augmented aggregate supply curve at y_1, P_1. This is exactly the same as in the closed economy except that the factors that shift the aggregate demand curve in this case are different from those responsible for shifts in the closed economy aggregate demand curve. Random fluctuations in actual demand around its expected value will generate procyclical price and output co-movements.

The balance of payments will be in equilibrium at the higher price and output levels, but the mix between the current account and capital account will be different from the full-employment mix. With a fixed exchange rate and fixed world price level, the higher domestic price level will mean that the real exchange rate will have fallen, so that imports will rise and exports will fall. The higher real income will also raise imports. Thus, the current account of the balance of payments will move into a smaller surplus or larger deficit. This change in the current account will be matched by an equal, but opposite, change in the capital account.

That is all there is to the determination of output, prices, and the balance of payments in a fixed exchange rate economy with perfect capital mobility under rational expectations. As in the closed economy case, anticipated changes in the exogenous variables that determine demand will have price level effects only, and unanticipated changes will have the effects traced out in Figure 43.3. Changes that are partly anticipated and partly not anticipated will have effects that combine the effects shown in Figure 43.3 with the pure price level adjustment that would occur in the anticipated case. Notice that the domestic economy is not immune from shocks occurring in the rest of the world. Other things being equal, an anticipated change in the foreign price level or a fully anticipated devaluation of the currency will raise the domestic price level by the same percentage amount. Fluctuations in world output, prices, and interest rates will lead to fluctuations in domestic aggregate demand, and if they are not anticipated, will lead to fluctuations in output in the domestic economy that are procyclical with fluctuations in the world economy.

Let us now go on to consider the more difficult, but perhaps more interesting, case of flexible exchange rates.

D. Determination of Output, the Price Level, and the Exchange Rate under Flexible Exchange Rates

We shall proceed in a similar way in analyzing the flexible exchange rate economy as we did with the fixed exchange rate. The first task is to determine the rational expectation of the price level and, therefore, the position of the expectations-augmented aggregate supply curve. This is not as straightforward in the case of a flexible exchange rate as it was in the case of a fixed exchange rate. The reason for this is that the exchange rate contains information that it will be rational for people to use in forming their expectation of the price level. There is a fundamental informational difference between a fixed exchange rate and flexible exchange rate economy. Under fixed exchange rates, it is the stock of foreign exchange reserves that adjusts on a daily basis to random shocks that hit the economy. These movements in the stock of foreign exchange reserves are not continuously reported and are unknown outside the central bank. In a flexible exchange rate economy, the exchange rate itself is constantly adjusting to reflect the random forces that influence the economy and is available for all to see at almost zero cost. There is, therefore, more widespread information available in a flexible exchange rate economy than in a fixed exchange rate economy, and that information may be used in order to make inferences about the shocks that are hitting the economy. Making complete sense of this will take a paragraph or two.

Pretrading Expectations

Let us begin by imagining that we are at the beginning of a trading period before any trading has begun. All the markets—labor, money, goods, and foreign exchange—are not yet open for business. We are standing at the beginning of the business "day" and trying to form expectations about all the variables in the economy. Figure 43.4 will be a useful vehicle for analyzing this situation.

Frames (a) and (b) of Figure 43.4 are exactly the same as frames (b) and (c) of Figure 43.2. The top left frame of Figure 43.4 is simply a device for turning the price level through 90° so as to read the same price level on the horizontal axis as we are reading on the vertical axis. Frame (c) is a device for determining the exchange rate. The way to read this is as follows: Recall that the real exchange rate θ is defined as

$$\theta = EP_f/P$$

Multiply both sides of this equation by P, so that you obtain

$$\theta P = EP_f$$

Now the foreign price level P_f is being treated as fixed, and if we hold the exchange rate constant, EP_f will be constant. This says that θP (the real exchange rate multiplied by the domestic price level) is equal to a constant, once we have determined the exchange rate.

For a particular value of the exchange rate, we could draw a rectangular hyperbola in frame (c) that shows the relationship between θ and P. Thus, for some particular exchange rate, shown in the diagram as E^e, and for a given world price level P_f, if the domestic price level rises, then the real exchange rate θ must fall by an equal percentage amount. That is all that the curve E^e traces out.

In principle, there is a whole family of such curves, all rectangular hyperbolas and all drawn for different values of the exchange rate. We don't need

Figure 43.4
Rational Expectations at the Commencement of Trading

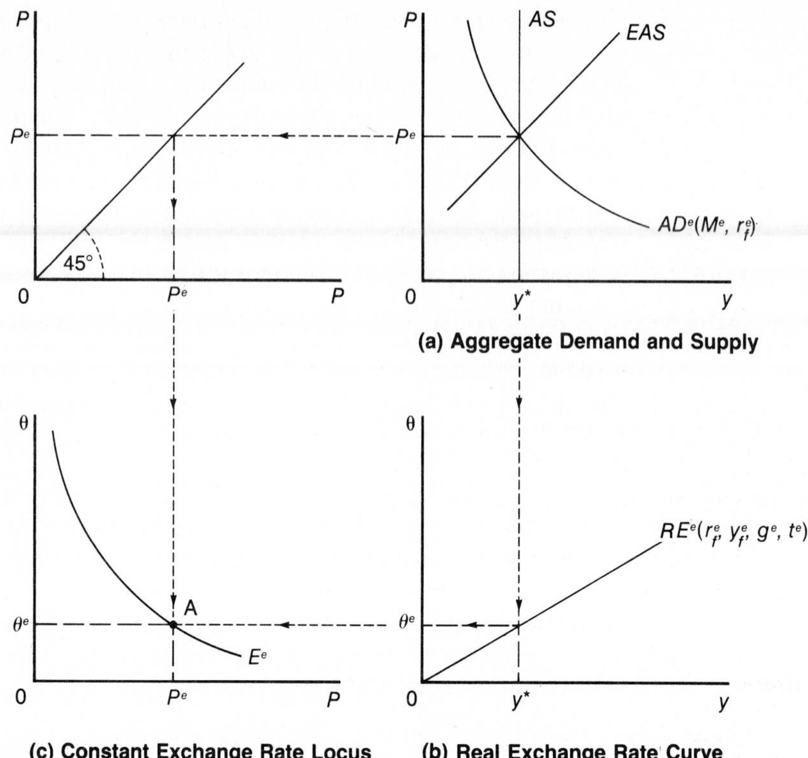

Before any information is revealed, the rational expectations of the price level, the (nominal) exchange rate, and the real exchange rate can be calculated. Where the expected aggregate demand curve (based on expected money supply and expected foreign interest rates) cuts the AS curve, the expected price level P^e is determined. Expected income is y^*, and this determines the expected real exchange rate θ^e. There will be one (nominal) exchange rate only, E^e, that is compatible with the expected price level and the expected real exchange rate. This is shown at point A in frame (c).

the whole family of these curves for the moment (although we shall need more than one subsequently). Now that you know how to read frame (c), the only slightly tricky part of the diagram, let us proceed to use the diagram to analyze the determination of the rational expectation of the price level and the exchange rate.

The starting point is in frame (a). The AS curve is determined by the basic model of aggregate supply and is located at y^*. The curve $AD(M^e, r_f^e)$ is the expectation of the aggregate demand curve for a flexible exchange rate economy, based on the derivation in Figure 43.2. Its position depends only on the expected money supply and expected world rate of interest. The rational expectation of the price level is determined where that curve cuts the AS curve. The rational expectation of output is y^*.

Next, calculate the value of the real exchange rate that is consistent with this value of output. To do this, simply read off from the RE curve in frame (b) the value of the real exchange rate consistent with the income level y^*. That value is θ^e. This same value may also be read off from the vertical axis of frame (c). To calculate the rational expectation of the nominal exchange rate, transfer the rational expectation of the price level from frame (a) through the 45° line to the horizontal axis of frame (c). Then join θ^e and P^e to give point A in frame (c). Point A will lie on a rectangular hyperbola, the location of which determines the nominal exchange rate. There will be a unique constant exchange rate locus, labelled E^e, that passes through point A. Any other nominal exchange rate would involve a different combination of the price level and the real exchange rate than what is implied by the rational expectations of these two variables.

Just prior to the commencement of business in this economy, the expectations of output, prices, and the real and nominal exchange rates are those depicted in Figure 43.4. A higher expected money supply would result in a higher expected price level, no change in the real exchange rate, and a higher expected nominal exchange rate (a depreciated currency). You can easily work this out for yourself by considering what happens in this diagram if we replace the expected *AD* curve with an equivalent curve located to the right of the existing curve. There would be no change in expected output or the expected real exchange rate. There would simply be a rise in the expected price level and a rise in the expected nominal exchange rate that would be proportional to each other.

Extracting Information from the Exchange Rate

Next, imagine that this economy has just started to do business. No one knows what the money supply is that underlies the actual aggregate demand curve, so no one can do any better, on the basis of information available about the economic aggregates, than continue to expect that the aggregate demand curve is in the position shown in frame (a) of Figure 43.4. There is more information now, however, than there was before trading began. In particular, everyone now knows the actual value of the nominal exchange rate that is being determined on a minute-by-minute basis in the foreign exchange market. In other words, as soon as trading begins, it is known whether or not the exchange rate expectation was correct. If the exchange rate expectation was incorrect, then it will be immediately clear to everyone that the initial expectation of the price level must also have been incorrect.

Let us think through the consequences of this, using Figure 43.5. The starting point is the initial expected values for the price level, the nominal exchange rate, and the real exchange rate, shown as P^e, E^e, and θ^e. Suppose that the actual aggregate demand curve turned out to be not $AD(M^e, r_f^e)$ but $AD(M, r_f)$, as shown in frame (a) of Figure 43.5. According to this theory, the actual levels of output and prices will be determined as y_1, P_1, where the actual aggregate demand curve cuts the expectations-augmented aggregate supply curve. Transferring this solution for output down to frame (b) shows the actual real exchange rate as θ_1. Transferring the price solution, P_1, from the vertical axis of frame (a) through the 45° line to the horizontal axis of frame (c) gives point B in frame (c) as the real exchange rate, price level point. Point B lies on the constant (nominal) exchange rate locus E_1 and so determines the exchange rate at that value.

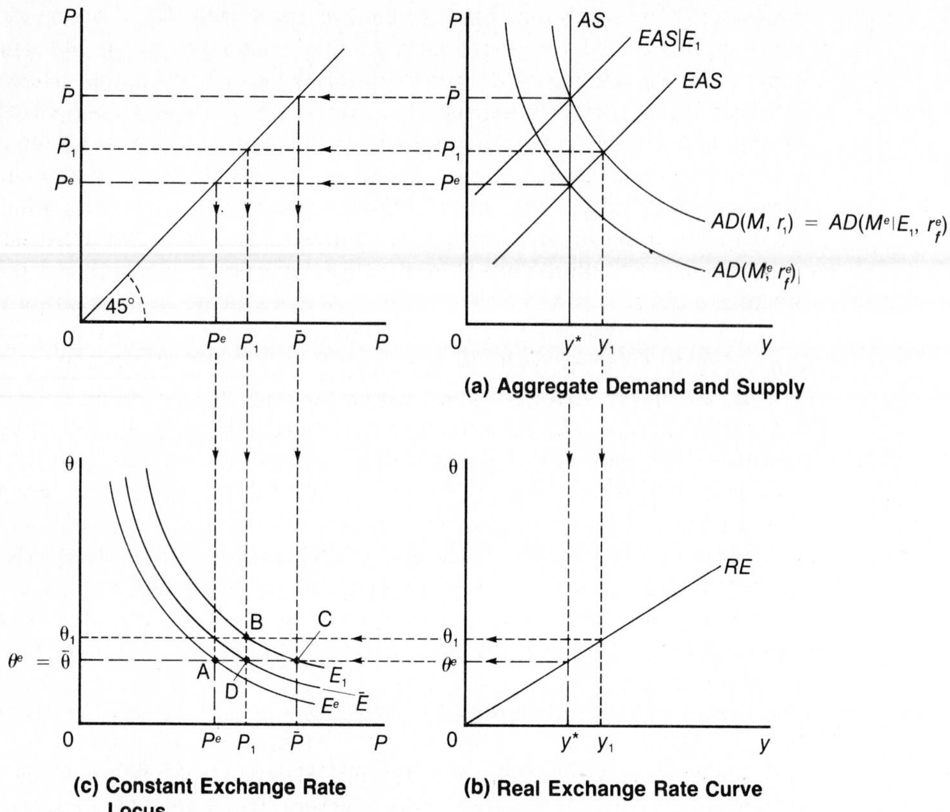

Figure 43.5
The Information Content of the Exchange Rate Influences the Rational Expectation of the Price Level

Before trading begins, the expected aggregate demand level is $AD(M^e, r_f^e)$. The expected real exchange rate curve is RE. The expected equilibrium for the economy is a price level of P^e, real income of y^*, real exchange rate of θ^e, and nominal exchange rate of E^e.
The economy is shocked: aggregate demand turns out to be higher than expected at $AD(M, r_f)$. The real exchange rate curve remains at RE. If the expected price level was P^e, it would generate an actual price level of P_1, an actual real income level of y_1, an actual real exchange rate of θ_1, and an actual (nominal) exchange rate of E_1. Since the expected exchange rate, E^e, is different from the actual exchange rate, E_1, and since the exchange rate is observed, people will know that their expected price level is wrong. The price level expectation will change. Only if the expected price level is $\overline{P}$ will the expected exchange rate equal the actual exchange rate (at point C). In that case, the actual price level will also be $\overline{P}$, output y^*, and the real exchange rate θ^e. (In this example, the equilibrium and initial exchange rates are the same—E_1. This is a special case and will not occur in general.)

Now the actual price and output levels, although determined by the analysis, are not known to the people in the economy. They only observe the prices of the small range of goods that they are currently engaged in trading, and they do not know the general price level or any of the other aggregates.

Everyone, however, knows the nominal exchange rate. It is observed on a continuous basis and is therefore available for all to see. In the situation depicted in Figure 43.5, everyone would know that the exchange rate was E_1 and that it was different from E^e. The economy is not at point A in frame (c), but at point B. No one would know that, however, for no one would know the *real* exchange rate. This is not a directly observed variable. People would, however, know that the nominal exchange rate was different from what they had expected it to be. That being so, everyone would know that a mistake had been made in forming expectations about aggregate demand. Aggregate demand could not be the curve $AD(M^e, r_f^e)$. If it was, the exchange rate would be E^e, and not E_1, which it has turned out to be. The price level P_1 and the output level y_1 cannot therefore be a rational expectations equilibrium.

If the exchange rate is higher than it was expected to be, then the aggregate demand curve must be higher than it was previously expected to be, and expected prices need to be revised upwards. By how much does the expected price level need to be revised upwards? To answer this question we need to see how a change in the expected price level affects both the expected exchange rate and the actual exchange rate. Only when the expected price level is such as to generate an expected exchange rate that is the same as the actual exchange rate will that price expectation be rational. That is, only in such a situation will all the information available have been incorporated into price level expectations.

We can examine how the rational expectation of the price level will be formed when information conveyed by the exchange rate is employed if we perform a conceptual experiment. Imagine that the expectation of the price level is increased from P^e to P_1—in frame (a) of Figure 43.5. (Be clear that this is not a description of the *process* that would go on in the world because P_1 is not observed and could not therefore be used to calculate an expected price level. This is simply an imagined experiment that will help determine the *amount* by which the expected price level must rise and not the *process* whereby it does so.)

What we need to do is to examine the effects of the higher expected price level on both the actual and expected exchange rates. Consider first its effects on the expected exchange rate. With an expected price level of P_1, the EAS curve will shift up (not shown in figure) to intersect the AS curve at P_1. In other words, the expected level of aggregate demand will remain constant at y^*. In turn, the expected real exchange rate will remain constant at θ^e. To see what this implies for the (nominal) exchange rate, all we have to do is to trace through as we have done before in frame (c) of Figure 43.5. Tracing the price level P_1 and the real exchange rate at θ^e into frame (c) shows that they imply a nominal exchange rate equal to $\bar{E}$ (meeting at point D on the equal exchange rate locus $\bar{E}$). Thus, raising the expected price level raises the expected exchange rate. In fact, although not transparent from the diagram, there will be a one-to-one correspondence between the change in the expected price level and the change in the expected exchange rate. If the expected price level rises by X percent, the expected exchange rate will rise by the same X percent.

Next consider the effect of a change in the expected price level of P_1. It is clear that with an expected price level of P_1 but with the aggregate demand curve remaining in its position, $AD(M, r_f)$, the actual price level will rise above

P_1. Further output will be above y^*. It will, however, be below y_1. (These values have not been shown in the figure.) With output between y^* and y_1, the real exchange rate will lie between θ^e and θ_1. With the price level above P_1 and the real exchange rate below θ_1, it is evident that the actual value of the nominal exchange rate could rise or fall depending on whether the price level or the *real* exchange rate effect is larger. The rise in the price level would tend to raise the nominal exchange rate, whereas the fall in the real exchange rate would tend to lower it.

Although there is ambiguity as to the direction of movement of the exchange rate, there is no ambiguity about the fact that the actual exchange rate will have moved closer to the expected exchange rate. How do we know this? We know, first, that in the initial experiment, the pretrading expected exchange rate was E^e and the actual exchange E_1. Thus, the actual exchange rate was higher than the pretrading expected exchange rate. We also know that a rise in the expected price level raises the expected exchange rate by the same percentage amount as the rise in the price level, but it raises the actual exchange rate by less than that and could even result in a fall in the actual exchange rate. Thus, raising the expected price level to P_1 closes the gap between the actual and the expected exchange rate. We can see, however, that the expected price level P_1 cannot be the rational expectation of the price level because it does not generate an actual value of the exchange rate equal to its implied expected value. You can see this by noting that with an expected price level of P_1, the real exchange rate will lie between θ_1 and θ^e. The actual price level will be above P_1 but below $\bar{P}$. (Verify that you indeed agree with the propositions just stated.)

With the real exchange rate between θ_1 and θ^e and the price level between P_1 and $\bar{P}$, it is evident that the actual (nominal) exchange rate locus must lie between E_1 and $\bar{E}$. Thus, the actual exchange rate implied by an expected price level of P_1 is higher than the expected exchange rate implied by this expected price level. It is evident that we could repeat the experiment just conducted with a higher price level (equal to the actual price level generated by the expected price level P_1). If we did perform such an experiment, we would discover that, with one exception, we repeatedly obtained the same type of result that we have just obtained.

There is just one price level, however, that would give a different result and that is $\bar{P}$. The price level $\bar{P}$ occurs where the actual aggregate demand curve cuts the *AS* curve. Expected aggregate demand remains y^*, and the expected real exchange rate of course remains at θ^e. With an expected price level of $\bar{P}$, this implies an expected exchange rate of E_1—point C in frame (a) representing the expected equilibrium. With the actual aggregate demand curve intersecting the *AS* curve at $\bar{P}$, the actual price level is also determined at $\bar{P}$. Thus, the actual exchange rate is also E_1. Point C becomes not only the expected but also the actual equilibrium position of the economy.

To avoid having to shift the constant exchange rate locus too many times, I have used a special set of assumptions to ensure that the final equilibrium exchange rate and the initial exchange rate implied by the initial expectation and shock are the same, E_1. There is, in general, no reason why this would be so. Indeed, for it to be so, the *RE* curve must be a straight line and the aggregate demand curve must be a rectangular hyperbola (have an elasticity of minus one).

In the setup in Figure 43.5, I have rigged things such that people are able to work out exactly what the actual aggregate demand curve is from the observation of the exchange rate. This has happened because, purely for the purpose of introducing you to the ideas involved, we have imagined that there is just a single source of random disturbance to the economy, namely, a random disturbance to the aggregate demand curve. That being so, from observing the exchange rate it is possible to infer exactly what that random disturbance is and, as a result, to correct for it by adjusting the expectation of the price level conditioned on the knowledge of the exchange rate. The expectations-augmented aggregate supply curve conditional on the actual exchange rate, $EAS \mid E_1$, moves to intersect the actual aggregate demand curve, which in turn becomes the expected aggregate demand curve conditional on the exchange rate $AD(M^e \mid E_1, r_f^e)$. If there were additional sources of disturbance so that the aggregate demand shock being analyzed here was just one of several random disturbances affecting the economy, then it would *not* be possible to make a direct inference from the exchange rate as to the position of the aggregate demand curve. Even though people might know that they had made a mistake, in the sense that the exchange rate had turned out to be different from what they had expected it would be, they would not know for sure the source of that mistake. That being so, they would not be able to correctly identify the actual values of the exogenous variables that are influencing the economy.

This will be seen better if we consider a case in which there are two sources of shocks—shocks to the aggregate demand curve (coming from the money supply or the world rate of interest) and shocks to the *RE* curve (coming from world real income, the world rate of interest, or fiscal policy). We shall consider two experiments. Both of them are highly artificial. Despite their artificiality, however, they are useful experiments for clarifying the concepts and propositions about the behavior of a flexible exchange rate economy under rational expectations.

An Unexpected Change in Aggregate Demand

The first experiment imagines that the economy has always had a completely predictable level of aggregate demand, so that expected aggregate demand and actual aggregate demand have always been one and the same. This could be put more directly as saying that there have never been any aggregate demand shocks in the economy. This economy has, however, often been subjected to real exchange rate shocks—shocks from world real income or interest rate movements or from fiscal policy. In fact, the normal state of affairs is for the real exchange rate curve to be constantly bombarded in a random fashion. Imagine that in a particular period in such an economy, an aggregate demand shock in fact occurs, but no real exchange rate shock occurs. This will be a very unusual circumstance for this hypothetical economy. It will in fact be something that by the hypothetical setup assumed has never happened before. Naturally, the nominal exchange rate will respond to the shock that has

Figure 43.6
The Effects of an Unanticipated Domestic Monetary Shock

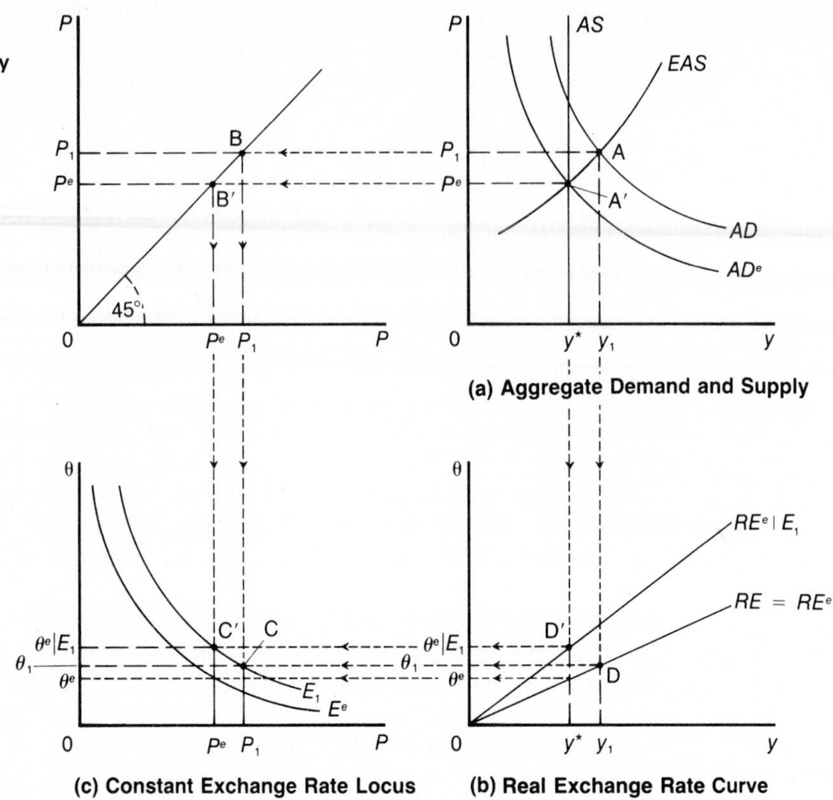

The economy is initially at y^*, P^e, θ^e, and E^e on the aggregate demand curve AD^e, the expectations-augmented aggregate supply curve EAS, the real exchange rate curve $RE = RE^e$, and the constant exchange rate locus E^e. There is then an unanticipated rise in aggregate demand to AD. This raises the price level to P_1 and raises real income to y_1. It also raises the real exchange rate to θ_1. At the price level P_1 and real exchange rate θ_1, the nominal exchange rate becomes E_1. The higher nominal exchange rate is incorrectly interpreted as a rise in the real exchange rate to $\theta^e | E_1$. The corners of the square ABCD describe the actual situation, and the corners of the square A′B′C′D′ describe the situation that agents rationally believe to be occurring. The effect of an unanticipated rise in aggregate demand is to raise prices, output, the real exchange rate, and the nominal exchange rate. The higher real exchange rate tells us that the nominal exchange rate rises by more than the price level does.

occurred. It will be rational in this situation for people to infer that there has been a real exchange rate shock. It will also be rational for them to infer that there has been no aggregate demand shock. They will be wrong, but they will not be irrational. To see what happens in this situation, let us use Figure 43.6.

The setup in Figure 43.6 is comparable to that of Figure 43.5. Before trading began, people formed expectations about aggregate demand and the real exchange rate and, as a result, formed their pretrading rational expectations of the price level, the real exchange rate, output, and the nominal exchange rate. These are shown in Figure 43.6 in the following way. The curve labelled AD^e in frame (a) is the expected aggregate demand curve. Where it intersects the AS curve is determined the rational expectation of the price level, P^e. The expectations-augmented aggregate supply curve EAS passes through point A′ where the expected aggregate demand curve cuts the aggregate supply curve. The real exchange rate curve, both actual and expected, is labelled $RE = RE^e$ in frame (b). At the expected full-employment output level, the expected real exchange rate is given as θ^e on the vertical axis of frame (b). Transferring the expected price level through the 45° line to frame (c), and transferring the expected real exchange rate also across from frame (b) to frame (c), we arrive at a point in frame (c) that lies on a constant exchange rate locus that determines the expected nominal exchange rate (E^e). This is the pretrading rational expectation for this economy.

The shock described above is an aggregate demand shock, but one that is completely misperceived. The actual aggregate demand curve that incorporates this shock is shown in frame (a) as the curve AD. Where the actual aggregate demand curve cuts the expectations-augmented aggregate supply curve (point A) is determined the actual price level P_1 and output level y_1. At the output level y_1, reading from frame (b), we may determine the real exchange rate as θ_1. If the price level is P_1 and the real exchange rate θ_1, transferring these two magnitudes to frame (c) takes us to point C on a constant exchange rate locus E_1. Thus, the actual nominal exchange rate in this situation would be E_1, the price level P_1, output y_1, and the real exchange rate θ_1. People will see that the exchange rate was different from what they had expected it to be. They will not, however, see any reason to revise their expectations of the price level. As far as they are concerned, there must have been a change in the real exchange rate. This is the normal state of affairs. Aggregate demand shocks never occur, so there will be no reason, based on observed regularities in the past, to revise opinions about the level of aggregate demand.

People will be able to reconcile the currently observed exchange rate E_1 with the currently expected level of aggregate demand AD^e and the currently expected price level P^e by adjusting their expectations of the real exchange rate to fall on the line labelled $RE^e | E_1$. To see this, notice that there is a square, the corners of which are A′, B′, C′, D′, that just touches the intersection of the curves AD^e and EAS, the 45° line, the constant exchange rate locus E_1, and the expected real exchange rate curve $RE^e | E_1$. Thus, the expected price level P^e, the expected real exchange rate $\theta^e | E_1$, and the actual (nominal) exchange rate E_1 are all compatible with each other and with an expectation that the economy is at full-employment output y^*. The other square, ABCD, represents the actual situation. That is, where the actual aggregate demand curve cuts the expectations-augmented aggregate supply curve, the economy is on the actual RE curve and again on the actual constant exchange rate locus. Both C and C′ are on the same constant exchange rate locus. Thus, the actual nominal exchange rate E_1 is compatible with the combined expectation of the price level and the real exchange rate.

In effect, people are making two offsetting mistakes. Aggregate demand is actually higher than they believe it to be, and the real exchange rate curve is actually lower than they believe it to be. In combination, these two mistakes generate the same expectation of the exchange rate as the actual exchange rate and therefore cannot be corrected simply by observing the exchange rate.

Before leaving this highly artificial economy that has frequently been bombarded with real exchange rate shocks, but never before with an aggregate demand shock, let us consider what would happen if there was no aggregate demand shock, but if the economy indeed did undergo a real exchange rate shock. Specifically, imagine that the aggregate demand curve had remained at AD^e, but that the real exchange rate curve had in fact changed, so that the actual real exchange rate curve was denoted by the line $RE^e \mid E_1$. If that shock had occurred, then the economy would have remained at full-employment output y^*, the price level would have remained at P^e, the nominal exchange rate would have moved to E_1, and the real exchange rate would have moved to $\theta^e \mid E_1$. The square A′B′C′D′ would describe the actual situation. Thus, by forming expectations on the basis of what usually happens, people would have correctly inferred the real exchange rate shock by using the information given to them by the nominal exchange rate. In the previous experiment, where there was an unanticipated change in aggregate demand leading to a rise in the price level, output, the real exchange rate, and the (nominal) exchange rate, it was the unanticipated nature of the aggregate demand change that caused the problems.

An Unexpected Change in the Real Exchange Rate

Let us now leave this highly artificial economy and go on to consider another equally highly artificial, but opposite extreme, situation. Imagine an economy that is always being bombarded by aggregate demand shocks, but which has never before known a change in its real exchange rate. Imagine that in some period that we shall now analyze, the economy suffers a real exchange rate shock but has no aggregate demand shock. Just as before, this is a very unusual event—something that has perhaps never happened before. The nominal exchange rate responds to the real exchange rate shock, but people rationally attribute the nominal rate adjustment to an aggregate demand shock—to something that commonly occurs—and not to the real exchange rate shock—something that has never before been known. What happens to output, prices, the exchange rate, and the real exchange rate in this case? Figure 43.7 will analyze this situation.

Let us first use Figure 43.7 to describe the pretrading rational expectations of the variables. The expected aggregate demand curve is AD^e in frame (a), and where this curve intersects the AS curve is determined the rational expectation of the price level P^e and the location of the EAS curve. The expectation of the real exchange rate in frame (b) is the curve labelled RE^e, so the rational expectation of the real exchange rate is θ^e. Transferring the rational expectation of the price level through the 45° line to frame (c) and transferring the expected real exchange rate to frame (c) gives a point on the constant exchange rate locus E^e. This, then, is the initial pretrading rational expectation for the economy.

Imagine that there is now a shock to the real exchange rate, and the actual real exchange rate curve becomes the line RE. If there was no change in the rational expectation of the price level, and if actual aggregate demand equals expected aggregate demand (as we shall assume it to do), the level of output and prices would remain constant at P^e and y^*, but the real exchange

Figure 43.7 The Effects of an Unanticipated Real Exchange Rate Shock

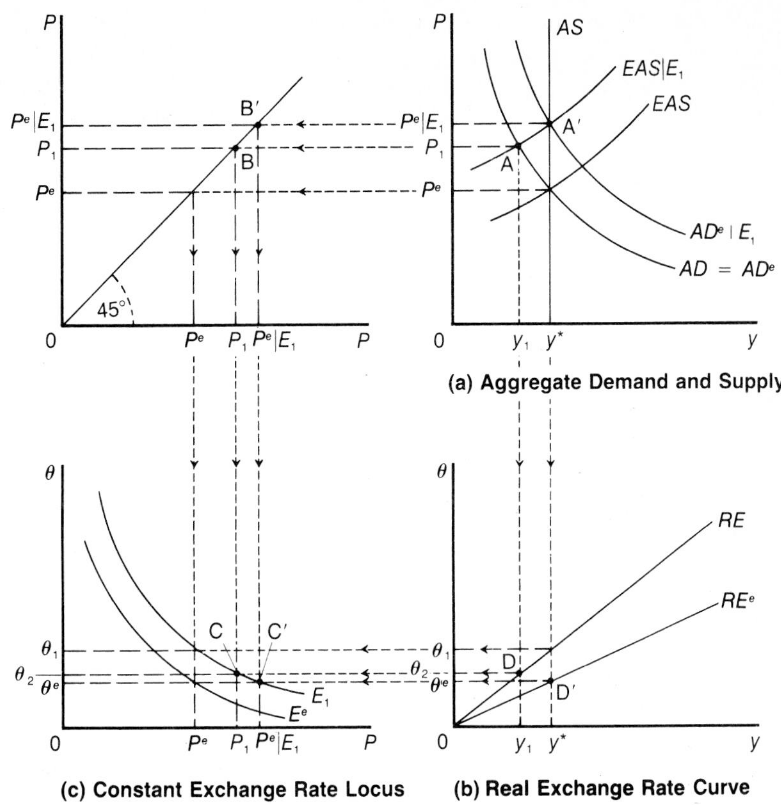

The economy is initially at P^e, y^*, θ^e, and E^e on the aggregate demand curve $AD = AD^e$, the expectations-augmented aggregate supply curve EAS, the real exchange rate curve RE^e, and the constant exchange rate locus E^e. There is then an unanticipated rise in the real exchange rate curve to RE. With no change in income and the price level, this would raise the nominal exchange rate to E_1 (the exchange rate compatible with the price level P^e and the real exchange rate θ_1). Since the real exchange rate shock is unanticipated, the higher nominal exchange rate will be read incorrectly as an aggregate demand shock. The expected price level will be revised upwards to $P^e|E_1$, which will shift the expectations-augmented aggregate supply curve to $EAS|E_1$. Actual output and the price level will be determined at y_1, P_1 and the real exchange rate at θ_2. The price level P_1 and the real exchange rate θ_2 are consistent with the nominal exchange rate E_1. The actual situation is described by the corners of the square ABCD and the expected situation by the corners of the square A′B′C′D′. The unanticipated rise in the real exchange rate raises the price level, lowers output, and raises the nominal exchange rate. The nominal exchange rate rises by more than the price level does, therefore the real exchange rate rises.

rate would rise to θ_1. At the price level P^e and the real exchange rate θ_1, the economy would be on a constant exchange rate locus E_1 shown in frame (c). Thus, the (nominal) exchange rate would be higher than expected.

Recalling that this is an economy which, by assumption, never has had a real exchange rate shock before, but often has aggregate demand shocks, it will be evident that people will read the higher (nominal) exchange rate as implying that there must have been an aggregate demand shock. As a result, they will revise their expectations of the price level upwards. Since they know the exchange rate to be E_1, and since they firmly expect the real exchange rate to remain at θ^e, they will believe the economy to be at the point C′ on the constant exchange rate locus E_1. They will read off from that point on the locus E_1 the rational expectation of the price level, conditional on knowing that the exchange rate is E_1. This is labelled in frame (c) as $P_1^e \mid E_1$. That is, given that people firmly believe that the real exchange rate has remained at θ^e, but that they know the (nominal) exchange rate to be E_1, they calculate a rational expectation of the price level that is compatible with these two facts.

Now transfer the rational expectation of the price level $P^e \mid E_1$ from frame (c) through the 45° line to frame (a). This takes us to the point A′ in frame (a). Passing through point A′ is an expectations-augmented aggregate supply curve, given knowledge of the exchange rate as E_1. This is the curve labelled $EAS \mid E_1$. Where this expectations-augmented aggregate supply curve intersects the actual aggregate demand curve (point A) determines the level of output y_1 and price level P_1. With the real exchange rate actually being determined by the *RE* curve, the output level y_1 determines a level of the real exchange rate of θ_2. (The real exchange rate θ_1 would be associated with full-employment output y^*.)

Now transfer the price level P_1 through the 45° line to frame (c) and transfer the real exchange rate θ_2 across to frame (c). These meet at point C on the constant exchange rate locus E_1. Thus, the nominal exchange rate E_1 that gives rise to an expectation of the price level of $P^e \mid E_1$, and an expected real exchange rate of θ^e (point C′) also gives rise to an actual price level P_1 and an actual real exchange rate θ_2 at point C. The actual equilibrium is described by the corners of the square ABCD, and the expected equilibrium by the corners of the square A′B′C′D′. The effects of this unanticipated rise in the real exchange rate curve has been to raise the domestic price level, raise the exchange rate (depreciate the currency), and lower output.[1]

Now consider what would have happened in this economy if it had been actually subjected to the shock to which it is normally subjected, namely, an aggregate demand shock. Imagine that instead of having a real exchange rate shock, the real exchange rate remained at its normal level RE^e. Imagine further that there was a shock to aggregate demand that took the actual aggregate demand curve to the curve labelled $AD^e \mid E_1$. Such a shock would have raised the exchange rate, and the higher exchange rate would have been interpreted as evidence of a positive aggregate demand shock. People would have adjusted upwards their expectations of prices, thereby building into their current expectations the information being given by the exchange rate. The only equilibrium to which this economy could have come would be the one described by the corners of the square A′B′C′D′. That is, the economy would

---

[1]In order to keep the diagrammatic analysis clean, we have rigged this experiment to yield a rational expectations equilibrium in "one iteration" by selecting convenient slopes for *EAS* and *RE*. In general, although the characterization of equilibrium shown in Figure 43.7 is correct, a lengthier iterative process would have to be followed in order to establish what the equilibrium is. Its defining characteristics are the two squares: ABCD, which describes the actual situation, and A′B′C′D′, which describes the expected situation. The points C and C′ are on the same constant exchange rate locus.

have remained at full-employment output, the price level would actually have risen to $P^e | E_1$, and the exchange rate would have risen to E_1. The real exchange rate would have remained at θ^e.

This serves to emphasize that the reason why the real exchange rate shock in this economy had an effect on output was because it was unanticipated. This is directly analogous to the reasons why the aggregate demand shock had output effects in the previous extreme example.

The Current Account of the Balance of Payments

Let us now briefly turn our attention to what is happening to the current account of the balance of payments during the administration of the shocks that we have just analyzed. In the first economy that was subject to an unexpected aggregate demand shock, there is a rise in the price level, in the output level, and in the real exchange rate. The higher real exchange rate leads to a rise in world demand for domestic output (exports) and a drop in domestic demand for world output (imports). Other things being equal, this tends to raise the current account surplus (or lower the deficit). Other things are not, however, equal. The higher real income level raises imports, thereby contributing to a lowering of the current account surplus (or increasing the deficit). We do not, in general, know which of these two offsetting forces is the stronger and do not therefore know in which direction the current account balance changes. The overall balance of payments would, of course, be maintained at zero as a result of the flexible exchange rate and the perfect capital mobility.

In the case of the economy that is normally subjected to aggregate demand shocks, but was unusually subjected to a real exchange rate shock, there is no ambiguity as to what happens to the current account balance. In this case, there is a fall in output and a rise in the real exchange rate. The combination of these two things is unambiguously to raise the current account surplus (or lower the deficit), since the lower real income level lowers imports, whereas the higher real exchange rate lowers imports but stimulates exports.

More General Shocks

The experiments conducted and illustrated in Figures 43.6 and 43.7 are excessively simplified. In practice, *both* the real exchange rate and aggregate demand will be shocked simultaneously, and there will be difficulty in disentangling the extent to which each of these two has been shocked. Nevertheless, the conclusions that we have reached using the simplified analyses apply to the more general case. The propositions made above concerning the effects of unexpected changes in aggregate demand and the real exchange rate, taken by themselves, apply to cases where there is a mixture of both shocks. Shocks that reveal themselves through changes in the exchange rate will, in general, be misinterpreted not completely, as in the two extreme examples used above, but partly. The more common is a particular type of shock, the more inclined will people be to infer the presence of that shock when there is a previously unanticipated change in the exchange rate. The smaller will be the real effects, and the larger will be the price level effects of such a shock. Notice that it is not possible, given that people observe the exchange rate, for there to be unanticipated changes in one variable that are not offset by unanticipated changes in other variables. At least two mistakes must be made.

Fixed vs. Flexible Exchange Rates Again

It is often said that flexible exchange rates give an economy insulation from foreign shocks. What does the above analysis say about this? Certainly we discovered when analyzing the fixed exchange rate economy that an unanticipated change in foreign prices, real income, or interest rates would produce a change in domestic output and prices. Does the same apply in the flexible exchange rate case? The answer is clearly yes. Even though these foreign shocks do not in fact affect the position of the aggregate demand curve, they do affect the position of the real exchange rate curve, and therefore they affect the nominal exchange rate. Through their observed effect on the nominal exchange rate, they lead to inferences about the position of the actual aggregate demand curve, which, in general, will be incorrect. Foreign shocks will partly be misperceived as domestic demand shocks. To the extent that they are so misperceived, they will lead to a shift in the expectations-augmented aggregate supply curve and, therefore, to a change in the actual level of output and prices. Interestingly, a foreign shock that raises the expected price level will, other things being equal, produce a stagflation style of result comparable to that which we saw when analyzing the effects of a supply shock in Chapter 34.

What the flexible exchange rate does offer is insulation from the effects of anticipated foreign shocks. Any such shocks will come out entirely in the exchange rate and will leave the domestic price level and output level undisturbed. Such shocks, of course, will be pretty hard to imagine occurring uncontaminated by unexpected components. Nevertheless, and importantly, flexible exchange rates *do* give insulation from ongoing, anticipated, trend changes in prices in the rest of the world.

Summary

A. The Need for a Rational Expectations Theory of the Open Economy

The need for a rational expectations theory of the open economy arises from the same considerations as in the case of the closed economy. The basic model accounts for some facts, and the Keynesian model for others, but neither accounts for all the facts. The rational expectations theory, which emphasizes the importance of the distinction between anticipated and unanticipated shocks, offers, in effect, a method of combining the best of both of those models into a single unified framework. There is a clear need to extend this framework to handle the determination of output and prices as well as the exchange rate and balance of payments in an open economy.

B. Aggregate Demand when Capital Is Perfectly Mobile

If capital is perfectly mobile, the rate of interest is determined exogenously in the rest of the world. In a fixed exchange rate economy, aggregate demand is determined purely by the *IS* curve and the world rate of interest. Shifts in aggregate demand therefore depend on changes in the world price level, world real income, world interest rate, and domestic fiscal policy. In a flexible exchange rate world, aggregate demand is determined solely by the domestic demand for money, supply of money, and world interest rate. Changes in aggregate demand in that case depend only on the world rate of interest and the money supply. In the fixed exchange rate setting, the *LM* curve determines the money supply via the balance of payments; and in the flexible exchange rate setting, the *IS* curve determines the real and the nominal exchange rates.

C. Determination of Output and the Price Level with a Fixed Exchange Rate

The expected values of fiscal variables and foreign variables determine the expected aggregate demand curve, which in turn determines the rational expectation of the price level. The actual aggregate demand curve intersecting the expectations-augmented aggregate supply curve determines actual output and the price level. Anticipated changes in fiscal policy or foreign variables will have price level effects only; unanticipated changes will affect both output and the price level. Fluctuations in the current account of the balance of payments will be countercyclical. Domestic output will be procyclical with world output. An anticipated foreign inflation or depreciation of the currency will raise the price level proportionately.

D. Determination of Output, the Price Level, and the Exchange Rate Under Flexible Exchange Rates

With flexible exchange rates, the continuous information given by the exchange rate has to be used to form a rational expectation of the shocks influencing the economy. If there was one, and only one, source of shock, then knowledge of the exchange rate would enable a perfect inference to be made and would ensure that the economy always operated at full-employment equilibrium. The effects of all shocks in that case would be exactly the same as in the basic model.

If there is more than one source of shock (for example, a money supply shock and a real exchange rate shock), then observation of the (nominal) exchange rate alone does not enable a complete identification to be made concerning the magnitudes of those shocks. In general, an unexpected rise in the money supply will be associated with an unexpected drop in the real exchange rate, and vice versa. That is, at least two expectational errors will be made that offset each other so as to give rise to an expectation of the exchange rate that is the same as the actual exchange rate.

An actual rise in the *RE* curve, with no change in the money supply, will, in general, be misinterpreted as a rise in the *RE* curve but of a smaller amount than has actually occurred, accompanied by a rise in the money supply. Its effect will be to lower output, raise the price level, raise the real exchange rate, and depreciate the currency. The current account of the balance of payments will move into a bigger surplus or smaller deficit since the fall in income and rise in the real exchange rate will lower imports and raise exports. A rise in the money supply, which raises the exchange rate, will partly be interpreted as a rise in the real exchange rate. Its effect will be to raise output, the price level, the nominal exchange rate, and the real exchange rate. Its effect on the current account will be ambiguous since the higher real income level will raise imports, but the higher real exchange rate will have an offsetting effect on imports and will stimulate exports.

Review Questions

1. What is wrong with the basic and Keynesian models of the open economy?

2. What determines aggregate demand in an open economy that faces perfectly mobile international capital flows:

(a) Under fixed exchange rates?
(b) Under flexible exchange rates?

3. Why does the exchange rate regime make a difference to the determinants of aggregate demand?

4. How is the rational expectation of the price level determined when the exchange rate is fixed and capital is perfectly mobile?

5. Work out the effects on the rational expectation of the price level (with fixed exchange rates and perfect capital mobility) of the following:

(a) An anticipated rise in the world price level of 10 percent.
(b) An anticipated rise in world income.
(c) An anticipated rise in domestic credit.
(d) An unanticipated devaluation.
(e) An anticipated devaluation of 10 percent.
(f) An unanticipated rise in domestic credit.
(g) An unanticipated tax cut.
(h) An anticipated rise in government spending.

6. Work out the effects on output, the price level, and the current account balance (with fixed exchange rates and perfect capital mobility) of the eight shocks listed in Question 5.

7. What is the fundamental difference between a fixed and a flexible exchange rate regime? Which generates the most information?

8. How is the rational expectation of the price level determined when the exchange rate is flexible and when capital is perfectly mobile:

(a) Before the markets begin trading?
(b) When trading is taking place?

9. How is the rational expectation of the price level affected by the eight shocks listed in Question 5 when the exchange rate is flexible and capital is perfectly mobile?

10. How are output, the price level, the exchange rate, and the current account balance affected by the eight shocks listed in Question 5 when the exchange rate is flexible and capital is perfectly mobile?

11. Do flexible exchange rates provide better insulation from foreign shocks than do fixed exchange rates?

44

The U.S. Economy and the Rest of the World

Most Americans pay little attention to the economic plight of other countries and don't often worry about how economic events in the rest of the world influence the United States. Of course there have been occasions when Americans have needed to worry about economic developments in the rest of the world. Notable examples from recent history are the two periods 1973 and 1979, when world energy prices increased dramatically, thereby having a massive influence on the United States. In contrast, citizens of the rest of the world do spend a great deal of time worrying about U.S. economic policy. Developments in the U.S. economy have a dominant influence on the economies of Europe, Asia, and the Third World. This chapter cannot pretend to take you through all the detailed connections between the American economy and the rest of the world. What it will do is to show you the highlights of how the U.S. economy and the rest of the world interact and how the United States influences economic developments outside its own borders.

This chapter will take you through four tasks, which are to:

(a) Know the main patterns of world output, prices, interest rates, and exchange rates in the 1970s.

(b) Understand the causes of world output, prices, interest rate, and exchange rate movements in that period.

(c) Understand how the United States has influenced the world economy in the 1970s.

(d) Understand the policy choices facing the United States in its relations with the rest of the world.

A. The Main Patterns of World Output, Prices, Interest Rates, and Exchange Rates in the 1970s

There is a mass of information available on macroeconomic developments in the rest of the world, and it would be quite impossible to do more than scan the highlights in this chapter. Excellent summary sources of information that you will find useful, mainly as reference sources, are the publications of the International Monetary Fund (IMF) and of the Organization for Economic

Cooperation and Development (OECD). The International Monetary Fund publishes each year its *International Financial Statistics, Yearbook*. This contains a wealth of macroeconomic data on most of the 143 countries that are members of the International Monetary Fund. In addition, the IMF provides up-to-date information on the macroeconomic developments in its member countries with the monthly publication of *International Financial Statistics*.[1] The OECD publishes a series of "country reviews" at periodic intervals. It also publishes an excellent semiannual (in July and December) appraisal of the world economy called *Economic Outlook*.[2] You will find these publications of the IMF and OECD in the government publications section of your university library and in the major public libraries.

Output Growth

In viewing the highlights of the macroeconomic developments of the 1970s, it will be convenient to consider the four groups of variables—output, prices, interest rates, and exchange rates—one at a time. Let us first consider output developments. Figure 44.1 illustrates the growth rate of output (measured by GNP or GDP) for three different aggregate entities: the United States, the "Big Seven" economies (Canada, France, Germany, Italy, Japan, United Kingdom, and the United States), and the OECD in aggregate. The OECD in aggregate consists of the Big Seven together with a large number of smaller countries. The striking pattern in the growth rates shown in Figure 44.1 is their similarity. There is a general boom in world economic activity in the opening years of the 1970s, reaching a peak in 1973. The period 1974–1975 sees the world plunging into recession, and 1976 sees the whole world recovering. From 1976 to 1979, output growth sags again.

The growth performance of the United States departs from that of the broad aggregates of the Big Seven and of the OECD in some interesting details. The amplitude of the fluctuations in the United States is slightly higher than that of the other aggregates. This is particularly noticeable in the depression of 1974–1975, when the United States sank to a distinctly negative growth rate for two years, whereas the other aggregates barely went below zero and then only for one year. Further, the slowdown in growth after 1976 is much more pronounced in the case of the United States than in the case of the broader aggregates. The U.S. growth on the average is slightly slower than the growth rates in the other countries. This is evident from the fact that, at its peak, the U.S. growth rate roughly equals the average of the other countries, whereas at its trough, the U.S. growth rate is below those of other countries. Nevertheless, aside from these differences of detail, the broad patterns of growth have been the same in the United States as in other countries throughout this period.

Prices

Figure 44.2 sets out the inflation rates of the United States, four other countries, and a world average. The four countries (Canada, Germany, Japan, and the United Kingdom) have been selected because they are the dominant

[1]International Monetary Fund, Washington, D.C.
[2]Organization for Economic Cooperation and Development, Paris, France.

Figure 44.1
Output Growth, 1970–1979

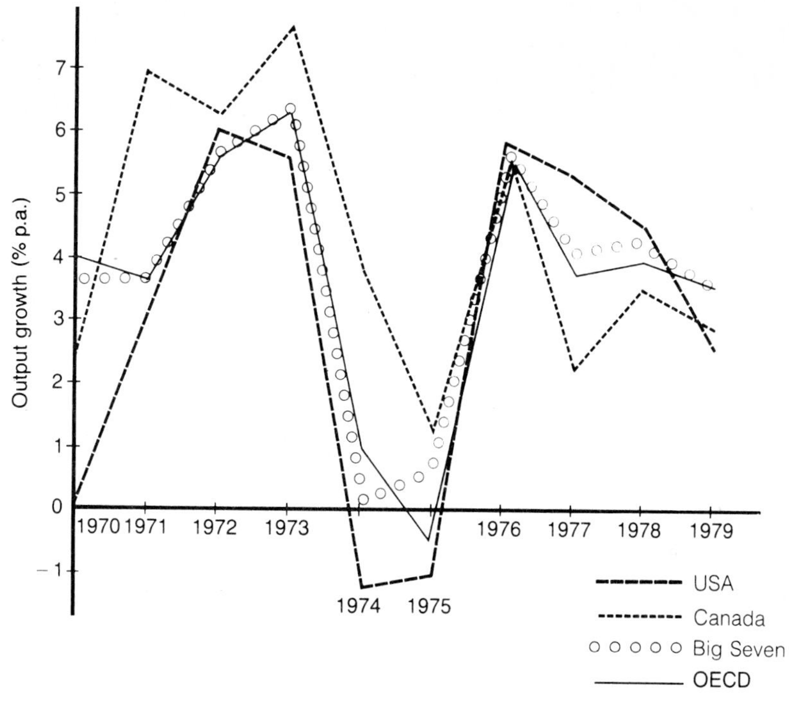

The output growth rates of Canada, the United States, the Big Seven, and the OECD as a whole have been remarkably similar throughout the 1970s. A boom in 1972–1973 was followed by a deep recession in 1974–1975, a recovery in 1976, and modest (slightly falling) output growth in the final years of the decade.
SOURCE: *OECD Economic Outlook*, December 1980.

countries in the world economy, viewed from the U.S. perspective. The world average is an average of the 143 countries that are members of the International Monetary Fund. In constructing that average, each country is weighted by its share in world gross output (converted into U.S. dollars). The most striking contrast between the inflation paths shown in Figure 44.2 and the output growth rates shown in Figure 44.1 is the way in which inflation rates *diverge* through the decade of the 1970s. As the decade opens, the five inflation rates shown in this chart are all clustered together, lying between a little over 3 percent per annum and about 7.5 percent per annum. This four percentage-point spread between the highest and lowest is roughly maintained through 1972. The divergence then begins. By 1974, the spread between the lowest and highest inflation rate is more than 17 percent (Japan being 24.3, and West Germany at 7.0). The inflation rates stay very far apart for the rest of the decade, although they do come closer together again by 1979 than at their peak divergence in the middle of the decade.

The second noteworthy feature of these inflation rates is the common cyclical pattern. All countries' inflation rates accelerated between 1972 and 1974–1975, all fell through 1978, and all began to rise again at the end of the decade.

Figure 44.2
World Inflation of Consumer Prices, 1970–1979

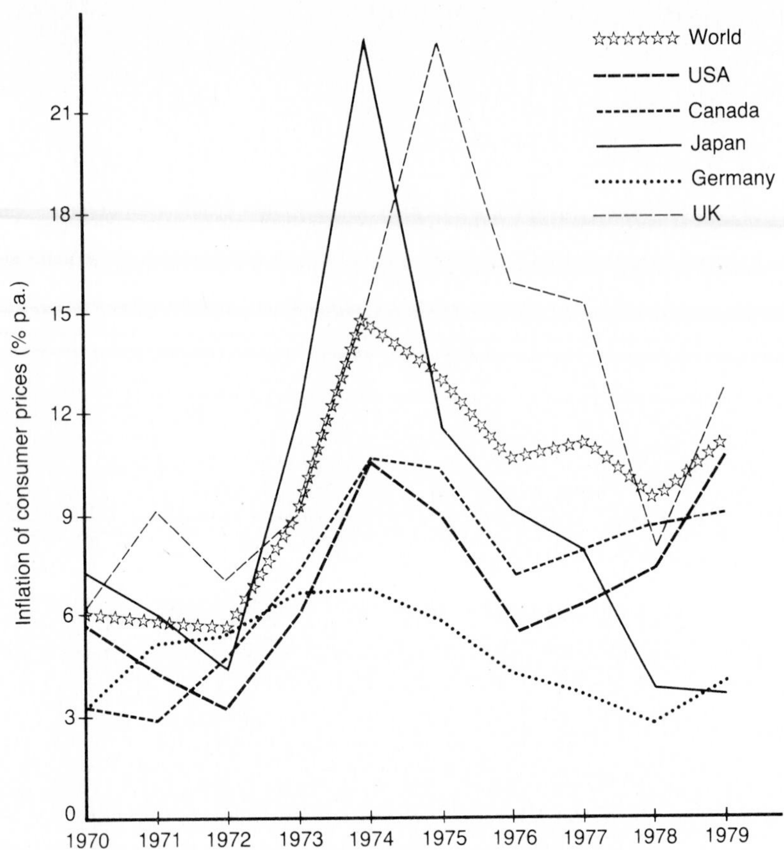

Inflation exploded in all countries in 1973–1974. After a brief recovery, there was a further rise toward the end of the decade. After being very similar to each other, inflation rates diverged after 1973.
SOURCE: *International Financial Statistics Yearbook*, 1980, p 59.

The U.S. inflation performance throughout this decade looks very average compared with the other major countries and with the world aggregate measure. The country whose inflation experience most closely resembles that of the United States is Canada. The inflation rates of these two countries may be seen as somewhat better than the world average.

Although macroeconomics is concerned with broad averages of prices, there is a particular price that took on a special significance in the 1970s, namely, the price of oil. The causes of that oil price rise and its consequences for the United States cannot be ignored even in a brief examination of world macroeconomic events of the 1970s. Let us therefore examine what happened to the price of oil over this decade.

There are several alternative measures of the price of oil, and only one has been selected as being fairly representative, namely, the U.S. dollar price of Saudi Arabian crude oil (Saudi Arabia is the biggest producer in the world).

TABLE 44.1
World Oil Price, 1970–1979

YEAR	SAUDI ARABIAN CRUDE, $U.S. PER BARREL	PERCENT RISE OVER PREVIOUS YEAR
1970	1.30	1.6
1971	1.65	26.9
1972	1.90	15.2
1973	2.70	42.1
1974	9.67	258.1
1975	10.72	10.9
1976	11.51	7.4
1977	12.40	7.7
1978	12.70	2.4
1979	16.97	33.6

SOURCE: *IFS Yearbook* 1980, p. 77, line 76aa.

Table 44.1 sets out the U.S. dollar price (column 1) of a barrel of Saudi Arabian crude oil on the average for each year in the 1970s. The second column shows the percentage rate of change in that price over the previous year. After opening the decade with a modest rate of increase, there is a tendency for the oil price to move upwards more quickly in 1971, 1972, and 1973. Then, in 1973–1974, there is what can only be described as an explosion—a near quadrupling of the price. Between 1975 and 1978, oil prices rise only modestly and especially so when viewed against the average rises in other prices. In 1979 there is another large increase.

We shall return to an examination of these oil prices when analyzing the causes of world macroeconomic activity. For now it is important to take careful note of the timing of the movements in oil prices. The key explosion occurred at the end of 1973 and was partly reflected in the 1973 rate of increase (42.1 percent) and in the 1974 rate of increase (258.1 percent).

Interest Rates

Let us now turn to examine the developments in world interest rates in the 1970s. It will be convenient to focus on those same countries whose inflation performances were highlighted in the previous section. Figure 44.3 shows both short-term [frame (a)] and long-term [frame (b)] interest rates in the five major countries.

The pattern in interest rate movements shown in this figure reflects one of the stylized facts about the business cycle that you have already reviewed in the specifically U.S. context. That is, the tendency for long-term interest rates to fluctuate less than short-term rates. Aside from this key difference between the movements of short- and long-term rates, the movements of both rates reflect the same pattern. Rates fall slightly from 1970 through 1973, then rise very sharply to a peak in 1974, fall to a new trough in 1977–1978, and rise again to the end of the decade.

National differences in interest rates reflect the national differences in inflation rates that we looked at in the previous subsection. The countries whose inflation rates rise most over the decade are those whose interest rates are highest at the end of the decade. The sharp decline in Japanese and

Figure 44.3
World Interest Rates, 1970–1979

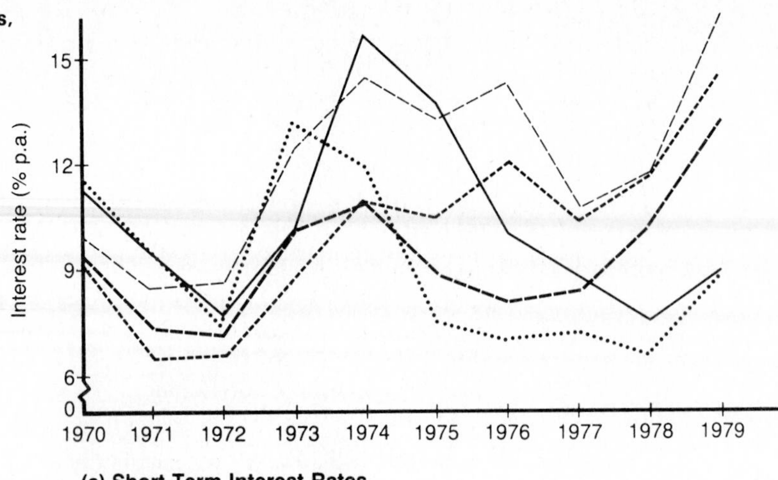

(a) Short-Term Interest Rates

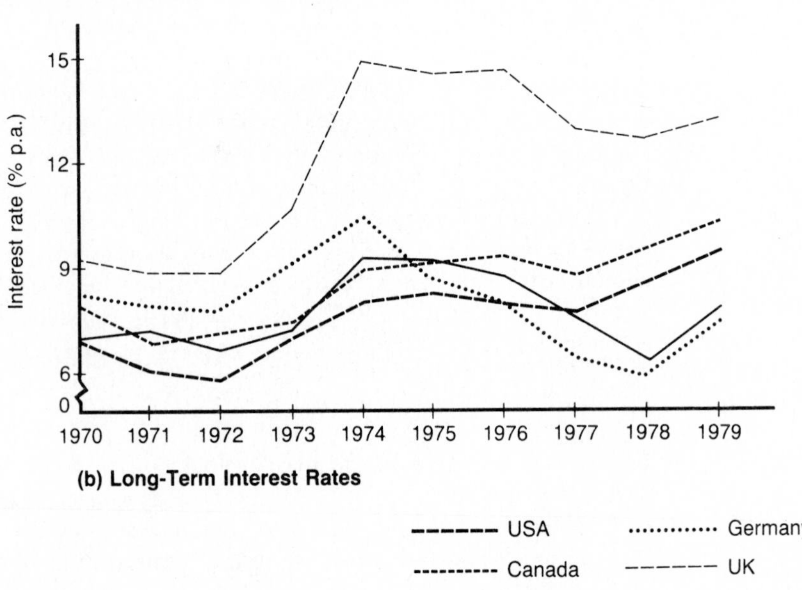

(b) Long-Term Interest Rates

USA
Canada
Japan
Germany
UK

Movements in interest rates broadly reflect movements in inflation. Short-term rates [frame (a)] fluctuate with greater amplitude than long rates [frame (b)]. Countries whose inflation rates rise most are those whose interest rates rise most. Like inflation, interest rates diverge after 1973.

SOURCE: *International Financial Statistics Yearbook*, 1980. Short-term interest rates: U.S.A., Canada, U.K., 3-month Treasury Bill rate, line 60c. Germany, Japan call money rate, line 60b. Long-term interest rates for all countries is long-term government bond, line 61.

Figure 44.4
The Value of the U.S. Dollar in Terms of Four Other Currencies

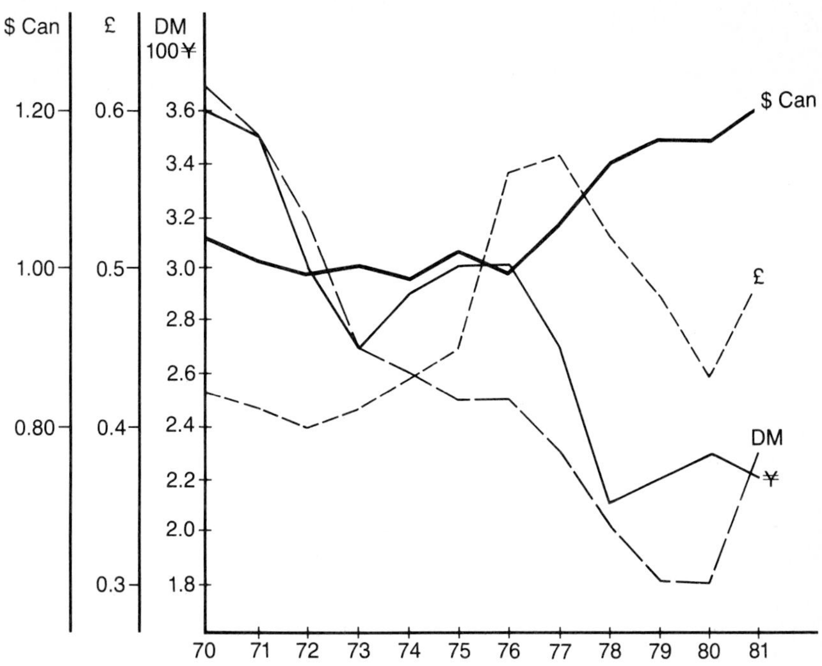

During the 1970s, the value of the U.S. dollar has trended downwards against the German mark (DM) and Japanese yen (¥) and upwards against the British pound (£) and Canadian dollar ($C).
SOURCE: *International Financial Statistics Yearbook*, 1982, pp. 137, 203, 271, 461.

German interest rates (both short- and long-term) between 1975 and 1978 is a clear example of this. Also, the sharp rise in United Kingdom interest rates and the persistent (although less sharp) rise in U.S. and Canadian rates are examples at the other end of the spectrum.

Exchange Rates

Finally, let us examine the behavior of exchange rates among the major currencies throughout this decade. Focusing on the major economies, Figure 44.4 shows the value of the U.S. dollar against the German mark—the Deutsche mark (DM)— the Japanese yen (¥), the United Kingdom pound—the pound sterling (£)—and the Canadian dollar ($C).

First let us be sure that you know how to read Figure 44.4. The vertical axis measures the units of each of the four foreign currencies per U.S. dollar. There are three separate scales—one for the Canadian dollar, one for the pound, and one that is to show the value both of the Deutsche mark (DM) and the Japanese yen (¥) (measured as 100 yen). When the line graphed is rising, this indicates that the U.S. dollar is becoming more valuable in terms of foreign currency. That is, the U.S. dollar is appreciating. Conversely, when the line is falling, the U.S. dollar is losing value or depreciating.

The trends in the foreign exchange value of the U.S. dollar clearly vary from one currency to another. On the average, there has been a tendency for the U.S. dollar to become more valuable (to appreciate) against the Canadian dollar and the pound sterling. There has been the opposite tendency in the case of the Deutsche mark and Japanese yen. Indeed there has been a fairly dramatic depreciation of the U.S. dollar against the Deutsche mark and the yen over the eleven years shown in the figure. Overall, the U.S. dollar is worth about a half as many Deutsche marks and yen in 1981 as it was worth in 1970. The appreciation against the pound and the Canadian dollar, although clear, is much less pronounced than the depreciation against these other two currencies.

The detailed movements of the foreign currency value of the U.S. dollar do not always follow the broad trend lines. For example, in the early 1970s, the U.S. dollar was falling in value against all four of the currencies shown here. In the middle of the decade, the U.S. and Canadian dollars remained fairly steady in relation to each other, and there was a strong appreciation against the pound and depreciation against the Deutsche mark. The yen fluctuated in value in both directions in the middle years of this decade. Then, by 1977, the dollar was losing ground rather strongly against all the currencies shown here, except for the Canadian dollar, against which it began to appreciate. The most recent experience, in the early 1980s, has seen the U.S. dollar appreciating against most currencies again.

This completes our brief description of the macroeconomic developments in the major countries of the world as well as in the United States over the decade of the 1970s. Let us now turn to the task of explaining and understanding the sources of these movements and also assessing the main influences of the United States on the rest of the world.

B. The Causes of World Output, Price, Interest Rate, and Exchange Rate Movements in the 1970s

First, let us try to understand the *world averages* of output growth and inflation. How can we account for the movements in the world averages of output and inflation set out in Figures 44.1 and 44.2?

In approaching this question it is helpful to begin by realizing that the world is closer than any national economy to approximating the closed economy, the behavior of which we have analyzed in the bulk of this book. It would seem instructive, therefore, to examine the forces that, according to closed economy macroeconomic analysis, are the principal determinants of output and price movements. According to this theory, aggregate demand is determined by the money supply, government spending, taxes, and other factors that influence the scale of investment spending. It would be a massive undertaking to compile world aggregate measures of all these variables. In principle, we would like to know what has happened to world aggregate government spending and taxes as well as to factors influencing world aggregate investment spending. However, such an exercise has not, as far as I am aware, been undertaken. What has been undertaken is the compilation of world money supply growth. The International Monetary Fund has constructed a world aggregate index of money and the growth rate of money (based on national money supply growth rates weighted by the share of each country in world output). It is possible, therefore, to examine the influence, if any, of world money supply growth on world economic activity. Although not a substitute for a careful and detailed statistical analysis, Figure 44.5 provides an overview of this relationship.

The world money supply growth rate is shown in Figure 44.5, along with world inflation and output growth. First, focus on the movements in world money growth over the period after 1968. As the figure shows, there is a steady decline in world money growth between 1968 and 1970, followed by three years in which the growth rate accelerates. Although money supply growth accelerates between 1970 and 1973, the rate of acceleration itself slows down. That is, the 1973 growth rate is bigger than that of 1972, but by a smaller increment than that by which 1972 exceeds 1971, which, in turn, is smaller than the increment with which 1971 exceeds 1970. By 1974, the world money supply growth rate is cut, and rather substantially so, to a rate less than that which prevailed three years earlier. Between 1974 and the end of the decade, money supply growth fluctuates, rising to a peak in 1976 and a trough in 1979, but it remains in the same high range that it had moved into in 1972–1973.

According to the theory of output and inflation, anticipated changes in the money supply growth rate lead to changes in the rate of inflation and to no change in output. Further, the inflation rate overshoots the money supply growth rate during the transition process to the new higher inflation rate. Also, according to this theory, an unanticipated change in the money supply growth rate leads to a change in both output and inflation.

Effects comparable to the predictions of the theory can be seen by examining the movements of output and inflation shown in Figure 44.5. The way that inflation and output growth have been plotted involves some adjustments in the *timing* of the variables. Instead of plotting inflation and output growth in each year corresponding to the growth rate of the money supply in that same year, the timing of inflation and output growth has been adjusted in the following way. First, up to 1975, money growth in each year is lined up with output one year later and inflation two years later. After 1975, the time lag is compressed. Money growth in each year is lined up with output growth in the same year and inflation one year later.

These data may be interpreted as saying that when a change in the money supply growth rate occurs, it is largely unanticipated and has its impact on output. Only after a period is the change in the money supply growth rate perceived to be of sufficient durability for inflationary expectations to be revised upwards. The patterns revealed in Figure 44.5 suggest that a change in the money supply growth rate has a strong effect on output, with about a one-year time lag, and a strong effect on inflation, with about a two-year lag. After 1975, the lags are shorter. The output lag is now less than one year, and the inflation lag about one year. The shorter lag may be interpreted as the consequence of people paying more attention to inflation when its rate is high than when it is low.

At higher rates of inflation and higher rates of money growth, the consequences of misjudging the inflation rate are more serious than at lower rates. It is, therefore, rational to pay more attention to, and become more responsive

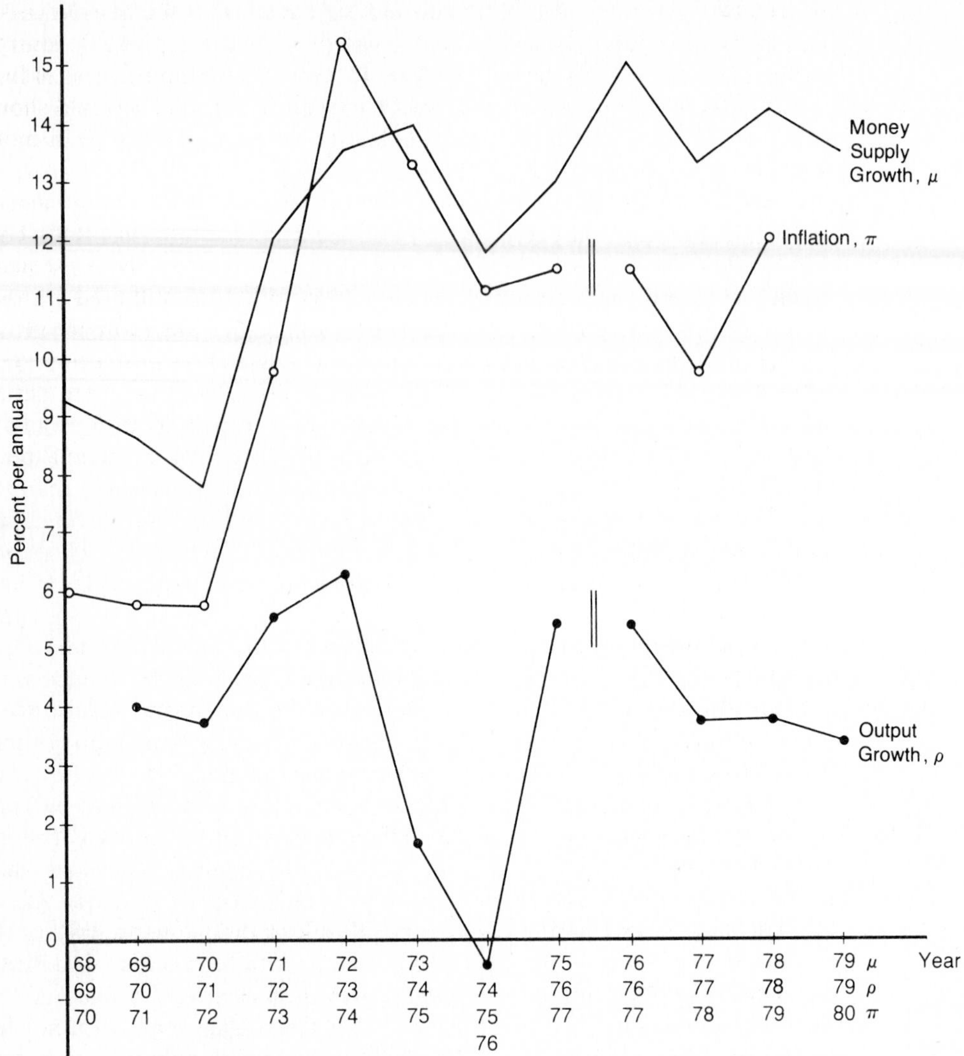

Figure 44.5
World Money Supply Growth, Output Growth, and Inflation, 1970–1979

World money growth, inflation, and output growth are well correlated. Before 1975, changes in the money supply growth rate preceded changes in output growth by one year and inflation by two years. After 1975, changes in money supply growth were contemporaneous with changes in output growth and preceded inflation changes by one year.

SOURCES: *IFS Yearbook* 1980, p. 55, line 1; p. 59, line 1. *OECD Economic Outlook*, December 1980.

to, changes in money supply growth rates. According to the new Keynesian interpretation of the aggregate supply response (recall Chapter 25), contracts would get shorter and/or would tend more to be indexed to the cost of living in high-inflation situations than in low-inflation situations. This would shorten the time lag in the response of both output and prices to a change in money growth.

Let us use the above interpretation to account for the movements in output and prices in the 1970s. The slight drop in inflation in the first two years of the decade and the slight drop in output are seen as the consequence of tightening money growth in the late 1960s. This slowdown in money growth is interpreted as being initially unanticipated, and as being subsequently, although only gradually, incorporated into inflation expectations. The surge of money growth in 1971 and 1972 is interpreted as having been initially unanticipated and, therefore, as the source of rising output with steady inflation. Eventually the higher money growth rate was built into price expectations and, by 1973, it was producing a strong inflation acceleration.

By 1974, the inflation acceleration is very strong. During this year, very rapid inflation coincides with a deceleration in money growth. By 1974, money supply growth actually falls. It may be reasonably conjectured that the drop in money supply growth in 1974 was unanticipated. It is even plausible to suggest that the slowdown of money growth in 1973 had also, to some extent, been unanticipated. This is seen as a principal determinant of the deep recession in world economic activity in 1974 and 1975. It is also seen as the source of falling inflation in 1975 and 1976. The renewed burst of money growth from 1975 through 1976—largely unanticipated—generates the big world recovery of real activity into 1976. The higher money growth rate of 1976 was built into peoples' expectations and was reflected in a shortening of contracts and a speeding up of the effects of a change in money growth on output and prices. The renewed acceleration of inflation toward the end of the decade is also the consequence of this higher money growth rate. Slowing money growth in the final year of the decade brings a quick slowdown of output growth and is predicted to moderate inflation in the opening years of the 1980s.

From this account of the 1970s, it is evident that although in principle it would be desirable to know what was happening to world fiscal policy variables throughout the decade, movements in world money growth alone seem to have been a dominant influence on the course of world output and inflation.

The other feature of world macroeconomic activity during the decade of the 1970s, evident in Figures 44.2 and 44.3, is the divergence in inflation and interest rates across the major countries. Why did these divergencies occur? In a deep sense we do not know the answer to this question, for it resides in some as yet not well understood differences in national tendencies to inflate. We do know that these tendencies have been present for many years. They were not, however, permitted to have full reign until the fixed exchange rate trading system established after World War II finally collapsed in 1972. Therefore, we can say that the proximate cause of the spreading out of world inflation and interest rates through the second part of the 1970s was the consequence of this collapse. As countries one after another abandoned the commitment to maintaining a fixed exchange rate against the U.S. dollar and gold, so national monetary policies became more diverse, and national inflation and interest rate experiences diverged from each other.

As we learned in Chapter 42, under fixed exchange rates, purchasing power parity and interest rate parity keep one country's inflation and interest rates broadly in line with those in other countries. (They will not, of course, be exactly equal, for differences reflecting differences in national risk and changes in the real exchange rates will be reflected in the aggregates.) The details shown in Figures 44.2 and 44.3 for the early 1970s are an interesting reflection of these propositions.

We further learned, in Chapter 42, that when the exchange rate is flexible, movements in the exchange rate and movements in interest rates and inflation rates all must be compatible with each other, and that all are generated by movements in national money supply growth rates relative to each other. Thus, an economy that is pursuing a high money supply growth rate policy relative to the rest of the world will be a country whose currency is becoming weaker, whose inflation rate is higher, and whose interest rates are higher than the world average. These patterns are clearly discernible in the figures presented in the preceding section. The low-inflation countries, Germany and Japan, are the low-interest rate and strong currency countries. The high-inflation countries—the United Kingdom, United States, and Canada—are the high-interest rate, weak currency countries. Study the patterns shown in Figures 44.2, 44.3, and 44.4. They provide a remarkable cross-country confirmation of the predictions of the basic model. Almost on a one-for-one basis, interest rates, inflation rates, and exchange rate movements line up with each other just as the basic model predicts they will.

You may by now be saying to yourself, "This all sounds very well, but what about the price of oil? Don't we all know that the world's macroeconomic problems of the 1970s, the inflation, as well as the recession of the middle 1970s, were caused by movements in world energy prices in 1973? Don't we also know that the renewed burst of inflation at the end of the decade, as well as the recession of 1979–1980, is also the consequence of a subsequent rise in the price of oil?" These are certainly fashionable propositions. They also almost certainly contain an element of truth. The burst of inflation in 1974, the recession of 1975, and the renewed inflation of 1979 were all made more severe than they otherwise would have been as a result of the *timing* of the oil price changes.

It is of some interest and importance to notice, however, that we have been able to explain the broad movements in world output and inflation, both on the average and across individual countries, without any need to refer to the price of oil as a separate item. It is also of some importance to note the *timing* of the movements of world money supply growth, output, and inflation. In the early part of the decade, changes in the money supply growth rate *preceded* changes in the output growth rate by one year and changes in the inflation rate by two years. In the later part of the decade, changes in the output growth rate and inflation rate continued to follow changes in the money supply growth rate, but the time lag has shortened substantially.

Although knowing that something happens *after* something else does not constitute proof that the former causes the latter, when combined with a body of detailed analysis as to *how* one causes the other, it amounts to fairly

TABLE 44.2
The Price of Oil, 1950–1979

YEAR	SAUDI ARABIAN CRUDE, $U.S. PER BARREL	WORLD CONSUMER PRICE INDEX	REAL PRICE OF OIL	TREND OF REAL PRICE
1950	1.71	28.7	5.96	5.96
1960	1.50	40.2	3.73	7.40
1970	1.30	62.3	2.09	9.19
1979	16.97	152.0	11.16	11.16
			Average Annual growth rate 2.2%	

SOURCE *and* METHODS: *IFS Yearbook* 1980: col. 1 is pp. 76–77, line 76aa; col. 2 is pp. 60–61, line 64; col. 3 is col. 1 divided by col. 2 multiplied by 100; col. 4 is the trend between the 1950 and 1979 points.

impressive evidence that a causal relationship is at work. The macroeconomic theory reviewed in this book sets out the links whereby changes in money supply growth influence output and prices. The combination of this theory with the facts shown in Figure 44.5, simple and highly aggregative though they are, seems to constitute fairly powerful evidence for the proposition that variations in world money supply growth have been a primary cause of variations in world output growth and inflation.

There are some further aspects of the oil price rises of the 1970s that reinforce this conclusion and that are worth considering here. The first of these arises from the fact that the price of oil is a *relative price*, whereas inflation is the change in the *absolute price level.* It is true that oil is an important commodity, and a large change in its relative price will have important consequences. It is also true that the relative price of oil changed dramatically in the early part of the 1970s. What is remarkable about the behavior of the price of oil is not that its price has risen relative to the prices of other goods, but that the rise came so suddenly, rather than gradually over a long period.

Table 44.2 gives some information about long-term developments in the price of oil. Interestingly, as shown in the first column, the U.S. dollar price of oil fell between 1950 and 1970. In that same period, as shown in the second column, world prices measured by the IMF world consumer price index more than doubled. Between 1950 and 1970, the real price of oil (the dollar price divided by the world consumer price index) fell to little more than one-third its 1950 level. In the next decade, the real price increased more than fivefold. The change between 1950 and 1979, not quite a doubling of the real price of oil, represents a 2.2 percent annual growth in the real price of oil. If oil prices had increased at that steady trend rate throughout the 29 years between 1950 and 1979, the prices in 1960 and 1970 would have been $7.40 and $9.14 a barrel, as shown in the fourth column in Table 44.2. If that trend line had been followed throughout the 30-year period, the prices of the 1970s would have been entirely unremarkable, and the *macro*economic effects of the oil price changes would have been negligible or even nonexistent.

The theory of relative prices (microeconomics) predicts that the price of an exhaustible resource will rise at a rate equal to the real rate of interest. The real rate of interest, of course, is the money or market rate of interest minus the rate of inflation, and generally is seen to lie between 2 and 3 percent per annum. Exhaustible resources prices are predicted to rise at the real rate of interest because, were that not so, it would not pay anyone to own the reserves of those resources. Rather, it would pay to extract them from the ground and consume them instantly.

You can see this by considering the choice between investing in, say, an oil well and investing in some other profit-seeking activity. A dollar invested in the oil well today will yield a rate of return only if the oil can be sold later at a higher price than it could be sold for today. If the rate at which the price of oil is predicted to rise exceeds the rate of return on other activities, then it will pay to invest in oil wells. This would drive up the price and drive down the rate of return on oil wells. Conversely, if the price of oil is expected to rise less quickly than the rate of return on other activities, then it will pay to try to sell oil wells. This will drive down their price and raise the rate of return on them. The price of an oil well today is nothing other than the price of oil today, adjusted, of course, for extraction costs. It is evident, then, that the equilibrium price of an oil well, which will determine the current price of oil, will be such that the expected future price of oil will rise at a rate equal to the real rate of interest.

Of course, looking backwards over any particular historical episode, it will not be the case that the price of oil has behaved exactly as predicted by the theory. The theory concerns expectations about future price changes, not realizations of past price changes. Nevertheless, it would be surprising if, over very long periods of time, the price of oil behaved differently from the predictions of the theory.

It is true that over the decades of the 1950s and 1960s, the price of oil behaved very differently from what the theory predicts. That is, the real price of oil fell successively through that 20-year period. Why it did so constitutes an interesting fact, one that requires an explanation. The explosion in the price of oil relative to the price of other commodities in the early 1970s can be viewed as an adjustment in the price of oil to place the price on the track that it ought to have been on during the 1960s and 1970s. Thus, the explosion in the price of oil in the early 1970s may be viewed as a sudden (and perhaps surprising) adjustment in the real price (relative price) of oil to place the price back on the trend that it would have been on by then had the price increased each and every year by an amount roughly equal to the real rate of interest.

Noting that the change in the price of oil was a relative price change, not an absolute price change, does not mean that it might not have been responsible for triggering the worldwide inflation explosion in the later part of the 1970s. If the rise in the price of oil generated additional money growth, then of course it would generate additional inflation. To some extent, on the average, this may well have happened. It has not, however, happened everywhere. The cross-country experience set out in Figure 44.2 shows that not all countries experienced high and accelerating inflation after the oil shock of 1973–1974.

Indeed, two countries, Germany and Japan, each of which had very different impact effects of the oil shock on their inflation rates, pursued policies that almost completely eradicated inflation by 1978. Furthermore, these are two countries that rely more than any others do on imported oil for their energy requirements. In the Japanese case, there was a very big impact effect of the oil shock on inflation, whereas in the German case, the impact effect was milder. In both cases, however, the subsequent trend in inflation was downwards.

If the oil shock of 1973–1974 was the primary cause of the inflation of the second half of the 1970s, it surely would have to be the case that national inflation rates would have been broadly similar to each other, and, if anything, those countries whose reliance on imported oil is greatest should have had the greatest inflation consequence. What we see is almost the exact reverse of this. First, national inflation rates displayed greater variety after the oil shock than before it; and second, the countries that relied most on imported energy had the lowest inflation. The conclusion to which this leads is that national monetary policy (trend growth rates in national money supplies) is, as it always has been, the principal cause of trends in national inflation rates in the 1970s. Furthermore, changes in world average money growth, preceding as they did, by almost two years, the world oil shock, were, as they too always have been, the major causes of the explosion of world inflation in the 1970s.

C. How the United States Has Influenced World Macroeconomic Developments in the Postwar Period

The United States has been a major factor in the world macroeconomy in the postwar years. Its influence began before World War II was over when it dominated the discussions that led to the establishment of the new Bretton Woods world monetary system. Its actions at that time were directed toward the establishment of a stable world monetary order based on a fixed dollar price of gold and on fixed exchange rates for other currencies in terms of the U.S. dollar. This monetary system served the world well for almost 25 years, but during the late 1960s, it began to become unravelled. It finally collapsed in the early 1970s and was followed by a period of generalized floating exchange rates. During the 1970s, the United States has indulged in alternating bouts of inflation and deflation with increasing severity as the decade wore on, and the rest of the world has been buffeted by, and in some cases has accentuated, these shocks. Let us look at this history in more detail.

The Bretton Woods Era

In the period from the end of World War II to the early 1970s, the Bretton Woods international monetary system was in operation. This was a system in which the United States declared that one ounce of gold was worth 35 U.S. dollars, and other countries defined the value of their currency in terms of the U.S. dollar. In order to ensure the gold value of the U.S. dollar, the U.S. government stood ready to buy or sell gold at $35 an ounce. Other countries ensured that their currencies stood in a fixed relation to the United States dollar by themselves standing ready to buy or sell their own currency at a price that did not depart by more than 1 percent in either direction of a declared par or central value.

For the most part, countries took the fixed exchange rate commitment seriously. It was regarded as a sign of abject failure if a country had to devalue its currency. It was also regarded as unsatisfactory if a country had to revalue its currency. Thus, rather than see the external value of its currency change, governments would take whatever actions seemed necessary. The way in which a government can peg the foreign exchange value of its currency is to hold reserves of foreign currency with which to buy its own currency in the event that its price falls too low. Conversely, the government can use its own currency to buy foreign exchange in the event that its own currency is becoming too valuable on the world markets. Thus, it is the stock of foreign exchange reserves that adjusts when a currency comes under pressure. When a currency comes under downward pressure, the stock of foreign exchange reserves fall, and if the currency comes under upward pressure, the stock of foreign exchange reserves rise.

A country that is attempting to prop up the value of its currency and is, as a result, rapidly losing foreign reserves clearly has to make some other policy change if it is to avoid running out of foreign reserves. Further, a country whose stock of foreign reserves is increasing as a result of an attempt to prevent the value of its currency from rising clearly will be under pressure to do something to prevent the accumulation of too many reserves. The policy changes that a country can introduce in such situations are straightforward and have already been reviewed in Chapters 41 and 42. If a country is suffering from a balance of payments deficit under fixed exchange rates, it has to cut the growth rate of domestic credit. If it is suffering from upward pressure on the value of its currency, it has to increase the rate of domestic credit creation.

With the above remarks as a background, let us now see how the U.S. economy was able to influence the rest of the world during the fixed exchange rate Bretton Woods era. Suppose the United States was to undertake policies that had the effect of stimulating economic activity in the United States. For example, an unexpected burst of monetary expansion in the United States would stimulate output and prices in the United States, thereby leading to a rise in the demand for U.S. imports and a rise in exports of the rest of the world. This would stimulate output and employment in the rest of the world. At the same time there would be a tendency for the rest of the world's balance of payments to move into surplus. In such a situation the governments of the other countries could allow their foreign exchange value to appreciate. However, the fixed exchange rate system would prevent them from doing this, and in order to avoid their currencies becoming too strong, other governments would stimulate domestic demand with their own monetary stimulus, thereby offsetting the tendency for their exchange rate to appreciate. Thus, all countries would stimulate domestic demand in a synchronized fashion with stimulation coming from the U.S. economy.

The same story could be told in the reverse direction. If the U.S. government undertook policies that had the effect of damping off economic activity in America (for example, unexpectedly tight monetary policies that led to temporarily high U.S. interest rates and low U.S. output, employment, and prices), this would tend to cut U.S. demand for imports and thereby cut exports from the rest of the world. There would be a balance of payments deficit in the rest of the world that would have to be countered by slowing down the rate of domestic credit expansion, thereby raising interest rates and lowering economic activities still further in other countries.

This cycle of economic activity, with each country expanding and contracting at more or less the same time, seems to have been a characteristic of the Bretton Woods era.

Over and above these cycles there were some very clear inflationary trends. The United States was able, through this period, to create additional U.S. dollars at a much more rapid rate than that consistent with a long-term maintenance of a fixed gold value for the U.S. dollar. At first, other countries were happy to accept U.S. dollars in increasing quantities as their demand for foreign exchange reserves tried to keep up with the growth in world trade. By the late 1960s, however, U.S. monetary expansion began to outstrip the rest of the world's demand for U.S. dollars, and the dollar itself came to be mistrusted. Many countries sought to protect themselves by ridding themselves of U.S. dollars (which they thought were likely not to maintain their value) and by acquiring gold instead. This, in turn, put pressure on the U.S. gold reserves and led, in August 1971, to the closing of gold sales by the United States.

With the United States creating more money than the rest of the world was willing to hold at existing prices, there was no alternative but for the general price level to be bid up at an increasing rate—that is, for there to be a rise in the rate of inflation. As this happened, problems that had been inherent in the Bretton Woods system intensified. Several countries were simply not willing to tolerate the inflation rate that went with the maintenance of a fixed exchange rate against the U.S. dollar. As a result, several of the more conservative countries such as West Germany began to appreciate their currencies against the U.S. dollar. As more and more countries sought to adjust their exchange rates with greater frequency, eventually the Bretton Woods system collapsed.

During this Bretton Woods era, the major countries of the world had been locked into a single monetary unit with the United States, and the whole world economy could be regarded as having behaved very much like a closed economy behaves. It is true that the world aggregate money supply was not being determined and controlled by a single central bank. It was, however, being strongly influenced by a single central bank—the Fed. When the Fed expanded the U.S. money supply, this put into motion a chain of events that led other countries to expand their money supplies. When the Fed contracted, this led others to contract. The link in this chain was the stock of foreign exchange reserves. If the Fed expanded the U.S. money supply, other countries found themselves with additional reserves and had to expand their own rate of domestic credit expansion to prevent the reserves from growing too quickly. Conversely, if the Fed ran a tight monetary policy, other countries lost reserves and had themselves to slow down the rate of domestic credit expansion to prevent reserves from falling to too critically low a level.

The Floating Exchange Rate Era

With the collapse of the Bretton Woods system and the introduction of generalized floating exchange rates, economists were, somewhat naively it turns out, predicting that the world would be able to move forward to a period of much greater macroeconomic stability. For most of the postwar period, many economists had doubted the appropriateness of the fixed exchange rate system that had been in operation. It was argued that, with floating exchange rates, countries would be free to pursue their own independent monetary policies, thereby avoiding the phenomenon of a world business cycle and also avoiding accepting the inflation rate dictated by U.S. policy. The events of the 1970s briefly revealed above make it clear that these predictions have not been borne out by the facts and were far too optimistic. If anything, the business cycle of the 1970s has been more heavily synchronized than that of the 1960s. It has, however, been possible for countries to pursue their own inflation trends, as we also saw above.

Why have countries shared the same real business cycle experience in the 1970s? What seems to have happened in this period is that, although in principle countries are free to pursue their own independent monetary policies, in practice they have found it beneficial to follow a policy that has been closely geared to the one being followed in the United States. Suppose, for example, that in a particular year, U.S. policy was disinflationary. Specifically suppose that the U.S. money supply grew by an unexpectedly small amount, thereby leading to low output and lower prices but also higher interest rates in the United States than elsewhere. If other things remained the same, this would tend to put downward pressure on the foreign exchange values and other currencies. With a floating exchange rate, there is no reason why this should not be allowed to happen. It has, in general, however, not been allowed to happen. The principle reason for this seems to be that countries have feared that if they permit their currencies to fall in value, this will lead to a sharp rise in import prices, which in turn will quickly feed into other domestic prices (especially the price of labor), thereby giving domestic inflation an unwanted upward impetus. To avoid this, governments have taken steps similar to those that they would have taken under a fixed exchange rate system. Thus they have followed the U.S. policy by adding additional disinflationary pressure to their own economy.

Similarly, if the United States has been experiencing unexpectedly rapid monetary growth with high output, higher prices, and lower interest rates, then this has put upward pressure on the value of other countries' currencies. Again, although in principle the other countries were free to permit an appreciation to take place, there has been a general reluctance to do so. The fear of allowing too rapid an appreciation of their currencies seems to be associated with the fear that their exports would be priced out of world markets if their national currency became too strong. Thus, again, although free in principle to permit the exchange rate to change, other governments have prevented it from doing so by mimicking the U.S. stimulatory policies.

There have been two extremely dramatic examples of this "follow-the-leader" behavior. The first occurred in the early 1970s, when U.S. monetary policy was strongly expansionary. The rest of the world, anxious to avoid seeing their own currencies become too strong against the U.S. dollar, joined the United States in monetary expansion. The result was the worldwide boom and worldwide inflation explosion in 1972–1973. The second dramatic example was in the opposite direction and occurred in the early 1980s. The U.S. monetary growth in 1980–1981 was unexpectedly tight, leading to a deep recession and high interest rates in the United States. Most other countries followed the behavior of the United States in order to prevent their own currencies from depreciating too much. On this occasion, however, U.S. monetary growth was so tight that no one was willing to go the whole way in preventing the change in the foreign exchange value of their currency. Thus practically all currencies were allowed to depreciate somewhat against the U.S. dollar in 1981.

D. Macroeconomic Policy Choices

The macroeconomic policy choices faced by the United States are fundamentally different from those faced by other countries. This difference arises from the U.S. central role as the major economy in the Western world. The United States cannot single-handedly impose a fixed exchange rate system on the rest of the world. It can, however, pursue its own monetary policies independently of whether the world has a fixed or floating exchange rate system. As we have seen in the previous section, regardless of the monetary system in operation, the United States is big enough to be able to call the tune.

The same is not true for other countries. The macroeconomic policy choices that face smaller countries, such as, for example, Canada, Japan, Germany, or the United Kingdom, fundamentally boil down to choosing an exchange rate or a money supply growth rate. At the pure extremes, small countries could have rigid monetary targeting (i.e., cause their money supply to grow at a known predetermined rate) and a flexible exchange rate determined on the foreign exchange market, or they could peg their foreign exchange rates (to the U.S. dollar, any other individual currency, or a basket of currencies) and let the domestic money supply and price level be determined by the rest of the world. Some combination of these two extremes could be achieved by some predetermined mechanism for a managed float for the country's currency. Yet, none of these policies avoids world shocks to the small open economy. You have seen *why* this is so in Chapter 43, and *that it is so* in the two preceding sections of this chapter.

It is commonly believed that monetarists advocate fixing the money supply growth rate and floating the exchange rate, and that to advocate a fixed exchange rate is the ultimate in interventionism and therefore an extreme form of Keynesianism. Nothing, in fact, could be further from the truth. A fixed exchange rate policy is a monetary policy and often the best monetary policy. The open economy version of monetarism says that for big countries, there is really no alternative but to control the growth rate of the money supply; for smaller countries, there always is the alternative of pegging the value of domestic money against the value of some other money. In selecting a currency against which to peg, it is of some importance to pay attention to the monetary policies that will govern the value of that currency in terms of goods. Fixing the value of, say, the Canadian dollar against, say, the Deutsche mark, would produce a very different behavior for the Canadian price level than would fixing it against the U.K. pound.

The lesson that we learn from economic theory and from the brief consideration of the facts in the previous parts of this chapter is that real fluctuations (fluctuations in output growth) seem to be very hard to insulate against. They are shared more or less uniformly by all countries, regardless of the policies they have pursued. They are shared by high-inflation and low-inflation countries, by countries whose currencies have been strong and those whose currencies have been weak, by countries with high interest rates and countries with low interest rates. The other lesson that is clear from theory and the facts is that it is possible to insulate a country from inflation arising in the rest of the world. By pursuing firm domestic monetary policies (which also are credible and engender a rational expectation of future firm monetary policies), low inflation, low interest rates, and a strong currency can be achieved. Furthermore, moderate inflation can be achieved even in the face of massive relative price changes such as occurred in the price of energy in the middle 1970s. Furthermore, low inflation does not seem to require low growth.

In order to achieve low inflation and low interest rates, it is necessary to float the exchange rate and permit an appreciation of the value of the currency against those of countries whose inflation rates are higher than that being attained domestically. Whether or not this worsens macroeconomic fluctuations of real variables such as output and unemployment it is not possible to say in the current state of knowledge. Certainly, we know that aggregate demand is insulated from foreign shocks (provided capital is perfectly mobile) in the flexible exchange rate case. We also know, however, that the rational expectations of the price level will be influenced by observations of the exchange rate, which will in turn be influenced by shocks arising in the rest of the world. Whether these shocks will translate into domestic output and employment movements that have bigger amplitude than those that would arise under a fixed exchange rate cannot be said on the basis of what we now know. For the time being, however, the gains to be had on the inflation front from pursuing a flexible exchange rate would seem to be so worthwhile as to push us very strongly in the direction of choosing the combination of a money supply rule, and a flexible exchange rate.

Summary

A. The Main Patterns in World Output, Prices, Interest Rates, and Exchange Rates in the 1970s

World output growth went into a boom in 1972–1973 and a deep recession in 1974–1975. It recovered in 1976 but trended downward slightly toward the end of the 1970s.

World inflation exploded in 1973–1974, moderated markedly in 1975–1976, and then accelerated again toward the end of the decade. Interest rates followed the inflation pattern very closely. The U.S. dollar was fairly steady against the Canadian dollar, depreciated slightly against the Deutsche mark and the yen, and appreciated against the British pound in the first half of the 1970s. It depreciated substantially against all major currencies except the Canadian dollar in the second half of the 1970s. Growth rates in output have been remarkably similar in all countries throughout the 1970s, whereas inflation and interest rates have diverged markedly, especially after 1974.

B. The Causes of World Output, Price, Interest Rate, and Exchange Rate Movements in the 1970s

The macroeconomic theory of the closed economy may be used to understand the movements of world average output and prices. Although, in principle, world aggregate fiscal policy variables play a role, it turns out that movements in world money supply growth are quite capable of explaining the main trends in both output and inflation. It is necessary to interpret that there is approximately a two-year lag before money growth is fully incorporated into inflation in the first half of the decade, and approximately a one-year time lag in the second half of the decade. The divergence of inflation and interest rates across the major countries in the second half of the decade is seen as arising from the pursuit of diverging monetary policies in a world of flexible exchange rates.

C. How the United States Has Influenced World Macroeconomic Developments in the Postwar Period

Under both the fixed exchange rate era (World War II to early 1970s) and the floating exchange rate era (the 1970s up to date), U.S. macroeconomic developments have had a major influence on the rest of the world.

With fixed exchange rates, countries necessarily found themselves linked to U.S. macroeconomic fortunes. Stimulation in the United States automatically led to stimulation elsewhere as countries sought to prevent their foreign exchange reserves from rising too quickly. Conversely, deflationary pressures in the United States led to deflationary pressures elsewhere as countries sought to protect their foreign exchange reserves.

In the floating exchange rate era, an unwillingness to see exchange rates move too quickly has led countries to continue synchronizing their monetary policies with those in the United States, although in the latest U.S. deflation, less than completely so.

D. Macroeconomic Policy Choices

The United States has more macroeconomic policy freedom than other countries. Although it cannot impose a fixed exchange rate system on the rest of the world, it can nevertheless pursue whatever monetary policies it chooses regardless of whether the world operates on fixed or floating exchange rates. Other countries have less freedom of choice. At the extremes, a small country may choose a flexible exchange rate with monetary targeting, or it can choose a fixed exchange rate, with the money supply and inflation being determined by the country (or countries) against whom the exchange rate is fixed. In the present state of knowledge, we cannot say definitively which one of the extremes is better than the other. It is possible to say, however, that world inflation may be avoided by firm domestic monetary policies that are pursued with long-term credibility. This requires that exchange rates be flexible.

Review Questions

1. Review the major movements in world income, prices, interest rates, and exchange rates during the 1970s.

2. Compare the performance of U.S. output growth, inflation, and interest rates with that of Canada, Germany, Japan, and the U.K. during the 1970s.

3. What are the broad facts about world money growth, output growth, and inflation in the 1970s? How might the fluctuations in output and prices be explained?

4. Why did national inflation rates and interest rates diverge in the second half of the 1970s?

5. Why are the high inflation countries also those with high interest rates and depreciating currencies?

6. Did the rise in world money growth in the 1970s occur before, during, or after the oil price shock? What bearing does your answer have on interpreting the causes of the 1970s inflation explosion?

7. Can the different national inflation experiences in the post-oil shock period be explained? What are the implications of that explanation for the widely held view that U.S. inflation in the 1970s was caused by the world energy shock and was inevitable?

8. What, according to the predictions of modern macroeconomic theory, were the main foreign influences on the U.S. economy during the 1970s?

9. How may a small country like Canada attempt to insulate its output movements from those occurring in the United States and the rest of the world?

10. What contribution did the U.S. energy policy make during the second half of the 1970s to the reduction of inflation and interest rates in the U.S.? Why would it be *de*flationary to allow the U.S. price of energy to *rise* to world levels?

Index

A

B

C

D

E

F

G

H

I

J

K

N

O

P

R

S

T

U

V

W